Anonymous

The Englishwoman's Review of Social and Industrial Questions

Anonymous

The Englishwoman's Review of Social and Industrial Questions

ISBN/EAN: 9783337891718

Printed in Europe, USA, Canada, Australia, Japan

Cover: Foto ©Andreas Hilbeck / pixelio.de

More available books at **www.hansebooks.com**

(... Withstand the beginning; after ... Kempis, Lib. i. cap. 13.)

LONDON:

PUBLISHED AT THE OFFICE OF THE "ENGLISHWOMAN'S REVIEW,"

22, BERNERS STREET, OXFORD STREET, W.;

AND FOR THE PROPRIETOR BY

TRUBNER & CO., 57 & 59, Ludgate Hill.

PUBLISHED MONTHLY.

JOHNSTON'S (THE OLD HOUSE)
CORN FLOUR

"Is decidedly superior."
Lancet.

IS THE BEST.

Englishwoman's Review.

CONTENTS FOR JANUARY, 1876.

All Communications to be addressed to the EDITOR, 22, Berners Street, Oxford Street, W.

Post-Office Orders payable to SARAH LEWIN, at the "Regent Street" Post-Office.

TERMS OF SUBSCRIPTION AT THE OFFICE.

Per Annum (Post Free), Six Shillings.
Subscriptions payable in Advance. Single Numbers posted Free on receipt of Six Postage Stamps.

MSS. are carefully read, and if not accepted are returned, on receipt of Stamps for Postage, but the Editor cannot be responsible for any accidental loss.

Contributions should be legibly written, and only on one side of each leaf.

THE

ENGLISHWOMAN'S REVIEW.

(NEW SERIES.)

No. XXXIII.—JANUARY, 1876.

ART. I.—ADMIRAL MAXSE ON WOMEN'S SUFFRAGE.

THE lecture which Rear-Admiral Maxse has lately delivered in several institutions in London, and subsequently in Croydon, has been republished in the *Beehive*, and we are thus enabled to review his arguments and weigh their worth, at some length. It is in many respects the best written essay which has appeared against women's suffrage. He does not fall into the illogical errors of Goldwin Smith, by whom women were stigmatised as Conservative and Revolutionary in the same breath, like the traveller in the fable, who blows cold and hot at once; he does not talk sentiment like Sir William Harcourt or Knatchbull-Huguesson, or discover a new reading in the Doxology like Mr. Leatham; but, nevertheless, his arguments are instinct with party spirit, and will not bear the test of impartial reasoning.

Admiral Maxse divides his lecture into the Counterfeit Woman Suffrage and the True Woman Suffrage. Women-householder suffrage, the only suffrage which is being now demanded, is, he declares, counterfeit—adult suffrage, whether for men or women, being the only true one. He accuses the lady advocates of the movement of "attempting to pervert the law and mislead the public," by limiting their claim to the demand that, *whatever the suffrage might be, a question with which they do not meddle—sex should form no disqualification.* Admiral Maxse acknowledges the evil and oppressive laws from which women suffer, but believes that "the single woman vote will confirm the bad laws and uphold the very restrictions that we desire to get rid of." He sees no remedy to oppression, but in changing entirely the basis of representation, the electoral districts, and the manner in which candidates are offered to those districts; and because Women's Suffrage does not imply these changes, and would, *in his opinion*, be inimical to them, it is therefore counterfeit. We affirm on the contrary, that the rapidly growing demand of a vote for women householders is based on the existing constitution, and is a change that would be in accordance with the method of voting in municipal and parochial elections. Is it a counterfeit right that Miss Smith exercises when she votes for a Town-Councilman, because Mr. Jones, who lives next door, votes also? Is it counterfeit that only the widow Mrs. Brown, and not her daughter who lives with her, has the vote in a School Board election?

Admiral Maxse declares that "widows, spinsters, and detached ladies are in an abnormal condition, the mere fragment of their sex." It is a large fragment. According to a recent estimate, two fifths of women of a marriageable age are unmarried. As a matter of fact, these abnormal voters would form from one tenth to one seventh of the entire constituency. He condemns the movement as a counterfeit claim to representation, "because it would raise only propertied single women to citizenship." It is not so many years since only propertied men had votes, and yet England was even then said to have a representative government.

The lecturer next complains that there are two faces to the movement, the one irreconcileable with the other. . . . "their course is politic. To the astute Conservative mind, the scheme is altogether deserving, it may be truly termed a 'constitutional' one, it is favourable to people who have 'a stake in the country' as it is called. The radical is also conciliated. Extension of the franchise is his one panacea for all ills. Then there is the concession of an abstract right. All his own pet arguments and declarations about the rights of every man

&c.,—why not every woman? are turned against him.
He thinks the measure is in favour of every woman; he
is told that this is the ultimate object, although the
Conservative is carefully told that it is not so." There
is much unfairness underlying this assertion. Admiral
Maxse should remember that there are among women
and the advocates of Women's Suffrage as many diversities of opinion as there are among men, and the
supporters of any other public movement. It was easy
when the friends of Women's Suffrage were but a few
hundreds, for them to be unanimous; now that they are
counted by tens of thousands, there are of course many
shades of opinion in their ranks. There are women who
are Conservative, women who are Liberal; women who
will support the Church in its extremest pretensions, and
women who will do hearty battle for Disestablishment;
there are women who wish for Adult Suffrage which
includes of course every man or woman, married or unmarried, and women who are contented with the present
basis of representation. The Suffrage party, as a party,
is firmly united on one point,—that whatever other
qualification for voting the Laws of England may insist
upon, sex shall not be a bar; but a movement which
embraces such various opinions, does not merit the charge
of insincerity, because the arguments used by some of
its supporters differ widely from those brought forward
by others: the wonder might rather be to see them
working so unanimously together as they do, than that
there should be minor differences. The Women's Suffrage party can no more be accused of insincerity on this
account, than can the Liberal Association, because some
of its members advocate manhood suffrage, and some
go no further than household franchise for counties.

No person, probably, has given so largely to charities
as Lady Burdett Coutts. We know of another lady
who has property, which in a man's hands would be
equivalent to seven votes. In view of such examples,
it is natural to women who are Conservative, to plead
the right of property to representation. It is equally
natural for the factory and working women to plead
that representation should be the correlative of taxation.
Admiral Maxse qualifies this last expression as "a

popular formula without any foundation; a mere phrase."
It may be so, but it was a phrase that a century ago,
was strong enough to make England lose her fairest
provinces. He stigmatises as supremely ridiculous,
"those women who mimic Hampden by refusing to pay
taxes and allowing their spoons to be sold." From a
certain point of view, the casting the tea into Boston
harbour was supremely ridiculous, yet eight years
afterwards the armies of Great Britain withdrew from
America.

The lecturer warns us to consider the character and
disposition of "average women who are now all at home
encompassed by a household horizon." If staying at
home be the rule for women, there are many exceptions,
for it is a fact that there are now more than three
millions earning their own subsistence. The theory of
a dependent protected sex if true "once upon a time,"
as the fairy tales say, is certainly not true now. He is
lavish of pity for those ladies who though they may
wish not to vote, will not be *left alone* and "have no
male at hand to intimidate canvassers." This picture
of threatening and bullying canvassers making house-to-
house visitations, evidences a lively imagination in these
humdrum days of the ballot. At the last general election
it is said that only half the electors in some of the
London boroughs voted. Were those who stayed at
home intimidated?

"It is claimed that women have voted well in School
Board elections; I do not know upon what ground this
claim is made; I am disposed to think that the Woman
School Board vote has been a clerical one. Their voting
in municipal elections has not so far been characterised
by much public spirit." Admiral Maxse here quoted a
letter from a friend living in a large town, which showed
that "women had voted Tory in a compact mass and that
they were actuated by the most frivolous considerations."
On what grounds does Admiral Maxse assume that
women who "vote Tory" cannot be actuated by public
spirit? If too, the Woman School Board vote was a
clerical one (though this fact appears a little doubtful),
how does he characterise the large support which the
Church received in both Houses of Parliament during

the discussion of the 25th clause? He quotes Gibbon, that "to a philosophic eye the vices of the clergy are less dangerous than their virtues;" and adds, "what with their doctrine, their virtues, and other accessories, they exercise great power over women." It might be wished that the generality of men would try if by imitating clerical virtues they might not share some of this peculiar influence. He protests against the enfranchisement of a merely Conservative section of women, and demands " as a set off, the simultaneous enfranchisement of the wives of town workmen." Are town workmen so invariably Liberal that the desired leaven of liberality is certain to be found in their wives? Is there not moreover a tone of exclusiveness, not only of sex, but of party in this distinction? If Admiral Maxse, in order to amend the laws, proposes to reconstruct the British system of representation, it follows that any class claiming the franchise in accordance with the present order of things, will be in his eyes inimical to his policy. He does not concede any natural right to vote: "it is all a question of expediency" (for men as for women?), and he quotes minors and foreigners as instances of exclusion on this principle. To our minds it is a question of right that every person shall have during his or her life a chance of self government. A minor can become of age, a foreigner can be naturalised, a pauper may become a man of substance, a criminal may reform, an agricultural labourer (supposing the law unchanged) can emigrate to a town; it is in the possible future of all of these to become a voter—only women have the franchise put out of their reach for life. If we argue the question as one of expediency, we urge that it is expedient that educated, respectable, responsible householders should vote irrespective of sex. Admiral Maxse believes that sex is the one indispensable qualification. His alteration of the law would, we venture to think, be more violent than ours.

Having disposed of the counterfeit Woman's Suffrage, he next considers the true Woman's Suffrage. He does not exactly explain whether this is every woman having a vote, or simply "wives of town workmen." Probably the former, because it implies, in his opinion, that the number of women electors would be equal or superior to men electors. He protests against any claim to political talent in women being based upon the lives of queens and princesses; royal personages are "fictitious" and "ornamental," and we really "know nothing about them." We should have thought that in "the fierce light which beats upon a throne," there was a fair amount of reality about Queen Bess, or Maria Theresa. Women, as a whole, are unfit, he says, to govern—"To vote means to govern, that is to say, theoretically; of course, under our constitution the real power of voting is slight, but the theory is that the voters elect the government, and it is with this object that the vote is claimed, it is a means of governing the nation. And women have no natural capacity for this task. Nature, he continues, appears to place women entirely at the mercy of men. Their independence is an artificial product, it is the outcome of civilization and the growth of sentiment, but we shall err in supposing that there are no natural limits to such independence. We cannot make women the equal of men in male strength, and there are certain male duties which result from this strength. Government must correspond to such strength in some degree. Rebellions occur sometimes under male legislation. People will submit to much vexatious legislation, rather than resort to rebellion, but when great questions are at issue, and there is national excitement, they will not submit to an oppressive law if they consider they are strong enough to resist. The knowledge, or even the suspicion, that such law is enacted by the vote of women, supplementing that of a minority of men, would be sufficient to provoke rebellion."

What sort of argument is this to use at the present time? Is moral force of no value unless backed up by physical force? If so, what does our law mean by disfranchising the exponents of physical force, policemen and soldiers? Are we to go back to the policy of savage times, when might was the only right, to frame our code? A very large proportion of our electors are men past the prime of life; are their claims to consideration to decrease with their strength of sinew? Is a cripple or a deformed man to be deprived of his vote for the same reason? or shall we be told that the law can deal only with generalities, and that sex forms the sole incapacity? On what grounds also does the Admiral assume that the feminine vote would all go one way? Are women apt to be so much more unanimous than men? To assume that women must necessarily be all of the same mind, is to concede far more than we claim; it is conceding that the evils and wrongs that women suffer are so universal and so crushing in their operation, that the whole sex will be banded together against their tyrants. Unanimity in the oppressed can only be obtained by extremity of oppression. Elsewhere he says, "The whole theory of the value of the vote rests upon the supposition that they will oppose male legislation." We look forward to supplementing and helping men, not to opposition.

"Would women," he further asks, "make wise laws if they had equal political power with men?" He believes not, but that they "fail to appreciate indirect causes, and only grasp the actual." If it be true that a tendency to *detail* is observable in many women, it is equally true that many men overlook necessary minutiæ in grasping the *whole* too roughly. Opticians tell us of two sorts of defective sight: that which can only see at a distance and blurs near objects, and that which is of the utmost delicacy near at hand, but can see nothing afar off. A perfect lens combines the good of both. A perfect government will have both manly breadth and womanly completeness of thought.

But Admiral Maxse affirms that "even superior women rarely have sympathy with the struggling principles which determine the life of a nation." What does he mean by this? If he means that political interests, party considerations, and doctrinal subtleties have been generally postponed by women to human sympathies, he may be right. If he means that women, always deprived of a part in the civic and legal life of a nation, have a slender appreciation of the benefits in which they have no share, he may be right too; we should not be surprised if, in process of time, Æsop's fox came honestly to believe that the unattainable grapes were green. "They are not to be counted," he says, "among the active supporters of the National Education League, they did not send us a single half-crown in support of Mr. Mill's Land Tenure Reform scheme. * * * * They care more for persons than for ideas." We emphatically protest against this assertion. In every movement which has sprung up on English soil, in every struggle for freedom, women have given their sympathy and help. Women suffered for American abolition, and whenever and in whatever country martyrs have shed their blood for principle, women have been among those martyrs. Miriam followed Moses to the Promised Land: women stood around the Cross.*

Admiral Maxse pleads that for the sake of "our children and those that come after us" women should not be forced into this position of antagonism. We, too, plead for those same children that they may have the nobler influences which juster laws and purer social life will give them. We believe, as Admiral Maxse owns he does not, in the certainty of progress, in the certainty that as the years go on our freedom will have "broadened slowly down," till another generation shall know neither ignorance nor bondage, neither the obtuseness which cannot see that there is but one law of justice and right for man or woman, nor the impulse to employ the physical force of the strong for the oppression of the weak.

C. A. B.

---

* *One actual experiment is worth a score of theories.*—In Wyoming, where women have had the vote for some years, this was Governor Campbell's testimony to their influence in 1871: "In this territory women have manifested for its highest interests a devotion strong, ardent, and intelligent. They have brought to public affairs a clearness of understanding, and a soundness of judgment, which, considering their exclusion hitherto from practical participation in political agitation and movements, are worthy of the greatest admiration, and above all praise. The conscience of women in all things is more discriminating and sensitive than that of men ; their love of order not spasmodic or sentimental merely, but springing from the heart. All these—the better conscience, the exalted sense of justice, and the abiding love of order—have been made by the enfranchisement of women, to contribute to the good government and well being of our territory." Governor Campbell repeated this opinion with still more emphasis three years later.

Art. II.—CO-OPERATION IN VIENNA.

A NUMBER of ladies have succeeeded in establishing a very flourishing co-operative society in Vienna for the purchase of household stores at wholesale prices, a movement which seems likely to have ulterior results even more important than improved domestic economy. The nature of these may be inferred from the treatment of the movement by the local press, which is certainly very suggestive of the need existing in Austria, as else-where, of enlightened views of the claims and position of women. Having premised that he does not object to the ladies meeting in public because they only do so to further home interests, a writer in the leading Viennese journals lately gave a detailed account of the association, and described its operations in a manner that is very amusing in another sense than that intended. The *naïve* astonishment with which he observes that persons in elaborately-trimmed dresses could actually develop an aptitude for business, could express themselves with ease and fluency, and generally conduct themselves like reasonable human beings, is evidently unaffected, recalling that expressed by Sir Henry James, on finding that ladies "fluttering in ribbons" attempted to answer the arguments of speakers in the House of Commons. Viennese ladies are, indeed, said to be very fond of dress, and may, possibly, devote so much attention to it as to justify their critic in being surprised to find that they had other pursuits, but the fact is that demonstra-tions in the way of trimmings and ribbons are not to be relied upon as evidences of imbecility, since many a woman who has better things to think about, allows herself to be made into a "Jack in the green" by her *modiste* from sheer force of habit. Meantime, the really admirable organization of the Viennese *Hausfrauen Verein* will go far to show that the exercise of the highest administrating faculty on a scale of national im-portance being well within the compass of female capa-city, it is but a poor joke to criticize a combined public effort on the part of women to advance an economical reform, in the same strain as the performance of a com-pany of trained canaries.

The only feminine representative of the plastic art in Vienna, Fräulein Minna Weitmann, died on the 19th of December, of a chest complaint of long standing. This artist, like her father, Joseph Weitmann, who was her master, confined herself to copying flowers and birds in biscuit and marble. Fräulein Weitmann twice received gold medals at art exhibitions, and her attainments were even surpassed by the amiability of her disposition, which endeared her to a large circle of pupils, by whom, and by Viennese society in general, her premature decease, at the age of thirty-six, is deeply regretted.

The Art School at Vienna is an important institution; it was established in 1869. During the six years of its existence, women students have shown their eminent capacity for higher art education. They have followed the same course of study as the men students, and the universal testimony of their teachers has proved them to be equal in industry and power of work, as well as natural gifts, to their men colleagues. Women of various ranks may obtain occupation through this school—a large field being open in various branches of art work—in designing patterns for manufactures, copies for school drawings, &c. A similar government school has been opened for instruction in art needlework—a previously neglected branch of employment.

ART. III.—HIGH PRESSURE.

AN "Anxious Mother" thus writes to the *Times* :—"My unfortunate daughter has lately been in for the Junior Cambridge examination; perhaps I ought rather to say fortunate, as she has survived it. She is still only a child, and yet she has had longer hours than my husband tells me he ever underwent even at Cambridge itself. . . . . In all seven hours and three-quarters, to say nothing of three hours' travelling. I am convinced that a slight re-arrangement of the time-table might make the pressure much less on the unhappy juniors."

This complaint is not by any means a solitary one. Another parent speaking of an examination for schoolmistresses says that the curriculum had been so severe that his daughter was rejected on account of her health having broken down under it. We must not forget that Dr. Clarke in America, and Dr. Maudsley in England based their chief objections to the higher education of girls, upon the early age at which the great mental strain was incurred. The first, at any rate, admitted that if the severe study were postponed till the system had become stronger, its evils would be greatly lessened. Much was said on all sides, and in particular it was pointed out that the ill effects of severe study at an early age were not confined to girls. A petition was lately presented to the School Committee of Boston, signed by more than 200 parents of the 250 boys of the Latin school, by 150 of the leading physicians of the city, and by 65 clergymen, in opposition to the cramming system of the school. Col. Higginson justly observes: " he does not know why the complaint of public school methods should be brought with respect to its effect on girls alone. . . . It would seem that if a system is at fault it should be modified, instead of forcing those who cannot meet undue exactions to avoid them by abandoning their aims." It is the same in England. Last year very serious complaints were made of the physical injury inflicted on the boys by the severe Naval Examinations and Civil Service Examinations: one report stated it was several months before some of the boys recovered their strength. These complaints are too widely spread to be quite ignored. The educational problem of the present is to secure a more thoroughly-instructed, and at the same time a better physically developed race than we have hitherto had. Increased mental force can never be obtained for a nation, though it may for an individual, by the sacrifice of physical strength. A sound body for containing a sound mind is a necessity of our organization. The brain has a certain amount of vital strength to carry on the mental and bodily processes of life. Of what avail will it be to try to increase this strength by sanitary improvements in houses, gymnastics, better clothing, &c., if we con_ tinue to take away more vitality than we add, by a system of early forcing. In former days the problem was solved by requiring only a very low standard of instruction for boys, and a still more miserably insufficient measure for girls. With this we can no longer be content. We demand a higher educational standard alike for girls and boys, but do we not make a mistake in not allowing more time for it? The standard will probably be still further raised each year, and far be it from us to wish to see it lowered, but cannot the strain be spread over a greater number of years?

It appears certain that the amount of study which will be injurious at the age of 15, might be safely undertaken at 18. Is there any satisfactory reason why our junior examinations should not be deferred for two or three years, and the senior examinations take place at 20 or 21? It was very well for a girl to consider her education finished at 18 or 19, when she only learned "Maugnall's Questions" and a superficial smattering of accomplishments; but it is different now that we require (and rightly require) that she shall know grammatically two or three languages, arithmetic, and mathematics, something of science, history, and a long string of etceteras. Is there any need that we should force our children as we do early fruit and vegetables? We much doubt if peas and strawberries are improved in flavour by the process—but do we not run a risk of overstraining the brain energies at a time when the bodily growth requires a large amount of vital strength? We would gladly extend this plea for the boys too. Why should the race of life which every year intensifies in speed, begin so very early. It may be answered that they cannot afford to wait; but at any rate our middle and upper class girls need not be pressed so early into the struggle, that two or three more years might not be allowed them with advantage. Every girl should ride, walk, climb, swim. When will she find the time for this, if by eighteen she must pass examinations which in former days would have been considered difficult for grown men. We would not wish to see the standard of examinations altered one iota—not one language or *ology* taken off—only to see our speed **a** little slackened, convinced as we are that we do not get the best out of our boys and girls by hurrying them on so fast. The finest intellects are often the slowest in coming to maturity, and we cannot be sure that either man or woman will be the fittest to fill any given post, because as boy or girl they may have gone through a system of cramming with most impunity.

Art. IV.—SUPPRESSION OF THE ASSOCIATION POUR L'AMELIORATION DU SORT DES FEMMES.

THIS Association, which our readers may remember to have been established in Paris in 1870, has just been suppressed by the French government, an additional proof—if any were needed—of the ceaseless tyranny and arbitrary interference with private rights to which our neighbours are in the habit of submitting. A circular has been addressed to the Associates by M. Leon Richer, President of the dissolved society, in the following terms:—

It is with deep regret I announce to you that the Society for Improving the Condition of Women, founded in April, 1870, and authorised by the government of that time, has been prohibited by order of M. le Ministre de l'Interieur.

Consequently, our society of intellectual propagandism is dissolved. Our sections for study and work are suppressed. Our quiet meetings in which we endeavoured to discover, apart from all political interests, the best means to improve the standard of education in girls' schools, to raise the wages of workwomen, to combat the incessant increase of prostitution, to suggest a revision of the principal laws which oppress women—all these meetings, in spite of the small number of persons who were present (on an average, ten or twelve), must now cease. Only one last meeting will be allowed, that of the Members of Committee on whom devolves the charge of receiving the accounts for the year 1875.

The Report which will be presented to them, will be printed and forwarded to all our associates.

But if we are forbidden in future to assemble to work together, each one will still be able to carry on *individually*, by annual subscriptions, the propaganda of our ideas of justice and of social reparation. You can pay each year the voluntary contribution you had agreed upon, and we trust none of our former members will refuse us this necessary help. The journal (the *Avenir des Femmes*) remains, and will carry on vigorously the work of reform for which it was established. This is, at present, most important.

Better days will come. A liberal Ministry will restore to us what the present Ministry has taken away, and a new society may then be founded. Let us have patience.

The subscribers who have not yet sent their subscriptions for 1875, are begged to send them immediately, in order that the accounts may be made up, and the report issued.

Let all the supporters of the cause of women remain united. I repeat once more that the journal, which for seven years has endeavoured to elucidate the many questions in which we are interested, will still continue its important work.

Signed, the President of the dissolved Society,

LEON RICHER.

We have not, fortunately, to contend with similar obstacles in England. Committees of ten or twelve persons may gather together to discuss plans for the amelioration of society, without being arbitrarily suppressed. We are sincerely sorry that this useful little society, which promised to do so much valuable and necessary work, should have been dissolved. Let women keep as quietly as they can in their social circle, politics will search out and interfere with them, and, as Madame de Staël once said, " It is natural women should ask why?"

In a letter in the *Avenir des Femmes*, M. Richer adds: "—This society had received from Victor Hugo, some months ago, a public testimony of sympathy, and Garibaldi was an honorary member. M. Buffet likes no societies which are not either Bonapartist or Clerical; if the association had put itself under Ultramontane protection it would not have been suppressed."

The decision of the supreme authority was given verbally, no reason whatever having been assigned. It has naturally caused indignation, and the *Avenir des Femmes* has received a large number of new subscriptions, as a testimony of sympathy towards the suppressed society.

ART. V.—EVENTS OF THE MONTH.

EDUCATION.

Girton College, Cambridge. — Notwithstanding the opening of Newnham Hall, Girton College is too small, the applications for admission far exceeding the accommodation afforded for ladies anxious for university instruction, and it has been resolved to enlarge it so as to accommodate a score more students and to provide two new lecture-rooms. This will cost £6,000. A subscription has been opened for the expenses of the new buildings, and by the date of the publication of the last *Journal* of the Education Union, £1,500 had been already subscribed. For a boys' school sufficient funds would at once be forthcoming; for women's education they are more difficult of attainment, yet still there is fair hope that among the wealthier friends of the good cause, they may be raised without too much delay.

A letter from Isa Craig Knox to the daily papers, called public attention to the present need of subscriptions. In it she says :—

The college was founded in 1869 by the gathering together of some ten or a dozen students in a hired house at Hitchin, from whence, with added numbers, it removed in 1873 to a permanent building at Girton, near Cambridge. This building was erected at a cost of £15,000, the friends of the movement identical with those who laboured to obtain for the country the acknowledged boon of the University local examinations, raising contributions to the amount of £13,000. Accommodation was provided for twenty-one students, with the necessary public and lecture rooms; the latter on a scale which would admit of the future extension of the other portions of the building. Such an extension has already become imperative. The number of students at present in residence is greater than the building was intended to receive, and unless additional accommodation is provided without delay it will be necessary to refuse admission to a number of candidates. Apart from the cost of the buildings, the college is self-supporting, and the friends of wealthy students have already contributed liberally to the building fund; but as it is not intended exclusively for the rich, its founders find that they must appeal to a wider public, and they do so on public grounds. Owing to the much-needed increase of a better class of girls' schools, through the action of the Endowed Schools Commission and other public bodies, the demand for highly trained and competent head mistresses is already greater than the supply, and adequate remuneration is beginning to be offered for their services, and nowhere, more certainly, can such training be received or such competence be tested than at Girton.

There is every guarantee that the work of the college is real. An entrance examination bars the way to the incompetent or trifling, and, through the generous help of members of the University of Cambridge, the high character of the teaching becomes indisputable. The list of lecturers at Girton includes no fewer than eleven names of high academical standing. The examiners in the various examinations for degrees have also given their assistance in testing the work of the students by University standards. The certificates given have thus the value, if not the name, of a University degree, and several of the students have acquitted themselves so as to have deserved honours. Such a certificate is, of course, a passport to the higher educational work, and it is to this work that the bulk of students look forward to devoting themselves. In order not to exclude any who, with the requisite ability and attainments, may be desirous of further advancement, scholarships and exhibitions are being founded in connection with the University local examinations and the entrance examination of the college. * * * * * The proposed addition to the building will cost £6,000, and would then contain rooms for thirty-eight students, the mistress, and two assistant lecturers (ladies), with four lecture-rooms, a small laboratory, dining-hall, prayer-room, reading-room, gymnasium, &c. Contributions may be paid to the Treasurer, Mr. H. R. Tomkinson, 24, Lower Seymour street, London, W.; or to the Girton College account, at the London and County Bank, 21, Lombard street, E.C.; or to Messrs. Mortlock & Co., Cambridge. The Report and other papers containing information may be obtained from Miss Emily Davies, 17, Cunningham place, N.W.

City of London College for Ladies.—The distribution of prizes to the students at this College took place on December 20th at the City Terminus Hotel, Cannon street—Sir Charles Reed in the chair. There was a large attendance of young ladies and their friends. The chairman was accompanied on the platform by Dr. Abbott, head master of the City of London School, the Rev. J. Harris, Miss Berridge, principal of the college, M. Schneider, &c. In opening the proceedings Sir Charles Reed said he supposed most of those present were interested in the girls there, but he believed that all of them, individually and collectively, felt an interest in the great and growing work of female education, and it was that feeling that had brought most of them there on the platform. It might be said to be almost a new thing in England that there should be so deep an interest in the education of women. He was glad to know that the obstacles in the way of women's education were gradually breaking down. They saw it on all hands, and there was no greater evidence of it than in the establishment of colleges like that. He could remember, 20 or 30 years ago, when it would have been thought a preposterous thing to have a college for girls. He did not know why it should have been so, for he found from his own experience that girls were as ready and as laborious as boys. In learning, and in teaching, young women achieved as satisfactory results as men did. He was speaking of the teachers in the infant schools, the primary schools, and the secondary middle-class schools. The question had still to be considered whether, in higher training, women would hold their own with men. He believed they would, and he should be quite prepared to commit the task of higher instruction to the hands of women, after his experience in America, where the teachers in the schools were to a large extent women of great training and of great courage, and whose influence among young men was far more remarkable than they in England could have supposed. After a few words of encouragement to those who had not won prizes, the chairman called upon the Rev. J. Harris to read the examiners' report, which was of a generally satisfactory character. The prizes were then delivered by Sir Charles Reed.

LADIES' COLLEGIATE SCHOOL, BELFAST.

On December 22nd a large and influential meeting was held in the lecture hall of this institution on the occasion of the closing lecture before the Christmas recess. The subject of the lecture was Tennyson's "In Memoriam." The chair was taken by David Taylor, Esq., J.P. The Rev. S. Andrews said, in commencing the lecture, some might think an apology needed for bringing such a subject before such an audience; but to the objection that it is difficult we at once reply that the minds of the young ladies in this institution are accustomed to be exercised on difficult subjects. Whatever may be the case elsewhere, the spirit of the school does not allow young people to be ashamed of putting forth in study their utmost mental energies. He then gave a full analysis of the poem.

Rev. Dr. Bryce, in moving a vote of thanks to the chairman, said he was particularly gratified to find a

B

gentleman of Mr. Taylor's high practical wisdom sanctioning by his presence an undertaking which required not only qualities of head, but qualities of heart—in which Mrs. Byers had manifested an enthusiasm as well as intellect. Dr. Bryce confessed he had a fellow-feeling in the matter—it had been the dream of his life to promote the higher education of women; and, though his arguments had met with some ridicule, he was consoled to find a practical triumph for them in the result of Mrs. Byers's noble and successful efforts. He (Dr. Bryce) had much pleasure in testifying to the high character of the institution.—*Northern Whig.*

LADIES' CLASSES AT UNIVERSITY COLLEGE, LONDON.

The Ladies' Classes at University College begin on Monday, the 17th inst., the second term of their eighth session. There was a slight decline in the number of students for the session 1874-5, but the first term of the session 1875-76 showed a considerable advance beyond the highest success hitherto attained. In the Michaelmas term, 1874-75, the whole number of individual students was 199; in the Michaelmas term, 1875-76, just elapsed, the number of individual students was 265. The whole number of tickets taken in Michaelmas term 1874-75, was 257; in the same term 1875-76, it was 367. The ladies' classes, which are all held by the professors and lecturers at University College, in their class-rooms, are now so familiar a part of the work done in Gower-street, that those who attend them find no reason whatever to feel out of place. This labour has been sustained now for seven years as an experiment, growing in importance, permitted and assisted by the council, but not yet formally recognised as part of the college work. Every year the doors are opened to women, and they are invited to many studies; but they do not always take all that is offered. Last year there was a deficiency of entries to the classes of Mathematics and Latin. This year there is a class of Mathematics, there are three Latin classes, and there is a class of Greek. Every subject taught in the Michaelmas term, 1874-75, was taught in the Michaelmas term, 1875-76. In two subjects there was indeed a change in each from two classes to one, but the additional work taken by this year's students raised the whole number of classes from nine to fifteen. Of the 265 individual students who attended these classes in the term just closed, 3 were attending 5 classes each, 2 were attending 4 classes each, 10 were attending 3 classes each, 63 were attending 2 classes each, 187 were attending one class each. The work that has advanced thus far owes what success it has attained to the quiet endeavour simply to meet such demand for a higher education as is found really to exist in London among ladies whose schooltime is over. The educational resources of a London college, attended by more than 900 regular students, apart from the six or seven hundred boys in the school associated with it, are being made available for the higher education of women, who may take, of all that belongs to their general culture, as much or as little as they are themselves really disposed to take. There are examinations for those who wish to be examined, and certificates to be earned by those who wish to earn them. There are courses of eighteen lectures and there are courses of fifty lectures. As to subjects, as to length of courses, as to examinations, in all that belongs to the liberal education there is a supply offered from year to year which more than meets the present demand, and is apt for expansion as demands increase. That some hundreds of ladies are studying at University College session after session is, no doubt, good evidence of a step in civilisation that has been made within the last ten years; but, so far as this experiment is concerned, the women of London have not yet won all that they can win by simply entering at all the doors that are thrown open to them and taking all they can get. The subjects now being taught are the languages and literatures of England, France, Germany, and Italy; Latin in elementary and more advanced classes; Greek, Mathematics, Logic, Physiology, and Hygiene: also English Constitutional History, to which will be added in the next term a course of General English History, and perhaps a course of Physics. Beside these courses, which are for ladies only, four classes in the college (those of Jurisprudence, Roman Law, Political Economy,

and Geology) admit ladies as regular students, and all
teaching in the Fine Art department is open to students
of both sexes.

REPORT OF THE COLLEGE FOR WORKING WOMEN.

We have received the first Annual Report of the
College for Working Women, 5, Fitzroy Street, Fitzroy
Square, and the account it gives of the year's work is
exceedingly satisfactory. In recalling the circumstances
connected with the origin of the Institution it says, that
when a majority of the Council of the Working Women's
College in Queen's Square, decided in January, 1874, to
throw open that College to men as well as women, and
this resolution was carried into effect in the following
October; some members of the minority who did not
concur in this change, were unwilling to express any
opinion on the subject of mixed education, but they saw
with regret that the only institution in London, devoted
exclusively to the improvement and culture of working
women was about to be closed to many of them. They
resolved, therefore, " to continue to offer to women who
are employed in labour for many hours in the day, and
often all the year round, an opportunity of gaining instruction and education when the day's work is over;
and to give them the stimulus and interest which are
to be found in social life, intellectual pursuits, and rational entertainment." They appealed for help "to all
those who are interested in the culture of women, and
who desire to make their lives brighter and better, not
only by the higher instruction, but the higher moral
development which it would be their aim to promote."
This appeal met with a warm response, and in October,
1874, the College for Working Women, 5, Fitzroy-street,
was ready for the reception of students. 431 students
attended the College during the four terms of the past
year; of these 153 are dressmakers and needlewomen,
93 carry on work at home, and the remainder are all, as
the name of the College announces, women engaged in
some profession or trade, gilders, hairdressers, machinists,
&c. A lending library was opened last January; it is
at present small, and donations of books will be very
acceptable. We are glad to see that physiology forms
part of the course. There was a slight falling off of

students after the second term, but the hours during which women are employed in the London season, are so long that a considerable number will at all times be compelled to discontinue their attendance at the classes during the third and fourth terms of the session; and diminished numbers during these terms prove that those who come to the College are really the Working Women for whom it is intended. There is great need of funds to carry on the College successfully, although the expenses of starting have been all covered. The hon. secretaries for the College are Mrs. Lionel Lucas, 11, Westbourne Terrace, W., and Miss Martin, 22, Regent's Park-terrace, N.W. D. Storrer is the chairman of the Committee.

Birkbeck Literary and Scientific Institution.—The winter term of this institution will commence on Monday next. The classes, which are open to both ladies and gentlemen, embrace languages, mathematics, natural, applied, and mental science, law, literature, history, drawing, painting, music, &c. In addition to the prizes which have been already announced, the Lord Chief Justice of England has kindly offered an English essay prize of 20 guineas, and Lord Francis Hervey, M.P., has intimated his intention of giving prizes of the value of £5 each for English literature and architectural design.

We have been informed that Mrs. Bligh Sinclair, (widow of Colonel Robert Bligh Sinclair, Adjutant-General of Nova Scotian Militia, and formerly of Her Majesty's 42nd Royal Highlanders,) 8, Royal Crescent, Notting Hill, receives young ladies as inmates of her house to educate with her own daughters. Under the charge of a governess they will attend the classes of the Notting Hill and Bayswater High Schools, Norland Square.

NATIONAL UNION FOR IMPROVING THE EDUCATION OF WOMEN.

Lectures to Teachers.—The course of lectures to teachers on the Method of teaching Arithmetic by Mr. Sonnenschein's scheme, begun on November 16th at the Rooms of the Society of Arts, has been very well attended. The following courses have been arranged:—

Three lectures on the Method of teaching English, by J. G. Fitch, Esq., M.A., to begin January 25th.

Three lectures on the Method of teaching Modern Languages, by A. H. Keane, Esq., to begin Feb. 15th.

Three lectures on the Method of teaching Physical Geography, by A. Sonnenschein, Esq., to begin March 7th.

To be followed by others. These lectures will be given on Tuesday evenings at 6 p.m. in Exeter Hall. The fees for each course will be for teachers 2s. 6d., non-teachers 5s. Tickets can be obtained from the Secretary of the Women's Education Union, 112, Brompton Road, S.W. These lectures are open to both sexes.

Scholarships.—The Women's Education Union again offers five scholarships of £25 each, to be awarded at the Local Examinations of 1876, by the following learned bodies:—The University of Cambridge. The University of Oxford. The University of Edinburgh. The University of Dublin. Queen's University of Ireland.

Instruction in Shorthand.—A class for instruction in shorthand will be held at the Rooms of the Women's Educational Union early in the new year. It will meet on one evening in each week, and will be taught by Mr. J. B. Rundell, who holds a certificate of efficiency from the London Shorthand Writers' Association.

THE PHARMACEUTICAL SOCIETY OF IRELAND.

We have received, by the kindness of a friend, the following full report of the proceedings of the Pharmaceutical Society of Ireland, on the occasion when the admission of women was under discussion:—

The motion of Professor Tichborne to admit women to the licence of the Irish Pharmaceutical Society on the same terms as other students, came on for discussion on the 1st of December.

Dr. Tichborne said he would not take up the time of the meeting by a long speech, as the merits of the question were very self-evident, and he reserved himself for any objections that might be raised. He had only heard at present of two objections, and they were soon disposed of.

It had been stated that it was too soon to introduce women into pharmacy, yet such an objection is about as reasonable as what is sometimes understood as a woman's reason.

It is either right or wrong to qualify women to act as pharmacians; if wrong, better not qualify them at all, but if it were right, it were better that it be done quickly.

A palpable reason for doing it, was that we were now about to inaugurate a change in the conduct of the pharmacy of this country, and, therefore, why not make that change perfect as far as we could, and not be re-arranging the matter in a year or so. The second objection had been conveyed to the speaker in the following manner. It had been said that there were a great number of our sons who could not get situations, and that the demand was in excess of the supply. Now it would generally be found that no good man had ever any difficulty in getting employment; that it was the quality that was deficient, not the quantity that was in excess; every employer was crying out that he could not get efficient assistance. The objection was that if there were men who could not get employment, why provide for the women? Now, we find that in this country there are 131,764 more women than there are men, and that if every man in the country was married, there would still be this superfluous community to provide for. These women must be a burthen to either brothers or fathers; in fact, it was a kind of genteel pauperism, hidden, perhaps, but none the less felt. When a woman is married, she had her part of the social partnership to fulfil; when she is not married, if she had no vocation, she must live upon some one. It was a most superficial idea to imagine that the agitation amongst females in Great Britain and Ireland was in any way connected with such twaddle as "Bloomerism" or "Women's Rights." It was merely the result of a pressure felt by the middle classes, a pressure produced by an advance in the cost of living.

Therefore, Professor Tichborne maintained that it was the duty of that council to open pharmacy to women, if it was a legitimate employment for them. He was strongly of opinion that it was an employment just suited and in keeping with their proverbial neatness. There was no demand for any physical exertion or great mental strain, and such an occupation was surely more suited to them than surgery. He, the speaker, proposed no revolution; his contemplated change provided that women should be properly educated for the calling—how they will get that education is their own business—so that they satisfy the council that they have acquired the necessary knowledge; and the result of my motion, said Professor Tichborne, is that at the end of a year's time it is quite immaterial whether the candidate that comes forward be a man or a woman.

Dr. Frazer spoke at some length against the admission of women. He said that the council had all heard of the boy who cried for the moon. If the women got pharmacy, they would only want something more— to be physicians next. The women had plenty of good pursuits open to them, and yet they had not taken advantage of them. Watchmaking, for instance, was just suited to them, why did they (the women) not take advantage of it? &c., &c. He proposed, as an amendment, that the consideration of the admission of women be postponed to that day six months.

Dr. Owens (the Lord Mayor elect) had much pleasure in seconding Dr. Frazer's amendment, although he must confess he could not agree with a word he had said; he, however, objected to see the women admitted to pharmacy at present.

Sir Dominic Corrigan, in a long speech, advocated the admission of women, and said that from personal examination into the question, he had found that the dispensing in some of the large foreign hospitals was in the hands of women, and that it was conducted in the most satisfactory manner.

Dr. Tichborne was about to reply, when he was met with a request to divide, as the hour was late, and as no argument had been brought forward against his motion.

Dr. Frazer said that as he saw the feeling of the meeting was against him, with the consent of his seconder, he withdrew his amendment.

The original motion was then put and carried unanimously.

ENGLISH PHARMACEUTICAL SOCIETY.

At the Major Examination of the Pharmaceutical Society in December, Miss Isabella G. Clarke, having passed the examination satisfactorily, was admitted a pharmaceutical chemist. There are several ladies on the register as "chemists and druggists," but this is the first instance in Great Britain in which a lady has passed the Major Examination as a pharmaceutical chemist.

The Board of Managers of the Queen's Hospital, Birmingham, have decided to admit female Medical students to the clinical lectures, and to permit them to enjoy all the privileges of male students.

REPORT OF THE VIGILANCE ASSOCIATION.

The fifth annual report of the Vigilance Association has been issued. It gives an account of a fair amount of work done during the year. The following papers have been published by the Association during the year:—

1. Fourth Annual Report.
2. Report of Fourth Annual Meeting, 1874.
3. Reprint of Mrs. Butler's Speech at Fourth Annual Meeting.
4. Reprint of Mr. Russell Carpenter's Speech at ditto.
5, 6, 7. Papers on the Punishment of the Lash.
8. How Soldiers are encouraged to neglect their Duties as Husbands and Fathers (Report of Debate on the Mutiny Bill).
9. Reprint of Article on the Lash from the *Manchester Examiner*, of June 16, 1875.
10. Circular on the Appointment of a Royal Commission on the Factory Acts.
11. Suggested Questions to be asked of Witnesses giving Evidence before the Royal Commission on the Factory and Workshops Acts.
12. Reprint of Mr. P. A. Taylor's Speech on Crime and Punishment in the Navy.

The Report commences with recording the rejection by the House of Commons of Mr. P. A. Taylor's proposed amendment of the Mutiny Bill. The object of these amendments was to render it impossible for a soldier to evade his just liabilities for the maintenance of his wife and children. The period allowed for consideration of the Bill, and also of the Marine Mutiny Bill, was even shorter than it has been in previous years. Mr. Taylor then moved the two amendments on Clause 107, of which he had given notice. The first was to leave out of the following Clause the word "may" (given in italics), and to insert the word "shall."

"When any order is made under the Acts relating to the relief of the poor, or under the Bastardy Acts, on a soldier for the maintenance of his wife or children, or for the maintenance of any such bastard child as aforesaid, or of any such persons, a copy of such order shall be left at the office of one of Her Majesty's principal Secretaries of State, and the said Secretary of State *may* withhold a portion not exceeding sixpence of the daily pay of a non-commissioned officer who is not below the rank of sergeant, and not exceeding threepence of the daily pay of any other soldier, and allot the sum so withheld in liquidation of the sum adjudged to be paid by such order."

This was negatived by 138 votes to 56. The next amendment was also negatived by 122 votes to 48.

The "Offences against the Person" Bill, introduced by Mr. Charley, M.P. for Salford, passed into law last session, but the Committee regret to say that its value has been diminished by the alteration of the clause affording protection to a girl of fourteen years of age, to *thirteen.* Whilst deeply regretting the rejection of the proposal to extend protection to girls up to fourteen years of age, the Committee cannot but acknowledge that the extension of protection for one more year is an important advance, especially as it renders still more apparent the absurdity of the law which permits the marriage of a girl of twelve years of age. The Committee feel that Mr. Charley is entitled to the thanks of this Association for his indefatigable exertions on behalf of the measure, and that thanks are also due to Lord Hampton, who took charge of the Bill in the House of Lords, and to Lord Lyttelton. The Bill became law on August 13th.

With regard to the punishment of the lash, the Committee resolved to oppose any measure for extending the punishment of flogging, and when the Home Secretary's Bill was introduced in May, the Association prepared a petition against it. The Bill was brought up for second Reading on June 14th, when Mr. P. A. Taylor in an exhaustive speech moved its rejection. The debate was adjourned. Subsequently the Government withdrew the Bill, Mr. Cross expressing the satisfaction he felt at the unwillingness he perceived in the House to recur to such punishments without clearly proved necessity, and distinctly declining to pledge himself to bring in such a Bill next session.

On the appointment, in March, of a Royal Commission "for inquiring into the operation of the Factory and Workshops Acts, with a view to their consolidation and amendment," the Committee determined to make vigorous efforts to obtain evidence of some of the women whose industry is affected by these Acts, and who had hitherto been afforded no opportunities of stating their opinions and wishes upon such legislation. A member of the Committee, Mrs. E. M. King, kindly consented to visit several of the principal centres of industry shortly before, or during the time of, the sitting of the Commission in those places. The result of Mrs. King's work was that important evidence was given by women employed in factories and workshops in Birmingham, Leicester, Nottingham, Sheffield, and Manchester. Further evidence has been obtained or promised from Belfast, Stroud, Luton, Dunstable (where the Workshops Acts press upon the straw-hat and bonnet workers with especial hardship), and other places. The Committee did not in any way attempt to influence the opinions of the witnesses, their main object being to establish the right of women to be heard upon the question of legislation so closely affecting their interests. Yet the general feeling expressed by the women who gave evidence before the Commission was against the Acts and their extension.

Several of the witnesses protested strongly against any special legislation with regard to the industry of married women, such as has from time to time been proposed. The Committee desire to direct attention to the notice given in the House of Commons on the 11th of August by Dr. Lush,—that he will introduce early next Session a Bill to amend the Factories' Act, 1874, "so far as relates to the employment of women and young persons after recent childbirth." For the reasons fully given in their Reports of 1873 and 1874, this Bill will meet with most strenuous opposition from the Vigilance Committee.

WOMEN'S TRADES UNIONS.

Under the auspices of the Women's Protective and Provident League, a meeting was held on December 2nd in the schoolroom, Bishopsgate churchyard, for the purpose of explaining the objects and advantages of Working Women's Unions. Two resolutions in favour of constituting such unions were unanimously adopted. The chairman, the Rev. William Rogers, promised to use his local influence in support of the movement, and offered the free use of the schoolroom for further meetings. The speeches delivered were generally to the point, brief, and of a practical character. An employer of labour on a large scale rose to support some remarks made by Mr. Adolphe Smith, to the effect that a union among women was necessary, so as to afford willing and kind masters a pretext for taking the initiative in raising the wages. However deeply they may deplore the low rate paid for labour, and especially female labour, no one tradesman can alone pay a higher scale unless, at least, the majority of his competitors consent to similar terms; and a union on the part of the workers is about the only way, it was urged, of wringing this concession from the various trades for which women work.

The *Labour News* says that a significant illustration of the need of a strong body to watch the interests of our women workers was afforded by the sudden and, as it turns out, mistaken reduction of wages lately in a large London house, an appeal to the magistrate having been found necessary before the rights of the women were recognized. It was almost equally significant for us to learn that for the fourteen machines vacated by the complaining parties, no less than 200 candidates for work immediately made application to the employers. "Elsewhere," it says, "much has to be done before our women workers have proper security afforded them in the investment of their too often scanty earnings.

" The extension of the new National Penny Bank with its great facilities for small deposits, ought to prove a great boon to women, quite as much as to men, and as the facilities for withdrawal are greater than in connection with the Post Office Savings' Bank, its popularity will depend almost entirely on the amount of publicity which is given to it."

We have already announced that measures are being taken for the establishment of a women's trades union at Sheffield, to confederate all the women employed in the various branches of the Sheffield trades—there are many thousands of them—in union. A meeting, with the same object, has also been held in Rochdale.

THE NATIONAL REFORM UNION.
CONFERENCE IN MANCHESTER.

A conference of members and friends of the National Reform Union was held in the Free Trade Hall, Manchester, on December 15th. The delegates appointed by the various Liberal Associations to attend the proceedings numbered some hundreds, and represented 173 associations in 128 towns. Mr. J. Slagg, chairman of the executive committee, presided. Among the subjects of discussion was the extension of the Suffrage and Redistribution of Seats.

Hon. E. Lyulph Stanley moved—" That this conference is of opinion that the National Reform Union should continue to agitate in favour of the reform of the representative system, by the extension of household suffrage to the counties and the equalisation of electoral power."

The resolution was supported by various speakers, and amendments were proposed, all of which, save one, were rejected. The successful amendment was moved by Miss Sturge, who, with Mrs. Ashford, appeared as a delegate from the Women's Liberal Association, Birmingham.

Miss Sturge, who spoke from a form in the area of the hall, said she wished clearly to know whether the words of the resolution were understood to include women householders. (" Hear, hear," laughter, and cheers.) Whether she as a delegate would be able to vote for the resolution depended upon the reply to that question. If she did not get an answer to the question she would move an amendment.

The Chairman : " I think the meeting will understand that the motion before us embraces exactly what it says, and anything that is not excluded from it is a matter for subsequent discussion and subsequent determination. It is quite impossible within the scope of these deliberations to include everything that the Liberal party may have to consider. We are met to determine those points on which we have the largest amount of agreement, otherwise, I think it will be impossible to proceed at all. I can assure Miss Sturge that at any rate her idea of the subject of household suffrage is clearly not excluded by the words of the resolution.

Miss Sturge : I move that for the words, "to the counties," the words "to all householders" be substituted.

The Rev. Lloyd Jones (Warrington) seconded the amendment which was submitted to the meeting and carried by a large majority.

In the evening a public meeting, under the presidency of Mr. Jacob Bright, was held in the Free Trade Hall. Mr. W. S. Caine, of Liverpool, moved the first resolution. In his speech, he said he was glad that Miss Sturge had introduced in the three words which she had added to the resolution the principle of granting the vote to all householders, male and female, and he was glad that the Conference had adopted the amendment unanimously.

After a vote of thanks to Mr. Jacob Bright, Miss Sturge, of Birmingham, said :—It was because she felt that she represented to some extent the women of England—(cheers), the women of England whose sympathies would be with them more largely still if they did not treat them too Conservatively. (Laughter.) It was an old saying and a true one that " as they sowed, so they must reap." Mr. Jacob Bright had done much to endear the cause of Liberalism to the women of England. (Cheers.) The National Reform Union had added that day to that debt of gratitude. She was proud to say that the Liberal Association of her native town three years ago adopted the same principle by a resolution moved by Mr. Joseph Chamberlain—now their worthy mayor. (Cheers.) Their Liberal Association had failed to carry it. It was an unsettled question, and she stood before them, like Mr. Joseph Arch, one of a highly deserving, yet unenfranchised class. (Laughter and renewed cheering.) Trust women with political power, and she could assure them they would become trustworthy. Distrust them, and what could they expect? Lord Hartington remarked the other day that whereas the Parliamentary elections had gone in a Conservative manner, they would find that generally, especially of late, the municipal elections had gone in favour of the Liberals. (Hear, hear.) She asked them to remark that in the Parliamentary elections women had no part; in the municipal elections they had. (Laughter and cheers.) There was to-day a stronger feeling in favour of religious equality, which must of necessity include women. By priestcraft she understood that profane assumption whereby one mortal would presume to step between another mortal and his or her God. So long as men assumed that they knew better than women what was right than women knew for themselves we must have priestcraft. (Laughter and cheers.) Sympathising with all the proceedings that day she felt that she would class them all under a simpler and less wordy heading than some gentlemen before her. She would have said that the grand object for which they had met and were likely so soon to proceed in the path of progress was the disestablishment of mancraft. (Laughter.) Sometimes, when she could not exactly find words to express her meaning, she was obliged to compose them herself. Therefore, perhaps, they would excuse the very inferior poetry of the lines—

> Disestablish the Church and Dissent cannot gain,
> If the priestcraft of man over women remain ;
> Disestablish all mancraft, and then we shall see
> The people in England both noble and free.

(Cheers.) She did not ask that women should be a law unto men any more than men unto women. She longed that they might both seek after a higher law, and in that unity of purpose there would be a better, a truer, a holier harmony than any we at present enjoyed. (Cheers.)

The resolution was passed with acclamation.—*Abridged from the Manchester Examiner.*

It is impossible to exaggerate the importance of the action thus taken by the National Reform Union in recognising the principle of the right of women citizens to vote in the election of members of Parliament. The *Women's Suffrage Journal* justly characterises it as a "signal step in the political progress of the question." It says :—

The significance of this resolution may be estimated from the fact that the Conference consisted of several hundred delegates representing 173 Liberal Associations in 128 towns, and this great representative body found it impossible to resist the logic of the claim of women citizens, householders, and ratepayers, for the electoral privileges which the household and ratepayer's qualification confers on men. The Women's Suffrage Associations, as such, were, of course, not represented at the Conference. They exist for the sole object of obtaining for women who are otherwise legally qualified, the right of voting in the election of Members of Parliament. Their platform is not a party one, and they could not appear at any gathering convened for party purposes. But though the Women's Suffrage Societies are of no party, their principle is one which commends itself to both parties. It recognises the necessity for the further enfranchisement of the people, and is therefore Liberal. But it seeks this extension of enfranchisement strictly on the ancient lines of the Constitution, and is therefore Conservative.

SUFFRAGE.

The meeting of Parliament is fixed for February the 8th, and Mr. Forsyth proposes to re-introduce the Women's Disabilities Removal Bill at the earliest possible opportunity.

A public meeting was held at Malton, Yorkshire, on Dec. 17th, the Hon. C. W. Wentworth Fitzwilliam, M.P. for the borough, occupied the chair. In opening the proceedings, the chairman said he must not be supposed to commit himself to the principles of the measure, but he would give the subject most careful consideration. Miss Beedy and Miss Becker appeared as a deputation on behalf of the society, and the usual resolutions were put and carried by a large majority.

A meeting was held in Lambeth Baths on January 11th, the Rev. G. M. Murphy presiding. The meeting was addressed by Mr. Hopwood, Q.C., M.P., Mr. Chesson, Miss Beedy, and others.

Meetings are announced in support of Mr. Forsyth's Bill, at Evesham, on January 19th. The Worshipful the Mayor (Alfred Espley, Esq.), the Rev. W. De Bentley, Joseph Masters, Esq., J. Colston, Esq., Herbert New, Esq., and others, have promised to attend.

DUBLIN.—A meeting will be held on January 20th, in Dublin. Miss Tod and Miss Becker will attend as a deputation from the National Society for Women's Suffrage. Further particulars in future announcements.

BELFAST.—The Fourth Annual Meeting of the North of Ireland branch of the National Society for Women's Suffrage will be held in the Clarence Place Hall, Belfast, on Monday, January 17th. at eight o'clock. The Mayor of Belfast will preside. M. R. Dalway, Esq., M.P., Thomas Dickson, Esq., M.P., James Sharman Crawford, Esq., M.P., and other friends are expected to be present.

BRITISH AND CONTINENTAL ASSOCIATION FOR ABOLISHING STATE-REGULATED VICE.

It was announced at a meeting in Liverpool of the Executive Committee of the British and Continental Federation for the Abolition of State-regulated Vice, that the first General International Congress of the Federation would be held at Geneva in 1877, immediately after the meeting of the Medical Congress there.

Many Swiss ladies have taken up this subject earnestly. In Vevey they propose purchasing a building, formerly a hospital, and establishing in it a complete home for women and young girls. Madame Mouriet is the soul of this undertaking, but it also depends largely upon Madame Couvren. A committee of ladies at Lausanne announce the opening of the *Secours*, or Home for young girls for that city. Another Committee of ladies has been formed at Locle; the President is Madame Esther Richard-Houriet, wife of Mr. Ferdinand Richard, watch manufacturer and deputy to the Grand Council; she is possessed of great energy, and strong practical sense.

C

In Geneva about 200 ladies of different classes of society assembled in the smaller Hall of the Reformation at the invitation of the Inter-cantonal Committee of Geneva. The meeting was opened with prayer by M. Frank Coulin, national pastor, one of the most eloquent preachers of Switzerland; he afterwards read the address of the ladies of Great Britain. M. Aimé Humbert then read the proposed rules for the "Home" at Geneva, which had been drawn up by the Provisional Committee, Mesdames de Gingins, Coulin, and Cellerier, and explained the recent proceedings and work of the Federation upon the Continent, and the special aim of the meeting, which was to elect a Definitive Committee. About forty ladies took part in the voting. Twelve ladies were nominated to form the Committee; Mdme. de Gingins, Mdme. Poulin, Mdme. d'Espine, Mdlle. Coulin, Mdme. Lenoir, Mdme. T. Coulin, Mdme. Filliol, Mdme. Hyacinthe - Loyson, Mdme. Tophel, Mdme. Julliard, Mdme. Ador and Mdlle. Cellerier. A special Committee for the "Home" will also be nominated.

In Italy the ladies are also working well; among the Milanese ladies special mention is made of Mesdames Ravizza, Pouti, and Venegoni; the latter has sought relief from terrible domestic affliction, in the effort to benefit her fellow-creatures. A stirring appeal has been addressed by Signora Beccari to her country-women in the pages of *La Donna* (Venice), and it has met with a ready and hearty response. This appeal of the editor of *La Donna* has called forth corresponding articles in the pages of other Journals, by Malvina Frank, Georgina Saffi, Madame Lo Sko, and other ladies.

EMPLOYMENT.

The late Employees in Tait's Factory, Limerick.—The *Irishman* of 11th December has the following:—"Provision is about being made for a large number of young women lately employed in the Army Clothing Factory of Sir Peter Tait, the closing of which was notified a short time since. The Messrs. Gardiner and Co., army clothiers, of London, who have lately entered into several large contracts, are making arrangements to take over 200 of Sir Peter Tait's hands to the metropolis.

In connection with this subject there was a meeting of Roman Catholic clergymen in the Northumberland buildings, Cecil-street, to take steps to provide suitable residences for the young women on reaching London, and also to provide for urgent cases arising out of the closing of the factory. But a brighter prospect seems clearing up for the young women nearer home. The eminent firm of Messrs. Tillie & Henderson, shirt, stay, and underclothing manufacturers, Londonderry, advertise for 100 hands, to whom constant employment and good wages will be given. There is a general feeling here that there is now an excellent opportunity for some of the Derry shirt factories to open a branch here, where they would at once secure the services of good workers at reasonably low rates."

The shameful payment doled out to girls who work for wholesale shops was made apparent lately, by a so-called respectable firm (Messrs. Frederick and Charles Bliss) having justified before a magistrate the offering of twopence halfpenny for embroidering a petticoat skirt! The following letter appeared in the *City Press*, Dec. 18th:—

Employer and Employed.—To the Editor of the *City Press.*—Sir, —Will you grant me a small space in your columns to correct some misstatements in reference to the above case at Guildhall, wherein my employer stated the mistake was mine? Truthfully I assert that all work was given out by me, the prices I copied from a written list kept in my room, and that Mr. F. Bliss agreed from the first that the price for the skirt in dispute should be 4½d., and which has been paid by them for five weeks, allowing 1½d. for deep embroidery and ¾d. for curling; there were two rows of each pattern. I can truly say I never received any intimation to alter the prices from any of the firm, and I have nothing whatever to do with the paying of the young women; there is a clerk kept. I must add that I have faithfully discharged my duties as forewoman for over twelvemonths. The number of hands returning to their machines was only five. I consider it an injustice that I was not called to give my evidence, having been suddenly dismissed for an error that was not mine.—I am, &c., F. Robinson, late forewoman to Messrs Bliss Brothers, Aldersgate-street.

Another instance of the miserable salaries given to women, and the indifference with which they are still further reduced is afforded by the guardians of the North Dublin Union. On December 15th, Mr. Thorpe moved "that the workhouse teachers should receive the results fees awarded by the Commissioners of Education, viz:—Male department, £40 14s. 6d., of which £20 7s. 4d. should be given to Mr. Griffiths; £10 3s. 7d., to Mr. Hetherington, and £10 3s. 7d. to Mr. Mahon. Female department, £19 15s. 3d., of which £9 7s. 7d. should be given to Mrs. Allen; £4 18s. 10d. to Miss Keogh; £2 12s. to Miss Giltrap, and £2 17s. 8d. to Miss Jenkins. Infant department, £12 3s. to Miss Sherlock." This pittance seems wretched enough, but it was to be still further reduced, as one guardian moved and another seconded that the amount of female salaries should be reduced by one fourth. It was subsequently proposed that the matter should be referred to a Committee to "see if a more equable distribution might not be made among the teachers;" but this was negatived and the resolution agreed to unanimously. One fourth taken off at once! but the Dublin paper dismisses it in a jaunty little paragraph.

MAINTENANCE OF WIVES.

This question lately received elucidation by the magistrates at Aldershot, as reported in a London paper:—

"At Aldershot, before the magistrates, Amy, the wife of an Officer of the Artillery, addressed the magistrates as follows:—Will you have the goodness to favour me with your advice under the following circumstances, as I am too poor to go to a lawyer? I am the wife of Major Ward-Ashton, Royal Artillery, now stationed at the permanent barracks, and to whose battery the Prince Imperial of France was attached during the late summer drills. I am unable to live with my husband, owing to his cruel treatment. I have been married to him ten years, and during the whole of that time have only received from him £150, notwithstanding that he is the possessor of £7,000 a year, and the owner of Gorstage Hall, Chester. Owing to the difficulties in which he has placed me, my own property is so nearly mortgaged that I am unable to pay the interest on the mortgages, and I have only £20 a year to live on. During the past five years had it not been for my mother's friends I should have often wanted the common necessaries of life. I owe Dr. Greenhalgh, of Grosvenor-street, £300, which my husband refuses to pay, and another large sum to one of the Queen's surgeons. I have placed this matter several times before the authorities at the Horse Guards, and the late Colonel Middleton, D. A. G., for artillery, who was most kind, and did all he could for me, but I could obtain no amelioration of my position, as my husband's conduct is not considered a *military offence.* The small debts I incurred for the common necessaries of life he refuses to pay, thereby subjecting me to the most cowardly abuse and annoyance; and to strangers he denies that I am his wife. During the last interview I had with him some five years ago, he offered to provide me with a home if I consented to receive his German mistress as a friend. I have, at least, a dozen penitential letters, in which he confesses that he has cruelly treated me, and that his remorse will cease only with his death. Yet he has done nothing for me.

"The Chairman: We can do nothing for you unless you go to the Union. Can you not engage a solicitor?

"Applicant: I cannot; I am too poor. I do not know to whom I should apply for advice. I have not committed myself in any way, and he is bound to support me. He refuses to do so unless I consent to live in the same house as his mistress, which I never shall. If I take out a summons, do you think I can compel him to support me?

"Major Birch: We do not think you can.

"The Chairman: We could do nothing without incurring considerable expense. It is a hard case. We are sorry that we can do nothing for you.

"Applicant: Then I must try some other course. I am much obliged to your worships.

"Applicant, who was accompanied by her mother, then withdrew."
—*Women's Suffrage Journal.*

MISCELLANEOUS.

Steps are being taken in Leeds towards the establishment of a training institution for nurses.

Mainly through the instrumentality of two ladies in Beccles, a working men's club has been established, which, judging from the interest taken in it by those on whose behalf it has been started, bids fair to be a success.

Instructors in Cooking.—Schools of cookery are being established in Warwickshire. Mr. J. C. Buckmaster lately lectured at Warwick on the subject. We understand that good appointments for ladies as instructors and superintendents in connection with these schools are springing up.

A Ladies' Debating Club is now holding its meetings at 22, Berners Street, W. The object of the Society is stated to be to give women practice in public speaking and debating. The meetings take place not oftener than once in three weeks. Each member present takes part in the discussion: no one, except in the case of the speakers who open the discussion, occupies more than ten minutes. No theological subject is appointed for discussion.

Schoolmistresses (Certificated) are wanted for the Convict Service. Candidates must be in good health, either unmarried or widows; salary £60 per annum, rising

by annual increments of £2 10s. to £80 with quarters
or allowance in lieu.—Applications, stating age and
experience, with references, to be sent at once to the
office of the Directors of Convict Prisons, 44, Parliament
street, Westminster, S.W.

Among the many appeals to the benevolent at this
season, Miss M. Lupton, 124, Lancaster-road, Notting-
hill, hon. sec. of the Gentlewomen's Self-Help Institute,
15, Baker-street, Portman square, appeals for aid. The
society numbers about 450 working members, all of
them ladies by birth and education, and necessitous.
The amount of distress that exists among them is little
known. At all times needy, the winter brings with it
much additional misery, and during the recent severe
weather the sufferings of many from want of proper
clothing, fire, and food have been truly distressing.
Assistance may be given by purchases of work, which
is always on sale at the institute, in every variety, and
at moderate prices, by orders for work, by gifts of cast-
off clothing, or by subscriptions or donations, which will
be gladly received by the treasurer, Mr. S. Morley, M.P.,
18, Wood-street, Cheapside; or by Miss Lupton.

The *Victoria Magazine* for January, contains a clever
little story by Miss Ramsay, of which the two heroines
are, respectively, a medical student and a secretary and
reporter. There is also an article by Mr. Gossan, author
of a "Plea for the Ladies," bearing testimony to the
excellence of the work done in the woman's cause in
Ireland.

The *Woman's Gazette* for January contains a second
article on Art Embroidery, by Miss Scott.

A writer in the same paper suggests a peripatetic hair-
dresser, who might be a lady, and would contract to do
the hair for poor married ladies who have been accustomed to maids of their own for such purposes.

Lady Missionaries.—The *Woman's Gazette* also reports
that St. Deny's Home, Warminster, has vacancies for
training ladies as missionaries for foreign countries.
The Warden is the Rev. Sir Jas. Phillips, Bart. There
is also the North London Training Home for Missionaries,
68, Mildmay Park, London, N.

Ladies as Elementary Teachers.—The appendix to

"The Year Book of Woman's Work" states that the practical value of the step at first recommended to ladies desiring to enter the profession, viz., to obtain a certificate as "acting teacher," is much doubted, and the value of a full college course of two years is strongly insisted upon. It is, therefore, good news that Otter College, at Chichester, has been enlarged, and now accommodates forty students.

Bookbinding.—Mary A. Tooke has an article in the *Art Journal* for January, on "The History of Bookbinding."

The testamentary trustees of the late Mr. A. H. Rhind, of Sibster, Caithness, have given £7,000 for the establishment of an institution in Caithness for the industrial training of orphan girls born in certain parishes enumerated in the settlements, the management to be vested in a board consisting of four trustees, to be appointed by the Commissioners of Supply for the county, and two by the Town Council of Wick.

The Girls' Refuge and King Edward Certified Industrial Schools.—The opening of a new house in connection with this excellent institution at St. Andrew's road, Cambridge heath, was celebrated by a Christmas fête given to the inmates. A number of visitors were present and inspected the new premises, which are comfortably furnished, and in every way adapted for the purpose to which they are designed. About fifty girls are already in the home. The homes are intended for the reception of outcast, destitute, and neglected girls, a large proportion of whom are sent by the magistrates of the various metropolitan and City police courts, and are detained by the managers, under the Industrial Schools Act, till they are sixteen years old. During the period that they are in the home they receive a thorough and practical training, which is intended to fit them for various branches of domestic service. In Home No. 1, which is in Albert street, Mile end New town, there are one hundred inmates, who, in addition to the ordinary school work, do that of housemaids, scullerymaids, laundresses, and cooks. The different departments of the home are models of cleanliness and order, and afford valuable testimony as to the efficiency of the mode of training.

Taking the new premises has thrown upon the committee the responsibility of providing for 110 additional inmates, and the necessary outlay is £2,500, all of which must be met by voluntary offerings. It is only needful to read a few cases of those admitted, which may be taken as fair samples of the whole, to see what the value of the work of the home is, and from what condition of life these girls have been rescued. The committee are greatly in need of further funds. The bankers to the home are Messrs. Smith, Payne, and Smiths, Lombard street; Mr. H. R. Williams, the treasurer, Oak Lodge, Highgate; and Mr. J. H. Lloyd, honorary secretary, 3, Lime Street, E.C., will also take charge of subscriptions.

PROTECTION TO SMALL BIRDS.

A letter has been sent to the newspapers, purporting to be from Lady Burdett Coutts, calling attention to the cruelties which have been practised lately in Hampshire upon small birds, with the object of obtaining a superior glossiness to their feathers for hats and trimmings. Some doubt has been expressed whether this special letter was authentic, but it is well known that Lady Burdett Coutts has consistently given her influence to endeavour to stop this destructive fashion. This is surely a matter in which every woman ought to help. To say nothing of the injury done to agriculture by the destruction of millions of small birds who diminish the ravages of insects, how can woman feel satisfaction in an ornament which has been purchased by the torture of a living creature? Cannot women enter their protest against such a practice? If they refused to countenance it, by discontinuing the use of the feathers, it must cease at once.

LECTURE NOTES.

Miss Fenwick Miller (of the Ladies' Medical College), lectured for the Sunday Lecture Society on January 2nd, on "Mental Epidemics; an account of some of the chief excitements and delusions of past times, and a consideration of their Philosophy."

Miss Miller has also prepared two new lectures for this winter:—"The poetry of women writers," and "Leigh Hunt and his writings."

A series of lectures on the "Metromanie," the French play which has been selected by the Cambridge examiners, were given by Mdlle. Maria Cellini, at the Eyre Arms during December. Mdlle. Cellini will repeat these lectures in the course of the spring.

ART NEWS.

A correspondent from Florence writes:—By special request of a Committee of the Centennial, Miss Margaret Foley, a New England sculptor, long resident in Rome, is sending from Italy to the exhibition in Philadelphia a marble fountain, about seven feet high. The subject represented is "children about to bathe." There are two boys and a girl, aged 4, 6, and 9. The figures are life-size. This work must convince all who see it of woman's power of excelling in art.

Miss Sarah Clarke, of Boston, (also for some time in Rome) exhibits in the centennial her "Pilgrimage of Dante," a series of exquisite drawings in pen and ink, sumptuously bound in vellum, adorned by illuminated medallions, &c. This artist has visited every spot connected with Dante's life; the result is a most beautiful voume, already, we believe, bespoken.

Florence. E. HADWEN.

Costumes for Artists.—It will be one of the "Specialités" of the Ladies' Dressmaking Association (42, Somerset Street, Portman Square, London), to make up historical and national costumes at moderate charges for artists who may furnish their own designs and materials.

Practical Cookery.—Mrs. McNair, of Croydon, has now a course of "General Practical Knowledge," including ironing and clear-starching, washing silk and wool, cleaning copper, brass, tin, &c., with the best possible thing to use for each. Mrs. McNair's address is Montpellier house, Oakfield Road, Croydon.

ART. VI.—CORRESPONDENCE.

MADAM,—Perhaps the few following notes on Spanish marriage laws may be interesting.

If a woman has money, and there be neither settlement nor will, at her death her property goes back to her family, if she has no children; if she leave children, her husband has the use of her property during their minority.

If the husband has money at his marriage, half of it devolves on his death to the wife, and also half of any he may acquire after his marriage. Besides these rights, he can benefit her by will in a third and fifth of the residue; in this her privilege is greater than that of her children, for one of them can only be benefitted in a fifth; otherwise the residue must be divided equally among them all.

Unfortunately, owing to a want of marriage settlements on the husband's side, often the money is spent, so that the wife in reality is not so well provided for as she is legally.

I am, Madam,

Yours obediently,

A READER.

21st December, 1875.

DEAR MADAM,—As in general I sympathize with the principles which the "Englishwoman's Review" advocates, I regret the more to find paragraphs in it approving of the Bill legalizing marriage with a deceased wife's sister. In Leviticus xviii. 16, a man is expressly prohibited from marrying his brother's wife, which, by parity of reasoning, certainly implies that a woman may not marry her sister's husband. And this is the accepted interpretation of the marriage law, both by the ecclesiastical and civil law, as the lists in the English Prayer Book and the authorized version of our English Bibles shew; and also the one that is accepted by the Church of Scotland.

It seems to me that this Bill is another instance of the tendency in the present day to make a difference in legislating between men and women, for by it a man may marry his wife's sister, but a woman may not marry her husband's brother.

Believe me,

Yours very truly,

Edinburgh. E. H.*

Art. VII.—POETRY.

Are we sad for the world's great sorrows,
    The toil, the pain, and strife,
And tired of the petty struggles,
    The wear and worry of life?

Do we wonder God hears not the crying?
    Is the suffering and sin unheard?
Will He let His little ones perish,
    Who could right the world with a word?

Vile? while it is His workshop,
    And we are His trusted tools?
Base? while we are His pupils,
    In divinely appointed schools?

'Tis ours to share the sorrow,
    'Tis ours to lighten the load,
'Tis ours to scatter the darkness,
    With the help and guidance of God.

And though by a breath He could banish
    The sorrow and shame and sin,
And make the whole world as perfect—
    As we trust to make it through Him—

He will not because He honours
    Us by a share of the task;
Because by loving and working,
    We gain far more than we ask.

---

* E. H. has read the paragraph in p. 569, vol. vi., too hastily. The "Englishwoman's Review" has never advocated the Bill for legalizing marriage with a deceased wife's sister. It has refrained from giving an opinion on the subject, believing that *no* legislation having reference exclusively to women is likely to be impartial, till women by a vote have a share in choosing their legislators. The paragraph in question is deprecatory of the measure.—*Editor's Note.*

Art. VIII.—FOREIGN NOTES AND NEWS.

France.

There are many complaints throughout France that the law forbidding the employment of children for longer than ten hours per day is constantly set at defiance. This new enactment should have come into operation on the 1st of September last, but a great number of children are still working more than ten hours, and to many, labour is imposed up till noon on the Sunday. A workman writes to the *Rappel* to suggest that if all the children under sixteen were compelled to attend evening school, the schoolmaster would be able to see that the manufacturer did not detain the youths too long at work. The child's attendance at school and at the factory could be registered in a book, and the law would thus be maintained.

A Lady Doctor.—Madam Brès, who some time ago was reported to have been appointed physician in ordinary and in *partibus* to the Grand Turk's harem, has now opened a *Cabinet de Consultation* for all points of pathology in Paris.

An association of dressmakers, milliners, and embroiderers, has opened a co-operative workshop in Paris—No. 13, Rue Beauregard.

Work for Teachers in France.—Mons. S. Monod, writing in the *Academy* from Paris, says, "France is utterly destitute of an educated womanhood, and the education of women is one of the first national requirements of the present day."

Switzerland.

The female teachers of primary schools in the canton of Berne, have addressed a petition to the Great Council demanding that their salaries shall be put upon the same footing as those of male teachers. The Swiss Working Union admits as part of its programme "equal wages for equal work," whether the workers be men or women: it recommends warmly, therefore, this petition. Since the last rise in wages, the poorest employée of the state is better paid than a woman teacher.

A Latin course is now open at the upper school for young girls in Zurich under the direction of Professor Schweizer-Sidler.—*Avenis des Femmes.*

Germany.

Weimar.—A new school has been started at Weimar, exclusively for men and women who wish to follow the profession of chorus singers. The students will be thoroughly instructed in singing and in reading music at sight, and will also be taught French, German, Italian, and English.

Italy.

The *Cornelia* says that two young ladies, Guiseppina Cattani and Giulia Cavallari, have passed a most brilliant university examination at Bologna.

All the university examinations in Italy are open to women on the same terms as to men.

At the last A.A. degree examination in Tasmania, twelve candidates out of sixteen passed, Mr. Neil Lewis securing the first position. Out of four female candidates three succeeded, Miss Beatrice Pike gaining nearly 1,000 marks above any previous lady candidate. The degrees were subsequently conferred at the annual meeting of the Council of Education, at which Dr. Bromby made an admirable speech.

Melbourne.—We are glad to hear that the Ladies' College at Melbourne, Victoria, over which Professor C. H. Pearson presides, has succeeded beyond the expectations of its promoters. It has 120 regular students, and 30 occasional ones. The principal, Professor Pearson, has taken the Lectureship on English Literature, and has delivered a course of lectures on Shakespeare. For the Mathematical Lectureship an ex-professor from Sandhurst, a high Cambridge wrangler, has been secured.

ART. IX.—PARAGRAPHS.

"WOMENS RIGHTS—THE FEMALE MAGNA CHARTA, 1776."

To the Editor of the DAILY POST.

Sir,—The following extract from an epilogue, written by George Colman, and spoken by Mrs. King in the character of "Dr. Anodyne," is interesting under present circumstances:—

"A female doctor, sirs! And pray why not?
Have men from nature a sole patent got?
Can they chain down experience, sense, and knowledge
(Like madmen in straight waistcoats) to a college?
Let us prescribe! Our wholesome revolutions
Would quickly mend your crazy constitutions.
Invest a female with a reverend cassock—
What spruce divine would more become the hassock?
Or robe her in a lawyer's gown and band—
What judge so sweet a pleader could withstand?
Into St. Stephen's palace let us go—
What power our 'Aye' would have! what force our 'No!'
Try us in all things! There are very few
We women would not do as well as you.
Break down your fences of a partial tribe,
And let us then preach, counsel, and prescribe.

Firm as Rome's matrons, bold as dames of Sparta,
Let British women form a female Magna Charta."

It is passing strange that the above poetic claim for women's rights is 100 years old, and yet even now thought too advanced for this progressive generation.

Yours, &c., O.

As few of the organs of public opinion omit, at some time of the year, to discuss the ever interesting subject to a home-loving nation, of the management of servants, it might be supposed that nothing new could be said on the topic. The *Queen*, however, has been favoured with a most original contribution to this perennial discussion; in the shape of a letter from an individual signing himself "Quick March," who maintains that as "few ladies are capable of managing servants with the necessary amount of nerve and judgment," it is desirable that the master of the house should undertake their supervision, especially as regards the cook, whom he holds to be "decidedly the gentleman's servant." His *reductio ad absurdum* has, indeed, the merit of being useful in pointing out a very common reason for the confusion and disorder reigning in too many homes—namely, that many men who most loudly declare their belief that woman's only legitimate sphere of action lies within the household, are apt to destroy her authority and efficiency therein by interference with her management. It is often the case that, as another correspondent of the *Queen* observes in answer to "Quick March," "the master attempts to rule supreme, the province of the wife being merely to echo his wishes and his orders; in fact, simply to play the part of an upper servant, with far more anxiety about her duties, and much less freedom of will than many servants can and do exercise." This is generally done thoughtlessly, but should any man make such a system his rule of life, we could only bid him, as the Irish beggar did an obdurate passer-by, think of "his own poor widow," or, at any rate, consider whether the assumption of incapacity during the greater portion of existence is not likely to entice the reality at times when the inevitable vicissitudes of human life demand the most vigorous exercise of "nerve and judgment" in women as in men.

The *Daily News,* in speaking of the Théâtre Français, says :—" The *Societaires* are twenty in number—ten of either sex—and a quorum of seven among them, all men, constitutes the managing committee, who regulate questions of finance and decide, under the manager's presidency, as to the acceptance or rejection of pieces. Formerly ladies were allowed to sit on the committee, but it was found that their judgments were not always dictated by luminous impartiality, or that when the judgments were in themselves sound, the style of expressing them was not so—as in the case of the lady who wrote on a voting ticket *je refuse cette piesse parcequ'elle est movaise.*" Would one instance of wrong spelling in a gentleman associate have been considered as sufficient reason for excluding all gentlemen?

The following is from a Wisconsin paper :—" Miss L. Goodell delivered a temperance address at the Congregational church in this village on the evening ot the 16th inst. Miss Goodell, is, we believe, the only practical lawyer of the feminine gender in Wisconsin. She has been admitted to the bar of Rock County, and during the sittings of our circuit court, may be found almost every day in attendance at court, occupying her seat with an easy nonchalance that gives the spectator an idea that she is not out of her sphere, and in our opinion she is not. Miss Goodell has tried a number of cases in Justice Court in this and other portions of the State, and has acquitted herself in a manner that admits of no doubt of her ability to conduct a case as successfully as any of her masculine competitors. Her lecture here was upon the prohibitory question. She made an able effort and adduced some logical arguments in favour of a prohibitory law and a third party, having for its object the incorporation of the temperance work into politics, and also made known her views on the Suffrage question, of which she is an ardent supporter.—*Janesville (Wis.) Gazette.*

We often find a more generous spirit prevailing towards women in the Colonial Press than in our own: witness the following paragraph in the *Australasian Sketches,* an illustrated paper, published at Melbourne. It is upon a man's right to leave his widow destitute by will :—" The law compels a man as long as he lives to support his wife and family. It he deserts them he can be followed from one colony to another, arrested, and brought back like a criminal. If he is possessed of means he must maintain his wife in a manner to which she has been accustomed, and the law takes the liberty of interfering with his private arrangements to the extent of compelling him to find sureties that he will do as he is ordered. While he lives, and as long as his money is of value to him, he has to part with it to support her ; but from the very hour of his death, the law allows him to leave her destitute. The sacred right of permitting a man to dispose of his property as he thinks fit only commences when he no longer lives to give an explanation of his conduct. He may have been for years a drunken debased sot, an object of mixed pity and loathing to everyone who was brought into contact with him ; in his diseased brain he may have harboured insane delusions regarding the conduct of his wife to which no human being would listen for a moment—his vile suspicions could not affect her character any more than the ravings of a madman ; but in a day's interval of sobriety he is allowed to execute a will which leaves her penniless, and places the guardianship of her children in the hands of strangers. This will, to the disgrace of justice, the law upholds, and the drunkard is able from his grave to work a wrong that he could not have worked living. The law is very tender in the view it takes of a dead man's wishes ; they may be unnatural, unjust, and such as, if living, he would not have been allowed to carry into effect ; but simply because he is dead they must be attended to. Among the things that ' they manage better in France,' is the legislative safeguard against posthumous malignity."

Englishwoman's Review.

CONTENTS FOR FEBRUARY, 1876.

All Communications to be addressed to the EDITOR, 22, Berners Street, Oxford Street, W.

Post-Office Orders payable to SARAH LEWIN, at the " Regent Street " Post-Office.

TERMS OF SUBSCRIPTION AT THE OFFICE.

Per Annum (Post Free), Six Shillings.
Subscriptions payable in Advance. Single Numbers posted Free on receipt of Six Postage Stamps.

MSS. are carefully read, and if not accepted are returned, on receipt of Stamps for Postage, but the Editor cannot be responsible for any accidental loss.

Contributions should be legibly written, and only on one side of each leaf.

THE

ENGLISHWOMAN'S REVIEW.

(NEW SERIES.)

No. XXXIV.—FEBRUARY, 1876.

ART. I.—THE HINDU MAHILA BIDYALAYA.

A paper read to former pupils and friends in the College for Men and Women, 29, Queen's Square, W.C., January 15th, 1876.

MANY of our readers will recollect a paragraph in last February number of our *Review*, p. 94, upon the school for young women in Calcutta, in charge of Mrs. Beveridge (then Miss Akroyd). To these, this cir-circumstantial description of a girls' school, so different in every respect from the schools of our own country, will have more especial interest. The object of the *Hindu Mahila Bidyalaya*, or School for Hindu Ladies, is to give thorough instruction in Bengali and English. The teaching is conducted by an English head-mistress (resident), second English mistress (also resident), and a Bengali pundit, and examinations are held at regular intervals. It was under the direction of a General Committee, of which H.H. the Maharaja of Vizianagram is the first name. The Managing Committee consisted of the Hon. Mr. Justice Phear and Mrs. Phear, Hon. Mr. Justice Romesh Chunder Mitter, Mrs. Bignold, W. L. Heeley, Esq., C.S., Mrs. J. B. Knight, Miss Akroyd (Mrs. Beveridge), Babu Durga, Mohun Dass, Manomohan Ghose, Esq., and Babu Hem Chunder Banerjea.—*Editor.*

I have been told that many of you would be interested in learning something about the work in which I have

D

been engaged during my absence in India. Some of you already know from my letters that all my practical interest centered in one school, in giving you an account of which I hope to interest you to-night.

This school is a boarding and day-school for Hindu girls, and is known as the *Hindu Mahila Bidyalaya,* or Hindu Ladies' School. It was opened in November, 1873, after almost a year of preparation, that is, of efforts to raise a sufficient sum of money to guarantee its existence for at least a year, and of enquiry as to the probability that pupils would present themselves for admission in numbers sufficient to justify the establishment of an institution so unfamiliar to Bengal. At length the Committee were satisfied that the school might be opened without risk of failure for a year. A house was taken and furnished, the first pupils were received on November 17th, and their number soon reached seventeen.

Throughout this paper I am speaking of Hindu women, not of Mahomedan, and only of those Hindus who are Bengalis. There are some circumstances connected with the Hindu Mahila Bidyalaya which are really remarkable in a Bengali school. In the first place, it is a boarding-school, and is (I believe) the only one of its kind in India. Amongst Hindus, the practice of sending girls or, indeed, grown women away from home, except on a rare family visit, or still rarer pilgrimage, is almost unknown. If of respectable families, they are kept secluded in their own houses, and in their own part of their own houses. Women of the poorest classes have much more liberty than those of greater means, because, having no servants, they must go to the tank to fetch water, and must do various kinds of household work outside their houses. Shopping is always left to the men, though one sees poor women in the bazars sometimes, and also one may see them working in the fields, or selling vegetables and fruit by the roadside, but these are generally widows who are compelled to earn their own living. It is quite contrary to native prejudice to send girls away from home, and by many orthodox Hindus, consequently, the new school was regarded with distrust. No girls are

ever likely to become boarders who are not ready to
break the rules of their caste.   Up to this time, no pupil
has ever wished to observe the rules about eating with
Hindus of other castes, &c., which bind orthodox
Hindus.   In the second place, it was remarkable
that there were unmarried girls in the school, as, in
the East, girls are married between the ages of
eight and twelve, and after marriage are secluded
at home.   Little girls of even strict Hindu families are
allowed to go out, and to go to day-schools, but
their freedom and their childhood soon end; it is,
therefore, a significant and remarkable fact that there
have been in our school as many as eight unmarried girls
between the ages of eight and eighteen.   Several people,
well acquainted with Indian customs, have said to me,
on hearing this, that the pupils must have belonged to
families which are not respectable.   Quite the contrary;
all of them belonged to families which are called respectable in India itself, where position depends mainly
on birth, and not on education or wealth, and several
were of the very highest—the Brahmin caste.

The third remarkable circumstance is that for each
pupil in our school a substantial fee is paid, amounting
to £20 per annum.   This is a very high fee for a girl's
schooling in Bengal, and is quite beyond the reach of
all but a few.   Provision was made for the admission of
really poor pupils, by granting scholarships which friends
had given for this purpose, or by the reduction of the
fees.   The Hindu Mahila Bidyalaya is not likely for
many years to be largely attended, because there are
very few Bengalis who realise that it is desirable to
educate girls, and who would therefore be willing to pay
the school fee, and there are really very few educated
men who can afford to spend so much on their daughters.
There has been a good deal said, both in native newspapers and privately, about the amount of the school
fees, but this was chiefly by Hindus whose orthodoxy
and love of old customs would never have allowed them
to send any pupils to a boarding-school.   One gentleman
went so far as to say that he should be willing to place
a pupil in the school if he could do so without charge;
he might have gone further, and have asked to be paid

for allowing his relative to be educated—for it is a fact that there have been schools in India which the children were paid to attend, and at the present time there is a successful day-school in Calcutta for little Hindu girls, where the fee is only sixpence per month, though the pupils are, in many instances, the children of wealthy parents. The fee for day-pupils in the Hindu Ladies' School is 6s. per month, but no day-pupil was ever admitted during the time I was acquainted with the school. The school was established in accordance with the request of a few educated Bengalis, and was, from the beginning, managed by a mixed committee of Bengali and English ladies and gentlemen. It certainly owed its existence to English influence, for the pupils were all the relatives or friends of Bengalis who had been in England, and who had therefore seen a mixed society of educated men and women. Five ladies who are the wives of Hindus who have studied in England, have been boarders in the Mahila Bidyalaya, and all the other pupils were relatives of men who wished to give women the freedom and education enjoyed by Europeans*.

The schoolhouse is white, with many green shutters, and stands in a walled garden, in which are a small tank or pool, and a good sized plot of grass, besides many flowering shrubs and some fruit trees. On two sides of

---

* The following form of questions to be answered by parent or guardian on the admission of any girl to the school, will give a better idea than any number of explanations, of the caution with which the friends of woman's education are obliged to proceed in India.

1. Do you wish that any special arrangements should be made for her private religious observances?

2. Do you wish her to attend a place of worship?

3. If so which? and under whose escort do you allow her to go?

4. What friends are to be allowed to visit her?

5. Do you consent to her going out under the charge of (*a*) one of the ladies of the Committee? (*b*) of the Head Mistress? (*c*) of the 2nd Mistress?

6. Do you object to her being taught the use of a spoon and fork?

7. Do you object to her practising English class-singing?

8. Is she a vegetarian?

9. Are there any special points, with reference to your daughter's education, which you wish to suggest for the guidance of the Head Mistress?

the garden, or compound, against the walls, are the kitchens, store-rooms, and servants' houses, for no servants sleep in the house itself. The roof of the house is flat, and is a favourite place for walking, as it gives a view over the town, and for many miles over the tree tops; not a hill is to be seen, only a perfectly flat country.

The dormitories are all on the first floor and are comfortably matted and furnished with English beds. The Bengali's fashion is to sleep on a mat, spread either on the ground, or on a hard wooden stand like a low table. Sometimes, too, they use a rough kind of bedstead laced with rope, which is called a charpoy, but this is, I believe, only used for out-of-door sleeping or in houses where the floor is the bare earth.

In summer the pupils rise at 5, breakfast at 8.30, and dine at 5. The lesson hours are from 10.30 to 1 p.m., and from 2.30 till 4.30 p.m., with preparation time in the morning and evening. In the early morning they take their books and walk about the garden, or sit in sunny corners to say their lessons aloud, and also to dry their long black hair. The hair receives much attention in a Hindu lady's toilet. It is washed at least every other day, and as it is very long and thick it always takes some hours in drying. One of the comical sights in the streets in Calcutta is the hair-dressing of the lower classes of both sexes. The women sit outside their houses in the sun, looking-glass in hand, and oil and coil up each other's heavy plaits amid a fire of gossip.

By seven o'clock everyone in the school is busy. The sound of the piano is heard, for there are several music pupils; some girls sit in the class-rooms writing, others carry stools to distant corners where they may indulge in the loud repetition which they believe must get any lesson into their memories; there is certain to be a committee on an English lesson in the verandah, where, too, the pet parroquet is getting his breakfast.

You would be amused if you crossed the garden to the Hindu kitchen. There is no table, some clean mats receive the food materials, dishes, etc.; the fire-places are made of earth and were prepared by the cooks themselves. There are two cooks who cook all the Bengali food. They profess to be Hindus

but are, we suspect, Mahomedans, for they keep all the
Mussulman holidays. They look picturesque with their
silver ear, nose, and toe-rings, and with patches of red
paint on the parting of the hair. They do all their
work in a stooping attitude and are remarkably clever
with their toes which serve them as well as hands for
some purposes of holding or picking up. In the
kitchen is also one of the pupils, keeping an eye on
the cooks or helping in the work. She is the cooking monitor of the week, and is responsible for the
cooking. She has a delicate office, for all her comrades
can cook well, and she gets her full share of ridicule and
criticism if any dish proves unsatisfactory. There is a
great deal of difference in the cooking of the same
materials by different girls, whether they come from
different districts or from different families only. The
seclusion of the women removes them from general influences, and so gives to those of each family a
marked individuality in domestic customs. There are
several vegetarians, who are all widows, amongst our
pupils, and they have their own fancies in cooking, and
especially in the spicing and flavouring of the dishes.
The peculiarities of the widows' cooking, doubtless, are
caused by the fact that in their own homes each usually
cooks for herself. So marked, however, were the differences of preparation and flavouring at first, before a
sociable medium was hit upon which suited all, that I
have often heard the girls on first tasting a dish, say,
sometimes with approbation, "So-and-so's week," and
sometimes have seen a hasty draught of water follow
the first mouthful, betokening the rule of a lover of
chilis and pepper. All our grown-up pupils could cook
better than the women-servants engaged to do the
work, because they all belonged to good families,
and as a rule the higher her caste the better a
woman can cook. The best cooks amongst Hindus are
of the Brahmin caste; orthodox Hindus, who keep up
their own old customs, will not eat anything which has
been cooked by a member of a caste lower than his own.
All can eat what a Brahmin has cooked, so the priests
get much practice and are greatly sought after
as cooks. When the school was opened a wish was

expressed to have a Brahmin man-cook and one was accordingly found. He was, however, very unsatisfactory; did not know how to be punctual, and used to sit smoking while the woman assistant did all the work; so that it was a relief when he said that he did not like to cook for Hindus who were so unorthodox as our girls.

Before breakfast the girls are subjected to very little restraint, and usually indulge themselves in the luxury of sitting in native fashion on a low stool or on the ground. At first it is a trial to women who habitually lounge as though they had no back-bones, to have to sit straight and upright. It is a great innovation for Bengali women to use tables and spoons and forks. This last is considered such a great change that no girl is allowed to use a spoon or fork without the written permission of her guardian. Fortunately all our girls were anxious to learn to eat with other tools than their fingers. Our girls eat meat and fish, but in small quantities, compared with the rice and vegetables they take. The girls, like English school girls, have in turn various monitor's duties—they cook, they dust, and arrange the class-rooms for lessons: they prepare the table for luncheon, and wash all the glasses, plates, &c., used at that meal; they also polish the spoons and forks, singing or chatting the while.

When I knew the school well, it was the custom of the head mistress to do her housekeeping of all kinds between breakfast and lesson time. Besides the ordinary ordering of dinner, paying of bills, and general inspection of servants' work which an English housekeeper has to do, there were often special worries and work. For instance, there may have been rain and the soil has washed down into the drains. The sweeper-woman and the gardener cannot decide who shall replace it. The gardener mutters about caste, and the sweeper-woman clasps her hands and says she has nothing to do with the soil of the garden. It is decided that she is right, when she retires in undisguised triumph. Or the milkwoman comes; she is not only unpunctual, but waters the milk, and has a trick of bringing a small vessel of good, and a large vessel of poor milk, and of sending the former to the head mistress for inspection. She has been often convicted, and is one day warned that she will be fined for her offences. She instantly becomes dramatic, and bringing forward a small boy of most comfortable plumpness, exclaims, " Then my child will die." He does not die, however, and accompanies his mother for many another month to the house. Or the cook spreads out her rice baskets to show how full of holes they are; she says the rats can walk up straight walls to the shelf where the baskets ought to be kept. Or white ants are eating the matting and must be driven back with carbolic acid, and sometimes, too, there is an alarm of a snake.

At twenty minutes past ten a bell rings, and all take their seats and wait quietly until the half hour bell announces the beginning of lessons. By this time the Bengali teacher has arrived—a sedate, oldish man in orthodox Hindu dress of white muslin, with shoes, but without stockings. Lessons continue, with a quarter of an hour's recess, until one o'clock, when there is rest for an hour and a-half, during which time tiffin is taken. The subjects taught are those which are taught in any moderately good English school, with English as the foreign language in place of French or German. There is, however, this great difference, that as soon as a pupil has learnt enough English to read an easy English text-book, she studies her geography, history, arithmetic, etc., in English instead of in Bengali. This is because there are so few good text-books in Bengali that it is not possible to get a good education from Bengali books alone. Our girls learn English history, some natural science, and the elements of the laws of health, besides the grammar of their own and our language, and all the ordinary requisites of a fair education. Bengali girls learn to write and to read a foreign language faster than English girls, and are decidedly quicker in learning to sew and darn. All our girls are taught to darn stockings; some darned without fault at the first trial, and all worked fairly. This is remarkable, as showing not patience only, but great aptitude for handiwork. Hindu women have clever but ignorant fingers, and, unlike Mahomedan women, do not learn to embroider.

Doubtless, this is because among orthodox Hindus no sewn garments used to be worn, a single long strip of muslin, wound round the figure, being the only garment for men and women. Now almost all Hindus of the respectable classes wear additional garments—*e.g.*, at least a jacket and socks, but their clothes are made by tailors, although only of muslin or calico, and quite within the range of women's sewing.

All the pupils whom I have known, were taught to make, and in some cases to cut out their undergarments and jackets. During the time fixed for sewing, it was the custom to read aloud some book either in Bengali or very easy English, or to sing English or Bengali songs.

No servants remain in the house at mid-day, an arrangement made to allow the girls to do some house-work. Those who have no monitor's work to do, amuse themselves with sewing or fancy work, story-telling, or reading aloud, etc. It is generally thought that Orientals all sleep in the middle of the day; but, except in the hottest weather none of our girls ever did so, and even then there was always some ridicule in store for the sleeper.

After the five o'clock dinner there is play out of doors until seven, when lessons are prepared during an hour and-a-half. The girls learnt two excellent things at play-time, to play games and to run about. The fancy that it is unfeminine to move quickly was soon banished with other conventional notions, and many a merry game at Cat and Mouse, or Tom Tiddler's ground, went on in the garden. At first there was great shy-ness about walking, probably because the genuine Bengali dress is quite unfitted for exercise, but soon no opposition was made to the rule of a daily fixed walk in the garden. I well remember when I first took the girls to the Botanical Gardens the exultation with which they heard that they had walked at least three miles. "It can't be," they said. One incredulously asked, "Have I, with my very own feet, gone three miles?" She was twenty-two, and had never been for a real walk before. In the gardens some of them walked very quickly and excitedly, exclaiming, "How nice to walk! come quickly!" They learned some indoor games—Post, Friends, etc., and sometimes played native games at cards. The day often ended by gathering in the drawing-room to chat with the mistresses or hear some music.

One distinctive feature about the Hiudu Mahila Bidyalaya is that there is no religious teaching whatever in the school. Not one of the pupils is a Christian nor is any attempt at conversion allowed. The school was established in accordance with the wishes of a few Bengalis, and those English people who gave their assistance were content to follow the example of the government in India, and to leave the people to settle their own theological opinions. In fact, the school would never have existed if there had been any purpose of interference with the religious opinions of the pupils. But although the school authorities were absolutely neutral, they allowed the pupils complete liberty to do what they thought right. An hour was set aside in the morning, generally from six to seven, immediately after bathing, for private reading or prayer. Most of the pupils belonged to a native church, and liked to spend this hour together. They usually went up to the roof where they had furnished mats for kneeling, and where they were safe from interruption. At night they almost invariably held a kind of service with much singing and prayer. They were very devout, and seemed to find genuine happiness in their devotions. Many of them, under the escort of their friends, went to their church on Sundays, but none of them were Christians, nor was the slightest attempt made to convert them to Christianity.

The pupils whom I knew intimately, showed some excellent traits of character. They were helpful to one another with their lessons in a self-sacrificing way deserving of the highest praise—the girls of a higher class cheerfully giving their time to help those of a lower class. They rarely quarrelled, they were uniformly considerate and affectionate to their teachers, and were unwearying in their care and attention to any one of their number who required nursing or help. For all the domestic affections, for helpfulness and kindliness, Hindu women are very loveable, and it is a source of great happiness to be able to help them. Our pupils have frequently said that they have never been happier than at school, and we may readily believe this, when we remember how much more varied and healthy is a life spent in regular work, than one which is stagnant and desultory. I have taught in several institutions in England, and have never seen a more industrious, even enthusiastic set of pupils than those of the Mahila Bidyalaya. Many of them felt their own deficiencies and ignorance keenly, and were ambitious to improve. Though they were, in many respects, in less happy circumstances than Englishwomen—for they are inexperienced, totally dependent, and painfully timid to the end of their lives—yet there were occasions during my acquaintance with the school on which my mind was turned back to my former pupils in the Working Women's College, for I saw in these Hindu girls the same perseverance, the same humble-minded desire for instruction, and the same affectionate effort to satisfy their teachers, which had smoothed my way in old days when I had the pleasure of teaching a few of the working women of my own country.

ANNETTE S. BEVERIDGE.

ART. II.—WOMEN'S WORK IN FLORENCE.

MISS JOHNSTON, lately editor of the *Espèrance*, Geneva, thus writes to us from Italy :—

"One of our visits which interested me most in Florence was that to the Giardino d'Infanzia, ably conducted by the Fraulein Birdushek, pupil of Madame la Baronne Maronholtz, and supported by a committee of Florentine ladies. There are about fifty children, all of good families, in this school, and a very bright, happy-looking party they were, both in the class-rooms and in the playground. I heard there a first music lesson given to a class of twenty children, by Signor Domenico Bertini, Professor of Music, after the Frœbel system, in a manner which fascinated the children's attention completely, so that at the end of an hour, without any kind of fatigue, they had learned the names and proportionate value in time of the different kinds of notes, semibreve, minim, &c., and could also for the time, sound them as, *do, re, mi, fa,* &c., in correct accord.

"Froebel's system is not introduced into any of the other schools of Florence, indeed, it seems very little studied in Italy, although there is a pervading feeling of the need of education, and a general effort in the large towns to provide it for *all* classes. But the teachers, and especially the female teachers, are so poorly paid that these salaries can only attract those of inferior attainments. I heard that many female teachers were only paid forty francs a month for such fatiguing services, rendered all the day long. I feel sure that superior women are needed to influence the young and to develop differently their moral sentiments.

"In the Piazza of St. Marco is a fine old building, used for centuries as a foundling hospital. The *custode* assured us that 4,500 infants had come in during the year 1875, but when we went over the hospital, under the guidance of a pleasant-faced, but not very intelligent woman, who had herself been a foundling reared in the hospital, she said only 2,500 had come in. Even the smaller number seems terrible in so small a city as Florence! We saw the bigger girls occupied in the kitchen, dormitories, &c., also in a sewing-class, but both my friend(who interprets) and myself were struck with the discontented, stupid expression on most of the faces of these; they seemed sadly to need Frœbel's teaching to waken up their intellects, and to give them interest and gladness in life.

"Madame Cimino di Luna da Foliero, editress of the *Cornelia,* was in Rome when I came here, though she usually resides in Florence. Having for years exchanged our journals, we met as old acquaintances, and spoke of the common work in which we had been engaged. She tells me that her journal is a great anxiety to her, on account of the heavy expense, and

still too small number of subscribers. I promised
to ask you to publish this fact; also. that she would
very gladly have advertisements to print on the
cover of the *Cornelia*—advertisements of tradesmen, or
of governesses, or ladies' maids. All these would be
useful to both parties, she thinks, as the journal circulates in Italy, almost entirely among the higher classes;
the Princess Margherita to begin with, is a shareholder.
Madame Cimino expatiated rather largely on the social
position which she and her supporters occupy, and told
me again and again, that for that reason it was necessary to be so careful of what was said in her journal, as
it would not do to offend prejudices, or rudely attack
the favourite vices of the upper classes! This no doubt
accounts for the negative character of the articles which
appear in the *Cornelia*, and of which I have heard many
readers complain as rendering them uninteresting. Still,
Madame Cimino appeals to the *solidarité*, which should
subsist among women, as a reason why she asks Englishwomen to support her, and assures me the articles are
written in thoroughly pure and good Italian, therefore,
good exercise for English readers.

" The municipal female schools of Rome have lately
had an exhibition of the work done by their pupils,
which bore testimony to the careful teaching of the
mechanical powers of the girls. Needlework—from knitting and samplers to the most exquisite point lace to be
worn by Princess Margherita, the patroness of the schools
—was exhibited for a fortnight in some of the large
rooms of the Capitol, besides which, there were maps,
drawings, specimens of writing as such, and of composition. All were most creditable to pupils and teachers,
and one cannot but look forward hopefully to the good
results which must follow such careful teaching of the
young. Those acquainted with Rome in former days,
remark with pleasure the absence of the swarms of dirty
little children who formerly infested the streets. All
parties seem to have united their efforts to get them
to school. The Protestants, Waldenses, Baptists, &c.,
have schools for children. And Mrs. Gould's well-known
schools are still continued by the teachers she had appointed, under Dr. Gould's superintendence, though as

yet no lady has come forward to replace her fostering
care of them. Dr. Gould hopes to find some one, however, who will do this. In the municipal schools on
Epiphany day, prizes were given to the best pupils,
and a large banner on the colonnade of the palace
announced that on that day 'the country gives to
the young girls the honour which it expects from its
future mothers.'

"A great want still existing in Rome is that of evening adult schools, where young men and women could
go, after the day's work, to learn to read. The spread
of instruction among the children makes them also
desirous of learning."

Art. III.—CO-OPERATION AMONG SHIRT-MAKERS.

Union is strength. This principle which men, mechanics
or artificers, have so long understood, and have brought
into use in every profession is now being applied by
women to their trades, and with every prospect of
great advantage, both to producers and consumers.
The labours peculiar to women, carried on, as they
used to be, by each separately in her own home,
were not susceptible of much improvement. Every
housewife had to be a "Jack of all trades;" brewer,
baker, dyer, and chemist to some extent, each following her own experience or family receipts, and no
great degree of perfection could be obtained in any of
the arts. Clothes which were spun, woven, cut out, and
made up by the same hands, were durable and serviceable no doubt, but would not answer our present requirements of elegance. Women now, however, are
beginning to find, like men, that their work can be better
done by combination; and also are learning that co-
operation, beneficial to men, is almost necessary to women,
who, with smaller wages, insufficient training, and (possibly) less physical endurance, are less able to support

themselves independently. They have more need of benefit associations, unions, and co-operative societies than men who have hitherto monopolised these advantages.

The present experiment takes its rise from a Society for the working women in the shirt and collar-making trade, which was established last year in London in connection with the Women's Protective and Provident League ; so far at least, that half-a-dozen of these trade-unionists, respectable and industrious women who were willing to run a little risk to secure future advantage, turned co-operators, and brought in their friends, so that there was the nucleus of a workroom of thoroughly skilled hands. The circular which Hamilton and Co. has issued tells the rest.

68, Dean Street, Soho, W.

Among the many attempts which have been made to raise the wages or improve the condition of women employed in needlework or other trades, we believe the experiment of co-operation has never been tried.

No class of operatives have more to gain by co-operation than shirt makers, because no trade suffers more from the sub-division of the price paid by the ultimate purchaser of manufactured goods amongst a number of retail dealers, contractors, and middlemen.

The question was : Would the women employed in the trade be willing to join a Co-operative Society if its advantages were brought before them ? The event has proved that a small number of intelligent and experienced workers for the west-end trade were fully able to understand the objects proposed to them, and willing and anxious to combine for their attainment.

Rooms have accordingly been taken at 68, Dean-street, Soho, where the co-operators are prepared to receive and execute orders for all descriptions of shirts, collars, and underlinen ; they invite a trial of their work with confidence, since it has already received the approval of private friends and professional critics ; and they submit that co-operative shirts must not be condemned beforehand as misfits because some former societies of tailors or shoemakers have been unsuccessful.

It has not been thought necessary to give the women employed a share in the management of the business ; but it is proposed, after paying them at the best current rate of wages, to distribute a fixed proportion of the profits amongst them at the end of the year ; and they are further invited and encouraged to invest their savings in small shares, or loan capital, payable by instalments, and giving their owner a proportionate share in the trade returns.

The promoters of the enterprise are anxious to explain that it is altogether independent of charitable assistance, and will be conducted as a *bonâ fide* commercial adventure ; at the same time, they are prepared to extend their operations as rapidly as the development of their business will allow ; and it is evident that the good effect upon the trade, to be exercised by the existence of such a concern, depends largely upon its scale, and this again, depends upon the amount of practical sympathy, *i.e.*, custom, received from the general public.

Any further information about the management and progress of the Society can be obtained by application to Miss Hamilton or Miss Simcox, at their office, 68, Dean Street, Soho.

Although this special scheme has been taken up for the sake of working women in the narrower sense, yet, should it prove a commercial success, it may encourage women of the educated classes who have a little money, but not enough to live on, and no especial talent for the professions, to try what co-operation and trade will do for them.

We had the pleasure, the other day, of visiting the light and airy work-rooms of Hamilton & Co.; they were warm and perfectly well-ventilated, and the work-women all looked comfortable, and interested in their occupation. In a room on the ground-floor were the makers of ladies' underlinen, while the shirtmakers, more numerous, occupied a large room on the first floor. The firm began by employing ten workers—it has already doubled the number. We understand that in the shirtmaking profession, the cutter-out is generally a man—cutting out being usually considered too profound an exercise for the feminine intellect. Here, however, the cutter-out is a woman, and we have already heard numerous testimonies of the accuracy of fit and delicacy of workmanship, of the work done by the newly-established firm. The workwomen were consulted, when the business was begun, on the number of hours a day that work should be carried on, and were unanimously of opinion that the work hours ought to be as long as those of other employers—one more proof that women, when they manage their own concerns, are not grateful for the shortenings of labour operations of the Factory Acts.

Hamilton & Co. were working at shirts, collars, cuffs, and every kind of ladies' underclothing, and the firm will on occasion purchase and make up sheets and blankets, so that ladies in the country will find great advantage in applying to them. The concern ought to have the hearty good wishes of all who wish to see women employed in independent, well-organised, and remunerative work.

ART. IV.—REVIEWS.

Correspondence of Dr. Channing and Miss Aikin. Williams and
Norgate.

It is exceedingly interesting to trace in the works of a
past generation, evidences of their sympathy with the
identical questions which are engaging us at the present
day. These letters, of two such distinguished writers,
not only afford us pleasant glimpses of rising literary
people whom we only know in the zenith of their fame,
or who have passed away from us, but discuss continually, subjects which our best women-thinkers of
to-day are discussing. The correspondence extended
over more than twenty years, and throughout the volume,
Miss Aikin expresses the deepest interest in the welfare
of women. Rammohun Roy had aroused her to
sympathy with the degraded condition of the Hindu
women, to which in our days Miss Carpenter has attracted
so much attention. The necessity of a broad and
thorough education of women is continually occupying
her thoughts. In 1832 she writes:—

Women are seldom taught to *think*. A prodigious majority never
acquire the power of reasoning themselves or comprehending the force
of arguments advanced by others. Hence their prejudices are quite
invincible, their narrowness and bigotry almost inconceivable, and
amidst a crowd of elegant acquirements, their thoughts are frivolous
and their sentiments grovelling. Exceedingly few have any patriotism, any sympathy with public virtue. Private feelings, private
interests engross them. They are even more insensible then you
charge our public men with being, of "the greatness of the times in
which we live." Rammohun Roy has been justly scandalised at
want of zeal for the Reform Bill amongst the ladies, and I sometimes
pensively ask myself whether the country could now supply many
noble Lady Crokes to exhort a husband to follow his conscience in
public matters regardless of the worldly interests of herself and their
children. * * * You look with some jealousy on the principle of
patriotism as hostile to universal philanthropy; but I am sure that
you will agree with me that it is better to love one's country even
partially and exclusively than to love nothing beyond our own firesides, and when public good and private interest interfere, to feel no
generous impulse to sacrifice the less to the greater.

In 1837 she mentions the scheme of a periodical devoted to the good of women of which Miss Martineau
was to be the Editor. We are not aware if this scheme

E

was ever matured. (It was not till 1857 that the *English-woman's Journal* began its career.) In 1837, she says:—

With regard to Miss Martineau's notions of the political rights of women, I certainly hold, and it appears to me self evident, that on the principle that there should never be taxation without representation, women who possess independent property ought to vote; but this is more the American than the English principle. Here it is, or was rather, the doctrine that the elective franchise is a trust given to some for the good of the whole, and on that ground I think the claim of women might be dubious. Yet the Reform Bill, by affixing the election franchise only, and in all cases, to the possession of land, or occupancy of houses of a certain value, tends to suggest the idea that a single woman possessing such property as unrestrictedly as a man, subject to the same taxes, liable even to some burdensome, though eligible to no honourable or profitable parish offices, ought in equity to have, and might have, without harm or danger, a suffrage to give. I vote for guardians of the poor of the parish by merely signing a paper—why may I not vote thus for members of Parliament? As to the scheme of opening to women professions and trades now exercised only by men, I am totally against it for more reasons than I have time to give.

If Miss Aiken had lived at the present day and been witness to the patient endurance shown by women desirous of entering the medical profession, she might have seen cause to modify this last sentence. In a letter, written in the subsequent year (1838), she says that though on comparing the Code Napoléon with ours, she is convinced that we have the advantage of French women—

There are two points in which our laws bear hard on women. The first is the want of a stricter hand against the inveiglers of girls for wicked purposes; the second in the full power which the father is still allowed to retain over his children when *his* offences have compelled an innocent wife to obtain a divorce from him. * * * *

Nearly forty years have passed and these laws have undergone but little alteration. We need many more Englishwomen yet, who like Miss Aikin will bravely raise their protest against injustice.

English Primer. By M. H. M., author of " Reading made easy in spite of the Alphabet." (Longman's). Price Threepence

We are exceedingly glad to see this primer for English reading, which, from its low price, places within reach of all, the system of teaching embodied in the larger work, " Reading made easy," which we reviewed three years since (*Englishwoman's Review* for January 1873.) Mr. Meiklejohn, late assistant commissioner of Endowed schools, in the admirable letter published some time since in the *Daily News*, set forth very distinctly the present difficulty of teaching children to read, saying that " out of 26 letters, only 8 are true, fixed, and permanent quantities; that is, are true both to eye and ear," that there are 800 of our commonest words in which the symbol and the sound are at variance—that " the letters of our alphabet mislead a child oftener than guide him; that " instead of finding a regularity and self consistency in the black marks, the child finds out, with much pain and weariness, that he cannot trust his letters at all." " He is troubled in a thousand different ways, perplexed and harassed, baffled and beaten, disappointed and dumbfoundered by the character, or rather want of character of this code of signals which he has to set himself to master. The wonder is, that he does learn it at last."

Mr. Meiklejohn adds: "It is as well that we should see that all our methods of teaching the subjects we have to teach are based upon ascertained facts, and are in accordance with the regular and legitimate procedure of the human mind."

In our opinion, the M. H. M. Primer meets the case, as far as teaching the present system of English orthography will allow.

It at least allows the pupil to employ what infantile logic and common sense his young brains may possess. Some simple accent marks are placed over each letter that has more than two sounds, as à, ò, for those vowels pronounced as *aw* in *tall* and *holly*, while *a* stands for the *ah* in father, and *ä* for the vowel in *cake*. All silent letters have a very thin mark drawn through them, which does not hide them from the child, but indicates their silence. The phonetic mode of pronouncing the consonants *le, me, se*, is, or should be adopted with this marking, as in that case the child, in spelling each word quickly, pronounces it naturally. We have seen the system in operation at the Infant schools of St. Barnabas, Earls Court Road, Kensington, and are ourselves satisfied of its suitability for young minds. The children are *not* puzzled, but can use their small logic in deciphering each new word, and find their code of signals a sure guide. They labour under one disadvantage, in that the inspectors of schools have not yet recognised their method of spelling, and oblige them to spell aloud for their edification on the old system, aitch—o—ar—es—ee, horse, be—o—why, boy, so that for the last few weeks before the visit of the inspectors, they have to be coached up in this old system of spelling, but notwithstanding this disadvantage, their progress in reading is very quick and satisfactory.

The stories in the M. H. M. Primer are simple and attractive, and we highly recommend it to any mother who is teaching her children at home.

Eggs all the Year Round at Fourpence the Dozen.
(Jas. Maclehose, Glasgow.)

This is the title of a useful little manual of fowl keeping, in which the author, who has evidently, practically considered the matter, shows that poultry farming, properly managed, would be a most profitable concern. We confess that the book has aroused in us a very great desire to go and do the same—to invest in Brahmas and Crevecœurs, hire a small farm, and try if we cannot also make it pleasant and profitable. But our chief reason for speaking of the book here, is the suggestion that people of very limited incomes might, by care and attention, find considerable advantage in it. According to Stephen's "Book of the Farm," "women only, in a farmer's estimation, are fit for such a charge, and doubtless they are the best, and would do it well, were they not begrudged of every particle of good food they may bestow upon poultry." We have elsewhere heard it suggested that as the eggs and chickens were pre-eminently the perquisites of the women of the family, it was not thought worth while by any farmer to incur an outlay towards making them profitable. We would gladly believe that the author of this manual is a lady who has found out a new trade in which women may profitably engage. A widow and her daughters, or two sisters living in the country, might, at very small expence, begin poultry farming on a small scale, to be enlarged as their experience or their market suggested. In the neighbourhood of our large towns, they would have no difficulty in disposing of their surplus stock, and the amplest directions for the management of fowls, now so little understood, may be found in this volume, which we cordially recommend to any ladies willing to try the experiment.

Miss de Rothschild has a paper on " Hebrew Women" in the current number of the *New Quarterly Magazine.* The *Examiner* says "It is a well-written survey of the great part which women have played in Jewish history. No other history contains such a roll of heroic women.

Our Laws and our Poor. By Francis Peek. (Published by John Day, Savoy Street, Strand).

THIS book is divided into three parts headed respectively, " The Influence of the Law, " The Orphan's Wrong," and " Just Principles of Punishment."

In each part information and suggestions of value will be found, but the first appears to us the most useful, as it calls attention to a subject which does not receive the consideration it deserves.

Mr. Peek opens the first chapter as follows:—

"There is scarcely an assertion more common than that " We cannot make men virtuous by an Act of Parliament, and this phrase is generally regarded as embodying an ascertained fact. Without at present controverting this statement or pausing to examine how much of truth and how much of illusion may be contained in it, it is proposed rather to show that whether or not good laws fail to influence for good, it is most indisputable that unjust and inadequate laws exert a powerful influence for evil."

At page 45 he gives an instance of the evil influence of our present laws.

" There is still another cause of pauperism that must not be overlooked—namely, the inadequacy of the law for enforcing the duties of men in regard to their wives and families. Its practical teaching is that men are only bound to prevent their becoming a burden on the parish, and thus, though the man may be earning large wages, he is at liberty to keep his wife and family in a state of pinching poverty and in rags, as well as compel them to herd together in one wretched room, while he wastes his money in dissipation and drunkenness, no existing law touching him. That this is a great wrong is evident, when it is considered that these children owe their existence to him, and that the woman, by the care of them, is deprived of the power of doing much for their support; and also, that by omitting to provide proper sustenance for these children their father will most likely cause them to become a burden and injury to society, as well as to endure a life of suffering. To present this wrong in a more forcible manner, let us compare the relative positions of the virtuous married women and of the abandoned outcast who lives at her own pleasure, bringing into the world a family of illegitimate children. The poor virtuous woman is really a slave to her husband, dependent upon his whim for everything except the barest necessaries of life, and exposed to suffer in herself and through her children from every freak of his bad temper or drunkenness; but for the shameless outcast (so-called) the law enforces very different treatment. It provides that for every illegitimate child she has, she can claim from its father from 2s. 6d. up to 5s. per week for its maintenance; and thus with a family of four or five illegitimate children, she may live in uncontrolled comfort and comparative luxury, while her virtuous sisters are toiling early and late to meet the wants of their legitimate family, and are, perhaps, suffering from the whims of a dissolute husband, being able only to claim the few shillings he has left of his wages after his drunken orgies. Let no one doubt the teaching power of the law. If we cannot make men good and virtuous by Act of Parliament, we can make them drunkards and paupers and educate them in vice, and with all our boasted freedom, enlightenment, and philanthropy, we are, it is to be feared, to a great extent, still allowing the law to do this.

"A striking and almost ludicrous example of the different treatment meted out by the legislature to the virtuous and the vicious, is afforded by the practical working of the law which forbids the marriage of a man with his deceased wife's sister. The woman living in illegal union with her late sister's husband, can obtain 5s. a week for each child she bears him, whilst her sister's legitimate children can claim nothing but the barest sustenance."

The other chief causes to which Mr. Peek attributes the wide prevalence of pauperism are drunkenness and improvidence, and to each of these he would apply a remedy. We are inclined to think that Mr. Peek ascribes to improvidence a larger share in producing pauperism than is really due to it. It is at least rarely possible for an agricultural labourer to lay by enough money to support him in his old age. A man who earns no more than 15s. or 18s. a week, with perhaps an extra £5 at harvest time, cannot save much.

The Poor Rates, to which he contributes while young, form practically a kind of benefit club, and when he is too old to work it is only fair he should derive a comfortable maintenance from this source.

The worn out labourer receives his weekly allowance

from the Parish as a matter of right without shame, nor do we think that he takes a false view of this matter.

It is true that a few labourers save money enough to take a small farm, and thus raise themselves into another class, but average men cannot do this.

A larger number of labourers subscribe to benefit clubs, and in some cases these clubs will maintain them in old age, but their wives are seldom, if ever, included in the arrangement, and it is no fault of the widows if at last they come on the parish for support.

Thus large numbers of respectable persons, both men and women, who meet with no special misfortune, and who have been guilty of no improvidence, are necessarily maintained by the rates in their old age, and have a just claim to be maintained in comfort in their own homes.

The second part of "Our Laws and our Poor," relates to the management of pauper children; the third part, to the treatment of criminals.

On the whole the book is a hopeful one, for though the evils pointed out are great, the remedies indicated appear practicable, and it irresistibly suggests the idea that, with good management, half the misery and wickedness of the world might be abolished. We heartily recommend it to our readers.

Art. V.—EVENTS OF THE MONTH.

THE UNIVERSITY OF LONDON AND DEGREES TO WOMEN.

AT a meeting of Convocation in this University, on January 18th, a debate arose on the admission of women to degrees in arts; Dr. Storer in the chair. The subject was introduced by Mr. A. P. Hensman, B.A , who moved the following resolution : "That it is desirable that a new charter should be granted to the University; and that no such charter will be acceptable to Convocation which does not enable the University to grant degrees in arts to women." With reference to the second part of the resolution, he said that a new class had been brought within the scope of the advantages of that University. In 1867 the Senate was empowered to grant certificates to women, and it was very noteworthy that since that time the examinations had been in precisely the same subjects as those which the other undergraduates of the University had been called upon to pass in. Now one could understand the opponents to the granting of the degrees to women saying that the subjects upon which the degrees were granted were not suitable to that section of the community. One might not agree with that view, but at all events it might be a strong position to take up. It was now agreed on all hands, not only by the practice of that University, but of all other Universities, that the subjects which were suitable for the education of men were suitable for women also. Now, what had been the effect of that extension of examinations to women, and of similar extension in the university of Cambridge? Colleges for women were springing up in all parts of the country, and at University College (London) the professors instructed a large number of young women. At Cambridge also the professors had courses on the very same subjects upon which they instructed the young men. In May, 1874, the House passed a resolution in favour of granting degrees generally to women. The Senate passed a resolution to the effect that that body was desirous to extend the scope of the education to women, but it was not prepared to receive a new charter giving power to admit women to the degrees. Perhaps it might be suggested that it would have been better if the resolution had not been limited to degrees in arts. It seemed to him, however, that by limiting that resolution to degrees in arts they were making, to a certain extent, a compromise with the opponents generally of the question. First they got rid to a great extent of what one might call the professional opposition of the medical graduates. It had hardly become yet a practical question of the admission of women to degrees in laws and science; and with respect to medicine it seemed not at all unlikely that before long a general Act of Parliament, applied to all Universities, will enable women to take degrees and other diplomas in medicine. The College of Surgeons, which he did not suppose was a very revolutionary body, or dedicated to change—(laughter)—had lately agreed to grant certificates to enable them to practise. The question of the admission of women to degrees in arts was a practical and a pressing one; and he would ask was it fair or just to deprive them of that encouragement for pursuing a regular and a liberal course of education? It was now nearly two years since they passed their resolution in favour of admitting women to degrees, and he would remind Convocation that the title of their University to consideration did not depend, as was the case with the old Universities, upon the possession of large revenues, or upon the prestige which must attach to ancient seats of learning. Their claim to respect was that, having been founded in the nineteenth century, they must adapt themselves from time to time to the advancing spirit of the age. It would be, he thought, discreditable to them if they allowed older Universities to outstrip them in that respect. He trusted that, inasmuch as the sense and justice of the country had come to the conclusion that where a woman had fairly earned a reward she ought not to be deprived of it, this University would be the first in this country to act in accordance with that view, and proceed to grant degrees to women. A long discussion ensued on an amendment moved by Mr. A. W. Bennett; but eventually the original motion was carried, with the omission of the words "in arts."

EDUCATION.

Women's Education Union.—The annual general meeting in support of this Institution was held on February 7th, in Willis's Rooms, St. James's square, and was numerously attended. The Princess Louise, the President of the Union, was present, and sat near the platform. On the platform were Sir Charles Reed, who presided; Lord Aberdare, Mr. Stansfield, M.P., Mr. Barber, Mrs. William Grey, the originator of the Institution, Miss Brough, the secretary, and a number of ladies.

Miss Brough read the report of the Central Committee,

which stated that the Committee had resolved to take
as their work for this year the formation and development of some scheme which should be at least the
beginning of a system for giving to teachers help in
gaining such instruction and training as would fit them
for their profession. They were, at the outset, greatly
assisted by a donation of £100 from the Baroness Meyer
de Rothschild, made specially to aid some scheme for
the assistance of teachers. This donation formed the
nucleus of a fund which will be used solely for the
purpose specified. The deliberations of the Committee
resulted in a scheme which was divided into three
branches:—1. The teachers' loan fund: 2. the students'
library; 3. lectures to teachers; each of which was
managed by a separate standing sub-committee. The
students' library was opened in November, but already
promised to be successful. Courses of lectures on
methods of teaching special subjects had been arranged,
the fees for teachers being exceedingly low. A second
School Board scholarship had been given this year of
£30 a year for four years, being £5 a year more than the
first. The increase of value was decided on in consequence of its having been pointed out to the Committee
that other scholarships given to the School Board were
of the value of £30 a year, and that it would be advisable for the Union to make their scholarships for girls
equal to those which had been offered to boys. Scholarships of £25 for one year were again offered in connection
with the local examinations of the following Universities:
—Cambridge, Oxford, Edinburgh, Dublin, and Queen's
University (Ireland), the Committee having been again
enabled, by the generosity of private persons, to make
the offer. All these scholarships have been awarded,
with the exception of that offered to Oxford, for which
there was no candidate. Two scholarships of the value
of £50 a year for three years had been given to Girton
College, the funds being raised by special subscription,
of which £208 7s. had been collected.

Mr. Barber, barrister, moved as the first resolution,
that the report of the Central Committee be received and
adopted; that her Royal Highness the Princess Louise,
Marchioness of Lorne, be re-elected president, and that

the vice-presidents and the members of the central committee be re-elected. He said the Public Schools company had grown out of the Union, and they had now 9 schools open in different parts of the metropolis and different parts of England, at which 1,000 girls were being taught, and which in the aggregate, were returning a good profit. The great want was, not of candidates, for there were too many of them, but of teachers who could teach because they had themselves learned. They wanted a training school or a training college for teachers in the metropolis.

Mr. Stansteld, M.P., in seconding the motion, said perhaps the best measure of the injustice shown as between male and female education was to be found in the report of the late Endowed Schools Commissioners, which showed that nineteen-twentieths of the educational endowments were for the education of boys, and only one-twentieth for the education of girls. Speaking for himself, he was not prepared to admit that permanently there should be any inferiority in the educational arrangements for girls as compared with those for boys. Each class had an equal right to the best education that the society could give.

The resolution was adopted.

Lord Aberdare moved the next resolution:

That this meeting, recognising that the supply of duly qualified teachers for schools above the elementary is the most pressing educational question of the day, pledges the Union to continue and extend its efforts to obtain for women the higher education following that of school, corresponding to the University education which confers so great an advantage on male teachers, and also special training in the principles and practice of teaching. He believed that the Endowed Schools Commissioners would gladly, if they could, apply a greater portion of the endowments to the education of girls, but they were resisted by the trustees. He was glad to say, however, that a feeling was growing up that more should be done for the education of women, and it was his duty to preside the other day at a meeting of Colston's trustees at Bristol at which they resolved to devote £200 a year for the education of women.

Mrs. Burbury, said she was not in favour of training colleges for female teachers, if the object could be attained by other means; Mrs. Grey, who pointed out that the public day schools Company which had been referred to was entirely distinct from the Union, said the committee had no idea of establishing a training college, but what they wanted to do was to supplement as far as possible the training which was given now, and that they hoped to do by lectures on special educational subjects, and also by getting admission for their students into schools where they would learn the principles of education. She moved a vote of thanks to Sir C. Reed for presiding.

The motion was seconded by Mr. Botley, and carried by acclamation, and the meeting then separated.

FRÖBEL SOCIETY FOR THE PROMOTION OF THE KINDERGARTEN SYSTEM.

As there is an increasing demand for trained Kindergarten teachers, the committee of the Fröbel society desire to make known to all who are occupied or interested in education, the following opportunities of training in the principles and methods of Fröbel's system:—

21, Stockwell road, S.W., Classes conducted by Fraülein HEERWART, £10 per annum, Boarding House £40. Course, eighteen months.

Girls' College, Southampton. Principal, Miss SHARWOOD. £10 per annum. Students board in families. None received for less than a year. Age 18 to 24.

Manchester Kindergarten Association. For particulars of Training Classes, apply to Miss SNELL, 4, Great Western street, Moss Side, Manchester.

An examination will be held at the end of next June, open to all students of the Kindergarten system (fee £1), to be conducted by examiners appointed by the Fröbel society; a certificate will be given to those that satisfy the examiners.

E. A. MANNING, Hon. Sec. of Fröbel society, 35, Blomfield road, Maida hill, W.

Women Teachers.—At the recent conference of teachers in London, Miss Millington, of Victoria Park College,

Manchester, read a paper on the "Training of Women Teachers."

The Women's Education Union (offices, 112, Brompton road), announces a series of Tuesday evening lectures in Exeter Hall, specially addressed to teachers of both sexes. The fee to teachers for each course of three lectures is 2s. 6d., to the general public 5s.

The school founded by Mazzini for poor Italian children, and for a time discontinued, is to be re-opened at 12, Red Lion square. The school will be open every Monday, Wednesday, and Friday, at 8 p.m.

Two scholarships have been founded to be competed for by the pupils of the Commercial Travellers' School for Girls at Pinner, and which will enable them to complete their education at a school or college chosen by their parents, subject to the sanction of the Board of Management.

BOARDING OUT IN IRELAND.

The third meeting of the twenty-fifth session of the Statistical and Social Enquiry Society, was held on January 18th, in the Leinster hall, Dublin; the chair was occupied by Professor O'Shaughnessy. Professor Ingram, F.T.C.D., who delivered the opening address of the session, devoting the larger portion of his address to the subject of the boarding out of pauper children, now read a supplemental paper dealing with aspects of the same question which he could not then consider within the time at his disposal. Since then he had, by further study, increased his knowledge of the history and working of the boarding out plan, and many valuable communications had reached him from persons who were able to supply information founded on personal experience. As discussed in England, the question had been mainly one between district schools and the boarding-out system—as means of training the permanent children, that was, the orphans and deserted, who came upon the rates. After making elaborate quotations from the report, &c., of Mrs. Senior (in relation to the London schools), Mr. Tufnell, Mr. Doyle, the well-known poor-law inspector, who supported the system established at Mettray; the Rev. Dr. Clutterbuck, school inspector, who gave powerful support, and that from an official source, to the opponents of the district schools; Mr. Nettleship, Mr. J. D. Llewelyn, the former chairman of the Swansea Union—a warm advocate of the boarding-out system—and others; throughout the professor elected the boarding-out system as the best. But after all had been done that could be done in the way of boarding-out, there remained in the schools a residuum of children, in most unions a small one, to whom that method was not applicable; and the question arose— How was that residuum to be provided for? To that Mr. Llewelyn replied: "Send them away from the walls of a union house to a country school more or less self-supporting, and assimilate, as much as possible, to the conditions which are found so successful in the cottages of our country districts." That pointed, he thought, to the right method. It fell in exactly with Mrs. Senior's proposal respecting the metropolitan schools—namely, that the schools should be broken up, and that whilst the orphans in them should be boarded out in cottage homes, for the remaining children, schools should be provided of a more home-like character, arranged on the Mettray system. That appears, without doubt, what they were coming to—and, so far, the plans of Mr. Doyle and Dr. Clutterbuck, seemed to tend in the right direction. But they certainly erred in discountenancing boarding out, as they understood it, for the orphans; the natural home, if well chosen, was the best of all, and fulfilled most completely all the ends to be attained; the artificial home was next best, and ought to be resorted to only for those who could not be provided with real homes. Boarding out, first, as far as it was available—this was what he would emphasize, as the most important point; and when it was not available, the nearest possible approach to it. Power, he thought, should be given to detain casual children for a certain period, if they had come several times with their parents into the workhouse—so that they might derive some benefit by a stay of a certain duration in the school. The schools, Mr. Llewelyn urged should be, in unions like his own, of a simple inexpensive kind—consisting, in fact, of a few cottages in a rural district, with pure air, abundant water, and plenty of free space, and with garden-land for spade labour. The drainage and ventilation should be thoroughly good. Literary instruction, though not neglected, should be subordinated to industrial training. There ought to be the necessary appliances, he added, for keeping cows and managing a dairy, and sheds where children might be taught some sort of artizan work—as tailoring, shoemaking, and the like. It would be important he thought, to follow these suggestions so as to prevent the proposed schools from becoming, in their turn, elaborate, costly, inelastic institutions, without the close resemblance they ought to bear, in all their conditions and surroundings, to real rural life, and from that point of view it appeared better that they should belong to the several unions, than be formed by counties or combinations of unions, as proposed by Dr. Clutterbuck and Mr. Doyle. What he was desirous of insisting on now was the adoption of the boarding-out system, as by far the best for the permanent children—the orphans and deserted; as the best means of developing their moral natures, cultivating their practical intelligence, training them for real life, and incorporating them with the honest and industrious mass of the labouring population. It was sometimes said that an adequate number of eligible homes cannot be found for the children. It was perhaps in the report of Dr. Clutterbuck that the existence of this difficulty is most strongly asserted. But it should be remembered that it was not proposed to scatter the children broadcast through the mingled good and bad of working society; but by a careful examination of the antecedents of proposed foster parents, through intelligent residents in their neighbourhood, who could thoroughly inform themselves on the subject, to choose those only who are worthy of the trust. Whenever this was not done, the system was not rightly managed; for the wise selection of homes was one of the essential conditions of its success. Having referred to the system as worked in England, he urged that this department of the Poor Law should be entrusted to persons resident in the locality, who would obtain personal supervision. To make the boarding-out plan permanent and really useful in Ireland, committees of supervising ladies would be absolutely necessary. It was in the highest degree desirable that such committees should be formed without delay in the several boarding-out unions, and that the guardians should recognise and countenance their action; and it was in the two Metropolitan Unions that it was natural to expect the first rise, as well as the fullest development of that much-needed institution. Having alluded to the growth of affection between the foster-parent and children boarded out, he urged the importance of extending the age to which the children might be kept out in Ireland from ten, at which it was now fixed, to sixteen, which was the limit in England.

The Chairman said it was universally felt that it would be well to procure an inspection of children boarded out by persons unconnected with the board of guardians, and that it was absolutely necessary to have the assistance of the ladies in that work.

Miss Sturge, of Birmingham, said she had had some experience of the boarding-out system as worked in England, and was a supervisor in the Bewdley district, in Worcestershire. She found that the ladies' committee had a very healthful influence over the board of guardians—that both, working towards the same end, vied one with the other as to which could reach it best. In her opinion the district school system, or even the keeping of children together in a workhouse, tended to "dull" their feelings, and to prevent the proper development of their natural qualities; and for that reason she hailed the advent of the other system of boarding out, which she thought must work with success, both for the present and the future. Something had been said about the disadvantage of voluntaryism; its slipshod nature making it uncertain. Well, they might try to obtain some legal organisation for such lady and voluntary workers, which would remove that, and render the system most perfect.

Miss Becker, of Manchester, made a few observations in the same direction. It had been said that it was difficult to board out pauper children in large cities for the want of suitable "homes." She would reply to such critics that in every community there were families in which the pauper poor might be brought up.

Miss Tod said a suggestion had been thrown out as to the propriety of appointing permanent inspectors of children boarded out, and it struck her that in many respects a lady would be best suited for such an appointment.

Professor Kavanagh said there were only 45,000 persons in Irish Workhouses, and not 15,000 of them were children under 16 years of age. Out of these there were not 5,000 or 6,000 suitable to be boarded out. They were dealing with this matter as if it was a mountain, whereas it was—as far as Ireland was concerned— a very small matter.

Dr. Hancock observed that the Irish boards of guardians were in favour of the boarding-out system—that Irish opinion was not divided on the subject, but almost unanimous, whereas in England it was divided, and at the present moment war was being waged between the advocates of the two systems, to which allusion had been made. In this country we were behindhand as regarded England and Scotland, for in these countries the age to which pauper children might be boarded out was 13, whereas in Ireland, by the act of 1869, it was limited to 10. In America, too, the question had made great progress, and all they wanted was to keep pace with the times, and to change the age from 10 to 13.

Mr. H. J. M'FARLANE said the Board of the North Dublin Union, of which he had been a member for the past thirty years, had, since the passing of the act of 1862, boarded out between six hundred and seven hundred children. He happened yesterday to see the girls who had been returned, and a few days ago the boys. They were very few in number—he believed only nine girls being at present in the workhouse schools, the remainder having been absorbed into society, and those who had returned being in preparation by a more liberal education to go into suitable situations in life. He believed that 10 years was a sufficient limit. Unfortunately the boarding-out system had not been properly tested in Ireland. Out of the 163 unions in the country, little more than a majority had adopted it, and in a great many cases they found that only one child had been sent out from unions; but of course in the metropolitan unions the numbers were very large.

F

Professor Ingram, in the course of a brief reply, quoted the opinion of Mr. Parker, of Cork—an energetic advocate of the boarding-out system in Ireland, who thought that the age for the boarding out of boys should be extended to 15, and that of the girls to 17 years— as against Mr. M'Farlane's observations.

The proceedings then terminated.—*Daily Express.*

The National Committee for Promoting the Boarding-out of Pauper Children have issued their fourth annual report, in which they express a belief that, with a very small expenditure, they have promoted the objects in view.

MEDICAL EDUCATION OF WOMEN.

The Admission of Women to the Royal College of Surgeons.—At a meeting held during the third week in January, the committee appointed by the council of the college to report on the question of the admission of women to the examination in midwifery, it was decided that no important change could be made in the regulations applying to candidates for this diploma until the conjoint scheme was absolutely settled. There was, we believe, a very general feeling on the part of those present, that after the conjoint scheme had become law, the college should take such steps as it thought desirable to make the curriculum for the diploma of midwifery suitable for women. It is also thought desirable to change the character of the examination to such an extent, that the licentiates may be able to practise midwifery as a branch of general medicine, not as a narrow department in which alone their knowledge had been tested. There is, moreover, a very general conviction amongst the members of the committee and council, that the registration of the female licentiates should be so distinct that they cannot by any reasonable possibility be mistaken for registered practitioners of general medicine. The council have not yet decided whether the certificates, presented by the three ladies now applying for examination, are sufficient to fulfil the requirements of the curriculum.—*Medical Examiner.*

Medical Diplomas for Women.—The *British Medical Journal* states that the Council of the Royal College of

Surgeons of England has arrived at the important decision to admit women to examination for its licence in midwifery. This diploma will entitle them to a place on the *Medical Register*, and will give them a legally recognised position in this country as practitioners in the obstetric department of medicine and surgery. The clause in the College Charter under which the right to admission has been claimed was, it appears, expressly framed, by the use of the word "persons," to meet the case of females as well as of male practitioners; and the College has been advised that it could not legally refuse to admit duly educated women to examination for this diploma.

The *Spectator* says:—"It would appear that women have always had a legal right to obtain a diploma from the Royal College of Surgeons authorising them to practise in midwifery. The College has been advised that a clause in its charter was expressly drawn to admit women, the word 'persons' being employed instead of 'men,' and according to the *British Medical Journal*, the council has decided on submission. This is a mere step towards the acknowledgment of a right, but it is a long one, as it places women among recognised medical practitioners, with whom surgeons must consult."

Registration of Women Doctors.—Mr. Cowper Temple has again brought forward in Parliament a "Bill to amend the Medical Act of 1858," so far as relates to the registration of women who have taken the degree of doctor of medicine in a foreign university. The Bill was read for the first time on February 9th. There can be little doubt that this question stands in a much better position this session than last year.

PROTECTION OF WOMEN. LAW OF HUSBAND AND WIFE.

The following case was reported in the *Times* of February 2nd. It was heard in the Court of Queen's Bench.

PHILLIPS *v.* BARNET.—This case raised a curious and novel question, arising out of the operation of the Divorce Act, the question being whether, after a divorce, one of the parties can maintain an action against the other for an assault or other personal injury during the marriage. The plaintiff, Sarah Phillips, complained that the defendant, assaulted, beat, and ill-treated her, whereby she was permanently injured. He set up the Statute of Limitations, alleging that the so-called assault was more than six years ago, and he also pleaded that at the time of the alleged assault the plaintiff was his lawful wife. To this she replied that since then the marriage had been dissolved by an absolute decree of the Divorce Court at her suit, to which the defendant, the late husband, demurred, maintaining that it was no answer to his plea of the marriage, and that in point of law the action could not be sustained, as the assault was committed during marriage, and while the plaintiff was his wife.

Mr. C. RUSSELL, Q.C., argued for the Defendant, the late husband, that the action was not maintainable, for by the Common Law, the husband might assault his wife, for he might use lawful correction, for which he cited "Blackstone's Commentaries," vol. i. c. 15. Moreover, he argued it was clearly contrary to the policy of the law that matters of this nature, occurring between the parties during marriage, should be the subject of actions for damages. If there was danger of undue violence, the wife could have protection by means of articles of the peace. If the violence amounted to a breach of the peace and an offence against the public, the husband might be indicted. If it was carried to such an extent as to endanger her health, or interfere seriously with the comfort of her life, a judicial separation could be effected, but it was contrary to the policy of the law that either party after divorce should be allowed to maintain actions against the other for personal injuries.

Mr. J. BROWN, Q.C., argued for the plaintiff, the late wife, that the action could be maintained. The assault, he urged, was a wrong, in itself a ground of action, and although during married life the wife could not sue her husband in an action, she might indict him, and that showed that the difficulty in the way of action was merely one of procedure, and the obstacle being removed by the dissolution of the marriage the action was maintainable.

Mr. Justice LUSH asked if the late husband could now sue his late wife for goods of his she had injured or made away with.

Mr. BROWN admitted that he could not, but denied there was any analogy between the cases.

Mr. Justice BLACKBURN referred to the ancient maxim that husband and wife are one person.

Mr. BROWN replied that this was not quite accurate. It was only true as to property, and was so laid down: as regards personal injuries they are different persons, and one may be indicted for assaulting or injuring the other. He urged that it was a mistake to suppose that the Divorce Act gave any remedy for past cruelty; it only made provision for the wife's future support; there was nothing in the way of compensation for the past.

Mr. Justice LUSH.—Suppose that during the marriage the husband has maimed his wife or so injured her as to prevent her from earning her livelihood, would not the judge take that into consideration?

Mr. BROWN.—No doubt, as to allowance for her future support, but not as to compensation for the past. The power of the Divorce Court is only as to alimony or provision for future maintenance. Unless such an action was maintainable there would be no remedy for the most atrocious injuries inflicted by the husband during marriage.

In reply it was urged that if the wife required protection from injuries by her husband, she could have articles of the peace, or could indict her husband ; but Mr. Justice Blackburn pointed out that these were proceedings only for prevention, and afforded no compensation.

The Court, however, gave judgment in the defendant's favour.

Mr. Justice BLACKBURN said the rule of law was that husband and wife were one person, which prevented a cause of action from arising between them. It was so laid down in " Littleton " and by Lord Coke. No doubt either might be indicted for an assault or injury to the other, but no action was maintainable between them, and no cause of action arose between them. It was true it was so laid down as to property or contract, but it was laid down as a rule that they were one person in law. Then the reason why the one could not sue the other for any injury during marriage was that they were one person. For this reason the wife could not be indicted for larceny from the husband, though the property of course was in him. Hence the dissolution of the marriage could not make that a cause of action, which was not so before. There was no cause of action during the marriage, and the dissolution of the marriage could not give a cause of action which did not exist before.

Mr. Justice LUSH concurred. The question was one of great importance, for many divorces proceeded upon the ground of cruelty, coupled with adultery. The effect of the decision would be that in every case of that class the wife could maintain no action against her late husband for injuries caused by his cruelty. It was the first case of the kind, and the consequence of allowing such actions to be maintained must be considered. The dissolution of the marriage produced no alteration in their *status* as to the past. It did not destroy the marriage *ab initio;* it only dissolved it for the future, and it worked no alteration in their *status* or their mutual civil rights while married.

A safe law is therefore laid down by this decision. A wife-beater has only to estimate how much "lawful correction" does not interfere "seriously" with the comfort of her life, and he is secure from even an indictment. If he forgets discretion, and "maims" her so as to "interfere with her earning her own living," he will be compelled to provide her a better maintenance; he may even undergo a judicial separation, but in no instance can the victim of his assaults get compensation for her past sufferings. The law may in extreme cases protect her—may even inflict an inadequate punishment upon the offender, but however free she afterwards becomes, it will never forget that she and her tyrant were at that time "one person," or accord her damages for her sufferings.

The *Echo* says:—

The husband pleads that the woman was his wife, and that, therefore, he had a perfect right to do what she was then attempting to get him punished for committing. The plea would seem a strange one in equity; but in law it appears to be a perfectly sound one. Indeed, there can be no doubt that the decision of the presiding judges was in strict accordance with the law of England. It is long ago since Blackstone laid it down that the wife and the husband were one person, and that the one could not sue the other for the recovery of property, or in an action for assault, though, indeed, if the assault was very aggravated, an indictment from the one against the other could lie. The great commentator even lays it down that it is quite in keeping with the letter of the Common Law that the husband might use " lawful correction to his wife."

The legal fiction that a husband and wife are one person, and that one, the husband, occasionally causes difficulty even to the one person in question. At the Salford police court, a woman was charged with assaulting her husband. After hearing the evidence, the judge said the case was extremely difficult to deal with, for if he bound the woman over to keep the peace, and if she failed to do so, the amount of her bond would have to be paid by her husband. The lawyer who appeared for the prosecutor agreed that such was the fact, and added that the result would be the same if a fine were imposed on her. Finally, the prisoner was discharged, after being cautioned to amend her behaviour, a caution which it is to be hoped will be observed so long as her punishment would be vicarious.—*Suffrage Journal.*

SUFFRAGE.

On February 7th Parliament was opened, and Mr. Forsyth gave notice to bring in the Bill to remove the Electoral Disabilities of Women. The Bill was read for the first time on February 8th. The second reading of the Bill is fixed for the first Wednesday after Easter week, April 26th. We can only exhort our friends who are willing to aid the movement for securing an equitable representation for women, to petition for the passing of the Bill. Petition forms can be obtained from—

Miss BECKER, 28, Jackson's row, Albert square, Manchester.

Miss BLACKBURN, 64, Berners street, London, W.

Miss Tod, 8, Claremont street, Belfast.

Mrs. McLaren, Newington house, Edinburgh.

or from any other committees and correspondents through the length and breadth of the country. The earlier a petition is sent in the more valuable it is, but in any case it should be forwarded before the Easter holidays.

The election, which will take place in Manchester in a day or two, is looked forward to with great interest by all the friends of this cause. The return of Mr. Jacob Bright to Parliament cannot be a matter of indifference to any supporter of this Bill, whether Conservative or Liberal. We understand from the active workers in this movement, that there is every prospect of an increased number of supporters in Parliament at the next division.

Important meetings have taken place during the past month—the two principal being in Ireland. January 17th was the fourth annual meeting of the North of Ireland Branch of the National Society; the chair was taken by the Mayor. Miss Tod read the report, which was the most encouraging one the Committee had ever presented. Mr. Johnston, M.P., Miss Becker, Mr. Dickson, M.P., Miss Tod, Mr. Biggar, M.P., and others, addressed the meeting. On January 20th another meeting was held in the large Concert Hall of the Exhibition Palace, Dublin, at which Mr. Maurice Brooks, M.P., presided. There were present also, Sergeant Shirlock, M.P., Mr. Fay, M.P., Mr. Sullivan, M.P., and many others. Miss Becker said, in the course of her argument:—

Suppose it were now the law that every Irishman were personally disqualified from voting, although taxes were levied alike from Irish and English. Suppose that Irishmen were deprived of the benefit of educational endowments originally intended for both nations, denied the right to enter lucrative and honourable professions, and whenever an Irishman and an Englishman went into partnership, the Englishman was held the sole legal representative of the firm. Would not every one say that such unequal laws were the result of a system of representation which gave one side only a voice in legislation? Until the year 1829 the vast majority of the Irish nation were by law incapable of voting at elections. They were disqualified on account of religious belief, and the result of the disfranchisement of Roman Catholics was the maintenance of atrocious penal laws. For the sake of political freedom the Irish Catholics were ready to brave civil war. To resist taxation without representation the American colonists did make a revolution. Women do not care less than men for personal freedom and political rights, because they do not resort to such desperate expedients to obtain them. They appeal not to force, but to reason and persuasion, not to men's fear, but their sense of injustice.

A crowded and influential public meeting was held in Brecon on January 27th, in the Town Hall, the chair was taken by Mr. Hugh Powell Powel, of Castle Madoc, and the meeting was addressed by Miss Sturge, Professor Morris, Miss Beedy, the Rev. J. B. Jones, and others.

Another public meeting took place in York, on the 31st of January, Lord Houghton presided. A very successful meeting has been held at Evesham.

On February 8th Miss Fenwick Miller lectured at the Lecture Hall of the Avenue road Church, Shepherd's Bush. The Rev. R. Macbeth presided.

Miss Miller's excellent reply to Admiral Maxse's lecture in the Eleusis Club, Chelsea, has been reprinted at full length in the *Beehive*.

We regret to record the death, under very painful circumstances, of Miss J. Luke, who for some years had filled the post of Secretary to the Bristol Branch of the National Society. The deceased lady had carried on her arduous duties with a zeal and ability which every one who had had correspondence with the Society acknowledged.

The Central Committee, 64, Berners street, W., is endeavouring to raise a fund of £5,000 to carry on the rapidly extending work of the movement.

Women Voters in Chili.—We learn from the public press that Chili can boast of being the first country in the world that has admitted women to the electoral franchise. Chilian law makes no distinction of sex, the only qualifications required for citizenship being the attainment of majority, and the ability to read and write. It has therefore been decided to register women, and they will vote at the coming election.

The Boston *Woman's Journal* asserts, however, that a project of law is being brought before the senate, to declare that neither friars nor women shall be allowed to vote. From the juxtaposition of "friars and women," we should infer the framers of this project had been reading Admiral Maxse's lectures.

OPENING OF THE SESSION.

OFFENCES AGAINST THE PERSON BILL.—On Feb. 10th, Mr. Charley moved the second reading of his Offences against the Person Bill, which he said would do away with the necessity of putting a woman on trial for infanticide in cases in which conviction on that charge was impossible, while it would provide for her trial on a minor charge and prevent the absolute defeat of justice. He contended that if the Bill became law the number of infanticides would decrease. The Bill was read a second time. Among the other items of interest to women, leave was also given to Sir Harcourt Johnstone to introduce a Bill to repeal "The contagious Diseases Acts, 1864, 1866, and 1869."

Also to Mr. O'Shaughnessy to extend the limits of age up to which with the assent of Boards of Guardians, orphan and deserted children may be supported out of workhouses in Ireland.

EMPLOYMENT.

THE QUEEN'S INSTITUTE, DUBLIN.

The Annual meeting of the patrons and supporters of the Queen's Institute, was held on January 21st in the Molesworth Hall. There was a numerous attendance of ladies and gentlemen. His Grace the Duke of Leinster presided. Miss Corbett read the report. This, which gave a most encouraging account of progress, we must, for want of space, defer to our next number.

Messrs. Cockerell and Co., the great coal merchants, have set apart one of their offices at their wharf, Earl street, Blackfriars, where lady clerks only are employed to do the accounts. The hours are from nine to six o'clock and the salary a guinea a week.

Pottery Painting.—Painting on pottery has been much revived of late years in England, and forms an excellent opening for ladies who are desirous of obtaining employment in art. The superior artistic skill and knowledge which are requisite, in order successfully to follow this branch, fully entitle it to stand first on the list of art industries.

The name of Messrs. Minton will always be associated with the production of this work, and until quite lately, this firm had a studio at South Kensington, and employed nearly twenty ladies in carrying out their designs. Owing to the destruction of their buildings by fire, and the prohibition of the Commissioners against their re-erecting the kiln, they have decided to discontinue the studio in London, and limit the production of the work to their factory at Stoke.   Several other firms, however, continue to find work for ladies in London, amongst whom may be mentioned Mr. Mortlock, of Oxford street; Mr. Brown Westhead, of Holborn; Messrs. Doulton, of Lambeth; and Messrs. Simpson in the Strand.   Messrs. Doulton employ a large number of young ladies on the premises, and a few at their own homes.   The terms and arrangements of these firms are very various, some paying by the time and some by the piece.   By the time is generally the most remunerative.   Some of the ladies thrown out of the employment by the removal of Messrs. Minton's studio have taken rooms at 68, Newman street, Oxford street, and started for themselves under the title of " The Art Pottery Painting Association."   In addition to these there are numbers who work at their own homes upon their own responsibility, and trust to the quality of their work for it to find a sale with the dealers.   Though they can thus command a higher price for an individual article, yet it is not, in the ag-gregate, so advantageous as regular work at a lower rate from a well-established firm such as Messrs. Minton, Mortlock, or Doulton.   The expenses of ware, colours, carriage, firing, &c., are very considerable, in addition to which they have to take all the risk of packing, forwarding the goods to the kiln, firing, &c., and sustain the entire loss should an accident arise without any compensation from those whose carelessness or mis-management may have caused it.— *Woman's Gazette.*

At the Artizan's Institute, 29, Castle street, Upper St. Martin's lane, of which the Rev. Henry Solly is principal, a class for the instruction of women in China and Tile Painting is held every Monday evening at 7 p.m.

Fees 2s. for six lessons. The *Circular* says:—The art of Tile-Painting is not only an agreeable accomplishment, but it is an occupation peculiarly adapted to women and girls, and, as such, is strongly recommended by many persons who take an interest in opening up sources of female employment. It is hoped that this attempt to promote a comparatively new branch of profitable and artistic occupation for a class of persons who often suffer from scanty work and low wages will meet with adequate support.

MUNICIPAL FRANCHISE IN CANADA.

In the Ontario Legislature a motion giving women the right to vote at municipal elections has been thrown out by a small majority.

Is it possible that this defeat may be through the public-house interest? The American newspapers go on to tell us that a petition of 8,220 women of Toronto, and a large number of other petitions from women were presented to the Ontario Legislature, recently, to restrict the liquor traffic. In all probability the influence of women if they enjoyed the Parliamentary, as they do already the Municipal, vote in England would be found to be in favour of temperance.

MISCELLANEOUS.

Textile Operatives.—According to "The English Census of Occupations, 1871," there were in that year 22,734 females engaged in the cloth manufacture of the West Riding of Yorkshire; 27,216 in the worsted manufacture; showing a great increase compared with the numbers engaged in 1851. In the silk manufacture there had been a serious decline.

Cookery in Board Schools.—The Bristol School Board, following the example of some other Boards, have resolved to introduce cookery as a subject of instruction in their girls' schools. Mr. Buckmaster delivered the inaugural lecture in Hamilton's Rooms, Park street, Bristol, on Monday. The Mayor of Bristol presided, and there was a large attendance, chiefly of ladies interested in the welfare of the poor. In the evening Mr. Buckmaster repeated the lecture to an audience of working-men's wives.

Bristol Dispensary for Women and Children.—A letter in the *Woman's Gazette* for February gives the following interesting report:

To the Editor of the Woman's Gazette.

As you take a very great interest in the social and physical well-being of women, you will be pleased to learn that a dispensary for women and children has recently been established in Bristol, and succeeds admirably. Women are required to pay on their first visit 1s., and children 6d., and on every succeeding visit the patients pay half these charges. This rate of payment it is to be hoped, will soon render the institution entirely self-supporting. This rate of payment and the slight self-denial it occasions on the part of those wishing to benefit by the medicines and the gratuitous advice of Dr. Eliza Dunbar tend to foster the spirit of independence and self-reliance so much needed among working women. Many collateral advantages are offered. I was much delighted to find that a series of lectures had been given by Miss Reed, the generous founder of the dispensary, on "The Conditions of Health." I had the pleasure of attending the last of the series on the subject of food constituents, and how best to preserve the nutritive qualities or ordinary food in cooking. Lectures of this description given with sufficient accuracy, and at the same time simple enough to command the attention of the audience addressed, are much needed. The exertions of Miss Reed and Dr. Dunbar are highly appreciated by the women themselves. I venture to trouble you with these few remarks, knowing that your paper is widely circulated among persons who take an interest in the subject.

E. Scott.

The Girls' Friendly Society.—At a recent meeting of the guardians of St. Saviour's, Southwark, the question came under discussion as to what was to be done with workhouse girls, who having gone from the Union school into service, were discharged from the latter. Mr. Williams urged the necessity of some special home being provided for girls so situated—they could not be sent back to school, and they ought not to mix with the paupers. Mr. Chubb suggested that application should be made to some Servants' Home, to ascertain if accommodation could be found there.

Mrs. P. A. Taylor's Home for Young Women Servants, at 1, Bessborough gardens, Pimlico, was established last year, precisely to accommodate this class of girls. The beneficial work of this Home has become well-known in the neighbourhood. The girls, while out of service, do the housework of the Home, and receive lessons in needlework, writing, and other useful arts; which training, supplements, in a slight degree, the wretched education—in a practical light—of the workhouse schools.

Temperance Movement in Berkshire.—A campaign against intemperance has been opened in Hungerford (Berks). On Sunday the subject was referred to from the pulpit in every place of worship in the town of Hungerford. There was also a Good Templars' meeting in the Town hall. Mrs. Lucas, sister to the Right Hon. John Bright, delivered an earnest address in support of Good Templarism. She expressed her belief that before long the Permissive Bill would be adopted. Referring to the movement for providing better homes for working men, she said that abstinence from drink would go far to render them more comfortable.

An asylum for dipsomaniac women has been opened in Scotland. A number of ladies in Scotland have taken a farmhouse in Peebleshire, remote from any drink shops, and thither they send women of a humble class, for a small weekly payment.

Liverpool Shopwomen.—The *Liverpool Albion* states that in consequence of the development of spinal and other diseases among ladies engaged as shop assistants, there is a movement amongst the Liverpool ladies in respect to this matter, and it is their object to inquire whether something can be done in the way of providing seats for the occasional use of the young women so employed. A numerous array of medical men have notified their approval of the scheme. We are glad to see this movement spreading; it is worth the attention of London ladies.

Club for Servants.—It is reported that a club for the special use of female domestic servants has been opened in the Queen's road, Bayswater, London.

LECTURE NOTES.

Sir Henry Maine began a course of public lectures on Saturday, February 12th, at 2 p.m., in Corpus Christi Hall, Oxford. The subject of the lectures will be the

" Salic Law," and that of the first was " The origin of the so-called Salic rule of regal succession."

Midwives and Monthly Nurses.—A course of lectures to midwives and monthly nurses will be given at the London Diocesan Deaconesses' Institution, Tavistock crescent, Westbourne Park, every Thursday at 3 p.m., during the months of February, March, and April, 1876. For particulars apply to the Head Sister.

Mrs. Buckton of the Leeds School Board is generously giving a weekly course of lectures, on subjects relating to Sanitary Science. She will treat of—1. Air; 2. Circulation; 3. Respiration; 4. Digestion; 5. Solid Foods; 6. Liquid Foods; 7. Mineral Foods; 8. Organic Matters. Four other lectures will be on the principles of Heat as applied to the Preparation of Food. These lectures present an opportunity such as is scarcely likely to occur again, and will be found invaluable to persons who are desirous of becoming instructors of cookery—indeed, to all who have the charge of a household, or who take any part in the efforts now making to improve and extend sanitary knowledge. These schools of cookery open a new branch of employment for women.

ART. VI.—CORRESPONDENCE.

To the Editor of the " ENGLISHWOMAN'S REVIEW."

MADAM,—A little while ago there was in the *Spectator* a review of Dr. Nichol's pamphlet: "How to Live on Sixpence a Day." Though all may not not care to follow the worthy man's advice, yet the subject is one of general interest, and some knowledge of the various properties of food is necessary for every woman trying to "make both ends meet." The problem of "Given £400, stretch it so as to cover the space once occupied by £1,000," is not uncommon in our day. The "Cost of Living," as the *Cornhill* told us last Spring, has well-nigh doubled during the last fifty years. It was remarked at the time that the item causing most difference

in daily expenditure, by rises in price, was the butcher's
bill.   Indeed the *Saturday Review* pronounced that
"meat alone costs some £75 out of £250."   It was
noticed, too, that "the consumption of butchers' meat
has enormously extended in the course of the last
quarter of a century, and keeps on increasing."   Comparing various dietetic tables by Dr. Edward Smith, it
appears that in animal and vegetable food, "carbon,"
or heat-giving elements, and "nitrogen," or flesh-forming
elements, are represented thus:—

		CARBON.	NITROGEN.	
One Penny-worth.	Bread	1,450	66	Total cost, 3d.
	Barley	2,500	93	
	Oatmeal	1,513	75	
		5,463	234	

		CARBON.	NITROGEN.	
One Penny-worth.	Beef	320	23	Total cost, 3d.
	Mutton	415	20	
	Pork	483	18	
		1,218	61	

The result is more than fourfold in favour of the fruits
of the earth, both as to economy and nourishment.
From about thirty scientific and medical opinions, all
resulting in the same confession; let me quote a few
specimens.   *Cuvier:* "The natural food of man, judging
from his structure, appears to consist principally of the
fruits, roots, and other succulent parts of vegetables."
Professor Lawrence: "The teeth of man have not the
slightest resemblance to those of the carnivorous animals, except that their enamel is confined to the external
surface.........Whether we examine the teeth and jaws,
or the immediate instruments of digestion, we find that
the human structure closely resembles that of the simæ,
all of which, in their natural state are completely fru-
givarous."   *Liebig* says: "Vegetables produce, in their
organism, the blood of all animals, for the carnivora, in
consuming the blood and flesh of the graminivora, con-
sume, strictly speaking, only the vegetable principles
which have served for the nutrition of the latter."   If any

suppose that although those in full health may dispense with meat and wine, yet that for delicate persons they are desirable, let him read what is said on this theme by Dr. Cheyne, Dr. Nichols, Dr. Buchan, and others. After trying both modes of living, and comparing the result both in my own case and that of others, experience proves, beyond doubt, the superiority of Vegetarianism.

Any one thinking of taking part in cooking clubs, soup-kitchens, or other attempts at improving the quality and preparation of food, would do well to study the publications issued at 91, Oxford street, Manchester, also by Isaac Pitman, Paternoster row, London (see "Fruits and Farinacea," &c. &c).

The first step towards reform in diet should be with regard to "our daily bread." What is usually sold by the bakers is deprived of much nutritive power, by the removal of the coarser parts of the flour. By this means it loses also its ballast, and the body needs ballast quite as much as the mind. Good "whole meal unfermented bread," can be had from Hill & Son, 60, Bishopsgate within, and 3, Albert mansions, Victoria street, S.W. If brain workers realised the immense gain to themselves and their work caused by a simple diet, combined with fresh air and exercise, we should see fewer morbid books, and hear of fewer break-downs of mind and body. Women have generally most influence in household matters, let them feel it a duty first to learn and then to practise the higher life even in "meat and drink."

Faithfully yours,

Florence.   E. HADWEN.

Englishwoman's Review.

CONTENTS FOR MARCH, 1876.

All Communications to be addressed to the EDITOR, 22, Berners Street, Oxford Street, W.

Post-Office Orders payable to SARAH LEWIN, at the "Regent Street" Post-Office.

TERMS OF SUBSCRIPTION AT THE OFFICE.

Per Annum (Post Free), Six Shillings.
Subscriptions payable in Advance. Single Numbers posted Free on receipt of Six Postage Stamps.

MSS. are carefully read, and if not accepted are returned, on receipt of Stamps for Postage, but the Editor cannot be responsible for any accidental loss.

Contributions should be legibly written, and only on one side of each leaf.

THE

ENGLISHWOMAN'S REVIEW.

(NEW SERIES.)

No. XXXV.—MARCH 15TH, 1876.

ART. I.—LEGAL CONDITION OF WOMEN IN MASSACHUSETTS.

A PAMPHLET has been recently published by a well-known American lawyer, the Hon. Samuel E. Sewell, upon the legal condition of women in Massachusetts. The tract was originally written in 1868, subsequently revised in 1870, and again altered, as additional improvements were made in the law, in 1874. Probably there is no state in America which bears so close a family resemblance in its social life to England, and none therefore which may so safely be held up as an example to us; some of the western states have achieved even greater equality between men and women, but the conditions of society owing to the smaller number of women, and the floating character of the population would make it impossible, if indeed it were desirable, which is very doubtful, to imitate them. But Massachusetts, in common with the rest of New England, started with English laws, and has proceeded in our British fashion, not violently changing, but mending, patching, and remodelling the old laws, till, as in the well-known story in which the silk stocking became worsted through repeated darnings with worsted, the fabric of the laws has been almost entirely changed through repeated amendments.

Up to 1855 the English common law prevailed, and as Blackstone says "so great a favourite is the female

G

sex with the laws of England" that the husband and wife were held to be one person, and that person the husband; but the last thirty years have brought more changes than the preceding four hundred, and these changes have all been favourable to women, recognising and enforcing their claim to their property, their own persons, and their children.

"Most people," Mr. Sewell says, "have a general idea of the disabilities of the female sex. But very few, except lawyers, understand in their full extent the annoyance and oppression to which our system subjects women, until some hard case directs their attention to a peculiar form of this injustice."

Foremost in this injustice Mr. Sewell places the exclusion of women from the franchise.

The denial of this franchise is the most serious wrong done to women, since granting them the ballot would, no doubt, lead eventually to the redress of their other wrongs.

This refusal of the ballot perpetuates the stigma of inferiority on more than one half of the whole population of the State. The effect is obvious. We look upon the ballot as one of the great educators of male citizens, because it interests them in public affairs, and leads them to consider and discuss important questions of legislation. Our Constitution not only shuts out this great avenue of education from our female citizens, but the legal inferiority tends in every direction to produce the mental inferiority which it presupposes.

It is hardly necessary to add, that to deprive any class of persons who pay taxes of the right of voting, violates the principle for which our fathers contended during the revolution, that taxation without representation is tyranny. Thousands of women pay taxes in Massachusetts, some of them very large ones. Yet women have no voice in directing the appropriation of their money, are compelled to submit to enactments from which their moral instinct revolts, and have no power to urge effectually reforms which they believe to be all important. Since women are not allowed to vote, they are generally considered ineligible to any public office, and incapable of holding any by appointment of the governor. Governor Claflin, in 1871, nominated several ladies for Justices of the Peace. Some of the Council, doubting whether women could hold the office, the opinion of the judges of the Supreme Court was asked on the subject. The judges delivered an opinion that women could not be Justices of the Peace. The ground of the decision appears to be that the office of Justice of the Peace, under the Constitution, is judicial and therefore cannot be held by a woman, according to the common law, which had not been altered by the Constitution.   *   *   *   *   Practically, women are disabled from holding many offices for which they are admirably qualified, even by the judgment of those who regard them as unfit for other positions.

Practically it is only within the last six years that
ladies have been on any board of education, with the
exception of that of Munroe, the smallest town in the
state, which has for many years had the honour of leading the van in this reform.   In 1868 many cities elected
women on their School Committees.

Three ladies were chosen members of the School Committee in Boston for 1874.   The School Committee declared them ineligible.   One
of the ladies applied to the Supreme Court to be reinstated.   But the
judges refused to decide the question of her right to a seat and dismissed her petition on the ground that the Charter of the city gave
the School Committee power to decide on the qualifications of members of the Board.   The Legislature, as soon as the decision was
known, passed with great alacrity and almost by acclamation, "An
act to declare women eligible to serve as members of School Committees."   There can be no doubt that within a few years women will
be members of School Committees in most of the towns of the State.
This year (1875), six ladies are members of the School Committee in
Boston.

No woman is to be found on the Board of State Charities, or as an
Overseer of the Poor, or as a Trustee of a Lunatic Hospital.   Yet the
warm sympathy which women feel for the sick and poor, to say nothing of their other qualifications, would make them very useful in
these positions.

The Legislature in 1874 passed an act to establish a reformatory
prison for women.   The deputy, superintendent, chaplain, physician,
and clerk of the institution are required to be women : and "either
men or women may be appointed superintendent, treasurer and stew-
ard, at the discretion of the governor and council."   *   •   *

Women are not allowed to serve on juries.   This may be regarded
either as an exemption or a disability.   Yet it is very clear that there
are cases in which women ought to be required to serve as jurors.
Where one of the parties to a suit is a woman, a portion of the jurors
ought always to be of her own sex.

The immunities which by some are considered a set
off against these political disabilities are that women
pay no poll tax and are not required to serve in the
militia.

"These," says Mr. Sewell, "are proper exemptions at the present
time.   When legal equality is given to the sexes, women ought to
pay a poll tax.   They can never perform military duty.

"The statute exempts from taxation property to the amount of
500 dollars, of a widow or unmarried female, and of any female minor whose father is deceased, if her whole estate not otherwise
exempted from taxation does not exceed 1000 dollars.

"With regard to labour, a statute passed in 1874 prohibits, under
a penalty, the employment of any minor under eighteen and any woman over that age, more than ten hours a day, except to make repairs

to prevent the stoppage of machinery. The act, however, permits a different apportionment of the hours of labour, for the sole purpose of giving a shorter day's work for one day of the week, but in no case allows more than sixty hours per week. This act, though no doubt well intended, is founded, as regards grown up women, on a false principle. It supposes women to be too weak and careless to take proper care of their health. The law as it respects minors is excellent. But men and women should be allowed to regulate their hours of labour for themselves. I cannot but regard it as an insult and injury to women to class them with children."

Inasmuch, however, as the law allows individual liberty in apportioning the hours of labour, it is superior to the English Factory Act. Mr. Sewell continues:

The unfortunate mother of an illegitimate child, enjoys at least one advantage over her happier sisters, she has the sole care and custody of her minor children, which the father can never interfere with.

The mother of a bastard child may compel the father to maintain the child, and assist her in such manner as the court may order.

So far Mr. Sewell has considered the law as it relates equally to married and unmarried women. He now comes to the law relating to married women, and here it is that the chief improvements have been made. The old English law, from which that of the eastern states of America has sprung, signified that after marriage the husband was the one person for both, and the wife nothing.

So entire was the annihilation of the wife, that an old law-writer, referring to Æsop's fable, calls marriage *leonina societas*, a leonine partnership, of which the husband has all the profits, and the wife none.

By marriage, all the wife's personal property, of every description, which belonged to her at the time of the marriage, and all which came to her afterwards by bequest, gift, or otherwise, became absolutely vested in the husband, even her clothes and jewels.

He became also the owner of all her real estate, so far that he was ontitled to the rents and profits of it, certainly during their joint lives ; and, if he survived her, he retained the real estate during his life, in case they had any child born alive, she could make no will, she could bring no action, make no contract, and the husband had the sole right to the custody of the minor children, and to the control of her person, though he was bound to exercise this power reasonably.

We know in what respects this law has been modified of late years in England. The first important changes in Massachusetts were effected in 1855, but subsequent alterations took place in 1862, and again in 1874. It now stands thus—

The property, real and personal, which any married woman now owns as her separate property; that which comes to her by descent, devise, bequest, gift, or grant; that which she acquires by her trade, business, labour, or services, carried on or performed on her separate account, or received by her for releasing her dower by a deed executed subsequently to a conveyance of the estate of her husband; that which a woman married in this State owns at the time of her marriage, and the rents, issues, profits, and proceeds of all such property—are, notwithstanding her marriage, her separate property, and may be used, collected and invested by her in her own name, and are not subject to the control of her husband, or liable for his debts.

A married woman, prior to an act passed in 1874, might sell and convey her separate property, enter into any contracts in reference to the same, carry on any trade or business, and perform any labour or services on her separate account, and sue and be sued in all matters having relation to her separate property, business, trade, services, labour and earnings as if she were sole. But no conveyance by her of shares in a corporation, or of any real property, except a lease for a term not exceeding one year, and a release of dower executed subsequently to a conveyance of the estate of her husband, was valid without his assent in writing, or his joining with her in the conveyance, or the consent of a judge granted for good reason.

The Act passed in 1874 enables the wife to convey her shares in corporations, and lease and convey her real property in the same manner as if she were sole, thus entirely relieving her from the degrading necessity of asking her husband's written consent as if she were a child. It also enables her to make contracts, oral and written, sealed and unsealed, in the same manner as she if she were sole, and to sue and be sued in the same manner as if she were sole, thus removing the annoying limitations expressed in the last paragraph.

The same great Act of 1874 provides that all work performed by a married woman "for others than her husband and children shall, unless there is an express agreement on her part to the contrary, be presumed to be on her separate account." This provision was necessary, because the Supreme Court had decided that work done by the wife must be considered as done on the husband's account, unless there was evidence to show that it was done on her separate account. The Statute further adds that nothing in it shall authorize a married woman to convey property to or make contracts with her husband, or authorize suits between husband and wife. All this is a mere iteration of the old law, and a very unwise one, as it seems to me. * * * To prevent a wife from calling in law to her aid in getting justice is no more reasonable than to deny a son or a sister the same privilege. Though ever since the Statute of 1855 married women have been enabled to carry on any business, yet, by an Act passed in 1862, any wife doing or proposing to do so is obliged to file a certificate in the office of the city or town clerk, giving her husband's name, the nature of the proposed business, and the place where it is proposed to be done. If she does not file a certificate, her property is liable to be taken for her husband's debts. The husband may file a certificate if she neglects to do it. If neither file a certificate the husband becomes liable for the debts that she contracts in carrying on her business. A married woman having

separate property may be sued for any cause of action which originated against her before marriage; and her property may be
attached, and taken on execution, as if she were sole. A married
woman may make a will of her real and separate personal estate, in
the same manner as if she were sole; but such will does not operate
to deprive her husband of more than one half of her personal property, without his consent in writing; nor can it take away his life-
interest in her real estate, if they have had a living child.

A wife abandoned by her husband, who has left the
State, or does not sufficiently maintain her, or whose
husband is in the State prison, may be authorised by the
Supreme Council to use his personal estate, and may
also sue and be sued as if unmarried. She may, under
the same circumstances, obtain an order prohibiting her
husband from imposing any restraint on her personal
liberty.

The next division of laws which Mr. Sewell examines,
have reference to the subject of divorce. Without
aiming at the extreme facility with which the courts of
the Western States grant divorce, it must be acknowledged that the tendency of recent legislation in Massachusetts, has been to render the legal separation of
man and wife more easy. But whatever we may think
of the wisdom of such legislation, it cannot be denied
that the American law gives almost total equality to
women; whereas, to quote Mr. Gladstone's words, the
English Divorce Act "introduced a new and gross inequality against women and in favour of men."

In the matter of intestate succession, the wife in Massachusetts is still inferior to her husband in some degree.

If the wife die, leaving no will, the husband has the whole of her
personal property, and, if they had a living child, her real estate
during his life. If she leaves no kindred, he takes her real estate in
fee. If the husband die without a will, but leaving issue, the wife
is entitled to one-third of his personal property absolutely, and
her dower, which is a life interest in one-third of all the real estate of
which he had been seized during the coverture. When a man leaves
no issue, the widow is entitled for life to one-half the real estate of
which he was seized with at the time of his death; and to the
whole of his personal property, to the amount of five thousand dollars, and to one-half of the excess of it over ten thousand dollars;
and if he leaves no kindred whatever, then she inherits absolutely
his whole property, real and personal.

By the act of 1874 a married woman may be an executrix and administratrix, and if appointed to any of

these offices when unmarried, her subsequent marriage does not deprive her of it; and when once appointed, she holds it entirely independent of her husband.

Another great improvement in the law has been in connection with the guardianship of children. By an act passed in 1870, in case of the father's death, the mother is entitled to the custody of the person of the child and the care of his education. Nevertheless there is room for further alteration, for while a father may appoint a testamentary guardian to his children, a widow cannot by will appoint a guardian to hers.

By the common law husbands and wives could not usually be witnesses for or against each other in any legal procedings. After various enactments diminishing this disqualification, the Legislature finally, in 1870, allowed their testimony to be received like that of all other persons in all civil and criminal proceedings, except that neither husband nor wife shall be allowed to testify as to private conversations with the other, or need be compelled to be a witness against the other.

One curious law which relates equally to husbands or wives, deserves notice, and we recommend it to the attention of our English Temperance Associations. The husband or wife of any person who has the habit of drinking intoxicating liquors to excess—call him A, may give a written notice to any person—say B, not to deliver intoxicating liquors to A. If B, within a year after the notice, deliver such liquors to A, the person giving the notice may recover by action not less than 100 dollars (£20), nor more than 500 dollars (£100), against B; and if it is a married woman who gives the notice, she may bring the action in her own name, and all damages recovered go to her separate use. In this particular the law treats both men and women alike.

In concluding his review, Mr. Sewell says very justly:—

The great difficulty to be overcome in effecting the complete emancipation of women is, not that most men are unwilling to do complete justice to the sex, or that the majority of women care nothing for this object; but it is simply a superstitious dread, lest a change so radical should unsettle all the foundations of society, and bring down the whole fabric in ruins. The history of the great legal reforms which have been accomplished in our generation shows how idle is this fear. So the great and fundamental changes already stated, which have been recently made in regard to the laws affecting married women, violently as they were resisted, are now, as admired by many of their former opponents, producing an amount of good which it is difficult to over-estimate, and no evil. When men and women are made equals in the eye of the law, and not before, shall we complete the foundations of a just commonwealth, which were laid by the Puritans, and strengthened by the Declaration of Independence.

Art. II.—THE NEW DOOMSDAY BOOK.

THE return of owners of land in England and Wales has received the popular name of the New Doomsday Book, although in a note to the preface the compiler expressly deprecates the comparison of his own work with the great book of the Conqueror, and points out its inferiority.

The note states that in the year 1085 serious apprehensions were entertained of an invasion of the kingdom by the Danes, the difficulty which the king then experienced in putting the country in a state of defence led him to form the notion of having a general survey of the whole kingdom, in order to ascertain the amount of military service which each man was bound to furnish in proportion to the extent of his holding.

To secure accuracy of results, commissioners were appointed with ample powers to ascertain upon the oath of the several "sheriffs, lords of manors, presbyters, reeves, bailiffs or villans, according to the nature of the place," what was its name, how many hides of land it contained, and how many and what landholders dwelt there.

The designations given to the various holders of land are now obsolete, and their precise meaning lost, so that it is not possible to distinguish which were landowners, and which occupiers only.

It appears, however, that 54,815 persons held land in some way or other, without reckoning villeins, many of whom, though only serfs, did, without doubt, occupy small portions of land by the permission of their lords. The number of serfs was 108,407.

The present compilation is of a very different character, and the means used to secure accuracy are very inferior.

In the place of commissioners from the king taking evidence on oath with power to summon the inhabitants of each district, and compel them to make a full disclosure of their property, we have humble clerks belonging to the various boards of poor-law guardians.

In 1862 an assessment committee was formed in every union for the investigation of the value of the rateable properties in each parish of the union, for the purpose of assessment; and as a preliminary step for such investigation the overseers of the poor were required to make out a list of all the rateable properties in each parish. These lists were deposited with the clerks of the guardians in each union.

In order to obtain the present return, application was made by the government to the clerks to furnish from these lists information as to the number of landowners in each union, the amount of land possessed by each, and its estimated yearly value.

The lists having been made in 1862, and the present return being called for in 1872, many changes had naturally taken place in the intervening ten years. The clerks were therefore requested to correct the lists as far as practicable from their own knowledge, or from information which might be received from parochial officers.

It is evident that absolute accuracy cannot be expected under these circumstances. The inaccuracy would not exist so much (if at all) in the numbers of landowners as in their names; and probably the names of many who have died since 1862 appear in the list instead of the names of their successors. I myself in examining the list belonging to a county with which I am well acquainted, perceive the name of a landowner who has been long dead. This amount of inaccuracy is, however, not sufficient to diminish its value materially.

The return was called for in consequence of a general

misapprehension which had arisen out of a statement in the census that only thirty thousand persons were land proprietors, and that half of those were women. A careful examination of the census itself would have explained the marvel. It there appears that if a land proprietor followed any other occupation, or possessed any office, he was entered in the census under the head of the other occupation or office, and not as a land proprietor.

A wealthy land proprietor who had been in the army would be returned as a retired officer. Another, if a justice of the peace, or a member of parliament, would be returned under one of those capacities. Among less wealthy land proprietors it is a common custom for a freeholder to take a neighbouring farm to cultivate along with his own land; a man thus circumstanced would appear as a farmer.

Small freeholders frequently follow a trade, and are blacksmiths, carpenters, &c. Some build an alehouse on their land, and follow the occupation of publican. Others grow vegetables, or breed poultry, and these would appear in the census as market gardeners and poulterers.

What the census really does shew is that 30,000 persons are landowners, following no other occupation, and possessed of no office.

The statement, however, was generally misunderstood, and erroneous reports arose in consequence.

In order to ascertain positively the facts of the case the late Government under Mr. Gladstone, undertook to institute an enquiry, and this enquiry was carried out through the Poor Law Officers in the manner described above.

Persons well acquainted with the country were always aware that the number of landowners must greatly exceed 30,000, for the following reason:—In every neighbourhood in every part of England, the number of men who own land is much larger than the number of women who do so; if, therefore, 15,000 women owned land it was self-evident that the number of men must be several times as great. Thus all country residents were prepared to find a larger number of landowners, but the

number given in the return is so great as to create surprise, even among country people.

It appears that there are in England and Wales
269,547 landowners who possess one acre of land and
upwards, and 703,289 who possess less than one acre.

The names and addresses are given of those who
possess one acre or upwards, and it will gratify our
readers to hear that one-seventh of the names are those
of women.*

The following table will show that more than 37,000
landowners, possessing one acre and upwards, the larger
part of whom are raised above poverty, while some enjoy great wealth—are deprived of all share in the
election of the parliamentary representatives of their
respective counties.

County.	Total Number of Owners of Land of one acre and upwards.	Number of Women Owners of Land of one acre & upwards.	Proportion of Women Owners omitting fractions.
Bedford	2,382 ...	309	One in 7
Berks	3,068 ...	432	,, ,, 7
Buckingham	3,288 ...	448	,, ,, 7
Cambridge	6,496 ...	1,085	,, ,, 5
Chester	6,029 ...	784	,, ,, 7
Cornwall	5,149 ...	639	,, ,, 8
Cumberland	5,896 ...	1,138	,, ,, 5
Derby	6,992 ...	995	,, ,, 7
Devon	10,162 ...	1,558	,, ,, 6
Dorset	3,409 ...	506	,, ,, 6
Durham	3,112 ...	363	,, ,, 8
Essex	7,472 ...	957	,, ,, 7
Gloucester	8,425 ...	1,326	,, ,, 6
Hereford	4,646 ...	829	,, ,, 5
Hertford	2,831 ...	377	,, ,, 7
Huntingdon	2,087 ...	235	,, ,, 8
Kent (exclusive of the Metropolis)	7,758 ...	1,031	,, ,, 7
Lancaster	12,558 ...	1,399	,, ,, 8
Leicester	4,927 ...	692	,, ,, 7
Lincoln	16,729 ...	1,690	,, ,, 9
Middlesex (excl. of the Metropolis)	2,875 ...	283	,, 10
Monmouth	2,841 ...	464	,, ,, 6
Norfolk	10,096 ...	1,338	,, ,, 7

* There is no reason to suppose that the proportion of women is
smaller among the freeholders who own less than an acre, and in that
case the number of women landowners would be above 137,000, but as
the names of these small freeholders are not published there are no
means of positively ascertaining this to be the fact.

County.	Total Number of Owners of Land of one acre and upwards.	Number of Women Owners of Land of one acre & upwards.	Proportion of Women Owners omitting fractions.
Northampton	4,455 ...	514	,, ,, 8
Northumberland	2,221 ...	294	,, ,, 9
Nottingham	4,628 ...	637	,, ,, 7
Oxford	3,344 ...	483	,, ,, 6
Rutland	564 ...	63	,, ,, 8
Salop	4,838 ...	776	,, ,, 6
Somerset	12,395 ...	2,209	,, ,, 5
Southampton	6,235 ...	891	,, ,, 6
Stafford	9,699 ...	1,248	,, ,, 7
Suffolk	6,765 ...	907	,, ,, 6
Surrey (excl. of the Metropolis)	4,581 ...	621	,, ,, 7
Sussex	5,059 ...	681	,, ,, 7
Warwick	4,622 ...	629	,, ,, 7
Westmoreland	2,662 ...	473	,, ,, 5
Wilts	4,378 ...	652	,, ,, 6
Worcester	5,796 ...	941	,, ,, 6
York, East Riding	4,564 ...	664	,, ,, 6
,, North Riding	6,198 ...	992	,, ,, 6
,, West Riding	17,417 ...	2,078	,, ,, 8
Anglesey	1,126 ...	181	,, ,, 6
Brecknock	1,219 ...	207	,, ,, 5
Cardigan	2,038 ...	358	,, ,, 5
Carmarthen	2,898 ...	520	,, ,, 5
Carnarvon	1,630 ...	245	,, ,, 6
Denbigh	2,272 ...	301	,, ,, 7
Flint	1,462 ...	232	,, ,, 6
Glamorgan	1,856 ...	271	,, ,, 6
Merioneth	651 ...	107	,, ,, 6
Montgomery	1,927 ...	324	,, ,, 5
Pembroke...	1,629 ...	293	,, ,, 5
Radnor	1,190 ...	136	,, ,, 8

Total numbers of owners of land of one acre and
  upwards in England and Wales (exclusive of the
  Metropolis) 269,547
Number of Women Owners   37,806
Proportion of Women Owners ... ...   1 in 7

                              JESSIE BOUCHERETT.

────────────────

ART. III.—WOMEN NEVER INVENT ANYTHING.

IT is a frequent complaint that "women never invent
anything," that they may be practical, painstaking, and
prudent, but they seem to lack the creative faculty to

be found in men, and this is sometimes asserted to be
a mark of decisive mental inferiority. It has been
more than once brought forward in the House of Commons as a reason for refusing them the elective franchise.
"Though women have almost invariably learned drawing and music," said one honourable gentleman, "they
have never produced a great artist. Women are wanting in the inventive and creative faculty."

Now whilst freely admitting that none of the great
discoveries of modern life have been made by women—
that printing, the steam engine, the use of anæsthetics,
&c., &c., are all due to men, we are not prepared to
admit that women are deficient in the organ of invention ; we deem that it is through no natural incapacity,
but through the trivial, and at the same time prosaic
nature of their education and life, that the vast majority
have been content to copy rather than originate—and
moreover that women have invented many things which
are ignored, or of which the credit has gone to the
men of the family.

Men have often devoted years of unrelaxed toil to
bring a machine to perfection ; or they have spent their
own fortunes and reduced their families to beggary to
carry out some improvement in science. Who, on reading the history of Palissy the potter, does not feel that
it would have been impossible for any woman, the
mother of a family, to have inflicted penury and starvation on her children for the sake of perfecting a
discovery, though it might hand down her name with
honour to future generations? A woman may love
science, but if the claims of her household interfere with
science, she will probably give up the hope of being an
inventor. The pressing daily need to look after the
comfort of father, brother, husband or children, takes up
far too much time with most women to permit of the
concentration required for invention. A man may shut
his study door, and calculate and experiment while the
baby is sobbing upstairs, or the meat burning to a
cinder in the kitchen, but no woman can. Even a
hard-worked man has intervals of more uninterrupted
leisure than his wife or daughters can command.

Secondly, women have been debarred from being

inventors by the want of money. If too scanty means
has paralysed the energies of many a clear-headed inventor among men, how much more may this be the
case with women? The theory that a woman should
not work unless compelled to it by actual lack of daily
bread, has from times "whereof the memory of man
runneth not to the contrary," reduced the purse-bearing
women to a very small minority. If a girl asked her
parents for more pocket-money to enable her to construct
a laboratory or workshop in which to try experiments,
she would be probably discouraged or refused—yet
parents complacently tolerate their boys cutting themselves with sharp tools, or infecting the house with
fumes of sulphuretted hydrogen, because "it is so nice
to see that George or Joe has got a mechanical or
chemical turn." Few women obtain even a partial independence or freedom to carry out their tastes till
middle life. No girl learns mechanics—till lately they
knew nothing of chemistry, but these are the very
groundwork of inventions.

This brings us to the want of education which has
hung like a dead weight upon women's creative faculties.
A discovery, an invention, may be the happy effort of a
moment, but it is the result of years of patient study
and research. A boy learns his lessons with hard drill,
which sharpens his observing and reasoning powers; a
girl slurs over her work, only employing half her mind,
learning nothing to the bottom, but satisfied if it makes a
show. The inaccurate and illogical habit of mind produced in women by the want of thoroughness in their
early education has been far more disastrous to them
than the actual want of knowledge. Besides this, comparatively few fathers have cared to instruct their
daughters in their profession ; even a painter or musician
seldom expects his girls to take up his career. The
women who have achieved eminence are almost self-
taught: Mrs. Somerville gave herself her education ;
Miss Herschel was almost the servant of all work of her
family, and could with difficulty even obtain a few music
lessons. Milton's daughters read Greek and Latin to
him by ear only, never being taught to understand what
they read. Instances of this sort might be multiplied
indefinitely.

The wonder is that with all these disadvantages women have been known to invent anything. Their efforts have of course been mostly in the direction of the fine arts, as is natural from the bias of their education; nevertheless, in America, where women are more self-dependent, many little discoveries and improvements have been made in machines of household economy by women, and the Centennial Exhibition, which reserves a special department for female work, will probably make these better known. But in literature, where women have stood more on an equality with men, there is no lack of invention on their part—rather, perhaps, we are disposed to hail with pleasure the production of any practical work of science or fact from their pens. In painting, though from the want of anatomical studies women have been placed at a disadvantage, we find no want of creative faculty in them; in sculpture, Miss Hosmer shows as keen inventive powers as any man. Two years ago, an Italian lady, the Marchioness Jannari, re-discovered the art of illuminating vellum which was forgotton in Italy; she received a prize at the Vienna Exhibition for the superb specimen of the art which she sent.

It has been repeatedly asserted that though women are good musical performers, there never was a female composer. This is not entirely true. Gretry who died in 1813, had a daughter, Lucilla, who died in her twenty-third year after having written two operas, which were considered successful. Mendelsohn wrote to his sister, "If you had the intention you certainly have the genius to compose." * * "If I had a baby to nurse I should certainly not write any scores." It is said, even, that she assisted him in some compositions.

Another instance of the inventive power in women is presented in a little pamphlet on the Tonic-Sol-Fa system, by J. Spencer Curwen. Miss Glover was the daughter of an English clergyman, and was living in Norwich, in 1812, and a young Sunday-school youth came to be instructed in singing. "It soon occurred to Miss Glover," to use Mr. Curwen's words, "that if she pasted letters over the keys of the pianoforte, and then wrote on a piece of paper the letters corresponding with those

placed over the keys, in the order in which they needed
to be touched to bring out the tune, the youth might
teach himself. So she chose the last twelve letters of
the alphabet, and pasted them over the black and white
keys. But O. P. Q. and the rest looked barbarous, and
the question came—"why not place the old Sol-Fa
syllables beneath the pitch notes, and slide them up and
down, following the key note of each tune?" It was
not long before *do, re, mi,* and the rest were thus added,
and then those who tried to pick up a tune in Miss
Glover's way told her that they never looked at O. P. Q.,
finding all that they needed in *do, re, mi.* She therefore
discarded the letters, except when they were necessary
in the beginning of a tune to tell where its pitch lay;
all that was left was a Sol-Fa notation of music. She
began a series of experiments with the Children of the
City Charity School, the Norwich Union, and the Parish
School of Pakefield, in Suffolk. The work was not all
encouraging, for many people said that the attempt to
teach music by a notation of letters was chimerical.
But Miss Glover's patient perseverance conquered, and
her work went on. She had received a thorough
musical education, and had obtained from Dr. Marsh the
idea of a family of keys—the principal major key with
its relative minor, and their offspring, the key of the
dominant with its relative minor, and that of the sub-
dominant with its relative minor. On this idea her
ladder of fame was based."

Mr. Curwen learnt and adopted the scheme, which he
carried on with so much energy that it is adopted by
many board schools, is largely employed by missionaries,
and has led to the establishment of a college. The
honour of the discovery however remains with Miss
Glover, which Mr. Curwen amply acknowledges in his
pamphlet. But how many Amerigo Vespucci's there have
been in science and art who have taken the credit to themselves. We can never tell how many men have been
aided or possibly guided in their discoveries by some
unknown silent helper in their own family. Wendell
Holmes says very truly :—

"You talk of the fire of genius. Many a blessed
woman who dies unsung and unremembered has given

out more of the real vital heat that keeps the life in human souls, without a spark flitting through her humble chimney to tell the world about it, than would set a dozen theories smoking, or a hundred odes simmering in the brains of so many men of genius * * I have known more than one genius, high-decked, full-freighted, wide-sailed, gay-pennoned, that, but for the bare toiling arms, and brave, warm beating heart of the faithful little wife, that nestled close in his shadow, and clung to him, so that no wind or wave could part them, and dragged him on against all the tide of circumstance, would soon have gone down the stream, and been heard of no more."

ART. IV.—REVIEWS.

Memoir and Correspondence of Caroline Herschel. (John Murray.)

"Caroline Herschel was one of the noble company of unknown helpers. She stood beside her brother William Herschel sharing his labours, helping his life. In the days when he gave up a lucrative career that he might devote himself to astronomy, it was owing to her thrift and care that he was not harassed by the rankling vexations of money matters. She had been his helper and assistant in the days when he was a leading musician; she became his helper and assistant in the days when he gave himself up to astronomy. By sheer force of will and devoted affection, she learned enough of mathematics and of methods of calculation which to those unlearned seem mysteries, to be able to commit to writing the results of his researches. She became his assistant in the workshop; she helped him to grind and polish his mirrors; she stood beside his telescope in the nights of mid-winter to write down his observations, when the very ink was frozen in the bottle. She kept him alive by her care; thinking nothing of herself, she lived for him. She loved him, and believed in him, and helped him with all her heart-and with all her strength."

H

Caroline Herschel was born in Hanover in 1750. As
a girl her chief occupations were scullery-work and knitting ; her mother seems to have feared to let her have
too good an education, and it was only occasionally she
got even a few music lessons. At 22 she joined her brother
William, then a popular musician in Bath. Here his first
discoveries were made, and here she began her astronomical education in the midst of housekeeping and
singing engagements, frequently breakfast being the
only time when she could get her questions solved. In
1782 she removed with her brother to Slough on his
appointment as Astronomer Royal, and her labours here
received their first recognition in being nominated as
his assistant with a salary of £50 a year.

It must not be forgotten, says Mrs. Herschel, that the progress of
astronomical science since Sir William Herschel's great reflector startled the world, has not been greater than has been the change both in
opinion and practice, on the subject of female employments and education. The appointment of a young woman as assistant astronomer,
with a regular salary for her services was an unprecedented occur-
rence in England.

In 1786 she discovered her first comet. "You have
immortalized your name," wrote Alexander Aubert to
her, and before the end of 1797 she had discovered eight,
to five of which the priority of her claim over other obser-
vers is unquestioned. In 1798 the Royal Society published two of her works, namely, "A Catalogue of 860
stars observed by Flamsteed, but not included in the
British Catalogue," and "A General Index of Reference
to every observation of every star in the above-
mentioned British Catalogue." Another work which was
not published was the most valuable, as it was the most
laborious of all her undertakings. This was "The
Reduction and Arrangement in the form of a Catalogue,
in Zones, of all the star-clusters and nebulæ observed
by Sir W. Herschel in his sweeps." It supplied the
needful data for Sir John Herschel when he undertook
the review of the nebulæ of the northern hemisphere ;
and it was for this that the gold medal of the Royal
Astronomical Society was voted to her in 1828, followed
by the extraordinary distinction of an honorary membership. This catalogue was not finished till she was 75
years old. This was followed by her election as hon.

member of the Royal Irish Academy, and by the presentation of the gold medal for science from the King of Prussia on her 96th birthday, which was accompanied by a letter from Humboldt to the "fellow worker of your immortal brother, Sir W. Herschel, in discoveries, observations, and laborious calculations." At 98 she died. For the last few years, we are told, she lived almost altogether in the past, in recollections of her beloved brother, to whom she had devoted the best years of her life. After reading the record of her loving, unselfish life, we feel as if we had found a personal friend.

Re-echoes. By Frances Power Cobbe. (Williams & Norgate.)

If it be true that "good wine needs no bush," neither does a book by Miss Cobbe require any commendation from the *Englishwoman's Review.*" There is sure to be in it good wholesome advice and words of hearty sympathy for women. "Re-echoes" is a reprint of some of the papers which Miss Cobbe for many years contributed to the *Echo,* those being selected which are on general subjects, rather than those exclusively on topics of the hour. It will suffice for our purpose to quote one or two passages.

"The reports of the directors of convict prisons in England for 1870 show, that out of 250 female convicts discharged during 1869, no less than 191 went voluntarily, on their release, to various Missions and Refuges, presumably reformed. It is this common but most false notion, this over-readiness to give up a woman as irretrievably disgraced, which is itself the cause why hundreds of hapless ones, who have only entered on the evil way, are never helped out of it and guided into better paths, but left to sink to the very bottom of the foul pool of vice into which, it may be, they have but dipped their feet. If the drunkenness of a woman be more disgusting than that of a man, it ought to be remembered that it has usually many more palliations."

The same generous pleading may be found in an article called "The Great Divorce Case:" "Women are of course in many points weaker than men; but it may be doubted

whether many men would behave as well as they do if
subjected from childhood to the unwholesome, heating,
stimulating atmosphere wherein they live, with pleasure
for their only business, and dress and music, and the re-
ciprocation of idle talk and flattery, for their occupation;
in short, without one healthy, bracing exercise for body
and mind, heart, will or intellect."

We recommend also a perusal of the "Chivalry of the
Period," about the probable loss of which we hear so
much when women try to render themselves self-dependent.

We fear it is a very enigmatical thing this same masculine chivalry
of the 19th century. In the humble ranks it never induces men to
prevent women from doing the coarsest and hardest labour. They may
sweep crossings, and fill coal trucks, and dance on tight ropes, and no
chivalry says, " Leave it for me !" But when women work so long that
their small strength competes with men, after the fashion of the tortoise
and the hare, then chivalry limits the hours of female labour; and when
women by chance discover that they can earn a good deal of money
in some new way—say by painting on china—then the chivalry of
their male companions induces them to seize their maul-sticks and
forbid them to do any work but that for which the smallest pay is to
be demanded. Chivalry is not in the least shocked at the sight of a
woman dressed in male attire dancing on a public stage with her legs
at right angles, but chivalry is disgusted beyond measure at the sight
of a modest lady attending the sick as a physician in a hospital.
Chivalry has not lightened any single tax, succession duty, or other
burden, in favour of women. There is nothing for which a woman
pays less and gets the same thing as a man. But there are a great
many things for which women pay as much (or from their ignorance
more) than a man, and obtain less in the way of accompanying rights
and privileges, without chivalry being in the remotest degree concerned with the matter. All this, to our thinking, is rather unchival-
rous chivalry.

The Practice of Medicine by Women. An Essay, by Sophia Jex
   Blake. Reprinted from the *Fortnightly Review*, of March, 1875.
   (J. Lindsay, 104, High Street, Edinburgh.)

AT the present day, when the barriers which have so
long excluded women from the study of medicine seem
breaking down with a rush on all sides, the publication
of this pamphlet—which gives a clear exposition of the
effects of the Act of 1858, and of the efforts which so
many ladies have made, during fifteen years, to obtain
professional education—will be found very useful.
When any Bill is brought before Parliament, it is intro-

duced to the attention of thousands, who read and desire
to understand it, but have never thought of examining a
"question", while it remained, so to speak, private property; and this pamphlet will be of real service to many
who wish to understand Mr. Cowper-Temple's motion
to admit women who have obtained a foreign diploma
to practice in England. Mr. Cowper-Temple said, last
session, "a large portion of the public were really
desirous that properly qualified women should be able
to practise medicine, and yet if women desired at present
to obtain degrees, they must go to France or to America
—anywhere rather than to their own land—because
England was the only one of the chief countries in
Europe where it was impossible for them to obtain
degrees." "The natural laws of supply and demand,"
Miss Jex-Blake concludes, "may well be trusted here
as elsewhere, and if women doctors do not meet a real
need, they will simply die out of themselves. At
present, it is certain that a definite amount of demand
for their services does exist, or sixteen thousand women
would hardly petition Parliament on the subject; and
seeing that 'an injustice is not small because it concerns
a small number,' I hold that if a single woman desires
to consult a physician of her own sex, and if one other
woman desires to qualify herself to be that physician,
no third person whatever has a right to interfere with
the accomplishment of such legitimate desires."

Workhouse Girls. By Margaret Elliot.

A LITTLE pamphlet which is a copy of a journal that was
kept by the author and her sister fifteen years ago,
before the subject of the advantages or disadvantages
of training girls in large schools was generally discussed.
Miss Elliot shows a way in which ladies might do much
quiet good where a committee does not exist. She
fully endorses Mrs. Senior's views on the unpractical
nature of the teaching; we sympathise with the kindly,
but overworked mistress, who says, "Lor, ma'am, the
girl don't know so much as to take the kettle off the fire
if it boils over, and as for the baby, would as lief hold it
upside down as not." "Small blame to them either,"
said another, "in them institutions they only think of

the children making a fine figure in reading, writing,
and such like, and drills them till they get stupid, and
are of no use to themselves or any one else."

Woman and a future Life. (Houlston & Wright.)

AN earnest little book, which aims in the form of a
vision, to show the help which men and women could
mutually render each other if united in the same pursuits and interests—if uncramped by the convention-
alities of ignorant prejudice and love of dominion.
Here and there are clear practical sentences: "It is not
love of womanhood, but love of self, which leads men
to oppose the possession by women of the commonest
political rights, and creates a jealousy of the slightest
division of that power which they so falsely imagine
they will eternally arrogate to themselves." And again,
"Men complain of the 'instinctive and emotional' in
women, yet they constantly allow these influences to
dominate the higher intelligences in themselves." The
volume, however, would be more likely to be generally
useful if its reflections had been embodied in a more
practical shape.

Our Magazine.

THIS is the first number—and a very good one—of a
school magazine issued by the pupils, with the exception of one or two articles contributed by the teachers,
of the North London Collegiate School for Girls. The
first magazine ever issued by a girls' school was published
the year before last at Milton Mount College, Graves-
end, and Miss Buss's scholars are following in their
steps. "Our Magazine" contains stories, poetry, notes
of travel, most useful articles upon education (we assume these last to be contributed by the teachers) reports of the work of various useful associations, and
local news. It is an excellent example for other girls'
schools to copy.

Good Words for March has an article on "Nursing as
a Profession for Gentlewomen" by Miss Florence S. Lees.

Miss Swanwick's Paper on the "Sunday Question,"
which was read at the Social Science Congress, has
been reprinted as a pamphlet.

The *Æsthetic Review* is the name of a new paper published by Madame Ronniger, and principally devoted to literature and art. Madame Ronniger's well-established reputation in both of these subjects is alone a sure guarantee that the paper, which for the present appears every two months, will be well conducted.

ART. V.—EVENTS OF THE MONTH.

EDUCATION.

CAMBRIDGE LOCAL AND HIGHER LOCAL EXAMINATIONS.

Mr. Phillips-Jodrell, M.A., late Fellow of Trinity College, offers two or more Exhibitions of £25 a year each, tenable for three years, to be given for proficiency in the Cambridge Local Examinations in December, 1876, to girls who are preparing for the profession of teaching.

Also, two or more Exhibitions of £25 a year each, tenable for three years, to be given for proficiency in the Cambridge Higher Local Examinations in June, 1876, to women who are preparing for the profession of teaching.

The Exhibitioners will be required to proceed to Cambridge and to conform to the conditions of residence and attendance on lectures laid down by the Committee of the Association for Promoting the Higher Education of Women in Cambridge. A further sum, sufficient, together with the exhibition, to defray the whole expense of residence and instruction in Cambridge, will be lent by Mr. Phillips-Jodrell, without interest, to any Exhibitioner applying for it who shall appear on enquiry to be unable to defray such expenses out of her own resources, on certain conditions of repayment which will be stated to the applicant.

Another gift of a somewhat unusual character has lately been made in recognition of the value of systematic education of the University type for women.

The proceeds for a year of an Oxford Fellowship are to be given in the form of a Scholarship of £100 a year for three years, tenable at Girton College from next October. The scholarship will be awarded to the best candidate in the June entrance examination, for which forms of entry may be obtained from the Honorary Secretary, Miss Davies, 17, Cunningham place, London, N.W. The now urgently needed extension of the building is to be set on foot without delay, more than £3,000 having been promised towards the estimated expense of £6,000. Among contributions to the Special Fund for this purpose may be mentioned grants of £100 from the Grocers' Company, £50 from the Mercers' and 30 guineas from the Merchant Taylors' Company.

LECTURES TO WOMEN IN CAMBRIDGE.

The lectures to women during the Easter term will be as follows:—

English Literature...Mr. Skeat & others...
English History......Mr. Prothero ......
Astronomy.. ....Mr. Ferrers ....Room A, Tu., Fri., 1 P.M.
Conic Sections ......Mr. Wright ....Room A, Mon., Thur., 3 P.M.
Mechanics ....Mr. Garnett ....Room A, Wed., Sat.,10.30 A.M.

The following are also continued:—

Divinity ....Mr. Stanton ....Lecture-Hall, Thurs., Sat., 11 A.M.
Modern History......Prof. Seeley ....　　　,,　Wed., 12 A.M.
Arithmetic ....Mr. Hudson ....　　　,,　Wed., Fri., 2 P.M.
　(Continuation)
Arithmetic ....Mr. Torry............　　　,,　Tues.,Thurs.,12M.
　(Elementary)
French I..............Mr. Boquel ....　　　,,　Wed., Fri., 4 P.M.
　(Confined to Stu-
　dents over 17.)
French II. ....　　　,,　　　　,,　　　,,　　5 P.M.
German ....Mr. Steinhilper......Room A, Tues., Sat., 4 P.M.
Early English ......Mr. Skeat ....At his house, Mon., Fri.,3 P.M.
Latin I. ....Mr. Lewis...........Committee Room, Wed., Sat., 3 P.M.
　,,　II. ....　　　,,　............　　　,,　　　,,　2 P.M.
Greek I. ....Mr. Archer-Hind...Room A, Tues., Thurs., 12M.
　,,　II. ....　　　,,　...　　,,　　　Wed., Sat., 2 P.M.
Political Economy...Miss Paley...........Lecture Hall, Wed., Fri., 10 A.M.
Logic ....Mr. Ward...........Committee Room, Tues., Thurs., 10 A.M.
Chemistry ....Mr. Main ....S. John's Laboratory, Wed., Fri., 9 A.M.
　(Laboratory Work)

Manchester New College. Admission of Women.—At an adjourned meeting of the Trustees of Manchester New College, held on February 9, the following resolution, moved by Mr. R. D. Darbishire (Manchester), and seconded by Mr. J. Lupton (Leeds), was carried by a large majority—"That this meeting of the Trustees of Manchester New College, recognising with sympathy and respect the growth of the demand now made by women for the opportunities of higher and systematic intellectual cultivation, declares with satisfaction that as the classes of the College have always been open to any who wish to attend them as occasional students on payment of the proper fees, they be not now closed against students who may be women."

A cookery class has recently been established in connection with the North London Collegiate School for Girls. The terms are very moderate, and place good cooking lessons within reach of any of the pupils. The teacher is a lady who was trained at South Kensington expressly to conduct this class.

The marked advance in the opportunities open for women to enter professions has received a great stimulus in the allotment of a salary of £1,000 a year to Miss Buss, of the North London Collegiate School for Girls. This lady is well entitled to this splendid recognition of her abilities, as this wonderfully successful school was founded and throughout managed by her. The head mistress-ship of St. Paul's school is equally well endowed. A lady, formerly connected with the Queen's Institute, has been appointed head mistress of one of the English public day schools for girls at £250 a year, and capitation on each pupil after the school numbers one hundred.

MEDICAL EDUCATION.

On March 2nd the Duke of Richmond and Gordon received at the Privy Council Office a deputation of ladies and gentlemen interested in the question of the registration of properly-educated women as practitioners of medicine in terms of the Medical Act of 1858. The deputation included Lord Aberdare, Mrs. Garrett Anderson, M.D., Miss Bailey, Dr. King Chalmers, Mr.

Forsyth, M.P., Miss Jex-Blake, Mr. A. T. Norton (Dean of the London School of Medicine for Women), Mrs. Pennington and the Right Hon. J. Stansfeld, M.P.

Mr. Stansfeld introduced the deputation as representing the London School of Medicine for Women, and also the other friends of the movement in Edinburgh and elsewhere. The object was to ascertain the intention of her Majesty's Government with reference to this question. Certain ladies had already spent much time and much money in preparation and study for the profession of medicine, and every year that passed added to the loss and injustice which they had already suffered. He believed that the question had now passed beyond the phase suitable to legislation by a Bill introduced by a private member, and that the time had come for action on the part of the Government. The question now was what that action should be. In answer to an inquiry addressed to his noble friend Lord Sandon, he had been informed last session that the Government would consider the matter during the recess, and the present deputation was anxious to learn the result of such deliberations. The letter addressed by order of his Grace to the President of the Medical Council had occasioned a three days' debate in the Medical Council, and at its close they reported in reply that they were "not prepared to say that women ought to be excluded from the profession." He rested the claim of women to enter the profession of medicine on two main grounds —1. The *à priori* right which all women had to gain their livelihood by an honourable calling, and the equal right which suffering women could advance to be attended, if they wished it, by physicians of their own sex; and (2) the interests of medicine itself as a science and as an art. It was no part of the theory of those whom he represented to assert the identity of the two sexes; on the contrary, they believed in essential differences between them as regarded faculties, instincts, and special kinds of activity. He believed that the sensitiveness, quickness, delicacy, and self-possession in which women so frequently excelled men were all qualities highly fitting them for medical practice. He could not doubt that the admission of women to the profession would result in some gain to medical science, and in still more gain to medical practice.

Mr. Forsyth, M.P., felt that there was a peculiar hardship in the exclusion of women from a profession for which they seemed peculiarly adapted. The point to which he desired specially to direct attention, was the fact that no law prohibited the admission of women to the medical profession. The Act of 1858 contemplated the admission to the register of all persons who had complied with certain conditions. The word "male" did not once occur in the Act; but a certificate of competency was required, and the 19 examining boards by whom such certificates were granted had, it seemed, combined to refuse to examine women with a view of ascertaining their competency for practice. Hence arose the whole difficulty. That women could successfully study and practise medicine had been abundantly proved in foreign countries, where no such obstruction existed, and he earnestly trusted that the Government would forthwith frame a measure that should meet and remedy the present condition of things here.

Dr. King Chambers felt sure that the Government could now deal with this question with less difficulty than at any previous time. The prejudices of medical men on the subject were gradually diminishing, and the study of medicine by women was becoming more generally popular. A majority of the medical journals were now either in favour of the women or at least neutral. This change of feeling on the part of the profession would certainly render the action of the Government easier.

Mrs. Garrett Anderson explained that a two-fold difficulty lay in the way of admission of women to the register. The only body that did not profess to be able to exclude women as women was the Society of Apothecaries, and they practically refused them admission, inasmuch as they would only examine those who were educated at the public medical schools already recognized, and from these schools women were excluded. It was true that on the Continent women could obtain an excellent education in medicine, but then no foreign diploma was now admitted to registration in this country.   The complete School of Medicine which had been organized for women in London was not recognized by the examining boards, and its students were refused admission at all the hospitals.

Lord Aberdare said he felt very strongly that this avenue of employment should not be closed to women, and that, in fact, it was only by accident that it was so closed.   On all sides there seemed a resolution to shut out the women.   He must say that, as a man, he felt profound shame at the proceedings of which he heard on the part of medical bodies with regard to this question.   He might remind the Lord President of a certain room in the South Kensington Museum which was expressly set apart as a refuge for those women who had been driven forth from the china painting works at Stoke by the jealousy of the male china painters.   He confessed that the injustice under which these women suffered seemed to him no greater than that now complained of.   The opinion was daily growing that women should be provided with the means of earning an honourable livelihood in this profession as well as in other ways.   He trusted that the Government would follow up the course they had begun by the letter to the Medical Council, and he could assure the Lord President that strong support would not be wanting from those on the opposite side of the House.

The Duke of Richmond and Gordon expressed his gratification at receiving the deputation, and his sense of obligation for the clear manner in which the facts had been laid before him.   It was true that the Government had the matter under consideration, but he feared that he could not at that moment state the course which they will ultimately adopt.   He quite saw the force of all that had been put forth by Mr. Stansfeld, and by Lord Aberdare, but he could not at present announce a distinct line of action.   The question seemed in the first instance to rest with the examining boards, as if they consented to admit the women, *cadit quæstio*, the need of legislation would disappear.   He desired to know whether he was correct in understanding that the women proposed to attend women only.

Mr. Stansfeld replied that he presumed the practice

of women would be among their own sex, but that they desired an education complete in all its branches, and a diploma qualifying them for general practice.

Lord Sandon inquired whether he correctly understood that no special privileges were desired, but merely the removal of special disabilities.

Mr. Stansfeld replied that this was exactly the case, and that if only women were placed on an equality as regarded examination and registration, the friends of the movement would see that all other facilities, such as hospitals, were provided, if necessary.

Mrs. Garrett Anderson remarked that several of the examining bodies seemed to doubt whether they had the power to examine women, and that an authoritative declaration of that power might be sufficient to solve the difficulty.

Miss Jex-Blake remarked that on the other hand it had never yet been decided that any of the examining boards had the power to refuse to examine women. It was true that they had assumed that power, but it had never yet been conceded to them by any legal tribunal, except in the case of the Scotch Universities, where a decision was given by a bare majority of the Lords of the Session, and on quite different grounds.

The Duke of Richmond and Gordon inquired whether no such case had ever come before the courts.

Mr. Stansfeld replied in the negative, and added that it would be quite out of the question to expect individual women to incur the expense of such legal proceedings.

Mr. Forsyth urged that the Bill should be a general one, including all the examining bodies, and referred to the fact that Mr. Playfair had opposed the Scotch Universities Bill on the plea of its limited application.

Lord Aberdare then expressed his opinion that the true way of meeting the difficulty would be to require all the nineteen examining bodies to examine candidates without distinction of person, just as the Act of 1858 expressly bound them to examine all candidates irrespective of their holding or not holding certain medical theories.

The Duke of Richmond and Gordon having promised his best attention to the subject, the deputation withdrew.

The second reading of Mr. Cowper-Temple's Bill is fixed for Wednesday, July 5th. This Bill is to enable women who have obtained medical degrees in the foreign Universities of Paris, Berlin, Leipzig, Berne, or Zurich, to be registered as practitioners in England.

THE REGISTRATION OF MIDWIVES.—Deputations from the Obstetrical Society, the Social Science Association, the British Medical Association, and the Society for the Protection of Infant Life waited upon the Duke of Richmond, Lord Sandon, and Mr. Sclater Booth, March 8th, to express their views relative to the instruction and registration of midwives. Among those present were Dr. Priestly, Dr. Arthur Farre, Sir Trevor Lawrence, Dr. Ryalls, and Mr. E. Noel, M.P. Mr. Lyon Playfair having introduced the deputation, Dr. Priestly, President of the Obstetrical Society, pointed out the large amount of infantile mortality caused and the injury done to women by improper attendance by unskilled midwives during confinements. The deputation urged that it would be a fitting function of the Government to see that, if possible, midwives should be better educated, and some form of registration provided by the State which should indicate who were qualified to practise. Mr. E. Hart and Dr. Curgenven having expressed their views, the Duke of Richmond said they were always very much indebted to any body of gentlemen who wished to place before them the knowledge they had acquired, and seldom was a deputation composed of men more thoroughly competent to speak upon a subject they had at heart. Every one must feel that this subject was one of great importance, and since a deputation had waited upon him last year he had written to the Medical Council on the subject. The question would not be lost sight of by the Government, but it must be remembered that its importance was scarcely exceeded by the difficulty of dealing with it.

The report of the Winter Session of the London Medical School for Women gives a most satisfactory statement of its progress. Five new students were admitted when it re-opened. The classes this year embrace anatomy, practical anatomy, physiology, surgery, practice of medicine, midwifery, forensic medicine, and ophthalmic surgery. The funds of the school do not admit at present of the simultaneous delivery of lectures on every subject required by a medical education, but by a rotation of classes it has been arranged that the whole curriculum will be embraced within a three years course of study. The winter session of 1876-77 will therefore include practice of medicine, clinical medicine, and clinical surgery, and pathology, and it is intended that the fourth year of study shall be devoted to practical work in a hospital or dispensary, to practical pharmacy, practical widwifery, vaccination, &c.

"The non-medical public are probably not aware that it is absolutely required by the examining boards that all students shall pursue the bedside study of disease in hospitals of not less than 100 beds (if in London) and with a distinct staff of medical and surgical officers. Almost all the metropolitan hospitals which have the requisite number of beds are already appropriated for the instruction of male students, and in most quarters great unwillingness exists to extend their benefits to women, although in many instances this might easily be done without in any way affecting the interests of the male students. In Edinburgh an effort was made to exclude the women students from the infirmary of that city, and for two years the attempt was successful. But when the question came fairly before the public, it was decided that the infirmary could not be considered as the appanage of students of one sex only, and its benefits were extended to women also, with the understanding that arrangements for their private instruction should be made by those doctors who were willing to do so, at separate hours. As this plan was found to work with complete success, although the numbers of male students was very much greater than in any London school, it is difficult to see why it could not also be carried out here. It cannot be doubted that sufficient public interest exists in the question to secure increased support for any hospital that will secure to women the needful facilities."

The recent decision of the governors of the Queen's Hospital, Birmingham, to admit women to its educational advantages, has decided this question. It cannot be long before one, at least, of the great London hospitals, follows the same generous policy.

SUFFRAGE.

A noteworthy incident of the Manchester election is thus recorded by a local paper as "showing that even under the present suffrage women cannot always be excluded from voting at Parliamentary elections." A lady householder voted in Oxford Ward. Her name, Christian

Donald, was unmistakably on the register. She claimed her privilege, and as her name appeared on the burgess roll the returning officer could not refuse her a ballot paper. She made no secret of the fact that she used it on behalf of the champion of the equalisation of the municipal and Parliamentary franchise. This is not the first occasion on which Mr. Jacob Bright has received similar support. At the election in 1867, when he was first returned to Parliament, before the last Reform Act, Lily Maxwell, whose name was on the register, recorded her vote in his favour.—*Woman's Suffrage Journal.*

The election of Mr. Peter Rylands, for Burnley, and of Mr. Blake, for Leominster, has had the effect of returning two warm supporters of the Woman's Disabilities Removal Bill to Parliament.

The number of petitions sent in by March 7th, amounted to 232, with 118,746 signatures. No petitions against the Bill have yet been recorded. At a meeting of the Healey Liberal Association, on February 19, a resolution in favour of Women's Suffrage was adopted.

On February 16th, the annual meeting of the Edinburgh National Society for Women's Suffrage was held in the Literary Institute. There was a good attendance. Amongst others present were—Professor Masson, Professor Hodgson, Mr. Macfie (of Dreghorn), Councillor Wellstood, Councillor Durham, ex-Bailie Lewis, the Rev. Mr. Seton, ex-Councillor Robertson, Mr. Duncan M'Laren, jun., Mrs. Duncan M'Laren, Miss Becker (Manchester), Miss Beedy, Miss Wigham, Mrs. Wellstood, Miss Stevenson, Mrs. Macqueen, Miss Craig, Miss Caldwell, Mrs. and Miss Hope (of Bordlands), Mrs. Nichol, Mrs. Lucas, Mrs. Hodgson, Mrs. Richardson, and Miss E. Kirkland. Professor Masson was called to the chair.

A series of very important drawing-room meetings have also been held in Edinburgh during the winter.

Bristol.—The annual meeting of the subscribers and friends of the Bristol and West of England branch of the National Society for Women's Suffrage was held February 17th, at the offices of the society, 53, Park-street, under the presidency of Mrs. Charles Thomas.— Miss L. Ashworth read the annual report of the society.

A large public meeting also was held in the Victoria rooms, Bristol, on Thursday, March 9th.

Hanley.—A public meeting was held in the Mechanics Institute, Hanley, on Feb. 21st.   The Mayor of Hanley (Mr. J. Baker) presided, and on the platform were Mrs. Lucas, Miss Beedy, Mrs. Leslie, Mrs. Ashford, and several gentlemen.

Stafford.—A large and influential meeting was held in the Lyceum on Feb. 22nd.

Mr. P. A. Taylor in the course of a speech to his constituents at Leicester, said :—

I will allude to two or three matters more interesting to you than the Suez Canal.   One is the question of Women's Suffrage.   I believe some of you feel a little disappointed that there has been a check in the progress of this question for the last three or four years, but if it be so I would recommend you to look back for 20 years, and I might defy you to point to any question of our time that has made such great advances.   This question of giving women a vote is getting matured, and in the year which has swept by I find that at Birmingham women are capable of taking degrees and occupying positions as surgeons in an institution there.   I need not point out to you that that would have been an impossible thing for us to have seen twenty or thirty years ago, and would have then involved a sacrifice of old ideas and prejudices infinitely greater than would be the case in giving a woman a vote now.   I think it is extremely desirable that women should have some political power, as, for instance, there has been an attempt to give women the right to their own property, and yet the mode in which this has been carried out has been of a most slovenly and ridiculous kind.

THE QUEEN'S INSTITUTE, DUBLIN.

The annual meeting of the patrons and supporters of the Queen's Institute was held January 21st, in the Molesworth Hall, Molesworth-street.   There was a numerous attendance of ladies and gentlemen.   His Grace the Duke of Leinster presided.   The report was read by Miss Corlett the secretary, to whose untiring exertions the rapid advance made by the Institute is mainly owing.   The following extracts from the report will be interesting.

"Two years have elapsed since an account has been rendered of the progress of the Queen's Institute, but in the interval twenty-nine meetings of Committees have been held.   The period has been spent in bringing some things to a close which proved inconvenient when brought into operation, and in the endeavour to place the work of the Institute on a basis in accordance with

I

the great advance to be observed in the progress of
what are termed 'women's questions.' These may be
taken to mean simply women's right to share in the
world's work, the world's responsibility, the world's
prosperity. Before passing in review the connection of
the Queen's Institute with these modern movements,
it may be fruitful to point out, that a vast change
seems rapidly approaching our benevolent organisations
and our institutions, and we shall soon see new modes
of dealing with poverty and vice ; new modes of reform :
new institutions for the prevention of misfortune and
crime. New ideas are every day taking shape. In all
efforts for promoting public good, women will be called
on to take their part, and we have no doubt situations
of usefulness, honour, and emolument will by these
changes be open to women. Voluntary workers will
soon come to be assisted by well-paid labourers ;
governors, superintendents, inspectors will be required ;
and we hope women will look forward to the possibility
of these things not being so distant, but that they may
prudently begin to prepare for them. Among the acquirements necessary in such positions will be a practical
acquaintance with figures, and in this subject ladies may
graduate at the Queen's Institute, by attending the
book-keeping courses; they will find arithmetic a good
foundation for all purposes, either as paid officers, members of committees, or mistresses of large establishments,
and always useful to themselves individually. We also
recommend the study of political economy, which has
been introduced at the Queen' Institute, as a necessary
branch of knowledge to women who look forward to a
career of usefulness for others and themselves."

"A statement of the progress of the Institute, from its
commencement, has been compiled and printed, which
it is hoped will give a clear idea of the work which has
been done by your society. The original draft was
made three years ago for the trustees of the Ladies'
Irish Work Fund (which is now an endowment of the
Queen's Institute for certain trusts), and which some
members considered it would be useful to print, not
alone for this society, but of others founded in imitation
of it. The Queen's Institute has come to be considered

the typical institution for women, and the associations
at Vienna, Berlin, Darmstadt, and in Italy, have been
founded on the model of the Queen's Institute,
and now in Georgia a similar society is in process of
formation. The society in Vienna has lately been enabled to erect magnificent buildings for its accommodation, and we may fairly hope the Queen's Institute will
soon, by the liberality of the public, be equally well
housed. The Female Professional Schools at Turin and
Milan have grants in aid from the Italian Government,
from the municipalities, also the liberal patronage and
support of the public. Our friends must be informed
that the growth of the Institute, from year to year, being
such, that what was regarded as suitable accommodation some years ago is now wholly inadequate to meet
our present necessities, and the inevitable requirements
of the future. All these societies abroad have now their
large educational schools, affording teaching suited to
their own purposes. This, no doubt, has been discovered
to be essential.

The music classes, originally at the Royal Irish Academy of Music, were removed to your own house; not
because better instruction could be given, but that
working mutual time-tables between institutions was
found to be an utter impossibility. The system of
teaching music at the Queen's Institute is identical with
that of the Academy:

The addition recently made to your curriculum of
science classes has arisen from a desire to open greater
advantages of education, and to enable teachers to
profit by the payment on results allowed by the Government. In Ireland we find during last year three female
teachers received such payments against seventeen in
England.

Your educational classes are directed with a view to
insure thoroughness in every branch, and we may hope
governesses educated at the Institute will continue to
command high salaries. There is here an opportunity
of acquiring accomplishments not usually taught elsewhere, or learned under less favourable circumstances.
Teachers can, through the School of Art, obtain the
Government certificates as drawing mistresses, and have
the same advantages in the Science Classes."

"Among contemporary movements to be regarded with gratification, is the opening of the Pharmaceutical Society of Ireland to women, to be trained as pharmacians. The Pharmaceutical Society is the first body in Ireland which has taken a thoroughly liberal view of the abilities of women. This promises to be a permanent occupation for ladies. The occupation of compounding is one eminently suited to educated women. Classes in preparation for the matriculation examination for the Parmaceutical Society are at work at the Institute.

The English Government having opened some of the Civil Service departments to ladies, classes have been formed at the Queen's Institute with a view to preparative instruction in the branches more specially required for the examinations. Some of these appointments are worth £170 a-year, and are filled by the daughters of men who have been well-known and eminent in public life. * * *

Two ladies have started in the specification and plan-copying business at the Queen's Institute, where lecture diagram making, architectural drawing, and similar work is carried on. * * *

Her Majesty the Queen has been graciously pleased to permit our educational schools to be named "Queen's College for the Education of Women."

The report went on to state that a fund is being raised for the extension of the building. A good exhibition room is greatly needed by the Institute.

Mr. John P. Adair, barrister-at-law, moved the adoption of the report. He said that amongst those callings which were generally considered as peculiarly belonging to the manly class were the medical and legal professions; and yet they had instances of the success and efficiency of females in both these avocations. He himself knew more than one judge who, when he was at the bar, and afterwards when on the bench, received valuable assistance from his daughter in the preparation of his professional work. Then ladies were found in the hospitals. He himself was governor of three hospitals, he could answer for the nerve and skill they bring to the performance of their duties as nurses.

Miss Tod next said that there was a large amount of

the work of female education which could only be done by large institutions like the Queen's Institute. To that institution belonged the credit of having initiated the system which it best represented in these countries, and braved many serious difficulties, which no private person could well undertake.

Miss Ashworth, Miss Becker and others next addressed the meeting, which then separated.

WOMEN'S PROTECTION AND PROVIDENT LEAGUE.

THE Women's Protection and Provident League is continuing its useful work most actively. It has commenced a monthly journal, which will be of great service to the members by making known the progress of the societies, and collecting and spreading information about the condition of the different trades engaged in by women. Friends of the movement should endeavour to circulate this little publication, whose office is 31, Little Queen Street, Holborn. It gives ample details of the meetings held by the various benefit societies.

It is also proposed to establish a Woman's Printing Company, and a preliminary circular has been issued. It says :—

The results of the experiments hitherto made, have shown that there is room for the special capabilities of women in some branches of printing ; and in many other occupations in which they are at present seldom employed. Their progress in such occupations appears, however, to have been retarded by the fact, that there are so few facilities for enabling them thoroughly to learn, and afterwards to carry on the work.

It is obvious, for many reasons, that such facilities can only be fully afforded in establishments where, although some of the instructors would necessarily be men, the general supervision would be in the hands of women. The success of the Queen's Institute in Dublin, conclusively shews, that, under this supervision, such establishments may be made thoroughly successful. Parents, however anxious they may be to give their daughters the means of earning their own livelihood, may yet shrink from apprenticing them in ordinary workshops where the majority of the employés are men ; and even if girls are so apprenticed, there are, and for some time must be, difficulties attending their entrance into, and employment in such workshops.

It is suggested, that, to meet the wants above indicated, workshops should be opened where girls might receive a thorough technical training ; and where, also, an opportunity should be given to test fully the business aptitude of women, by the gradual formation of a

Co-operative Trade Establishment in which the workers should be at liberty, if they desired, to become, by small payment, shareholders and participators in the profits.

It is proposed that the training should be thorough, that good work should be insisted upon, and that it should be paid for at the ordinary trade rate; since it is not at all intended to introduce women into an unfair competition as regards wages, such as that to which workmen have hitherto naturally objected.

Temporary Office,
31, Little Queen Street, Holborn.

February, 1876.

Already printing is being done by women in the office of the League, while new premises are being sought for. The establishment of a good school where girls can receive the necessary technical training to fit them for being skilled printers, will greatly facilitate the practice of this profession for women.

ANOTHER TRADE SOCIETY FOR WOMEN.

A MEETING was held at the infant school, Bishopsgate-churchyard, on the evening of February 16, under the auspices of the Women's Protective and Provident League, in order to form a society amongst female machinists for the protection of their trade interests, and for making some provision against sickness and want of employment.

The chair was taken by Mr. Verney, a member of the league.

Mrs. Paterson, the hon. sec., read a letter from Mr. Harcourt Johnstone, M.P., who regretted his inability to attend.

Mrs. PATERSON said that what they wanted was not so much to increase women's wages as to prevent their falling lower than they were at present. The interest in the formation of the society had been considerably quickened by a case which had occurred lately, in which a reduction of wages without notice had been successfully resisted. They had representatives present from two very successful societies, the bookbinders' and the upholsterers'. They wished to promote a fair remuneration for their labours, and to prevent the undue depression of wages. They did not want machine work to drift into the disastrous position which most other trades followed by women occupied. They proposed to have a sick fund, and to open an office for registration of vacancies, so that girls should not have. to go about from shop to shop when they required employment. The committee of the league would render every assistance to the society in their power.

Miss SIMCOX moved the first resolution, which was, " That in order to protect their trade interests and to make provision against sickness and want of employment, all women working for wages should unite together in protective and benefit societies."

Miss SIMCOX spoke of the rise of the sewing machine trade, and entered into the economic reasons on which a trade society is based. She warned them against any illegal interference with the rights of those outside their society. It was to the interests of employers to be guarded against ruinous competition by having the prices of work kept up by such a society as this. The public would have to wear the same number of garments, and the price the public paid for those garments depended on the price the workers chose to put on the goods.

Mr. GRAINGER said he was glad the Lord Mayor had acknowledged the usefulness of trades unions, particularly for women.

Miss BROWN urged that no improvement was likely to come from consumers, because if they patronized the dearer shops in hopes of benefitting the machinist, the profit would only go to the shopkeeper. Again, no improvement would come from the shopkeepers and manufacturers, because they were bound down by competition. All that was left then was for the workers themselves to take the matter up, and raise their wages as men had done.

The resolution was carried.

It was then moved that a provisional committee should be formed, and this was unanimously adopted. Many of those present enrolled themselves as members, and a committee was chosen.

The National Union of Working Women, of which the President is Mr. Alan Greenwell, Clifton, Bristol, has issued an "Urgent appeal for funds." The circular records successful meetings at Rochdale, Wigan, Blackburn, and Bury.

THE "OFFENCES AGAINST THE PERSON" BILL.

On March 1st, on the order of going into committee on this Bill, Mr. P. A. Taylor, Sir Edward Watkin, and others opposed its further progress. Mr. P. A. Taylor said that while the Bill purported to mitigate the punishment in cases of infanticide, it left capital punishment to be inflicted when the murder, wilful or premeditated, was proved, and would subject the woman to seven years' imprisonment when all that could be proved was that the child unhappily was killed. It sought by establishing a lower penalty in cases where wilful murder could not be brought home to the unhappy mother, to induce juries to bring in a verdict of guilty in cases where they would not otherwise do so. It had been described by the hon. member for Leeds as a Bill to imprison a woman for being out of her mind. Women, he believed, in these cases, suffered from temporary mania, and he had received a number of letters from ladies in support of that view, who regarded the proposed change of the law as wicked and cruel. One lady wrote that a woman in her great agony was not responsible for her actions, and that her doctor told her of many cases where women at child-birth had unconsciously injured their children. Another had asked her doctor what he would do with a woman who killed her child under these circumstances, and he replied that he would hang her to show that such things should not be done. That was to say he would hang her in order to show that when in a condition of mania she could not act with common sense. This condition of mind was produced by brooding over shame and probable ruin for months before the birth of the child, and was most likely to arise in the cases of poor women who had been seduced. The House should be especially careful in legislating on that subject. They were an assembly of men chosen by men, and there was something most painful in the idea of their legislating with this terrible severity towards the other sex. The theory that severe Acts of Parliament were alone sufficient to "stamp out" a crime, the roots of which were deep laid in social immorality, was fallacious. The crime of infanticide was brought about by a false code of morality, which treated the sin which

resulted in the birth of an illegitimate child as trivial—
if not blameless—in one sex, but as one which society
could neither condone nor forget in the other. It was
only fair to the women, who were not represented, that
the House should reject this Bill.

Mr. CHARLEY submitted that the Bill came with the
authority of a Royal Commission, and the approval of
distinguished members of both Houses of Parliament.

Sir E. WATKIN said it was not a question of precedent
or authority, but whether this was a humane Bill, or
was one brought forward in that fussy spirit which affected so many lawyers in that House. Public opinion,
he believed, was against the Bill, none of the women's
organizations were in favour of it, and its monstrosity
was not generally known.

The House divided—

| | For going into Committee | ... | 108 |
| | Against ... | ... ... | 82—26 |

The result was received with slight cheering by the
Opposition at the small majority.

The House went into Committee *pro forma.*

In the House of Commons on February 8th, Colonel
Egerton Leigh asked the Home Secretary whether the
government intended to take any steps to prevent
aggravated assaults on women. Mr. Cross replied that
he was now waiting for further reports from the judges.

THE FOOTT CASE.

A STRIKING instance has lately been furnished by the
Irish law courts of the indifference with which the law
regards a mother's claims. A child of nine years of age,
whose father is dead, has been separated from her mother,
not because the father had made a will to that effect, but
simply on the ground that the mother was a Catholic,
and the father had been a Protestant while he was
alive. In the Irish Court of Chancery, on February
17th, Mr. Foott, J.P., county Cork, presented a petition
praying that his granddaughter, a child nine years of
age, might be transferred from the care of her mother,
a Roman Catholic, and placed under the care of her
guardians, two aunts, who are Protestants, with a view

to her being brought up in the Protestant religion. The mother claimed to have the possession of the child on an agreement between the father and herself that the child was to be a Roman Catholic, and she had taken the child to her brother's residence, and openly declared that she would have it educated a Roman Catholic. She said that the marriage settlement of February 6th, 1862, as originally draughted or prepared, contained provisions that the issue of the marriage should be brought up and educated in the Protestant faith, to which she objected, and her husband, Edward O'Callaghan Foott, concurred in her objection thereto, in consequence of which the settlement was altered, and all the provisions expunged therefrom, because the understanding and agreement between her and her husband upon and previous to the marriage was that the male issue, if any, were to be brought up Protestant and the female issue were to be brought up Roman Catholics. With regard to the deed of April 16th, 1862 (a deed which secured the family estates on the child only on condition it should be a Protestant), she said it was prepared and executed without her consent and knowledge, and she was in complete ignorance of its contents until May 8th last. The child had been baptized during its father's lifetime both by a Protestant and a Catholic clergyman. The petitioner, the grandfather, said his son had not been cognizant of the second baptism. The mother brought the certificate of a doctor in Cork that the child " has always been an extremely delicate child, of nervous constitution, easily excited or depressed, and greatly attached to her mother, and he thought her removal from her only parent, from whom she had never been separated, might be of serious consequences to her." There were also certificates from Dr. Harvey, Dr. Edward Townshend, jun., and Dr. O'Sullivan, of Cork. Counsel would go to the full length of sustaining the proposition that the father had in some way renounced or abdicated his right of having the child educated in his own faith. Mrs. Foott stated that her husband's family were unkind to the child. The Vice-Chancellor said he quite agreed that this was a very painful case, but it was made still more painful by the charges brought

forward by the widow of the deceased gentleman in
reference to her husband's family. The rule of law on
the subject of religion in such cases where these painful controversies arose was clear, and he thought it was
of the highest importance that it should not by unnecessary exceptions be infringed upon, that was, that
the religion of the father was to govern that of the
child. To that rule there were undoubtedly exceptions
—if the father had given expressed directions, or
waived his rights, it might justify the court in making
exception to the general rule—but in his opinion those
circumstances .ought to be dealt with as exceptional,
and the person who relied upon bringing up the child in
a religion different to the father's was bound to prove
the affirmative. He had not the slightest doubt in
coming to the conclusion that there must be a direction
that the child should be brought up a Protestant member of the Church of Ireland. He considered that the
lady proposed by the petitioner ought to be appointed
guardian of the person of the minor, and Mr. Spratt
hould be appointed guardian of the fortune. Of
course they would give directions that free access
to the minor, should at all times be afforded to the
mother and members of the mother's family. The
Vice-Chancellor ruled that the residence should be with
the aunt.

It is hard enough when a mother is separated
from an only child by the claims of a living father;
harder still when it is a dead father's will which thus
divides mother and child; but the hardest case of all is
when in default of such a will the family of the deceased
parent may step in between the two whom nature
would seem to have joined together by ties impossible
to be loosed.

Obituary.—On March 8th, the friends of Women's progress have had a heavy loss to lament in the death of
Mr. Thomasson, of Bolton. Probably no man not in the
House of Commons has done more than Mr. Thomasson
to help forward the cause of women. His hearty
sympathy and munificent generosity were never appealed
to in vain. Amongst the many movements which
received his unfailing help, were the Medical Education

of Women, Women's Suffrage, and the Married Women's Property alteration. His death is as yet almost too recent for the workers in these questions to realize the vacancy that it will cause.

MISCELLANEOUS.

THE FEMALE SCHOOL OF ART.

ON February 25th the prizes were given away to the successful students by the Duke of Edinburgh, in the theatre of the London University.

The report stated that the year just expired had been one of the most successful that had passed for the school since its management had been undertaken by the present committee, in 1859. The principal, Miss Gann, had gained a premium of £40, coming in second in the list of principals of 130 competing schools. During the summer season the number of students on the books amounted to 209, and during the winter they reached 196, as compared with 141 and 142 respectively in 1869. During the year 1,962 drawings and models had been sent in to South Kensington for competition, these productions being the work of 134 students. Seven of the national awards open to all the schools in the Kingdom had been won by students in this school, the highest, a gold medal, had been won by Susan Ruth Canton. This young lady had also won the Princess of Wales's scholarship, value £25. In the second division the Queen's scholarship, £30 and gold medal, had been awarded to Ellen Isabella Hancock. The Gilchrist scholarship and £50 had been awarded to Frances Harriet Newton, of the Durham School of Art, winning against seven competitors. In conclusion, the report thanked her Most Gracious Majesty the Queen for her continued patronage and condescending personal interest in the working and progress of the school.

The reading of the report having terminated, the list of the successful students was called over by Professor Donaldson, and the prizes were distributed by his Royal Highness. He congratulated the committee of management and the principal of the school, Miss Gann, on the success which the school has attained. It is now 35 years since it was first established, and its complete success is pretty plainly indicated by the large number of competitors who have striven for this year's prizes.

National Training School for Music.—The following is a list of the successful candidates at the recent examination at South Kensington for scholarships in the National Training School for Music :—Scholarships: Miss Bénard, Miss Bradwen, Miss C. Davis, Miss Heale, Miss Hughes, Mr. R. Jefford, Miss Riley, Miss Sturmfels, Miss E. Turner, Miss Wardroper. The following is a list, in order of merit, of candidates reported by the examiners as qualified for scholarships had they had more to award: 1. Mr. Alcock. 2. Miss Twist. 3. Miss Akroyd. 4. Mr. Mull. 5. Miss Westmacot. 6. Mr. Dove. 7. Miss Warman. 8. Miss Brickwell.

Croydon Literary and Scientific Debating Society.—The February meeting of this society was opened by Miss Ramsay, who moved the resolution that " The phenomena known as spiritualism are worthy of investigation by scientific men" in a most eloquent and able extempore speech. She related some incidents within her own experience and argued that the phenomena, if genuine, opened a wide and interesting field of psychological inquiry which might prove to be of the greatest value, and protested against the indifference and ridicule of scientific men who were qualified to investigate this subject but rejected it without inquiry. We were pleased to see a considerable number of ladies present and trust that they will attend and take part in future meetings.—*Croydon Advertiser.*

The Victoria Club for women has been opened at 25, Regent street, London, W.

Female Shop Assistants.—The *Leeds Mercury* has the following—A memorial, which has been numerously and influentially signed, has been sent to us for publication: —" We, the undersigned, being ladies resident in Bristol, Clifton, and the neighbourhood, are on the best authority assured that in the shops in which we are accustomed to make our purchases, the comfort of the female assistants is much interfered with, and great injury done to their health, by their being obliged to stand so many hours continuously. It is said that this custom has, to a certain extent, been adopted out of deference to the supposed wishes of customers. Without any desire to interfere unduly in business arrangements, but solely out of sympathy with those of our own sex, we beg to submit to the masters of all retail shops in which women are employed as assistants, that it would very much add to our comfort when we are making our purchases if we saw these young women relieved from this unnecessary strain upon their constitution by seats being provided for them, and permission given to sit and take a few minutes rest at the various intervals, in which, as we be-believe, they might, when not serving, do so without neglecting the interests of the employers. We further beg to record our conviction that, with great (both physical and moral) advantage to masters, as well as assistants, as much business would be done, and as much profit secured, if all shops were closed at a much earlier hour than is now the case. Customers would soon, and in most cases without inconvenience, get into the habit of making their purchases before the hour, however early, prescribed for the closing of shops; and the assistants of both sexes would have the opportunity of making use of the evening classes, and other instrumentalities, now plentifully provided in Bristol and Clifton for their mental improvement. The chief thing wanted is unanimity among masters."—A meeting of ladies was held at the Trevelyan Hotel, Corporation street, Manchester, on Tuesday, to consider what steps could be taken in order to procure a mitigation of the general rule by which shopwomen during the whole of their working hours are compelled to stand. A provisional committee was formed, and it was resolved to take measures for procuring signatures from ladies living in and about Manchester in favour of the proposed reform."

Lecture Notes.—The Sunday Lecture Society announces that Miss Fenwick Miller, will deliver the lecture in their course at St. George's Hall, Langham Place, on March 26th, the subject being "The 'Woman Movement;' its History, its Present, and a glimpse of its Future." The Society's lectures commence at four o'clock. This will be Miss Miller's second lecture there this season.

Art. VI.—SONNET.

Let no one ever idly deem it vain,
 That woman's head should with her heart keep pace;
 Let her but bravely join the onward race,
For wider thought and action—larger brain.
Even should she fall at first, no dust shall stain
 Her pure white robe, or soil her gentle face;
 Kind mother earth shall lend her strength and grace,
To rise refreshed and struggle on amain.

And, should she carve herself a deathless name;
 It shall not mar her grave sweet modesty,
So she remember; Work is more than Fame:
 So her true heart enshrine in memory,
The dear old days before her laurels came,
 When childhood's stars were shining in her sky.

E. Hadwen.

Art. VII.—PARAGRAPHS.

Sir David Salomon on Women's Work.—Sir David Salomon, in a circular "addressed to the ladies," considers the following avocations easily learned, well-paying, and adapted for ladies to teach:—Photography, photographic-printing; wood carving; fret-saw work; frame-making by means of a mitring-machine; parquetry work; buhl-work; inlaying; making designs for wall-papers or carpets; preparing girls for the Post Office Telegraph examinations, accountant's work; surveyor's work; drawing plans of grounds or buildings; architectural drawing; landscape gardening (for consultation); preparing skins and stuffing animals; drawing machinery; chemist's or laboratory assistant's duties; secretary work; watch cleaning and mending; gilding; electrotyping; electro-silvering and gilding; compositor's work, etc. The majority, if not all, the arts and trades thus enumerated, are pronounced not only to be suitable for every class, "from the highest lady down to the poor and most wretched, but to be soon learnt, well-paid, light, and pleasing.

ENGLISH ABOLITIONISTS.

Many years ago some ladies came over from America
to the Anti-Slavery Conference and wanted to speak.
The gentlemen, as some gentlemen are now, were
afraid of the women, and did not wish to hear them
speak. Mr. Forster asked one lady why she came, and
she replied, "This is a conference of persons interested
in the suppression of the slave trade; am I not a
person?" The recent Admiralty Circular touching the
claims of fugitive slaves to protection as soon as they
reach an English ship, is a question which must thrill
the hearts of Englishwomen and of Englishmen. Women
were among the earliest abolitionists in America; in the
meetings which are now being held through the length
and breadth of the land to protest against this desecra-
tion of the English flag, women ought to take their part
side by side with men.

A Woman Banker.—The following appeared in the
Boston Women's Journal:—I know one girl, Miss Grace
Alexander, who has managed the business of a bank in
a country village, Winchester, New Hampshire, for many
years. Nominally there is a man at the head, but the
real work is nearly all done by the woman, the man of
course receiving the salary, and giving her the pay of
an ordinary clerk. I wrote to this girl, asking her for a
few items in regard to her work. She replied: I
doubt if I can give you many items of interest, but will
say that I commenced my labours in this bank four
years ago, and have been here, with the exception of
short vacations, ever since. I act as book-keeper, tel-
ler and clerk, and in the absence of the cashier, transact
all the business of the bank. My salary is small, not
one-fourth of the cashier's, and much less than they
would pay a man for the work. It is only 400 dollars
per year, and I board myself. I think I can honestly
say that the work is done as well as any man would do
it. I work six hours per day, and, on the whole, find it
pleasant employment. I do not know of any other
women who hold situations in banks, but see no reason
why they cannot fill such places just as well as men, if
they properly prepare themselves for the work.

𝔈𝔫𝔤𝔩𝔦𝔰𝔥𝔴𝔬𝔪𝔞𝔫'𝔰 𝔕𝔢𝔟𝔦𝔢𝔴.

CONTENTS FOR APRIL, 1876.

All Communications to be addressed to the EDITOR, 22, Berners
Street, Oxford Street, W.

Post-Office Orders payable to SARAH LEWIN, at the "Regent
Street" Post-Office.

TERMS OF SUBSCRIPTION AT THE OFFICE.

Per Annum (Post Free), Six Shillings.
*Subscriptions payable in Advance.   Single Numbers posted Free on
receipt of Six Postage Stamps.*

MSS. are carefully read, and if not accepted are returned, on receipt
of Stamps for Postage, but the Editor cannot be responsible for any
accidental loss.

Contributions should be legibly written, and only on one side of
each leaf.

THE

ENGLISHWOMAN'S REVIEW.

(NEW SERIES.)

No. XXXVI.—April 15th, 1876.

Art I.—THE WOMEN SUFFRAGE MOVEMENT AS AN EDUCATIONAL INFLUENCE.

It appears from an account given in the *New York Herald* of an interview with Miss Louise M. Alcott, the authoress of "Little Women" and other charming stories, as much valued in England as they are in America, that this excellent writer must be included among the large proportion of literary women who are interested in obtaining the suffrage for their own sex. "She (Miss Alcott) had just come in from a long walk," says the reporter of the *Herald*, "and as she sat down to the table, turned toward Miss Horey—a lady who is doing and has done much for the freemen, and is an advocate of the woman reform movement—and said something to her about being in Syracuse last October. It was an excellent chance for my tongue to free itself, and I said:—'I understand, Miss Alcott, that you are interested in that Woman's Congress?' 'Yes, I was and am decidedly,' she replied, 'and although I can't hope for any immediate good result, still, before long, I expect that women will have some few rights.' 'Why, Miss Alcott!' I answered, quite surprised, 'I never supposed that you cared or thought much upon woman's rights; certainly, your looks never give one that idea.' 'They don't? Well, then, I must say they're a failure. But what objection do you have? Don't you think a

K

lone woman has just as much right to vote as any lord of the creation? I live in the little town of Concord. Why shouldn't I have just as much right to vote? I have to pay taxes the same.'" Here the reporter confesses that he "didn't attempt to put forth any bold argument why he thought it unnecessary for women to vote," but made use of the usual commonplaces instead, suggesting that he should object on coming home from the office to find his "wife in hot discussion with some other woman concerning politics while the baby was squalling like mad in the wash-tub." To this Miss Alcott simply replied—"But we don't intend that they shall neglect other duties for politics. I don't believe that it will be anything out of woman's sphere, and the next book I issue I shall have something to say to the girls upon this subject, and see if I can't exert a good influence that way."

We are glad to hear of Miss Alcott's resolve, at the same time we feel that our obligations to her as an advocate of women's suffrage date from a period anterior to her present declaration. Every writer, who, as she has done, teaches girls to think and act for themselves, to love work and the independence which is best secured by work, fosters a state of mind which disposes a woman to resist by all fair and constitutional means the law or custom that deprives her of individual rights. It is an agreeable reflection that the work done by such books as Miss Alcott's must be still more effectually performed by the improved methods of education now brought to bear upon an ever increasing proportion of the rising generation of women in this country. Every woman who has been taught to make full use of her faculties, to think as well as to feel, and to reason no less than to persuade, will have become competent to gauge the extent of the wrong which law and custom have hitherto inflicted on her sex, and will feel no hesitation in claiming political and professional privileges as a matter of course.

That all work done by women for women will in the end forward the cause we have at heart we feel no doubt. The proof of this fact, however, lies in the future. Meantime, it is interesting to consider how much the claim put forward by certain Englishwomen

to exercise the franchise on the same terms as men has
done to improve the condition of the women of this
country. There can be no question, and, considering
the comparatively short period during which the movement has been in progress this is scarcely wonderful, that
many women regard a claim to the suffrage as a very
large, not to say exorbitant, demand upon the justice and
fair dealing of men. At the same time the extent of the
claim impresses their imagination, and induces them to
think, whether after all there is not a good deal which
women could or ought to do that they are debarred from
doing, no one seems to know exactly why, unless it is
that they have not done such things before. Thus, as
the enamoured copyist of some masterpiece of ancient
art produces not the grand work itself, but a not
unpleasing sketch recalling its beauties, these timid
reformers, though shrinking from equal participation
with men in the business of life, acquire some notion of
self-help, and by taking advantage of all existing means
of employing their abilities in active occupations, acquire
a certain degree of intellectual independence.

It would be interesting to collect from the newspapers
and periodicals proofs of the great difference which has
arisen during the last twenty years in the opinion of
women themselves as to their position in the social
economy, and even, barring some fanatical partizans of
the old system, in that of men on the same subject. It
is but fifteen years ago since Miss Martineau published a
spirited protest against the line taken by the chairman
at the annual meeting, in 1861, of Queen's College,
Harley Street, with regard to the object of educating
girls. She then, commenting on his speech, said—" Mr.
Cowper has not got beyond the notion of the majority
of the friends of female education who think they have
said everything when they have recommended good intellectual training as fitting women to be 'mothers of
heroes,' 'companions to men,' and so on. No great
deal will be done for female improvement while this sort
of sentiment is supposed to be the loftiest and most liberal.
Girls will never make a single effort. in any length of
school years, for such an object as being companions to
men, and mothers of heroes. If they work, and finally

justify the pains taken for them in establishing such colleges as these, it will be for the same reasons that boys work well and come out worthy of their schooling, because they like their studies, and enjoy the sense of moral and mental development which is so strong in school and college years; and because their training is well adapted to educe, develope and strengthen their powers and render them as wise and good as their natures, years, and circumstances permit. Till it is proposed, in educating girls, to make them, in themselves and for their own sakes, as good specimens of the human being as the conditions of the case may allow, very little will be effected by any expenditure of time, pains, and money."

Now, although the sentiment of which Miss Martineau complains might still find expression in the speeches of the Mr. Bouveries, Mr. Leathams, and Mr. James's should they undertake to advocate female education at all, we can safely say that it is no longer expected at the head-quarters of the movement in favour of that great object. This is so much gained, and this gain we regard as mainly due to the suffrage agitation, which, based as it is on the fact that women are as interested in public questions as men, are potentially as competent to understand them, and are therefore entitled, if duly qualified, in another sense, to have a share in their solution, has, besides raising a large body of powerful supporters of the cause, insensibly leavened the whole of society with some rudimentary notions of the principles on which it works. The phrase to which Miss Martineau objected has become obsolete now that most people have awakened to the fact that women may have interests and occupations on their own account whether they are or are not " companions of men " and mothers of heroes."

There are many unsuspected ways in which the efforts now systematically made to obtain the franchise for women, have assisted the existing agencies for benefiting them in other ways to which it is unnecessary to do more than allude, so obvious are they to any candid observer of the tone of modern thought on the subject even in circles in which the suffrage question itself is

little discussed or understood. Our space will, indeed,
only permit us to mention one great result of the movement—the formation of a nucleus round which all who
desire justice done to women may gather, and draw
from more or less direct association, the strength which
comes of union with sympathetic minds. All who agree
with us in the main may be unable to work at details
with us, but we, nevertheless, assist and support them
by presenting a firm front to the common foe. In short
we hold up a standard bearing a definite motto, and in
some sense may lay claim to the position which the
admirable writer, from whom we have last quoted, had
in view when she penned the following lines :—"Meantime in the midst of the groping among sympathies and
sentiments and imitations, and ambitions and imperfect
views of all sorts, let us only have some few who uphold
the claim of every human being to be made the most of,
in all the provinces of its nature, and the female sex is
redeemed."

A. DRUMMOND.

ART. II.—CONGRESS AT SYRACUSE.

THE papers read at the Third Congress of women held
in the United States last October, which have been
since published, are replete with interest. These congresses of women, held at stated intervals, are a peculiar
feature of the "woman's movement" in America. In
England we prefer to adopt the theory—which seems
to us the true one—that men and women work best
together, at the same time and on the same subjects.
The Social Science or British Association gatherings,
where men's papers are read, also welcome women's
papers. Combined work of men and women appears to
us better than separate work, and we have, therefore,
never tried the experiment of a conference composed
only of women. It cannot be denied, however, that in
America these congresses have been productive of great

good. At this last one, the most eminent woman in
science in the States, Maria Mitchell, was president, and
the leading women writers, speakers, educators, and
physicians gave their aid; standing committees had
been appointed to consider and report, during the past
year, on matters connected with science, art, literature,
or practical work, and the result is a mass of useful
facts, practical suggestions, and, most rare of all, reliable
statistics concerning the work and status of women,
which will be of great value to all interested in those
questions.

The President, in her opening address, enforced the
necessity of carefully collecting and methodically ar-
ranging statistics on subjects connected with women.
A solid phalanx of figures is a formidable opponent to a
flourish of rhetoric. " We can then find," she said, " if
certain methods of education are really fatal, if certain
industrial methods are really failures." It had been
suggested that the " Woman's Aid Association " would
be a good name for them, as they were to aid women in
finding work, and to aid work in finding women. She
would like to have the influence of the Association felt
in every town in the land, in art enterprises, in scientific
associations, in moral reforms; she would like to see it
establish courses of lectures, art schools, industrial
occupations, and business enterprises.

Mrs. Ednah Cheney followed with a paper on the
future of women in our public schools The total
number of teachers in the United States is 216,000, of
these 104,000 are women; but this does not represent
fairly the proportion of their influence, for in the best
schools the female teachers are greatly in the majority.
In St. Louis, for instance, whose schools stand in the
highest rank, there are only 52 men to 549 women
teachers, or less than one tenth. The average time
that a woman teaches is only three years, so that an
enormous number of newly-trained female teachers is
annually required to fill up the deficiency. Not only as
teachers, but as supervisors and managers women were
obtaining influence. In many states the payment for
supervision was only 400 dollars yearly, at which price
it was almost impossible to secure men of intellect,

consequently in many States the friends of education had secured the passage of laws authorising the employment of women on School Boards, and as superintendents of schools. Such laws had been passed in Connecticut, Ohio, Rhode Island, Massachusetts, Michigan, Pennsylvania, and New Hampshire, and several women are now engaged in the work. Three women were chosen for school offices in Kansas, nine in Iowa, and eleven in Illinois.

"The public school system also bears upon this question of labour in another way. By the fitness of women for teaching and the great demand for teachers, a blow is struck at the long established fallacy that women should not be paid as much as men for the same work, and already in ten states or territories of the Union, the monthly salaries of female teachers is reported the same as that of men, while it is less in only sixteen or seventeen according to the reports. Many States have not reported on this point. It is in the oldest States that the greatest inequality still exists, and in Massachusetts it is the greatest, the average of men's salaries being 93 dollars 63 cents per month, and that of women only 34 dollars 14 cents. We must remember, however, that in Massachusetts the number of male teachers is very small, and that they are generally principals of large schools.

Mrs. Cheney reviews the advantages and drawbacks of the public school system. While believing in the preponderance of the former, she urges women to associate for the purpose of discussing and fully comprehending the system, as by devoting themselves to the improvement of the schools in every town, they would do more for the future moral, intellectual and industrial improvement of the country, than could any other agency.

The next paper was also upon "Education," by Miss Eastman. She dwelt on the necessity that women, who are supposed to understand better than men the management of children, should have the control of the schools. The long hours that education lasted, which were injurious to the children, the inflexible school system which permitted no adaptation to individual children, even the construction of the magnificent schoolhouses, with their painfully fatiguing flights of stairs, sometimes nine in number, without a "lift," though all the teachers and half the pupils were women —all this required to be organized and controlled by qualified women.

In a paper on "Marriage and Work," the Rev.
Antoinette Blackwell combatted the assumption that
married women should be exempt from taking a practical interest in matters outside their own homes. We
needed their depth of thought, the warmth of their
sympathies, their superior practical experience for the
world's highest work, and they had, moreover, more
leisure than any other class of Americans.

The Rev. Phebe Hanaford followed with "Statistics
of the Women Ministry." Though the idea of women
preachers is contrary to popular feeling in England, the
historical details of their work are interesting. "The
early Church from the apostles' own times, set the seal
upon the ministering functions of women, by the
appointment of a female Diaconate, strictly excluded
from the priestly functions of public teaching and
worship, but nearly co-equal with the male diaconate
as respects the exercise of active charity." In the
seventeenth century the Quakers admitted women as
preachers, and they are now admitted and ordained by
many other denominations in America.

Mrs. Croly, of New York, contributed a paper on
"Women in Journalism." The first newspaper ever
published by a woman in America, was at Newport, in
1742. James Franklin, brother to Dr. Franklin, had
been the publisher, and at his death his widow continued
it, her two daughters did the type-setting, and her
servant girl worked the press. During the next fifty
years individual instances occurred of women being
connected with journalism, and at the present day there
are many well-known and honourable instances of
women editors. But, as a rule, Mrs. Croly doubts if
their connection with the newspaper press is of a solid
practical character. "The majority are correspondents,
or writers of occasional articles. They are rather
amateurs than workers; they come without being
wanted—they fall off without being missed—they take
little share in the hurry, the late hours, and the confusion
of editing.

As a promise for the future, I would rather see girls and young
women admitted into newspaper offices to run errands and do the
lowest drudgery of the reporter and *itemizer*, than flourishing at the

head or tail of columns of fashion and gossip. Such beginnings would
give less individual prominence, but infinitely better opportunity for
future advancement. To obtain a permanent foothold in a strange
community, we must enter it upon terms of equality and remain in it,
or we must begin with beginners, and work our way up. I do not
know what the lives of these women journalists may have been, but
I know that in my nearly twenty years of journalistic life, I have not
had one entire week of leisure, and have often waited months and
months for the chance of making a call upon a friend. I have risen
at seven o'clock in the morning or earlier, and have written in an
office or at home till twelve o'clock at night. Fashions and market
reports, editorials and paragraphs, gossip from Paris and letters from
London, book reviews and dramatic criticisms, mail reading, and
reports of state fairs, have all been in my line of duty. I have written
the reports for my paper behind a bar counter (the only quiet corner
I could find) in Chicago, and run after the train to deliver it to the
baggage master. I have been called up at a moment's notice to fill
nearly every place upon the staff. I have read the telegraph reports,
edited them, that is, written in head-lines, and made up the paper.
I have answered few of the hundreds of private letters received from
strangers, because it was simply an impossibility, but I have replied
to thousands through periodicals.

She adds—" the dangers and temptations to women
in journalism do not come from its work or its hardships,
they come from the partial success built upon false
foundations. . . . This is no evidence of advancement.
It does not help women to a higher or more assured
place in the active or the intellectual world."

(To be continued.)

ART III.—THE FORTHCOMING DEBATE ON THE " WOMEN'S DISABILITIES " BILL.

ON the 26th of April, the first Wednesday after Parliament
resumes business, the Women's Disabilities Bill will come
on for second reading. It may seem a bold thing to
give a report of a debate which has not yet taken place,
but there has hitherto been such a curious similarity in
all the Women's Suffrage debates that we cannot go far
wrong in being wise before the event, and giving a *resumé*
of the speeches which will be uttered against the Bill on

this occasion. With the arguments of our friends we have
nothing to do; they have been repeatedly reported in the
Review—nor do we pretend to foresee how the tug of
war when Greek meets Greek will end on the 26th. We
will "limit ourselves to reviewing" some of the arguments
which are so certain to be produced by our opponents
that we view them as old acquaintances, endowed as
old acquaintances frequently are, with the power of
making themselves temporarily disagreeable, but not
of doing any permanent harm.

It is said to be seldom that the speeches uttered
during a debate influence the number of votes given
pro. or *con.* Members speak for the reporters and not
for each other; and if this is the case in debates affecting what men are apt to call distinctively "great national
questions," how much more so on a measure for the
political recognition of women only, which has been discussed and voted on seven times already, and on which
members have pretty much made up their minds from
facts or opinions acquired outside the House. We are
safe in prophesying what kind of chaff will be given us
instead of wholesome corn: if we could hope that our
predictions would be falsified, and that a new line of
opposition would be invented, we would gladly put up
with the mortification of being proved wrong, for the
sake of so welcome a surprise.

It is impossible to foretell what line of argument will
be taken by the young member who has come forward
as the David of the opposite party against the feminine
Philistines. He has never even yet recorded his vote
against the Bill. There are several sorts to choose
from; there is the "physical inability" argument, the
"overturning of the decrees of Providence" argument,
the "danger to the Constitution" argument. He can
select the sentimental, the abusive, the sneering, or the
facetious style. He may either rate woman as "too
pure and good for human nature's daily food," or he may
credit her with dangerous instincts which can only be
kept in due subordination by man-made laws.

"The world is all before him where to choose."

It may, however, be confidently predicted that he and

his supporters will share the following arguments among them.

One member will have a clear insight into the "inscrutable" ways of Providence which has created woman smaller and weaker than man, and which there is considerable danger will be entirely thwarted if the present Bill becomes law. The British House of Commons must by every means in its power enforce the intentions of Heaven which are too weak to stand alone. Man was ordained to be woman's protector, so he is perfectly justified in refusing her any rights.

Another speaker will object to the Constitution being tampered with. "English law should be that of the Medes and Persians, majestic and unalterable." The franchise was already extended, perhaps too diffusely, to men, and they must "draw the line somewhere" like the barber in Nickleby. He draws it at women. "The movement in question was not one which was popular with women. There are 16,260,213 females in the United Kingdom; what though 430,000 persons had petitioned for it? there were still presumably 15,830,213 women, female children and babies who were indifferent to the measure! A reform where men only are concerned may be granted, even if unclaimed by them, on the simple grounds of justice or expediency, but a different standard must be applied to a woman's demand—it needed unanimity among the sex."

Another member will thrill with indignation at the accusation that Parliament makes unjust laws for women. Were they not doing what men had always done? Had they not the best intentions, and are they to be dictated to by a parcel of discontented women who think they know better what they want than men do for them? Let any law, really remedying an injustice to women, come before the house, and he would *not* vote for it. Women are discontented precisely because they do not know what is good for them. The rule which nurses apply to fractious children was the safest for them—"If you ask you shan't have; if you don't ask, you don't want." A woman's only real right was to be married! If she missed this by any infelicitous chance, such as an unaccountable overplus of the female population, the backwardness of men to marry, or, having married, suffered from the unfortunate liability of husbands to die and leave their wives widows with young families depending upon them, the law could not provide for such contingencies. An independent woman was a social failure, and *deminimis non curat lex.*"

Next, a speaker will rise to show that it is on record that *some* women have been seen drunk at a municipal election ; so have a *good many* men. Intemperance is so shocking in a woman that, in his opinion, the only way of checking it is to deprive her of any franchise at all.

Another will begin by throwing a slur upon the motives of the women who conduct the agitation. They are seeking to thrust themselves into notoriety to attract men's attention, or they are hopelessly unattractive man-haters, whose opinions are disavowed by the rest of their sex. The movement is only carried on by a small number of agitators, he will say, forgetful that no movement continues for nine years with an ever-increasing vote in the House, hundreds of public meetings, and hundreds of thousands of petition signatures unless it is supported by the approval of a large section of the community.

Another member, more outwardly courteous, will begin his speech with a compliment to the ladies of his acquaintance, possibly to his mother (a man is never in so good a position for decrying the whole female sex as when he has just acknowledged his obligations to them). Having thus cleared his conscience he will proceed to demonstrate that the entire feminine population with whom he is not acquainted are silly and trifling, readers of novels, not of newspapers, studiers of fashions, not of politics, unfit to form an opinion on so momentous a subject as the election of their Honourable selves, the mightiest deliberative assembly in the world—a self-congratulatory sentiment which always elicits cheers from the gratified House, reminding one forcibly of the response which met O'Connell, when at a popular meeting he asked, "Are you not the finest peasantry in the world?" and "We are! we are?" was the delighted chorus. It is galling to the pride of men to think that

their future position and consequence might depend
upon the coolly-judging estimation in which they were
held by some women constituents.   Judge Kingman
says in his testimony respecting woman's suffrage in
Wyoming that "frequently the men set aside certain
applicants for office because their characters would not
stand the criticism of women."   Is it possible—we do
not ask with levity—that this consciousness affects any
English members in their unwillingness to have female
electors ?

Another member will denounce the measure in eloquent accents because it proposes only to enfranchise
women householders.   As a "rough and ready test,"
the property qualification works well for men, but women proprietors may be, he says, the least endowed of their
sex.   A man may be illiterate, drunk or incapable, and
yet vote so long as he pays his rates, but a woman voter
should be refined, educated, and unexceptionable in
conduct.   At the same time he will predict that the
Bill means something quite different from what the
lawyers who drew it up thought it meant, and that unknown possibilities of "domestic fury and fierce civil
strife" menace us in the future.

Yet another speaker will rise and with lugubrious
tones deplore the revolutionary character of the Bill.
The representation of property is supposed to be a constitutional measure, but Cassandra sees that it has a
socialistic origin.   If women ever meddle with politics,
they will overthrow every time-honoured institution
and will precipitate us into the worst horrors of social
revolution.   *Varium et mutabile semper femina.*   Look at
the French Terrorists of 1793—there were poissardes in
France.   Look at the Communists of 1871—there were
petroleuses.   Wherever we find a nation going to destruction we may be sure that women form part of that
nation :—It was Eve who first ate the apple.

For our own sakes we have avoided entering upon
the coarse vituperation and vulgarity which too frequently disfigure the "Woman's Disabilities Removal"
debate. It would be too much to hope that the next reading will be suffered to pass without some speech which
raises a blush of indignation in every woman who hears of

it.   Last year Mr. Forsyth uttered his belief that in an
assembly of gentlemen, no member would descend to
low and vulgar ridicule.   How this expectation was
answered those who read the speech of the member for
Cambridge will too well remember.   It is easier to fling
a coarse taunt at a woman than at a man; easier to
raise a laugh in the House at a joke than to win
applause by clear logic or forcible oratory; easiest of all
to attack a class who, precisely because they are not
constituents, are deprived of one important means of
retaliation.   We have but enumerated some of the
hackneyed arguments which are brought forward with a
"sad constancy" against the measure.   We do not
believe that these arguments have the weight even with
the speakers which they profess.   We are tempted to
think we have never yet got to the real grounds of their
opposition of the Bill, and that there must be some underlying sentiment, some deep-rooted feeling, which
when they "permit reason to repose," as the member
for Huddersfield would say, influences their resistance.
But the arguments, such as they are, though, as we have
said, they may not influence votes, will serve to pass the
time away during the debate.

The world is full of Aladdin's magicians, who offer
"old lamps for new," and the very old lamps of argument which have served Mr. Bouverie and his successors
in seven debates are not, because they are hollow and
worthless, to be hid under a bushel, but through the
medium of *The Times* and *The Telegraph* are to illumine
every breakfast-table in England the next morning.

Art. IV.—REVIEWS.

How to Influence Little Children.   By H. F. Lord.   (London: John
    Bale and Sons, 87, Great Titchfield Street.)

Miss Lord gives us in this pamphlet some valuable
lessons on "how to influence little children," acknow-
ledging at the outset the sources whence are drawn, to

quote her own words, "most of the ideas I have so
roughly put together." The lecture before us was sup-
plementary to a three months course of practical work
started by some of the leading Kindergarten teachers in
London, and intended chiefly for an audience of nurses
and nursery governesses.

Kindergarten work, though as yet not nearly enough
practised and appreciated in England, has begun to occupy some of the most thoughtful and practical among
the great body of teachers in this country. We have
still to hope for the day when every town will possess
its Kindergarten, whence children may be passed on to
the larger schools we see growing up even for girls in
town after town. But that so pleasant a hope may be
indulged in without fear of ultimate disappointment, a
pamphlet like the one before us abundantly proves.
People will not write and work for a subject in which
they have no real and growing interest, nor will new ad-
herents be found on all sides for a faith destined to be
labelled "fancy" at last. In spite of the ridicule too often
heaped on Fröbel and his work we boldly confess ourselves believers in the truths he taught. The results he
promised may seem to some of us a little out of proportion to the means he used and would have us use too,
but we believe that to a worker as patient and obser-
vant as he those results were real and attainable and
that close imitators of the work will find them after
all no mere vision. Little children have, at least, as
much to teach us as we have to teach them. One of
the things they have to teach us is the intense reality to
themselves of their actions, even of those which to us
have seemed involuntary or mechanical. For example,
the pamphlet before us draws attention to the insignifi-
cant baby action of kicking and crying. We refer our
readers to Miss Lord's remarks on these matters, but
we must especially point out what she has said of the
mother's instinct, which is often (so ignorantly) to our
thinking, supposed to be more than equal in prescience
and divination to anything that thoughtful men and
women may tell us of a young child's world. It is
always worth while, as Miss Lord says, to learn from
other people's thoughts as well as from our own

observation, even about baby-deeds. We hope that
in these days of "Science Primers," "Practical Physiology," and "Health in the House," there is an
ever-decreasing number of mothers who think that the
mere fact of *being* a mother puts them far above the
necessity of thinking and learning in order to be able to
govern a household well and to bring up healthy,
vigorous children, and that the number of those who
take a delight in learning what may add to the well-
being of their children is increasing. As Miss Lord
writes—"Better days are coming; we are setting to
work to *learn* little children." It would be a long task
to discuss in detail all that Miss Lord has written, and
the best thing our readers can do is to go to the
pamphlet itself for her views on influencing little children. We are grateful to her for having so forcibly put
before us the fact that children can be influenced even
in babyhood, as the too generally received opinion is,
that they are only capable of being fed or amused at so
early a stage.

The "logical" style in baby development is also insisted on. "Whatever happens once will, we think,
happen again." This is true, not merely of babyhood
but of the later stage when, in listening to an oft-told
tale, a child refuses to hear the slightest variation of it,
often to the tale-teller's discomfiture. A child always
loves to go over sensations again and again, and hence
finds endless amusement in what appears to older folk
to be monotonous repetition.

We like Miss Lord's definitions of a smile and of play;
"a smile is his (the baby's) first social act," and "play is
his great spiritual development." The endless uses to
which a baby will put the same toy is also insisted on
as showing the steps by which babyhood grows in experience. It is only a late, and we fear morbid
development which insists on new materials for pleasure, being constantly provided. Miss Lord gives us all a
valuable hint when she bids us nourish a baby's fancy
by keeping in contact with Nature, nor is what she says
less true when she speaks of a baby's "first link with
humanity" and widening by degrees into "the idea
of a circle wider than the family, an idea which, as l

said, is a religious idea." The idea of prolonged punishment is also touched upon to be very earnestly deprecated.

> " Whatever you do, do not keep up for days together the sense of
> sin. Pray at any time keep up the thrill of goodness, energy, plea-
> sure, but never dwell on wrong, pass on as soon as the question is
> settled to new opportunities for doing right."

And again—

> " After giving reproof or forbidding anything, never stand still to
> be argued with, you only tempt a child ; always begin to talk about
> something else, so as to give the child an idea that he and his little
> sins are not the whole business of your life."

While encouraging a child to create for himself and
to act with others in concert with others, neither mother
nor nurse are to interfere unnecessarily with him.
" Mother or nurse is to a child's game like a ray of sun-
light on some particular point." If we overstep that
point we make our children stupid and dependent on us
for their amusement. " The difference between love of
approbation and love of vain applause is, that love of
approbation is content with a silent look or touch
unseen by others—it is the love of love, while love of
applause insists on everybody knowing," is a quotation
for which, we think, readers will be grateful. The plea
for the " dear, open-hearted children who do not mean
to be vain when they rush round the house begging
everyone to take an interest in what they have achieved"
comes in opportunely at the end. We have always had
a sympathy for them, and think Miss Lord's advice as to
how to treat them the only true way of preventing them
from becoming tiresomely self-asserting.

We cannot agree with Miss Lord's feeling that "there
is no harm but great good in getting a child to do things
to please you, assigning no higher reason." A child is
hardly ever too young too begin to learn the great lesson
of doing right for right's sake. Anything which prevents him from seeing clearly the simple beauty of this
precept puts him in a false position, morally and lessens
his chances of happiness in after life. Again, to admit
that corporal punishment should ever be resorted to,
opens the door to a mass of wrong we would fain shut
out. However low a child's nature seems to be sunk,

L

there is a lower depth to which a slap or a blow may
sink it, and on this point we cannot too strongly assert
our opinion. In conclusion we have to thank Miss Lord
for all she teaches us and for the many suggestions she
gives us in this very useful pamphlet.

A. W.

The Book of Noble Englishwomen. Edited by Charles Bruce. (Nimmo).

"England has been richly blessed with noble women"
says Mr. Bruce, and the following record of martys, beginning with Anne Askew, patriots like Lucy Hutchinson,
literary celebrities, and queens of society goes far to prove
his assertion. The book is an interesting one for girls,
and might be an instructive one for those writers and
statesmen who are apt to assert that the history of the
world's progress has been acted out only by men.

ART. V.—EVENTS OF THE MONTH.

EDUCATION.

The Women's Education Union propose to establish a
Society for the Training and Registration of Teachers
for Schools higher than Elementary, and have issued a
circular inviting support. It says :—

1. The Central Committee having by the formation
of the Girls' Public Day School Company, promoted one
of the first objects of the Union, *i.e.*, the establishment
of good and cheap Day Schools for Girls of all classes
above those attending the Public Elementary Schools,
desire now to direct their efforts towards the accomplishment of another of its objects, *i.e.*, to provide means
for Training Female Teachers, and for testing their
efficiency by Examinations of recognised authority,
followed by Registration according to fixed standard.
The demand created by the rapid increase of the
Company's and other similar schools, endowed or pro-
prietory as well as private, makes the supply of duly

trained and qualified teachers one of the most pressing
educational questions of the day. It is well known that
the Government Training Colleges are restricted to
teachers in elementary schools, and that with the
exception of a department of the Home and Colonial
Society's Training School in Gray's Inn Road, there is
no public provision for the training of teachers for
higher grade schools, or for their examination and
registration. This is equally true of male as of female
teachers, but the former have the immense advantage
over the latter of access to a University education,
following that of school, by which they not only gain
larger knowledge of the subjects they will have to teach,
but learn in some measure how to teach them, by being
well taught themselves. Even in their case, however,
it has been admitted by the leading educational authorities of the day, including a large number of Head
Masters, that special training in the principles and practice of teaching is requisite in addition to their
general training. Still more, then, is it requisite
for women, who are excluded from the Universities,
and of whom only a very small number can obtain
in such institutions as Girton College, and Newnham Hall, Cambridge, the only equivalent for a University course now open to them. As a step in
this direction, and with a view to feel their way, the
Central Committee instituted last year Lectures on
Methods of Teaching special subjects, open to both
sexes, and the result has been so encouraging that they
now propose to form an Institution which shall do the
work of a Training College for first grade teachers,
minus collegiate residence, and secure to student teachers
enrolled under its provisions:—

I. Instruction by lectures and classes in the subjects
comprised in a liberal education, continuing
and completing School instruction.

II. Instruction, similarly given, in the principles of
education as a science and an 'art, and in the
methods of teaching special subjects.

III. Admission to schools for study of School organization and management, and for practice
in teaching.

IV. Periodical and progressive examinations testing proficiency in study and practice.

V. A final examination of recognised authority for giving Certificates entitling the holders to be registered as trained teachers.

VI. Registration of the Certificates so obtained.

In order to carry into effect these objects, and to raise the funds required for the first establishment of this Institution and its maintenance until it can be reasonably expected to become self-supporting, it is proposed to form a Society, under the Companies' Act 1867, entitled The Teachers' Training and Registration Society.

The Extension of University Teaching. — The London Society for the Extension of University Teaching have elected at their first annual meeting three ladies upon the Council, Mrs. William Grey, Hon. Organising Secretary of the Women's Education Union; Miss Mary Gurney, Executive Committee of the Women's Education Union; and the Dowager Lady Stanley of Alderley, Council of Girton College. The following ladies have also been nominated by other educational bodies in London: by the College for Men and Women, Mrs. Malleson, hon. sec.; and by Bedford College, Miss Smith, School Board for Oxford.

Student Teachers at Kindergarten Schools.—The Southampton Girls' College has vacancies for ladies not under 18. Fee, £10 and board in private family at £40 a year.—Address, The Lady Principal, 8, Sussex-place, Southampton. (*Times*, 22nd March.)

The Council of the Leeds Girls' High School Company, Limited, will shortly appoint a Head Mistress. Salary £200 per annum, board and residence, and capitation fee of £1 per pupil over fifty. Applications, with copies of testimonials, to be sent to the Secretaries, Claremont, Leeds.— *Woman's Suffrage Journal.*

The Girls' Public High School will shortly be established at Brighton.

Schoolmistresses in Marine Schools.—Schoolmistresses

in marine schools are in future to be placed under naval regulations as to pay, pensions and allowances, instead of following the regulations of the army as hitherto. An Order in Council has been obtained for carrying out the proposed regulations.

SUFFRAGE.

The Bill for removing the "Political Disabilities of Women" will come before Parliament for its second reading on Wednesday, April 26th. Notice of opposition has been given by Viscount Folkestone, one of the members for South Wilts. Mr. Leatham and Mr. Chaplin appear to have soon tired of the front of battle, and their opposition to the measure, should they see fit to continue it, will be carried on as supporters not as movers of the amendment. The *Suffrage Journal* points out that the Parliamentary changes during the past year have been, on the whole, favourable to the prospects of the Bill, and that there are good grounds for hoping that the next step will be one of substantial progress.

The petitions presented up to the 4th of April were 540, the number of signatures were 213,324, a greater number than have been presented for any other measure this year. The Town Councils of Huddersfield, Lincoln, Denbigh, Batley, Northampton, and others have petitioned for the Bill.

On March 18th a crowded meeting was held in the Music Hall, Barnstaple. At Ipswich a public meeting took place on April 4th, Miss Ashworth and Miss Becker attending as the national deputation; and on the same night another was held at the Penrhyn Hall, Bangor.

THE RIGHT OF WOMEN TO ACT ON DEPUTATIONS.

An additional proof has been lately given of the desire which some men, high in office, have of restricting the scanty political privileges of women. We have been informed that the National Health Society (whose aim is certainly not political), which was started by, and is worked chiefly by women, asked leave to send a deputation to one of our ministers. He consented to receive the deputation *provided* ladies formed no part in it. He knew of no precedent for receiving ladies on deputations, he added, when subsequently questioned on this point, and expressed his distinct determination not to do so. We might point out that many of the ministers in the present Government as well as in the preceding Government have repeatedly received deputations in which women took their share. We do not suppose that even this minister will be able to establish his precedent free from question, but we quote the circumstances to show the necessity of some legal recognition of women as citizens, if the recognition hitherto accorded to them by usage is to be shut from them.

HOSPITAL FOR WOMEN, 222, MARYLEBONE ROAD.

THE Fourth Annual Report announces that the beginning of 1875 saw the new hospital burdened with a debt of £500, but that this debt is now paid off, and the Committee has moreover been able to invest a further sum of £35 in the purchase of the lease of an adjoining house, No. 220, Marylebone Road. The Committee have no immediate intention of adding to the number of beds in the hospital, and propose sub-letting the new house for a time. In view, however, of the rapid development of the hospital since it was started, it was thought wise to secure the opportunity for its extension. The number of in-patients received during the past year was 194; out-patients made 7,946 visits to the hospital. The working staff of the hospital has this year been increased. It has hitherto consisted of two ladies, Mrs. Anderson and Mrs. Hoggan; to them has now been joined Mrs. Atkins. Mrs. Atkins received the M.D. degree at Zurich in 1872, and since that date she has enjoyed special opportunities of gaining experience as the resident house-surgeon of the Women's Hospital, Birmingham. Another change has been the appointment of a lady as resident pupil; ladies who are waiting for the final examination for the M.D. degree at Paris, where the curriculum of study is long, and examinations numerous, are qualified to fill this post. Miss Anna Dahms was the first resident student; she has been succeeded by Miss Rorison, a student who has completed her medical curriculum, and who is waiting in the hope of some one of the English medical examinations

being shortly open to women.   Failing this, she intends
to graduate at Paris.

To the annual report is also added a statement of the
general progress of the movement for the admission of
women to the medical profession during the year.   The
cheering circumstances may be briefly summed up as:
—the decision by the College of Surgeons—that the
special licence in midwifery may be held by a woman,
and that the college may be compelled to admit women
to the examinations for this licence—The resolution
passed by the convocation of the London University
favourable to granting degrees to women—The admission on the part of the General Medical Council that it
could not advise that women should be excluded from
the profession—The spontaneous decision to the same
effect on the part of the Gloucester branch of the
British Medical Association—The admission of papers
by Mrs. Anderson and Mrs. Hoggan on medical subjects
at the annual meeting of the association in Edinburgh
last August—and the resolution passed by the Governors
of the Queen's Hospital, Birmingham in favour of
admitting female students to that hospital, and allowing
them to receive clinical instruction from any members of
the hospital staff who are willing to give it.

*Election of a Lady Candidate for the Office of Guardian of
the Poor.*—Two ladies candidates for seats at the St. Pancras Guardian Board.   In No. 8, or Gray's-inn-road Ward,
Miss Margaret Collett, of No. 22, Upper Woburn place,
"gentlewoman," Secretary of the Charity Organisation
Society, has just been returned at the top of the poll.   In
No. 1, or Kentish-town Ward, Mrs. Amelia Howell, of 12,
St. John's-gardens, Haverstock-hill, received a large
number of votes, but nevertheless, has not been elected.
The importance of having well-qualified women in this
office cannot be over-estimated.

In Kensington, Miss Merington who has served during
the past year will again come forward.

REPORT OF THE FACTORY ACTS COMMISSION.
THE Report of this Commission is now published.   It is
signed by six out of the seven members of the Commission.   The seventh Commissioner, the O'Conor Don

M.P. has declined to sign, and gives a separate report, being unable to concur with his colleagues in their recommendation on certain points, the most important of which, as affecting women, are the proposed extension to all workshops, of the factory restriction which limits the work of adult women within a certain fixed period of 12 hours, and the proposal that the Factory Inspectors should be assisted by the Police.

The Commissioners make 113 recommendations of alterations in the existing law. Some of the most important of these are:—

The word "Factory" should be defined so as to include the Factories now under the Factory Act of 1874 (textile factories), and the word "Workshop" used to cover all other places of work within the Act.

The definition of work to be regulated by the Act should include labour in or incidental to the washing, cleaning, or furbishing any article. (Laundries, hitherto exempt from regulation by the Act, would then be brought under it.)

The Act should not interfere with employment by the occupier of a room used also for the purposes of a dwelling house, if there are no protected persons but adult women employed, and if they do not, in addition to inmates, exceed two in number.

The limits of the hours of labour should be, in all Factories and workshops, 6 a.m. and 6 p.m., 6.30 a.m. and 6.30 p.m., or 7 a.m. and 7 p.m. all the year round.

Of the 12 hours within which the hours of labour must be included, two hours shall be reserved for meals in Textile Factories, and one hour and a half in workshops, thus making the hours of labour ten in the former and ten and a half in the latter.

The meal hours should be so distributed that not more than four and a half hours in Factories, and not more than five hours in workshops, should elapse between them.

The rules as to distribution of meal hours should not apply to domestic employment; that is, employment in business carried on by the occupier in a room used for the purposes of a dwelling house, and employing none but inmates.

There should be a relaxation allowing the twelve hours' limit of work to be fixed as late as 8 a.m. to 8 p.m. in the following trades:— Printing, Bookbinding, Tailoring, Dress and Mantle Making, Millinery, Shirt and Collar Making, Straw Hat and Bonnet Making, Fringe and Trimming Making, Skirts, Stays and Underclothing Making, and warehouse occupations; and the Secretary of State should have power to extend this relaxation to all occupations in which earlier hours are not customary: also, in any trade where this same condition exists, to allow the limits to be as late as from 9 a.m. to 9 p.m.

Alternative relaxations giving power to employ young persons over

16 and women for 14 hours a day, or else young persons over 14 and women for 13 hours, upon not more than five days in the week or 48 days in the year, subject to the limits of 6 a.m. and 9 p.m., and to the giving of half an hour extra for a meal after 5 p.m., should be permitted to all trades liable to emergency from sudden press of orders; *such over time to be subsequently deducted, within six months, from the legal 60 hours per week, at the rate of not less than half an hour per day.*

Permission to work under any relaxation of the law in respect of hours of labour, should be made conditional upon the adoption of sanitary provisions to the satisfaction of the inspector. All working overtime should be registered and reported to the inspector.

Assistance by way of information and evidence should be supplied to the inspector by officials with local knowledge, engaged in kindred duties, such as sanitary officers or school board visitors, and also by the Police.

It is not likely that any Bill will be brought forward this session by the Government in consequence of these recommendations, but before this time next year, those women who disapprove of these attempts to limit and control female industry, must work hard to enlighten public opinion upon it. The *Scotsman* says, very wisely :—

When the Factories Acts were passed, it soon became clear that there were women in workshops who worked as many hours as women in factories, and at as exhausting occupations. If the law had for its object the protection of women, those of them who were in workshops had as good a right to it as those in factories. The women in factories, however, took another view of the subject, and insisted, as far as they chose to make their voices heard, that it was unfair to fix the hours they should work, and leave the workshop women free to do as they pleased. Then the workshop legislation came, and forthwith jealousies arose between large employers who were handicapped and small employers who were free, and between women whose hours of work in workshops were fixed, and women who could work as long as they pleased in their homes. Further restrictions were demanded and granted, and, as matters stand at this moment, the power of women to earn their living honestly is made as difficult and embarrassing as restrictive laws can very well make it. . . . . . The evidence to which the Commissioners had to listen indeed showed that the evils which the workshop legislation had been passed to meet were to a large extent imaginary. The hours of work are not unduly long even in the cases where the women can virtually regulate their own hours. The Workshop Acts, however, do not always allow them to work as many hours as they desire, and in these cases they take their work home to finish. That was made a matter of great complaint by some of the male witnesses who were called, who were very anxious for further restrictions on the work of women. What do women themselves say? Take the evidence of three working dressmakers at

Manchester. They said, "We do not want to be tied down to any time; we want to come and go at our own pleasure." The Factory Act would not suit them. And that is the burthen of the evidence of many women. Further, it was shown that the restrictions on the hours of work in workshops led to more night work. Three women in London testified, "If the people are prevented from working at the workshop they take home the work to do, and if you stop the working in the workshop, you only make the work get on under more unwholesome conditions." Manifestly, then, in proportion as work is driven out of roomy and healthy workshops to crowded and unhealthy homes. an injury and not a benefit is done to those who are affected by the law. The truth seems to be, that well-meaning philanthropists have got on to a wrong line in seeking to restrict the labour of women. Something might with advantage be done by the State in the way of seeing that workshops are in a sanitary condition; but beyond that there can be little safe interference with workpeople. It would be far better and more kindly to leave women to take care of themselves, than to injure them by what is called taking care of them.

EMPLOYMENT.
FEMALE CLERKS IN THE POST-OFFICE.

On April 4th, Lord. J. Manners, in answer to Mr. Anderson, said the classification of the female clerks in the Post Office would shortly be made, and they would be promoted according to their proved proficiency during their period of probation.

A Lady Pharmaceutical Chemist.—Miss Isabella S. Clarke, who passed the full examination as a pharmaceutical chemist last January, and is the first woman who has done so, has begun business at 18, Spring street, Paddington.

Lessons in Pottery Painting.—Mr. Mortlock has opened an Art Pottery Studio at his gallery, under the superintendence of several lady artists from the late studio at South Kensington. The pottery galleries are at 203 and 204, Oxford street, and 31, Orchard street, Portman square, London, W.

Letter from Lord Aberdare.—It will be remembered that Lord Aberdare, on the occasion of a deputation to the Duke of Richmond on March 2nd, reminded the Lord President that some years ago a room near the South Kensington Museum, on the property of the Exhibition Commissioners, had been set apart for the reception of female painters on china, who were prevented by the jealousy of the men from pursuing their work at Stoke on equal terms. " To this statement," he says, in a letter to the *Daily News*:—

Mr. Copeland and Mr. Campbell give a distinct contradiction. Mr. Campbell, in a courteous letter, informs me that the premises at South Kensington were erected by his firm, at the suggestion of Sir H. Cole, "for the purpose of affording technical instruction in china painting to students at the South Kensington School of Art, and most assuredly not in consequence of the tyranny of the men, &c." He adds that when he joined the establishment of Messrs. Minton, more than 30 years ago, he remembers his uncle, the late Mr. Herbert Minton, saying that the men objected to the women using a "rest." or piece of wood fixed to the table, on which the arm could be rested; but Mr. Campbell is strongly of opinion that "although at that time it may have been the idea that the men objected to the use of it on the part of the women, such a rest could not have been required by them;" and states that for more than 20 years, during which he has had the entire management, he can most conscientiously assert that there has been no such oppression on the part of the painters and decorators; and that, on the destruction by fire of the premises at South Kensington, he offered employment at Stoke to the female artists, who, for various reasons, declined it, but who, he assures me, would have been treated by their fellow-workmen with the utmost courtesy and consideration. Nothing can be more satisfactory than this contradiction to my statement; and although I regret having made a charge thus proved to be erroneous, I am glad to have given Mr. Campbell the opportunity of removing a misapprehension which I find to prevail widely, even among persons usually well informed on such subjects.

Perhaps, sir, you would kindly allow me space to explain the reasons for believing in the prevalence of the shameful—I wish I could say unmanly—custom to which I referred. In 1849 a Select Committee on Schools of Design was appointed by the House of Commons, and sat under the presidency of Mr. Milner Gibson. One of the most important witnesses examined was Mr. Herbert Minton, of Stoke-upon-Trent. I extract his answers to questions put to him by Mr. Beresford Hope:

Question 2,801. Am I correct in the information I have had that in painting flowers the females are not allowed to use a rest for the arm?—Yes; the men have the rest, the women not.

2,802. Can you give the Committee any reason for that?—It is an arbitrary rule; just the same as another rule, that the women are not allowed to use gold to gild.

2,803. By whom is that arbitrary rule enforced?—By the workmen entirely.

2,804. (Mr. Milner Gibson): What has suggested such an ungallant proceeding?—I cannot say. It is a most tyrannical thing, but such is the fact.

And Mr. Minton adds, in answer to question 2,805, "In years

gone by there has been an attempt [on the part of the masters] to
upset this arbitrary rule, and the men have turned out, and people
[*i.e.*, masters], considering their own private interests, have rather
given way than contest the point. There has not been any attempt
for the last fifteen or twenty years to renew the question; the women
are so accustomed to it that they never think of using the rest; they
are not brought up to it.

But this, it will be said, was so long ago as 1849. True, but Sir
H. Cole assures me, and I have his authority to use his information,
that such was his conviction of the continued prevalence of this
arbitrary rule, that he has frequently, in comparatively recent times,
referred to its existence in terms of condemnation at public meetings
at Stoke, which he attended as representing the science and art
schools, and that his statement was never disputed. Such being the
case it is no wonder that the charge has been generally believed. I
do not for a moment wish to set up this merely presumptive evidence
of the continuance of a disgraceful custom against the clear and positive statements of such competent authorities as Mr. Campbell and
Mr. Copeland. But even these gentlemen will see that the charge
was not altogether unfounded, and will understand why I, in common
with others, believed in the existence of a custom which all will rejoice
to hear has become obsolete.

The *Labour News* writes, after giving a list of places
in London where women workers or apprentices are
wanted:—" but what I do say is, that for young girls
anxious to get an honest living, there appears to me to
be any amount of openings as learners in this great hive
of industry; as learners, they must be content with
small remuneration, the future depending entirely on
their own steadiness and perseverance. Many women
in this quarter are now earning first-class wages; others
again a bare pittance."

PROTECTIVE AND PROVIDENT LEAGUE.

We are glad to see that the excellent little Journal
of the League has this month doubled itself in size; we
hope it will go on and prosper.

The Women's Societies are holding their quarterly
and half-yearly meetings, and their reports continue
very satisfactory. The Society of the Machinists is
fairly established. It is impossible to over-estimate the
advantage which these unions for registration, arbitration, and benefit funds, afford to the hard-worked,
under-paid, and hitherto scattered and solitary women.

The beginning has been made; they have now only to persevere.

THE PRACTICE OF VIVISECTION.

ON March 20th, a deputation from the Society for the Protection of animals liable to Vivisection, waited upon Mr. Cross, the Home Secretary, to ask the Government to introduce some legislative measure for the restriction of the practice of vivisection. The deputation consisted of the Earl of Shaftesbury, K. G., Mr. Cowper Temple, M.P., Sir F. Elliott, Colonel Evelyn Wood, Dr. Hoggan, Admiral Sir Charles Eden, Colonel G. Wrottesley, Sir Rutherford Alcock, Mr. Mundella, M.P., Mr. Leslie Stephen, Cardinal Manning, Mr. Froude, and the Rev. Thomas Hugo.

The Earl of Shaftesbury, in introducing the deputation said that, speaking for himself, he should be much disposed to ask for total prohibition of vivisection; but as he was sure that at the present moment this was unattainable he wished to join in the common action, and to ask that something should be done to restrict the present state of things, which was altogether abominable. He then read the following memorial of the Society :—

The Committee, and the large body of friends and subscribers whom it represents, must respectfully ask her Majesty's Government to grant without any unnecessary delay the object which this society has been formed to obtain, namely, the utmost possible protection for animals liable to vivisection. Various opinions exist, both in this society and generally throughout the nation, respecting the extent to which the practice of vivisection ought to be permitted, but this society is unanimous in desiring that such efficient protection be extended to all animals subjected to physiological experiments, as that (in the words of one of the members of the late Royal Commission) "an end shall be put to all torture, and to everything approaching thereto." This Committee is also entirely agreed in adopting the recommendation made by the same gentlemen, that, in any legislation on the subject, experiments upon the higher and more sensitive animals should be altogether prohibited. The Committee are fully aware that no Government in this free country can introduce a legislative measure without inquiring in the first place whether public opinion on the subject be sufficiently matured to afford them the requisite support: and, secondly, whether more time will be consumed by the discussion than can be spared from other important questions. On the first head, the Committee would point to the wide-spread agitation of the public mind on the subject of vivisection, and may mention that in 1875, 145 petitions against the practice were presented to the House of Commons, with 27,814 signatures, and that already, up to March 10th, 1876, 112 petitions have been presented, with 29,315 signatures. A large number of petitions have also been presented in both sessions, to the House of Lords, among which, it should be noticed, was one presented by the Archbishop of York, signed with scarcely a single exception by all the heads of Houses in Oxford, Cambridge, and Dublin Universities, and by the head-masters of the great public schools. On the second point, the Government, it will be remembered, included in their Commission eminent men well understood to represent the conflicting views and interests which claimed consideration; and those distinguished persons have unanimously concurred in certain practical conclusions. This fact affords a presumption that any Bill embodying their recommendations will, so far as it goes, be an unopposed measure: although to prove satisfactory to this society, the law must be framed with extreme care and stringency, lest while seeming to forbid, it should undesignedly shelter cruelty and¦ abuse. Even at the present moment such cruelty and abuse may too possibly prevail and since the highest authorities have admitted that precautions against them are required, the Committee earnestly appeals to her Majesty's Government for that effectual prompt legislation which alone can tranquilise the public mind.

Mr. Cross made a reply to the effect that it was an extremely difficult subject to legislate upon, and that Government desired to come to a satisfactory conclusion upon it—a reply which might almost be stereotyped from its universal applicability to any deputation upon any subject.

The Society for the protection of animals liable to vivisection has issued its statement on the report of the Royal Commission. The Commission reports that experiments on the living animal are largely on the increase; but that if prohibited altogether our medical professors and students would leave the country to pursue their investigations abroad. All existing laws are inadequate to deal with the difficulty. The Commission recommends a law by which experiments upon any living animals shall be placed under the control of the Secretary of State who shall grant or withdraw licenses, and institute efficient inspection; the owner of the license being bound to avoid inflicting suffering wherever it can be avoided. Mr. Hutton, one of the Commissioners, would in addition entirely exempt the household animals, dogs and cats, from experiment, because endowed with greater sensibility than other animals, and because they are often stolen from their proper owners, to meet the demand.

The Committee regret that the language of the Commissioners has not been stronger in condemning the abuses of the practice, and does not adopt the opinion that the benefits to be derived from Vivisection justify it when the pain to the animal is serious. They further regret that there is no proposal in the Report of the Commission to prohibit the use of Vivisection for purposes of mere demonstration as distinct from research.

Petitions to repress Vivisection have been already presented to the number of 189, containining 55,140 signatures.

This is emphatically a woman's as well as a man's question. It is one which the women through the length and breadth of England should investigate, and when they have made up their minds on it, work for with all their strength.

It is a too common assertion that vivisection has been the chief means by which the science of medicine has been advanced, " The three most notable discoveries ascribed to experiments on living animals are the circulation of the blood, by Harvey; the double functions of the spinal nerves, by Sir Charles Bell ; and the use of chloroform as an anæsthetic, by Sir James Simpson. . . . . The use of chloroform was the result of an experiment tried by Sir James Simpson *upon himself.*" Harvey discovered the circulation of the blood by observation, and he only made use of experiments to remove the obstinate prejudices of his day against the discovery. Sir Charles Bell's method was precisely similar. He himself wrote:—"The results have been considered as in favour of experimenting on living animals. They are, on the contrary, deductions from anatomy, and I have had recourse to experiments, not to form my opinions, but to impress them on others. It must be my apology that my utmost powers of persuasion were lost while I urged my statements on the ground of anatomy alone. . . . . Experiments have never been the means of discovery." Even greater names can be now quoted against the practice.

MISCELLANEOUS.

A Lady Commander of a Brig.—The *Scotsman* says, "the brig Clitus which was recently condemned by the Board of Trade surveyors, has just been sold at Salt-coats. The Clitus has a peculiar history, having for twenty-two years been commanded by the late Miss Betsy Millar, of Saltcoats, who (says our correspondent) managed the vessel with great skill. While Miss Millar was in charge, the vessel was on two separate occasions driven ashore, and in both mishaps she evinced a considerable amount of courage. Her sale deprives the two surviving sisters of the late commander, who died in 1864, of a means of livelihood.

The Dean of Westminster has, it is said, commissioned Miss Grant to execute a bust of the late Lady Augusta Stanley, to be placed in Dunfermline Abbey. Lady Augusta Stanley is buried in the chapel of Henry VII. in Westminster Abbey, which rarely receives a female tenant—a special honour due to her high personal qualities.

Royal School of Art Needlework.—On the 22nd ult. the rooms at South Kensington were opened for a display of needlework, principally destined for the Philadelphia Exhibition. The examples shown were good, both in execution and design, and well deserved a visit.

SCHOOL BOARD IN EDINBURGH.

The elections for the School Board are just over; out of the fifteen successful candidates two are ladies.

National Training School for Music.—The Northampton Scholarship has been awarded to Miss Eliza Cosford, aged eighteen years.

It is announced that the National Temperance League, 337, Strand, will hold a conference in London early in June, "to consider what plans would be most likely to prove effective in extending and consolidating women's work in connection with the temperance reformation."

Joint Stock Enterprise.—Two ladies' names appear as signatories to the Memorandum of Association of the newly constructed Aberdare and Plymouth Company, Limited.

A home has been opened at 21, Greville street, Holborn, for the reception of young women who are engaged in business during the day.—*Labour News.*

Lady Pembroke has provided a free library for the girls employed in her carpet factory at Witton.

The late Mrs. Hugh Miller.—Mrs. Miller, *née* Lydia Fraser, widow of the distinguished geologist and literary man, Hugh Miller, died at Assynt, Sutherlandshire, on the 11th ult., at the age of 64. She possessed literary talents of no mean order. At the time of the Disruption of the Scottish Establishment she published a novel entitled "Passages in the Life of an English Heiress," in which the views of the "non-intrusion" party were enthusiastically advocated. A book for young people, with the graphic title "Cats and Dogs," was more successful, and has been frequently republished within the last twenty years. She took a chief part in editing her husband's works after his death, and her prefaces and additions display extraordinary vivacity and no small imaginative power. She gave much assistance to Mr. Peter Bayne in the preparation of the biography of Hugh Miller, and deserved credit for the intrepid honesty with which she published documents essential to the illustration of her husband's life, but which a pusillanimous regard to the sensibilities of some influential persons might have prompted her to hush up.—*Daily News.*

DISABILITIES OF MARRIED WOMEN.

The *Women's Suffrage Journal* says:—"The inconvenience of the disabilities, with regard to property and contract, which the common law of England attaches to marriage in women, lately received an illustration in the Police Court at Westminster. An order had been made against one Elizabeth Hemmings, on the complaint of Mr. Phillips, for the payment of £1 4s. and costs, she having been a machinist in his employ, and having left her work without notice. In default of payment a dis-

M

tress warrant was issued, but this was returned *nulla
bona*, and consequently the plaintiff took out a summons
calling on defendant to show cause why she should not
be dealt with according to law. Defendant pleaded
that she was a married woman. Mr. Arnold said it had
been decided, in the case of Tompkinson appellant and
West respondent (39 Justice of the Peace, 293), in the
Court of Queen's Bench, that a married woman could
not be convicted under the Master and Servant's Act
(30 and 31 Vic. cap. 141) for leaving her employment
without notice, on the ground that she, as a married
woman, was incapable of contracting, and that consequently there was nothing to bind her as between her
and her employer. And in Hodgkinson appellant and
Green respondent (39 J.P., 372), the Court held that an
order on a married woman under the same Act to pay
money by way of compensation, under similar circumstances, could not be made. The summons was then
dismissed.

"A case of this kind usually calls forth from a certain
portion of the press comments to the effect that the disabilities in question are to be regarded as some special
privilege accorded to women, which is to compensate
them for the denial of political and personal rights, and
yet women who avail themselves of these disabilities in
order to avoid their just debts, whether of money or
service, are taunted with not acting honourably.
Women are reproached because the laws that men have
made for them deprive them of the status of persons
legally reponsible for their actions, and men are slow to
understand that a removal of this condition of non-
responsibility is as much an object of those who seek to
amend the property laws for women at the establishment of their right to hold property on the same terms
as men. Fortunately for employers who depend largely
on the work of married operatives, women have consciences as well as laws to guide them; at the same
time the relation between such workpeople and their
employers is one of unstable equilibrinm, and in the interests of the labour market it would seem desirable that
some inquiry should be made with a view to the amendment of the present unsatisfactory law."

The *Manchester Guardian*, March 31, gives the following:—*A Wife's Control over a Wedding Ring.*—At the Sheffield County Court, the Judge (Mr. T. Ellison) gave judgment in a case which involved the question of a wife's control over a wedding ring. A married woman died at her mother's house, and shortly before her death gave her mother her wedding ring. The husband now claimed the value of it as a set off against a claim brought against him for his wife's board and lodging.— In giving judgment His Honour said a wedding ring came under a class of articles which the wife had separately and independently of her husband, and she had power to keep them, but she had no power to give them away. On the other hand, the husband had power to give them away even during her life. In this case the wife had no power to give away her ring, and his judgment must be accordingly.

The National Training School for Cookery.—A deputation from this institution waited upon the Lord President of the Privy Council and Lord Sandon, on March 9th, to ask that the encouragement of the Government might be given to the school. The deputation urged the Government to send scholars from the female training schools, say at the rate of ten from each training school. The National Training School for Cookery, the deputation stated, was supported entirely by voluntary contributions, subscriptions, and the fees of students; and they thought that they could not extend its sphere of usefulness without further aid.

The cookery school in Hurlford, Ayr, has proved a great success. The institution is established on a thoroughly practical and common sense basis. The charge to the girls is 1d. per lesson, and their instruction embraces purchasing provisions, cookery, and setting table, with the inculcation of neatness in person and celerity in serving.

The Petition List is always instructive. Up to April 4th there had been sent in—
For alteration of Married Womens' Property Laws— Petitions 5, Signatures 427.

Against Restrictions on Female Labour—Petitions 2, Signatures 259.

For Repeal of the C. D. Acts—Petitions 40, Signatures 4,908.

Against Mr. Charley's Offences against the Person bill (infanticide)—Petition 1, Signatures 94.

One Petition has also been presented for granting Medical Degrees to women.

The *Rinkomania* has one good result if the following advertisement in the *Daily Telegraph* of March 15 is any real evidence that another employment is open to women :—"Roller Skating.—Several young ladies required to be trained for teachers of skating.—State height and age, by letter, to Rink, care of Messrs. Squire & Co.. Advertising Agents, 7, Burleigh street, Strand, W.C."

LECTURE NOTES.

On April 2nd, Miss Vickery gave a lecture on the "Political Status of Women," at the Eleusis Club, Chelsea.

On April 5th, the adjourned debate on Admiral Maxse's paper on "Women's Suffrage: reasons for opposing it," was resumed at the London Dialectical Society, Langham Hall, 43, Great Portland Street, W.

The same Society announces a lecture by Professor Hunter, M.A., on "The Relation of the Sexes as governed by Legislation"—a historical comparison of the laws of the Jews, Romans and English, on Wednesday, April 19.

The lectures of the National Health Society commenced on the 11th of April. The list of lecturers includes the names of Dr. H. C. Bartlett, Miss Florence Lees, Dr. S. Wilks, Miss M. Hill, Mrs. Buckstone, and Mr. Eassie.

THE ADVANTAGES OF BOARDING OUT.

We have been kindly permitted to print the following excellent letter from a lady upon the advantages of boarding out pauper children :—

St. Asaph, March, 1876:

" I wanted to tell you how deeply I sympathise with

your efforts in the cause of pauper children. Now I must tell you that though I am not able to take any active part in the management of pauper children, yet my heart "leaps up" with sympathy whenever I hear of efforts to remove them from the deadening and morally killing influence of large establishments, where there is none of the natural teaching of natural life, which is in reality of more value than any possible amount of artificial teaching, even if it were conducted by angels in human form, which alas! is far from being the case in large establishments. A little creature left to run with others, even in a street, soon learns to take a little care of a younger one, and then tries to sweep the floor, and next to mend the fire, and peel the potatoes, and so on, and so on, till without effort and *with good will* it at last is trained for household work, or, if a boy, for whatever work is going on outside, and thus is ready for further instruction in gaining a livelihood. No one can watch the constant efforts of little children to "help" those older than themselves, and their delight in thinking themselves useful without seeing that the constant quenching of such desires must destroy their very nature and so it proves. The desire to "help" dies away, and most of the cruelty exercised on unfortunate workhouse children, no doubt, arises from vain efforts to force them to yield that "help" which years of enforced uselessness has driven out of their nature. Without proper superintendence in boarding out, no doubt cases of neglect would occur, for parents often alas! neglect their own children, but at the worst the poor orphans would have their chance with the rest of the working population. Another evil fostered by large establishments where there cannot be individual love and care, is intense selfishness, and this alone is enough to cast a blight over every virtue.

> "I care for nobody, no not I,
> For nobody cares for me,"

is practically the motto of each poor little creature, and thus they learn to care only for themselves, and not even for themselves in a rational manner, but only in the way of getting all they can, and doing as little as possible in return.

I hope you are not tired by my long letter, but " out
of the abundance of the heart," &c.

Yours very truly,

_____

_____

ART. VI.—FOREIGN NOTES AND NEWS.

FRANCE.

The question of woman's work is still engrossing the attention of
some thoughtful Parisians, and a committee of ladies have opened a
workshop, No. 13, rue Beauregard, to be managed on co-operative
principles, where employment will be given to sempstresses, etc.,
who are out of work. A registry of demands for work and workwomen will be kept in this workshop and copies sent to various trades
unions, so that they may also assist in finding employment for the
women who depend on their own exertions.

The sempstresses' union has on its side issued a circular demanding
support for the realisation of a most ambitious project. It is argued
that most needle-women desire to work at home so that they need not
entirely neglect their domestic affairs. On the other hand the employers object to giving out small quantities of work, and it is necessary for several women to unite together in a workshop where such
wholesale orders are given. To meet this difficulty, it is proposed to
construct a special building which will at once combine the home with
the workshop. There will be, I presume, private apartments adjoining
common workrooms. Such an establishment, properly managed,
would have the extra recommendation of affording an excellent home
for apprentices, where they might be properly watched, instructed,
and protected from the dangers and temptations which generally beset
this class. Mlle. Henriette Floch, 12, Avenue Parmentier, has undertaken to collect money for this purpose, and the French papers
interested in such questions are giving due publicity to the project.—
Labour News.

The French papers report that a young lady, daughter of M.
Benoist, principal of the school of Fontenay-le-Comte (Vendee), has
just passed a brilliant examination for the degree of bachelor of letters,
at the University of Poitiers. Among twenty-two candidates, she
obtained the first places for French dissertation and for Latin composition, and the second for Latin translation. She was warmly
congratulated by the Dean. An elder sister is said to have already
obtained similar honours.

The *Avenir des Femmes* says that ladies may now be present at all the lectures of the Sorbonne, even without any special permission, and the number has much increased of late.

The *Avenir des Femmes* also announces that it is probable that the interdict which was laid on the Association for the Amelioration du sort des Femmes by M. Buffet, will be taken off by the present Government, and that the Society may soon recommence its labours.

The results of the examinations last year for the *brevêt de capacité* required in France for private teachers, give, of 2,259 men candidates, 801 admitted, 1,758 postponed; of 4,508 women, 2,487 have received certificates.

The Examiner says—"The Countess d'Agoult, who, under the the name of "Daniel Stern," has been a prominent French writer, and whose decease was mentioned in our last issue, was a German by birth, of the Bethmann family at Frankfort-on-the-Maine. Brought up in France, she produced some works of sterling quality in the tongue of that country. Her strong political spirit came out in a 'History of the Revolution of 1848,' which passed through two editions. It is. perhaps the most serviceable work for those who wish to make themselves acquainted with the events of the stormy epoch in France, from the proclamation of the Republic, in February, 1848, to the terrible street battles of June of the same year, when General Cavaignac was raised to power. In trustworthiness of details, and in graphic description, Daniel Stern's work has scarcely its equal, so far as the epoch alluded to is concerned.

"The real name of the French authoress, Louise Colet, who has just died at Paris, at the age of sixty-six, was Réovil. Besides various lyrical productions, novels, and dramatic attempts, in one of which she brought the figure of young Goethe on the stage, she wrote some strong anti-clerical books; for instance, 'Les Derniers Abbés.' Among her political writings are to be noted, 'Naples under Garibaldi,' and 'The Italy of the Italians.' She was an ardent Republican; and, though characterised by some eccentricities, has done much to promote free thought in France."

ITALY.

A book on the Duties of Women (dei doveri della donna) has been published in Naples by Signore Adalfisa Costa. The *Pungolo* announces it to be "worth reading."

SWITZERLAND.

Miss Franziska Tiburtius, a German lady, who had studied at Zurich for the last four years and a half, has received her degree of "Doctor of Medicine, of Surgery, and of Midwifery," after having passed an examination in a highly satisfactory manner. On the day of her promotion, she gave a lecture on a medical thesis, and was afterwards complimented by the Dean of the Faculty.

GERMANY.

Karl Blind says that in Germany, the movement for the higher education of women, and for the opening up of new avocations, is making head by means of the foundation, in various towns, of first-rate grammar-schools for girls, equal to those for boys, as well as by the exertions of the different Frauen-Vereine, or Women's Associations, which recently met in a Delegates' Conference.

Within this month the German Women's Associations for the Promotion of Industrial Pursuits and of Intellectual Culture will hold a delegates' meeting at Hamburg. The subjects to be discussed are, the protection of single women intending to emigrate; the aims of the societies for house-management; the question of the training of lady-teachers; and the training of lady-assistants in chemists' shops. Meanwhile, the tenth general meeting of the " Patriotic Women's League" has taken place at Berlin, in the great hall of the Board of Trade. From forty-four branch unions which the League had in 1867, its affiliated societies have risen to the number of 383, with 32,219 members, belonging to all classes of society. The establishment of orphan asylums, of houses of rescue from poverty and vice, of infant schools, the formation of a staff of sick nurses, and so forth, have been the beneficent objects of this Patriotic Women's League. The capital at present in the hands of the Association is 700,000 marks, or £35,000. Last year it had been a little less than £12,000. This useful movement is spreading very rapidly all over Germany.

Russia.

The Semaine, published at St. Petersburg, gives the following particulars concerning lady doctors in Russia : During the scholastic year 1874-5 the number of female students reached 171 - 102 of whom belong to the noble class, 17 to the mercantile, 14 o the shop-keeping, 12 to the families of the clergy, and the remaining 24 to mixed classes. Among the number are 23 Jews, 1 Armenian, and 3 Lutherans the majority belonging to the Orthodox Church Twenty-three are married. Fifty-three had before received their diplomas as teachers ; and the Professors of both Schools of Medicine and Surgery express themselves as much pleased with their progress.

An official Russian ukase has been promulgated forbidding the exercise of the functions of barrister by women.—*Labour News.*

Ten young Jewish ladies of Odessa, who finished their education at the gymnasium of that city. have gone to St. Petersburg to study medicine at the university of that city.

America.

Poor Law Reforms.—Miss Schuyler, President, and Miss Putnam, Secretary of the State Charities Aid Association, of New York, have just issued a highly instructive report condemnatory of out-door relief as conducive to the pauperism which it professes to remove. A system of judiciously applied migration is recommended as against merely palliative assistance in the crowded centres, where the poor have such a fatal tendency to remain.

A Woman's Suffrage Bill passed the Senate in Massachusetts, but has been defeated in the Legislature.

The Massachusetts Senate is also favourable to a Bill granting the Municipal Suffrage to Women, in the following terms :—

SECT. 1.—Every woman who is a citizen of this Commonwealth, of twenty-one years of age and upwards, and has the educational qualifications required by the twentieth article of the amendments to the Constitution (excepting paupers and persons under guardianship), who shall have resided within this Commonwealth one year, and within the city or town in which she seeks a right to vote, six months preceding any meeting of citizens, either in wards or in general meeting for municipal purposes, and who shall have paid by herself, or her parents, or guardian, a state or county, city or town tax, which within two years next preceding such meeting has been assessed upon her in any city or town, shall have a right to vote at such town and city meetings for town and city officers, and upon all questions concerning municipal affairs, and to hold any city or town office to which she may be elected or appointed. ·

We have just received the Annual Report of the New England Hospital. The progress which that institution has made in usefulness and public estimation is very great. There are now many similar hospitals in the United States. The New York Infirmary for indigent women and children was the first, the New England Hospital the second, the Philadelphia Hospital for women and children was the next, then the Chicago Hospital. In Providence, Rhode Island, there is a dispensary started by·a woman doctor, and in Detroit a hospital begins to flourish under the charge of an able woman physician. The New York Medical Society admits women as members and equals.

A lady has just died in Virginia, at the age of ninety-six, who grew up to womanhood in the State of New Jersey. where she was born, and when just twenty-one gave a vote for Thomas Jefferson as President —a property qualification in that State then entitling a woman to vote.

Boston University.—The President's Annual Report for this university says that the University is divided into eight colleges and schools, viz., —the College of Liberal Arts, the College of Music, the College of Agriculture, the School of Theology, the School of Law, the School of Medicine, the School of Oratory, and the School of All Sciences. The number of students was 1745 during the year, and of these 102, as compared with 64 in the previous year, were young women. Nearly half of these, that is 52, were students in the School of Medicine, and one quarter, that is 26, in the School of Oratory.

The Professions in the United States.—Michigan University has 117 female students, of whom four have chosen law, 47 medicine, and 56 literature and science.

CHILI.

At the Santiago Exhibition a lady, Alice Gordon, has received a medal of the second class for a system of telegraphic communication on railroad trains in motion.

A lady has also done much to improve the cultivation of cotton.

Senora Carmen Alvarez de Araya, of Quillota, sent to the recent
Chilian Exhibition samples of cotton raised on her estate. This lady,
animated by a progressive and patriotic spirit, wished to make a test
to learn if it be advisable to give an impulse to the cultivation of cotton in Chili. The samples were very complacently examined by the
judges, and the lady awarded a medal of the first class. The *Mer-
curio* presages that from the trials and lessons of the lady the farmers
will be led to imitate her example and thus develope a profitable cotton growing industry in Chili.

AUSTRALIA.

A new review has been lately published in Victoria under the title
of the *Melbourne Review* : it is modelled on the *Fortnightly*, and will
probably do much to elevate the tone of literary thought and free
opinion.

The *Melbourne Argus* says that while competent house-servants are
greatly sought after, governesses are only offered about the same
terms as domestic servants, and are required to be very highly accomplished. It is a mistaken view to suppose that educated women will
find employment more easily in the colonies than here.

INDIA.

A Hindu lady, Mrs. Sanacummah Ragaviah, the first Hindu lady
who came to England from Madras, has written a work entitled
Pictures of England.

An American school for native ladies has been opened in Bombay.
It will have classes for general instruction, music and drawing, and
will be open for such Parsee, Mahomedan and Hindu ladies as may
wish to receive private instruction for a few hours during the day.
Several ladies take a special interest in the work, and it is expected
that many native ladies will avail themselves of the benefits offered.
Journal of the Indian Association.

A Cottage Hospital for sick women and children, the first of the
kind, has been opened in Bombay.

ART. VII.—CORRESPONDENCE.

The Editor is not responsible for the opinions of Correspondents.

MADAM,—In the March number of the ENGLISH-
WOMAN'S REVIEW reference is made to the undeniable
fact that women have never taken a place among composers. It does not appear to be generally known that
composers do not at first invent an air and then invent
the harmonies which form the orchestral accompaniments; but that the air *with* its harmonies offers itself to

their minds, although many changes are afterwards elaborated. But for an air thus to present itself, a very intimate knowledge of the capacities of the various instruments of an orchestra is required, which can only be obtained by passing much time in an orchestra, either as a performer or otherwise.

This was stated to me by one of the greatest and best known of living musicians, and may explain the fact, that though women can write pretty ballads they have never shewn a talent for music in its higher forms.

I enclose my card, and am,

Your obedient Servant,

A. G.

To the Editor of the "ENGLISHWOMAN'S REVIEW."

MADAM,—In your February number a vegetarian diet was advocated by me, both on physiological and economical grounds; may I state here another reason in its favour, viz., its great use in curing intemperance.

Many years ago Liebig remarked that "most persons found they could take wine with animal food, but not with farinaceous or amylaceous food." Following up this idea, Mr. C. O. Groom Napier, F.G.S., Member of the Anthropological Institute, &c., proved its truth in 27 cases of intemperance, and detailed these cures to the British Association in 1875. Dr. Turner, of New York, achieved the most happy results in upwards of 1000 similar cases, nearly all of which were cured by abstinence from a meat diet. Considering that Great Britain spent, in 1874, on intoxicating drinks, £128,469,848, surely it is worth trying whatever may lighten the curse of drunkenness.

In Germany, the use of Schrot-brot, or Graham bread is recommended in cases of intemperance; its nourishing yet unexciting properties render it peculiarly valuable in such instances.

Yet not merely as a cure, but as the most important part of our daily food, wholesome bread is absolutely necessary, in order to preserve or regain good health. Millers and bakers, when asked for "whole meal," often concoct a fancy mixture of bran and flour, yielding an insipid bread, differing widely from the aromatic and

delicious Graham bread, which is really a "staff of life."
All who can bake at home should do so, even at the cost
of some inconvenience. Nothing can be simpler than
bread-making when properly managed.

After the corn has been carefully cleaned let it be
ground, the coarse and the fine meal being left together:
This can be done by a miller, or in Nye's hand mill [373,
Oxford Street]. Then mix this flour with warm water,
knead it till it no longer clings to the hands, form into
loaves four inches high or so, and bake at once in a hot
oven for about an hour. A natural and sweet fermen-
tation takes place, very superior to that caused by any
addition to the flour. Bread raised by yeast, baking
powders, &c., undergoes an artificial change, certain
starchy particles being thus decomposed and converted,
first into sugar, and then into alcohol. A waste of
material occurs, small in each single loaf, but estimated
at a million lbs. daily, when we reckon up the two or
three millions of persons who eat leavened bread.
Moreover, all bread in which yeast is used swells considerably after being swallowed, and surely it is better
one's loaf should be heavy in the hand (as is Graham
bread) than elsewhere.

Vegetable salt, more fitted to the organism than
mineral salt, exists in due quantity in the coarser flour.
Professor Johnston found the following relative proportions :—

Whole meal,	28lbs.	for flesh.
,,	156lbs.	for muscle.
,,	170lbs.	for bones and salt.
Sum total...	354lbs.	
Fine Flour,	20lbs.	for flesh.
,,	130lbs.	for muscle.
,,	60lbs.	for bones and salt.
Sum total...	210lbs.	

1,000lbs.

With the growth of luxury arose the practise of
separating the bran from the fine flour, thus depriving
the bread of much of its nutritive power, and also of its
ballast. According to Liebig the coarser meal contains
most material for forming flesh and blood and bones,
and most salt, the finer most respiratory material. Each
part gains in strength through the other, so that both

must be used together. Four hundred years ago Tryon set forth the waste and folly of removing the bran and taking the fine flour alone for bread. In our own day Dr. Graham showed how a most nutritious and pleasant-tasted bread can be made from whole-meal flour, and much has been spoken and written on the subject. Dr. Müller says, that in order to keep in order the bowels and digestive organs, a certain amount of indigestible material is absolutely necessary in the food. This has been abundantly proved on various occasions, when animals fed only on concentrated food have gnawed wood and eaten shavings, thus instinctively seeking the ballast needed. On a ship provisioned with the finest ship's bread, the sailors were stricken down with weakness and loss of appetite, so that they were obliged to run into port. The captain gave as a reason for the sickness the fineness of the bread. Countless disorders of mind and body arise from constipation, chiefly induced by the habit of using only fine flour. This folly seems the stranger when we know that Graham bread is far more tasty than that usually sold, as well as more wholesome. The most delicate constitution in a few days becomes adapted to the change from white bread to the coarser looking loaf. Until the staple article of food be right, we are, indeed, poorly fed. Let us look to this matter. Amongst the many pursuits now open to woman, she still remains, as ever, the guardian of the hearth. Let her study the laws of health in regard to " our daily bread."

Faithfully yours,

Florence.   E. HADWEN.

ART. VIII.—PARAGRAPHS.

The *Times* says:—The female population of London exceeds the males by more than two hundred thousand (220,158). At the Census of 1871 there were 226,393 women and girls, or more than one-eighth of the whole, occupied in domestic service; while the milliners, dressmakers, and sempstresses amounted to less than half that number. A popular novelist has lately made a vigorous appeal to the latter class to engage in competi-

tion with the former; and the Registrar General says
that the needlewomen are probably as unhealthy as the
servants are healthy.   We do not know of any evidence
with regard to the comparative salubrity of the ordinary
female employments; but it is evident that household
servants should be exempt from the many diseases
which arise, directly or indirectly, from various kinds of
privation.   The excess of women over men appears to
be due to an incursion of the former in search of work;
for, as influenced by births and deaths alone, the sexes
would be nearly equal.   The number of males born is
greater than the number of females, and the difference
is almost exactly corrected by the greater male mortality.
The efforts which have been made to open new kinds of
industry to women have probably added to the inherent
attractiveness of a great centre of population; and it is
even possible that these efforts may tend, for a certain
time, to increase the keenness of the competition which
it may be hoped they will ultimately abate.

   Women in the Civil Service of Massachusetts.—The
Woman's Journal says:—Nine years ago, General Burt
took charge of the Office.   Never before had women
been employed in prominent places therein.

   The clerks being all men, the general delivery boxes
had become in Boston, as in many other cities, a
favorite resort of disreputable persons of both sexes, so
that respectable ladies and gentlemen were often annoyed
by improper behaviour, for which some of the delivery
clerks were in part to blame.   Mr. Burt at once dismissed several of these, and employed women in their
places at the general delivery.   The scandal instantly
ceased, and has never occurred since.   At first only three
or four women were introduced into the office, but their
services proved so acceptable that the number has been
gradually increased, and more than thirty female clerks
are now employed in the main station and in the branch
offices in Boston.   They are mostly in the Money Order,
Registered Letter, and General Delivery departments.
The women have proved superior to men in looking up
missent and misdirected letters, and in making returns
to the dead letter office.   They have also proved entirely reliable.   There has not been a single instance,

in nine years, where the accounts of any woman have shown a deficiency of one dollar, in the Boston Post Office.

Four ladies have been elected Guardians in Leamington.

The Malton Bench of Magistrates have just appointed Sir Charles William Strickland, of Hildenly, near Castle Howard, and Miss E. Thompson, overseers for the parish of Hildenley, Yorkshire.

Agassiz and Woman's Rights.—"The liberal man deviseth liberal things." Mr. Agassiz did many a kindly, gracious thing for women, for which we hold his memory in very grateful remembrance. During his journey through Brazil, he gave lectures in some of the large cities. Thinking of the pleasure, and profit of the Brazilian ladies, he desired specially that they should be invited to attend the lectures. "At first," says Mrs. Agassiz, in her published account of the journey, "the presence of ladies was objected to, as too great an innovation on national habits; but even that was overcome, and the doors were opened to all comers; the lectures being in the true New England fashion.'"

And again she writes: "It is worthy of remark that the appearance of ladies on such occasions no longer excites comment. There were many more sennoras among the listeners, than at previous lectures, when their presence was a novelty."

The admission of lady students to the school at Penikese, is another instance of Mr. Agassiz's kindly interest in women, and his active desire to extend to them as far as he could, a wider opportunity of scientific culture.

The Saturday Review, in an article upon Working Women's Clubs, after describing the wretched homes of the young shopwomen and workgirls, says :—"It seems to be the opinion of a considerable number of people who have the interests of the working-classes at heart that the establishment of Working Women's Clubs would be a desirable step. They think that the cheap theatres, the dancing saloons, the music halls, the public-houses, offer temptations too attractive to be resisted by

young women, who, having worked hard all day, have
only a poor lodging, or a crowded, noisy, or ill-kept
home in which to spend their evenings. They argue
that a girl would be better employed in reading a story-
book, or playing a game of bagatelle in an airy, well-
lighted room, where she could have a cup of tea at cost
price, than in going about with young men of questionable character to entertainments of a debasing description, where she learns to drink gin. The advocates of
clubs for working women do not offer anything to induce
those who have already a home to leave its comforts
and its duties. They simply wish to enter into competition with the places in which they see female modesty
corrupted, and a craving for unwholesome stimulants
for mind and body encouraged. We may lament as we
will the changes that are taking place in the constitution of society, and deplore that women are thrown unprotected into the temptations of large towns. The
fact unfortunately remains that women will soon be obliged to enter the labour market on much the same
footing as their brothers, and the question is now to
help them to resist the allurements to vice which must
await those cut off from the restraints and protection of
family life. The fatigue and hurry of a long day in a
crowded shop, the exhaustion from mechanical work,
the giddiness caused by many hours of monotonous
mental exertion—all these often produce a craving for excitement rather than a desire to repose. . . . . . .
what seems to us much more needed by working-
women than either clubs or reading-rooms are respectable
lodgings in central situations at reasonable rents.
These might be combined with a coffee-room. There is
no intelligent reason why such a scheme, properly
managed, should not be quite safe, and pay a reasonable
percentage on the money which might have to be
borrowed for the purpose. At present parents who live
in the country and who would like their girls to learn a
trade, are often obliged to relinquish the idea because
they cannot find respectable lodgings at a price which
they can afford to pay. Cannot the Peabody trustees
move in the matter?

Englishwoman's Review.

CONTENTS FOR MAY, 1876.

All Communications to be addressed to the EDITOR, 22, Berners Street, Oxford Street, W.

Post-Office Orders payable to SARAH LEWIN, at the "Regent Street" Post-Office.

TERMS OF SUBSCRIPTION AT THE OFFICE.

Per Annum (Post Free), Six Shillings.
Subscriptions payable in Advance. Single Numbers posted Free on receipt of Six Postage Stamps.

MSS. are carefully read, and if not accepted are returned, on receipt of Stamps for Postage, but the Editor cannot be responsible for any accidental loss.

Contributions should be legibly written, and only on one side of each leaf.

THE

ENGLISHWOMAN'S REVIEW.

(NEW SERIES.)

No. XXXVII.—MAY 15TH, 1876.

ART. 1.—THE ARGUMENT OF CUSTOM.

"IMMEMORIAL custom is transcendent law, approved in
the Sacred Scripture and in the code of Divine legislators." So say the laws of Menu, and, in different
phrase, a similar thought was repeated by honourable
members in the House of Commons, when last month
the merits of women's suffrage was discussed. On that
day it was repeatedly demonstrated—on the premise
quod semper, quod ubique, quod ab omnibus—that women
never have had, never can have, never should have
direct political influence.

If the *quod semper, quod ubique* argument contains any
truth, it is this: that the sharpness of demarcation
between the sympathies and pursuits of men and women
always and everywhere diminishes *pari passu* with the
advance of civilization. The customs of mankind in
regard to eating, furnish a curious illustration of this
To ourselves, as to all the most enduring civilizations
of earlier ages—Egypt, Rome, Mexico—nothing has
seemed more natural and desirable than that men and
women should partake of their meals together socially,
nevertheless immemorial and sacred custom has taught
large masses of mankind differently. In Greece, whose
short-lived civilization herein bore an Oriental taint, men
and women only ate together in private domestic life,
the presence of guests was the signal for the wife to

N

retire from her husband's table.   In stationary China,
Barrow states that "a wife must never eat at the same
table, nor sit in the same room as her husband;" albeit,
an old voyager relates*, that in the Corea wives did
sometimes go to feasts, but sat by themselves facing
their husbands. On the other hand, the laws of Menu
forbade a Brahmin to eat with his wife or even to see
her eating.   And to make the descending scale, both of
action and of civilization, still more complete, the Ta-
hitians, when first visited by missionaries, strictly prohibited a wife from partaking of the same kinds of food
as her husband; moreover, "sacred custom forbade that
she should eat in the same place, or prepare her food at
the same fire."†

Thus a complete gradation from our social unison to
absolute separateness, has existed amongst the time-
honoured customs of various races of men; yet how can
we afford to be amused at even the extremest of these,
when we ourselves still sunder our boys and girls in the
enjoyment of their mental food, and make them partake
of separate courses of intellectual nourishment in separateness?

Among certain tribes of American Indians, the women
speak almost a different dialect from the men; others
have so many different expressions appropriated to the
use of men and women respectively, that a learner is
apt to be laughed at for talking like a man or like a
woman, as the case may be.‡ Nevertheless, other things
being equal, there is not much to choose between the
wild Sioux who expects his wife to use different names
for the same things, and the civilized Saxon who expects
her to use the same language, but to follow different
mental processes—emotion, she; reason, he.

Although
            "Adam delved and Eve span,"
a recent traveller relates that in certain parts of the
Himalayas—ignoring these remarkable ancestral exem-
plars—"every man you meet is invariably spinning;

* "Pinkerton's Voyage," VII., 533.
† "Ellis' Polynesian Researches," I., 221
‡ "Schoolcraft's Indian Tribes," III., 234.

they work very slowly, but incessantly, carrying a
bundle of loose short wool in the breasts of their
blouses;"* whilst in Angola "a male slave cannot be
made by his master to cultivate the ground, which is
women's work, and the mistress and her slaves till the
ground together."†

Can we doubt that our great-grandchildren will look
back on the horror which Members of Parliament now
express at the idea of women voting, with feelings akin
to those with which we regard the horror of the Red
Indian if a woman dares to ride on his horse, nay, even
to bridle it—sure omen to him that misfortune is
impending over some one belonging to him.‡

Surely these uncultured notions read like a parody
on ourselves. Might they not help us, not exactly to
see ourselves as others see us, but to see ourselves as it
were, so to say, other than ourselves?
      " As if from afar we took our point of sight,"
and perceived that the "transcendent law" is to pass
from distinct towards common sympathies, from separated towards united action.

HELEN BLACKBURN.

ART. II.—CONGRESS AT SYRACUSE.

(Continued from page 153.)

MRS. GRACE ANNA LEWIS, from Pennsylvania, read a
paper upon "Science for Women." The American Association of Science meets from year to year in different
cities. A number of its members are women. The
American Philosophical Society for the Promotion of
Useful Knowledge, which owed its origin to Benjamin
Franklin, admits women as members. Mrs. Somerville

---

* *Spectator*, March 4th, 1876 (Review of from Hebrides to
Himalayas.)
   † " Monteiro's Angola and the Congo," 1876, I., 58.
   ‡ " Schoolcraft's Indian Tribes," III., 230.

was a member, and Miss Mitchell and other ladies now
are.   The Academy of Natural Sciences of Philadelphia
admits women to memberships with the privilege of
other members ; and other scientific institutions in
Boston, Chicago, and San Francisco offer them equal
advantages.   Scientific courses are now common in the
best schools and colleges, and already a number of
women have distinguished themselves in this department of knowledge.   Professor Baird mentions in his
"Annual Record of Science and Industry" Mrs. Mary
Treat and Lady Hooker in connection with the study
of botany; Miss Christine Chart, of mathematics; Miss
Oimeiod, of zoology ; Madame Seiler, in general physics;
Lady Napier, in pisciculture; Mrs. E. Vale Blake, in
geography; Mrs. de Selle, in mineralogy.   Miss Bodley,
long a devoted student of plant-life, occupies the chair
of chemistry in the Woman's Medical College of Philadelphia.   Other ladies have made important microscopic studies.   Miss Annette Buckle. M.D.. of Boston,
is eminent in embryology.   Among the recent additions
to the list of Women Professors in America are Miss
Hallowell, Professor of Natural History in Wellesley
College, Massachussetts; and Miss Breslin, Professor of
Mathematics at Vassar College.   In several other colleges
women occupy professional chairs, and the number of
such is yearly increasing.   Thus, women in America are
gradually coming to share the honours and emoluments,
as well as the duties, of education.

The next paper was by Mrs. Livermore. Massachusetts,
on "Superfluous Women." The theory, she says, that
marriage offers to woman her only career of usefulness
leads us to do injustice to the great army of the unmarried.   They not only drop down in general estimation, so that we speak slightingly of them as old maids
and superfluous women, but neglect to provide for them,
and to give them the training necessary for their successful living and proper development.   Mr. Greg, the
charming English essayist, calls unmarried women
"redundant" and "superfluous women," and has
written an elaborate paper in answer to the question,
" Why are women redundant ?"   He not only attempts
to answer this question, but he raises another—" What

shall we do with these superfluous women?"   And after
a full discussion of the whole subject in a kindly spirit
he is unable to suggest any other provision for these
superfluous women than exportation.   You must do
with them as you do with any other commodity with
which the market is overstocked.

"There is no way by which provision can be made for
superfluous women," continues Mrs. Livermore, "except by
training them intellectually, morally, and industriously, so
that they can make their own way in life whether married
or single.   A very large number of women do not marry.
Of those who do marry a large proportion are obliged
still to earn their own living entirely or in part.   The
majority of widows bear the burden of their own maintenance thrown upon them and that of their children.
It is therefore an absolute necessity of our present social
condition that women should have as free admission to
professional and industrial training as men; that there
should be no monopoly of sex, and no protection duty
on either side.   *   *   *   No girl should be considered
educated for life till she is in possession of a trade, profession, or business that will give her a living."

Some essays on "Art Culture" and "Art for Women"
followed.   In the course of the latter Mrs. Doggett
urges the establishment of additional art schools, in
which women might learn to draw on wood or stone,
and to carve.   A thorough general knowledge of drawing would do much to extend the sphere of woman's
work.

Mrs. Chase, of Rhode Island, contributed an article on
"The Relation of Women to Crime and Criminals."   In
England the average of female prisoners is about one-
third compared to male prisoners; in America, by Mrs.
Chace's report, the number of women convicted of crime
is even less.   In the Massachusetts State prisons in 1874
there were 763 men and 188 women.   In Rhode Island
in the same year 333 men and 145 women; and in other
prisons an even smaller proportion of women.   The
causes of this disproportion are, she suggests—that girls
are exposed to fewer temptations than boys; that, being
less called on to provide the means of subsistence, they
commit fewer depredations on property; and that having

less physical strength and more tenderness they commit
fewer brutal assaults. She complains, however, that
women are not as well or comfortably provided for in the
prisons as men; that prisons are universally consigned
entirely to the control of men. Boards of State charities,
boards of inspectors, trustees of juvenile reformatories
are all men, who, feeling their deficiencies in the management of the women, leave them pretty much to themselves. Women in Rhode Island have repeatedly petitioned the Legislature to appoint them on the boards of
direction of the penal and correctional institutions of the
State. As yet they have been refused on the ground
that the Constitution forbids the appointment to any
civil office, except school committees, of any person
who is not an elector. The Legislature, however, has
appointed an Advisory Board of Women to visit the
prisons and reformatories, and prepare reports and suggestions; and these have been able to accomplish some
changes productive of much comfort to the prisoners.

Finally, Mrs. Bond, of Boston, gave an account of
some employments open to women. Her own speciality
is an unusual one for a woman—watch and chronometer-
making—including manufacturing, as well as importing,
watches, clocks, and scientific instruments; and her
business is of such repute that she has supplied the
Russian Imperial Observatory and two observatories belonging to the English Government. Since her husband's
death she has carried on his business for the sake of her
children, and has maintained it for nine years. "I could
not have done it," she says simply, "without previous
training, not only mathematical but mechanical, which
training I went through from choice, when there was no
reason to apprehend that I should ever be obliged to put
it to practical use, simply from the desire to understand
and share my husband's pursuits. When I knew the necessity, it would have been too late to acquire it."

Even from the present short and imperfect notes it
will be easy to imagine how interesting the topics chosen
for the Congress were to anyone engaged in promoting
the higher life of women. We have been compelled
from want of space to do but scant justice to the ideas
—none at all to the language—which is often clear,

concise, and vigorous. The committee engaged in the
collection of the papers last year invited the co-operation of friends from the Old World. It may be that this
autumn we shall hear of English contributors to the solid
and thoughtful suggestions which will in all probability
mark the Congress of their centennial year.

<hr>

ARTICLE III.—WOMEN AS A "CLASS."

IN a recent debate in Parliament Mr. Bright said,
"Nothing could be more monstrous or absurd than to
describe women as a class. They were not like the
class of agricultural labourers or factory workers. There
were women in the highest ranks, women in the middle
ranks, and others in the humbler ranks. Who
were so near the hearts of the legislators of our
country as the women of their own families. It was a
scandalous and odious libel to say women were a class."
  It is quite true that there is a careless and inaccurate
generalization in the manner in which it is often said
"women as a class do this or that," as if they formed
only a small division of the world's *personnel*, and could
be "lumped together" as men are into their various
professions. Men are spoken of as soldiers, physicians,
tradesmen, labourers, and it is presumed that each section has distinct characteristics : women are spoken of as
if they all had a professional likeness to each other, or as
if womanhood were some "common denomination"
which effaced individual peculiarities. We hear them
classed legally with criminals, idiots, and minors among
the unrepresented divisions of English humanity; writers,
who are mostly men, attribute to men fine distinctions
of character, the effect of education, nature, or circumstances, while they classify women in one or two
broad types.

> Men, some to business, some to pleasure take,
> But every woman is at heart a rake,

said Pope long ago, and, though it is expressed with more

courtesy, there is still a very prevalent notion that
women form a group by themselves, not subjected to
the minuter classification accorded to men. It is sometimes difficult to believe that such writers know that in
all times half, and now-a-days more than half, the population of the British Isles are women.

But there is another sense in which we are justified in
talking of women as forming one class, whether in " the
highest, the middle, or the humbler ranks of life ;" a
sense in which women whether seamstresses, factory hands,
servants, authoresses, countesses, or even the women of
" the families of our legislators," do form one common
class. There may be every variety of education, of
thought, of habit ; they may differ from each other by
nature or by social custom, as much as a prince differs
from a peasant; but so long as there is "class" legislation, so long as the law makes an insurmountable
difference between men and women, women must be
spoken of as a separate class.

This is the only "class" legislation remaining in
England. We may justly boast that there is no law to
prevent the son of a labourer or artizan from rising to
the highest offices in the State. We have abolished the
slavery of colour a century ago in our own land, and
for nearly half that time in our colonies. We have
thrown our universities open to men without distinction of birth or religion. We have opened our hospitable gates to aliens of every race. We have lowered
the franchise till it is within the power of any well-
conducted man who cares about it to be placed on the
register. Our tribunals mete out justice to rich and
poor, if not with absolute equity, with a nearer approach
to it than any other nation has attained. Class legislation (with the exception of one or two lingering ghosts
of its former greatness, the game laws, law of entail,
&c., may be said to have ceased as between man and
man. It is still in full force between woman and man.

We should have to go back to the dark ages to find
so absolute an interference exercised by the law over a
man's property as the common law of England asserts
over that of every woman who marries. By that law
every woman who commits the act (we had almost said

the crime) of matrimony forfeits control over her
property; she cannot dispose by will of any real property, nor give it away; she cannot sue or be sued,
contract or be contracted with. Her husband on dying
can will away not only his own, but her property : even
her apparel and ornaments are at his disposal, though he
may not leave them away by will, and even her right of
dower may be taken from her. Marriage settlements to
some extent modify, or rather " hamper" the action of the
law for the rich, but the Queen is the only woman
whose legal capacities remain unaffected by matrimony,
and who may therefore be considered out of the "class"
of women. Even if unmarried, a daughter cannot
inherit real property so long as there are any sons alive :
all her brothers having a prior claim to herself.

Class legislation has ceased in America by the extinc-
tion of slavery during the civil war; black and white
men are now equal, they have long been so in England,
but women still suffer many of the disabilities that
negroes suffered in America. They are liable by law
to be severed from their children. A parent, if a man,
has inalienable rights which the law ignores, if the
parent be a woman. She has no right to instil into the
children her own religion, she has no right to appoint a
guardian over them, she has no right to keep them with
her if the father choose to remove them. Wealthy
people in this, as in the former case, patch up the law
with settlements and agreements and appeals to the
High Court of Chancery, but the inequality of legislation
as between men and women remains the same.

Class legislation no longer exists between differing sects
with regard to their admission into the universities, but it
has not yet been removed for women. We are told
that ninety-five per cent. of the educational endowments
of the country are reserved for boys. Is there any
other monopoly of such magnitude and value that is
enjoyed by one class of men and not by another?

In early Rome a plebeian could not aspire to the high
offices of State; in France up to the close of the last
century none but a noble could attain place and dignity.
In England lowly birth has long ceased to be any
obstacle to public power or eminence. There is no law

to keep back a boy, though he be a pauper's child ; he
may become Lord Chancellor, bishop, or Court physician
if he will.   But to a girl, though she may be an heiress,
the offices of government are for ever closed ; the doors
of the learned professions are shut upon her, and if she
is in the humbler walks of life the hours of her labour will
be defined by law for her.

A woman criminal is never tried by her peers—judge,
jury, counsel for the accusation and defence are all men.

There is " class " morality, too, which entails class
legislation.   Society pronounces that to be an unpar-
donable offence in a woman which in a man is easily
condoned, and a whole series of offences against the
law have arisen from this assumed difference accompanied by penalties which men escape, but in which
women are the sufferers.   Divorce is granted to a man
more easily than to a woman ; simple unfaithfulness on
one side will procure it ; on the other, unfaithfulness only
if coupled with cruelty.

Such laws affect women both in high and low stations,.
though not of course with equal severity, but they are
enough to set a broad line of demarcation between them
and men.   It avails little to inquire how this state of
things came about ; whether unequal laws are the relics
not yet effaced of ancient barbarism, or the Parliamentary outcome of new opinions upon manly superiority
and feminine need of protection.   The fact remains that
by the law all men in England are equal, and by the
law all women are inferior to them.

But Parliament has of course the kindest intentions
towards this class, which is thus set apart ; we have no
wish to deny it, but occasionally from want of knowing
what this disabled section do actually need, they make
strange blunders, just as we might suppose a well-
intentioned House of Lords to do, if English electors had
no House of Commons to look after their interests.   An
alien can be naturalized in England, and, if a man, enjoy
a right which is permitted to no Englishwoman.

The same right hon. gentleman whose remark headed
this paper said that though a man might feel it a stigma
to be deprived of a vote, because other men voted, a
woman could not feel disfranchisement as a stigma,

because no women voted, and therefore there was no
inequality. We once knew a little boy who had a
regiment of tin soldiers, one of which had its head
knocked off; he at once decapitated the ninety-nine
others that there might be no inequality between them.
The argument appears to us somewhat similar:—because
it is expedient that no woman should feel her "disabilities"
as an insult, therefore all women should be disabled alike.
In France the penalty of civil death is sometimes pronounced for state crimes; it consists in deprivation of
voting, inability to hold office, &c. A parallel sentence
is pronounced in England, simply because the offender
is a woman.

In one respect, however, "caste" might be a better
word than "class," because it conveys the idea of im-
mutability. For as no woman can by any merit or
exertion of her own transfer herself into the privileged
rank of Man, so in India caste is unchangeable.
A Soodra must remain a Soodra, and a Brahmin a
Brahmin to the end of his life. Learning, riches, and
virtues cannot lift a Hindoo out of his native caste, nor
can talent, energy, or wealth, under our present laws
raise an Englishwoman to be the legal equal of an
Englishman.

ART. IV.—REVIEWS.

Marriage Law Injustice; Objections to the Divorce Act. By
Frederick Binney. (Manchester.)

AN eloquent pamphlet upon the abuses, shortcomings,
and unfairness of the present English law of divorce.
As the law stands now, it leaves room for occasional in
justice towards the husband, and for very frequent hardship for the woman. Mr. Binney first points out the inequality towards women:—

Absolute divorce is granted in all cases where the husband can
prove that his wife has been guilty of adultery (since the marriage)
whilst a wife who seeks for a divorce must prove something more than

the mere unfaithfulness of her husband. Adultery on the part of the
man is considered by a parliament of men to form no sufficient excuse
for a dissolution of the marriage tie, but the same offence in a woman
is sufficient to render her no longer a wife. Thus we have one law for
the wife and one law for the husband. In the case of a wife seeking
divorce it is required by the legislature that she should afford proof,
*in addition to the adultery, of cruelty, or a desertion of two years with-
out a reasonable excuse.* In judging of the justice of this state of the
law, it becomes necessary to enquire what, in the eye of the law,
amounts to " cruelty " on the part of a husband such as would justify
his wife in seeking for a divorce.

It then appears that what the legislature calls cruelty
must "be either actual violence committed, attended
with danger to life, limb, or health, or there must be
reasonable apprehension of such violence." And Mr.
Pritchard says in a "Digest of the Law and Practice of
the Divorce Court," "The Court has never, as far as can
be gathered from reported cases, granted a divorce
without proof given of a reasonable apprehension of
bodily hurt."

Here, then, we have at once evidence that one crime
in a woman is to be visited with a penalty which is only
accorded to a double crime in a man. Mr. Binney
claims that habitual drunkenness, confirmed insanity, or
transportation for life should be made sufficient grounds
for divorce on both sides. As it is, no amount of brutality or cruelty, unless coupled with adultery, are
considered sufficient to enable a woman to obtain a
divorce; the utmost she can hope for in such a case is
a judicial separation.

Mr. Binney argues for a freer as well as more equal
law of divorce, and thinks that insanity of seven years'
duration, cruelty, desertion for three years, or felony
involving seven years', or upwards, imprisonment, should
be held to be sufficient cause. He adds:—

Unhappy marriages might undoubtedly be prevented to a large extent by the exercise of increased caution in the first instance ; but who
is to insist on it? Any law which is directed against unsuitable matri-
monial unions would be at once denounced as an " interference with
the liberty of the subject," and as to expecting a young girl of eighteen or twenty, fresh from school, and with little knowledge of
life, to forsee the life she will lead with a man of twenty-five or
thirty, versed in all the ways of the world, and perhaps merely court-
ing her for her money—the expectation is unreasonable and contrary
to common experience. To tell such a woman, when deceived, heart-

broken, and abandoned, that she ought to have known better, and she must content herself with being 'a warning to others,' is simply heartless mockery."

The New Abolitionists: a Narration of a Year's Work.
(Dyer, Brothers. London.)

We can do little more than direct our readers' attention to this work by Professor James Stuart, of Cambridge. It contains the record of the mission undertaken by himself and by Mrs. George Butler to the Continent, to inquire into the various Government systems for the state regulations of vice. This journey has resulted in the International Federation. The system in France and Italy more especially, is demoralizing the very core of society, but there are not wanting noble men and women in both countries to protest against it. One instance of the encouragement given by the government of Italy to vice, will suffice. By an order dated 1860, any prostitute who shall present a certificate proving that she has deposited a sum in the savings bank, receives a premium in money equal to a twentieth of the amount she has paid in. There is now a widespread association in Italy embracing every town of importance, and counting among its members many deputies to Parliament, and women of the highest rank, as well as delegates from all the working men's societies. In France the evil is so wide-spread, that a meeting of working men against the government regulations was deprecated as too dangerous, as out of every 100 men, 30 or more had a daughter or sister in St. Lazare or other government prisons. Thoughtful and religious people in France have largely joined the association in order to combat this growing evil. In Germany, petitions have been presented to the Reichstag by the Inner Mission of the Evangelical Church, against the extension of the present system. In Switzerland, where as yet it prevails only in two or three cantons, amongst which Geneva has a fearful pre-eminence, fatal to its reputation as an University city, the very centre of the Federation exists. It is supported by well-known thinkers and workers, M. Loyson (Père Hyacinthe), Pastor Borel, M. Aimé Humbert, M. Budé, President of the Society de l'Utilité Publique, and others. The objects of the Federation are to combat the increasing immorality of the age, to prevent the State from tolerating or supporting vice, and to open refuges for young girls, giving earnest attention to the question of honest industries for them, and the raising of women's wages.   On all this work the book gives careful and valuable information.

The *Westminster Review* of April has a good article upon the "Legal Position of Women," not in this country only or at the present day, but from the earliest times and among all races.   One remark about a woman's sphere is well worth quoting.   It says, "It is important to notice, not only with reference to our immediate subject but with reference to the popular generalities about the capacities of women, and the 'sphere' or 'mission' marked off for them by nature, that in early societies which approach nearer than our own to a state of nature, it is precisely the women who do all the hard work in addition to their duties as wives and mothers. The men all the time if they are not fighting, sit at home at their ease.   So that, as Plato long ago observed, it is rather existing customs that are contrary to nature than nature which forbids any changes.   From the absolute power of a savage over his slaves flow all those rights over a woman, from which the marital rights of our own time are the genealogical descendants.

A short history of Natural Science for the use of schools and young persons, is the title of a work by Miss Buckley.   We are glad to see women day by day taking a greater part in the world of science and fact.

Lady Lubbock has a careful review of Dr. Darwin's latest work in the *Academy* of the 22nd April.

The *Theological Review* for April contains an able article by Miss Frances Power Cobbe on the "Fitness of Women for the Ministry."

The *Langham Magazine* for May, has an article on "Fröbel and Infant Education."

ART. V.—EVENTS OF THE MONTH.

EDUCATION.

The Ladies' Educational Association, in connection with University College, London, announced additional subjects for Summer Session.—Greek (Talfourd Ely, Esq.). 1. Elementary—Tuesdays 3.45, and Wednesdays 2.30 ; beginning April 25. 2. Advanced—Tuesdays and Thursdays 12.30 ; beginning April 25.——Latin (Talfourd Ely, Esq.). Mondays and Wednesdays 12.30 ; beginning April 24. — French Grammar (Professor Cassal). Mondays and Fridays 3.30 ; beginning April 24.

Prospectus at the office in the College, or of J. E. Mylne, Esq., 27, Oxford Square, Hyde Park, W.

The Committee of Queen's College, London, announced supplemental courses of Higher Lectures for Women during the Easter term, each course to consist of eight lectures. The courses are—English Language, by the Principal, on Thursdays. English Literature, by the Rev. Stopford A. Brooke, to begin in the third week of the term. (The day and hour can be ascertained on application to Miss Grove, secretary.) English History, by Henry Craik, B.A., on Mondays. Roman History, by A. Rankine, B.A., on Fridays. French Literature, by M. Kastner, on Tuesdays.

Sir Titus Salt., Bart., has expressed his intention to found two scholarships of the value of £100 each, in connection with the Bradford Girls' Grammar School.

Endowed Schools for Girls.—The following memorial to the Charity Commissioners on the subject of the omission of any provision by which women are to be represented on the governing bodies of girls' schools, created by the reform of the old endowments, is being numerously and influentially signed by members of the Union :—" We beg permission to address the Endowed Schools Department of the Charity Commission on a point nearly concerning the interests of the Union for Improving the Education of Women, to which we belong. We have seen, with great regret, a marked change in the schemes providing for Girls' Schools, which have emanated from the new Endowed Schools' Department, as compared with those framed by the late Commission. In all the schemes for Girls' Schools of the former Commission, provision was made for securing that women should be at least partially represented on the governing bodies; and in most of them there is an express general proviso that women may be governors. But in the * five schemes relating to Girls' Schools which have been framed under the new law, no provision is made for insuring that a single member of the governing body, whether representative or co-operative, shall be a woman. It is merely enacted that the governors "may" (not even "shall") appoint a Ladies' Committee to assist in the internal management of the school in such matters as the governing body may entrust to them. It seems hardly necessary to observe that these Ladies' Committees, even if appointed, will not in the very slightest degree make amends for the entire absence of any representation of female interests in the governing body. The Ladies' Committee can, in fact, do nothing but what they are told, and will have no voice in regulating the school routine, appointing the teachers, and, above all, apportioning the endowments. In endowments which are to be shared between the sexes, this is obviously a very important matter. Past experience gives too good reason to fear that if the girls' schools have no women to represent and defend them on the governing bodies, their interest will be systematically and most unjustly sacrificed. We would further observe that the proviso inserted in former schemes that women may be governors is omitted in the new schemes. It is possible that, in the absence of any limitation the other way, this proviso may not be absolutely necessary; but it is extremely probable that in practice its omission may operate as a reason or pretext for excluding women who might otherwise have a chance of obtaining seats on governing bodies. We would, therefore, respectfully, but most earnestly, urge on the Commission the

---

* Burlington, Thetford, Clerkenwell, Newcastle-upon-Tyne, and Crediton.

necessity of making provision for ensuring to women some share in the government of all girls' schools in schemes which are now, or may hereafter be, under consideration of the Commission, and the advisability of leaving no room for doubt as to the eligibility of women to be governors, whether representative or co-operative." Signatures—Douglas Galton, Janet Mary Douglas, Anna Bidder, E. C. Tuffnell, Fanny Hertz, Frederica Micholls, R. N. Shore, Mary Gurney, G. C. Bell, E. Wilton South, George C. T. Bartley, H. M. Stanley of Alderley, Aberdare, Lawrence, Julia A. E. Roundell, A. P. Stanley, Napier and Ettrick, James A. P. Kay-Shuttleworth, J. London, Lyttelton, Lucy C. F. Cavendish, Frederick Cavendish, Helen Taylor, H. W. Eve, William Barber, Airlie, Edwin A. Abbott, Joseph Payne, L. T. Mallet.—*Journal of the Women's Education Union.*

BISHOP OTTER'S COLLEGE FOR TRAINING LADIES AS ELEMENTARY SCHOOLMISTRESSES.

The new wing of this College is now finished, and the Committee are ready to receive applications from candidates for the Queen's Scholarship examination, which will take place in July. Applications should be made to the Lady Principal, Bishop Otter's Memorial College, Chichester.

The Notting Hill and Bayswater Kinder-Garten and Preparatory School, 9, Norland Place, Notting Hill, conducted by Miss E. Lord (late Assistant Mistress in the High School).—The Kinder-Garten and School opened on Tuesday, May 2, 1876, and are mainly intended to prepare pupils for the Notting Hill and Bayswater High School of the Girls' Public Day School Company (Limited). Girls and boys under eight years old will be taught together, and will receive such a thorough grounding as will pass the girls by entrance examination into the High School, and the boys into any school their parents may select. Fees, three guineas a term. Any Tuesday morning Miss E. Lord will be happy to see parents, and visitors interested in the Kinder-Garten.

SUFFRAGE.

THE Women's Disabilities Removal Bill has been again

o

lost this Session.   On the 26th ult. Mr. Forsyth moved
the second reading in an able speech, and he was supported admirably by Mr. Jacob Bright, Dr. Ward, Mr.
Fawcett, Sir Robert Anstruther, and Sir C. Legard.
Viscount Folkestone moved the rejection of the bill in a
somewhat weak address, which however was the more
excuseable as it was his maiden speech. · Mr. Leatham
seconded him, vindicating his continued opposition to
the measure.   Mr. Newdegate again deplored the revolutionary character of the movement.   Mr. Smollett repeated the abusive coarseness of last year, which roused
Mr. Fawcett's eloquent indignation.   With this one exception the debate was characterised by much more
earnestness than it has usually possessed.   Enemies as
well as friends are by this time aware that there is a
hard struggle before them,   The majority this year is
greater than last, being 239 against 152 ; or, counting
tellers and pairs, 247 against 161.   Only a small proportion of these are new voters—that is, men whose
opinions were still to learn ; they represent for the most
part votes which were *latent* in the House, having been
given already during one or other of the now numerous
debates.   There is nothing, therefore, in the increase of
the hostile majority as compared with last year to alarm
or discourage the friends of women's suffrage ; they see
only that the opponents are fully on the alert.   There is
however subject for regret that the Right Hon. John
Bright should have departed from the traditions of a
life-time, and spoken at considerable length against the
extension of the suffrage.

The debate is given *verbatim* in the *Women's Suffrage
Journal*, which this month appeared later than usual.   It
is a double number, and should be read by all those who
want to know how the subject now stands in Parliament.

Mr. Leatham has republished his speech in opposition
to the bill, in pamphlet form (price sixpence, Effingham
Wilson, Royal Exchange.)   It is advantageous to women
that they should have an opportunity of carefully weigh-
ing the arguments of their opponents, and we are glad
that it should be republished.   We would, however, respectfully suggest that sixpence is rather dear for one

speech, as the whole debate of thirteen speeches, of supporters and adversaries alike, is given *verbatim* in the *Women's Suffrage Journal* for May, price one penny. We suppose however, that quality in this instance makes amends for want of quantity.

Up to the report of May 2nd the number of petitions sent in were 1,063, containing 363,694 signatures. Some of the petitions deserve especial notice. Twenty-one English and Scotch Town Councils petitioned for the bill, and one (Kilmarnock) petitioned against it, being the only hostile petition that was presented. Ten thousand people, 2,400 of whom were electors, petitioned from Huddersfield; 4,000 from Newcastle. The Birmingham Liberal Association sent a petition to Mr. Bright; so also did other Liberal Associations. Ireland sent between 4,000 and 5,000 signatures. One petition was from 43 Cambridge professors and lecturers; another from 24 Scotch University professors. The entire number of signatures amounts to more than three-and-a-half times the number presented for any other object this Session. Putting together all the signatures for every object, exclusive of Women's Suffrage, enumerated on the Parliamentary Petition List this Session we find, up to May 2nd, 542,294. The Women's Suffrage signatures, therefore, amount to more than seven-tenths of the whole. It would be instructive to know what limit Parliament will fix on before it admits that the demand for Women's Suffrage is a national movement.

The principal meeting of the month was in St. George's Hall, Langham-place, W., on Saturday the 13th instant. The Right Hon. Russell Gurney, Recorder of London, took the chair. The speakers were among the most eminent of the supporters of the movement. It has occurred, however, too late to permit us to give any report of it in this number.

Other meetings have taken place. Mr. Hare presided at a well-attended one in Camden Road, and a large meeting was held at Bridport during Easter.

An important conversazione was given to the friends of the movement in the Westminster Palace Hotel on the 11th. All such meetings, as well as the drawing-room meetings which have from time to time taken place this

spring are very useful in bringing the workers in this
question together.

MEDICAL EDUCATION OF WOMEN.

*Registration of Midwives and the Royal College of
Surgeons.*—At the quarterly meeting of the Council of
this institution, on the 13th of April, the announcement
was made that the whole of the Midwifery Board of this
College had resigned except the chairman, rather than
examine women who had not gone through the regular
curriculum for the registerable licence in midwifery. It
was resolved:—"That Mesdames Jex Blake, Thorne,
and Peachey should be informed that the members of
the Board of Examiners in Midwifery having resigned
their offices, the Council are obliged to postpone the
holding of examinations for certificates of qualification
in midwifery. That the President and Vice-Presidents
be deputed to request an interview with the Lord President of the Privy Council, for the purpose of stating to
his Grace the difficulty which their Council finds in fulfilling the duty imposed on it by the 17th Clause of the
Charter of the 15th Victoria; and of suggesting that the
names of persons holding no other qualification to
practise than that of a certificate or licence in midwifery
should be placed in a separate list in the Medical
Register."

The following letter, addressed by one of the examiners to the medical papers, is to be considered their
own explanation of this step:—

"To the President, Vice-Presidents, and Council of the Royal
College of Surgeons, England.—(Gentlemen,—The duty imposed upon
the Midwifery Board to examine for the College Licence in Midwifery 'persons' who shall not be required to submit to an adequate examination in medicine and surgery has compelled me to re-
consider my position as a member of that Board. The Council calls
upon the Board to aid in placing on the medical register 'persons'
possessing only fragmentary medical skill, but who will, notwithstanding, acquire a practical, if not legal, right to practise far beyond
the limits of their qualification. Knowing as I do that obstetrics is an
integral part of medicine; knowing that it cannot be rightly understood or safely practised without a fair knowledge of the other parts
of medical science, and feeling deeply the injustice and danger of
making women and children the subjects of inferior medical skill, I
cannot reconcile it to my sense of right to assist in carrying out the
College charter in the spirit expounded by counsel. With extreme

regret, but without hesitation, I resign the office of Examiner in Midwifery to your college.—I have the honour to be, gentlemen, your most obedient servant, ROBERT BARNES."

The other two examiners who have also resigned are Dr. Arthur Farre and Dr. Priestley.

"It is now about three months, says the *Scotsman*, since it was announced that the Royal College of Surgeons of England had been advised by their own Standing Council that it was not in their power to refuse admission to the Licence in Midwifery to any "person" who complied with their ordinary conditions, and who could pass the usual examinations, and that, consequently, this licence would henceforth be open to women on the same terms as to men. This opportunity of obtaining admission to the register was at once embraced by three ladies who seven years ago began their studies at the University of Edinburgh, and who have since then passed through the full curriculum of study required for its degree, to examination for which, however, they have been refused admission under circumstances which will not soon be forgotten. These ladies now sent in their certificates of attendance on all the classes required, and a month's delay took place for the thorough examination of these certificates, which were ultimately declared to be satisfactory, and accepted by the College. It is worth remark that no candidate can be admitted to the Licence in Midwifery who has not gone through the full curriculum required for the membership of the College of Surgeons, and it appears that in this instance the certificates sent up were considerably in excess of the usual number, as these ladies had fully followed out the more extensive requirements for a University degree. It is not surprising, therefore, that the Council of the College of Surgeons decided in favour of their claim to examination and notified the fact to them in due course. As soon as it was announced that the ladies' certificates were perfectly satisfactory, and that they would consequently be admitted to the next examination, forthwith. and with truly edifying unanimity, the whole Board of Examiners resigned *en masse*. . . To read the well-turned sentences about the writer's "sense of right" and "deep feeling of injustice" (and "injustice to women"),

the innocent reader might suppose that here were the
words of a champion of chivalry instead of those of an
arrant trades-unionist. In the first place, the "duty
imposed" is assumed to be quite novel, and altogether
different from that which was from the first attached to
the office of Examiner in Midwifery. Will it be believed
that no change whatever has been made in any of the
College regulations for the licence, that the requirements
laid down and the advantages offered do not differ by
one jot or tittle from what they have been for the
twenty-four years that have elapsed since the examination was first established? The only novelty—and it is
one to which the writer has not thought it expedient
to refer in plain terms—is that both sexes are now declared eligible for examination, whereas hitherto this
privilege has been carefully reserved for one only.

The next point that troubles the Examiner's conscience is the "fragmentary medical skill" of the "persons"
who are now to be examined. It is a little difficult to
see how this scrupulous gentleman arrives at the conclusion that those who have taken the full curriculum
prescribed by a University are sure to be so much more
ignorant than the candidates he has previously examined,
who may have complied but barely with the more
limited requirements of the College of Surgeons. One
would at least have thought that the best way of setting his mind at rest would have been to examine the
"persons" in question, and find out the extent of their
"fragments" of knowledge; but then this course might
hardly have suited his ulterior, though less ostensible,
objects, and, besides, it might actually have aided these
most obnoxious "persons" to place their names on the
Medical Register on the same terms as other people."

Earl Granville, as Chancellor of the University of
London, yesterday presided at the presentation of
degrees, which took place in the theatre of that institution. In the women's general examination for 1875
twenty candidates passed, of whom seven were in the
honours division. The noble earl, in the course of his
observations, expressed a hope that more ready means
would be found for the acquirement of medical degrees
by women. It was clear that female doctors were get-

ting into practice, and that many women were studying medicine abroad. The subject was, he knew, a difficult one; but he trusted that the senate would give it its careful consideration. Mr. Lowe, the representative of the University in Parliament, rejoiced at the admission of women into the medical profession, as whatever might be said of the "rights of women" elsewhere, there could be no doubt of their fitness for presiding in the sick chamber.

This expression of opinion from two men of eminent authority in the London University will not fail to have great weight on the question.

LONDON SCHOOL OF MEDICINE FOR WOMEN.

The Earl of Shaftesbury yesterday afternoon distributed the prizes at the annual gathering of this institution, in Henrietta Street, Brunswick Square. The statement of the Dean showed that the classes in the various subjects had been well attended since the foundation of the institution in October, 1874, and that every facility was afforded to female students to gain in the school a sound medical education, its only drawback being the necessarily somewhat prolonged curriculum. Notwithstanding the strenuous efforts that had been made for the accomplishment of that object, it had hitherto been found impossible to gain admission for the students in any hospital containing the number of patients requisite to enable them to comply with the regulations of the legally-constituted examining bodies. The prizes were then distributed as follows:—Botany, anatomy, comparative anatomy, surgery, and physiology, Miss Shove; chemistry, materia medica, and practice of medicine, Miss Ker. Certificates of honour were awarded in the various branches to Misses Waterton, Clark, Shove, Butler, Ker, Bartholomew, and Hammond, and Mrs. Hart. Mrs. Hammond further gained Mr. Hart's scholarship of £25 per annum. On the conclusion of the distribution the meeting was addressed by the Right Hon. James Stansfeld, M.P. He said that the question of the right of women to practice medicine was one of great national importance, placing a double obligation on the Government, and he should not allow the session to expire without himself asking in Parliament whether it was intended to introduce a Bill to remove the medical disabilities of women. He trusted that there was no great reason to anticipate an unfavourable reply. As far as the legislative side of the matter went, he thought he could bid the institution be of good cheer, and hope with assurance for a favourable end to their difficulties. But there were other serious stumbling blocks in the way that seemed at present more difficult of removal. Three ladies had proposed to present themselves for examination at the Royal College of Surgeons for licences to practise in midwifery. What had occurred? Why, the examiners had at once tendered their resignation rather than undertake the duties of conducting their examination. So far for the prospects of the general question. He now came to the consideration of the special prospects of the institution. The executive committee had endeavoured to tide over a time of financial difficulties, and it was hoped they would yet be able to do so, but if necessary more funds must be sought. It was hoped that they would have been before this able to announce the provision of sufficient hospital accommodation for the students, but hitherto, as they had all heard, the metropolitan hospitals had met their requests with closed doors. If they did not meet with better success, the institution would have to come to a standstill, for young women could not be expected to come up to study year after year, without any prospects of ever getting their names on the register. He proposed the first resolution, " That this meeting sees with much pleasure the satisfactory success of the London Medical School for Women, both as regards its staff of lecturers, and its number of students, and earnestly trusts that its efficiency will speedily be made complete and secure by the necessary facilities for qualifying hospital study." The motion was seconded by Miss Jex Blake, who believed that the institution would compare favourably with any medical school in London, and remarked that though admission for the students had not been gained in any of the "qualifying" hospitals, they were nevertheless not entirely without clinical study. The second resolution was proposed by the Right Hon. W. Cowper-Temple, M.P., "That in the opinion of this meeting, legislative movements should be taken to secure the removal of all existing hindrances to the practice of the medical profession." Mrs. GARRETT ANDERSON in seconding it, said that she had not much hope that the Bill which was now before Parliament to enable women who had obtained diplomas in foreign universities to be registered as medical practitioners, would pass. There was some mistrust in England about foreign diplomas. She thought that what ought to be brought forward was a Bill to compel the examining bodies to examine anyone, man or woman, who possessed a foreign diploma.

Dr. KING CHAMBERS proposed a vote of thanks to the Chairman, which was seconded by Lady Stanley of Alderley.

LORD SHAFTESBURY replied, expressing his astonishment at the determined opposition shown by the members of the medical profession to a step which he was convinced would conduce to nothing but good. None were more fitted than ladies for the discharge of medical duties—as, indeed, we knew from every-day experience of their gentleness and skill as nurses of the sick. He could see no valid reason why they should be shut out from following a useful and noble career.

WESTMINSTER HOME FOR NURSES.

On May 3rd a public meeting was held in the Jerusalem Chamber of Westminster Abbey to consider the best means, in co-operation with the central committee of the Westminster Nurses Home, of placing the institution on a solid and permanent foundation as an enduring memorial of the late Lady Augusta Stanley, and thus perpetuate her name in association with a work of beneficence in which she took the most earnest interest in her lifetime. Lord Hatherley took the chair, and the meeting was largely attended.

Of all the charitable work undertaken by Lady Augusta Stanley, there was none to which in her later years she devoted more time and trouble than that of establishing a home for nurses in connection with Westminster Hospital, under the superintendence of the Misses Merryweather, whose success in Liverpool seemed to her to offer a guarantee for their success in London, if the opportunity of their offer of assistance was properly used. For this purpose she desired to have the home placed on a footing that should render it self-supporting. The Westminster Training School and Home for Nurses has only been in full working order for a year. Its objects are twofold—firstly, the provision of an adequate supply of trained nurses for the hospitals and for the public, and secondly, the opening of a new and honourable career to women endowed with education and refinement. No difference of opinion appears to exist on the importance of the first of these objects. In building new hospitals or in making additions to old ones—as occurred recently at the London Hospital in the Whitechapel road—due space is set apart for the nursing staff and "probationers." As yet the supply of nurses is drawn from comparatively uneducated women, but hopes are entertained that by the influence of Nurses' Homes where some degree of comfort and refinement can be secured, that women of a higher class might be induced to adopt the profession. To provide funds for the establishment at No. 8, Broad Sanctuary a subscription list was opened, with the result of securing upwards of £2,000 in donations, and annual subscriptions to about the tenth of that sum. The Duke of Westminster, Lord Hatherley, the Dean of Westminster, the late Lady Augusta Stanley, Mr. P. P. Bouverie, Mr. W. H. Smith, M.P., and Madame Christine Nilsson contributed large sums—the amount realised by the valuable efforts of the last-named lady having reached £942. Excellently organised by Miss Merryweather, whose previous experience in Liverpool and elsewhere admirably fitted her for the post of lady superintendent, the Westminster Training School and Home for Nurses has proved so completely successful as to justify the project now entertained for its extension on a permanent basis. The amount required to build and furnish on a freehold site a house capable of accommodating fifty probationers is estimated at £10,000. The present Home is small, only accommodating twelve nurses; the Home they propose to establish will not only accommodate a large staff, but will soon, as previous experience has shown, become self-supporting.

Mr. C. S. Parker moved the first resolution:—"That it is the desire of this meeting that an enduring memorial should be founded to perpetuate the honoured name of Lady Augusta Stanley; and it is their opinion that such object may be best accomplished by associating that name with a work of beneficence originated by her, in which to the close of her life she evinced an active and sympathising interest. They therefore suggest that means be immediately taken in connection with the Committee of the Westminster Training School and Home for Nurses to obtain the funds required to place that institution on a solid and permanent foundation, in association with her name, in such form as may hereafter be determined by that Committee." He said Lady Augusta was not better known to those connected with the hospital than she was to the poorest of her neighbours; and it was the universal desire of all classes in Westminster that there should be some memorial of her, and he thought there was none that could be placed in competition with this. The second resolution, which Dr. Rutherford Alcock moved, authorised the Committee of Management of the Westminster Training School to receive subscriptions. The donations announced at the meeting amounted altogether to about £1,300, including £500 from the Duke, of Westminster and £300 from Lord Hatherley.

Training for the office of Nursing is offered at the newly established Deaconess Home in Cheltenham.

BELFAST LADIES' TEMPERANCE UNION.

On April 21st, a conference of ladies and gentlemen interested in the Temperance movement, was held in the Clarence Place Hall in Belfast, Mr. J. G. Richardson in the chair. The main object of the meeting was to give a welcome to Mrs. Stewart, the leader of the women's temperance movement in America.

Miss Tod moved the first resolution which was that "the conference presented its grateful acknowledgments, and accorded a hearty welcome to Mother Stewart, the noble hearted and devoted leader of the women's temperance crusade in America, and expressed its earnest hope that her mission to this country for promoting the work of temperance reformation, especially among women, might be crowned with a large and distinguished success." There was no great cause in which there was a greater variety of work possible or desirable than the cause of temperance, and one of the ways of working for it was pleading, especially with professing Christians, to abstain totally from intoxicating drinks for the sake of others. Paley made a remark that it was much more difficult to get people to see an evil than to see the remedy for it when once the evil was perceived. Their first and greatest work was to awaken the consciousness of other women, and to convince them that much lay in their power in promoting temperance.

Mrs. JOSEPH RICHARDSON, in seconding the resolution, said that she took it that they were there to be stimulated to see and do what was their individual duty in regard to this great matter. None of them should think that they were without influence because this great evil of drinking was not brought immediately into their own household. They had each and all influence, and they should resolve to throw it on the side of temperance.

Mrs. J. G. RICHARDSON proposed the second resolution, which was—" That the conference deeply deplored the extensive use of intoxicating liquors amongst women, regretted the increased facilities which existed for obtaining them, and, in view of the appalling miseries caused by the drinking customs, and remembering the great value of example, undertook to use its influence in promoting the cause of temperance, and earnestly called upon all Christian ladies to aid the movement by personal abstinence for the removal from the social circle of those pernicious drinks."

Mrs. BYERS seconded the resolution, which was passed unanimously. Mrs. E. D. (Mother) STEWART then addressed the conference.

In the evening a large public meeting was held in the same hall, Mr. T. S. Mayne presiding, and Mrs. Stewart again spoke, pointing out the necessity of an organization on the part of the ladies of this country, in order that they may successfully promote the cause of temperance.

The Woman's Temperance Convention.—A woman's conference has also been held at Newcastle, under the presidency of Mrs. Parker, of Dundee, for the purpose of appointing delegates for the International Women's Convention, to be held in Philadelphia in June. About 150 delegates from various parts of England and Scotland were present. Ten delegates were appointed to attend the Transatlantic convention, and the assembly then resolved itself into the British Women's Temperance Convention, with Mrs. Parker as its president.

It is proposed to hold a National Bazaar during Whit Week, the proceeds of which are to be devoted to building a Temperance Hospital, of which the site is already fixed in Hampstead Road. Every town will have its stall in the bazaar, which appears to be intended to be on the model of the Anti Corn Law Bazaar of thirty years ago.

THE LADIES SANITARY ASSOCIATION, 22, Berners Street, Secretary, Miss Rose Adams, has lately published its eighteenth report. It contains an account of valuable work done, lectures undertaken, pamphlets (to the number of 76,000) printed and distributed during the past year, mother's meetings encouraged, &c., &c. The Liverpool, Leeds, Clifton, and Paisley branches contribute their report of work; its influence has spread to foreign countries; in Rome, day nurseries for children are to be established; in Neuchatel, Switzerland, considerable interest is excited. Miss Chessar's lectures to ladies last summer were particularly useful. The Committee observe that "Members who have witnessed the carelessness which is occasionally to be seen in houses where infectious disease is present; washing, ironing, mangling, making up of garments &c., being carried on in the same rooms where patients lie ill with fever, will be glad to hear that it is proposed to establish public workshops in various parts of the metropolis, properly built, warmed, and ventilated, in which for a small payment work can be carried on."

" The efforts to secure efficiently trained midwives will be anxiously watched, while the endeavour to establish a system of District Nursing must commend itself to all.

When nursing is made a fairly remunerative profession it will attract to its ranks well-educated women, and by this means sickness among all classes will be more intelligently treated."

"It will, perhaps, not be known to all Members that in schools formed under the Endowed Schools Commissioners' Scheme the study of Physiology and Domestic Economy are obligatory." The Committee urges Members to aid in the movement for obtaining seats behind the counter for young shopwomen; it also calls attention to the suffering of another class, viz., barmaids. Public-houses are open from 6 to 12 in London, and from 7 to 11 in the country. Now 17 hours on week-days with Sunday labour in addition is far too great a strain on the physical powers. Public-houses surely should be worked on the relay system. The Committee, in commending this subject to the consideration and influence of Members, quote the following letter:—

"Being a barmaid myself for nearly seven years, I speak from experience; and what I write I affirm to be the truth. I live in a city house with six others, and we all work very hard, our hours being seventeen a day. We open at 5.30 a.m., and close at 12.30 p.m. (midnight). Two of us take it in turns to get up for a week at half-past five o'clock, and retire at 10 p.m., the rest of us get up at 8 a.m., and are up till we close. We are supposed to have two hours' rest each a day, but this we only get three days out of six, the other three days we have but an hour. We are supposed to go out every third Sunday. Several of us have asked to be allowed to go out in rest time to get a breath of fresh air, but we have been refused for fear we should exceed our time. Therefore, from week's end to week's end, we have to inhale smoke, gas, and the foul breath of the numbers crowding at our bar, and have no comfort, release, or relaxation from this dreary, wearing toil. I assure you we all feel fit to drop with fatigue, long before the period comes for our short rest."

EMPLOYMENT.

The Society for the Employment of Women (22, Berners Street, W., Secretary, Miss King) has just printed its seventeenth annual report, which gives a satisfactory account of steady progress. Several of the items of employment which it mentions are new during the past year, and others have been confirmed and established on a more permanent footing. During the year 2,879 visits have been paid at the Office; 2,002 letters have been received, and 2,733 written; 183 visits of inquiry have been made by the Secretary; 72 applicants have obtained regular employment; 35 have commenced learning trades, and 158 orders for temporary work have been executed.

The Report further says—

Though the higher professions still close their doors to female students, women are no longer excluded from Public Offices. A large number of women and girls are engaged as clerks in the various departments of the General Post Office. During the year a new branch has been opened to them, and between 60 and 70 young women, the majority of whom are gentlewomen by birth and education, have been appointed clerks in the Savings' Bank department.

China Painting.—In the autumn of last year the studio of Messrs. Minton, at Kensington, where gentlewomen were employed, was burnt down. For various reasons Messrs. Minton decided not to rebuild it, and they consequently ceased to employ women in London. Of those women who had worked for them, some obtained employment from other firms, but a few resolved to endeavour to establish themselves in an independent business. To do this with a fair prospect of success, it was important to secure a studio in a central position, and as they needed a small capital to enable them to take and fit up a studio, they applied for help to the Committee. From the high character of their work, the Committee were convinced that the ladies had every prospect of ultimate success. Accordingly they determined to make an effort to give them a fair start, and without any appeal to other supporters of the Society, subscribed a sum amply sufficient for the purpose. A studio was taken at 68, Newman Street, where they commenced work in November last. They are ready to execute any orders which may be entrusted to them, and also to give lessons in all kinds of pottery and porcelain painting, and in water colour drawing.

Plan Tracing.—In February last an Office for tracing the plans of engineers and architects was opened at 42, Queen Anne's Gate, Westminster, under the auspices of the Society. It is superintended and managed by Miss Crosby, who has acquired a thorough knowledge of her work in the office of an eminent firm of engineers, where she and the three ladies who commenced work with her were trained, and have been employed for a considerable time. Owing to a change in the arrangements of the firm, the rooms devoted to these tracers were required for other purposes, and the head of the firm suggested that they should open an office for themselves, promising them both employment and support. Being unable to incur the responsibility of rent and office expenses without assistance, the present manager applied to the Society. Specimens of tracings executed by them were submitted to the Committee, who, seeing the excellence of their work, and being convinced that this was a means by which women might earn a respectable living, resolved to help them. A special subscription was opened, which in a short time amounted to £17 5s. 6d., and the Committee desire to thank their friends for their support in this matter. After some difficulty, and by the kindness of the head of the

firm by whom the ladies had been employed, suitable premises were
found at the address given above and the office was taken for one
year, during which time the experiment will receive a fair trial.
Hitherto orders have come in most satisfactorily, and one new worker
has been added, who is now receiving instruction with a prospect of
work. It is calculated that if regular employment can be obtained
for eight or nine workers, the office will be entirely self-supporting.
Ten can be accomodated comfortably in it. Those who desire to
learn this art must be willing to give three months' time without
earning any wages at all, and during the following three months the
earnings will be small. Great neatness of hand and accuracy are
essential. Specimens of the tracings may be seen, either at 42, Queen
Anne's Gate, or at the Society's Office, 22, Berners Street.

Art Decoration.—During the year the Society has placed two fresh
pupils with Miss Collingridge, of 13, Dorset Street, Portman Square
(formerly of 20, King Street, Baker Street), one as a regular appren-
tice for three years, the other, who is upwards of twenty, and has
had good elementary training in design, merely to receive a course of
lessons. The latter has already, through Miss Collingridge's recommendation, obtained regular employment at Stacy's, in Duke Street,
Manchester Square. The young ladies who were placed under Miss
Collingridge's instruction last year have made great progress, and
work diligently. One, having completed her term of apprenticeship,
has obtained regular employment at Messrs. Simpson's, in the Strand.
Miss Collingridge informs us that since March, 1875, she has received
commissions for panels, heads, and floral designs, from firms in Bond
Street, Finsbury Pavement, and Tottenham Court Road, and has
executed four large designs for tapestry curtains for one of the principal manufacturers of Glasgow. *   *   *   *

Dispensers.—It is now eight years since a woman first began to
study this business at a Dispensary for Women and Children, then
in Seymour Place, now the New Hospital for Women, 222, Marylebone Road. When qualified she was appointed dispenser to that
Institution. In the following year a second woman was appointed
dispenser to the Hospital for Women and Children at Bethnal Green.
In both cases women continue to fill the same positions, and at
Bethnal Green a third acts as assistant. Others have since been
trained, one of whom has just obtained an appointment at the Eye
Dispensary in the Marylebone Road. Another has just finished her
course of study.

The book-keeping class still continues, and there is no
difficulty in obtaining situations for its certificated
pupils. Miss Pritchard, 83, Edgware Road, is a shorthand writer, who will be happy to give lessons in her
art, report meetings, &c. The commercial school for
girls, established in 1860, which has been hitherto
carried on at Miss J. Boucherett's expense, fits girls to
become telegraph clerks, saleswomen, &c. It will
continue to be carried on on the same principles by the
head mistress.

A new employment, which bids fair to occupy women,
is that of silk reeling. The Report gives an interesting
account of Mrs. Bladen Neill's experiments in growing
silk, of which our readers have elsewhere seen an account. One girl has already found permanent employment in it.

Hair Dressing.—Miss Minnie Moore has started on her own responsibility, and is working up a business connection satisfactorily.
She has at present only a small room at 11, Charles Street, Kensington Square, but it is nicely fitted up, is very clean indeed, and
contains all that is essential to the comfort of ladies, for either sham-
pooing, cutting, or dressing of hair. She understands the arrangement of artificial hair, and the Committee take this opportunity of
recommending her to ladies residing in the neighbourhood of Ken
sington. * * * *

Among the "temporary work" may be mentioned the addressing
and issuing of circulars, large orders for which have been executed for
the Charity Voting Reform Association, the Provident Life Office,
merchants and others. The Committee are always glad to receive
such orders, as they provide a means of helping ladies who are unable
to undertake regular situations, and also those who are waiting for
appointments. Last year a lady who had been repeatedly employed
in this work through the agency of the Society was engaged by the
proprietor of some directories to prepare and send out the circulars
necessary in his work. The idea of employing a woman for this
purpose first suggested itself to him when he heard how women were
employed in work of a similar character by the Society. This lady
has been regularly engaged throughout the year, and has now four
young women clerks working under her.

The *Woman's Gazette* says that Glasgow is taking a
foremost place in the movements for women's work of
all kinds. An office is open at 365, Bath Crescent, for
the registration and assistance of female workers of all
classes, and an organised system of district nursing
among the poor has been started under the auspices of
Mrs. Higginbotham, and is in active work.

WOMEN'S UNIONS.

A meeting of Women employed in trades was held on
Monday, 1st May, in Sheffield, to consider the desirability of forming women's unions in Sheffield. Mrs.
Wood, president of the Dewsbury and Batley Woollen
Weavers' Union, and Mrs. Paterson, of London, took
part. A society has been formed there with every prospect of success.

P

Society of Upholstresses.—The first annual meeting of this society was held last evening in the Cambridge Hall, Newman-street, Oxford-street, the Hon. Auberon Herbert in the chair. The association was established last year under the auspices of the Women's Protective and Provident League (Holborn) for the purpose of affording advantages not hitherto enjoyed by the women engaged in the trade. The report stated that satisfactory progress had been made during the year, the income having exceeded £50. The chairman addressed some practical remarks to the meeting with reference to the principles of association. Miss Frances Power Cobbe said that the difficulties that men had to contend with in their struggle for life were as nothing compared to those of women. Some of the latter were compelled to work at the miserable business of constant needlework, by which they earned a small pittance. She thought that in many cases they did not even have enough to eat during the day, and it was to be hoped that the Society would enable them to improve their condition. They had heard that they must not speak of women as " a class," but she might say that nothing that concerned a woman was alien to her. The subsequent speakers included Mr. Hodgson Pratt, Miss Wilkinson, Miss Mears, and Mr. F. W. Verney, M.A.

WAGES OF WOMEN.

The disproportion between the wages of men and women is no where more shown than in the payment of the teachers and assistants in the board schools. The mininum commencing salary of a head master is £110, and that of a head mistress £90, and may be gradually increased, according to the teacher's deserts, to a maximum of £210 in the one case, and of £150 in the other. The assistant teachers are of various classes, and receive salaries of from £55 to £80 in the case of males, and from £50 to £75 in the case of females, which sums may be gradually increased to a maximum of £110 for males and £20 for females. Pupil teachers, who do not receive any share of the Government grant, are paid, if males, 9s. a week in the first year of their apprenticeship, increasing gradually to 16s., and if females, 5s. a week in the first year, increasing gradually to 10s. Candidates for pupil teacherships are paid, after a month's probation, 6s. a week if males, and 4s. if females.

The same disproportionate pay of the two sexes is seen in the Post Office. In the Savings Bank Department of the General Post Office we find that the Assistant Controller (male) receives £600 per annum; whereas the Superintendent (female) is only paid £165; the principal male clerks from £425 to £500; but the principal female clerks from £110 to £150; the first-class male clerks from £300 to £400; females from £80 to £100; and the second-class men from £200 to £300; whilst the women clerks of the same class only receive £40 on entering the service, and cannot rise beyond £75 per annum.

In the chief towns of the departments of France, M. de Foville tells us the wages of workmen in the year 1853, averaged 2f. 6c.; in 1872 the average had risen to 2f. 96c. It was a rise in the 20 years of about 45 per cent. In the same period, and in the same towns, the wages of workwomen rose from 1f. 7c. in 1853 to 1f. 51c. in 1872, showing a rise of no more than 41 per cent. It will be seen that women on an average earn throughout France but very slightly more than half the wages earned by men. M. de Foville is of opinion that to place women on a footing of equality with men they ought to earn at least two-thirds as much. For, he argues, if they eat less, they dress more expensively; and, moreover, when they work at home, they require both fire and light. On the other hand, it is to be observed, that men usually have a family to maintain. No doubt there are also many widows who are the sole support of their children, as there are likewise not a few wives, with drunken, criminal, or invalid husbands.—*Labour News.*

MISCELLANEOUS.

Conference of Women's Associations in Hamburg.— Among the German Women's Associations, whose delegates met at Hamburg towards the close of April, were: The "Lette Union;" the "League of German Lady Teachers;" the "Society of Housewives;" and the "Society for Co-operative House Management"—all of Berlin. From Brunswick and Breslau there were delegates of "Leagues for the Promotion of Culture among Women;" from Bremen, a delegate of a "League for the Promotion of Industrial Pursuits among Women;" from Darmstadt and Mainz, delegates of a similar society which combines with its programme the promotion of intellectual culture, as well as delegates of the "Alice Union for the Care of the Sick;" from Stettin, delegates of the "School of Trade and Industry for Girls;" from Hamburg itself, delegates of the "Hamburg-Altona Society of Lady Teachers;" of the "Fröbel Union;" of the "League for the Enlargement of Female Avocations;" and of the "Society for the Relief of the Poor among Women." Mr. A. Lammers, of Bremen ; Mrs. Lina Morgenstern, of Berlin ; Miss Louise Buchner, of Darmstadt ; Miss Marie Simon, of Berlin ; and Dr. Kinsky, of Belgard, read Committee reports on the various questions referring to the higher education of women, to the promotion of their industrial pursuits, and to the better protection of their various interests in life.

Another Lady Guardian.—Miss Lloyd has been elected a guardian of the poor at Wolverhampton.

A Lady Member of Parochial Board.—Miss Margaret Foulton has been elected a member of the Managing Committee of the Inverkeithing (Scotland) Parochial Board.

The *Woman's Gazette* for May, gives the welcome intelligence that an association of ladies is being formed at Brighton, to secure to young women serving in shops the use of seats behind the counters. A society is also being formed in Birmingham for this purpose.

Convalescent Home.—Lady Bourchier has established a small convalescent home at Hampton Court, for women servants, needle-women, shop-women, &c., needing change of air from London after illness. They either pay a small sum weekly for themselves, or a lady sending a case pays a slightly higher charge. Information may be obtained from the housekeeper, Hope Cottage, Hampton Court, S.W.—*Echo.*

The Exhibition of Works of Art in aid of Mrs. Salis Schwabe's Model Schools in Art in Italy, is now open at 25, Old Bond Street, W. In the spring of 1873, M. Scialoja, the Italian Minister of Public Instruction, conceded to Mrs. Schwabe for a long term of years a large building, with extensive gardens, at Naples, with a grant of 24,000 francs (since then 3,000 francs from the Minister of Commerce, and another 3,000 francs from the Minister of Public Instruction), for the establishment of a Kindergarten and Elementary Schools on the system of Dr. Fröbel. Mrs. Schwabe's School is also an industrial school, and intends to include a training school for pupil teachers. Her work has great claims upon every one interested in promoting the education of the poor and ignorant. The exhibition contains contributions from the Empress and the Crown Princess of Germany, the King of Bavaria, the Princess Alice of Hesse, and many other eminent supporters of the scheme. It will be closed on the 24th inst.

The late Mr. Joseph Payne.—We regret to announce the death of Mr. Joseph Payne, who for many years has been a warm and earnest worker in the cause of both primary and secondary education. He was elected in 1873 to the Professorship of the Science and Art of Education at the College of Preceptors—the first chair devoted to that subject in any chartered institution of this country. When the question of the higher education of women was first brought into prominence, Mr. Payne devoted much time and energy to the work, and much of the success achieved by the Women's Education Union and Girls' Public Day School Company may be traced to his unflagging zeal. He was Chairman of the Council of the latter body until the close of last year, when failing health forced him to give up active occupation. Mr. Payne was the author of "Lectures on Education," and other lectures and pamphlets on similar subjects.

Prevention of Vivisection.—The number of petitions sent into Parliament up to May 2nd, amounted to 241, with 64,397 signatures.

A Brave Woman.—At the recent terrible fire which

consumed the theatre at Rouen, there were many instances of bravery and heroic self-devotion. The conduct of one woman was noticed even in the horror and confusion; she had let herself down on to a jutting ledge, where she crouched for nearly ten minutes. From this position she helped the other girls to reach the ladders which were held towards them from the balconies, and it was not till her companions were rescued that she thought of her own safety. A rope was thrown to her, and with astonishing deliberation and coolness she fastened it about her, and then swung off into space. The people thought she was saved, but the shock on the rope was too great, the cord snapped, the woman fell on the balcony of a club house, and rebounding thence, she struck the ground, breaking her thigh, and fracturing her skull.

A Girls' Club.—A Girls' Friendly Club has been proposed in Marylebone. Mrs. Symes Thompson, 3, Upper George street, London, W., will give all necessary information.

Sericiculture in Australia.—At an ordinary meeting of the Society of Arts held on April 26th, under the presidency of the Duke of Manchester, Mrs. Bladen Neill read a paper on the subject of "Sericiculture in Australia." The authoress, who has devoted considerable time and energy for several years past to the promotion of the silk-growing movement in Australia, commenced by referring in complimentary terms to the prolonged scientific labours in connection with silk culture of Mr. Charles Brady, of Anthony Tweed River, New South Wales. The mulberry tree flourished throughout Australia with great vigour, and the ease with which it could be reproduced and multiplied both by seed and by cuttings was a circumstance beyond all others favourable to the rearing of silkworms, and accordingly the "Victorian Ladies' Sericicultural Company (Limited)" —a company formed under Mrs. Neill's direction —had been enabled to introduce the best varieties, and to spread them widely throughout the colony. The selection of suitable "grain," as the silkworm eggs are technically called, was another point of vital importance, as some worms were more liable to disease than others.

A silk farm and plantation had been established at Mount Alexander, about 70 miles from Melbourne, where a grant of 1,000 acres of land had been obtained from the Government of Victoria; Lady Bowen kindly consented to become patroness; shares were issued at £4 4s. each, and were all taken; 20 acres were fenced in and planted with the best varieties of mulberries, and cuttings put in for 200 acres more; and a large silk house, manager's cottage, and offices were put up, and the results had hitherto been so successful that an assured market had been opened up in Italy for as many cocoons and eggs as the means of the company enabled them to produce. It was not, however, in Italy alone that Australian silk produce had earned high commendation. Various articles of clothing, stuff, and woven fabrics, had been made for experimental purposes here in England. Samples of some of these goods were shown on the table, and the authoress asked the noble chairman to accept, as a specimen of their work, a pair of socks made by some of the gentlewomen working with her, out of silk "refuse" from the "sunny land of Victoria." The work was carried on by a band of ladies who had no other means of living, and the undertaking was therefore one deserving of support, if only from a philanthropic point of view. Considered, however, in a financial aspect, the undertaking was one which must be productive of steady and increasing profit, and it was therefore hoped that numerous friends would be found in England to embark in it sufficient capital to enable it to extend the valuable work which it had already begun, and to develop not only into a truly philanthropic but also into a sound commercial success.

Mrs. Thwaites is giving a course of lectures at Warrington on "Artisan Cookery." The lectures are of a strictly practical kind.

Miss Elizabeth Thompson, the artist, has been elected a foreign member of the Academy of Florence.

A Lady School Inspectress.—The *Echo* states that the Bengal government has appointed a native lady inspectress of the female schools in Calcutta. She is a daughter of a Bengalee clergyman. This is the first instance of any appointment of the kind.

Art. VI.—CORRESPONDENCE.

The Editor is not responsible for the opinions of Correspondents.

LONDON, May 8th, 1876.

DEAR MADAM,—It is easy to believe that it was a
sympathy with Mr. Mill rather than agreement with his
opinions on the Woman's Franchise Bill, that led Mr.
Bright into the lobby of the House of Commons to give
his first vote for it. Between Mr. Mill's " Subjection of
women" and Mr. Bright's last speech against the franchise,
there is a wide difference, a great gulf! which I would
fain attempt to bridge over, however feebly and lightly,
neither quite accepting nor quite denying the facts and
foundations of both their arguments. Having long ago
attempted to criticise *appreciatively* Mr. Mill's admired
essay, I should like with your permission to study
(also appreciatively) and contrast with it Mr. Bright's
remarks on the vexed subject of women's rights and
wrongs. Are we to believe with Mr. Mill that men were
and are always by their nature disposed to be
cruel and unjust towards women, or with Mr. Bright
that they are no more unjust towards women now,
than they are still, in special instances, towards their
own sex. What "struck" Mr. Bright most was the
"millions of men" making "sacrifice" for the comfort
and happiness of women connected with them. This is
a very agreeable reflection, and not I hope generally an
observation untrue in married life, but he might have
doubled his delight in it by the simple addition of the
" millions " of women who are responding by sacrifices
on *their* side " for the comfort and happiness" of men!
The Bill he said was "based on an untenable proposition"—"an assumed hostility between the sexes."
Here he seemed to take strong ground! but hastened
to admit that the men who were about to vote for it
did not take this view of it. In "familiar conversation"
however, he had become aware that the Bill " as it was
offered to them by its supporters *out of doors* was a Bill
based upon an assumed and *irreconcileable hostility* between
the 'sexes." Here, in strengthening his expressions, he
weakened his case! The property franchise for widows
and spinsters could certainly be powerless against " **an**

irreconcileable hostility between the sexes." One is at a loss to conceive all the possible negative results of such a state of things! It would be decidedly what our American cousins might call a *fix*. I rather wonder at a statesman condescending to repeat those womanish words, but he was particularly provoked that "words about men's tyranny and injustice," and "women's degradation were found in the speeches and conversation of *women* who were the chief promoters of the Bill; and this was not said of women in savage nations, but of (and by) women in general in this civilized and Christian country!" Now this was a very pertinent remark of Mr. Bright's, and might have been more dwelt upon as the key to the situation, and capable of with those of the more ordinary and matter of fact and yet even somewhat reconciling the views of the philosopher true observer. For it is generally admitted that women of savage nations have much to complain of from savage men, and yet (good creatures) they do not complain, or, at least, we do not know, or do not imagine that they complain as women do in this "civilised and Christian country!" There is an anecdote worth quoting on this savage subject, and believed to be authentic. Byron, grandfather of our poet, on occasion of his shipwreck in the South Sea Islands, near Chili, 1774, "Here," he writes, "I must relate a little anecdote of our *Cacique* (or Chief). He and his wife had gone off, at some distance from the shore in their canoe, where she dived for some sea eggs; but not meeting with great success they returned a good deal out of humour. A little boy of theirs, about three years old, whom they appeared to be doatingly fond of, watching for his father and mother's return, ran into the surf to meet them: the father handed a basket of sea-eggs to the child, which, being too heavy for him to carry, he let fall; upon which the father jumped out of the canoe, and catching the boy up in his arms, dashed him with the utmost violence against the stones. The poor little creature lay motionless and bleeding, and in that condition was taken up by the mother, but died soon after. She appeared inconsolable for some time, but his *unnatural* (the query is modern, and,

in fact, mine) father* showed little concern about him.
A day or two after we crossed the sea again, &c., &c."
It does not appear that this squaw complained, and it
is not likely she did, as she had herself been " dashed
against the stones" a short time before, "and afterwards beaten in a cruel manner." The wife's crime was
having been *suspected* of giving Byron a bit of stinking
seal—only suspected. Christianised and civilised mothers
and wives, would you have restrained your lamenta-
tions or your reproaches? Mr. Bright's observations on
you are just. The manners of wives and mothers have
changed, aye, and *pari passu* husbands and fathers
too. Thank God, Mr. Bright himself, might be made
an illustration of the latter, for he admitted that he
differed in opinion from his nearest and dearest (*women,
of course*), and yet we are sure that no honourable gentleman in the House can suspect (and we hope that *out of
doors, also,* no dishonourable female can imagine for a
moment) that he lays violent hands on the dissention of
his family. No, not even in the way of correction, by
using a stick only, and that no thicker than a man's
thumb! Mr. Mill writes in explanation of men's blind-
nesss and backwardness to emancipate women† " that
people of the present and the last two or three generations have lost all practical sense of the primitive
condition of humanity, and only the few who have
studied history intimately, or have much frequented
the parts of the world occupied by the living representatives of ages long past, are able to form any
mental picture of what society then was. People are
not aware how entirely in former ages "the law of
superior strength was the rule of life, &c., &c." Captain
Byron's peculiar and terrible experiences of life among
semi-savage Indians enabled him to relate " The good
Indian women,—(we must allow their attraction to
the Englishman and stranger as a slight offset to their
goodness, but it will leave a trace of tenderness still in

---

* Page 103, Byron's Narrative of the Loss of the Wager Man-of-
war. Dublin, 1819.
† P. 12 of Essay.

savage women. He had previously said "the men showed themselves unconcerned at our greatest distresses), but the good Indian women, whose friendship I had experienced before, continued their good offices to me. Though I was not suffered to enter their wigwams, they would find opportunities of throwing in my way such scraps as they could secrete from their husband. The obligation I was under to them on this account was great, as the hazard they ran in conferring these favours was little less than death. The men, unrestrained by any laws or ties of conscience, and being both ignorant and barbarous, exercise a most despotic authority over their wives, whom they consider in the same view as they do any other part of their property, and dispose of them accordingly: even their common treatment is cruel, for, though the toil and hazard of procuring food lies entirely upon the women, yet they are not suffered to touch any part of it till the husband is satisfied, and then he assigns them their portion, which is generally very scanty, and such as he has not a stomach for himself.' This hardy Byron, and bold seaman, was not only able to observe but moralise and generalise his observations made 136 years ago in the following words :—"This arbitrary proceeding with respect to their own families is not peculiar to this people only. I have had occasion to observe it in more instances than this I have mentioned, and among many other nations of savages I have since seen, and I *was always able to tell the character of each nation* from the condition *of the female sex there, that* country being barbarous or *advanced in civilisation according as women were treated with cruelty or kindness.*"

One great English lawyer has made the same discovery from the history of law, and has, of course, carried the idea farther. In his lecture on married women's property, we read "It has been said that the degree in which the personal immunity and proprietary *capacity of women are recognised in a particular state or community is a test of its degree of advance,* and, with the qualifications necessary, is far, indeed, from being a mere gallant commonplace.

I thought to lighten the dulness of this letter by

stringing together the argumentative jokes of the
enemies of the Franchise Bill, but time and space do
not allow.—Sincerely yours,

M. T. **M**

May 9th, 1876.

DEAR MADAM,—The following facts, which have just
come under my notice, are amusing, and I think instructive.

At a certain office in Fleet street two religious papers
are issued weekly; both have the same proprietor, who
is also the editor of one of them; both find most of
their readers in the same religious communities, and so
closely are the two connected, that most weeks they
have whole columns—sometimes pages—of matter
common to both. One is a high-priced paper, whose
readers are mostly clerical; the other is a cheap penny-
worth, numbering its readers by the hundred thousand.
Not long ago both these papers bitterly opposed the
Disabilities Bill, but of late the cheap one has become a
very jealous advocate of our cause. Now for the suggestive part of the story. Both the current numbers
have leading articles on the recent debate. The dear
paper talks about "Class Representation," and repro-
duces with approval the very crudest of Mr. John
Bright's fallacies on the subject. The cheap one has a
spirited notice of "Mr. Bright's Bugbear," and as effectually disposes of his arguments as could be done by
our most energetic advocates. You must draw your
own conclusions from the facts, but my interpretation
of them is as follows. It is well known that Mr. ———
conducts his business on the principle of *making it pay,*
and of course puts into his papers what he thinks their
readers will like. It is presumable that the select constituency which support the dear paper like to have
reproduced the wretched twaddle which does duty for
argument against the Bill; while the much larger circle
of readers who make the cheap paper one of the most
valuable literary properties in London, have rather more

sense or more manliness, and therefore prefer a more reasonable view of the question, whereat I thank God and take courage.

Yours very truly,

T. G. C.

Art. VI.—PARAGRAPHS.

Right of Women in America to Practice Law.—The Supreme Court of Wisconsin has lately uttered a decision adverse to a woman practising law in that State. Miss Goodell, a lady who had already followed that profession for some years, had a case in the Circuit Court, which was appealed to the Supreme Court. When this appeal was made Miss Goodell applied to the Supreme Court for the right to go with her case to that Court. She argued her own cause, and based her claim in part upon a statute which provides "That words of the masculine gender may be applied to females; unless, in either case, such construction would be inconsistent with the manifest intention of the Legislature." Also upon another statute, which provides that "Male and female students shall be admitted to all departments of the State University, under such regulations as the Board of Regents may deem proper." She claimed that the Legislature had thus provided for graduating females by the law school, with the implied understanding that these students would have a right to practice the profession which the State had allowed them to study. Miss Goodell also made other good points to establish her claims.

The following precedents are in favour of the admission of women:—

Iowa.—In 1869, Mrs. B. A. Mansfield was admitted to the bar of Iowa under a statute providing that "any white male person" with the requisite qualifications, should be licensed to practice; by virtue of a statute providing that " words importing the masculine gender only, may be extended to females; " and the Court held that the affirmative declaration that male persons may be admitted, is not an implied denial of the right to females." (See *Legal News*, Feb. 5, 1870; Mrs. Bradwell's case.)

Missouri, under a statute providing that "any person" possessing certain qualifications may be licensed, admits women. (See case of Miss Barkaloo, in *Legal News*, April 3 and April 9, 1870.) Miss Barkaloo was also admitted to the Supreme Court of Missouri.

Michigan, under a statute using the word " citizen" as the statute of Wisconsin uses " person," admits women to practice.

Maine, under a statute similar to that of Wisconsin, admitted Mrs. C. H. Nash to Supreme Court in 1872. (See *Legal News*, Oct. 26, 1872.)

District of Columbia, Charlotte E. Ray was admitted, about 1872, on graduating from Howard University.

Ohio, under a statute similar to that of Wisconsin, has admitted a woman to practice.

The Federal District Court of Illinois has admitted women. See *Legal News*, May 29, 1874.

Illinois and Iowa have recently made legislative provision for the admission of women.

It took two months for the Judges to render their adverse opinion. They admit the personal excellence of Miss Goodell as follows :—

" This is the first application for admission of a female to the bar of this court. And it is just matter for congratulation that it is made in favour of a lady whose character raises no personal objection; something perhaps not always to be looked for in women who forsake the ways of their sex for the ways of ours."

But in spite of this admission the judges of the Supreme Court sum up with the oft-repeated statement that " The law of nature destines and qualifies the female sex for the bearing and nurture of the children of our race, and for the custody of the homes of the world, and their maintenance in love and honour."

The argument is, that because the majority of women are mothers, therefore no woman shall practice law. Not

because they are not able to do it, for Miss Goodell and
other women have proved that they are able, but simply
because they are women.

The Court goes on to declare that "it would be
revolting to all female sense of innocence and sanctity
of their sex, shocking to man's reverence for womanhood, and faith in Woman, on which hinge all the better
affections and humanities of life, that Woman should be
permitted to mix professionally in all the nastiness of
the world which finds its way into courts of justice; all
the unclean issues, all the collateral questions of sodomy,
incest, rape, seduction, adultery, bastardy, legitimacy,
prostitution, infanticide, obscene publication, libel and
slander, divorce; all the nameless catalogue of inde-
cencies, *la chronique scandaleuse* of all the vices and
infirmities of all society, with which the profession
has to deal. . . . Reverence for all womanhood
would suffer in the public spectacle of woman so
interested and so engaged."

We would ask, as the American women do, how is it
possible that womanhood can suffer through female
lawyers more than it suffers at present?

The crimes above mentioned are impossible without
the participation of women; they necessitate in the
majority of cases the evidence of women, whom the law
compels to be present as witnesses, who have to answer
every indecent or insolent question which lawyers may
ask. The "delicacy" of her sex is no shield to her;
how would the matter be made worse by the presence
of another woman who had legal knowledge or authority to come to her help. When the co-education of
women with men in their medical and surgical professions is talked of, the constant argument heard is, that
the delicacy of women will suffer by such education:
so long as more than half the patients in the world are
and must remain women, who, under present circumstances, can only be attended by men physicians, we
fail to see that delicacy is in anyway preserved by excluding women from intelligent participation in the profession. So long as the law has to deal with the indecen-
cies which the Supreme Court of Wisconsin enumerates,
which all involve the action and testimony of women,

feminine delicacy is not preserved by merely excluding her from the honourable and lucrative position of a member of the Bar. The Supreme Court of Wisconsin has taken two months to consider the matter, and then renders a decision which forbids her presence in the Court as a lawyer, because such a place will, in the opinion of the Court, be destructive of her purity and delicacy! We believe that we need the presence of qualified women in law courts in order to give an additional safeguard to members of her own sex.

Miss Goodell very ably stated in her plea the reasons why women should not be excluded from the practice of law. She said

1. That a class wholly unrepresented in courts of justice, can never obtain full justice in such courts; and that when that class is so numerous as to include one-half the human race, the promotion of "the proper administration of justice" requires that they be represented.

2. That a union of the peculiar delicacy, refinement and conscientiousness attributed to women, with the decision, firmness, and vigour of man, are not only desirable but necessary in promoting "the proper administration of justice" in our courts.

3. That in excluding women from the practice of law, an injustice is done the community, in preventing free and wholesome competition of the best existing talent.

4. That a great injustice is done to one-half the community, by shutting them out arbitrarily from an honorable and remunerative field of industry for which many of them have both taste and ability.

If the decision of the court of Wisconsin has any lesson for us, it is that it shows afresh, how every new avenue to honorable and remunerative occupation for women has to be contended for, and is yielded only at the last moment, when it can no longer be withheld.

Englishwoman's Review.

CONTENTS FOR JUNE, 1876.

All Communications to be addressed to the EDITOR, 22, Berners Street, Oxford Street, W.

Post-Office Orders payable to SARAH LEWIN, at the "Regent Street" Post-Office.

TERMS OF SUBSCRIPTION AT THE OFFICE.

Per Annum (Post Free), Six Shillings.
Subscriptions payable in Advance. Single Numbers posted Free on receipt of Six Postage Stamps.

MSS. are carefully read, and if not accepted are returned, on receipt of Stamps for Postage, but the Editor cannot be responsible for any accidental loss.

Contributions should be legibly written, and only on one side of each leaf.

THE

ENGLISHWOMAN'S REVIEW.

(NEW SERIES.)

No. XXXVIII.—June 15th, 1876.

Art. 1.—THE CENTENNIAL OF AMERICAN INDEPENDENCE.

Benjamin Franklin wrote in 1768, "That every man of the commonalty (excepting infants, insane persons, and criminals) is, of common right, and by the laws of God, a freeman, and entitled to the free enjoyment of liberty. *That liberty, or freedom, consists in having an actual share in the appointment of those who frame the laws, and who are to be the guardians' of every man's life, property, and peace,* (the italics are ours) for the all of one man is as dear to him as the all of another, and the poor man has an equal right, but more need, to have representatives in the Legislature than the rich one. *That they who have no voice nor vote in the electing of representatives, do not enjoy liberty; but are absolutely enslaved to those who have votes, and to their representatives; for to be enslaved is to have governors whom other men have set over us, and to be subject to laws made by the representatives of others, without having had representatives of our own to give consent in our behalf.*" (Sparks' Franklin, II. 372.)

In this Centennial anniversary when every American is looking back with pride towards the commencement of his country's political existence, these words, and the corresponding passage in the Declaration of Independence

Q

which sets forth that "Governments derive their just powers from the consent of the governed," have double significance. American women, to the number of many thousands, are asking whether these words are to have a broad foundation on the principles of justice and human equality, or are to be twisted and restricted to meaning only one half of the race.

We cannot too clearly point out how different is the stand-point taken by Englishwomen who claim the parliamentary suffrage from that which is adopted by the American speakers and writers on this subject. In England, women point to ancient national institutions, the Saxon Witenagemote, and the feudal courts of justice in which women have had their seats—and the parliamentary elections in which they used to take part; or they can urge the similarity between this electoral franchise, from which they have only been legally excluded in comparatively modern times, and the municipal and parochial franchises, from which nobody has ever thought of excluding them. But American women have no history of this kind to appeal to; so far from having achieved the condition of political supremacy depicted by Professor Goldwin Smith in his imaginative and denunciatory pamphlet, they have, with the exception of about thirty years in New Jersey (from 1776 to 1807), and two western and comparatively unpeopled territories at the present day, none of our franchises. They have not yet got the municipal vote.*   They are

---

* It may be observed that when Mr. Sewall, last January, brought in a Bill before the Massachusetts Legislature to give female citizens the right to vote for city and town officers and on municipal affairs, he reverted for precedent to the time when English law would have permitted such a vote in the colonies.

The Province Charter granted by William and Mary, in 1691, after directing how the "Great and General Court of Assembly" is to be organized, namely: by representatives from the towns, chosen by "the major-part of the free-holders, and other inhabitants of the respective towns," proceeds as follows:

"Provided always that no freeholder or other persons shall have a vote in the election of members to serve in any Great and General Court or Assembly—who at the time of such election shall not have an estate of freehold in land within our said Province or territory of

only gradually and after many contests obtaining the
School Board vote. Taking the states, as a whole,
women enjoy less *political* recognition than in England,
though in many cases the laws affecting them are
better.

It was from no wish to be exempt from the lawful
burden of citizenship that in 1876 the American men
destroyed the tea in Boston harbour, but from the fixed
determination that those who paid the money should
have an authoritative voice in its expenditure. The
same feeling now is prompting some American women
to resist the payment of taxes, preferring to see their
farm stock, and in some instances the land itself sold to
pay the fines. The sisters Smith and Mrs. Foster are
instances of this practical application of the principle
which caused the national revolution a hundred years
ago.

Even in 1776 there were not wanting those who deeply felt the injustice shown towards women, and the applicability of the same principles which justified the resistance of the men, to their own case. A letter is still
extant from Abigail Adams, the wife of one President
and mother of another: writing to her husband, who
was in his seat in the Congress, she says:—

' I long to hear that you have declared an independency. And, by-
the-way, in the new code of laws which I suppose it will be necessary
for you to make, I desire you would remember the ladies, and be
more generous and favorable to them than your ancestors. Do not
put such unlimited power into the hands of the husbands. Remember all men would be tyrants if they could. If particular care and
attention is not paid to the ladies, we are determined to foment a
rebellion, and will not hold ourselves bound by any laws in which we
have no voice or representation. That your sex are naturally tyrannical is a truth so thoroughly established as to admit of no dispute ;
but such of you as wish to be happy, willingly give up the harsh title
of master for the more tender and endearing one of friend. Why,
then, not put it out of the power of the vicious and the lawless to
use us with cruelty and indignity with-impunity ? " * * * *

---

the value of forty shillings per annum at the least, or other estate to
the value of forty pounds sterling." Act and Resolves of the Province of Massachusetts Bay, Vol 1, p. 11.

It is worth remarking that this provision does not exclude women
from voting either as freeholders or inhabitants.

"I can not say that I think you are very generous to the ladies, for while you are proclaiming peace and good-will to men, emancipating all nations, you insist upon retaining an absolute power over wives."

The *Standard*, the other day in commenting on the Conference of Agricultural Union delegates on the 24th ult., said that the chief object of Government was the attainment of a good national council. "It is desirable that the franchise should be distributed with as much evenness as possible, but nobody is really injured by electoral inequalities. The object is to secure a good deliberative assembly, and if that end is attained, the part which each unit contributes towards effecting it cannot signify very much either to himself or to anybody else." Now, parenthetically, we might remark that if the holders of landed property, or the *Standard* itself were among the "*units*" who were left out, when a deliberative assembly, representing only the working and agricultural classes was established, they would probably be far from finding it good, and would doubt, as women at the present day wonder, whether no one is really "injured by electoral inequalities." Such a paragraph is only possible in an English publication; no American paper, least of all in this centennial anniversary could write so complete a denial of the principle of their declaration of independence.

We may safely predict that in America the declaration of Independence will not have more weight in obtaining a concession of the franchise to women than constitutional consistency has in England; when the franchise ceases to be withheld it will not be for the sake of either logic or justice, but from motives of expediency, and as a measure of compromise, acting upon an already favourably prepared public opinion; but there is little doubt that the meetings and discussions which take place in Philadelphia during this year, will, make the principles of the movement better known, and bring the workers in it together, and thus tend to its more general appreciation, and accelerate the period of its accomplishment.

Art. II.—SELF-HELP IN THE HOUSEHOLD.

THE institution for lady helps in Seymour-street is, we hear, prospering. Employers and employed are both forthcoming: many ladies without means are found willing to do household service, and many ladies with means are willing to employ them; so far, therefore, the scheme may be considered to have filled up a gap, and a home and quiet work is provided for many poor gentlewomen. This is, we believe, the entire aim of the foundress, who does not intend to call a new class into existence, but only to supply a present want. There can be no doubt that the permanent introduction of women of culture into the ranks of housekeepers and nurses would be found equally advantageous to both classes, employers and employed. In Sweden the custom of employing as housekeepers ladies who, not only belong to the educated, but frequently also to the noble classes, is very general, and is found to be an excellent plan. As the Kindergarten system spreads also, the introduction of carefully trained lady nurses will become very popular and advantageous to the children. Mrs. Crawshay only advocates "lady helps," when there can be at least two or three who can make a little society of their own: this necessarily restricts the adoption of the plan to a few wealthy families, and neither the servant difficulty nor the general demand for remunerative employment for cultivated women can thus be really settled. It is at best only a palliative.

But if women with no means are obliged to do service as lady helps, seeing that the hardest work is more honourable to them than indolence or dependence on charity, it is probable that a little more self help in households might be the means of economising the resources of many a family, and enabling them to keep together. Many a household with small means would be able to maintain itself in freedom from care, and comfort if the expense of hiring service could be avoided. And this was never so practicable as now.

In former days a housewife had to wash, wring,

brew, bake, make candles, distil her household medicines,
and spin and weave, and the mistress of a family had
not only to understand how these things were done,
but did a large part of them with her own hands. It
was no wonder if at such a time a large train of household "helps" were required; and yet even under these
circumstances, a fair amount of literary culture was
found compatible with these multifarious duties, as the
"faculty" possessing housewives of New England could
show. Now that housekeeping is simplified so greatly
by the discoveries of science, and the co-operation of
independent trades, it seems a pity that it should not
be more generally undertaken by the daughters of the
house. In families where means are scanty and daughters plentiful, the lighter portions of the housework
should be invariably undertaken by them—the family
income would be made to go further, and their own
health benefited at the same time.

We are inclined to think also that the daughters of
rich men would be all the better for having a little
vigorous exercise in household work before sitting down
to long hours of music or study. Making beds is both
healthy and easy; exquisite china might always be
washed by the mistress of the household, and dusting a
room need not roughen the most delicate hands. There
are so many appliances now towards making household
work easy. In all large towns the washing is done out
of the house, the bread is baked and brought to the
door, home-made wines and medicaments are things of
the past; preserves and pickles may be bought as
cheaply as they are made; the household work has
been already reduced, we were going to say to a minimum, only there is one point in which it might be reduced still further.

Cooking remains a serious difficulty; despite the
popularity of schools of cookery, gas stoves, or dainty
saucepans, it will only be a small proportion of women
who will care to spend their mornings at a kitchen
dresser rolling paste, or beating eggs. Since the days
when Eve " on hospitable thoughts intent " to entertain
the angel, tempered " dulcet creams," our banquets have
undergone considerable expansion, and even "neat-

handed Phillis" might find it difficult to prepare her savoury messes. Three, and sometimes four, meals a day would leave but scanty leisure for the other employments of an educated woman. It is common enough on the occasion of a dinner party for a family of only moderate resources to supplement the home-prepared dishes by others from the confectioner, but nowhere in England are complete family dinners sent out as a matter of course. Yet this is very simply managed in Rome and other Italian cities, where the master of a *trattoria* undertakes to send out the dinner, or, if required, two meals, daily at a very moderate cost. It is a daily sight in Rome to see the boxes kept hot by charcoal or a hot water tin carried round to neighbouring houses at dinner time ; a man calls for orders in the morning with the *menu* of the day, a very comprehensive one, and plates as well as dishes are provided, if required, to be replaced in the empty box when it is called for. An arrangement of this kind need not be expensive, the cost of distribution being covered by the economy of cooking large quantities of food together, and in the absence of waste, no food being spoiled by unskilful cooks or inexperienced housekeepers. The system, too, would in no way intrude upon the domestic privacy of English households, as eating at a general table d'hote might be supposed to do. Viewed also in the light of another employment for women, these cookery establishments are not to be rejected hastily, as many a woman who had good abilities for cooking, and yet would think it beneath her to take a situation in a private family, could carry on successfully such a profession, and make a fair income by it. The chief repast of the day being thus supplied, the other meals could be prepared with very little trouble, and the diminution of labour in each household would be great. Families who now want two servants would keep but one, and those who now have one, would hire a charwoman for half a day—two families, as is often the case in France, thus dividing her services.

If a lady lives alone and requires but one servant, she might engage a "lady help" and share the work of the house with her, if she has time for it ; she would thus have companionship as well as service. A different method of building would also enable us to simplify our family life greatly. Wherever houses are built in flats or single floors, the work of the house is greatly decreased. The absence of stairs not only lessens the work of the servants themselves, but many little details of household work can be done naturally by the mistress, which she would hesitate about going down two or three flights of stairs to perform. Co-operative house-keeping is now tried in several quarters : each family has a separate suite of rooms, the service, cooking, &c., being managed in common. As wages and the cost of food increase, all these methods of lessening household expenses will infallibly receive further trial.

We have sometimes wondered why three or four ladies do not club together, one taking charge of the house-work, one doing the cooking, another the dress-making for the rest, another perhaps occupied with her profession away from home during the day, but contri-buting her fair share to the home expenses and comfort. Such a household would be infinitely happier than if it passed its days in the weary idleness now distinguish-ing the lives of ladies. Solitary women have generally scanty means—they often need to club together to procure luxuries or even comforts, and how dreary are now many women's lives of indolent leisure and small incomes, where want of money prevents any variety of amusement, extension of education, or even much society, and where small worries and petty anxieties fill up the day. Many households, now straightened for money, would be able to maintain themselves in com-fort if the additional expense of hiring service could be avoided, and this might be done with comparatively small sacrifice of time, but for the fancied gentility of donothingness. It is not given to every woman to be artistic or literary, or to have acquired business habits enough to earn her bread comfortably in a trade. These must be acquired young, but every woman could learn enough of simple household arts to enable her to do her part in a community of housekeeping which we are convinced would bring interests to lighten and vary her life, besides making the most of scanty incomes.

ART. III.—THE MEDICAL STUDENTS AT ZURICH.

IT is now ten years since the gates of Zurich University opened to women, and since that time thirteen ladies have received degrees as Doctor of Medicine, Surgery, and Midwifery (six Russians, two English, two Germans, one Scotch, one American, and one Swiss). Professor Hermann has lately taken occasion to review the long struggle on the one side and the professors and lady students on the other. He appears to hint at some future change in the regulations of the university with respect to the female students, but affirms that the thirteen ladies who have received degrees have showed an undoubted vocation for the profession, and that he and the other professors will gladly welcome all young women who come with like preparation and earnestness.

ON the occasion of the birthday of M. Charles Fourier on the 7th of April, a fête was held in Zurich, at which Madame Gneiss Trant proposed the following toast to the lady students of the University. It will have great interest for all our readers.

AUX ETUDIANTES!

Aux étudiantes de toutes les contrées, à celles de Zurich, à celles ici présentes! A ces vaillantes jeunes femmes, dont le courage et l'intelligence ont su aborder et vaincre les difficultés qui leur barraient le chemin de la science! Les dangers, les veilles, les préjugès, les fatigues, elles ont tout bravé, tout enduré, pour conquérir par le travail et par la science, cette noble indépendance si précieuse aux âmes fières et qui seule peut assurer la dignité de l'être humain. Jeunes, elles ont renoncé aux plaisirs de leur âge, aux vanitès attribueès *traditionnellement* à notre sexe, et sans orgueil comme sans faiblesse, elles ont subi les épreuves imposées pour l'obtention des diplômes. Souvent elles se sont eleveés au-dessus du niveau de leurs condisciples masculins traçant ainsi d'une main ferme une ligne d'égalité intellectuelle entre l'homme et la femme à culture intellectuelle égale on équivalente.

Grâce aux efforts de leurs nobles devancières, les deux

sœurs Blackwell, les Garret-Anderson, les Barré, les Heim-Voeigtlin, les Daubié, auxquelles nous donnous ici un tribut de respect et de reconnaissance, la route qu'elles ont tracée, ouvre à l'humanité des horizons nouvcaux, car de grands .penseurs, et notre maître Fourier en tête, ont proclamé cette verité basèe sur l'expérience des nations, où la femme est asservie, que les progrès et le bonheur des sociétés sont en raison du développement intellectuel et de la liberté des femmes.

Art. IV.—REVIEWS.

English Female Artists by Ellen C. Clayton. Tinsley Brothers.

In these volumes Miss Clayton has given us a valuable contribution to our knowledge of celebrated women, and we may congratulate her upon the judgment with which she has handled her materials—sometimes tantalizingly scanty, sometimes bewilderingly voluminous. In reading the work our first feeling was of astonishment at the number of women who had obtained eminence in various branches of the art, especially when we take into consideration that, as the author says, " the earlier female artists almost invariably follow in the footsteps of a father or a brother, the reason being in all likelihood the impossibility of studying under other instruction." If this be so, we only know of the talents of those women who were exceptionally well placed in having talented male relations and being allowed to study under them. There is too much of interest in the multitude of names which are here collected, to permit us to do more than mention some of the best, of whom Miss Clayton has been able to gleam scanty particulars.

No evidence exists before the 16th century of any Englishwoman attempting any pictorial work beyond tapestry, and the first names found in these records are not English, being those of Susannah Hornebolt and Lavinia Teerlinck. The former, was known as an

admirable illuminator with her brother Luke. Durer
said of her ,"It is wonderful that a female should
be able to do such work." She was born in 1503, and
came to England in the reign of Henry VIII. Lavinia
Teerlinck was also invited to England by the same
king. She painted exquisite miniatures, some of which
have been attributed to Holbein, and her talent was so
much appreciated that she was in receipt of a Court
salary higher than that of Holbein by £6. She died
rich and much respected.

During the reign of Charles I. art received a new impetus.
Anne Carlisle was a portrait painter, and finished copyist
of the works of Italian masters. Old fashioned writers
speak of her as an "ingenious lady," and she obviously
occupied a very distinguished place in her profession.
She died about 1680.

Artemisia Gentileschi, a pupil of Guido, accompanied
her father to England in 1635. She painted portraits
of many members of the Royal Family and other persons. In historical painting she quite equalled her
father, and far excelled him in portraits. Several of her
works are in England though she only remained here
two years. She died in 1642. Several female artists
are mentioned of this date. Anna Maria Carew, a
miniature painter, received a pension of £200 a year in
1662. Elizabeth Neale was an excellent flower painter
at the same period. Mary More and Elizabeth Creed
painted portraits, but Mary Beale, who probably
began painting about 1662, is better known than
either. She chiefly excelled in portraits, charging
(such was the difference in the value of money in those
days), £5 for a head, £10 for a half length in oil. Nevertheless her exertions enabled her to earn about £200,
and once £429 a year. She appears to have been an
excellent wife and devoted mother.

Maria Varelst was a Flemish painter of historical
subjects who died in 1744; but during this century
portrait painting was the most lucrative branch of art,
that in which we find female painters most proficient.
Amongst those was Sarah Curtis, of whom Walpole said
when she gave up painting on her marriage "that the
art lost as much as she gained." Elizabeth Blackwell

(name of happy augury) was on the contrary a careful
flower painter and engraver. Her husband was imprisoned for debt, and she had to fight the battle of life
for him, herself, and their child.

"She could draw flowers carefully and with taste. Aware that there
was an acknowledged want of a good herbal, she calmly determined to
try her fortune in planning and executing one. She established herself
and child in a house near the garden of Medicinal Plants at Chelsea
to have the advantage of obtaining the necessary plants and flowers
in a fresh state as she required them. Not only did she make drawings
of the flowers, but engraved them on copper, and when printed,
coloured them herself. Her husband aided her so far as writing the
Latin names of the plants, together with a short description of their
principal characteristics. The first volume of this large folio work
appeared in 1737. It contained some two hundred and fifty plates,
each representing a distinct flower or plant, faithfully and character-
istically done, though not perhaps with that delicate minuteness now
required. * * * On the completion of the first volume, the
College of Physicians publicly distinguished her industry and ability
by a handsome present, as well as a testimonial, signed by the president and censors of the institution, characterizing her work as "most
useful," and recommending it to the public. * * * The second
volume of Mrs. Blackwell's book appeared in 1739; it contained 250
plates. The drawings are for the most part accurate; the style of
the engraving, though hard, is quite equal to that of the average
engraving of the period. The five hundred plates were all done
within four years.

The author lingers with loving minuteness on the
well known figures of Mary Delany, Frances Reynolds,
Maria Cosway, Angelica Kauffman, and Mary Moser. The
two latter were elected members of the newly-formed
Royal Academy. In the last decade of the 18th century
more than a dozen female artists were considered sufficiently distinguished to be enrolled among the hon. members of the Academy, among these were Miss Serres, and
Miss Heatley. But in recording the life of Mrs. Carpenter, the gifted portrait painter who died at an advanced age only four years ago, the author makes the
following just observation:—

It was a matter of indignation that so eminent and able an artist
should have been debarred the honour of becoming an Academician.
The *Art Journal* makes some severe, but justifiable remarks on the
subject, "Had the Royal Academy abrogated the law which denies a
female admission to its ranks, Mrs. Carpenter would most assuredly
have gained, as she merited, a place in them; but we despair of ever
seeing the rights of women vindicated in this respect; the doors of
the institution are yet too narrow for such to find entrance." It

cannot be denied that since the days of Angelica Kauffman and Mary
Moser, and the female honorary members of the same period, the
Academy, has studiously ignored the existence of women artists, leaving
them to work in the cold shade of utter neglect.   Not even once has
a helping hand been extended, not once has the most trifling reward
been given for highest merit or industry.   Accident made two women
Academicians—the accident of circumstances and the accident of
birth.   Accident opened the doors to girl students—accident aided
by courage and talent.   In other countries women have the prizes
fairly earned, quietly placed in their hands, and can receive them
with dignity.   In free, unprejudiced, chivalric England where the
race is said to be to the swift, the battle to the strong, without fear
or favour, it is only by slow laborious degrees that women are winning the right to enter the lists at all, and are then viewed with half
contemptuous indulgence.

The female painters of landscapes, flowers, &c., were
very numerous at the end of this century; others such
as Mrs. Pearson and Mrs. Lawrie were proficient in
painting on glass; there were also many successful
miniature painters.

As the present century opens, the crowd of women
artists thickens; flowers, miniatures, water-colours (the
Institute of Painters in Water Colours partly owed its
existence to Mrs. Harrison, called "the Rose and primrose
painter"), seem all to have invited their successful efforts.
The second volume, which is occupied entirely with
artists of the present day, is divided into chapters,
classifying figure painters, landscape painters, portrait,
miniature, and enamel painters; animal painters, decorative artists, humorous designers and amateurs.   It is
frequently asserted that women are not humorists; Miss
Bowers, however, now designs nearly all the hunting
subjects for *Punch*, besides contributing to other Magazines.   Miss Adelaide Claxton and Mdlle. De Tessier are
also caricature artists.   The decorative artists include
Miss Collingridge, Miss Edwards, Miss E. Harrison, Miss
M. Capes, and Miss Crawley.   Miss Clayton has shown
great taste in the short memoirs that compose this
volume; most of the artists in it being still living, little
except artistic notes would have been in place, and
these she has faithfully given.   Many of the ladies here
mentioned are writers as well.

We cannot better conclude than by quoting the passage in which she describes how Miss Herford practically

opened the schools of the Royal Academy to women.
Readers of the *Review* probably already know the incident, but its repetition will still be of interest to all who
value steady work and quiet perseverance.

Lord Lyndhurst, in a speech at the Royal Academy dinner, spoke
of the advantages offered by the Academy Schools to "*all* her
Majesty's subjects." Miss Herford thereupon addressed a letter to
him, in which she pointed out the anomaly that half of her Majesty's
subjects, those, namely, of her Majesty's own sex, were entirely
excluded from these Schools. This led to representations to Sir C.
Eastlake, the President, and interviews with him, which, together
with a circular addressed to all the Members of the Royal Academy
petitioning admission for the women students, and signed by numerous
lady artists, eventually gained the object which Miss Herford had at
heart. Sir C. Eastlake told Miss Herford there was no *rule* against
the admission of female students, and partly from his advice she sent
in a drawing, signed "L. Herford," receiving in due course a letter
to "L. Herford, Esq.," which granted admission to the Schools.
Much discussion ensued, but, supported by Sir Charles and one or
two other Academicians, the daring intruder was allowed to enter the
Academy Schools, where for some months she had to' endure the
discomfort of being the only representative of her sex, and was, no
doubt the object of curiosity and criticism more or less severe . . .
Opposition, prejudice, wonderment, the shower of *pros* and *cons*,
gradually faded away, and in these privileged later days, a fair proportion of female students are regularly admitted. In the ten years
that have since elapsed, some forty have passed as probationers. Miss
Herford died October 28th, 1870, aged 39.

Women in the Reign of Queen Victoria, by Madame R. A. Caplin,
        author of "Health and Beauty." Dean & Son.

In criticising this work we must observe that we
somewhat object to the title as giving an erroneous idea
of the book, and, in conjunction with its pretty green
and gold binding and very elegant style of printing,
making it appear an ordinary volume for the drawing-
room table, while it is in reality a very serious work,
containing many chapters on physiology and health, out
of which a mother will undoubtedly select much to read
to her daughters, but which are not to be placed un-
reservedly in the hands of young people.

Having recorded this protest, we can say that there
is very much that is worth reading in the book, both
upon health and on a variety of subjects most important
for women. Professional and artistic work, the training
for this work and the difficulties in the way of acquiring

this training; the want of good schools either for intellectual or technical education, and the unfair distribution
of the educational resources of the country in favour of
boys, are all here discussed.   Madame Caplin also
devotes much attention to the faultiness of the present
system of education in its relation to women's duties in
life.   In connection with this subject, we cannot do
better than quote her own words.

" The great defect in all this pretence of culture is, that young
women are taught to live for display : they are to be able to do
certain things.   That is all very well and commendable in its way ;
the great thing, however, that is required is, that they should be
noble and able beings ; and it is the *being* instead of seeming which
is so much overlooked in our schools, and, indeed, in our whole
social life.

" In a lady's general education, then, it should never be forgotten
that a time may come when her accomplishments have been displayed
in the mart and been withdrawn without a bid, or she may have been
married and left a widow ; or banks may break, or fortunes be dissi-
pated, even with those who have them—and they are comparatively
speaking, few. ' Then comes the tug of war.' The father, husband,
or other pillar of support being gone, the world has to be faced in the
autumn or winter of life when the sere and yellow leaf is on the tree,
or it may be the ground, ice-bound and desolate.   The glowing
hopes of early life have all faded ; those on whom she has depended
are gone, without youth or beauty the woman has to commence
her struggle for independence.   It is in such times as these, of all
others, that a woman of energy and spirit feels the value of some
profession or calling which will enable her to live without eating the
bitter bread of charity."

The *Spectator* of May 27th, in an article upon *A Plain
Guide to Good Gardening*, concludes with the following
sensible suggestions to women :—

" We hear a great deal of the need of employments for women,
why should not young girls develop their muscles, strengthen their
constitutions, and embark in the pleasing as well as useful occupation of gardening, having first, of course, made a special study of
what they are going to undertake ? We know that there are plenty
of amateur lady gardeners, and that they are usually most successful
cultivators; to these we say, ' go on and prosper ;' but there is room for
other and distinct classes.   Many of the operations of gardening are
especially suited to women, for they require neat-handedness, careful
manipulation, and minute and delicate attention.   The sowing and
the saving of seeds, the raising of cuttings, budding, grafting,
hybridism, the training of bush, pyramid, and espalier fruit trees,
the gathering and packing of fruit and flowers for the market, and
most of the multifarious operations of the propagating and plant-

houses, might be most efficiently done by women ; and granting that men would be required for the severer labours of digging, trenching, manuring, and draining, and for any other heavy work, it would very seldom be necessary to employ skilled gardeners, for the lady-workers would of course possess sufficient knowledge to be able to direct and superintend every operation. There would certainly be nothing menial in such an occupation, and we do not see why the daughters of gentlemen in reduced circumstances should not seriously undertake it, not merely to the very great advantage of their own families, but also, perhaps, later, in some profitable organisation where young women of the poorer classes could be trained and em-ployed under them. If some one would bring systematic gardening into fashion, we should not only hear very little of the need for stimulants and the other weaknesses of young-ladyhood, but we should no longer see so many weedy borders, unpruned and ' un-fruitful vines, neglected and unproductive kitchen-gardens, and greenhouses devastated by aphides and thrips.

"Schools of cookery have been instituttd with a considerable amount of success ; we recommend a school for practical gardening, with lectures upon agricultural chemistry, at which young women might learn, at all events, the rudiments of what they would require to know ; and we throw out the suggestion to those ladies who so anxiously desire to benefit their own sex, and also to our horticul-tural societies, which could so easily undertake the experiment on a suitable scale. In the meantime, however, instructors are by no means wanting. Books on gardening are multitudinous and con-tinually on the increase, and the one which has just been put for-ward by Mr. Wood, and which he calls "a plain guide to good gardening," is one of the best and clearest which we have met with for some time."

ART. V.—EVENTS OF THE MONTH.

EDUCATION.

WE hear that it has been resolved to admit as teachers in the Cambridge system of instruction by correspondence women who have satisfied the examiners in the exam-ination for one of the tripos.

Girton College.—The examinations for Entrance and Scholarships at Girton College will be held on the 20th of June. There are twenty-seven candidates, and but ten vacancies.

Women's Schools in Ireland.—Mr. Vere Foster thus

writes to an Irish newspaper:—" It will be in the recollection of your readers that, in a letter published in the *Irish Teachers' Journal* of February 13, 1875, I made the following announcement—

I propose to give annually one prize of £6, two prizes of £4, and six prizes of £3 to the principal teachers of those schools in Louth in which the greatest number of passes shall be obtained in proportion to the number of pupils examined, the application of this scheme to be limited to schools having an average daily attendance of at least 35 pupils during the year preceding the inspector's annual examination.

Having made inquiry at the Education Office as to the schools which have fulfilled the above named conditions, I append a list of all those National schools in Louth which had the required attendance during the twelve months preceding the Inspector's Results Examination for the year ended March 31, 1876, showing the number of pupils examined, and the number of passes obtained in *all* subjects.

(The list of schools in the county, male as well as female, is subjoined, and Mr. Foster continues).

In fulfilment of my promise, I have now much pleasure in awarding prizes as follows to the teachers of the undermentioned schools—

Fieldstown, £6; Knockbridge (Female), and Mullaharlin (Female), £4 each; Hacketscross, Tullyallen (Female), Darvir (Female), Dromiskin (Female), Tenure (Female), and Louth (Female), £3 each.

You will observe that, in almost every instance, the passes obtained in female schools were much more numerous than those in male schools, and the amounts earned were much greater, showing that if efficiency were, as it ought to be, altogether substituted for classification as a basis of payment, the pay of female teachers would be much higher than that of male teachers, instead of being very much lower, as has hitherto been the case.—I am, yours truly,—VERE FOSTER.

University College, London.—The graduates of the University of London have met in Convocation to fill up a vacancy in their senate. The choice in some degree turned on the readiness of the candidates to admit women to academical degrees.

Otter's College.—The formal opening of the new wing

R

of Bishop Otter's Memorial College at Chichester for
training ladies as elementary teachers, took place on
June 6th. It was preceded by a special service in the
cathedral. The very Rev. the Dean of Chichester
preached the sermon.

Brighton High School for Girls.—A meeting was held
on June 8th, in the upper room of the Town Hall,
Brighton. Its object was to explain the principles on
which the school (which was to be opened on the 13th)
would be conducted, and the character of the education
it provided. Mrs. William Grey addressed the meeting.
In the course of her speech she said:—" Class teaching
was far more efficient; there was more life in it, and
more stimulus to the pupil. That this was so, was
pretty generally recognised. Miss Sheriff, who was
travelling in Germany, had informed her that the
Princess Louise of Baden, believing in the superiority
of class teaching, had started a school in the Palace so
that her daughter might be taught with those of the
nobility. By their having day schools they had another
advantage—that of home influence, unbroken and uninterrupted. That was a great advantage, especially in
the education of girls. It might be interesting to know
what was said about these ideas in Germany. Amongst
others, the Princess Louise of Hesse—our Princess Alice
—felt great interest in the work; and a professor, who
had a training institution in the same country, whom
Miss Sheriff went to see, said that a great many of the
English girls who went to that institution had been
very badly prepared, especially in arithmetic and grammar; but he could say this of them, that when they
saw what work was put before them, and what they
had to do, he was greatly struck with the wonderful
energy and determination they displayed, and this
carried them through, enabled them to hold their place
in the class, and even enabled them to beat the German
girls, who had gone there much better prepared.
Several other German professors and others interested
in education also told her sister that though the German
girls were very much better taught, yet through its
being considered that at 16 they had learned enough,

they fell far short of English girls who stayed at school two years longer."

Miss Creak is the head-mistress of the school at Brighton. She was distinguished before any of the candidates who have come before the council, in arithmetic and mathematics. She is also well-known in literature.

The Plymouth High School for Girls has advertised for an assistant-mistress, who must be accustomed to prepare candidates for the Cambridge Local Examinations. Application is to be made before June 24th.

LORD CARNARVON'S BILL TO PREVENT CRUEL EXPERIMENTS ON ANIMALS.

The Bill introduced into the House of Lords by Lord Carnarvon has been printed. The Bill proposes to prohibit painful experiments on animals, except subject to the following restrictions :

"(1) The experiment must be performed with a view only to the advancement by new discovery of knowledge which will be useful for saving or prolonging human life or alleviating human suffering ; and (2) the experiment must be performed in a registered place ; and (3) the experiment must be performed by a person holding such licence from one of her Majesty's principal Secretaries of State, in this Act referred to as the Secretary of State, as in this Act mentioned ; and (4) the animal must during the whole of the experiment be under the influence of some anæsthetic of sufficient power to prevent the animal from feeling pain ; and (5) the animal must, if the pain is likely to continue after the effect of the anæsthetic has ceased, or if any serious injury has been inflicted on the animal, be killed before it recovers from the influence of the anæsthetic which has been administered ; and (6) the experiment must not be performed as an illustration of lectures in medical schools. hospitals, colleges, or elsewhere ; and (7) the experiment shall not be performed for the purpose of attaining manual skill. Provided as follows, that is to say :—(1) experiments may be performed under the foregoing provisions as to the use of anæsthetics by a person giving illustration of lectures in medical schools, hospitals, or colleges, or elsewhere, on such certificate being given as in this Act mentioned that the proposed experiments are absolutely necessary for the instruction of the persons to whom such lectures are given, with a view to their acquiring knowledge which will be useful to them for saving or prolonging human life, or alleviating human suffering; and (2) experiments may be performed without anæsthetics on such certificate being given as in this Act mentioned that insensibility cannot be produced without necessarily frustrating the object of such experiments ; and (3) experiments may be performed without the person who performed such experiments being under an obligation to cause the animal on which any such experiment is performed to be killed before it recovers from the influence of the anæsthetic on such certificate being given as in this Act mentioned ; and the so killing the animal would necessarily frustrate the object of the experiment, and provided that the animal be killed as soon as such object has been attained ; and (4) experiments may be performed not directly for the advancement by new discovery of knowledge which will be useful for saving or prolonging human life, or alleviating human suffering, but for the purpose of testing a particular former discovery alleged to have been made for the advancement of such knowledge as last aforesaid on such certificate being given as in this Act mentioned that such testing is absolutely necessary for the effectual advancement of such knowledge." The use of urari as an anæsthetic is prohibited. Painful experiments on dogs and cats and the public exhibition of painful experiments are also absolutely prohibited. Other clauses in the Bill provide that the license is to be granted for such time as the Secretary of State may think fit, and may be revoked ; that licensed persons are to make such reports as may be required, and all registered places are to be visited by inspectors ; scientific bodies are to grant certificates, and the judges are given power to grant a license for an experiment when it may be necessary in a criminal case. The penalty for offences against the Act is a fine of not more than £50 for the first offence, and for the second offence a fine of not more than £100, or imprisonment for a period not exceeding three months.

On May 22nd, the Bill was read a second time. The Earl of CARNARVON in moving the second reading, said, the first Act on the subject of protection of animals was the 3rd of George IV., and that had been followed by other Acts for preventing the torturing and ill-treatment of various animals, including all domestic animals ; but, while giving insufficient protection to domestic, it left all other animals quite unprotected, and it was quite necessary to lay down some new rules on the subject. He admitted that the practice of vivisection had been imported from the Continent. The existence of the practice abroad had been abundantly shown not only in the report of the Commission, but in books and newspapers. The experiments had not been confined to experiments for the purpose of scientific researches, but had been made for various other purposes, and sometimes for no purpose at all, and had been carried on with a barbarity which had scandalized the public mind. He then quoted the evidence of the Royal Commission, and concluded by reminding the House that it was with the commencement of the era of Christianity that cruelty to animals began to decline, and it had continued to decline just in proportion as civilization progressed. That great philosopher, Sir Humphrey Davy had acknowledged that he had been won over from scepticism by observing the intellectual qualities of animals. It was impossible to redress all the evils in the world, but it would be a great gain if they succeeded by this measure in reconciling the laws and necessities of modern science with the still higher laws of Christian morality and religion.

The Duke of SOMERSET opposed the Bill, fearing it would prevent all original research.

The Earl of SHAFTESBURY warmly supported it. He was in favour of complete prohibition, but he felt that a Bill for total prohibition would be a dead letter, while a restrictive Bill would be attended with much benefit.

Lord HENNIKER explained the reason which induced him to withdraw the Bill on this subject last year— namely, the appointment of the commission and the evidence of the growing opinion of the country on the subject. At the same time he pointed out that it was wise to propose a moderately restrictive rather than a prohibitory measure.

After further speeches from Lord Airlie, Lord Stanley of Alderley, and others, the Bill was read a second time.

THE Society for Protection of Animals liable to Vivisection has issued a circular calling attention to clause 5th, prohibiting all physiological experiments on dogs and cats. "This exemption was recommended by Mr. Hutton in the Report of the Royal Commission, and the Society deems it to be eminently just and reasonable. In the first place the creatures in question are exceptionally sensitive; insomuch, that the same experiment inflicted on a dog and on a rabbit may be estimated to involve twice or three times as much pain in the former case as in the latter. And in the second place the familiar relations in which these "Household Animals" stand to human beings renders cruelty towards them doubly demoralizing. Lastly, in favour of this clause it may be remarked that it will afford the only safeguard against the abuses of vivisection, on which much reliance can be placed. Other provisions—whether respecting licenses, inspection, or the use of anæsthetics—however judicious, may too probably be evaded, with more or less facility; but the vivisection of a dog or cat (generally stolen from its owner for the purpose) will constitute an offence not beyond the reach of successful prosecution.

The only Amendment which the Society for Protection of Animals liable to Vivisection would at present suggest is, that the immunity granted to the Household Animals should be extended to Horses, Asses, and Mules. These creatures are likewise extremely sensitive, and if not protected by law would become, when old, or disabled, the customary subjects for the most painful class of experiments. Such a conclusion to their lives of faithful service to man appears grossly unjust and inhuman."

Friends of this movement are therefore earnestly requested, 1st, to support Lord Carnarvon's Bill, especially the clause exempting dogs and cats from experiments. 2nd, to support (should it be introduced) an Amendment including Horses, Asses, and Mules in similar exemption.

A general meeting was held on June 2nd, at Westminster Palace Hotel, at which it was resolved not only to call attention to this Amendment, but in event of the Bill becoming changed or seriously crippled in its provisions in passing through the House, not to rest from its efforts till a satisfactory Bill has been obtained.

LADIES' NATIONAL TEMPERANCE CONVENTION.

A crowded meeting, convened by the Committee of the Ladies' National Temperance Convention, was held on the evening of May 22nd in the Memorial Hall, Farringdon street. The chair was taken by Mrs. LUCAS, President of the Convention, who explained that the meeting had been called to hear ladies, many of whom had come from a long distance, to speak on the subject of temperance.

Miss ROBINSON related her experience of the spread of the temperance movement in the army and navy. In

Portsmouth it was most successful, and mainly because
the women of the regiments there took it up so heartily.
She felt sure that if they could only get the women
heartily to enter the temperance movement, its success
would be secured. One reason of this hope was that
women were more tenacious of purpose than men; and
it should be also remembered that they were more
numerous. The women had in this kingdom a majority
of 900,000 for any cause they earnestly adopted.
Another advantage the women had was that they had
the training of the children. Above all things, she protected against the inconsistency of total abstainers, who,
whilst they kept their pledges themselves, winked at
the drinking of others. She had recently had to lecture
in the Soldiers' Institute, Portsmouth, at a concert and
entertainment held in support of the Sailors' Home.
The Duke of Edinburgh was to preside, and previous to
the meeting the committee of naval officers came and
asked her to give a room to which the Royal chairman
might occasionally adjourn for his brandy and soda.
She positively refused, saying that there was only one
principle for all, and the Duke supported her, declining
to have any room in the building used in violation of
total abstinence principles.

Mrs. JOHNSON (Brooklyn, New York) was the next
speaker, directing her attention more especially to what
had been done in her own country in the cause of
temperance. She described the labours of Mrs. Thomson
in the little village of Hillsborough, in the State of Ohio.
From Hillsborough a band of women, headed by Mrs.
Stewart, spread the movement all over the Union, until
now there were in the States nearly 1,000 Temperance
Unions. In the first year of the work 1,013 breweries
were closed, and in Brooklyn out of 2,500 drinking
saloons 1,300 had been closed within the year.

After a few words from Miss Le Geyt, Mrs. CLARA
BALFOUR said she firmly believed that women were
destined to be the agents of temperance reform all over
the kingdom. Mrs. HINDE SMITH urged the Christian
responsibility of women to devote their whole energies
to this movement without complicating it by the introduction of any political element. She feared that the

women were largely in favour of drink. In the public-houses in Leeds and other large places the proportion of women entering public-houses as compared with men was as two, and sometimes three to one.

Lady Jane Ellice had presided at the afternoon sitting, which was held previously to the public meeting; papers were then read by Miss M. Firth and others on "Alcoholic liquors in relation to health," the main object of which was to show that the use of alcohol was by no means necessary to nursing mothers.

The following morning a conference was held in the same hall, presided over by Mrs. J. Whiting, of Leeds, and papers were read by Mrs. C. L. Balfour and Miss Webb, on "The Drinking Customs—Domestic and Social." Both ladies deprecated the sale to women of stimulants in pastrycooks' shops, the use of strong drink at weddings, funerals, and other family gatherings, and laid great emphasis on the importance of female agency in banishing drunkenness from the land. A conversational discussion followed, in which the ladies participating pledged their best exertions in the cause of temperance.—The afternoon sitting was presided over by Mrs. Fielden Thorp (York), and the papers were read by Miss C. M. Ricketts (of the School Board, Brighton) and Miss C. Ellis. Both readers dealt with "Spheres of effort for individual workers," and pointed out the various ways in which women might do good work in the temperance cause. They might use persuasion—1st. Towards restoring the drunkard; and 2nd. For the prevention of drunkenness.

The President remarked as the result of her own experience that coffee stalls were powerful aids to the cause of temperance, wherever the coffee and other refreshments were good and cleanly served. She knew one case in which a coffee-stall having been started near a large public-house, the proprietor of the latter offered the stallkeeper a large sum to remove. In the course of the discussion that followed, Mrs. Meredith deprecated the too demonstrative interference of organised teetotallers with drunkards. She preferred prayer meetings for the latter, who were always remorseful and penitent after a drinking bout. Mrs. Balfour warmly defended the teetotal organisation, and cited several remarkable instances of conversion dating from public meetings. The discussion was continued for some short time by Miss Steel (of Dundee), Mrs. Johnson (Brooklyn), and other speakers, after which Mrs. Lucas informed the meeting that at Newcastle lady delegates had been appointed to the International Temperance Convention to be held in Philadelphia during the Exhibition. Those were Scotch ladies, but she trusted that some English ladies would allow their names to be proposed as delegates. She herself had been named, but unfortunately she was unable to go. The suggestion was approved of, and a committee was nominated to ascertain whether any ladies were willing to be delegates.

The following day the convention resumed proceedings, under the presidency of Mrs. Balfour, and papers were read by Mrs. H. Cadbury, Mrs. Dawson Burns, and Mrs. Parker on "Ladies' Temperance Associations, Local and National." The papers mainly dealt with the best method of future organisation. Some of the ladies present were in favour of a fusion with the British Women's Temperance Association. Mrs. Hilton moved, and Mrs. Sturge seconded, a proposal that the meeting should at once resolve itself into a committee of organisation, to decide on the name of such an organisation, and to elect its officers. This motion was supported by Mrs. Lucas and several other ladies, but was ultimately negatived. A resolution was passed to the effect that Mrs. Burns' and Mrs. Parker's papers should be taken into consideration by a committee to be named, and also that any lady who wished should be permitted to attend the preliminary meetings of this committee, and to have a voice in its proceedings.

Mrs. Hinde Smith, of Leeds, took occasion to express the gratitude of English ladies to Mrs. Johnson, of Brooklyn, for having crossed the Atlantic to participate in their discussions, and to give the invaluable support of her American experience. The resolution was seconded by Mrs. Thorp, of York, who wished to give her personal testimony to the aid of Mr. Rae, Secretary of the National Temperance League. Mr. Rae made his acknowledgments, and at the same time complimented the ladies on the quality of their papers, and the admirable order of their proceedings. After an earnest exhortation by Lady Jane Ellice to the ladies present to strengthen their exertions in the temperance cause by prayer, the proceedings of the convention terminated with a prayer and hymn.

The Bazaar in aid of the London Temperance Hospital was opened on June 3rd in Exeter Hall by Lady Aberdare. The purpose in view is to raise the sum of £20,000, with which to purchase the freehold site of the hospital and the furnishing of a suitable building for the accommodation of 100 in-patients. Since the opening of the present hospital in October, 1873, the in and out patients treated at the hospital have been 3,231 in number. Of the 325 in-patients, 41 per cent. had been discharged cured, and 121 relieved, whilst the deaths have been only 18. The principle of treatment at the hospital was, when possible, to dispense with alcoholic stimulants; and in only one case had it been found necessary to violate the principle. £10,000 of the whole sum required has been already subscribed, and it is hoped and confidently expected that the bazaar would produce the remaining moiety. Of the great provincial cities and towns, Edinburgh has been the most liberal in its contributions, and after it Manchester and Glasgow. Some of the stalls contain articles to upwards of £600 value.

At the annual meeting of the Women's Temperance Association in Belfast on June 2nd, the strenuous efforts made by many of the ladies in the cause of Temperance Reform, were referred to by the Rev. Mr. Mac Intosh.

EMPLOYMENT.

THE Brighton Society for the Employment of Women has issued its report of proceedings. It has been decided to commence a book-keeping class, as in London, the payments of the pupils to be in most cases supplemented from the funds of the Society. The expenditure of the Society during last year was only £38 10s., the receipts being £96, so that there is a fair balance in hand; but this was in great measure owing to the gratuitous services rendered by the two hon. secretaries, Miss Moon and Miss Macdonell, both of whom are no longer in Brighton, so that the expenses next year will be somewhat increased.

Manchester Women's Union.—We learn from the *Women's Union Journal* that since the large meeting of the sewing machine hands in Manchester, on May 2nd, 230 names have been already enrolled as members of the Society.

On May 17th, the first quarterly meeting of London machinists was held; Mr. Hodgson Pratt presiding.

Silk-Growing.—An Australian silk grower's depôt has been started at 7, Charles-street, Grosvenor square, where full particulars of the Victorian Ladies' Silk-Growing Association can be obtained.

Penmaking.—Joseph Gillott and Sons, of the Victoria Works, Birmingham, are continually advertising for female hands from 13 to 22 years of age, for the above business.

Watchmaking.—We hear from the *Woman's Gazette,* that Madame Lina Muller (from Geneva), is a practical working watchmaker and jeweller, 104, Lisson Grove, near Edgware-road station. She repairs all kinds of clocks, watches, and jewellery. This is a trade that many women might practice with advantage.

China Painting.—Miss Victoria Levin, who is steadily winning an acknowledged reputation as an artist in china-painting, has recently completed a figure subject on a large *plateau.* Miss Levin has also some smaller works on hand—consisting of charming studies and adaptations from nature of flowers and foliage. The characteristic and effective treatment to be observed in these, speaks well for the young lady's future success. —*Æsthetic Review.*

Women in the General Post Office.—The *Civil Service Review,* says, " The female clerks in the Post Office being aggrieved by what they consider the unfair promotion of one of their number, a committee, consisting entirely of females, has been appointed to enquire into the matter.

ANOTHER PROPOSED LADIES' CLUB.

It is proposed to open a Club, for Ladies only, in the neighbourhood of Westbourne Grove. It is hoped that it will meet the requirements of ladies wishing for a place in which they can read, write, study, or practice in quiet, as well as of those who would be glad of the usual advantages of a Ladies' Club and it is thought that the Club will recommend itself much to ladies living out of town, when coming up for a day. There will be different rooms for study, and for music, and other recreations and a drawing-room ; also a library in connection with Mudie's.

The Secretary, of whom full particulars can be obtained, is Miss Carole E. Steevens, 24, Hatherley Grove, W. We understand the club will not be started unless a sufficient number of ladies, to guarantee its success, testify their wish to become members.

LADY COMMISSIONER OF STATE CHARITIES IN AMERICA.

THE New York *Evening Post* says that Mrs. Charles Russell Lowell was appointed by Governor Tilden to fill the New York city vacancy on the Board of State Charities caused by the retirement of Mr. C. H. Marshall. Governor Tilden had the pleasure of learning that the appointment was instantly confirmed by the Senate, and that Mrs. Lowell is henceforth a Commissioner of State Charities. It is a most excellent appointment, though the office is not one of those to which politicians aspire. The term of office is seven years, and its services are performed without salary. This is, we believe, the first public office ever conferred by the Governor of New York upon a woman. At all events it is the first office thus bestowed involving large responsibilities, and requiring the exercise of high qualities both of mind and heart.

Mrs. Lowell was an efficient member of the New York branch of the Sanitary Commission which rendered such important service during the late civil war, and is now one of the best workers in the State Charities Aid

Association. At the annual meeting of this association, Governor Tilden heard Mrs. Lowell's Report upon Vagrancy in this state—a very valuable contribution to the discussion of the subject. He knew also of the efforts made by her to secure a safe passage through the Legislature for the Tramp Bill proposed by the association. Besides the report to which we have referred, she made another to the same association on the subject of the employment of the poor, and collected and summarized much information upon the methods of relieving them.

The appointment of Mrs. Lowell is quite unsolicited— a circumstance which makes it more welcome to the State Charities Aid Association, conducted as it is by women, all of whom, her fellow members, are much gratified by it, and it has the approbation of all who take an interest in the objects which that association has in view. She is a daughter of Francis G. Shaw of Staten Island, and sister of Col. Shaw who fell at Fort Wagner while leading his black regiment the 54th Massachusetts volunteers. Her husband also fell in battle during the civil war. She lives in New York and gives her time and exertions to the humane and useful labours of which we have spoken. On such a work as that to which she has been appointed, the proceedings of which relate to the treatment of the poor of both sexes and include the care of children, it seems a most proper and fitting arrangement that women should be called upon to counsel and assist.

LAW OF DIVORCE.

In the House of Commons, on Monday May 15th, Colonel Egerton Leigh asked the Attorney-General whether it was true that a woman, should her husband commit adultery, is not allowed by the law to marry again, a husband not being prevented marrying again should his wife commit adultery; and whether, should such be the case, a Bill would be brought in to remedy the injustice to women.

The Attorney-General said, "The question of the hon. and gallant Member seems to assume that if a man's wife commits adultery, he can immediately marry again. That is not so. By the law, as it stands, a husband is enabled to obtain a divorce if his wife commits adultery, but a wife cannot obtain a divorce on that ground. She must go on further, and prove cruelty and desertion, as well as adultery. I do not admit that the law, as it stands, works any injustice to the woman, and therefore I do not admit that a Bill on that subject is necessary."

The Attorney-General's verdict that the present law works no injustice, by its inequality, to women, will probably fail to strike conviction to the women themselves. Meantime, the illiterate classes carry still further their estimate of the privileges of a husband. It used to be a current opinion in France, and may be still for ought we know, that English husbands were permitted to sell their wives in Smithfield. That this belief is not confined to foreigners, the following extract from the *Liverpool Post* all too plainly shows:—

Selling a Wife for Half-a-gallon of Ale.—At Warrington, on Friday, a young man, named Wells, sold his wife, a good-looking young woman of some six-and-twenty summers, for the small figure of the price of half-a-gallon of beer. Wells, who is a forgeman has lived apart from his wife for about two years, on account of her conduct; and a labourer, named Clayton, who lodged with her mother in Stamford Street, Warrington, having become smitten by the lady's charms, conceived the idea that if her husband sold her to him there would be no lawful impediment to her becoming Mrs. Clayton. Accordingly, the pair proceeded to a public house, and a messenger was despatched for Wells. Clayton told him that he would buy his wife if he would sell her. Wells replied that he could have her for "nowt" if he liked; but Clayton did not wish to obtain her so cheaply, and requested the husband to name the price. Wells then said he could have her for half-a-gallon of beer, which was at once brought in and drank, and the transaction sealed to the apparent satisfaction of all parties. Clayton said she was a good wench to him and he loved her. He would like to marry her, he said, and asked Wells if he would "hurt" her. Wells replied, "No, theaw can mairy her as soon as theaw loikes; to-neet if theaw's a mind. I won't hurt either of you. Clayton also offered to keep Wells's little girl by his wife, which was accepted. Upon the declaration of friendship Clayton treated Wells to another pint, and Mrs. Wells, who was evidently pleased with the bargain, paid for another half-a-gallon of beer, which the company drank. The husband returned to his work, and the wife left the house with her purchaser, and avowed their intention of getting married as soon as the tardiness of legal formality permitted.

Here the husband evidently intended to do fairly by the woman, but carried out the common belief of marital supremacy. It is doubtful whether this belief would be modified even were he as well versed in English law as the Attorney-General, although he might no longer put it into practice with such rough unscrupulousness.

BOARDING-OUT OF PAUPER CHILDREN.

A Bill has been printed, bearing the names of Mr. O'Shaughnessy, Mr. O'Reilly, Mr. Bruen, and Mr. Redmond, which proposes to "extend the limits of age up to which, with the assent of boards of guardians, orphans and deserted pauper children may be supported out of workhouses in Ireland." The Bill provides that children may be placed out at nurse until the age of thirteen.

FEMALE MEDICAL PRACTITIONERS.

A Bill in the Commons bearing the names of Mr. Russell Gurney and Mr. Bright, has just been printed, to "remove restrictions on the granting of qualifications for registrations under the Medical Acts on the ground of sex.

PUBLIC LIBRARIES.

A Day for Women.—The Committee of the Nottingham Free Public Libraries have, at the suggestion of Mr. Briscoe, the Librarian, decided that on Tuesday in each week the branch library and reading room, which is to be opened shortly after Whitsuntide, shall be open to women only.

The Nottingham Libraries, it may be observed, are all open to women equally with men; at the new branch library one day is set apart *exclusively* for them.

Considerable discontent was lately felt by the lady-readers in the British Museum at the discomfort of the arrangements made with reference to them. A letter to one of the daily papers, May 16th, stated that:—

Literary women as a rule have a sufficiently hard struggle to achieve anything like success in their profession without petty insults and small irritations being forced upon them, and the British Museum, of all places in the world, ought to be the one where they might expect to be most free from them. Unfortunately such expectations are not realised, and the lady readers have recently been treated rather as wicked and rebellious children who must be condemned to a dark cell— the birch not being permitted by public opinion—than as refined, intelligent, and educated women. The offence which they unintentionally gave seemed simple enough. The cloak-room, which in 1857 was built for them, was in June, 1872, thrown open also to the female art students, and the overcrowding became so great that in March, 1876, thirty ladies signed a letter addressed through the superintendent to the principal librarian and trustees, asking that a suitable room should be provided for the art students and the reader's room kept for its original purpose. The reply to this could not be termed courteous; then came the punishment. On the 8th of May, the Museum having been closed for a week, the ladies were not allowed to return to their old quarters, but were directed to a passage by the side of the great staircase which was at one time the entrance to the readers' refeshment room. In this cell, cold, gloomy, and dimly lighted, the walls covered with dirt, amidst rows of uncovered pipes, broken brickwork and mortar, unpainted deal boards, and other unpleasing sights, they are condemned to dress, rest when they are over-fatigued with their work, and if they can do so, swallow their luncheon. After this treatment it cannot be unfair to ask—Does the British Museum belong to the nation, or is it the private property of one individual? If the former, will it be tolerated that the literary women ·of England shall be treated like this, while, according to a printed statement never denied, £899 in the course of five years—1869 to 1875—has been spent in fitting and furnishing the room of one of the officials?"

We are informed that most of these bad arrangements have since been remedied. If women would sooner make their complaints clear and public, this result would frequently follow.

MISCELLANEOUS.

Women's Peace and Arbitration Auxiliary of the London Peace Society.—The second anniversary meeting and conversazione of this society was held at the Memorial Hall, Farringdon-street, on May 26th, Mr. Mundella, M.P., in the chair. Mrs. Southey, the secretary, read a report of the operations of the society during the year, which consisted partly of the distribution of tracts and leaflets bearing on the subject. Communications had also been kept up with friends on the continent, and invitations from Signora Pieromaldi to the members of the committee to assist with contributions to a bazaar, to be held in Florence on behalf of the Association Cosmico Umanitaria had been responded to by the Auxiliary, and also by the ladies of the Manchester Peace Society.

THE EVANGELICAL PROTESTANT DEACONESSES' INSTITUTION.

The annual meeting of this institution took place on May 20th, at the Hospital, which is situated in the plea-

sant and healthy suburb of South Tottenham. The
institution is at once a hospital and a training school
for nurses. It has beds for forty-five patients, several
of which, however, are now vacant, the state of the
funds not being such as to justify the Council in permitting them all to be occupied at present. 303 patients
were admitted into the hospital during the twelve
months, of which 167 were surgical and 136 medical
cases, besides which 5,512 visits were paid to out-patients.
The number of nurses, or " sisters," as they are called, is
34 in all; but of these only eleven are attached to the
hospital at Tottenham. There are other hospitals to
which they give their services, two of the sisters being
at the workhouse at Cork, eight at the City and County
Infirmary at Perth, eight at the Infirmary, Sunderland,
two at the Cottage Hospital, Enfield, and one at the
Girls' Orphan Home, Tottenham. The sisters also, when
their public engagements permit, devote themselves to
nursing in private families, and the report stated that a
great number of applications had been received from
persons desirous of procuring their assistance in this
way. Mr. Samuel Morley, M.P., took the chair at the
meeting. In the course of his address he said he
believed this institution deserved to be more widely
known and supported. Sister Crissy, by which name
the lady superintendent chose to be known, was one
who was devoting her life and time in the service of
One whom she gladly recognised as her Master and
Lord, and she and the other ladies who were associated
with her in this work were doing service of the highest
kind.

Miss Rye and the Pauper Children.—An interesting
exhibition took place lately at Miss Rye's " Home for
Destitute Little Girls," Peckham. The attention of
visitors was not drawn to this collection of six hundred
photographs for their artistic excellence, though many
might be commended on this ground, but as an
example of what good conditions of life may do for the
very poorest and lowest waifs and strays from our
workhouses and streets. It was almost impossible to
believe in looking over the albums filled with the por-

S

traits of healthy-looking. well-dressed girls, that they
could have been taken from the workhouses of St. Pancras, Lambeth, Stepney, Chelsea, Neath, Merthyr, and
others, as also from our London streets. The ·photo-
graphs have been sent from Canada to Miss Rye. some
by the girls themselves, others by the adopted parents
and mistresses of the children, and in every case it has
been done voluntarily. Those interested in Miss Rye's
movement would do well to inspect this collection.—
Daily News.

A NEW park has been presented to Birmingham by
Miss Ryland. The intrinsic value of the gift is £30,000.
The same lady has already been the donor to the town
of Cannon Hill Park, and other splendid local gifts which
are estimated at £70,000.

The movement for enabling shopwomen to have seats
behind the counter, has now, we are glad to hear from
a correspondent, formed another association in Liverpool,
this association even undertaking to supply the seats.
There are now associations in Bristol, Brighton, (where
more than 900 members have joined) Leeds, Liverpool,
and Manchester. For what reason is London behind-
hand in this bit of practical benevolence? Ladies should
be just as much awake to the hardship of standing nine
or ten hours a day there as elsewhere. We hope to see
the commencement of a similar organisation in the
metropolis before the end of the season.

The *Examiner* calls attention to the usefulness of Mrs.
Weldon's Orphanage in Tavistock Square. "Among
the many institutions which compete for the assistance
of the public, a cause like Mrs. Weldon's, which she has
worked at for eight years with next to no help from
outside, deserves to be mentioned with honour. The
children taken charge of in the Orphanage are educated
with a view to their afterwards earning their living in
the musical profession, and the well-known reputation
of Mrs. Weldon is a guarantee that the education given
them is of the best possible kind. The growth of such
an institution depends, of course, on the support, in the
way of money as well as of sympathy, which the public
is willing to give."

The *Athenæum* says that the Countess of Charlemont, who lately contributed a paper on Lady Macbeth to the new Shakespeare Society, has in contemplation another paper.

Lecture Notes.—Miss Miranda Hill lectured on 24th May on "The Influence of Beauty on the Life and Health of the Nation," at 1, Adam street, Adelphi.

Miss Carpenter gave an address on her recent visit to India, at the Society of Arts, Adelphi, London, on May 11th.

ART. VI.—CORRESPONDENCE.

The Editor is not responsible for the opinions of Correspondents.

SECOND LETTER ON MR. BRIGHT'S SPEECH.

DEAR MADAM,—I take up my pen again on the same subject with a remark as old I suppose as the time of the Romans, "Tempora mutantur et nos mutamur cum illis." I hope your readers may remember my calling attention to the fact that Mr. Bright himself in his own person might be made an instance of the change of manners which has taken place (by slow degrees, no doubt, but very perceptibly) from savage to civilised life; since the women now have learnt to complain, while the men have learnt not to give them so much cause of complaint. Civilised life *in towns* has long made the use of rocks and stones for the treatment of refractory females impossible, but the use of a stick as a lawful instrument wherewith men might correct their wives brings us down to later days, and when I first attempted to study Blackstone's admired commentaries I there read that the husband's stick should not be thicker than his own thumb! *Very civilised* persons will be apt to perceive a trace of barbarism here, but it is fair to observe also that there is likewise proof of progressive civilisation in the caution given as to the size of the stick! Laying violent hands on a woman to hurt her is now punishable equally with the same offence against a man, but the right of property in a wife is so far maintained still that though cruelty *added to infidelity* on the part of a husband may by a recent alteration of English law procure a wife a divorce, it does not otherwise punish the husband. I am not lawyer enough to distinguish by the right name the privilege specially accorded for the protection of wives by their going individually before a magistrate to declare on oath that their husband beats them and starves them, and that they have supported themselves six months by their own labour, when

the law as administered by the magistrate kindly allows them to
continue as they have been doing, and even declares that what
they can make by their own hands or brains is *after this* time to be
their own and not their husband's. "Feminine" men and strong-
minded" women would be apt to call this protection *hard lines*, but
I prefer to look on it rather in the way of progress, for these improvements have taken place in Mr. Bright's time and mine. We
can both remember when law in England took no cognizance of conjugal infidelity in a husband, nor of cruelty either. He had power
to divorce his weaker companion. Not she him in any case. In this
respect English law is still behind Scotch law, and I think I may
say behind our age.

The traces of the paramount *right* of men to treat their wives ill
or well exactly as they pleased may still be observed in the lower
classes even when sober. When cross with drink it is no wonder if
this abiding belief of their rights takes the form of active injury, and
it is only what we ought to expect that the lookers on hesitate to
interfere with the husband's *rights*, as they believe them still to be.
Socially also we have all been taught by maxims spoken or printed,
if not by experience, that it is dangerous for ourselves to meddle in a
conjugal quarrel. Moliere has pleasantly shown us that even the
weaker party has little gratitude.

> " *De quoi vous melez vous,'*
> *Je veux qu'il me botte, moi,*"

is the faithful wife's first idea or expression to the intermeddling
stranger, and she goes on thus till she is in fear of her life.

I can relate a scene not very unlike in its commencement the anecdote of the South Sea islanders that Byron has commemorated in his
"Shipwreck of the Wager." I did not witness it, but it happened
in my own time, and among my own people—in a country village
where I often visited my maiden aunts I was one evening walking
with the youngest and liveliest of them when she startled me by
calling out "There's the deil." I looked and saw a tall, fair, young,
and handsome man leading a lamb on one side, and a lovely
child on the other. The deil's surroundings were certainly not
in character. I questioned my aunt about him, being unwilling to
believe he deserved this epithet, but she persisted in it,
saying "this was what his neighbours called him." I asked if he
drank. She said "No, he was only ill-tempered." Some time after
this, another of my aunts (one that well deserved the name of strong-
minded, though she had the tenderest heart for others that ever a
woman possessed to afflict herself with), was returning home
through the village when she found herself in a crowd sur-
rounding the deil's house, from which screams of pain were
issuing. The neighbours were sympathising in murmurs of pity and
indignation outside, but nobody tried to get in, though everybody
was quite aware from previous knowledge that the deil was be-
labouring his wife. On ascertaining that the door was locked, my
aunt Janet called out to the men to break it open! *They would not
stir.* Perceiving that two of them were her own gardener and
ploughman, she said to them, "Fetch me an axe." The poor fellows
then admonished her, "Eh, Miss Jeenat, wad ye interfere atween

man and wife."   "Cowards, bring me an axe," was her reply, and it
had its effect, for though, doubtless, she *would* have used it herself if
necessary (not being a "feminine" woman in the way of helplessness)
the men now fell heartily to work, knocking open the door, and dis-
closing the wife, whose cries had ceased, as she lay by this time
senseless on the floor, where her husband was still in act to kick her.
He offered, however, no resistance, when the mob entered his one
room, and by aunt Janet's command Robin and John carried off his
wife on the door to a place of safety, the house of an old widow who lived
a good way off under my aunt's protection.   There very soon another
lovely infant was born to the deil, which I had frequently an opportunity
of seeing as I walked in Milheugh garden, for my aunt employed the
poor creature on her recovery in the light occupation of weeding,
and the baby (it being fine, dry, summer weather) habitually lay
in the *creel* that held the weeds beside its mother.   The *Bright* style
of observer will wish to know what became meantime of the father
and husband.   He expressed no compunction, and, of course, got no
punishment.   His wife was supported by my aunt for three months.
The deil took care to avoid *her*, my aunt, but succeeded after a time
in getting hold of his wife again.   I think I am entitled to observe
that my aunt here represents the *courage of progressive humanity* in
rather a solitary manner, but it is pleasant to observe her feelings are
spreading. Still it hardly seems to me quite fair that now-a-days magistrates take upon them to rate severely the *non-interfering public* and
at the same time *feel their own withers quite unwrung.*   Judges are per-
petually apologising (see the *Times'* reports) for the unfairness of the
law! which these men feel themselves very unfortunate in being born to
administer, but not to correct.   It was a *woman* who brought to light the
scandalous injustice to women shown in the Mutiny Act with regard
to children legitimate or illegitimate born anywhere to soldiers, and
it was *a man* in the character of our Minister of War who, when told
of it, remarked it was *shocking, if true,* and who, having found it
true has not been able to set it right yet.   The person who has
done the most for women's rights according to my judgment is a lady
who has collected and printed the "Laws of England as they regard women" *without comment,* merely observing that, without becoming legislators, "women can show where the shoe pinches."   I
quote from myself now as my nearest if not my best authority.*

"We are, indeed, fully persuaded that the progress of civilization
will discover, nay, has discovered, many faults and defects in the laws
which concern women, and it would be hard indeed to adhere to the
wisdom of our ancestors *only with regard to them.*   While any causes
of complaint remain, it ought not, we think, to be a subject of regret
that they are liable to be exaggerated.   And it is also satisfactory
that the persons who suffer, or who fancy they suffer, injustice, are
now able, by means of pens and printing presses, if not in public
assemblies, to make their wrongs known.   How these are to be
redressed is another question.   Eventually, we think, this must

---

* Page 4, "Woman and her Social Position," reprinted from *Westminster
Review,* No. 68, 1841.

become the business of the legislature, and the redress of female grievances must proceed on the same grounds of a more impartial justice for all, which have brought every other reform in law, although the principle of absolute equality must always, in the case of women, be modified by their different situation (we need not call it inferior position) from men."

Here again I join issue with Mr. Bright. When I ventured to remark that the manners and customs of both men and women change by civilization, *pari passu*, I had not leisure to dwell on the importance of this parity of steps in the change. To make it effectual, the steps must be taken at the same time by both sexes. They must make the same progress on the same subject. We hardly need say this is far from the case at present between, for instance, those women who "work" the franchise, and the men who represent us all in Parliament, and who are supposed to represent civilized humanity in the three kingdoms and colonies ; some think all over the world! The franchise for women is an abstract question, actually concerning a few women only, and it has come to mean—not a simple act of justice to a few women, such as men would have had (according to my belief) no reason to repent of had they granted it a quarter of a century ago—it has come to mean a great many possible and, I do think, also impossible things. It is only natural that men, especially young men, should not be able to enter so easily into the interests (somewhat abnormal we shall call them) of single women and widows, and that they should use what they still feel their, *man's*, right to *think for them*, even more than they do for their wives and daughters. It is pleasant again to agree with Mr. Bright that in the intimate union of married life a perfect equality of power and influence seems to prevail (in spite of law) between two persons amenable to reason and moral obligation, and who are each disposed to do for the other, not only the part belonging to their sex, but to contribute every separate natural quality or acquired endowment to the common stock, so as to constitute a perfect communion of thought and action, and thereby producing the highest type of humanity, as seen in the family life. Very amiable men may be found, therefore, who cannot perceive inequalities which *they* would never permit to exist or to continue. I here offer an excuse for *unenlightened* men! Let me say a word for the *over-enlightened women*, named in scorn and sarcasm " strong-minded," " Social Failures," " Working Bees," Hommes-Femmes, " Monsters," &c. I go back to my motto. Not only are *we* all changed, but times and *things* are changed. Circumstances over which not one of us have any control, and yet by which we are guided, if not controlled, have procured for many women of the present day a vast amount of leisure, considerable opportunities of education, and a single life, capable, *they* think and feel, of being now turned to better account than ever before as mere hangers-on in families! They have studied the subject of their own actual situation only too well, and they have seized on the franchise as a means of improving it ; they *may* have over-worked it, at any rate they have outrun the sympathies of men about it. *Their* great expectations from it have had the effect of exciting in manly bosoms great alarms. It is in vain to preach moderation of hope and fear in present excitement. Some allowance must be made for the fanaticism of both parties, yet I rejoice that the single women can boast of the generous sympathy of many happy wives who feel no want of franchise for themselves, and of the support of a majority, I believe, of liberal men. I add a word of comfort to the alarmists. The witty French have long ago classed the sexes as the *Bête Feroce*, and the *Animal Domestique*. I have taken some pains to show that the former creature dies out with difficulty, may we not hope that the latter species will still survive in sufficient numbers to serve their would-be masters.

M. T. M.

DEAR MADAM,—Last October my friend, Mrs. C——, a district visitor, was obliged to go to London on business, on the very day that something of the nature of a crisis arrived in the affairs of a poor woman who had lately been recommended to her special care. Mrs. C—— begged I would go and see her *protégée*, whom I shall call Mrs. A——, and take whatever steps I thought best under the circumstances. Mrs. C—— informed me that Mrs. A—— was now suffering from a most painful disease in the bone of her knee; that this disease came in the train of a rheumatic fever, from which she had scarcely recovered; and that the fever came from neglect, Mrs. A——'s husband not allowing her money for the ordinary necessaries of life, Though in receipt of good wages—25s. to 35s. per week. For a long time—perhaps a fortnight, perhaps longer—all the money he had given her had been 8d. Poor people have not unlimited credit with tradespeople, and it was hard for her to get food for herself and her little child. A—— had sold all his wife's clothes during her fever, except one silk dress, two petticoats, a shawl, and a very little linen. He wanted to take some little ornaments a favourite brother of his wife's had given her, and when she objected and tried to send them to be kept for her by a sister, A—— became very violent. He had repeatedly struck her, and on one occasion he had threatened her life, and a brother of her's has waited more than one night outside her window till 1 a.m., in the expectation of a cry of murder. A—— announced that there would be an explosion should his wife's mother or sister go to the upper rooms in his house, as he had laid gunpowder for the purpose of blowing up intruders.

The doctors ordered Mrs. A—— to encase herself in flannel. With A——'s sanction some flannel was ordered from a shop. When it came A—— either tore it up, sold, or pawned it. Some charitable people sent Mrs. A—— grapes or jelly, or both, and A—— eat them, or gave them away in her presence.

When I went to Mrs. A—— I found a pretty, lady-like little woman, of twenty-two, I believe, but not looking more than seventeen. She was extremely weak; almost entirely unable to move herself; and suffering a great deal of pain at times when others moved her. She was too ill to speak much, or to be sensitive to almost anything except *terror* of her husband.

A bed had been secured for her at a country hospital, and arrangements had been made for taking her there. A—— had been informed of these facts by his wife. He did not wish her to go to the hospital, but the morning of the day I first saw her, he had said, alluding to the hospital-plan, "I suppose I shall not find you here when I return this evening." Meanwhile, Mrs. A——'s doctors said they regretted she should be removed from their care, as a critical point had been arrived at in her case, and they were anxious to keep her under their management to see if an operation on her knee might not be avoided, and also to tide her over her confinement, which was expected in four or five months. Mrs. A——'s doctor, in answer to my question, told me he thought I "would be actionable" if I removed his patient from under her husband's roof (it was expected the husband would forcibly put a stop to her going if he returned before it was executed), but the doctor advised me to "risk it," deeming her removal of great importance to the poor woman. A bed was found at the house of a kind, good woman of the neighbourhood; the doctor promised to lend his operating table to carry his poor patient upon; and Mrs. C——'s house was taxed to supply bedding—the remaining bedstead in the A——'s house fortunately belonging to Mrs. A——'s brother. We dared not take any of her own things, as the law had already dispossessed her of them by making them over to her husband at their marriage—particularly hard in the present case, as Mrs. A——'s industrious mother had laid out her life's savings to furnish her daughter's house. We feared that A—— would prosecute us if we took away anything that could not be proved not to be his. Once at her kind neighbour's, Mrs. A—— began to get better. In March her second child was born. It is likely to live, but will be partially, if not wholly, blind. The dreaded amputation of Mrs. A——'s leg is obviated, but she will be a cripple for life in consequence of the disease of the knee. An operation (the removal of the diseased bone) is contemplated, but as the doctors have not been paid for past attendance, they hesitate about giving their services gratuitously now.

A —— found out where his wife had moved to, and came to see her. She had now become a charge on a charitable parish fund, and on private benevolence. Her husband occasionally paid something towards her maintenance, and he discharged some of his old debts. His bounties were fitful. Sometimes, for weeks at a time, he behaved very well towards his wife and his creditors, but these good dispositions were not enduring. About three weeks ago, Mrs. A—— dragged herself and her little baby to London to see him, and if possible to get him to make some arrangement for paying the doctors' bill. She offered at the same time to return to him, being stronger, and being now unable to depend on the continuance of charitable support which had been eked out by her husband's doles. I need not attempt to describe my poor thing's pilgrimage. It resulted in her husband's telling her to go back to the lodging that had been found for her, he did not want her in London; he would allow her 16s. per week for herself and the two children. One week he gave her 16s., but he only gives this generously promised 16s. when it seems good to him to do so. He is now earning from 36s. to 40s. per week.

He has never struck her. He has been very cruel, but I cannot say if his cruelty would be *cruel in the legal sense of the word.* The law would uphold him in using his power over the small properties of his wife—her little presents, her few possessions. She is now unfit to support herself, which comes from the stiff knee-joint, which was induced primarily by neglect and parsimony on the husband's part.

The charitable fund has done almost its last and utmost now for Mrs. A. If A. reflects about it, the lesson the distribution of this fund will teach him is this: that provided he treats his wife badly enough, he will be relieved of the necessity of supporting her; or that, in proportion as his contribution is small, the funds share in her maintenance will be large. Even if the funds be now exhausted, private charity *must* come forward to teach A. the same lessson if he likes to learn it.

We have legal authority for saying that it is very unlikely the Poor Law Guardians would relieve Mrs. A., and sue A. for her support.

Supposing we can find a solicitor to take up her case, and risk some £30 or so, costs in a case of separation, may it not happen that A—— may prefer to go to prison than pay these costs (supposing the verdict be in Mrs. A——'s favour), or her maintenance; and in this case, Mrs. A——would be quite without resources—worse off, even, than now. A——has little or nothing in the way of property which could be turned to the purpose of her support, or to defray the legal costs.

If I could give any idea of Mrs. A——'s patience and forbearance (no one, perhaps, has heard her say one hard word of her husband; at rare intervals, and under examination she has related bare facts), or the *charm* there is about this delicately pretty, helpless, child-like looking little woman, I should not despair of making this sad case interesting. It *will* be interesting, I trust, however badly stated, as illustrating those hardships of women for which the law affords only partial redress, if even *that*. Mrs. C—— says her experience tells her that there are *thousands* of cases parallel to Mrs. A——'s amongst the poor, and they are not unknown either among the educated and prosperous.

ART. VII.--FOREIGN NOTES AND NEWS.

FRANCE.

Sewing Schools in Paris.—The *Globe* says that in one of the principal streets of Paris a school has been started where ladies of the highest social position can learn the art of making their own dresses. Instruction is given them in the art of cutting out first the patterns, and then the stuff itself, of making up the materials, and, in fine, the whole mysteries, however intricate, of the dressmaker's art.

Women Compositors.—M. Emile Martinet, the proprietor of a large printing-office in Paris, has also, at Pluteaux, an extensive typographical training institute for women. Girls of ordinary education are admitted here from 13 to 15 years of age. M. Martinet states that of the sixty women now remaining with him, he can only say that their work is highly satisfactory.

Elementary Teachers.—Miss Oppenheim, a daughter of the well-known financier, has followed, the example of Madlle. Rothschild, by undergoing, at the Luxembourg, Paris, the examination which has to be passed before a certificate of ability to teach is granted.

SWITZERLAND.

Another lady has recently passed her examination as doctor of medicine at Zurich; she is the thirteenth who has done so. Two ladies have also taken their degrees in the philosophical faculty. There are several lady-students at Berne, and their diligence and capacity are highly praised by the Professors of that University.

ITALY.

A correspondent mentions that there is some thought of establishing a college for women at Florence, on a similar plan to Girton College, in connection with the Pisa University. The Italian Universities are all open to women, as is only natural and fair, considering that women in former days not unfrequently held professional chairs in them.

The *Nuova Antologia* for May, contains a very interesting article by Signora Caterina Pigorini Besa on the popular songs of the Marca. She has collected a large number of these songs herself, writing them down as they were repeated to her by the peasants. She gives many instances of the different kinds, all remarkable for their simple beauty and pathos.—*Academy.*

GERMANY.

German Factory Women.—According to the returns published by the German *Bundesrath*, close on 226,000 female hands above 16 years of age are engaged in German factories; nearly 24 per cent. are married. Of this number, 128,500 hands are engaged in the German textile industries.

The *Woman's Journal* publishes an account of the work done by certain women in Berlin in reducing the price of living in that city. "In 1866, Mrs. Lena Morgenstern, with two or three other ladies of wealth and influence, finding that the cost of provisions was enormous, established several Volk's Kuchen, or people's kitchens—restaurants where meals could be had at the retail cost of the materials alone. In 1873 these women determined to bring their charity into their own homes by forming a Housekeeper' Association, whose object should be the reduction of the cost of living, the promotion of plain and economical habits, and the improvement of the condition of servants. In 1874 there were 250 members. Co-operative laundries, bakeries, intelligence offices, and stores for groceries, meats, and provisions were opened, all under the supervision of women. At the present time the membership embraces 6,000 families, and issues a weekly paper of a high order, containing its price lists, etc. The central bureau imports its supplies direct from China, France, Java, the United States, etc., and is thus enabled to supply the co-operative trade throughout Europe. Coal is also purchased wholesale by the association, and sold in accurately measured cars, an improvement on our own system which every householder in New York or Philadelphia will appreciate. The whole of this vast business enterprise is managed—and accurately managed—by women. Their last annual statistical report is as suggestive and forcible a commentary as any sermon on Woman's duties, work and opportunities."

DENMARK.

The Countess Danner, widow of Frederick VII. of Denmark, has left her property, valued at nearly 4,000,000 dols., for the maintenance of an institution for orphan and deserted girls of Denmark. The castle of Jagerspris in North Zealand will be the central building of the institution, and accomodation for 600 or 800 girls will be provided.

NORWAY.

There is a Reading Club for ladies in Christiana, called "Laeseforeningen for Damer." It is situated at 25, Öfre Slotsgaden, Christiana.

RUSSIA.

The Russian Government has lately begun to throw many obstacles in the way of professional employment for women. Lately, in Moscow, a lady, Madame Kaschawarow Rudnew, having sent into the Faculty of Medicine at the University a dissertation, by means of which she hoped to gain her degree as an M.D., the Faculty appointed a committee of professors to examine her paper. This had hardly been done when the Minister for Public Education entered his veto, declaring that Russian law forbids women to follow the medical profession. The dissertation of Madame Kaschewarow Rudnew was thereupon sent back to her without having been examined. It is to be hoped that a more liberal policy will shortly be pursued.

AMERICA.

The Minnesota Legislature last winter accorded women the right to hold the office of School Director, and to vote for candidates for that office. Last month the ladies took their part in the local elections wherever School Board vacancies occurred.

Employment of Women in Chicago.—The Chicago *Times*, after recapitulating the number of women employed in the various departments of business in that city, concludes that the problem of female employment is rapidly nearing a solution. In Chicago there are 7,875 women employed in the following named businesses and vocations :—Dry goods, millinery, essence and candy manufactories, ready-made clothing, printing houses, type foundries, binderies, shirt manufactories, tobacco factories, tin workers, and cashiers. It says further that there is a lady residing in that city, who has erected a marble front residence out of her earnings, as a travelling saleswoman or commercial drummer. Female compositors find employment to the number of about 100. Several offices like that of the *Inland Monthly*, a publication most ably dedicated to the cause of

ument

woman, and nearly all the religious papers employ female compositors, and others that are not religious quietly further the cause of women's employment. From two to half-a-dozen may also be found in each of the morning paper offices, where they serve as "distributers." Seven hundred women are engaged in teaching.

The Natural History Society of the Kansas State University, has ladies for its Vice-President, Secretary and Treasurer. It publishes a monthly journal, called the "Observer of Nature."

At the annual meeting of the New York Ophthalmic Hospital, a diploma was awarded to Emma B. Ryder, M.D., of San Francisco. Mrs. Ryder is the second lady who has received the diploma of this institution. They are thereby authorized to practice ophthalmic and aural surgery.

BUENOS AYRES.

The Argentine Minister to the United States has received from the Minister of Public Instruction of his government, Dr. Leguizamon, a commission to engage four first-class lady normal-school teachers, for the new institution recently established in the Republic. The ladies must be well versed in English, French, grammar, general literature, hygiene, geography, history, natural sciences, music, drawing and teaching. They will make a contract for three years, and will be furnished with free passage to Buenos Ayres, and paid a salary of 1,800 dollars a year in gold, the salary to begin on the day they sail. Several American ladies have already been very successful in teaching in the Argentine Republic. The principal of the Normal School at Buenos Ayres is Mrs. Emma Frigent, of New York, who has been there for the last six years, and met with very gratifying success.

NEW ZEALAND.

The speech of Sir Julius Vogel, one of the principal members of the New Zealand Parliament, to his constituents at Wanganai, is reported in the the *Otago Daily Times*. Sir Julius Vogel has publicly stated that he is in favour of extending the franchise to women.

CAPE OF GOOD HOPE.

The *Cape Argus* has the following excellent article on women's employment:—"The subject of the employment of women in handicrafts and other industrial pursuits is one that has caused considerable discussion of late years in every civilised country. There are people who consider that to exclude women from workshops would be beneficial to society, but the number of this class is, we are glad to know, getting less every day. In Europe, America, and Australia many employments, formerly restricted to men, are now open to women. Every year the number of wage-earning girls and women is increasing, and how to employ them profitably becomes a serious matter. It may be said, we know, that here at the Cape there is no difficulty in finding employment for females, either as domestics or at needlework ; but there are many girls and women who are not willing to serve as menials nor strong enough to labour either with a needle or sewing-machine from morning till night. Women of this kind would willingly earn their bread at any other suitable employment, and in other parts of the world their services are utilised in factories and workshops of various kinds. We cannot think of any employment more suitable for an intelligent girl than a good deal of what is done in connection with a printing-office, and we find that in almost every country, women are engaged in such work as bookbinding and composing type. The heavier labour in these trades is done by men, but such light employment as folding and stitching sheets of paper together and setting type have been opened to females with great success. In Great Britain, France, and America, women are now earning large sums of money as bookbinders and compositors, and are thereby enabled not only to support themselves respectably, but also to contribute to the maintenance of members of their families.

We are glad to say that the employment of women in the manner indicated above has been tried at the Cape with the best results. Some three years ago Messrs. Saul Solomon and Co. engaged, as an experiment, a number of girls for the bookbinding branch of their business. The girls, as might be supposed, took readily to the work, consisting, as the part allotted to them did, of folding and stitching. They were quick, clean, and careful; and the result more than justified the most sanguine expectations that had been formed. A great deal of the success of the experiment is due to the Lady Superintendent, Miss Fairlie, whose knowledge of the business is only excelled by her tact and power of management. Encouraged by the success of the first experiment, Messrs. Saul Solomon and Co. recently resolved to make another, and a few months ago they engaged some girls to learn the art of setting type. The progress made by these girls has been so great that a larger number will be employed, and, in our advertising columns this morning, the firm calls for applications from girls willing to learn the trade. It may be well to state that the hours of work are from 8 a.m. to 5.30 p.m., with an hour for dinner in the middle of the day. The workrooms are airy, well-lit, and cheerful, and every care is taken for the comfort and health of the girls. We have little doubt that the latter will be as successful as the earlier experiment, and that the example set by Messrs. Saul Solomon and Co. will soon be followed by other employers of labour. There are numbers of women here who could be usefully and profitably employed in the lighter trades. At least one example has shown that they made excellent telegraph clerks, even at the Cape; and we have often wondered why, as in London, New York, and Melbourne, they are not employed in the General Post-office. Probably it has been from want of adequate accommodation. However, we hope the success achieved by Messrs. Saul Solomon and Co. will stimulate the Government and private persons to further the cause of the employment of women in this colony.

ART. VIII.—PARAGRAPHS.

Medicine as a Profession for Women.—Dr. Eliza W. Dunbar, in an article on the above subject in the *Ladies' Edinburgh Magazine*, says: "In the present day it is quite possible for a girl of sense, who can command a small income, to obtain a thorough medical education. The Universities of Paris and of Zurich admit women to all their classes without reserve, and a school of medicine for women has lately been established in London. Four or five years are required to complete the curriculum of study. Four to Four and a-half years suffice to acquire the knowledge necessary to obtaining a degree, and some six or twelve months should afterwards be spent in visiting the various schools of medicine at home and abroad.

"The first two years of study are devoted, by common consent, to the natural sciences, including Anatomy and Physiology. The student attends lectures on Botany, Zoology, Comparative Anatomy, Natural Philosophy and Chemistry, and is expected to work for some months in a chemical laboratory. The lists of subjects will doubtless appear formidable to the uninitiated. It would not be fair to say that only the most superficial knowledge of the sciences named can be acquired in two years, for with average ability and common industry it is possible in that time to learn more than the mere outlines, and at all events it is possible to know as much as is needful for practical purposes, and to satisfy examiners. The more attention is given to Natural Philosophy and Chemistry, the more thorough and the easier will be the study of Physiology; while the dry facts of Comparative Anatomy gain much interest when viewed from the standpoint of Physiology.

"The anatomy of the human body is learnt partly from lectures and books, but chiefly by dissecting; and microscope anatomy demands dexterity in handling the microscope, and fine handiwork which need not be here described. After the student has been introduced to the natural sciences, and knows the structure of the human body (Anatomy), as well as the manner in which its functions are performed in health (Physiology), she is then fitted to begin the study of Pathology, *i.e.*, the science of disease, and therapeutics, or the treatment of disease. General Pathology and special Pathology, or diseases of special organs, are treated of in lectures and illustrated at the bedside. The various methods of discovering and determining diseases are to be carefully acquired from oral instruction and by constant practice. Medicine is divided into two branches: Surgery and Internal Medicine, a division determined by separate modes of treatment. Neither branch should be neglected for the other. Diseases of the eye, ear, throat, and skin have recently developed into separate and large departments, and the student must not consider her education complete without a knowledge of all the departments of disease. When the last examination is passed and the degree obtained, the new-made doctor must rely upon her own powers of observation and her faculty of learning from experience, as well as of making intelligent use of the experience of others, if she is to be truly successful as a medical practitioner.

"It is possible to board, lodge, dress plainly, pay fees, and all the expences of education, for £100 per annum, in Paris, and in Zurich, and I believe in London also. For examinations and expenses in connection with them, about £30 extra must be reckoned.

"It is very important to acquire the habit of study and some preliminary knowledge before commencing the medical curriculum, as it will otherwise present great difficulties. Besides a good English education, which should be a *sine quâ non*, Mathematics, Latin, German, and French are especially useful to the medical student. Mathematics trains the mind to habits of accurate thought, and facilitates the study of Natural Philosophy and Physiology. A little knowledge of Latin is essential, and every doctor ought to be able to read French and German works on medicine. The matriculation examinations of the London University, and of the Apothecaries' Hall, are open to women; and every girl who intends to be a doctor should pass one or the other—if possible, the London University examination, as its requirements are much higher than that of the Apothecaries' Hall. Information respecting these examinations may be obtained from the Registrar of the University, and from the Secretary of the Society of Apothecaries."

Women as Steel Engravers.—At the present time there
are only two women in the United States notable for
first-class engraving on steel. These are Miss Sartain,
daughter of Mr. John Sartain, chief of the Art Department of the Centennial Exhibition, and Mrs. Wormley,
of Columbus, Ohio. Miss Sartain had the good fortune
to be educated in her art by her accomplished father,
whose task of engraving Rothermel's latest picture, the
"Battle of Gettysburg," she lately returned from Europe
to assume in part, that he might accept the honourable
appointment offered him. Mrs. Wormley, who first
became expert in drawing, devoted herself to the illustration of a large work which her husband, a distinguished chemist, wrote on poison. After she finished
the drawings they were sent to some Eastern city to be
engraved. A difficulty arose—no engraver could be
found willing to undertake the microscopic work
required. It was the opinion of engravers who were
consulted that only the artist who drew the pictures
could successfully engrave them. Thus compelled to
finish the work, the wife of Dr. Wormley learned the
art of engraving, engraved the plates, and enjoys the
honour of having contributed so largely to the beauty
and completeness of a celebrated scientific treatise.
The work in progress at the wood-carving school at
Cincinnati, under the direction of Mrs. Pittman, has been
highly praised, and will be a unique contribution to the
Women's Department from Ohio.—*Colorado Springs Gaz.*

Women and Savings' Banks.—The first savings' bank
was started by Miss Priscilla Wakefield in the parish of
Tottenham, Middlesex, towards the close of the last
century, her object being mainly to stimulate the fru-
gality of poor children. The experiment proved so
successful, that, in 1799, the Rev. Joseph Smith, of
Wendon, commenced a plan of receiving small sums
from his parishioners during summer, and returning
them at Christmas with the addition of one third, as a
stimulus to prudence and forethought. Miss Wakefield,
in her turn, followed Mr. Smith's example, and, in 1804,
extended her work so as to include adult labourers,
women servants and others. A similar institution was
formed at Bath, in 1808, by several ladies of that city.
—"Thrift," by Samuel Smiles.

Englishwoman's Review.

CONTENTS FOR JULY, 1876.

All Communications to be addressed to the EDITOR, 22, Berners
Street, Oxford Street, W.

Post-Office Orders payable to SARAH LEWIN, at the "Regent
Street" Post-Office.

TERMS OF SUBSCRIPTION AT THE OFFICE.

Per Annum (Post Free), Six Shillings.
*Subscriptions payable in Advance.   Single Numbers posted Free on
receipt of Six Postage Stamps.*

MSS. are carefully read, and if not accepted are returned, on receipt
of Stamps for Postage, but the Editor cannot be responsible for any
accidental loss.

Contributions should be legibly written, and only on one side of
each leaf.

.THE

ENGLISHWOMAN'S REVIEW.

(NEW SERIES.)

No. XXXIX.—July 15th, 1876.

Art. I.—HARRIET MARTINEAU.

One of the greatest women that our generation has known, an able writer, a deep thinker, a warm-hearted philanthropist, has gone from us. At the age of seventy-four Harriet Martineau has passed away. When she was in the zenith of her fame, few English writers, certainly no other woman, exercised so great an influence on public opinion. We have had many writers of more genius, but none perhaps have excelled her in the power of clearly putting before her readers, what she believed to be the truth. Her talent lay in her simple un-exaggerated style, her practical clearheadedness, her unswerving integrity, her intense sympathy with all that appertained to progress, even though she might incur obloquy and danger in maintaining it, and her enormous capacity for work.

Miss Martineau was born at Norwich on the 13th of June, 1802. Her family was originally of French Protestant origin but had settled in Norwich in 1688. She was educated with her brothers, but even in her childhood her health was delicate, and there is said to have been no evidence of her subsequent abilities. She began to write before she was twenty. Many of her first works were of a devotional character. One of these "Traditions of Palestine" first drew public attention to

T

her. In 1829 she and her sisters lost their small property, but she continued to write with unabated energy. In 1832 she brought out, after discouragement, and anxiety caused by such repeated rejection from the publishers, as would have driven a less energetic spirit from the field of literature, the first volume of her "Illustrations of Political Economy." To many, these tales gave a first idea of what is meant by political economy, hitherto supposed to be a harsh uninviting science. These tales, rapidly followed by "Illustrations of Political Taxation," and "Poor Laws and Paupers," secured her reputation not only because it was so unusual a subject for a woman's pen, but from the intrinsic excellence of the work. The "Girl in Norwich" of whom Lord Brougham wrote that she did more to make the principles of political economy understood than any other writer, became at once famous.

As a writer of fiction, she was not pre-eminent, and never estimated herself highly in this branch: though there is a simple charm and pathos about her books for children which few have surpassed. "Miss Martineau's are the only books which do not make me frightened at reading about God," said a little nervously-sensitive girl, one day, and the childish criticism bore testimony to the sweet and tender piety which underlies her writings. Another powerful fascination in her works was her intense appreciation and ability to reproduce natural scenery. Whether in Egypt, the tropical islands of the western seas, or the Norwegian fjords, the scene rises vividly before our eyes as we read.

Popularity brought both social and literary engagements, and after the publication of her "Tales" her life was of the busiest. In 1834 she went to America, where she remained two years; her work there is thus described in the *Daily News*: "She hoped to learn some secrets of success in the treatment of criminals, the insane, and other unhappy classes, and in the diffusion of education. She succeeded in her aims to some measure, but the anti-slavery question just at that time absorbed every other ... For some months preceding her return, she was subjected to insult and injury, and was even for some weeks in danger of her life, while travelling where

the tarbarrel, the cowhide, and the pistol were the
regimen prescribed for and applied to abolitionists, and
threatened especially in her case."

It is in her book on " Society in America " that, so far
as we know, she first gave utterance to her belief that
women needed political representation—a doctrine of
which she was the firm adherent to the close of her life.
She says in chapter iii. section vii:—

" The interests of women who have fathers and husbands can never
be identical with theirs, while there is a necessity for laws to protect
women against their husbands and fathers. This statement is not
worth another word.

" Some who desire that there should be an equality of property
between men and women, oppose representation on the ground that
political duties would be incompatible with the other duties which
women have to discharge. The reply to this is, that women a·e the
best judges here. God has given time and power for the discharge
of all duties, and if he had not, it would be for women to decide which
they would take and which they would leave . . . . The truth
is, that while there is so much said about the 'sphere of woman,' two
widely different notions are entertained of what is meant by the phrase.
The narrow, and to the ruling party, the more convenient notion, is
that sphere appointed by men, and bounded by their idea of propriety—a notion from which any and every woman may fairly dissent.
The broad and true conception is of the sphere appointed by God, and
bounded by the powers which he has bestowed. This commands the
assent of man and woman, and only the question of powers remains
to be proved."

About this time (1835) Miss Aitken writes of her as
likely to undertake the direction of a newspaper intended
solely to discuss women's questions. This, however,
was never started. On her return from America she
was at once occupied in literary undertakings, which
were principally of an historical and social character.
Her " Household Education " was one of the most popular, and contains the germ of many suggestions upon
girls' education which are being fully elaborated at the
present day. Her condensation of Comte's " Positive
Philosophy " was another successful attempt to popula-
rise a difficult subject. Her histories were clear and
condensed ; she made no pretension to deep research,
but what she told, she told with such simplicity and
clearness, that it is impossible to forget it.

The mere titles of her works as drawn up by herself
for the *Daily News*, is complete evidence of her unflag-

ging industry; the more when we reflect that so large a portion of her life was passed in ill-health, and under the shadow of a malady which it was feared, though groundlessly, would end her life thirty years ago. Many of her books being written for specially temporary purposes have been forgotten; many others are household words with us all. We subjoin the list:—

"My Servant Rachel," 1827, 1 vol.; "Christmas Day," and "The Friends" (continuation), 2 vols.; "Principle and Practice," and "Sequel," 1827, 2 vols.; "Devotional Exercises," 1 vol.; "Addresses, Prayers, and Hymns," 1 vol.; Prize Essays (on Catholicism, Judaism, and Mohammedanism), 1830, 3 vols.; "The Children who Lived by the Jordan" (a Sunday School tale), 1836, 1 vol.; "Five years of Youth," 1830, 1 vol.; "Seven Tracts for Houlston," 1830, 7 vols.; "Traditions of Palestine," 1830, 1 vol.; "Illustrations of Political Economy," 1832, 25 vols.; "Illustrations of Political Taxation, 1834, 5 vols.; "Poor Laws and Paupers," 1833, 4 vols.; "The Playfellow," 1841, 4 vols.; "Letter to the Deaf," 1834, 1 vol.; "Society in America," 1837, 3 vols.; "Retrospect of Western Travel," 1838, 3 vols.; "Deerbrook," 1838, 3 vols.; "Guide to Service," 4 vols.; "The Hour and the Man," 1840, 3 vols.; "The Billow and the Rock," 1846, 1 vol. "Dawn Island," (Anti-Corn Law League Bazaar), 1845, 1 vol.; "Sketches from Life," 1856, 1 vol.; "Forest and Game Law Tales," 1845, 3 vols.; "Eastern Life. Present and Past," 1848, 3 vols." "Life in the Sick Room," 1843, 1 vol.; "Household Education," 1848, 1 vol.; "Miscellanies," (an American reprint of Essays, Reviews, &c.), 1836, 2 vols.; "How to Observe Morals and Manners," (one of a series); 1838, 1 vol; "Letters on Mesmerism," 1844, 1 vol.; "History of the Thirty Years' Peace" and Introduction, 1849-50, 3 vols.; England and Her Soldiers," (written for F. Nightingale's objects), 1859. 1 vol.; "Letters from Ireland," for "Daily News," 1852, 1 vol.; "Positive Philosophy" of Auguste Comte (translation and abridgement of lecture), 1853, 2 vols; "Guide to the English Lakes," 1855, 1 vol.; "British Rule in India," 1857, 1 vol.; "Future Government of India," 1858, 1 vol.; "Letters on Man's Nature and Development," (the greater part by Mr Atkinson). 1851. 1 vol.; "Health, Husbandry, and Handicraft," 1861. 1 vol.; "Endowed Schools of Ireland," (pamphlet), 1859, 1 vol.; "Biographical Sketches," (from "Daily News"). 1869, 1 vol.; "The Sister Brides," Poem in Miss Faithfull's ("Welcome to the Prince of Wales"), 1863; Annual Papers for "The Liberty Bell," Boston; Articles in "Cornhill," 3; Articles in "Chambers' Journal," 3; Articles in "Macmillan," 2; Articles in "Daily News," 1,642; Articles in "Edinburgh Review," 12; Articles in "Westminster Review," many; Articles in "Quarterly Review," 1; Articles in "Once a Week," 175; Articles in "Anti-Slavery Standard," 96; Articles in "Spectator," 19; Four Letters of an Englishwoman, "Daily News," 1870.

The last work she wrote was a preface to Pauli's "Simon de Montford."

Her sympathy with whatever was right and just remained her strongest characteristic. She was, from the time of her visit to America, a firm abolitionist. In her little cottage at Ambleside she gave lectures to the working people of the neighbourhood. Her interest in education, particularly in that of women, was unfailing; her sympathy could be relied on in every effort to get women freer employment and better opportunities of culture. The last work of her hands was a worsted-work ottoman, destined to be sold, through Mrs. Josephine Butler, as her contribution to the Society for the Suppression of Vice. Some one would buy it, she thought, as being her work. In fact there was hardly a subject of practical social usefulness to which she had not at some portion of her life given diligent and appreciative attention.

Harriet Martineau was buried, on July 1st, at the Old Cemetery, Birmingham, where her mother, one of her brothers, and other relatives are interred. Her funeral, according to her wish, was of a very private character, and there were not above fifty persons present. Her name is, and long will be a revered one wherever the English tongue is spoken, and wherever persevering energy and unwavering rectitude are valued at their true worth.

Art. II.—WOMEN'S DEPARTMENT IN THE PHILADELPHIA EXHIBITION.

THE *New Century for Women* is a weekly journal of eight pages which is published by the Women's Centennial Executive Committee at Philadelphia; all the work in it is done by women. Its object is to show what part women have taken and are taking in the work of the world, and to receive suggestions for bettering that work. Its first numbers contain very interesting accounts of the Women's Department in the Philadelphia Exhibition. This department by no means represents

the entire share which women have had in the Exhibition.
Much female work, from the painting of delicate china
to the burnishing of guns and the making of cigars, is to
be found in the other buildings by the side of men's
work, and many women exhibitors have preferred to
send their work to the general departments—their
ploughs to the Agricultural Hall, and their pictures to
the Art Gallery. Many others who have patiently
elaborated ideas and developed mechanical ability which
would have given them a high place in the Exhibition,
have been prevented by circumstances from sending
anything. Even the admirable preparations in Materia
Medica, made by the students of the Philadelphia
Woman's College, could not have occupied their place
had it not been for the thoughtful and liberal appropriation made to them by the Woman's Commission. The
object of the Committee in making a special women's
department was not to show to the world all that women
workers were able to do, so much as to help them to
gain a more definite place as workers, and increase their
opportunities of doing good work. Imperfect as it is, it
forms a complete refutation of the assertion which is so
often made, that women are not inventors.

The Women's Department covers about an acre in
extent, and is very simply built. In the South-east
corner are the Patents, Inventions, and Needlework, and
in the North-east corner of the building, the space is
filled with looms and their women workers.

One of the most important inventions which the *New
Century for Women* mentions, is the system for night
signals for the use of the Navy department, by Mrs.
Coston; it has complete apparatus for the saving of life
or property at sea or on the coast. The idea of the invention originated with her husband, Benjamin Coston, who
so long ago as 1840 made trial of it by order of the Hon.
Sec. of the Navy. He died before he had perfected it
for practical purposes, leaving his widow in possession
of a rough plan of the idea, but without the complete
combination of chemicals necessary for its perfection.
The system consists in the combination of different
coloured pyrotechnical fires in a case to represent certain figures or numbers, according to a pre-arranged

chart. They have been tested in various ways and in different states of the atmosphere. The small-size signal can be well seen at a distance of from four to six miles, and the large-size of from six to ten or fifteen miles, with perfect distinctness. The Secretary of the United States' Navy has ordered three hundred sets of Coston's Telegraphic Signals for distribution to vessels of the United States' Navy, after several very successful trials at Washington by ;boards of officers convened for this purpose. The most favourable reports were received after a period of from one to two years, from all the United States' squadrons in different parts of the world to which the above-named three hundred sets of Coston's Signals had been distributed, and upon these reports Congress based its action in purchasing the right to use the patent for the Navy of the United States.

In another section of the building is a small tank of water, in which are floating models of the Life Preserving Mattress, invented by Mrs. B. Mountain, of New York; this is used as the ordinary berth mattress, and is reversible so as to make no difference which side is uppermost when thrown into the water. This invention has been officially approved by the Board of United States' Supervising Inspectors of steamboats, and adopted for use as an auxiliary life-saving appliance, in lieu of boats or rafts, an allowance being made of two persons to each mattress. It is expected that a trial of its efficiency will be made this summer.

Mrs. Edson, Massachusetts, exhibits an India-rubber life-preserver, self-inflating, and adjusted in half a minute.

An invention called a horse-protector is exhibited by Mrs. Ruth, of Philadelphia. It is a horse blanket lifted slightly from the body by a slender wire frame extending over the head, and is of great use in protecting the animals from the fierce summer heat.

In scientific branches we find the Pharmaceutical collection from the Woman's Medical College, of Philadelphia; of its merits experts must judge, as determining woman's fitness for this new field of business. Specimens of artificial teeth are deposited by Dr. Annie D. Ramborger, dentist, Philadelphia, and noteworthy as the work of the only woman dentist in Philadelphia,

regularly graduated in the Dental College. Fish preserved in alcohol, and glass vials with other contents
interesting to those engaged in fish culture, come from
Miss F. W. Webber, New Hampshire. Mrs. French, a
Philadelphia physician, also exhibits a glass case full of
patent electro-magnetic appliances for the human body,
bands, lung protectors, &c.

In household economy a mangle and ironer, patented
by Mrs. S. Short in 1873, claims to do its work rapidly
and well without a skilled worker, and even to polish
collars and cuffs in a superior manner. The same inventor shows a blanket washer, which appears to be
very good, and a frame for stretching and drying lace
curtains, evidently well adapted to facilitate this trouble-
some process. Another dish-washer made of galvanized
wire, is invented by Mrs. Charlotte H. Sterling, Ohio;
and a dust-catcher by Elizabeth M. Page. This last is
a large pan on rollers, into which the house-maid sweeps.

A neat little tin lunch-box, with divisions inside,
heated by a spirit lamp beneath is patented by Mrs. M.
Bradley, New York; and a gridiron for beefsteaks, with
receptacle for gravy, by Mrs. Grahame, Pennsylvania.
Also a magic rolling-pin, made of tin, holding various
conveniences inside, by Mrs. Hunkins, of the same state.
Mrs. A. S. Sherwood's fountain griddle-greaser and
scraper looks ready to make easy work of baking hot
cakes, so important a part of American household
economy. A sewing machine, invented by a woman,
which threads its own needles, is shown; a model for
cemetery allotments, with ornamental recessed rail, for
the growth of flowers, is shown by Mrs. Stigale, Philadelphia, sole inventor and patentee; and a combined
travelling bag and chair, by C. Lammonier, New York;
a mathematical measurement system of dress and garment cutting, invented by Miss L. E. Robbins, which
is stated to be taught with great success in the public
schools in Boston. On a platform stands a very large
and comprehensive library desk, which can be folded
into narrow space, invented by Mrs. Styles, of Philadelphia. It includes three patents, the inkstand, paper
file, and combination desk. The lady had no thought
of becoming an inventor. Her improvements grew out

of the exigencies of her position, because nothing could be found in the market to meet her wants. We were informed that the government office opposite has ordered one of these desks, thus endorsing their merit. The same inventor shows some hanging ink-stands and bouquet-holders. Here is also a bedstead, used to show off two patents—rods for mosquito netting, and iron brackets on which the mattress rests, instead of the old fashioned wooden slats, which every housekeeper knows are unsatisfactory things. Miss Woodward, Vermont, sends a work-table of her own invention, very convenient, neat, and compact.

Two cases of great interest to botanists exhibit the Native Flora of Illinois, in a herbarium prepared by Mrs. P. V. Hathaway. Here are grasses, wild flowers, the blossoms of shrubs, varieties of ferns—the subject seems to be treated exhaustively. North American mosses are treated in the same thorough manner, judging by the number and wonderful variety of the specimens, dried and neatly arranged on cards, by Miss Jennie Watson.

A case of birds, life-like in appearance, is stated to have been *shot* and stuffed by Mrs. Sarah E. Bonny, of Mass., Taxidermist, who also exhibits feather work, a muff and tippet, and fans skilfully put together. Some articles made by Indian women, of Indian Territory,— bead-work, with which all are familiar, a quiver made of fur, a trunk cover embroidered, and other things of very primitive construction, find place in the exhibition. In another case is a muff and cape manufactured by a Maryland lady from the silky soft contents of the seed- pod of the silkweed *asclepias syriaca*. Hair jewellery of very fine workmanship is exhibited by Madame Schmitt of Philadelphia. Wax flowers of great beauty are exhibited by another Philadelphia lady, and natural flowers preserved by a chemical process which is patented by Mrs. Ware, also of the same city. A Danish lady in New York who takes pupils in the art, sends specimens of spatter work, remarkable for tasteful design and skilful execution.

The Schools of Design from Massachusetts flank the Art Gallery on its western side, with their fine painted tiles, tile and wood-work, crayons, decorated china, a table-top in painted china, with delicate hare-bells and wild-roses, designs for wall-paper, carpets, oil-cloths, and lace-work. At the northern end is the Cincinnati School of Design, with lovely paintings in china, and fine carved furniture, all by women.

Among the American lady artists who have contributed pictures to the Exhibition, Miss Anne Lea, Mrs. C. A. Fassitt, Miss Granbery, (flower painting), Miss F. Bridges, and Miss Ellen Hale are mentioned with especial commendation. A picture by Miss Maria Oakey of a "A woman serving" is also said to be excellent

In the dress and needlework departments may especially be mentioned the improved under-clothing for women and children, by Mrs. Flint of Boston. This, while making no change in appearance of the dress, removes the weight of dragging skirts which is so injurious to health. Madame Brosse, of Philadelphia, exhibits models for fitting ladies' dresses by self-measurement, for which she can show a silver medal awarded her at the state fair of California, in 1872. Silk embroideries, tapestry pictures, oil paintings on silk, specimens of trimming and of ornamental needlework of all kinds, are in great profusion as might be expected. Beautiful specimens of needlework, embroidery and lace have also been sent from England. The women of Sweden send embroidery ornaments made of fish scales, and picture frames of a snow-white substance, which looks like leather. They also show figures dressed in the national costume. Canada sends embroideries, painted velvet, and laces, which are very fine, though not quite equal to those of Belgium. From Brazil come embroidered cushions and great bouquets of feather flowers; and Turkey sends squares of dark cloth, embroidered in gold and silver. From Madeira there is some beautiful work.

We must congratulate our friends in America on the success which has attended their efforts: doubtless the immediate result of this portion of the Exhibition will be to open new fields of exertion to women workers, and eventually it may lead to the more generous recognition of their work in the labour market, and their juster remuneration. There is frequently too much truth in

the accusation that women play at work, but the success
of this Exhibition shows that their productions will bear
a favourable comparison even with the first-class work
of men, in those branches of labour where they have had
equal chances and education.

The *New Century for Women*, mentions another profession for women, which we will notice here, though it
is not connected with the Exhibition. A lady in New
York is training a number of women for the business of
life insurance, making the insurance of women's lives a
speciality. The examining physicians are women, and
it promises to be a success.

ART. III.—ANOTHER NOBLE WOMAN.

THE news that George Sand was dead did not surprise
any one, for it had long been known that she was slowly
wasting away, but to many, even here in England, it
was a sad reflection that as the last quarter of the century was beginning, the gifted writer to whose powers
of fascination they had owed so many hours of enjoyment had passed from the world. For to many of us
George Sand has been more than a novelist, she has
been a teacher of political and philosophical truths.
When she began to write Europe was entering on the
era of democratic agitation. which, after thirty years
duration, has changed the face of society in France,
consolidated Germany, and freed Italy from foreign
despotism. There were great moral uprisings even
where there was no actual fighting. It was a time of
social earthquake, and the more brilliant novelists of
the day naturally addressed themselves to the sentiment
of democracy and revolt against old conventional
tyrannies. George Sand herself was, if we may for a
moment coin an English word, a "revolt" against the
spirit in which her ancestors had been born and lived.
Yet this "revolt" began not with her, but with her
father. The Baron Dupin, the descendant of princely,

if not royal houses, threw himself with the ardour of a young crusader into the ranks of the Republican army, preaching democracy and fraternity by his own example. He lived among his soldiers, he chose a wife from the people, but he manifested the chivalry and loyalty of his ancestors in standing firm by his young wife when all the power of his aristocratic relations was exerted to annul the marriage. From such a father the daughter could inherit only a loyal and noble nature, but she lost him early, and her education was carried on by her warm-hearted but plebeian mother and her aristocratic grandame, who was herself a strange product of the French Revolution and the *ancien régime,* a mixture of the theoretical democracy of Rousseau with the courtly instincts of the old aristocracy. The two women quarrelled over the child, and the child saw the difference between them and reflected upon it, and perhaps from this conflict of castes and natures so widely different she learned that wonderful insight into the common humanity of the high and the lowly that makes her books not only the most fascinating of brilliant novels, but also works of profound philosophy. When, in answer to the Baroness Amelie de Rudolstadt's supposition that the queenly beauty of the Zingara Girl indicates remote descent from some illustrious house, Consuelo asks if it is impossible that virtuous peasantry can transmit beauty and dignity to their children, we seem to feel a denunciation against known quantities of unconfessed flunkeyism, or secret pride laid up in our own inward soul, which is not soothed by the reflection made in the caverns of the Illuminati that all who count old nobility among their ancestry are the descendants of men stained with the blood of the poor and oppressed, who have suffered under them. This, however, is the assertion of the Illuminati, not of George Sand; but throughout her books there are scattered sentences that contain the sense of whole pages of philosophical and psychological discussion, and give us, along with intellectual enjoyment, sudden revelations of truths unknown as yet to ourselves. The brave old peasant flogging the young noble for wantonly killing his pet owl, fearless of the terrible revenge the young tyrant

might exercise upon him; the boy aristocrat, vindictive
and savage as a young wolf, yet too conscious of the
obligations of chivalry binding on his race to take
revenge by any other hand than his own, and both boy
and old man suddenly recognising that the chastisement
had been but the assumption of the despotism of brute
force, though they only occupy a few pages in the extraordinary tale of Mauprat, are considerations not profitless
to any mind, nor easily forgotten. The faults of decorum
in George Sand's books will be pardoned, for they were
the reaction against cruel and false social relations, and
would probably never have been written had she lived
in England, where marriage is more or less a consequence
of love, and had she not been a witness of the heartless mercenary marriages of France. When she has to
speak of real conjugal affection her ideal is as pure as it
is high. But her ideas, right or wrong, upon marriage,
occupy but a small part of her greatest works and will
not be remembered. It is for her real sympathy with
the poor and hard working, for her great insight into
human nature, for the truth so honestly spoken, that
humanity is the same in the rich as in the poor, in the
learned and wise, and in the ignorant and fearful; in
man, powerful in arm and honest by reason of his brute
strength; in woman, weak and suffering, and slavish
from that weakness; in the wicked and the good; in the
king and in the peasant; in the robber and the priest;
it is for stating that truth, as few writers have dared to
state it and few still have been able to place it so vividly
before us, that Aurore Dupin will be loved and venerated
while Europe keeps its memory for the great men and
women who have worked and suffered for its regeneration.

S. S.

Art. IV.—EVENTS OF THE MONTH.

EDUCATION.

NORTH LONDON COLLEGIATE AND CAMDEN SCHOOL FOR GIRLS.

THE distribution of prizes of this school took place on June 15th, in St. James' Hall. James Wyld, Esq., J.P., Master of the Clothworkers' Company, occupied the chair, and Mrs. Wyld distributed the prizes.

The report stated that there were 842 pupils in the two schools; that a grant of a hundred guineas had again been made by the Clothworkers to found Scholarships, and that the leaving Scholarship had been gained by Miss Hester Armstead, and the other Scholarships by Miss Mary Pailthorpe, Miss Florence Williams, Miss Ellen Anderson, and Miss Edith Jackson; that in the London University Examination for Wouen Miss Armstead had also obtained the Gilchrist Scholarship, 50 guineas for three years, tenable at Girton College; that since these examinations were established 16 girls had obtained certificates, 8 in honours, and 8 in the 1st class, and 9 special certificates of higher proficiency; that the Reid Scholarship had been awared to Miss Mary Greig, the R. W. Buss Scholarship to Miss Anette Crowdy, the Crane Scholarship to Miss Maude Meger. the Maclean-Fraser Scholarship to Miss Edith Miall. In the Cambridge Examination out of 53 seniors two only had failed in preliminary arithmetic; and that in this examination Miss Sara Burstall had obtained half the prize offered to the best senior girl by the Cambridge Syndicate; also a prize for geography, political economy, and Shakespeare paper; that two old pupils, Miss Eliza Baker and Miss Alice Betham, had succeeded in obtaining at Cambridge a certificate of having passed an examination equivalent to the B.A. degree; that a large addition has been made to the library; and that Professor Henslow had kindly contributed several gifts of botanical and geological specimens, and Mr. Vacher of mineralogical specimens.

The REV. D. ABBOTT moved the adoption of the report. He congratulated the schools on the result of the Cambridge Local Examinations, because any school that could pass so large a number as thirty-seven in those examinations must be doing a very great and noble work. He had heard it whispered that the schools had passed most creditably as compared with schools for boys; but comparisons were odious and he would say no more.

The REV. PHILIP MAGNUS said that he found the proficiency in arithmetic throughout the school was exceedingly satisfactory, and he thought that praise was due, not only in respect of this, but other things, to Miss

Elford for the excellent manner in which she conducted
the Camden School for Girls. He had not inspected
that school except by results, which testified to the
admirable way in which it was conducted, it being now
an efficient training school for the Higher Schools in the
Camden road. One of the most important features of the
school was that it involved the burning question in University circles as to the desirability of admitting women to the
University examinations. That was a question much discussed at the present time, but from the experience he had
had of the mental faculties of women he felt sure that there
were many who would be able to distinguish themselves
at the universities if admitted. Besides, the admission
of women to degrees would stimulate the cause of female
education throughout the country. It was said by some
that women ought to be admitted to the medical professions, but that art and law were too difficult for the
capabilities of women; but others dissented, thinking
the medical profession was one too shocking for women
to take up. It would, perhaps, be best to open the
degrees to women on both sides. He was the inspector
appointed by the University of London to examine the
pupils in those schools, and he might state that recently
Lord Granville, as the Chancellor of the University, in
presenting some degrees spoke about the results of the
inspection of the North-London Collegiate School in
very high terms of praise.

The Report of the Cambridge Local Examinations,
senior class, is very encouraging in its comparative tables
of the proficiency of girls and boys. The North-London
Collegiate School for girls sent in 53 pupils of whom 37
passed; 16 failed, (these were not picked candidates but
entire classes belonging to the Upper Middle and Middle
of the School; of these only 2 failed in arithmetic, and 2
in grammar). Of boy schools entered at the same time,
one sent 23 pupils, 12 of whom failed (4 in arithmetic
and 3 in grammar); another boy's school sent 14 pupils
of whom 6 failed, (1 in arithmetic and 4 in grammar);
and a third sent 21 pupils, 9 of whom failed (7 in arithmetic). Thus, in subjects considered usually essentially
masculine, arithmetic and grammar, the girls have done

better than the boys. It may be added also that those girls of the North-London Collegiate School who have passed the Cambridge Local Examinations were working in the course prescribed in the London University Examination for women.

BELFAST LADIES' COLLEGIATE SCHOOL.

On June 29th the annual distribution of prizes took place in the lecture hall of the school Lower Crescent, Belfast. Sir John Savage took the chair. Mrs. Byers, the lady principal, read the report which was a very gratifying one; the school now contains 220 pupils. She said, "money given as rewards, and also to enable girls of limited means to obtain a higher education, and thereby fit themselves better for the practical struggle of life, is a new feature in the history of girls' education. At the recent sitting of the General Assembly everyone interested in this subject must have felt gratified when an eminent professor advocated the formation of scholarships to prepare those noble women for their work who are now devoting themselves to the elevation of their degraded sisters in India. In connection with our own work, I have also an interesting announcement to make. A Southern lady, whose daughter was educated here, has placed at my disposal a cheque for £10 to encourage education in this school. A Belfast lady very recently gave me a £5 note, to be used in a similar way. Another £5 has since come into my hands for this purpose. An additional £100 would be given to be funded for a scholarship to help struggling worth, on condition that £300 more would be raised for this purpose, and that two or three gentlemen would volunteer to take charge of the money and award the prize."

The REV. W. JOHNSTONE said among the many important changes passing over the town there was none more important or more interesting than the provision within a comparatively few years past for the higher education of ladies. In our own times, as they were all aware, there were a large number of reverses and vicissitudes of fortune, and the report suggested that some provision should be made to help those suffering under the misfortune of adversity to have their mental faculties and powers properly developed. They should, therefore, found a bursarship, and give a scholarship for one or more of the daughters of professional men or merchants who have been unsuccessful, and are labouring under difficulties in social life. In their General Assembly a similar movement had been made to educate the sons and daughters of poor ministers; and he was sure if the present movement were properly ventilated it would commend itself to a very large number, not only in Belfast but in the provinces.

Several other gentlemen also spoke in favour of the bursarship, and by the close of the meeting, a large portion of the necessary £300 had been promised:—*Abridged from the Northern Whig.*

UNIVERSITY COLLEGE, LONDON.

The annual distribution of prizes in the Faculties of Arts and Laws and of Science in connection with University College, took place on June 22nd. Among the recipients of prizes were a good number of ladies, namely:— Political Economy: Prize, Ada Heather Bigg, of London. Roman Law: Prize, Eliza Orme; ditto, Third Certificate of Honour, Mary Eliza Richardson, of London. Geology: Prize, equal, Catherine Raisin, of London; C. Eardley-Wilmot, of London. Fine Art.—Painting from Life: £10 and Silver Medal, Eliza A. Lemann, of Bathampton: Drawing from Life: £5 and Silver Medal, Ellen M. Woods, of Cardiff. Drawing from the Antique: Prize Louisa G. A. Jackson, of Southport. Anatomical Drawings: Prize, Ellen M. Busk, of London. Fine Art Anatomy: Prize, Ellen M. Woods, of Cardiff.

The Chairman, Mr. GOSHEN, M.P., said he was particularly interested in observing that not only had the ladies distinguished themselves, as they had done greatly, in fine arts, but they had also taken prizes in political economy and in Roman law—studies which were not always pursued by ladies. As regarded political economy, he was glad to find that ladies were taking up what men were too much neglecting in these days.

Bloomsbury College for Men and Women.—The annual summer social meeting of the teachers and students of

U

this college was held on June 23rd at the rooms in
Queen square. The institution, which was originally
known as the Working Women's College, was established with a view to affording persons who are occupied
during the day an easy access to the higher branches of
culture. For the most part the classes are taught
gratuitously, and one of the objects of the promoters is
to foster a system of mutual help and fellowship between
the students and teachers. The social comfort of the
former is secured by means of a coffee-room, where discussions are held on subjects which are calculated to
interest the debaters. At present the students number
about 300, but in the winter term the attendance is
larger. The Saturday lectures are a special feature of
the college curriculum, which includes, besides, special
subjects, the fees for which are exceedingly moderate.
The list of occasional lecturers and examiners includes
Professor Sheldon Amos, Miss Frances Power Cobbe,
Mr. Hughes (Principal of the Working Men's College),
Professor Morley, Professor Seeley, and others.

Kinder Gartens.—The *Times* says : "Now that the Kinder Garten
system of education is beginning to attract wider attention in England,
and, through the School Boards in London and other large towns, is
becoming an object of public interest, readers may be glad to know
that a Fröbel Society exists in London, devoted, as its name indicates,
to making known the principles of the founder of the Kinder Garten,
and to extend the work through the country. The society, which
has existed but a short time, has not the funds necessary for publishing good translations from the German or good English tracts on the
subject, which would, perhaps, be the most useful office it could perform. It has confined its operations hitherto to two points—
encouraging the training of Kinder Garten teachers, and holding
monthly meetings at which some paper connected with the subject is
read and discussed. Teachers, who are now in considerable request,
are trained in several different places. Manchester has had a training
institution for some years, and the Stockwell Training College has
also a class under the able superintendence of Miss Heerwart; but
the London society was anxious to provide a centre to which all candidates could come up for examination and receive a certificate according to their capacity. The first examination under this arrangement
will be made next month, and will be conducted by Madame de
Portugall, a German lady who has devoted many years of her life to
the propagation of Fröbel's doctrine, and who has lately been
appointed by the Government of Geneva to the post of Superintendent of all schools for young children throughout the canton. She has

accepted the invitation of the London Fröbel Society, and will thus give to their first examination the sanction of her name and authority.

On July the 5th a Petition to Parliament was presented by Mr. W. E. Forster, from the North of England Council for promoting the Education of Women, praying that clauses be inserted in the Oxford and Cambridge Universities Bills empowering the Commissioners to make due provision for the higher education of women.

National Training School for Cookery.—The Annual Meeting of the National Training School for Cookery was held at South Kensington, on June 27th, the Duke of Westminster, as President, in the chair. The meeting was mainly composed of ladies, amongst whom were the Princess Louise, the Countess Cowper, Lady Alford, &c. It appeared from the report, which was read, that the school was doing public service effectively. The working of the school with regard to the attendance of students, the increasing payment of fees, and the establishment of local schools was satisfactory. The number of pupils who have passed through the school from April 1875 to March 31st, 1876, is 1503, as compared with 766 pupils of last year. The executive committee have asked for the introduction of cookery into the code as a branch of domestic economy in elementary schools, but whilst hoping for the assistance of the Government, they pressed on the public the importance of sending persons to be trained as teachers. There have been Schools opened for instruction in cookery, taught by Teachers trained at South Kensington, in Liverpool, Leeds, Oxford, Leamington, Shrewsbury, Birmingham, Edinburgh, and Glasgow, and from all these satisfactory reports have been received; whilst other towns, such as Hereford, Bristol, Sheffield, Rugby, Dundee, and Wickham, will shortly have Teachers sent to them to open Schools in those towns also. A class of practical cookery had lately been started at Whiteland's Training College, Chelsea, the lessons being given by one of their staff of Teachers. This is a beginning of a connexion of the School with the Female Training Colleges which it is hoped will largely extend itself. The School Board of London had for some time past been actively aware of the need for instruction in cookery among the working classes from which their pupils are taken, and there are now established four Cookery Centres, at work in London with great success and giving satisfaction, both to the pupils and the Board.   The Cookery Class held last year at St. Mary's Vicarage, Soho, had been successfully carried on up to the present time.   The Society of Arts had lately given five free Scholarships of £10 10s. each, which were competed for at the School of Cookery at South Kensington, and it is hoped that this proceeding will be imitated by other Corporations.   The Hon. E. F. Leveson Gower, M.P., chairman of the Executive Committee, expressed his satisfaction at the progress the school was making.   In Liverpool, Leeds, Oxford, Leamington, Shrewsbury, Birmingham, Edinburgh, and Glasgow, cookery schools have been established, and the most satisfactory reports have been received, whilst to other towns teachers would shortly be sent to open schools.   During the past year £250 had been paid off, which was very much owing to the vigilant economy of Miss Nichols.   He thought the Government might introduce cookery into the national schools, and suggested an increase of fees in their own school.   Dr. Lyon Playfair, M.P., moved a resolution in favour of the adoption of cookery as a part of the instruction to be given in State schools.   Mr. Mundella, M P., seconded the motion, which was unanimously adopted.   On the motion of the Duke of Beaufort, seconded by Sir H. Cole, the report of the executive committee was adopted.   On the motion of Earl Sydney the thanks of the meeting were unanimously accorded to the Princess Louise for the interest which she had taken in the cause.

Lord Aberdare on Endowed Schools.—At the recent distribution of prizes to the students of the Galligaer Endowed Schools, Lord Aberdare said, he thought it "a matter of the utmost importance that the girls of this locality should receive a better education, not only upon their own account, but because it contributes to the general cause of education.   To have a good school you must have good masters and good buildings.   But there is another thing you want, and without which you will never have a good school.   You must have the parents of children interested in education not being educated themselves. Besides, it is but justice to girls themselves, who have to make their own career in the world, that they should receive the best education."

MEDICAL EDUCATION OF WOMEN.

On Wednesday, July 5th, Mr. Cowper-Temple moved the Second Reading of the Medical Act Amendment (Foreign Universities) Bill, which proposed to open the Medical Profession to women in this country by providing that the production of a certificate or degree from certain foreign Universities, of reputation in medical studies, shall entitle them to be registered as Medical Practitioners.

Amongst other arguments in favour of the Bill, he said, " In the University of Paris there were now 20 lady students, of whom 12 were British subjects, and several had passed with honours. At Jena the University authorities had passed a resolution admitting women to study just as men did. At Leipsic there were many female students, and at Zurich there were 20, while many had taken their degrees and become M.D's. In America similar facilities were given ; and Russia, which was regarded as the youngest European nation, had gone beyond England in what was a special mark of civilization —the fair and generous treatment of women. Great facilities were given at St. Petersburg for the study of medicine by Russian women, these facilities originating in the demand for female doctors among the Asiatic subjects of the Czar. It was not necessary to discuss the physiological question, raised by some persons, whether women had such a proportion of brains as fitted them to acquire the knowledge necessary for the study of medicine. There was the fact that at Paris, at Zurich, in America and elsewhere, women had passed not only a theoretical but a practical examination, and had received diplomas certifying to their knowledge and skill. Nor need the House discuss whether female doctors would have patients, because three or four who were now practising in this country had patients ; and in the female hospital in the Marylebone-road and the female dispensary at Bristol there were as many patients as could be satisfactorily prescribed for. It was a great hardship that female doctors should have to practice in this country, if at all, without legal sanction. To remedy it, the Bill proposed that if women could show by the diplomas of certain foreign Universities that they were qualified to practise medicine they should be allowed to do so. One objection was that if you admitted women to practise on the authority of foreign diplomas you must admit men also. (Hear, hear.) But it was hardly consistent in one breath to urge that you must have equality between the sexes in respect of foreign degrees, and then in the next breath to refuse equality in the grant of medical degrees at home. There was a vast field for female medical practitioners in India, which would of itself absorb more women-doctors than were likely to present themselves. There were in India 50,000,000 Mahomedan and Hindoo women who would never allow a man to come into their apartments to prescribe for their ailments. And the want of women-doctors was felt so strongly by the Indian Government that at Madras and Bareilly various attempts had been made to educate a body of native young women in order to give to their own sex the benefit of surgical and medical treatment. If the opportunity were given, large numbers would avail themselves of it, and no question of competition with men would arise. The Bill would open this field. It would also enable women who were now practising in England to do so legally, whereas at present their certificates were irregular, they were not acknowledged by the profession, and, whatever their education and training, the were classed with the most ignorant quacks. The Medical Council could not deny the justice of admitting women, but were averse from interfering with the functions of the examining and licensing bodies. They therefore proposed a new examination, distinct from any now in force, and a new class on the register. Such a plan, though now merely suggested, might be effectual, and if the Government would undertake to bring forward a Bill he would withdraw this measure. Another plan proposed was to enable examining bodies to treat their charters and statutes as though they applied to both sexes. This, however, was merely an enabling, not a compulsory power, and experience showed that such a plan might not, after all, attain the object which was desired. The Bill recognised the wish and the right of women to enter a profession for which they were pre-eminently qualified, and it would do something to remove what was really a discredit to the medical profession.

The rejection of the Bill was moved by Mr. WHEELHOUSE, on the ground that it would treat women and men in England in a wholly different manner. The medical career and the previous education were unfit for women. He was sorry that three or four ladies in England had somehow got upon the Register, but he hoped that the number would in no circumstances be increased. If they were once to allow women to slip into the profession by a side door opened to them by law, every branch of the public service would be in danger of being overflowed with candidates for office against whom no allegation with regard to sex could be brought to bear.

Dr. WARD, who seconded him, dwelt on the objections to the joint education of the youth of both sexes in such a study as anatomy. His own experience had shown him that the atmosphere of the dissecting room was dangerous in the case of young men, and how much greater would be the danger in the case of young women.

The Bill was supported by Mr. HENLEY, who thought that, as the population was increasing, the death-rate stationary, and the number of medical men decreasing, it was wise to take any steps which would give us a larger number of Medical Practitioners ; he should vote for the Bill, for he believed it might do some good in promoting the health of the people, and was thus a step in the right direction, although it would not, he was afraid, open the door to a very large number of female candidates ; by Dr. LUSH, who, though he did not believe that women-doctors would ever come into general rivalry with men, was

not disposed to resist the wish for the services of women ; and by
Lord ESLINGTON, who declined to be a party to closing any career to
women. As to the question of morality, he said that was a point on
which women were quite able to protect themselves.

Dr. CAMERON and Dr. PLAYFAIR joined in urging the withdrawal
of the Bill in favour of Mr. Russell Gurney's Bill, which it was
understood the Government would support ; Dr. PLAYFAIR said, that
although there were upwards of 3,000 medical men in his constituency,
he had not received a single letter asking him to oppose the Bill,
although he had received one from the College of Physicians in Edinburgh pointing out serious difficulties in the way of putting its provisions into operation.

Mr. STANSFELD said, that the Medical Council having reported
that, while there were special difficulties in the matter which could
not be safely disregarded, they were not prepared to say that women
ought to be excluded from the medical profession, the practical question for the House was, not whether women in large numbers should
study and practise medicine, but whether Parliament was justified in
maintaining a law which prevented women from following the practice
and rendering service to any who might desire to employ them. After
what had passed he hoped the House would receive such an indication
of the intentions of the Government as would obviate the necessity
for dividing on this Bill.

Lord SANDON said the discussion had shown that the subject was
one of general interest, and that the substantial proposal was one
that the House was not at all in the humour to scout entirely. It
was not necessary for him to discuss the fitness or unfitness of women
to enter the medical profession, but he desired to enter his personal
protest against some opinions that had been expressed as to the injury
it was supposed the female character would sustain from being mixed
up with surgical and medical matters. He could not forget the services rendered by women of the greatest delicacy and refinement at
the time of the Crimean War, nor, as representing Liverpool, could
he forget the reorganization of its workhouse infirmary by Miss
Jones, while it was well known that some of the best surgical nurses
in the country were women ; and he had never heard that the delicacy,
refinement, moral sense, and higher feelings of these women were
injured by their engaging in these works of mercy. As to this particular Bill, the Government could not concede the principle of admitting women with foreign qualifications to practise without extending
it to men, and on that point the Government were neither prepared
nor called upon to express an opinion. That the Government were
not neglectful of the question was shown by the fact that they referred the Bill last year to the Medical Council as an important body
representing the profession of the three kingdoms, and it was impossible to ignore the force of the reply of the Medical Council ; but if
they were admitted the Council desired to make certain recommendations, one of which was that it was desirable that the education and
examination of female students should be separately conducted. The
Government further consulted privately several leading members of
the profession and also the ladies who had prepared themselves, and
who were well qualified as individuals to adorn any profession. The

Government then became aware that the Recorder proposed to bring in a Bill to enable the Corporations and the Universities, if they chose, to admit women to the profession. That was referred to the Medical Council, who still adhered to what they had formerly said, did not object to the Bill itself, and proposed two or three amendments in it. The Government then came to the conclusion that it was their duty to assent to the Bill of the Recorder, taking care to make it clear that it was permissive and not compulsory, and that women were not to be admitted to the governing bodies of the Corporations or the Universities. He was afraid there was no chance of passing the Recorder's Bill this Session; but, as the Government were prepared to support it, he hoped the measure now before the House would not be pressed to a division.

Mr. BRIGHT urged that legislation should not be delayed. The question was not one of difficulty or detail, and, with the unanimity that prevailed, the Government could easily pass a Bill this Session. Delay would inflict great injustice, not only upon those who desired to study or to be examined and qualified to practise, but also upon the women who desired to have the assistance of medical advisers of their own sex.

Sir H. JACKSON having also spoken to the same effect, Mr. COWPER TEMPLE expressed his satisfaction with what Lord Sandon had said on behalf of the Government, and intimated his willingness to withdraw the Bill, which was accordingly done.—*Abridged from the Times.*

The Bill introduced by Mr. Russell Gurney and by Mr. John Bright, which the Government now stand pledged to support is to "remove restrictions on the granting of qualifications for registration under the Medical Act on the ground of sex." It consists of only two clauses, as follows:—1. The powers of everybody entitled under the Medical Act to grant qualifications for registration shall extend to the granting of any qualification for registration granted by such body to all persons without distinction of sex. 2. This act shall be taken to be incorporated with the Medical Act as amended by the act of the 22nd year of Her Majesty, cap. 21, and the Medical Act as so amended, and any other act amending the Medical Act, shall be construed and have effect accordingly. The speech of Lord Sandon is of immense importance, as the Government is now bound to support this measure. Although this Bill is only an enabling measure, permitting the nineteen examining bodies to do justice to women, and many a hard battle must be fought before women can enter the profession as easily as men, yet the debate had a much juster tone than we

have been accustomed to hear, and the right of women
to be attended, if they prefer, by physicians of their own
sex, was almost universally acknowledged.

BOARDING OUT (IRELAND).

Mr. O'SHAUGHNESSY moved the Second Reading of
the Orphan and Deserted Children (Ireland) Bill, on
July 5th, the object of which is to extend from 10 to 13
the age at which Boards of Guardians may board out
pauper children.   He said: " The experience of rearing
children in the workhouses in Ireland was not satisfactory.
The contamination of the minds of boys and girls was
terrible to think of, and this state of things existed in
spite of all the care and classification they could exercise
and devise.   The only remedy in Ireland was boarding-
out.   In England the difficulty was met by district
schools; but in Ireland these children had to be sent to
the workhouse school.   The peasantry to whose care
these children would be committed were sober and
moral people who had the respect of their ministers of
religion and of the landlord, and he held it would be
to the interest of the persons who had charge of the
children to educate them properly, feed them, and not
overwork them.   The system had been a great success
in Scotland, and in parts of England the power of
boarding-out had been used with good effect.   No doubt
in connexion with the system, so far as it was carried in
Ireland, there had been abuses, but he did not wish to go
into them.   He should be glad to see powers taken to
prevent abuses.   He looked forward to seeing ladies in
Ireland visiting these children, because he knew a great
deal of good would result.   Mr. Bruen and other Irish
members spoke in favour of the Bill; and Sir M.
Hicks-Beach also approved it but suggested that provisions should be introduced into it similar to those in
force in England to prevent ill-treatment of these children by their foster parents.   Mr. Forster also supported
the measure, and it was read a second time.

DRAWING-ROOM MEETING.

A numerously and influentially attended meeting was
held on June 16th, at the house of Mr. and Mrs. T. Taylor,

Hyde Park Gardens.   The subject under discussion was
the "Legal and Social Condition of Women."   Dr. Rae,
F.R.S. presided, and Mrs. Fawcett, Prof. W. A. Hunter,
and Miss Becker were the chief speakers.   In the course
of his remarks Mr. Hunter said : " out of 2½ millions of
women who have to maintain themselves, one million
are engaged as domestic servants or waiters. and one
million are engaged in factories, in agricultural and
industrial pursuits. That accounts for two millions. Then
100,000 are put down as engaged in professional life, but
when we enquire in what forms of professional life they
are embarked, we find that they are chiefly actresses,
singers, and school teachers.   So that if we take the
higher branches of professional life, or the more advanced
positions in the industrial world, we find that these, and
these alone, offer the kind of work from which women
are excluded.   I venture therefore to think that, looking
at the present distribution of the sexes, those who say
that women should not be allowed any avenue, any
career, except that of marriage in order that they may
not be drawn away from their domestic life, are presenting to women a somewhat cruel and bitter mockery."

EMPLOYMENT.

PROPOSED ASSOCIATION OF PERSONS INTERESTED IN "WORKING GENTLEWOMEN."

The *Woman's Gazette* announces that a conference of
ladies representing various institutions took place at 42,
Somerset Street, W., at which a paper was read by Lady
Mary Fielding, on the subject of a proposed Association
for promoting co-operation amongst all who are interested
in the welfare of working ladies.   An appeal is made
for " Associates" who will take interest in the various
institutions and centres of industry connected with this
class.   The special objects which need assistance are
" Help in *training* girls" (for without good training future
independence becomes almost impossible) and help for
orphans, and special cases of young friendless girls during
the period of training, as their earnings are only about
half the cost of their maintenance.   Homes for them are
very desirable, as they are now often alone, ill, and uncared for in lodgings.   It is hoped that a Training Fund

may be raised from which loans (and in special cases gifts) could be granted as may seem best. This is done with success by the "Society for the Employment of Women," the loans being generally repaid. Persons desirous of helping the proposed Association are requested to communicate with the Editor of the Woman's Gazette, 42, Somerset Street, W.

Book-keeping.—A letter in the *Sussex Daily News*, June 21st, by Mr. Lascelles, suggests the importance of book-keeping as a branch of every woman's education. A book-keeping class for girls is at present being held in the office of the Brighton "Employment for Women" Society.

"English girls' schools have much to learn from the way in which a simple system of book-keeping is taught to French girls. It would surprise anyone not before aware of the fact to see the admirable manner in which the books of French shopkeepers, especially what I would call small traders, are kept, and the neat, clean, and orderly manner in which, as a rule, this is done by French women. I know that the exigencies of the French code require this, and something may be ascribed to that pressure, but no law will work out such a system as prevails in France unless the people are sensible of the benefits which such a law brings and co-operate heartily with its enactments. That French women should be such good book-keepers is the more remarkable because, as a rule, they are educated by religieuses—that is nuns or sisters, and as a consequence their education is very faulty—the fact is, as I have before intimated, the people know the advantages arising from their daughters being good book-keepers, and that they shall be this is at all events required. If any school-manager or teacher really wishes to see for himself the difference between the two countries in this respect I would suggest to him to attend any County Court in England, and see the books produced there to verify the position of debtor and creditor, and then to pay a visit to any court of first instance in France for the recovery of small debts ; and he will, I think, be convinced that owing to the system the women have been taught to keep their husband's books, and the admirable manner in which they do it, the Judges of this class in France have seldom any difficulty in arriving at a just decision. But above, and far beyond this, they will find that the debtors themselves bow to the books, as I may say, or rather to the order, regularity, and system which they show, and are convinced accordingly. At the risk of being thought insular, I cannot see why if a French woman can do a thing well an English woman should not do it better— they have only to be taught, not merely that the book-keeping of the house or the shop or the farm is desirable in itself and for themselves, but that to keep good accounts for their shops or business is part of a great system which will tend materially to the order and well-being of the community."

Wood Engraving and Drawing on Wood.—Various attempts have been made to teach these arts to ladies, but we believe Edinburgh may boast of having made the only successful one. For several years a class has been conducted in Edinburgh by Mr. R. Paterson, one of our most eminent wood engravers, for instructing ladies in engraving and drawing on wood. It has been completely successful. One lady has been engraving for publishers for the last year, and her work always gives entire satisfaction. Two or three other engravers are now ready for publisher's work, and one or two drawers on wood. These employments having been hitherto monopolized by men, it is a work of difficulty for women to make their way into them. If the friends of women's work would remember this, and when they have any employment of the kind, give it to ladies to do, they would be giving valuable assistance and encouragement to those who are endeavouring to open a new profession to educated women. Mr. Paterson, the very able teacher of the Edinburgh class, has now commenced business in London, and if 10 or 12 pupils could be found, we believe he would easily be persuaded to open a class there similar to the Edinburgh one. The Edinburgh class is still continued by an experienced assistant, under the superintendence of Mr. Paterson. The thanks of all those who are interested in women's work are due to Mr. Paterson for having so nobly come forward, notwithstanding opposition, to help to open the profession of wood-engraving to women. Enquiries may be addressed, or work forwarded to Miss E. P. BURTON, Criag House, Lothian Burn, Edinburgh.

WOMEN'S PROTECTION AND PROVIDENT LEAGUE.

The second Annual Meeting of the above Society was held in the large hall of the Quebec Institute, Seymour Street, W., on June 29th : Sir Harcourt Johnstone took the chair. The report that was presented gave a very encouraging account of the past year's work. Seventeen meetings have been held in London during the year, and six in Glasgow, Sheffield and Manchester. In Sheffield the meeting was well attended by women in the silver polishing trade, and though no immediate result in the formation of a society followed, it is believed to have been very useful in spreading a knowledge of the subject. In Manchester, the meeting of sewing machinists on May 2nd resulted in the establishment of a Protective and Benefit Society, which now numbers 260 members. In London the members of the Bookbinding Society number 325; of the Upholsteresses, 130; of Shirt and Collar Makers, 60. This latter Society has decided to invite workers in the ladies' underclothing trade to join. The Society of the London Sewing Machinists is also prospering. In February the *Women's Union Journal* was started, as a medium for making the progress of the work of the League and the Unions better known, and calling attention to facts relating to the wages and work of women. The Committee further reports that delegates of three of the League Societies gained admission to the Trades Union Congress, at Glasgow, this being the first occasion on which women had been present as delegates. A further step is the establishment of corresponding members in various towns: Mrs. Mason and Mrs. Fray (Seamers and Stitchers' Union, Leicester); Mrs. Wood (Dewsbury Woollen Weavers' Union); Miss Sturge (Birmingham); Miss Carbutt (Leeds); and Mr. Chapman (Manchester). The Committee suggests that in many women's trades, especially those in which the "sweating system" exists —the establishment of co-operative workrooms (such as the Co-operative Shirt Makers' Association, carried on by Miss Simcox and Miss Hamilton) would bring about a great improvement in the condition of the workers. The League's receipts of the year amount to £133 7s. 4d., the expenses to £127 1s. 5d., so that there is a balance remaining of £6 5s. 11d.

Trained Nurses.—The *Woman's Gazette* mentions an Association for providing Trained Nurses for the West of Scotland. Its object is threefold—1st. To provide properly trained women who as District Nurses, shall attend the sick poor in their own homes. 2nd. To train a certain number of respectable women between the ages of 25 and 35, who shall be employed as district nurses. 3rd. To provide for those who have need of their services and can afford to pay for them, nurses of high character and proved capacity. It is proposed to train some in the Western and Royal Infirmaries, and that all should have experience in some Lying-in Hospital, hoping by this means to prevent the great mortality among women and children of the lower classes.

WOMEN'S PRINTING SOCIETY LIMITED.

The Women's Printing Society, 38, Castle Street, Holborn, is formed for the purpose of thoroughly training, and giving employment to women, in type setting and other light branches of printing, for which there is reason to believe that they have special capabilities; but in which their progress appears to have been retarded by the fact that there are so few facilities for enabling them thoroughly to learn, and afterwards to carry on the work. Provision is made by the Articles for the acquirement of shares by the workers, and it is hoped that ultimately the business will be largely in their hands, and that the introduction of this Co-operative element will render success more certain than in any ordinary commercial undertaking. Those who desire to assist women to enter more generally into this employment which appears to be particularly suitable for them, can do so by taking Shares in the Society.

Directors.—Miss Browne, 58, Porchester Terrace, W., Miss Mary Louise Bruce, 28, Hyde Park Square, W., Rev. S. D. Headlam, 135, Waterloo Buildings, Tito Pagliardini, 75, Upper Berkeley Street., T. Paterson, 2, Brunswick Row, Queen Square, W.C., Miss Williams, 9, Porchester Square, W., Arthur J. Williams, 4, Harcourt Buildings, Temple. *Secretary.*—Mrs. Paterson. *Bankers.*—London and Westminster Bank, Bloomsbury Branch, 214, Holborn. Capital £2,000, in Shares of £2 each, to be paid 10s. Deposit, 10s. on Allotment, and the remainder at intervals of not less than Three Months, by calls of 10s. The whole Amount of any Share or Shares may be paid on Allotment. The Liability of Members is limited to the Amount of their Shares.

Miserable Wages of Women.—The *Womens' Union Journal* gives the following particulars about file scouring by women in Sheffield. One of the branches of women's work in Sheffield is that of file scouring. In answer to inquiries about the payment for this work, made by the Honorary Secretary of the League when visiting some Sheffield workshops, one woman said that she had been in the trade for twenty years but that her payment had remained nearly stationary. At the present time it was *threepence for scouring and tempering fourteen dozen files* (fourteen to the dozen, making 196 in all). The tempering is done by dipping the files into molten lead, and it is not every scourer who can temper also. So expert had this woman become that she could turn out eight three pennyworths of work in the day, giving a total of 12s. per week. The work involves standing close to furnaces of considerable heat.

LIABILITY OF A WOMAN TO SUPPORT HER HUSBAND.

"On June 21st, Mrs. Collins, a lady of independent means was summoned before the Lydney magistrates to show cause why she should not support her husband who had been receiving relief from the parish. The defendant who conducted her own case, argued the matter with the Bench in a manner that would have done credit to a qualified legal practitioner, but she was nevertheless ordered to pay the amount demanded, and advised to make a weekly provision for her husband."

The Married Woman's Property Act of 1870, enables Justices to enforce upon a wife, for the maintenance of her husband, such order as by former Poor Law Acts they could enforce on a husband for the maintenance of his wife. But as the Act of 1870 did not secure to a wife her own property, it follows that a man may acquire by marriage the whole of his wife's property, and may spend it on himself or out of his home, and may force his wife to maintain him afterwards. This is another instance of class legislation for women, and of legislation which could only be imposed on an unrepresented class.—*Women's Suffrage Journal.*

VIVISECTION.

Lord Carnarvon's Bill for Preventing Cruelty to Animals was passed through the House of Lords, with considerable restrictions, which however it is understood, would not be accepted by the supporters of the movement. It is unlikely however that at this advanced period of the session, any legislation can take place this year. It remains to be seen, now that public opinion has been attracted to this subject whether prosecutions in proved acts of Vivisection might not take place under existing Acts for the protection of animals.

The most forcible article against the system of Vivisection which has appeared this spring, was written by Mr. Edward Maitland, in the *Examiner* of June 19th.

A New Home for Women and Girls.—A new House of Refuge at 205, St. John's Street Road, Islington, London, E.C., has lately been established for girls or women desirous of avoiding the temptation or escaping from the degradation of prostitution, whether in garrison towns or elsewhere. Mr. and Mrs. Hampson who have already had many years of experience in Rescue work have volunteered to undertake the management of this Home, and the Managing Committee have secured a very suitable house, where the inmates will receive such care and training as shall fit them to maintain themselves by honest industry. The girls and women under Mrs. Hampson's care will be trained in household work, needlework, and economical cookery, and instructed in reading, writing, and arithmetic.

No coercion will be used in order to retain any of the inmates in the Home. Those who undertake its management believe that in the great majority of cases it will be seen that kindness begets confidence, and goodwill creates goodwill. The Rules of the Home will be as few as possible, but to these implicit obedience will be required. The religious instruction given will be simple and unsectarian, and especially directed to rouse into activity those latent qualities of purity and morality which are inherent in womanhood, and to develope a sense of responsibility and duty. It is not to be expected that the advantages offered and the care bestowed upon the women and girls admitted will in every case produce permanent moral benefit; but it is held to be a duty to make the attempt, and it is believed that in the majority of cases lasting good may be effected, especially among the younger inmates of the Home.

.Mrs. Hampson will take charge of the sick, and when
needful, gratuitous medical and surgical aid will be
given.

Funds are much needed to carry it on.   The Treasurer
is W. Shaen, Esq., 8 Bedford Row, W.C.

MISCELLANEOUS.

A Woman as a Trustee.—Mrs. J. Kane, widow of the
late Secretary of the National Association of Ironworkers, has been appointed one of the trustees of the
Centralised Funds of that Association.   Mr. David Dale,
of Darlington, and Mr. Joseph Chamberlain, of Birmingham, are her colleagues in the Trust.   This appointment is well merited.

MR. JOHN KANE, the late Secretary to the National
Association of Ironworkers, whose recent death has been
so deeply and widely lamented, received from his wife
much valuable assistance in the arduous duties of his
office.   On one occasion when a large meeting of members of the Association had been called, at some important trade juncture, and Mr. Kane was detained on a
journey so that he could not be present, Mrs. Kane
addressed the meeting, expressing as far as she could,
what she knew to be his views upon the subject under
discussion.

THE Royal Society gave on Wednesday, June 14th, a
Conversazione, to which for the first time ladies were
invited.   The experiment was eminently successful.—
Nature.

LADY Herbert of Lea, is writing a book on the position
of the wife and mother in the fourth century, in which
she traces the resemblance between the domestic life of
the present day and that of the early Christians.—
Athenæum.

MRS. FAWCETT contributes an article on Communism to
the new volume of the " Encyclopædia Britannica."

Macmillan's Magazine for June had an article on "Domestic Service."

Good Words for July contains a good article by
Octavia Hill upon District Visiting.

W

The *Victoria Magazine* for July has a tale by the well-known author, Miss Ramsay, called, "A Summer Morning's Frolic."

Another Swimming Feat.—Miss Agnes Beckwith swam from Chelsea Bridge to Greenwich, on July 5th, a distance exceeding ten miles, in 2 hours 46 minutes. She is fifteen years of age. Her father accompanied her in a boat.

Female Servants' Home Society.—The 39th annual meeting of this society was held on June 21st in the Metropolitan Tabernacle, under the presidency of the Rev. C. H. Spurgeon. From the report it appeared that last year had been financially a good one for the home. The standard of merit had been higher; two gold and five silver medals had been earned, against three in all the previous years. The society had received in donations and subscriptions during the year £73. The home had been well patronised by employers in want of servants paying in fees £321. The servants themselves had paid in lodging and fees £446, making the total receipts of the Society for the year £870. The average number of female servants in London was about 100,000, and of those 10,000 were at one time or another out of employment. The society had during the year received 1,069, and all these young women had been protected and provided with situations at a cost out of the public funds of £150. Amongst those present that day were 50 young women who were to receive prizes for having retained their situations for periods ranging from two to fifteen years. The prizes consisted of gold and silver medals, books, and testimonials.

Sailors' Orphan Girls' School and Home, Hampstead.—The annual examination took place on June 27th. This home—like the kindred and neighbouring institution, the Soldiers' Daughters' Home—has been founded through private instrumentality, because of the absence of any Government institution for the daughters of sailors equally with the daughters of soldiers, but the Admiralty authorities recognise the value of the institution by maintaining about 50 girls in the home out of the Greenwich Hospital Funds, which leaves room for

50 more fatherless girls to be admitted by election, belonging either to the Royal Navy or British merchant service. They are received between the ages of six and twelve years, and in the training which they obtain it is particularly borne in mind that most, if not all of them, are destined for domestic service.

National Training School for Music.—Thirty-eight scholarships have been founded in the National Training School for Music by the City of London. To three of them scholars were directly appointed. In the examination of candidates, 314 in number, for the remaining 35 scholarships with the elections for which they were entrusted, the examiners—Mr. John Hullah, Herr Otto Goldschmidt, and Mr. W. G. Cusins—were occupied from April 24th to May 20th. The candidates varied greatly in age, accomplishments, and promise, and the election had been largely governed by the necessity for balancing these qualifications one against the other. In two scholarships there were no awards made, but of the 9 male and 24 female candidates elected 18 were pianists, organists, or composers, 2 violinists, and 13 vocalists. With regard to future elections the examiners suggest that some limit as to the ages of candidates be insisted on, for instance, that instrumentalists be not less than 12 or more than 20 years of age, and vocalists not less than 17 or more than 23; and, secondly, that as a condition of examination each candidate should produce a certificate of recent date from some musical professor of recognised talent and character to the effect that he or she is sufficiently advanced in musical practice to profit directly by the instruction given in the Training School.

Miss Julia Sinclair has just been admitted as Doctor of Medicine at the University of Zurich.

Orphan Pauper Children.—A drawing-room meeting was held on June 10th, at the house of Sir Charles Trevelyan, Grosvenor Crescent, on the subject of the boarding out of pauper children. Sir Charles Trevelyan explained that the purpose for which the meeting was held was not to promote the interest of a single orphanage, but to make suitable provision for all pauper orphans

in England and Wales. He read letters from various
parts of the country, showing the great success which
had attended the boarding out of orphan childen in the
improvement of the children morally, physically, and
mentally, and the advantages to the ratepayers in lessened pauperism, and to the state in adding to the wealth
producers. Mr. Geig gave practical details of the plans
pursued under the Poor Law Board of Scotland, and
said the results proved that the children thus boarded
out were more fitted for the work of life than those
brought up in such charities as George Heriot's at
Edinburgh. The Rev. H. Wood, of Calverton, where
children of St. George's, Hanover Square, are boarded
out in different families, said good had been done on
both sides; for the children, by the enforced regular
attendance at school, were an example to others, and,
on the other hand, they had all been cured of ophthalmia
with which they were afflicted when they came. Mr.
Tallack, of the National Committee for Boarding-out
Orphan Children—of which Mr. Francis Leek is chairman—gave his experiences in favour of boarding-out.
Miss Florence Hill read an interesting account of
boarding-out in Ireland, which dated, she said, from
early times. Colonel Freemantle, as a guardian and
chairman of the Committee of Guardians for Boarding-
out, said that the system should not be attempted on a
general scale, or in regard to other than orphan children.
He deprecated sending deserted children out to board,
for he said he had known the most heart-rending cases
of the child and the foster parent being torn apart after
the affections had become strong on both sides, in order
that the guardians might do the duty which the law
enforced upon them, of restoring the child to some
depraved and wretched parents in the worst dens of
Westminster or St. Giles's. It was stated that a clause
had been introduced into a Bill which it was hoped would
be passed this session, to give discretion in such cases;
for the guardians had to send the children even of
criminals to meet their parents as they came from the
risons. Miss Johanna Hill and Miss Matthews, two of
 ᴧ hon. secretaries of the Birmingham Committees for
    ᴧding-out, gave details of the work in that town, and

said that it certainly led to no increase of pauper children. The Rev. W. P. Freemantle, the Rev. R. J. Simpson, and others, also spoke.

The *Labour News* says :—

Kirkby Stephen.—The number of women offering for hire was much smaller than in past years. This year the wages were not quite so high as they have been for the last few years, but good, well-known men got as much as £18 to £20 for the half-year, and others in proportion. The wages of women servants were as high as ever, good dairy women asking and receiving £11 and £12 for the half-year, and young girls, about 18, £7 to £8.

Kendal.—At the recent hiring fair girls and women ranged from £4 to £10. In some instances first-class dairy maids topped the latter rate.

Embroideresses.—The following appeared in the *Standard* for 28th June :—"To Ladies requiring Employment. Wanted immediately, a few good embroiderers, chiefly for ecclesiastical work ; work must be done on the premises.—Apply, by letter only, to A. S. T., care of J. Morley, 27, Tavistock-street, Covent Garden."

Certificated Schoolmistress and Girls' Industrial Trainer.—Salary £30, with such further sum (if any) as may be advised by the Local Government Board, rations, &c. Age, class of certificate, with recent testimonials (not over three), endorsed "Schoolmistress," to Clerk to Guardians, Ludlow, by June 29.

Assistant Mistress.—For the Grey Coat Hospital (Endowed) Day School for Girls, Westminster. Must be a member of the Established Church. Some experience of class teaching essential, and a knowledge of drawing and needlework desirable. A lady holding the Women's Cambridge Certificate preferred. Salary £80 per annum, non-resident. Written applications, with copies of testimonials, and full particulars as to qualifications, experience, and age, are to be sent on or before July 12, addressed to the Head Mistress, at the Hospital. Duties to commence in September.

Nurses and Probationers.—Wanted for the Leeds Trained Nurses' Institution. Wages for nurses, £25, with uniform. Application to be made, in writing, to the Superintendent, the Leeds Trained Nurses Institution, 16, Hyde-terrace, Leeds.—*Times*, 27th June.

The inability of a woman to bring an action herself in those circumstances wherein she is the sole injured party, received a forcible illustration the other day in Ireland, in a case thus quoted in *Sanders' News Letter*:— "MURPHY *v.* FARRELL.—This was an action brought by a man, named James Murphy, for the seduction of his servant. The parties reside in the county Wexford, the defendant, Michael Farrell, being a farmer. Mr. David Lynch, on the part of the defendant, sought to plead a traverse of the seduction, a traverse of the woman being servant of James Murphy, and a general traverse to the cause of action. Baron Dowse said he was very doubtful about this motion. He considered it a very anomalous state of the law that this woman could not bring this action in her own name. Under the present state of the law, the money, if recovered, should be given to the master and not to the injured woman who was subjected to one of the greatest abuses. If this was not an age of unpracticable, and not practical, legislation, some enterprising barrister might bring in a bill in Parliament to redress the state of things. He would not give leave to plead the defences in the case unless there was a special affidavit denying the seduction and averring that the woman was not the servant of the plaintiff. Mr. Lynch said he would mention the matter on the next motion day.

AMERICAN ITEMS OF INTEREST.

Women Physicians in California. — The Board of Censors, to whom was referred the application of the ladies holding diplomas regularly conferred upon them for membership in this society, report that they know of no valid reason why the society should not admit ladies to full membership, and therefore recommend their admission. The following ladies were elected as members of the society:—Mrs. Dr. C. Brown, E. P. Stone, S. E. Brown, E. S. Meade, M. E. Bucknell.

MRS. E. E. HUTTER, of Philadelphia, has been "Female Inspector" of the Soldiers' Orphan Schools, since 1867, and we have no doubt has been of great service to the orphan daughters of the State. She has a yearly salary of 1,000 dollars and all expenses paid.

A WOMAN, Mrs. Erika C. Jones, has been for the last four years and a half Warden of the Hudson County Jail, New York; she is probably the only woman in the world who holds such a position. Some years ago her husband obtained the appointment of jailor, and from the time of their arrival a marked improvement in its administration was apparent. For six months before his death his wife practically performed the duties of his post, and when he died she was appointed warden of the jail by the unanimous vote of the freeholders. It is said to be admirably managed.

A LETTER from Iowa says :—" We have also a lady lawyer. Her husband is a lawyer. They are in partnership as 'Foster & Foster.' Through Mrs. J. E. Foster's indefatigable zeal in the temperance cause, a low saloon with theatre attached—a late importation—has been brought into the courts. A search warrant was taken out, and the sheriff found both whiskey and gin. The proprietor had to stand trial. 'Foster & Foster' won the case for the State, and the saloon-keeper was brought to grief. Still another low saloon in Lyons—an adjacent city almost one with Clinton—has been searched, and nearly one hundred gallons of whiskey captured. Again 'Foster & Foster' won the case for the State. Both have appealed to a higher court, but they are under bonds, and their unlawful traffic is being made more and more disreputable and a purer sentiment being strengthened in our midst. Mrs. Foster is also a warm advocate of Woman Suffrage. She has lectured on Temperance and Woman Suffrage all through Iowa and part of Illinois."

MRS. FOOTE, says the New York correspondent of the *New Century for Women,* one of the most successful artists in the department of wood drawing, will soon take up her residence in California. She has illustrated some of the most popular of the Messrs. Osgood & Co.'s Christmas books, as the "Hanging of the Crane" and "Mabel Martin." It is not her intention to allow her

talent to lie idle, for she has engaged ahead enough
book and magazine work to keep her busy for several
years.

—————————————

ART. V.—NOT UTOPIA.

I saw in a morning vision,
　A far-off beautiful day,
When earth was purged from darkness,
　As spirit is purged from clay.

No longer swarmed around me
　A desolate Pariah throng,
With mingled groans and curses,
　Dragging its chain along.

There were poor men still in my vision,
　But poverty's sting was gone,
For each man loved his brother,
　And rich and poor were one.

The highest beings in nature
　Slew harmless creatures no more,
They left to wolves and tigers
　A banquet stained with gore.

The human race of my vision
　Lived gently on fruit and grain,
And form and mind were nobler
　Than when they ate the slain.

No longer the tears of angels
　Fell over the piteous days
Of helpless little children—
　Thwarted in all their ways—

For every girl and mother
　Now humbly studied the law
Of sacred infant spirits,
　With reverential awe.

Rarely, if ever, now wielded
　Pale students the bitter knife—
Seeking, 'mid death's distortions,
　The mysteries of life.

No longer the slaves of Mammon
　Sold body and soul for pelf,
Men worshipped something better,
　Better even than self!

And I beheld in my vision
   How war, twin-brother of death,
Himself must die by inches,
   Slowly yielding his breath.

Faded the lingering echo
   Of women moaning for light;
Hushed the last of the voices
   Muttering that might is right.

In my vision man reigned with woman,
   Right royally, side by side,
And some one whispered softly,
   " See, love is wisdom's bride!"

No longer the seers of progress,
   All earlier insight slighted,
While hapless faith, weak-eyed,
   Stood trembling, affrighted.

I might not read in my vision
   The perfect unspeakable name
Underlying faith and science,
   But I saw both had one aim.

No longer raged in the Churches
   The maddening battle of creeds,
Forgetting, in human passion,
   The deepest human needs;

The Church of my happy vision
   Was as free and large as time,
And gathered in her bosom
   The good of every clime.

Shall these things be day-dreams, only?
   Dear sisters, brothers dear,
Be it ours to hail such future,
   Be it ours to bring it near!

             E. Hadwen.

Art. VI.—PARAGRAPHS.

Under the title of "Men, Women, and Animals," the *Pall Mall Gazette* of June 22, remarks upon the evils which are likely to accrue to the common-sense and scientific interest of the age, if legislation is to be interfered with by sentimental feminine agitators. The Bill to restrict vivisection is, according to their views, not

introduced from a conviction of the moral duties of man
towards animals, nor the debasing influence on ourselves of seeing cruelty inflicted, but as part of a systematic attack by women and philanthropists on the
medical profession, "which is held together by the
desire and design of abating suffering." The paragraph is long but very instructive.

"To say the truth, it was quite time that the medical profession
bestirred itself. For the present attack on a limited number of
experimentalists engaged in contributing to the extention of its knowledge is only a sample of a class of semi-popular movements from
which the medical profession primarily and the human race
secondarily are likely to suffer the deepest injury. It ought not to
escape notice that the new feminine and sentimental agitations
are almost exclusively directed against the doctrines or the practices
of physicians and surgeons. Such movements are not, indeed, confined to our own day. We are sometimes brought into contact with
the dregs of a popular prejudice which in its day was on the point of
preventing one of the chief scourges of mankind from being suppressed. There is still an Anti-Vaccination Society, which we all
laugh at, but few of us know that it represents an extinct power, that
there exists a whole literature of fierce attack on Jenner and his
system, and that nothing but the firmness of a minority, of masculine
firmness and sex, saved it from legislative prohibition. If it were
worth while, we might point out the strong analogies of this outcry
to more modern movements; for both religion and sentiment were
enlisted against vaccination, and stories of the horrors resulting from
it were part of the ordinary gossip of society. The old prejudice has
all but given way before practical experience, but it is to be observed,
and it is a highly important fact, that antipathies of the same class
have enormously gained in activity and dangerousness. Doubtless
the women were in the main against vaccination, but they had not
yet learned to organize public meetings, nor had men begun to
court their favour by sacrificing to them the better knowledge of the
more experienced sex. We have said that the new feminine movements have the singular characteristic in common that they are either
directed against doctors or have doctors for their natural antagonists.
The very claim for greater professional opportunities and a greater
share of political influence is advanced in the teeth of the bulk of
medical opinion. It is the doctors alone who know what the real
objections to allowing women to enter the same fields of labour and
action with men, and what are the real dangers incurred by the community which gives the permission, or allows it to be freely used. All
men may be conscious in a general way of these dangers, but to
medical men they are matters of elementary knowledge. The contagious disease agitation—the most popular and disgusting of the
new feminine combinations—is, of course, avowedly directed against
the doctors; it is avowedly founded on a denial of the right to abate
terrible physical evils, unless the same equality is maintained at
every stage of the process between the sexes which a court of justice

would observe in trying a man and a woman for a crime. The vivisection movement is even more plainly an attack on the medical profession; it forbids its members to violate one of the most doubtful, visionary, and ill-supported of all ethical hypotheses, the assumption that the lower animals have moral rights. This might, perhaps, be thought the extreme point to which the feminine interference with the liberty of professional action might go; but anybody who will turn over in his mind the daily necessities of medical practice will see that there are yet wide fields for the female objector to explore. The simple truth is that the whole of medical and surgical practice is based from one end to the other on the assumption that, in the cure or alleviation of disease, the end justifies the means. Without such an assumption made at the outset and firmly adhered to, medical science would either retrograde with extreme rapidity or become extinct. That the end must be a good one, and from the medical point of view a good one, is a rule insisted upon by the profession with an extreme and consistent sternness; but, if the physician or surgeon is condemned to keep himself fiddling and fidgeting over the means, if he is to think of the moral reasons for or against every step of the curative process, the hand which writes the prescription or holds the lancet will be at once paralyzed. The science will at once fall back into something like the condition in which it was when it was doubted whether the dissection of the dead body was not a deadly sin, whether the Bible did not contradict the circulation of the blood, and whether the weight of ancient and classical medical authority did or did not command the use of a particular remedial agent. Of all the members of the human race those who will suffer first will be women; for among the foremost doubts suggested those relating to the admission of women into consulting rooms will be the most pressing."

If our opponents assume that humanity, morality and justice, are concomitants of a feminine spirit in legislation, we are willing to take up the gauntlet. For our own part we do not despair of finding for them equally powerful advocates amongst men, but we know also that these men, in their championship of the oppressed, are everywhere desirous to have their hands strengthened by women's help.

THE *Saturday Review* of July 1st says—" The happiest life of a woman is perhaps attained when she adopts the opinions of a reasonably intelligent husband and conscientiously thinks they are her own. But all women cannot be happy in this way." We fear the *Saturday Review* has made an admission which will be destructive to its future peace of mind. From conceding that all women cannot be happy, either by having an intelligent man for a husband, or by merging her opinions in his, or finally by having a husband at all, the next step must be to admit that these unreasonably constituted women ought to have some other way of being happy put within their reach. *Facilis descensus.* The *Saturday Review* may already have entered on the broad road that leadeth down to "women's rights," although another sentence, quoted from amongst many similar from an article in a previous number on "Emancipated Women," proves that the conversion will not be a speedy one. "It is impossible," it says, "to shut our eyes to the symptoms which are visible on every side that one of the most forcible and dangerous currents of modern society is the impatience, and even mutiny, of a large class of women, not only on the continent, but here among ourselves, at the conditions of life which have hitherto been imposed upon and accepted by the majority of their sex. Many women would seem to be getting tired of what they call the tame and monotonous sphere in which they are confined, and demand that the same range of active life and personal freedom should be opened up to them which is allowed to men." How dreadfully unreasonable of these silly women to get tired of being taught their duties by the *Saturday Review.*

In the *Hour before the Dawn* (Trübner & Co.) we find a touching account of the effort made many generations ago by noble French ladies to redeem and raise the unfortunate of their own sex. Might not, as the author suggests, some example be taken from it by those who know that industrial training is required to fit these poor women for self-dependence and honest work, and who have at heart their rescue and rehabilitation?

"A happy picture of what might be done is presented in some broken and fragmentary accounts I have seen of a work accomplished in France, after that country had been scourged and desolated by the long wars of the Fronde. The fathers and brothers and husbands of the poor population of some of the provinces had been almost destroyed by that sanguinary war. Villages were depopulated and families broken up; famine and pestilence succeeded; orphan girls and young widowed mothers wandered about barefooted and ragged, a prey to hunger and misery. One of the noble ladies of that period, while travelling to her chateau in the country, was penetrated with grief at the sight of so many forlorn girls and women, and when she observed that many of them were offering to sell themselves to any comer in order to obtain bread to allay the agonies of famine, she said to herself, " It is time that women who are raised above this terrible alternative should hasten to the rescue of these." She asked of these girls, " Are you willing to work ?" Willing, even eager, they all were. The laborious and humble beginnings of the enterprise which arose from this necessity it is not needful here to record. Suffice it to say that an *Industrial Colony* was founded through the energy and perseverance of the men and women actuated by a desire to save these victims. The colony was situated in the country remote from any large cities. Hundreds were gathered there. " Industry " was the motto of the community. After some years, the place had the appearance of a large and flourishing village ; the sounds of busy labour, of the laughter of childhood, of singing and praise were heard by those who passed through it. The family life was truly realised here. Only while at work in the factory, which formed the main industry of the place, were the women assembled in one place. After work hours they returned to their homes—little cottages with gardens, some standing alone, others in rows, facing the central green of the village, shaded by luxuriant trees, and to these cottage homes were brought from many parts the aged poor and orphaned and deserted infants to be cared for and ministered to, and in their turn to bless those who tended them. Many a poor Hagar turned her wandering feet with her starving child to this abode of industry and peace, leaving behind her the great wilderness of the city.

" The mothers of this community lived in its midst, constantly and lovingly superintending, advising, and influencing, yet leaving abundant freedom to the citizens of this little colony. When some of these mothers—the ladies devoted to the work—were called away others took their place. A place of worship arose in the midst, and a schoolhouse for the little ones. Every varied form of ministration was here presented to the poor fallen ones, thus calling out such gifts of heart or mind as each might possess, while the alternation between the regular hours of industrial labour and the ministering of the cottage home filled the affections and the mind, at the same time employing the hands in a degree hardly attainable under any other conditions. We catch a glimpse in the broken record of this enterprise of the happy evenings when the girls, trooping back to their little cottages, would wrangle amicably for the first embrace of the baby or the tottering little ones, who came forward to meet their adopted young mothers, clinging round them, chasing far away, with their pure sweet kisses and innocent talk, all memory of unholy and unwomanly act and thought. We see, in the happy scramble for the embraces of the babes, defeated candidates among the young girls pressing forwards towards the cottage doors ; one throws her arms gaily and tenderly around the silvered head of a stooping, feeble, aged man, saying, 'This is my *baby.*' He was her special charge, and long did the hours seem to the aged man till his beloved nurse returned from her daily work to bring sunshine and gladness to the little room where he dwelt. She, once 'a woman of the city and a sinner,' now poured forth all the womanly tenderness of her poor heart on this old man, seeing, it may be, in him a father long dead,

whom she seemed now to serve again, as in childhood. Another
would be entrusted with an aged woman, in whom she found again the
mother long ago grieved for as lost. In some cases the patience and skill
of the young women were tried and tested, but bore the trial. Some
had an aptitude for teaching, and their evenings were spent in the
school. A library was established; books were read and exchanged
in the little homes. The poor women who approved themselves
by long service, or by devotion to the young, or sick or aged, became
promoted by degrees to the position of mothers of the colony. A
preacher would sometimes visit the place, when a crowd of all ages
and conditions would gather from many a porch of the industrial
colony to hear the glad tidings of the Gospel of Peace preached under
the open sky on the village green, whence hymns of praise ascended
evening by evening. The products of the industry of the colony
were sent to the nearest manufacturing city, and in the course of
years the colony became more than self-supporting.

* * * * * * *

"In travelling over our own healthful Yorkshire moors, or through
some of the beautiful secluded parts of rural England, I have sometimes
thought, 'Is the realisation of such an enterprise as this an impossibility in our own time and country?' God grant that ingenuity
and courage, as well as charity, may be brought to bear on this
matter, so that thousands (now, humanely speaking, without a straw
to catch at for life) may be withdrawn from that great gulf-stream
which is whirling them downward to destruction. Even in the heart
of our cities industrial enterprises might be established with success,
where the principle of self-dependence and the home element might
alike be secured. In work such as 1 have imperfectly recorded,
women must be the chief agents; but they cannot accomplish so
great a work unaided by men.

In an article in the *Christian Union* of June 2nd, Miss
Tod says—"One of the suggestive sayings of the late
Dr. Arnold, of Rugby, was that, 'in a fallen world, Con-
servatism was always wrong, because the tendency of
human nature was to fall back, if it was not steadily
and energetically advancing.' Of course, there is another
side to the question; but it will always be found that,
when serious efforts at reform have led to revolution, it
has been where reform has been delayed too long. It
is just as true in social matters as in political, and perhaps most of all in such matters as the claim of women-
householders to the suffrage, which affects both the
world of public and of private action. When an alarm
is raised, that grave consequences may follow from a
proposed change, the friends of peace should consider
whether the repression of the elements which lead to
change, or their regulation, is the wiser course. Such

a crisis has come now, in the external position of women in this and other civilized countries. The claim to share in that self-government which is the boast of a free people is part of a wide-spread movement by and for women, of which the claims to a larger and sounder education, and to a wider range of remunerative employments, are also parts. The latter are more popular, but they cannot obtain reasonable and sufficient support until women can make their views known with the emphasis which belongs to a represented class. It is very common for people to accept these claims fully, and yet to dislike the idea of women stepping, as they think, into a new sphere by touching politics. In this, as in many other cases, they are deluded by words. To give qualified women the parliamentary franchise would neither take them out of an old sphere nor into a new one. It would neither lessen their interest in, nor their qualification for, their private duties (in some points it would probably increase them), nor would it present to them any subjects in which they have not already a rightful interest. The change it would cause substitutes a direct sense of responsibility for an indirect hope of influence—a change which would be altogether for good, as a characteristic of thought for those who have practical work to do in the world. Now, all women have such work, but many of those who would be enfranchised by the Women's Suffrage Bill have an unusual share of it. They are, for the most part, widows, who have had experience of the vicissitudes of life, and who have to do the duty of both parents to their children, as regards both their moral and material welfare. Unmarried women who are householders have, in many cases, young relatives and others dependent on them; and it is among them, also, that we find the greater number of those quiet and earnest workers who carry religious teaching and charitable help, in every form, into the abodes of the poor and suffering."

The same writer says upon the subject of Vivisection in a letter to the *Northern Whig ;* No progress will be made towards settling this difficult question till the defenders of vivisection acknowledge that their opponents are quite as capable of forming a just opinion on the matter as they are themselves. They must also acknowledge that they have an equal right to do so. Scientific men are not judges in the cause; they are only one of the parties concerned. The whole nation has an interest in it, and must decide according to their consciences. In certain countries it would be thought preposterous for a by-stander to interfere with a man who was illtreating his horse or his dog. The animal being his own property, no one else had anything to do with it. But here, any one who saw such cruelty would feel it a duty to look for the nearest policeman and charge the man with an offence against the community. We have reached such a stage of civilisation that we cannot acknowledge the absolute ownership of anybody in the higher animals, but insist that his treatment of them shall, roughly at least, be in accordance with the national sense of responsibility towards sentient beings. No doubt that sense of responsibility stops short at a varying and capricious line, according as the animals are of a size or nature to attract much attention or not. But it exists, and it is growing, and it must of necessity keep pace with the growing sensitiveness of the public conscience with respect to preventable human suffering. Indeed, one large element in the horror with which cruelty to animals is regarded is the dread of its brutalising effect upon the character of those guilty of it. It is quite impossible to "turn back the clock of time," and restore the days when the sufferings of prisoners, of paupers, of slaves, were little cared for, and the sufferings of animals not at all.

CRIME IN THE WESTERN CIRCUIT.

The *Times* says that in the Criminal Court "the business promises to last some time, as the charges are generally of a serious character, including as they do no less than nine cases of criminal assaults on women and children." One might be tempted to wonder what becomes of the "respect and deference" which, according to Lord Folkestone, the stronger sex invariably pays to women.

Englishwoman's Review.

CONTENTS FOR AUGUST, 1876.

All Communications to be addressed to the EDITOR, 22, Berners
Street, Oxford Street, W.

Post-Office Orders payable to SARAH LEWIN, at the "Regent
Street" Post-Office.

TERMS OF SUBSCRIPTION AT THE OFFICE.

Per Annum (Post Free), Six Shillings.
Subscriptions payable in Advance. Single Numbers posted Free on
receipt of Six Postage Stamps.

MSS. are carefully read, and if not accepted are returned, on receipt
of Stamps for Postage, but the Editor cannot be responsible for any
accidental loss.

Contributions should be legibly written, and only on one side of
each leaf.

THE

ENGLISHWOMAN'S REVIEW.

(NEW SERIES.)

No. XL.—August 15th, 1876.

ART. I.—THE LAW WITH REGARD TO THE POSSESSION OF PROPERTY BY MARRIED WOMEN.

THE following is a short statement of the law as to the position of a married woman, where no settlement has been entered into on marriage, with regard to property of which she may be possessed at the time of marriage, and of which she may become possessed during the continuance of the marriage, to her rights and powers of disposing of the same, and to the liabilities attached to her rights of ownership.

Property is divided into two classes, real *Division of property into real* and personal, the former consisting of lands, *and personal.* houses, &c., wherein the estate or interest of the owner is at the least an estate for life which is the smallest estate of freehold; the latter consisting of money, goods, cattle, shares in stocks and funds, &c., and also including lease-hold property for any term of years, however long, and (with very few exceptions) shares in railway, canal, and joint-stock companies.

All freehold property of which the wife is *Freehold property.* possessed at the time of marriage, or of which she afterwards becomes possessed (subject to the exception afterwards mentioned) is vested in the husband and wife during their joint lives in right of the wife, during

x

Husband entitled to profits and sole control which time the husband is entitled to the profits, and has the sole control and management, but he cannot convey or charge the lands for any longer period than while his own interest continues, except by way of a lease for a term not exceeding 21 years. Where the wife has been during the marriage in actual possession of an estate of inheritance and there has been a child of the marriage born alive and capable of inheriting the property, the husband—upon the decease of the wife—becomes solely possessed of the property for his life. Subject to these limited rights of the husband, the freehold property of the wife is not affected by the marriage.

Leasehold property. As to leasehold property of which a woman is possessed at the time of her marriage, or which accrues to her during marriage, the husband becomes possessed of it in her right. He is entitled to **Husband entitled to profits and sole control** the profits and management of such property during their joint lives, during which time he **He may dispose of it.** may dispose of such property in any way. It is liable to be taken in execution for his debts, and if he survive her it is his absolutely, but he cannot, in her lifetime, bequeath it by will. If she survive him and he makes no disposition of such property before death, it remains to her by virtue of her original title, and does not go to his executors or administrators.

Personal property (other than leaseholds). Personal property (other than leaseholds) belonging to the wife at the time of marriage, or accruing to her afterwards during the marriage, **Becomes absolutely the husband's.** becomes in general the absolute property of the husband. *Choses in action** do not in general become the husband's until he recovers them by law, or reduces them into possession. If he die before this is done they remain to the wife. The rights of the husband do not extend to property held by the wife *en autre droit* (as in the capacity of executrix), but only to property of which she is possessed in her own right.

---

* A chose in action is a thing of which the owner has not the enjoyment, but merely a right to recover it by an action, as, for example a sum of money due on a bond.

If the wife survive the husband, her para- Paraphernalia.
phernalia (her bed apparel and ornaments suited to her
degree), if not disposed of by him in his lifetime, remain
to her, and do not go to his representatives. It may be
as well to mention here, that where any person has
power of disposition over any property during his or her
lifetime only, such person has no power of disposition
by will, for a will speaks from the testator's death, and
has no force during the testator's lifetime.

If the husband desert the wife without Desertion.
reasonable cause, at any time after such desertion (which
may be proved by a variety of circumstances, such as
leaving the wife with a declared intention never to
return; marrying another woman, or living in adultery
abroad; absence for a long time, not being necessarily
detained; making no provision for his wife and family,
he being of ability to do so; providing no dwelling or
home for her, or prohibiting her from following him) she
can obtain an order protecting any money or property
she may earn by her own industry, or become possessed
of after his desertion, and which will belong to her as if
she were a single woman, and such order endures until
it is discharged.

The husband, where the marriage took place before
the 10th August, 1870, is liable for all the Compensatory
debts of the wife contracted before such advantages.
marriage;   the   Married   Women's   Property   Act
1870, relieved the husband in any marriage contracted after the passing of the Act (the 9th August,
1870) of this liability, which, however, was by the Married Women's Property Act (1870), Amendment Act
1874, re-imposed on the husband if married after the
30th July, 1874, but such liability was limited to the
amount of property received by the husband from the
wife by reason of the marriage. The hus- Husband liable
band is also liable, during his life, to main- to support the
wife.
tain the wife, providing her with necessaries according
to his station in life, and her contracts made for the sole
purpose of supplying herself with such necessaries, will,
in general, be binding on him, though not on herself.
If the wife survive the husband she is en- Dower.
titled, unless her right has been defeated, to dower, that

is, to one third part for the term of her life of all the lands of which her husband was possessed at any time during the marriage, and of which any issue that she might have had (whether she actually had any such issue or not is immaterial) could have been heir. The Wife's equity to a settlement. wife has also what is termed her equity to a settlement that is to say, where during the marriage the wife becomes entitled to any equitable property* not settled to her separate use, she is (unless already enjoying a competent settlement) entitled to have a portion of such property settled on herself. But this right has become of much less importance since the passing of the Married Women's Property Act, 1870, which in many instances gives to the wife for her separate use property accruing to her during marriage, as will be seen later.

Proceedings in the Divorce Court.   In the Divorce Court a married woman is a privileged suitor, both as to costs and as to alimony. As regards costs in suits instituted either by the husband or the wife, the latter is entitled to have her costs paid by her husband as the proceedings go on, on the principle that the whole property is supposed by law to be vested in the husband. Where the wife has a separate income sufficient for her own expenses and for the necessary expenses of the suit, this right to costs during the continuance of the proceedings does not hold good. But the wife is entitled to her costs from her husband if the ultimate decision of the Court is in her favour.

Alimony, which is the allowance directed by the Court to be made to the wife when cohabitation has ceased is of two kinds, *pendente lite* and permanent. With regard to the former in suits instituted either by the husband or the wife after proceedings have been commenced, the Court will, on the application of the wife, direct an allowance to be paid to her by the husband during the continuance of the suit. Permanent

---

* Equitable property is property of which the owner's title is recognised in equity but not at law, as in the case of an ordinary mortgage; the mortgagee has the legal estate, and at law is considered the owner, but the mortgager has the right in equity of redeeming the mortgaged property, and this is an equitable estate.

alimony is the provision awarded to the wife by the
Court when the case is finally decided.   The amount of
alimony granted is in the discretion of the Court, which
is guided in its decision by the circumstances of the
case before it and the conduct of the parties.

A married woman may always act inde- Transactions.
pendently of her husband *en autre droit* as where she is
executrix. She can, with the concurrence Can dispose of
of her husband, make free disposition by freeholds and of
future interests
deed of her freehold property, and can, with in personal property with hus-
the like concurrence, dispose by deed of any band's concur-
future or reversionary interests in personal rence.
property to which she may be entitled under any deed
made after the 31st December, 1857 (and which does
not restrain her from so doing). She cannot make a
will either of lands or goods, except (1) of goods Can only make
in her possession *en autre droit* (2) of personal a will in the four
cases enumera-
estate settled to her separate use (3) of any ted in text.
property where an express power has been conferred on
her so to dispose of it, (4) of goods with the assent of
her husband. The wife can freely dispose of Wife can dispose of property
all property settled to her separate use unless settled to her
she be restrained from so doing by the deed separate use, unless expressly
under which she is entitled to such property. restrained.
She is incapable generally of contracting or Incapable of
contracting in
of doing any other act which will bind her- general unless
by husband's au-
self or her husband, unless by his authority thority.
or as his agent. She is also in general inca- Incapable of
suing in her own
pable of bringing any action in her own name unless by
name unless by leave of a judge. leave of a judge.

By the Married Women's Property Act, Married Women's Property
1870, the rights, powers and liabilities of mar- Act, 1870.
ried women have been somewhat extended. By that Act
where any freehold or copyhold property shall descend
upon any woman married after the passing Its operation
of the Act (9th August, 1870) as heiress or with regard to
property inheri-
co-heiress of an intestate, the rents and pro- ted from an in-
fits of such property shall, subject and with- testate.
out prejudice to the trusts of any settlement affecting
the same—belong to such woman for her separate use,
and when any woman married after the passing of the
Act shall during the marriage become entitled to any

personal property as next of kin to an intestate, or any

And to any
sum of money
not exceeding
£200 under ceed
or will. sum of money not exceeding £200 under any deed or will, such property shall, subject and without prejudice to the trusts of any settlement affecting the same—belong to

the woman for her separate use. The earnings of any married woman acquired by her, after the passing of the Act, in any employment in which she is engaged separately from her husband, and any money or property so acquired by her through the exercise of any literary, artistic, or scientific skill, and all investments of

the same, and all deposits in savings' banks in the name of a married woman are to be

deemed the separate property of such woman to be held by her independently of any husband to whom she may be married. Also moneys in the

Funded, &c,
property can be
registered in
married woman's
name. public funds, fully paid up shares and stock in incorporated or joint-stock companies, and shares and benefits in friendly and benefit societies, can be entered, registered, and certified on the application of any married woman, or woman about to be married, who may be entitled to such moneys, funds, &c., in the name or intended name of the woman as a married woman entitled to her separate use, when they will be deemed the separate

And are deem-
ed her separate
property. property of such woman, provided that such deposits, shares, investments, and benefits have not been obtained by a married woman by means of moneys of her husband without his consent, or have not been made in fraud of the husband's creditors.

A married woman is by the Act empowered to effect a policy of insurance on her own or her husband's life for

Can bring action
to recover sepa-
rate property. her separate use; and to maintain an action in her own name for the recovery of any property by the Act declared to be her separate property, or of any property belonging to her before marriage, and which her husband shall by writing under his hand have agreed with her shall belong to her after marriage as her separate property, and to have in her own name the same remedies, both civil and criminal, against all persons whomsoever, for the protec-

tion and security of such wages, moneys, and property
by the Act declared to be her separate property, as if
such wages, &c., belonged to her as an unmarried
woman. A married woman having separate Made liable to
property is made liable to the parish for the parish for maintenance of hus-
maintenance of her husband, and also for band and child-
that of her children, the husband, however, ren.
not being relieved in any way of his liability for the
same.

As to debts contracted by the wife before Wife's debts.
marriage, the husband and wife can be both sued, the
husband's liability being now limited to the amount of
property he received from his wife in respect of the
marriage, and the wife is liable in respect of property of
which she may be possessed to her separate use. After
marriage the wife is in general incapable of contracting
or of doing any other act which will bind herself or her
husband, unless by his authority or as his agent, and
such acts done by her are merely void.

Briefly, then, a woman on marriage loses Summary.
the rents and profits of freehold property during the
marriage (except the profits of such property as descends
to her, if married after the 9th August, 1870, during
marriage as the heiress of an intestate), she also loses
the power of disposing of such property by will during
the marriage, and can only do so by deed with the concurrence of her husband; she loses the profits of lease-
hold property during marriage, and loses such property altogether, if the husband either survive her
or dispose of it during their joint lives; and loses practically all her personal property, except, if married after
9th August, 1870, any personal property to which she
may become entitled during the marriage as next of kin
of an intestate, or any sum not exceeding £200,
under any will or deed, or where deserted by
her husband she obtains an order protecting all money
and property earned or acquired by her after such
desertion, or any money or property earned or invested
in accordance with the provisions of the Married
Women's Property Act, 1870; all of the property coming
within this exception being considered property to her
separate use, of which she can dispose in any way by

will or deed.   Her powers of making a will are limited,
and she is in general incapable of contracting.

Settlements.   It should, however, be borne in mind that
the husband's rights to the wife's property, as above
stated, can be defeated by settling such property to her
separate use, and that property can be so settled that
not only the husband, but his creditors even, cannot
deal with it, while absolute powers of disposal of the
same may be reserved to the wife.

ROWLAND W. D. HILL.

ART. II.—LEGISLATIVE MEDDLING.

When Alice in Looking-glass Land says that she is very
thirsty, the queen goodnaturedly offers her a biscuit.
"Alice thought it would not be civil to say no, though
it was not at all what she wanted, so she took it, and
ate it as well as she could, but it was very dry, and she
thought she had never been so nearly choked in all her
life." The proposed extension of the Factory Acts from
which we have escaped this session, but which is
threatened to come forward next year, places women who
subsist by their own labour much in the position of poor
Alice. They have already too few occupations, and
those few are overcrowded, and consequently underpaid,
and when they complain of the difficulty of self-main-
tenance, a paternal legislation answers the complaint by
setting additional restrictions on their labour, cutting
off some employments altogether, and curtailing the
hours of others. At the risk of being thought uncivil
in saying No, working women must protest that any
extension of the Factory Acts is as little adapted to
their necessities as the red queen's biscuit was to Alice's
thirst.

There is some danger that, as nothing with reference
to this subject has been discussed in Parliament
during the session just concluded, the alarm which
working women naturally felt last year at the proposed

interference with their right to labour will have subsided,
but there is no doubt that the attempt to enforce additional restrictions on female industry is only postponed,
not abandoned, and we should wish to see the measure
taken into serious consideration by all women who are
likely to be included in the regulations. We give full
credit for good intentions to those men who are trying to
alter the laws, they believe the restrictions to be not
only in the interests of women themselves, but also,
and chiefly, in the interests of the future generation of
which these women are to be the mothers; but we claim
the right of hearing the opinions of those who are to
be legislated for, and we think that on three separate
points they may raise grave questions as to the
advisability of any change in the law. Firstly, would
not the necessary reduction of wages consequent
on any further restrictions imposed on their labour, be
quite as injurious as over-long hours of work? Secondly,
are not the trades which are considered exclusively
feminine—machining for instance—as trying to the
constitution as those which legislation prohibits?
Thirdly, is not the well-being of the future generation
as dependent upon the health of the fathers as of the
mothers of the community, and yet, though there are
numerous trades in which men are employed injurious
to health, and even shortening to life, no arbitrary
legislation restricts the rights of men to be employed.
It is curious to see the distinction which is drawn
between men and women in this respect. To quote the
words of a witness before the Factory Commission at
Belfast last year, "Legislation has never interfered with
the labour of adult men unless it was in some way
injurious to the community. They must confine themselves at present to women and children." The rights
of the individual man as opposed to the imaginary
benefit of the community are allowed to be of weight;
not so the rights of the individual woman.

Women may in some instances need the same protection as the law accords to minors, but in the majority of
cases the power of doing as one chooses is a more
efficient help than enforced protection. Personal right
would be a real privilege and protection for women, and

the state is bound as undeniably to accord it to them as to men. By regarding them in the light of children, the legislature really interferes with their power of acquiring property. One or two hours more labour may mean for a woman better food or lodging, or it may mean the possibility of providing for an aged parent, or of keeping her children with her if she is a widow. If nine hours work obtains for her good and sufficient food, which eight hours work must necessarily diminish in quantity, is she likely to be any the better for the additional rest and leisure?

It may be assumed that women's wages are seldom at present high enough to afford them superfluities. On the subject of their obtaining inferior wages to men, Mill says, in his "Principles of Political Economy:"—

While men and women work at the same employment, if it be one for which they are equally fitted in point of physical power, they are not always unequally paid. Women in factories sometimes earn as much as men, and so they do in hand loom weaving, which, being paid by the piece, brings their efficiency to a sure test. When the efficiency is equal, but the pay unequal, the only explanation that can be given is custom, grounded either in a prejudice, or in the present constitution of society, which, making almost every woman, socially speaking, an appendage of some man, enables men to take systematically the lion's share of whatever belongs to both. But the principal question relates to the peculiar employments of women. The remuneration of these is always, I believe, greatly below that of employments of equal skill and equal disagreeableness carried on by men. In some of these cases the explanation is evidently that already given, as in the case of domestic servants, whose wages, speaking generally, are not determined by competition, but are greatly in excess of the market value of the labour, and in this excess as in almost all things which are regulated by custom, the male sex obtains by far the largest share. In the occupations in which employers take full advantage of competition, the low wages of women as compared with the ordinary earnings of men, are a proof that the employments are overstocked; that although so much smaller a number of women than of men support themselves by wages, the occupations which law and usage make accessible to them are comparatively so few that the field of their employment is still more overcrowded. It must be observed that as matters now stand a sufficient degree of overcrowding may depress the wages of women to a much lower minimum than that of men. The wages, at least of single women, must be equal to their support, but need not be more than equal to it; the minimum, in their case, is the pittance absolutely requisite for the sustenance of one human being.

It is well known however that this "minimum" is

sometimes decreased below the point necessary to their sustenance; viz., the lately reported case of the employer in Manchester who told a woman who complained of a reduction of wages, to supplement them by selling herself. Many a poor needlewoman in London could tell the same tale of starvation-wages; but the worst paid are not those with which Government proposes to meddle.

Mr. Mill elsewhere points out that "all laws and usages which favour one class or sort of persons to the disadvantage of others, which chain up the efforts of any part of the community in pursuit of their own good, or stand between those efforts and their natural fruit— are (independently of all other grounds of condemnation) violations of the fundamental principle of economical policy." Not only women themselves, but the whole country is the poorer when their labour is restricted or turned into less profitable channels. Women have already overstocked the labour market in the few occupations open to them; the law proposes still further to restrict the number of their occupations, either directly, by making them illegal, or indirectly, by causing employers who must work long hours, or keep their shops open late, to prefer the services of men who are free to make their own contracts. If women were recognised by the law to be as responsible and free agents as men, we should no longer hear of the need to protect their labour.

The Americans are not behind the English in their efforts to restrict the work of women. In the statutes of 1874, no minor under the age of 18, and no woman over that age can be employed in labouring. by any person, firm or corporation in any manufacturing establishment more than ten hours in one day; in no case are the hours of labour to exceed sixty a week. Any one wilfully employing a minor or woman above this time, or any superintendent or overseer of the work, may be punished by a fine not exceeding fifty dollars. Under this law a manufacturing company of Lowell, Massachusetts, was last summer fined twenty dollars and costs for employing Mary Shirley, a single woman of twenty-one years of age, for sixty-one hours in one week. Now, we ask on what principle or pretext was Mary Shirley not considered as capable of making her

own contracts as if she had been John Shirley? Why
could she not be the judge of the amount of work she
was able to do, and being twenty-one years of age and
single what possible pretext has the State, to place her
in the same category as a minor. But this law does
not go nearly far enough for some of the reformers.
The Sixth Annual Report of the Massachusetts Bureau
of Statistics of Labour devotes some of its attention to
the effects which some forms of employment have on
women's health. It considers the question relatively to
the health of the individual and also to the injury to the
State by the permanent ill-health of its women; it
reviews factory employments, in which it finds that for
the younger portion of the female operatives employed
therein, there is a degree of toil disproportionate to the
condition and capacity of those engaged; "it is unremit-
ting and monotonous, and the Report avers that most
women break down under it. The Report is equally
desponding upon type-setting; "an employment exacting
an unusual degree of mental concentration and energy
with great rapidity of manipulation, and as such if our
previous hypotheses have been correct, cannot fail to
have a marked effect upon the health of its female
operatives." Upon Telegraphy they become even more
lugubrious; it has "a most positive and rapidly injurious
effect on the youthful lady-operatives." Sewing machine
labour is found to be specially injurious to women. The
continuous counting of money, which occupies a great
many women in the State Treasury in America is declared to be "rapidly prejudicial to the health of the
young women engaged in it," and the manufacture of
cigars, the last trade specially considered, has "a most
pernicious effect" upon the girls. Among the remedies
suggested in the Report we find that no girl under 15
should be suffered to labour at all; that no girls or women
should be employed in work injurious to their health,
and it is suggested that a *council of salubrity* as in France,
should decide what such employments are; and that
special sanitary supervision and well-established examination and certification of all employés, male and
female, should be established, and only such as are certified to be healthy to be employed at all.

It appears to us there is a kind of medical mania now
raging both in the old and new worlds which seeks to register and examine and test everything by purely sanitary
standards; and as very few doctors can be found precisely to agree in a standard, these arbitrary regulations
have not even the merit of offering a certain good in
exchange for their inevitable evils; they are at best
experimental. *Fiat experimentum in corpore vili,* said
the old proverb, and it would seem that it is in compli-
ance with this maxim, that women's work and women's
convenience are the sole subjects of these theories and
practical experiments. It would seem as if the doctors
were of opinion that women were alone concerned in maintaining the health of the future community and the health
of men might be entirely ignored. One other difficulty
strikes us in reading the Report. The causes of ill-health
amongst women are, it says, *severe overwork,* and more
rapidly *overwork accompanied by innutrition, and non-
hygienic surroundings.* Might not the additional degree
of innutrition brought on necessarily by the cessation of
work, and consequently of pay, more than counterbalance
the benefits of rest. It is undoubtedly not in accordance
with nature that women should be overworked; but it
is in accordance with nature that women must eat, be
clothed, and live under some kind of roof. Let the
American statisticians who are so zealous to stop up
their present paths of labour, find some other remedial
way. Unless they can establish some National Reserve
Fund, to which all men must be contributors, and from
which all women, by virtue of their sex, have an unlimited claim to draw, (and of such a scheme we think
men would tire first), the problem of remedying overwork among women must be solved in some other way
than by diminishing the number of their occupations.

It is not by throwing additional difficulties into the
way of women who are earning their livelihood, that the
hard problems of health, happiness or morality will be
solved. If every branch of labour were left absolutely
open to every adult, whether man or woman, and the
same facilities for acquiring education and skill therein,
so far as the law can give them, offered to both, individual strength and capacity would soon decide which

was men's and which was women's work. If it were
acknowledged that women, whether married or single,
have the same freedom as men to make contracts, it would
rapidly develop the power to manage for themselves,
acquiring a sufficient knowledge of law to make them
valid, and appreciating the benefits of union among
themseves, to give them better "vantage ground" in
dealing with employers. It was not very long ago that
guilds and monopolies threw the same fetters upon men's
work, as the law now throws upon women's. We have
seen the folly of it, in the former case; we have now to
learn that equal disadvantages are entailed upon the
country, socially and economically, by retaining, still
more by increasing, the industrial disabilities of women.

Art. III.—HOMES FOR DOMESTIC SERVANTS.

It was not one of the smallest services conferred by Mrs.
Nassau, Senior, on our poorhouse system, during her
short term of office that the attention of the public was
to a great extent directed to the friendless and often
worse than friendless condition of the large number of
girls and young women who form the under-stratum of
our domestic serving class. Mrs. Senior's figures fully
showed that a large number of girls who begin life
respectably though with no very fair start, drift away
into the unknown from sheer neglect and friendlessness.
To remedy this enormous evil as far as London is concerned, many Associations and Institutions have sprung
up within the last five years. The Metropolitan Association for befriending young Servants, undertakes the
supervision of a number of young girls : it has volunteer
helpers in various parts of London whose duty it is to
look after the girls in their own neighbourhood, advise
and encourage them, help them to find new situations
when out of work, and represent to these poor social
orphans that "motherly" element in life which in these

days of drilling, teaching, grinding, and police-setting-to rights, seems somehow unaccountably left out of our social economy. Industrial schools for those who need training, convalescent homes for those who are weary with the "march of life," registration offices for those out of work, as well as committees of ladies who supervise and visit the girls when in place, all form part of the same scheme. The Society for promoting Female Welfare 31, Weymouth Street, W, and Miss Townsend, hon. sec., to the Metropolitan Association for Befriending Young Servants, 7, Great College Street, Westminster, are ready to give counsel and help to any one willing to join in so kindly a work. Of all these methods of helping friendless girls however perhaps, the most effective is the establishment of a home where they can take refuge when leaving one place, if they are not yet provided with a new one.

A few notes from a quarterly record of one of these homes which was established by Mrs. P. A. Taylor at 1, Bessborough Gardens, S.W., will show better than pages of argument the usefulness of its plan. The house looks on to the green square in front, is open to the fresh breezes from the river, and is airy and light. A small charge of 6d. a day, which is insufficient even to cover the expense of the food, is made, but no girl, if respectable is refused admission whether she is able to pay it or not, and it is to be recorded to the credit of the girls, that when once again in receipt of wages, they are eager to repay what they owe. The instances we shall select are not those of girls of the pauper class, who, it must be remembered are even more destitute, helpless, and friendless,—these are not by any means the most hopeless of their class.

No. 3 was seventeen years of age : she had no parents or friends and had been in service ever since she was eleven. She came to Bessborough Gardens from a convalescent home, and twice had rheumatic fever after coming there. A situation was subsequently found for her.

No. 4 ; a poor destitute girl twenty years of age who had provided for herself since she was a child. A suitable place was found for her; she keeps up communication with the Home and is doing well.

No. 10 ; aged twenty-four : has no friends or relations in the world. She has been out of health for some time, and had been in a hospital.

She was very badly off at the time she came, and had very little clothing; while at the Home she made herself new clothes, and was afterwards able to get into a good place as general servant. She frequently visits the Home and expresses great gratitude for the help it has been to her.

No. 11 was a native of a small town in Devonshire, and had lived for ten years as servant in a farmer's family. She had been tempted away by some people called A———, who were paying a visit to acquaintances of hers to come and live with them as general servant, offering her higher wages. She agreed to come to them and travelled up to London alone, never having seen a railway or been a day's journey from her old place; she found that the A———s kept a lodging house not of a respectable kind. She was very miserable there and dreadfully overworked, but she dared not leave, not knowing her way about London, or having the least idea where to go. A lady whom she met by chance told her of the Home, and she came to it. She was afterwards found to be subject to fits, and the doctor who attended her said she must go back into the country. She was sent back to her father, and has since been twice heard of as much better; and meaning when quite recovered to go back to her old situation at the wife of a farmer's.

No. 12 was brought by the wife of a clergyman: She had been brought to his church during morning service by a gentleman who found her wandering about the streets, not knowing where to go. She had come from Ireland three weeks before with a mistress with whom she had subsequently quarrelled. The Lady Superintendent persuaded her to return to her employers, but as she was really not treated well, another situation was subsequently found for her, and she promises to become a valuable servant.

No. 13 had come up from the country in the expectation of getting a situation as attendant on a sick lady. She was not engaged by this lady and after spending all the money she had in lodgings, looking out for a situation, pawning most of her clothes and being reduced to great straits, a friend brought her here. After staying a month, and refitting a little, a place was found for her and she is doing well.

These half-dozen cases of distress are not among the incapable class of the workhouses: they are girls who have been in service before, and some are good workers. All have been found respectable places, and yet any one of these cases might for lack of friends, distance from home and want of means have fallen into temptation; and, but for the opportune assistance given to them in the Home be now leading wretched and reckless lives.

Workhouse girls are of course even more in need of assistance. "The Gods help those who help themselves" said the old proverb, but Christian charity has to do more than this, and assist those who cannot help them-

selves at all. The pauper girls belong in all probability
to an under-vitalized ill-fed and hopeless class, in whom
habits of vagrancy and dependence are too ingrained to
leave them any longer capable of honest energy. The
doctrine of the "survival of the fittest" would long ago
have obliterated the permanent pauper class : poor
things, these girls have been trained in masses, drilled to
attend, though frequently not to understand, school and
church, to walk in time, and to read or write after a
fashion; their highest industrial teaching has been to
scrub a floor; their moral training has, in some instances
at least, been enforced by a cane; they have no
comprehension of self discipline or self management,
mending clothes, minding baby, cooking the commonest
food, washing up, have all to be taught by the hard-
worked mistress. If she is painstaking and good
tempered, and the girl strong and willing to learn, she
may yet do well; she may grow up to do valuable work
in the world. But if these elements of success be wanting
or if the girl has low relations hanging about her, or
doubtful associates who can only offer her an evil home,
her fate is certain. She must either drift back to the
workhouse, or swell the fearful tide of misery that rolls
through our streets, unless she can be taken by the
hand by some one of these Associations, or guided to a
House like that in Bessborough Gardens. The material
help is much, the human sympathy and advice even
more: the work is often very difficult, for some of the
girls have violent tempers, wretched constitutions, and
evil tendencies. Accustomed to a state management
which may almost be characterised as a "system of
coercion tempered by neglect," they resent advice, and
are distrustful of kindness. It is often up-hill work and
discouraging—but the Lady Superintendent of the
Bessborough Gardens Home, (and such must also be
the experience of the Ladies' Committees of the Associations for Befriending girls) finds that the influence
does tell even when least expected, and even unpromising
girls are better and happier therefrom. Could not similar
Associations be made in other towns, where the ignorance
and friendlessness are nearly as deep as in London? It is a
task in which all women might join according to their

Y

means, establishing industrial schools, or homes, or visiting
the girls when in service: so that none even of our incompetent "little ones" be left uncared for.

ART. IV.—EVENTS OF THE MONTH.

EDUCATION.

GIRLS' PUBLIC DAY SCHOOL COMPANY, LIMITED.

The schools of the Company at present in operation
are the following:—

Name.	Address.	Head Mistress.
Bath High School	5, Portland-place, Bath	Miss S. Wood
Brighton High School	Milton Hall, Montpelier-rd., Brighton.	Miss Creak
Chelsea High School	Durham House, Smith-street, Chelsea, S.W.	Miss M.A. Woods
Clapham Middle School	Clarence Ho., Clapham-com., S.W.	Miss Alger
Croydon High School	The Chestnuts, North End, Croydon	Miss Neligan
Hackney High School	275, Mare-Street, Hackney, E.	Miss Pearse
Norwich High School	St. Giles's, Norwich	Miss Will
Nottingham High School	1, Oxford Street, Nottingham	Mrs. Bolton
Notting Hill and Bayswater High School	Norland-square, Notting-hill, W.	Miss Jones
Oxford High School	16, St. Giles's, Oxford	Miss Benson
St. John's Wood High School	Winchester Ho., Winchester-rd, N.W.	Miss Allen-Olney

KINDERGARTENS are open in connection with the Chelsea, Notting Hill, and Norwich High Schools.

"Sixty Kindergarten Songs and Games," are edited by
Mrs. Edward Berry and Madame Michaelis of the Fröbel
Society. *Novello, Ewer, & Co.* Price 1s.

MISS HESTER ARMSTEAD, who had the Clothworkers'
Scholarship in the Girton Entrance Examination, is the
head girl of the North London Collegiate School. She
gained, also, another scholarship of fifty guineas, given
by the Gilchrist Trustees in connection with the London
University Examination.

AT the recent examination for exhibitions in connection with the Salford School Board, the list of candidates
in the order of merit was headed by a girl, Isabella
Cookson, aged 12, of Christ Church Upper School.

Seven exhibitions were offered but only six were awarded. The clerk stated that the best arithmetic paper was one by the first girl on the list. The exhibitions are of the value of £25 each, tenable for three years. They are open for competition among the children at public elementary schools within the borough; and are to enable the successful candidates to pursue their education at higher schools.—*Women's Suffrage Journal.*

COLLEGE OF PRECEPTORS.

At the Midsummer meeting of this College, Dr. Lyon Playfair, who presided, congratulated the College on the attention they paid to the education of women, who, he thought, "should be directed to the modern languages, the liberal arts, and the moral sentiments and duties."

It will be a welcome change when attention to "moral sentiments and duties" are confessedly part of the curriculum of boys' schools; at present they are supposed, like Dogberry's reading and writing, to "come by nature!"

CITY OF LONDON COLLEGE FOR LADIES.

The Rev. E. A. Abbott, D.D., head master of the city of London School, presided, on July 27th, at the distribution of prizes to the successful competitors in the recent examination of students of the Ladies' College, which is situated in the City road. The distribution took place in one of the upper rooms of the City Terminus Hotel, Cannon Street. The Rev. Dr. Abbott opened the proceedings with a brief address, calling attention to the growth of the school, which, in the course of six years, had increased its numbers from 70 to 140. The reports of the examiners—in the main not only favourable but complimentary to the principal of the school, Miss Berridge, and her assistant teachers—were then read, after which the prizes, consisting of handsomely bound volumes, were distributed. As each prize taker appeared to receive the reward of her merit (and some there were who had to answer to their names four, five, and even six times) she was warmly applauded by her less fortunate class fellows. These prizes were awarded for efficiency in English, French, German, Latin, music, singing, history, general literature, Euclid, algebra, arithmetic, &c. Amongst the prize winners, perhaps, those who attracted the largest amount of attention were three children—one boy and two girls—whose combined ages could not have exceeded 16 years, and whose intellectual culture had evidently in no way impaired their bodily vigour, for they were each a picture of blooming health. The prizes having been distributed, the Rev. Dr. Abbott again addressed the company, and expressed his opinion that the City of London College for Girls was doing a good and brave work. Like all other schools of course it had its faults, but the improvements suggested by the examiners would no doubt be carried into effect here as elsewhere. He trusted that such continuous progress would be made that ten years hence the examiners would not be satisfied with the standard of efficiency of which they at present approved. Of course girls' schools laboured under a great disadvantage as compared with boys' schools, because, save in the case of certain City companies—and especially the Clothworkers' Company—they were not favoured with those endowments which the educational institutions for male students enjoyed. He hoped, however, that this as well as other deficiencies would gradually disappear. A vote of thanks to the rev. gentleman closed the interesting proceedings.

On July 24th the Board Schools at St. Peter's Quay, Newcastle-on-Tyne, were opened, a tea being given by Mrs. Scholefield, of Windsor Crescent, who entertained 500 scholars and 200 mothers. Mrs. Scholefield, in expressing her pleasure at seeing so many of the parents of the children present, impressed upon them the necessity of sending their children early and regularly to school, for well educated men, she said, in this country might rise to any height. She was sorry there were not equal opportunities for the girls, but a good education would eventually bring about a better light, and she hoped an equally good time for the two. At some length she deprecated the evils of drunkenness. It had destroyed the finest intellects, and it was the means of bringing many to the lunatic asylums, prisons, and

workhouses in the country. She urged strongly upon
the mothers of the children, as she believed it was a
woman's work, the importance of becoming teetotalers,
and by this means also getting their children and husbands to abstain, and in a feeling manner she related
the evils of intemperance, and the misery attending
upon it.—From the *Northern Daily Express.*

WOMEN'S SUFFRAGE.

The *Women's Suffrage Journal* announces five lectures
on the Political Disabilities of Women, by Miss Becker.
On August 1st at Rhyl, John Rhys, Esq. in the chair;
August 2nd at Llandudno, H. D. Pochin, Esq., presiding;
August 3rd at Llanrwst; August 10th at New Brighton,
and August 17th at Harrogate. These lectures are undoubtedly the means of introducing the subject to many
persons who are unable from circumstances to attend
the public meetings of the winter and spring.

A pamphlet has been published by Miss Arabella
Shore in answer to Mr. Bright's speech upon Women's
Suffrage. It was written immediately after the debate,
but its appearance has been delayed from various causes.
It bears as motto an extract from the *Fortnightly Review,*
written by Leonard Courtney. "The special movements
that have hitherto prevailed, the admission of Jews to
Parliament, the Secularisation of the Universities, the
Ballot, the Abolition of Church Rates, and the like, have
been instances of victories over privilege, and the
Women's Disabilities Bill will in due time become law
through the power of the same principle."

MARRIED WOMEN'S PROPERTY COMMITTEE.

The seventh annual meeting of the above committee
took place on Friday, July 28, at Adam street, Adelphi,
Mr. Jacob Bright, M.P., presiding. A report was read
by Mrs. Venturi, describing the efforts which had been
made in Parliament and elsewhere to obtain greater
security for the property of married women, and announcing that Lord Coleridge had promised next session
to introduce a protecting Bill into the House of Lords.
The adoption of the report was moved by Mr. P. A.
Taylor, M.P., and seconded by Mr. A. Arnold, and car-

ried unanimously. The second resolution, proposed by Mr. H. Palmer, and seconded by Miss Downing, thanked Lord Coleridge for his promise ; and the third and last was a vote of thanks to the chairman of the day. Both votes were carried unanimously.

THE WAR IN THE EAST.

Several ladies of high rank have gone from Odessa to superintend the Servian hospitals. The Ladies' Hospital Aid Society of Servia, under the patronage of the Princess Natalie, has issued an appeal to the women of all Christian lands for aid for the wounded. They require surgeons, instruments, and appliances of all kinds for hospital service. Eight Russian female medical students have arrived at Belgrade. Miss Pearson and Miss MacLaughlin, so well known for their services to the wounded in the Franco-German war, have, with other doctors, started for Belgrade. These ladies addressed the following letter to the *Daily News* on July 31st :—

Sir,—The kindness and charity of our English friends during the last war encourages us once more to ask for their kindness and sympathy. We start on Tuesday next for Belgrade, having placed our services as trained nurses at the disposal of the Archbishop Michael. The experience we gained in the last war will, we trust, be of singular use in this. No words can describe the terrible state of the wounded in this war. We go to nurse and care for all alike, irrespective of nationality and creed, but we want a small sum, very small, as compared with the wealth and charity of England, with which to purchase medical stores and surgical instruments. We nursed 1,700 wounded in Orleans during the winter of 1870-1871. The medical and surgical stores used during five months cost under £50. From £100 to £150 would enable us to start such an ambulance as would greatly relieve the present distress and do honour to England. We may, we think, fairly appeal to past work as a guarantee for the efficiency of present efforts and of their economy. We may add that our services are unpaid. We only ask for what will enable us to relieve the fearful sufferings of the wounded in Servia.—We are, Sir, yours very truly,

EMMA MARIA PEARSON.
LOUISA E. MACLAUGHLIN.

Contributions of money and stores may be sent to Mr. Lewis Farley, 12, Great Winchester street, London, E.C.

EMPLOYMENT.

Embroiderers.—In Ireland, the production of embroidered muslin employs upwards of half-a-million

persons, much of the work being done by females at their
own homes.   No less than fifty firms in Belfast are connected with the production.   The *Draper* states that
many of the Glasgow houses send work to the schools
in the County Mayo, the especial aptitude and skill of
these female workers—qualities accompanying celerity
of execution—constituting a strong attraction.—*Labour
News.*

Pottery Painting.—George Jones & Sons, Stoke-on-
Trent, are advertising for Biscuit Paintresses.

Machinery.—Harper's *Bazaar*, New York, says:—"The
steam-engine in the Women's Pavilion is under the care
of a Miss Allison.   She has been a lover of machinery
from a child, and has received a thorough scientific education.   In answer to a question in regard to women
running engines as a regular business, she said that
there were thousands of small engines in use in various
parts of the country which women might manage.   The
work was less tedious than many of the usual avocations
adopted by women, and an engine required far less
attention than a woman gives daily to a child under her
care."

Machine Printing.—An envelope embossing machine,
which can be worked by a girl or lad, at the rate of
6,000 an hour, has been introduced by Hely & Co., Dublin.

Match Makers.—At the match factories in the East-end
of London, women, we are told in Mr. W. Glenny Crory's
"East London Industries" (Longmans, Green, and Co.),
can earn about ten or twelve shillings weekly if they
work steadily; little girls are paid in proportion.   All
are paid by the piece.

Manufacture of Clothing.—Tailoresses in the East-end
of London can earn with the assistance of a little girl,
fifteen to twenty shillings a week.—*Labour News.*

MISSION HOME FOR YOUNG ENGLISHWOMEN.

The Mission Home, 77, Avenue Wagram, Paris, has
just issued its Report.   The growth of this much needed
institution from small and utterly inadequate beginnings
is very noticeable.   It was on the 17th December, 1861,

it says, that the first visit was paid to an English shop-girl in the Faubourg St. Honoré, which has led to the formation of the Mission Home for Englishwomen in Paris. The first gift towards it was of one franc by a Scotch girl. "Close upon this came the gift of a friend, £100, to aid the opening of the first apartment taken at 77, Avenue Wagram, for the Mission Home for English-women in Paris. It was opened December 20th, 1872, with twelve beds, each of which found an occupant in five days. As applications increased, the Home was enlarged to accommodate thirty-six persons, and was still insufficient. Just at this time circumstances occurred rendering the purchase of the house a necessity. The responsibility for the amount required (about £10,000) was undertaken in faith that the same loving Hand which had hitherto supplied the daily needs of the Home would be sufficient, and an agreement was accordingly signed, August 11, 1874. Four months later, the first instalment on behalf of the purchase was paid down. On the same day that the government acknowledgment for the receipt of the money was passed, one of the co-vendors died; so, had there been any delay in the purchase, additional law expenses would have been in-curred. The second instalment was paid March 9th, 1875; the third and last on May 9th, 1875; thus happily completing the purchase. The necessary alterations in the house were commenced in July; they have unavoid-ably been very protracted, and it was found advisable to take other apartments for a time, so as to continue the work of the Home without interruption."

Among the separate compartments are a Home for Daily Governesses; to admit 12, or 14. This compart-ment has been full ever since it was opened. A children's Home for such as are orphaned and deserted, of whom forty-six have already been received. Of these, several have been either adopted, or given to the care of their nearest relations; others have been placed in schools or orphanages in England, and fourteen remain in the Home.

The total number of inmates since the Home was opened (Dec. 20th, 1872) is 577. Of these, 105 have returned to England; and the number of visits upon the Home books, mostly from such as require advice or assistance, is 11,670.   There is also a Sanatorium or Home for such as are sick and need rest and care, ere they continue the, too often, single-handed struggle for daily bread.   This part of the work is under the direction of the Mission nurse, who has just completed her training at the Middlesex Hospital.

It is a suggestive fact, showing what numbers of English girls are scattered in different parts of the habitable globe, that very recently one was directed to the Home when in the bush in Australia (by the first inmate of the Home who left it for that country); another from Moscow; a third was told of it by a monk when crossing an African desert; a fourth found her way to it from China; and only a few days ago a gentleman from Toronto, Canada, recognized one of his own countrywomen, whom the Home had sheltered for over two years, whilst she was pursuing her studies in the Paris Hospitals.   In each case the applicant was an orphan, without home,—of whom there are a sad proportion in Paris,—and with few who cared to claim relationship.

They who "*know* the heart of a stranger," can easily conceive the mighty power of influence for good such a work as this brings, especially to a girl thrown for the first time upon her own resources, in a city whose restless gaiety mocks the loneliness of her isolated life. Probably she is the victim of some unprincipled agent, or comes over to a situation already filled or grossly misrepresented, or she is discharged at a moment's notice, by her capricious mistress (as was the case a few days ago), within half an hour of midnight!   Unacquainted with the locality, debarred from the sympathy of speech, every man and woman seems to her an enemy, while she sees around her almost the only thing which bears the marks of success in Paris—the attraction of sin.

Within the last three days the story of such an one, found in the early morning by the gentleman who kindly left the following note at the Home, may speak for itself:—" J ai trouvé une jeune Anglaise hier soir dans la plus grande misère, ne sachant parler Français, mourant de faim.   Je l'ai conduite dans un hôtel pour la nuit, lui ayant donné du pain et du vin, pour ne pas la laisser dans le plus grand besoin.   Je suis sûr que vous ne la laisserez pas dans la triste position où elle se trouve."

Perhaps of all girls, an English girl is the least able to cope with the emergencies of such a position.   The homely simplicity of her early days, the want of practical education and knowledge of life, render her an easy prey to those into whose hands she may fall—for good or evil.

The Young Women's Christian Association, which has always been connected with the Mission Home is at 88, Faubourg St. Honoré.   Two of the associated lady-helpers, Miss Shaw and Miss Hensley, are resident here, and have always sympathising words and a welcome for those in need. A Mission Service is held here every Sunday evening. A soup kitchen was opened last winter, and a crèche, which has long been a great desideratum for the children of poor English widows and others who work by the day, is ready to be opened when some lady-helper can be found willing and able to undertake its charge. The crèche is entirely apart from the Home. The honorary secretaries are Miss Leigh, 77, Avenue Wagram, Paris, and A. H. Heywood, Esq., Windermere.

LADIES' ASSOCIATION OF THE UNIVERSITIES' MISSION TO CENTRAL AFRICA.

This Association has lately issued its report. It appears that last year an appeal was sent forth for a Ladies' Association in connection with the Universities' Mission to Central Africa, to raise a Special Fund for the sending out and support of ladies, nurses, and teachers, for the hospital and school-work of the Mission. £500 was asked for. £50 of that sum having been already secured. The result was £338 16s. 9d., of which by far the greater part was in donations. The funds thus raised were at once applied to the need especially urged upon subscribers in circular letters and appeals, that of the hospital work in Zanzibar. Before last autumn no lady had been found to undertake the post of superintendant, and no funds were forthcoming for the necessary expenses of such a work.

Miss Allen, the eldest daughter of Archdeacon Allen, vicar of Prees, Shropshire, resigned her post as Hon. Lady Superintendent of the Convalescent Home for Ladies, Scarborough, and nobly offered herself for the work. She accepted no salary, but her passage and preliminary expenses in England were to be paid, and the salary of the two trained nurses she took with her, being £25 and £28 a year. It was also agreed, that, as long as the funds could supply it, £100 per annum, paid half-yearly, should be placed in Miss Allen's hands to pay the nurses' salaries before stated, and to relieve the Mission of some portion of the hospital expenses. The generosity of Miss Allen in refusing to accept any salary, enabled the Ladies' Association to offer this.

The work of the Girls' School of the Mission presses
heavily on the one English teacher who, through unfortunate circumstances, has been left single-handed at
her post. Hitherto the Ladies' Association has been
unable to help this part of the work, though it naturally
falls within its province.

Funds are much wanted to continue this work. Subscriptions to the Ladies' Association should be paid to
Lady Campbell, Barham Cottage, Cupar, Fife, N.B., or
to Miss Uthwatt, Buckingham.

MISCELLANEOUS.

The *Shield* records the death of a much esteemed
friend and fellow-worker in Edinburgh, Miss Hope B.
Wishart. Her death has deprived the Repeal Cause of
one of its most faithful and zealous friends; she was
extremely earnest and energetic in her endeavours to
influence people's minds on that great moral question,
and though physically very delicate, contrived to get
through a greater amount of work than many strong
men could have accomplished. The influence of her
earnest spirit remains, though she has entered into her
rest.

Greycoat Hospital Female School.—August 4th being
prize day at the above institution, the children and their
friends assembled in the large school-room, when the
prizes were distributed by Mr. D. Smyth, chairman of
the board of governors, in the absence of the Bishop of
London. The number of pupils had increased from 100
to 140, but progress had not been so rapid as in the
boys' schools. The fact he believed to be that parents
had not as yet learnt to appreciate the fact that a good
education was as important to girls as boys. It had
been proposed to introduce dressmaking and cooking
into the teaching, and the subject was under consideration. Permission had been obtained from the Charity
Commissioners to extend the school term to 15 years,
and calisthenics had been introduced into the school.
One greycoat girl had already passed the Cambridge
examination, and the school generally had been placed
under the Cambridge syndicate.

THE *Æsthetic Review* for August, edited by Madame

Ronniger, contains a good article upon the Right Hon. John Bright's arguments against Women's Suffrage.

THE *Radical Review* issues its second number this month. It proposes to commence, in September, a series of articles on the Social Condition of Women and Children in England.

"The subject, it says, has not hitherto received merely the attention its importance demands, and when it has been discussed, the principles involved have been too frequently lost sight of. For a proper examination of this question it will be necessary to consider the home relations of parents and children, and of husband and wife; the marriage institution; women's suffrage; the various laws especially affecting women and children; and prostitution, with the laws relating thereto. The first article will indicate the general principles to be worked upon, and those succeeding will deal with the subjects just named. The object is to point out existing evils, and to suggest the direction in which remedies should be sought."

The *Radical Review* also contains a most appreciative article on Harriet Martineau.

THE *Women's Gazette,* for August, continues its excellent articles upon Nursing as a profession for Women. The London Hospital which contains 800 beds, employs sisters, sister-probationers, nurses and nurse-probationers, who are all under the superintendence of a lady who holds the office of matron. The candidates for the first-named are educated women only; their probationary term extends over three years, their salary begins at the end of the first six months, and is at the rate of £25, £30, and £35 per annum for the first, second, and third years respectively. Candidates for the post of nurse are drawn from the class of domestic servants; they also sign an agreement for three years, but their wages (£12, £18, and £21) begin at once. The sisterhood of St. John the Evangelist train their staff of nurses in two hospitals, King's College, 200 beds, and Charing Cross, 180 beds. In addition to the practical work in the wards, lectures on anatomy and physiology in application to nursing are given weekly to the pupils and probationers. There is room at present in St. John's House, 8, Norfolk-street, Strand, for about twenty lady-pupils. Ladies can be received as pupils for three or six months, but a year's training is necessary to obtain a certificate. When the projected Maternity Hospital has been built they will be able to give an equally thorough training in midwifery.

THE pupils of the North London Collegiate Schools have published two more numbers of *Our Magazine.* The composition, which is entirely that of the young ladies of the school, does them infinite credit.

THE *Women's Gazette* says the "Victoria Club" for ladies, 25, Regent-street, W., lies in a central position, and is within easy distance of the chief shops, theatres, railways, &c. It contains refreshment and waiting-rooms, and there is a buffet with light refreshments of the best quality, and at cost price, fitted up in the dining-room. Ladies wishing to dress for an evening engagement can have the assistance of a maid without extra charge, except for hairdressing. The terms of membership are—£3 3s. for a family ticket; £2 2s. for single tickets, and £1 1s. entrance fee. Only those are admitted who are introduced by an original member, *i.e.,* those who joined before the 1st January, 1876. We are very glad to hear of the establishment of this club, as few things are more wanted in London than places where ladies coming up from the country or suburbs can go for rest and refreshment.

MISS ELIZABETH THOMSON, who has joined the Roman Catholic Church, has, it is said, forsworn the painting of battle pieces, and will henceforth devote herself to sacred art.—*Athenæum.*

Australian Silk Depôt.—We have recently paid a visit to Mrs. Bladen Neill's depôt at 7a, Charles-street, Berkeley Square, and were astonished to find how much progress her work has made in the last few months. We were shown excellent samples of gentlemen's socks, ladies' neckties, &c., made in knitting-machines by the ladies working on the premises. The silk is made in white and colours, from what is commonly called the "rubbish," or outside waste from the cocoons. The price is therefore reasonable, and the material at the same time strong and durable. The workers are paid by the piece, and at present their earnings are not large; but they must recognise the fact that every business requires time for apprenticeship, and increased skill and dexterity will command larger pay. If ladies and gentlemen will patronise the depôt by giving orders for stockings and socks, Mrs. Neill will be able to employ more workers, and her praiseworthy efforts to promote employment for ladies deserve every encouragement. Beautiful silk for knitting and embroidery is sold at the depôt in a variety of colours.— *Woman's Gazette.*

ART. V.—WOMEN IN INDIA.

THE accounts given by Miss Carpenter of the progress which has been made among the native women in India, which have been published in the *Journal of the Indian Association*, are very interesting. The following extracts are from her lectures, and will be new to all who have not read the *Journal*:—" Among other things, on leaving Scinde I went to Poona, a very ancient city. There I found that the work of female education had been carried on well. In the Female Normal School a number of native young women had been trained with such success that about a dozen of them were actually keeping schools of their own. Of course, the tone of the instruction they imparted was not very high ; still, one of those engaged in the Normal School gave her lessons in a highly intellectual manner, and another displayed as much skill in teaching as any young English woman could have done. A proof of the progress which education is making in India is furnished in the fact that the native princes are getting such teachers to assist in the instruction of the ladies of their household. One of the young pupils of the Normal School was already established as a teacher in the court of a native prince, and another was now invited to go to the court of the Rajah of Kolapore. This is a very good augury. Besides the schools I saw, I was most gratified at the number of ladies, nearly sixty, who assembled in one of the ancient palaces which I visited, in order to meet me ; one of

the young women trained in the Normal School was
able to act as interpreter, and explained everything
which I wished. It was quite remarkable to see the
interest which all the ladies took in education, as the
fact of their coming out to see me conclusively proved.
*   *   *   *   *   From Poona I went to Madras.
Here I observed many features of interest, and signs of
progress in many ways, since my first visit to the place
nine years previously. I may mention in the first place
the erection of a large new hospital, the nursing department of which is under the supervision of two ladies who
had had long experience in the management of institutions in England, and they are instructing a number of
East Indian women in the duties of trained nurses. I
regard this as a most important movement; you can
hardly realise the distressing condition of the hospitals
when I first went to India; no nurses could be found,
and the management otherwise was defective; since
then great progress has been made. Not only are the
means of training for nurses provided; but in the medical
department arrangements have been made for the
instruction of ladies in medical science. At Madras I
saw four ladies taking their lectures with the gentlemen
students; the examiner questioned them with the others;
and I was proud to see that they answered equally well.
It is a most important thing in India,—where the
customs of the country make it most objectionable to
native ladies to be attended by doctors of the other sex,
—that there should be a number of ladies trained to
medicine, who would be able to instruct native women.
It is not sufficient that English ladies should go out
who have not learned the vernacular,—the difficulties
they would have to encounter would be at first great.
In addition to the training of nurses in this hospital is
another institution in Madras where this work is even
more valuable, I mean a large poor-house, the Monnegar
Choultry, which is under excellent management. I saw
it on the occasion of my former visit in company with
Lord Napier and Ettrick, and very much admired it;
since then it is greatly improved. There is a large
hospital attached, where a number of Eurasian women
are trained scientifically; a doctor heads the establish-

ment, and takes the women round the ward himself,
giving them instruction; after six months they are
trained in a midwifery and in a children's hospital and
then receive a certificate as qualified nurses;—medical
men are very well satisfied with the training they receive
in the institution.

At Bombay "Dr. Hunter had been training native
women in midwifery, and his classes were very well
attended; only those who were able to read and write
were eligible, and the fact that a number of them had
taken out their certificates is a sign that progress has
been made. I received from Dr. Hunter a list of what
had become of each, and I was pleased to find that they
were all employed, and that their skill was highly
appreciated."

"In Benares the movement for promoting female
education has made progress. That is the result of the
efforts of the Maharajah of Vizianagram, a most
enlightened and cultivated native prince, who, I am
informed, spends nearly half his whole income in
benevolent objects. He employs an English lady, Mrs.
Etherington, to superintend his schools, he taking the
whole cost of their maintenance. This lady has also
been appointed by the Government as female inspector,
and that is a very important thing in India; it would
be a good thing in England, but in India it is specially
important on account of the social prejudices which
exist with regard to the female portion of the population.
Mrs. Etherington has arranged suitable buildings for the
schools,—without any male attendants. She has also
engaged a number of female assistants, and the result is
that a number of young widows have been induced to
attend, and take lessons with the other pupils; as only
female teachers were employed, these young widows
were glad to attend and obtain instruction. An institution has also been established for training native women
to be medical practitioners; the women attending these
classes prove themselves as clever as the male students,
and it was most remarkable to see the ability which
they displayed in taking notes of lectures, and mastering
the contents of scientific books. After leaving the
classes they attend the hospital until they get a diploma,

and then are prepared to practice for themselves. If they had not had the opportunity of gaining instruction in the first instance without the presence of male teachers, they would never have been able to do this; —it was therefore of the greatest advantage to them that such schools had been established."

"In Ahmedabad there is much advance in female emancipation. A native lady with her husband met me at the station on my arrival, and I found that the ladies generally were permitted to walk about attended only by a servant, a custom which has not yet been allowed in any other part of India with which I am acquainted. A short time before my visit the daughters of a native judge actually delivered an address on the worship of the one true God to their countrywomen; on seeing the account of this in the newspapers I could hardly believe it, but the judge assured me that it was perfectly true, but he had wished the fact to remain private."

With respect to female education, it appears to me that the time has now arrived when there can be no real improvement without Government help towards providing proper teachers. In the first place, in all the Normal Schools for girls there ought to be regularly trained European female teachers. The Government adopted this plan when commencing Male Normal Schools, and good teachers were provided for the schools. This has been very successful. It can no longer be supposed as it was formerly, that encouraging female education is interfering with the native population. The natives have proved that they desire it, but it is out of their power to obtain good female teachers; native gentlemen cannot do this for themselves; nor can English voluntary effort accomplish it unaided. The circumstances of India are such that I would not advise any lady to go out there alone without proper introduction, support, and protection, which she cannot obtain without Government help. If any independent body were to form a fund to send trained teachers to India, they would be exposed to the greatest dangers unless they were under the protection of the Government. At the same time, any ladies who

z

wish to do good to their fellow creatures could hardly do a greater good than to qualify themselves as teachers, and go out to India to assist the native women to elevate themselves by education. * * * The Government recognise the importance of the Female Normal Schools; so much so that in Hyderabad, when a school was established and a lady teacher engaged to conduct it, the Government took upon themselves the whole of the expense. But in no one of the Normal Schools is there a regularly trained female teacher. There are excellent ladies superintending the schools at Madras and at Poona, but they have not been trained scientifically for teaching. That is the point which requires to be brought before the Government.

Art. VI.—FOREIGN NOTES AND NEWS.

France.

There are 75,000 women and 25,000 men engaged in laundry work in the neighbourhood of the capital. A Washerwoman's Union has been established. The address of this association is 89, Rue de la Reine, Boulogne-sur-Seine.

Five per cent. is deducted by the French Government from the salaries paid to clerks, &c., engaged in the telegraph offices. At the age of sixty, and if they have been in the service thirty years, they receive a pension amounting to half the average salary earned during the last six years of service. After their death their widows receive a third of this pension, but should the clerk die in his twenty-ninth year of service, his widow will receive no pension whatsoever, notwithstanding the deductions which have been punctually made from her husband's salary. Active protestations have, however, been made against this system, and a deputation recently waited on the Minister of Finance to discuss the matter. It is therefore probable that some alteration will be made, based on a more equitable principle.—*Labour News.*

Switzerland.

The *National* of Berne states that Mdlle. Isola Van Diest, of Louvain, has been appointed assistant professor of chemistry in the University of the Swiss capital.

Germany.

Princess Alice of Hesse has founded the following societies:—

1. "*Alice Frauenverein fur Krankenpflege*," under the Presidency

of H.R.H., with the object of training nurses for general practice in time of peace, and for nursing the sick and wounded soldiers in time of war. Its Central Committee is at Darmstadt; Branch Committees are spread over the whole Grand Duchy of Hesse.

Its institutions are :—

   a. A hospital (small) in Darmstadt.
   b. A School and a Home for Nurses.
   c. A Ladies committee for superintending the condition of the
       poor orphan children, who are boarded out of private
       families.

2. "*Alice-Verein fur Frauen-Bildung und-Erwerb*" (Society for women's work, and for improving the condition of women). It is also under the Presidency of H.R.H.

Its institutions are :—

   a. " *The Alice-Bazar*," a permanent place for selling women's
       work.
   b. " *The Alice-Lyceum*," in which courses of lectures are delivered.
   c. A school for educating girls to become teachers in the indus-
       trial schools.
   d. An industrial school.

3. The Princess has founded an asylum for the idiotic children of the Grand Duchy of Hesse, which is governed by a Committee of Gentlemen under the patronage of H.R.H.

A correspondent from Homburg says that an important conference of the friends of Women's Education and Employment will be held in Frankfort in October. Fräulein Bötte, of Stuttgart, and many other distinguished ladies will be there.

ITALY.

Signora Giorgina Saffi has lately published an excellent little pamphlet called the "Moral Law and Human Laws." It is reprinted from the ably-written journal, *La Donna*, a newspaper devoted to women's rights and interests, edited by Signora Gualberta, Adelaide Beccari. Madame Saffi, wife of Aurelio Saffi, formerly co-Triumver with Mazzini at Rome, is a well-known and popular writer, and her contributions to the literature on the question of state-regulated vice in Italy are likely to make a deep impression on her countrymen and women.

There is at present in Rome an Italian lady sculptress, Madame Maraini, whose works are said to be full of talent and originality.

Many Italian benefit societies for the working classes admit both men and women. The women's division of the working society at Imola is said to be in a peculiarly prosperous condition, though only of recent growth. Upon this Signor Fornione remarks, in the Emancipazione:—"The awakening of our working women to the principles and sentiment of association, is full of hope for all who have the well-being of the working classes at heart, when we see our sisters, wives and daughters, who form so great a part in our lives, joining with us in provident, economic and moral efforts, and sharing now, not only our home life, but also our associated life. The advance made this year has been great, although it has not reached the point we may hope to attain; it is made in spite of all efforts to the contrary on the part of that class which has hitherto dominated the feminine conscience, and it is precisely on account of their overthrow that the advance of the women's section is so valuable a result of our efforts."

In Rome a lecture was lately given in the Sala Mazzini upon "Woman's Mission." The lecturer, Ettore Ciolfi, exhorted women to free themselves from superstition by means of education and the study of good books. He showed how the co-operation of women as mother, sister and wife is absolutely necessary to the regeneration of society.

SWEDEN.

The *Women's Education Journal* gives the following account of the professional and commercial position of women in Sweden:—

"The Royal Decrees of September 29th, 1853, and October 21st, 1859, gave women the right to hold the post of teachers in the Primary Schools; the Royal Decrees of January 18th, and June 18th, 1861, admitted them after undergoing the necessary examinations, to exercise the professions of Surgery and Dentistry, whilst a series of measures passed by the Legislature in 1862—1863, granted them the right to superintend post-offices, to enter the telegraphic service under certain restrictions, and to hold places connected with the General Medical Service. Finally, the Royal Decree of the 3rd June 1870, admitted them to pass the necessary matriculative examinations in the higher Government Schools, which entitles them to enter as students in the State Universities and further to practise as physicians after undergoing the regular tests. Two exhibitions in aid of female students have already (in 1873) been founded, the one of £68 confined to the Upsala University for a student in any one of the faculties; the other of £333, is reserved for female students in the Carolinian Medical Institute of Stockholm. During the years 1871—1873, four women passed the Matriculation Examination, of whom two are pursuing their studies in the Philosophical and two in the Medical Faculty of Upsala. Schools of Midwifery exist in Stockholm, Gothenburg, and Lund, where gratuitous instruction is imparted in obstetrics in general, including the use of blunt and sharp instruments, vaccination, bleeding, the treatment of young children, &c. Much opposition had to be encountered before these privileges could be granted, but it has been so completely overcome that it is only in the most difficult cases surgeons are called in, nor has there been, since 1829, when former restrictions began to be removed, a single complaint of negligence or incapacity.

The number of teachers in the Government establishments is now 2,856, of which number sixteen teach drawing, and three music in schools for boys. In most branches of trade and industry women are beginning to hold a better position since they were granted full liberty in this respect by the law of 1864. They occupy important places in banking and insurance offices. There is more than one example of a branch bank managed solely by a woman, and in one provincial town the municipal funds have been under female management since 1871. In 1871, there were 4,055 women engaged in trade, of whom 2,675 had sole control of their own affairs. In the same year Sweden numbered 504 separate industrial establishments and workshops belonging to, and managed by, women. One woman has distinguished herself by mechanical inventions which she constructs in her own workshop ; two sisters are successful as goldsmiths, and one female watchmaker obtained a favourable notice at one of the London exhibitions. Several printing offices are also conducted by women. Women are largely employed wherever skilful fingers and delicacy have the advantage over muscular strength. In the porcelain manufactories of Gustafaberg and of Yorstrand, 329 women are employed, many of them in designing and enamelling. They monopolise all the branches of industry popularly supposed to be the peculiar property of women, amongst which is hair-dressing, and are employed largely in all shops.

INDIA.

Mr. Ananda M. Bose has exerted himself to establish a boarding school for the education of the young Hindu ladies at Calcutta, and, a large house with garden and tank having been secured, the school was to be opened on June 1st. Lord Northbrook has given 250 **rs.** towards it, and in the letter enclosing his donation expressed his deep interest in the movement. The school is intended to fill up the void caused by the closing of Miss Akroyd's (Mrs. Beveridge) school, in which Mrs. Phear, who has now left Calcutta, took such an active interest. Advanced and progressive education will be given in English as well as Bengali, including instruction in needlework, sewing, drawing and music. The school will admit boarding pupils and day scholars, and will be under the direction of a competent English mistress. One of its objects will also be to train up properly qualified female teachers with a view to remove a serious want felt in numerous girl's schools.—*Journal of Indian Association.*

The *Indian Mirror* says that several Brahmo ladies visited the Art Gallery at Calcutta early in May. Special arrangements were made with the superintendent for this visit, and the ladies much enjoyed seeing the collection of paintings.

Mrs. Wheeler, daughter of Rev. K. M. Banerjee, has been appointed Inspectress of girls' schools in Calcutta, the 24 Pergunnahs, and Hooghly.

NEW ZEALAND.

Several daughters of agricultural labourers, who went out to New Zealand a short time since, are now getting £35 a year and all found.

AMERICA.

Women Artists' Lending Fund.—At a meeting held to organize a Centennial Fund for the aid of women art-students, last month, at the studio of Mrs. Eliza Greatorex, No. 115, East Twenty-third Street, a subscription was begun which is to establish a fund from which shall be lent to women art-students sufficient means to begin, continue, or perfect their art education.

Mrs. Hackett Stevenson has been received as a member of the American Medical Association, the most important scientific body in the United States.

Law in New Jersey upon the Property of Married Women.—
1. Her wages and earnings in any employment carried on separately
from her husband, or any investment of such wages shall be her sole
and separate property.

2. She may bind herself by contract in the same manner and to the
same extent as if she were unmarried—these contracts to be obligatory
both in law and equity and to be enforced against her in her own
name apart from her husband, but she may not become an endorser,
or surety, or be liable on any promise to pay the debt of another.

3. Any married woman whose husband is an idiot, lunatic or of
unsound mind, or imprisoned in States Prison for crime, may during
the continuance of any of these contingencies, release, transfer or
convey any interest or right she may have in real estate as if sole;
but this shall not affect any right her husband may have in such
property.

4. If she acquire real or personal property, she may give a valid
receipt for it, which may be recorded if necessary.

5. She may, if of age, make a will, but she cannot affect her
husband's title to her real estate.

6. She may sue, and be sued in her own name.

7. She cannot execute a conveyance or mortgage of her real estate
without her husband joining her, nor can she deprive him of his
courtesy.

Women are employed in the Patent Office to make original
drawings; to trace these drawings on oiled muslin to be sent to the
lithographer; in sorting and pasting together prints and specifications.
They receive from four hundred and thirty dollars a year to one
thousand.

Art. VII.—QUESTION AND ANSWER.

"Women's Rights!" we have heard men saying
  With angry scorn in the word,
"The Right to argue and bluster!
  The fair print of nature all blurred!
To press in the crowd and stumble,
  To jostle and shriek and complain—
Are these Rights worth fighting for? answer,
  Do you hope in such to find gain?"

"Rights?" they are duties we ask for;
  We name *duty* what you name *right*—
The right to freedom and labour,
  To truth and justice and light!
If duty meant ease and pleasure,
  To fold our hands with no word—
If Rights meant but what you think them,
  We women would never have stirred!

The strength to have suffered is ours,
   Be it also our right to be strong—
Pain to soothe, truth to speak, laws to straighten—
   The strength to annihilate wrong.
We hear them moaning and crying—
   The little, the helpless, the weak,
We feel that their wrong is our own wrong,
   Do you wonder that we must speak?

That the struggle for life be made lighter;
   That toil and reward may be fair;
That the wasted form and shrunk feature
   May not fall to the worker's share.
That the faltering steps may walk firmer,
   That the wrinkles be smoothed from the brow,
That we may not weep for our daughters
   As we weep for our sisters now.

Though the night be yet dark around us
   Through the length and breadth of the land,
We have faith that the very darkness
   Is a sign that the dawn is at hand.
Our eyes may not see the glory—
   Our feet may have fallen by the way—
But others will rise up, ready
   To work as we're working to-day!

ART. VIII.—FURTHER REPORT OF THE MARRIED WOMEN'S PROPERTY COMMITTEE.

(*Continued from page 358*).

(*Continued from page 358*).

THE Seventh Annual Meeting of this Association was held on Friday, July 20th, in the library of the Social Science Association, 1, Adam-street, Adelphi, Mr. Jacob Bright, M.P., in the Chair.

The hon. CHAIRMAN, in opening the proceedings, said: Ladies and Gentlemen—We are here met to-day rather as a business meeting than for prolonged discussion, and my remarks will therefore be very few. The object of this association is to alter the law which confiscates the property of a woman when she marries; or, in other words, our object is to give a woman the same proprietary rights after marriage that she has before. This question was first heard of in Parliament in the year 1857, and was then introduced by Sir Erskine Perry. Since that time until the year 1868, nothing was heard of it in Parliament. In the year 1868 Mr. Shaw-Lefevre introduced a Bill upon the subject, which was carried by the casting vote of the Speaker.

The question was then referred to a Select Committee. The evidence was taken of witnesses from our own and other countries. The Committee decided in favour of the principle of the measure, but nothing further was done during that Session. In the Session of 1869, Mr. Russell Gurney introduced a Bill, and it was read a second time without a division. The feeling in the House in its favour was very strong. The Bill was referred to a Select Committee, and that Committee made some alterations in it. On the third reading it was opposed, but was carried by a large majority. In the House of Lords it was taken charge of by Lord Penzance, but it was too late to make any progress during that session. In 1870 Mr. Russell Gurney again introduced the Bill; it passed through the House of Commons without a division, and was taken charge of in the House of Lords by Lord Cairns. The Lords removed the principle from the Bill, and altered it so as to give protection to the wages of women, but little or none to their property; and the Bill was passsd in so complicated a shape that it led to great confusion, and very few persons, even of those for whose protection it was intended, understood how to obtain protection under it. At its next stage the Bill was in the hands of Mr. Hinde Palmer. He brought in a Bill in 1873, and probably he will himself give us some information on the subject. He got it into Committee, and struggled very hard and gave an immense amount of labour and time in order to get it through the House, and he was subjected to six "counts" in the course of the session. The Bill, of course, perished. However, the Association is still in existence, and it hopes by persistent labour to ultimately accomplish the object which it has in view. Unfortunately, there has been no Bill in the House this session, but still a good deal of work has been done, especially by the secretary, and I think, before sitting down, I should say that whatever progress of opinion has taken place on this question, and whatever improvements have been made in the law, are more due to the labour, the thought, and the influence which Mrs. Elmy has brought to bear upon the subject, than to any other cause. I will call upon Mr. Taylor to move the first resolution.

Mrs. VENTURI then read the Annual Report, which continued as follows:—

"During the Autumn of 1875 your Committee were in communication with Mr. Shaw-Lefevre, who introduced the original Married Women's Property Bill, and who undertook to introduce in the session of 1876, a Bill to Amend the Law with respect to the Property of Married Women. Mr. Shaw-Lefevre wishes it to be stated that he was unable to fulfil his promise, owing to the unusual pressure of other private members' Bills, which, even on the first night of the session had appropriated every available day.

"The Committee are glad to be able to announce that the Right Hon. the Lord Coleridge purposes, early next session, to introduce a Married Women's property Bill, and they earnestly appeal to their friends for such active support as may ensure the passing of a just and comprehensive measure."

Mrs. JACOB BRIGHT having read the treasurer's accounts, said:— We have to thank many friends for the generous pecuniary aid they have afforded us during a period of two years of activity. The mem-

bers of this Committee were encouraged to continue their.labours by
the offer of Mr. Shaw Lefevre to take up the matter.   At this time
they found themselves embarrassed with a debt of £158, but through
the prompt response made to their first appeal they were enabled to
discharge all their liabilities, and in two months from that date they
recommenced their work.   I have to report an increase in the total
subscriptions of £80 over the amount raised in any previous year;
and what is still more satisfactory, a proportionate increase in the
number of subscribers.   I trust this increase will continue, and that
the Committee may find themselves with sufficient means at their
disposal to prosecute their work with vigour and effect.   I would
urge those interested in the Married Women's Property Bill not to
refuse to give because they are only able to give small sums.   Until
this year the largest number of subscribers did not exceed 64.   This
number is now raised to 90, but considering the large interests at
stake one is surprised at the small number of those willing to aid a
cause so deserving of assistance.   I wish to call attention to this
point, because a few generous friends of justice towards women have
hitherto borne the whole of the burden which should be more widely
distributed.   Our grateful thanks are due to all those who have so
ably and generously given their time and strength to this cause.

The CHAIRMAN called upon Mr. Taylor to move the first resolution.

Mr. PETER A. TAYLOR, M.P., said: I have been quite unexpectedly
entrusted with this resolution, and I should have remonstrated at the
inappropriate prominence given to me in proposing the first resolution,
were it not that I am obliged to leave in a short time, and further,
that being merely a formal one, it requires no argument in support
of it.   Our excellent Chairman has told us that this is a meeting for
business only, and therefore you do not expect any explosion of oratory, and I shall exhibit that brevity which is said to be the soul of
wit, outside at least the House of Commons, and merely renew the
expression of my entire allegiance to the principle which our friends
here have so perseveringly and usefully vindicated, and to say that I
hall be happy to place at your disposal any humble services of mine
which at any rate may perhaps be effective, to the extent of being
one against a "count out" on this question.   I beg to move that the
report and statement of accounts just read be adopted, printed, and
circulated.

Mr. ARNOLD said: I have the greatest possible pleasure in seconding the resolution, because after hearing the report which Mrs.
Venturi has read, I felt that I, in common with other people, had a
good deal to learn on this subject.   I never heard a report which
contained in so short a space, so much valuable information.   I think
that the more widely that report is circulated the better; it will no
doubt be extremely beneficial to the cause.   I think that men, whether
married or unmarried, are deeply interested in this question, from
three points of view.   I should prefer, for my own part, dealing with
it from the moral point of view—in other words, from the point of view
of the general interests of society.   In that point of view, a wrong done
to any individual is an injury to society at large—that a person
should at one time of life possess or manage property, and that she
should be debarred from the use or exercise of that privilege after

marriage, must militate very seriously against the interests of society.
I think that every man is interested in this question, not only because
it relates to a partnership the most serious and most solemn any man
or woman can enter into, but because it is perpetuating in English
law a great disability, and a great wrong. He is interested, also, in
a lower point of view, because the law, as it stands at present, oper-
ates in the direction of inducing women possessed of property to
abstain from marriage. Now, it would not be desirable in the lowest
interests of men that women who possess property should be those
who have the strongest objection to marriage. The law is seriously
defective from that point of view. From a third point of view, men
are at disadvantage when they have entered into the marriage partnership—the property which they possess together cannot be generally
used to the utmost advantage by the married people. It often happens that when a woman has, to her own great injury, surrendered
all her property into the hands of her trustees, the hands of the
married pair are injuriously restrained, owing to the fact that the
possession of the property has been virtually surrendered, and that
they are unable to deal with it to the best account. So far, then, all
men, as well as all women, are deeply interested in this matter. I
have one word more with regard to the nation at large on this
question. I am not supposed generally to have a very great affection
for the Turkish Empire, and it does seem to me somewhat disgraceful
that we should be held in every part of the world to be giving our
moral support and friendship to the Turks; but on the other hand, I
am inclined to think that the friends of Turkey might retort upon us
that it is somewhat disgraceful that in this one respect the law of
Turkey should be so superior to our own—that in Turkey a woman
does retain possession of her property after marriage.

The resolution was carried unanimously.

Mr. HINDE PALMER then moved the second resolution. He said :
I have great pleasure in moving this resolution, because it records
one of the most important steps that this movement has achieved—
the fact that Lord Coleridge has undertaken to introduce a Bill in the
House of Lords on this subject. I have supported this Bill as a great
measure of law reform. I have taken it up on that ground because I
have not the slightest hesitation in saying that the branch of law with
regard to the property of married women is in a most disgraceful
condition, taken in a legal aspect. Scarcely anybody knows the rights
of married women, or how they can be carried into effect. You, sir,
have been good enough to allude to my exertions in the House of
Commons in the year 1874, and I may say that if it had not been for
your assistance that I doubt whether I should have got the Bill so
far as I was able to do ; but it was a great step, considering the indifference in that House to the rights of married women. If it had
not been for you, sir, coming down when the Bill was read a second
time, and when the Bill was in committee, and for the extremely
valuable assistance of Mrs. Elmy, we should not have achieved the
partial success we did achieve, notwithstanding all our efforts. However, we were prevented from carrying it that session ; but I should
mention this that the Bill was carried on a second reading by a very
considerable majority, and we should have got the Bill through com-

mittee very well if there had not been certain lawyers who took a prejudiced view of the matter, and they were enabled by the machinery of the House to prevent its getting further, although it did get through the committee. Some amendments were made to the Bill in committee, and consequently it had to be reconsidered afterwards, and at that stage there was always a motion to postpone it for three months or six months, as the case might be; and therefore we could not get it through the House of Commons. The law is in such a condition that it requires to be dealt with very carefully; and it is not in a condition to be remedied by one simple enactment. There are various matters connected with it which require careful consideration. As you know the Bill introduced by Mr. Russell Gurney in 1869 was referred to a Select Committee, and carefully settled by that committee, which contained several lawyers and men of eminence in the profession; and as it came out of the committee it was really a good Bill. But when it went to the House of Lords they so mangled it that when it came back to us it was an impracticable measure in many respects. All the good passages were struck out; and what were left were in such a state that nobody could tell how it could be carried into effect. We hear of the great advantage of the House of Lords in correcting the mistakes of the House of Commons; but in this case they did a great deal of mischief, and there, great doubts were entertained as to whether the Bill should not be rejected altogether. But it contained provisions protecting the earnings of persons in the poorer ranks of life, and it was therefore thought better to take it even as it was. That was the origin of that Act of 1870 which left the law in the unsatisfactory condition it now is. My great object has always been to point out that while persons in the higher class of life can by means of those marriage settlements secure to the married women a certain amount of the rights of property for their separate use—there is a large number of persons in this country in the middle classes engaged in business who have made considerable property and who never think of marriage settlements at all; and they are perfectly astonished when on their daughter's marriage they find that their share of property is confiscated to the husband. I wish to see a law enabling those in a more humble class of life to possess their property, as a matter of right and of law, instead of being compelled to resort to the scheme of marriage settlements. I desire to extend that wise principle of making a married woman entitled to her own property, not by means of marriage settlements, but by the general law of the land. I was going to suggest that the subject should be referred again to a Select Committee of the House of Commons so as to have the matter thoroughly sifted, but as Lord Coleridge is going to take it up, I think that will be by far the best step, because the evils are now so great that even lawyers say that they scarcely know what the state of the law is. It is a matter of congratulation that we have an increased number of subscribers to this Society. It is a question which affects a large class of society; and I think that if this most able report is circulated, so as to make the matter more generally known, the numbers of subscribers would be vastly increased. I beg to move the resolution, "That this meeting hereby expresses its hearty thanks to Lord Coleridge for his promise to take up the matter in the House of Lords early next session, and the meeting pledges itself to renewed activity to secure the passing of a comprehensive measure which shall establish for all women the same rights and liabilities as to property and contract as appertain by law to men."

Mr. H. N. MOZLEY said: I have great pleasure in seconding the motion. It is very gratifying to find that so great a legal luminary as Lord Coleridge has shown so warm an interest on behalf of a much needed change in the law. I entirely agree with the learned gentleman who has preceded me as to the unsatisfactory state of the law. The facts as to the passing of the Act of 1870 were these: The change in this law was first promoted by the Social Science Association. I speak especially as to what occurred at the Belfast Congress of 1867, on which occasion there was a very numerously signed memorial presented to the Congress praying them to urge Parliament to take measures for the amendment of the law on this question. The result of that was, that in the year 1868, Mr. Shaw Lefevre was induced to bring in a Bill. That Bill was a fairly exhaustive measure. It was introduced in 1869, and again in 1870. Of course, as this Bill took the property of a married woman from her husband, it was proper to provide that the husband should not be responsible for his wife's debts before marriage, and accordingly this clause was introduced as the 6th clause: "The husband shall not by reason of his marriage be liable for the debts of his wife before marriage." That provision was clearly just with reference to the Bill as brought in in 1868, 1869, and 1870. When the Bill of 1870 went to the House of Lords, the House of Lords mangled the first five clauses, substituted eleven others, and kept the last part of the measure as it was; thus putting new cloth to the old garment, and destroying the sense of the measure. Six years ago, prior to its passing, we had a meeting in this room to debate whether the Bill known since as the Married Women's Property Act of 1870 should be accepted or not. After some consideration we decided, notwithstanding the evil and uncertainty and obscurity of the Bill, that on the whole it was better to accept than reject it. We thought that the first section, which secures the earnings of a married woman to her for her separate use, was enough to counteract some of the faults of the Bill; and, moreover, we felt that the confusion and uncertainty which it was sure to introduce into the law would compel further legislation at a future time, while, owing to the Franco-German war it appeared improbable that an opportunity of achieving even that small amount of good would soon occur again. Therefore, this measure was accepted; but in the first four years of its operation, it acted so injuriously towards creditors that in 1874 an Act was passed patching up the Act of 1870. Here you have one Act patching up the mangled remains of another; and under those circumstances one can understand that the measure does not throw much light upon the subject. I think we all hold that nothing will be satisfactory except an entire reconstruction and renovation of the law on the proper basis of leaving to a married woman her own property entirely. There are one or two points to which I should like to make reference. I do not know whether Lord Coleridge proposes to touch a certain question—it is not necessary to touch it, but it ought to be mentioned,

—that is, that a married woman has no legal power without the consent of her husband to bring an action for wrongs done to her. I
think the right of suing for wrongs done would be included in the
power of suing and being sued as a *femme sole.* Suppose, for instance,
a woman is shut up in a madhouse, as sometimes happens, by her husband's connivance, or at his instigation; as the law stands she has no
civil remedy. Of course she has the right of a criminal prosecution,
for what it is worth, but she has no civil remedy for the wrong done
her. Another matter is this—a woman ought to be liable to bankruptcy. There is a case which I am sure Mr. Hinde Palmer knows,
the case of *Ex-parte Holland in re Heneage,* L. B. 9 Ch. App. 307,
where two of the judges held that a woman could not be made a bankrupt even as to her separate property, but the third judge, as this
woman had no property, was not prepared to go that length. We
know that by the custom of London a married woman can carry on
business and can be made a bankrupt. There was a case of a married
woman trading under the custom of London being prosecuted crimi-
nally for some offence against the Bankruptcy Law. I do not know
what was the end of that case, but no doubt seems to have been raised
as to the legal validity of the prosecution, or as to the legal status of
the woman for all purposes, civil or criminal. As present the law as
regards married women's contracts after marriage is in a very con-
fused state, and I am not quite sure whether we can remedy that
confusion, because every contract made after marriage must be
considered necessarily with regard to the circumstances of the
particular case. Some authorities go so far as to say that a
husband is not liable for necessaries supplied to his wife; some
authorities seem to go the other way, and I do not think that a
fair and satisfactory statement of the law can possibly be laid
down in that matter. There is another subject which has already
been spoken of to-day, and that is the right of a woman in reference
to her ante-nuptial property. That right is a very important one,
and the changes which have been made are utterly and wholly inadequate for her protection. I doubt whether they can be said to protect
a married woman's ante-nuptial property at all. I say that these
three main grounds—first, to enable a married woman to obtain a
remedy for her personal wrongs; secondly, to enable her better to
secure her ante-nuptial property; and thirdly, to make her liable to
the fullest extent to the law of bankruptcy;—on these points I hold
that a very great extension of the law in reference to this matter is
urgently needed. I therefore have the greatest possible pleasure in
seconding this motion. (Cheers.)

Mrs. DRUMMOND: I beg to move that the following persons be
appointed the Executive Committee for the ensuing year:

Mrs. Addey, Mr. Jacob Bright, M.P., Mrs. Jacob Bright, Mrs.
Butler, Mr. T. Chorlton, Sir C. W. Dilke, Bart., M.P.. Rev.
A. Dewes, D.D., L.L D., Mrs. Gell, Rev. S. Hansard. Mr. T.
Hare, Professor Hodgson, Mr. J. Boyd Kinnear, Mr. William
Malleson, Mrs. Moore, Mr. H. N. Mozley, Dr. Pankhurst,
Mrs. Sutcliffe, Mr. P. A. Taylor, M.P., Mrs. P. A. Taylor,
Mr. Thomas Taylor, Mrs. Hensleigh Wedgwood, Miss Alice

Wilson, Miss Lucy Wilson, and Mrs. Venturi, with power to add to their number.

Miss DOWNING : I must express my very great pleasure at being present at this meeting. Of course, this is a question to which I have given some attention, and from the report which has been presented to us I think it ought to be an encouragement to all working in any women's movement to take a great interest in this. It seems that a very great amount of valuable work has been done with an expenditure of funds which is very small indeed as compared with the expenditure of other public movements. I think any committee having upon it the names which have been submitted to us to-day would meet with the cordial approval of anyone connected with the work. I am very glad to hear that even lawyers themselves do not quite understand the Married Women's Property Act. I confess, in speaking upon women's questions, this is just the one subject upon which I am utterly and completely at sea. I have read over very carefully the laws connected with the subject, but I laid them down in a greater fog than I was in before. But as Mr. Mozley and Mr. Hinde Palmer have both said that even lawyers are in a fog upon the question, I am not ashamed to confess that I do not understand it. I should be very glad for any gentleman to tell me whether, if I put money in a bank it is my own property, or whether, if I happen to get married a month or two later, it goes to my husband. Certainly I should not think of entering into the married state without knowing something more definite than I do at present upon this subject. I need scarcely say that I and all who know anything of this question at all, are delighted to think that Lord Coleridge is about to bring in the Bill next session. It is such an opportunity for us that all who are interested in the movement ought to make every effort they can to try and aid him. That can be done by everyone, however small the subscriptions that we can afford to give to the association. It can be done by helping the cause in private, by speaking to one's friends, and in other ways, and I can only promise that, although this is my first attendance, I shall do my very best by giving my small subscription to help the association, and to endeavour to see this great measure of justice—perhaps one of the most important measures of justice for women—carried, probably next session.

Mrs. Arnold and Madame Venturi, having spoken, the meeting concluded.

<hr>

ART. VIII.—PARAGRAPHS.

AN American paper, devoted to the interests of women, gives the following biography of a musical composer who was not without celebrity in her day :—
Maria Theresa Priaduis, one of the most remarkable

musical composers and pianists of her time, was born at
Vienna, May 15, 1759. At five years of age she became
blind, but found consolation in music, for which she
displayed great aptitude. She had wonderful facility
in learning languages, and was familiar with Italian,
French, German, and English; very fond of sciences,
well instructed in geography and history, danced
gracefully, and was a fine chess-player. She had
various teachers, among them Salieri with whom she
studied dramatic composition. She was but eleven
years of age when the Empress Maria Theresa, after
having heard her play Bach's sonatas, granted her a
pension of 250 florins. In 1784 she visited several cities
where her musical performances excited the greatest
interest. The most celebrated artists of the epoch,
Abel, Fischer, Solomon, felt honoured to aid her with
their talent. In 1785 she gave concerts in London.
In 1786 she devoted herself to composition, published
various works for musical instruments, and brought out
several operas at Vienna and Prague. The house,
visited by the most distinguished personages of Vienna,
was the rendezvous of foreigners who admired the
charm of her conversation and her unwonted kindness.
This remarkable woman died at Vienna, February 1,
1824, at the age of sixty-five years. Besides several
operas she wrote a grand cantata upon the death of
Louis XVI., also a cantata upon the death of the
Emperor Leopold, and several sonatas, canzonettes, etc.

In Austria women are classed with minors, infidels,
and idiots in their inability to be witnesses to wills, and
in Spain with thieves or murderers in the same incapacity; in both countries they can make wills independently of their husbands.

Intemperance.—In the Commission Court, Dublin, on
August 10th, Chief Justice Morris said, the experience
of the present Commission had disclosed a terrible
increase in the drinking habits of women of the humbler
ranks; "it really seemed as if they were becoming as
bad as the men." In America women are almost unanimous in their opposition to intemperance. In some
cases their votes have been taken on this subject. If

Englishwomen had also this opportunity to enter an efficient protest against intoxication, it seems probable that their self-respect would produce a wholesome reaction.

OUT-DOOR LABOUR FOR WOMEN IN TYROL.

The annual total emigration of the male population of this valley compels the women to do the work of the men. There is probably not a single man above 18 or 20, and below 60 or 70 years of age, in that (Defferegger) valley for four of the spring and summer months. You see women fell trees, drive their heavily-laden carts, till the ground, gather fodder, chop wood, and if you enter one of the village inns you will see rows of women, their short pipes in their mouths, and elbows leaning on the table, drinking their pint of Tyrolese beer after their hard work. * * * * Hardworked as women are in the Tyrol, their lot is by no means an unenviable one They are uniformly treated in a kind manner by their husbands, and wife-beating or brutal handling of women is entirely unknown in the country.—*Tyrol and the Tyrolese,* by W. A. Baillie Grohman.

Country Life in Syria, by Harriet Rattray.—One can never sufficiently admire the patient fortitude with which the women go through their daily task of severe manual labour, never relaxed for sickness as long as it is possible to move about, and living upon the most wretched diet that can keep body and soul together. * * * * In every family the women and girls content themselves with what the lords of the creation choose to leave, when they do leave anything at all. They (the women) satisfy the cravings of hunger with dry bread, among the poorer classes, with uncomplaining cheerfulness, only considering themselves in a pitiable condition when they have been without bread at all for a day or more. How these women can perform hard labour, and walk from thirty to forty miles a day, scarcely ever sitting down to rest, from sunrise (or rather from break of day), and usually nursing a small infant, upon such scanty nourishment, seems so incredible that I can hardly expect you to believe it. * * * *

Englishwoman's Review.

CONTENTS FOR SEPTEMBER, 1876.

All Communications to be addressed to the Editor, 22, Berners Street, Oxford Street, W.

Post-Office Orders payable to Sarah Lewin, at the "Regent Street" Post-Office.

Terms of Subscription at the Office.

Per Annum (Post Free), Six Shillings.
Subscriptions payable in Advance. Single Numbers posted Free on receipt of Six Postage Stamps.

MSS. are carefully read, and if not accepted are returned, on receipt of Stamps for Postage, but the Editor cannot be responsible for any accidental loss.

Contributions should be legibly written, and only on one side of each leaf.

THE

ENGLISHWOMAN'S REVIEW.

(NEW SERIES.)

No. XLI.—September 15th, 1876.

Art. I.—REGISTRATION OF WOMEN MEDICAL PRACTITIONERS.

History has frequently had to record the fierce bombardment of some fortress, which after mine and countermine, assault, retreat, and perils in the "imminent deadly breach," has been quietly and pacifically yielded up by treaty, with not even a flourish of trumpets to chronicle its surrender. Thus the Bill to admit women students of medicine to examination was passed so quietly last session, that many did not know till they read in the *Times*' summary of the work accomplished during the summer, that the point which had been so hotly contested for successive years was at last decided. It will be remembered that this Bill was brought forward by the Rt. Hon. Russell Gurney and the Rt. Hon. John Bright. It enacts that "the powers of every body entitled under the Medical Act to grant qualifications for registration, shall extend to the granting of every qualification for registration granted by such body to all persons without distinction of sex, provided always that nothing herein contained shall render compulsory the exercise of such powers, and that no person who, but for this Act, would not have been entitled to be registered, shall, by reason of such registration, be entitled to take any part in the government,

A

management, or proceedings of the Universities or
Corporations mentioned in the said Medical Act."

It will be remembered that Mr. Cowper Temple had,
earlier in the session, introduced a Bill to enable women
who had obtained degrees in certain foreign Universities
to be registered as medical practitioners. This measure
was brought forward in consequence of the failure last
year to pass a measure enabling Scotch Universities to
examine women students. The matter was then hotly
contested, the old and time-worn argument of the
indelicacy of women studying medicine being varied on
the part of those who conceded the abstract reasonable-
ness of the claim by the plea that it was an unwarrant-
able and partial interference with the prerogatives
of the Universities of one country, because it left
those of the other countries untouched. Last July
the matter was discussed in a much more tem-
perate spirit. Very little was said of the indecorum
of women wishing to be doctors, but the main point of
objection rested on the unfairness of admitting women
to a special privilege, while men possessing foreign
diplomas were still excluded from registration, thus at
once establishing a distinction between male and female
students. Mr. Cowper Temple did not press for a
division, as Lord Sandon, on the part of the Government, promised to give their assent to the Bill brought
forward by the Recorder and Mr. Bright to enable
English Corporations and Universities to admit women
to examination if they desired to do so, taking care to
make it clear that the Bill was permissive and not compulsory. He added that he was afraid there was no
chance of passing the Recorder's Bill at that late period
of the session, and though Mr. Bright deprecated any
additional delay as inflicting great injury both on the
ladies who were studying, and on patients who desired
their services, yet most of the friends of the movement
feared that this tardy measure of justice would not be
meted out till next year. The supporters of the Bill,
however, were indefatigable. The principal opponent
of the Bill, himself in the profession, was satisfied when the clause was added that women were
not, by virtue of this Bill, entitled to take part in the

government and management of the Corporations which registered them.   The Bill was read the second and third time without a division, and during the "small hours" when newspaper reporters have generally abandoned their gallery; consequently it excited little, if any, public attention.

The measure, of course, is only permissive, not compulsory. Many of the Corporations, probably, were in no need of it, and might have examined women always if they had chosen to do so.   The Society of Apothecaries had always had the power till they disabled themselves from doing it by providing that if any part of the education of the students were privately conducted (an inevitable condition of women's medical instruction then), those students should not be qualified for admission.   The Edinburgh University only discovered its inability to examine lady students after two or three years had passed in educating them.   The charter of the College of Surgeons required them to examine any candidates; they acknowledged there was a legal claim, but when ladies did come up for examination a new impediment was thrown in their way.   The three examiners

—stood calm and silent
And looked upon the foes,

and resigned their situations rather than examine the lady candidates.   The "strike" still continues: the College is bound by law to examine (not merely *permitted* to do so), but they have no examiners, having none to replace the gentlemen who resigned.   But there is good reason to expect that the same spirit of ungenerous exclusiveness will not animate all the seventeen Examining Bodies.   It has been repeatedly declared that one, at least of the Scotch Universities is ready to do this act of justice, and the London University has during the last two years shown signs that it will not lag far behind. We may look upon the legal difficulty as conquered— the hard fought battle as won; but there still remains one most serious difficulty—no general hospital containing the requisite number of beds (100) in London admits women students.   All the London hospitals of the necessary size, with the exception of two, are already connected with a school for men.

The new hospital for women in the Marylebone Road, fails to meet the requirements of the examining bodies; it has only 26 beds instead of 100, and it is not a general hospital, as it is confined to women and children. Various ways may be found out of this difficulty. A new hospital of the requisite size may be founded, but it is doubtful if sufficient funds can be forthcoming, as the estimate of expense is £5000 a year, and a building fund to begin with of £16,000; or it is possible that some London hospital may yet open its gates to lady students, which might be done without interference or injury to the present students. Or some country hospital may permit their attendance. The Governors of Queen's Hospital in Birmingham some months ago passed a resolution to this effect, and other hospitals will probably show themselves equally liberal now that Parliament has distinctly expressed its opinion, that women students should be allowed equal facilities with men. The matter must quickly be decided, for the lady students cannot go on much longer learning the theory of medicine without having the opportunity of seeing it put into practice. The Medical Council having decided that "women ought not to be excluded from the profession," must next take into consideration how they may best be qualified to enter it, with advantage to themselves and safety to their patients; women, having permission to be examined, must also have permission to learn, and that speedily. It has taken three years to convince Parliament of the first—we must trust that the medical authorities will take a shorter time to learn the second lesson.

Art. II.—WOMEN PRINTERS AND EDITORS.

IT is a statement commonly received as fact, that it is only within the last decade and a half, that women have been admitted into the printing trade. This is only exactly true with reference to England. In other countries, and especially in America, where the arbitrary distinctions between masculine and feminine employments were not so rigidly drawn, women had been known as printers for two hundred years, conducting not only the business details of the printing establishment, but performing the manual operations of the art with great dexterity. Their connection with literature dates indeed earlier than this. The first daily newspaper, *The Daily Courant*, printed in England, is said to have been established by Elizabeth Mellet, in London, during Queen Anne's reign, in 1702. In the same reign too was established the first paper for women, called "The Ladies' Diary or Women's Almanack." Its contents are curiously meagre compared with the voluminous items in our modern magazines. Its prospectus announced that it contained "directions for love, marriage, preserving, cookery, perfumery, bills of fare, and many other concerns peculiar to the fair sex." There was poetry, the calendar, with the common notes of the year and eclipses. A picture of the "Queen" in copper, very well engraved. The rest of the almanack consisted of "delightful tales;" the editor having tried but failed to obtain the biographies of celebrated queens. The existence of such a magazine scanty as it was, showed however, that women were beginning to take an interest in literature. The earliest newsvendors appear to have been known as "Mercurie Women," they dispensed the papers among the hawkers. In France, when in 1681 the *Gazette de France* was first issued, women were the chief distributors.

But returning to women actually engaged in printing, we shall find them chiefly in America. Nearly every State of the "Old Thirteen" could boast of its woman printer during the eighteenth century, and some, indeed, practised the art much earlier. They were generally widows who carried on successfully their husbands' business, or daughters initiated into their fathers' trade, but it is evident from their success that they must have thoroughly understood their work.

Women printers were known first in Boston, with the sole exception of the wife of Benjamin Harris, a Canadian, who was in 1680 confined in the pillory in England, for publishing a petition; during his absence his wife con-

tinued his business. In Boston, Mrs. Green, the wife of
Samuel Green, a printer, is known to have been fully
engaged in the business as early as 1686. During the
same year a Mrs. Wilkins, also of Boston, commenced
printing and publishing various matters. The *Boston
News Letter* the first regular newspaper published in
America, was carried on by Margaret Draper, from 1774
to 1776. She went to England when the English troops
abandoned Boston and received a pension from the
government. Mrs. Penelope Russell succeeded her
husband in printing the *Censor*, also at Boston, in 1771.
She was an active, clever woman, and could not only
set type rapidly and well, but often while at the case
would compose short sketches and notes without any
written copy whatever. She educated two industrious
young women to assist her in the work of printing.
Mary Crouch, another widow, carried on her husband's
printing establishment in Charleston some time, and then
removed to Salem, Massachusetts, where she started a
Gazette which proved so prosperous that after some
years she retired with a comfortable fortune.

New York was not far behind. Mrs. Zenger, the wife
of John Zenger, who published the second newspaper
established in that city carried on the business most
successfully, as well during her husband's life-time as
after his death. This was about 1750. She published
the *New York Weekly Journal* for three years. The same
paper was, 45 years later carried on by Mrs. Mary Holt.
Her publication performed such marked services for the
revolutionary cause, that as a reward Mrs. Holt was
appointed printer to the State of New York, the only
woman recorded as ever having filled this post. The
paper was afterwards purchased by Thos. Greenleaf,
and on his death, in 1798, his wife published both a daily
and bi-weekly edition for some time.

The Rhode Island women were equally enterprising.
The original Declaration of Independence was printed
by Mary Catherine Goddard. She was a sister of William
Goddard the first printer in Providence. He was deeply
engaged in public matters, and his sister meanwhile
conducted the affairs of the printing office with great
ability, personally performing the duties of a printer, and

she was energetic and methodical in her management of
the business.   There seems to have been another woman
printer of similar name in Providence, in 1776—Sarah
Goddard, a well-educated and clever woman, who conducted a newspaper for two years with ability.   On the
death of James Franklin, brother of Benjamin Franklin
in 1735, his paper, the *Rhode Island Gazette*, was conducted
by his widow till her son was old enough to assume
control.   This lady is described as being a woman of
vast energy, industry, and experience.   She had entered
the printing office in 1732.   She became printer to the
colony and published pamphlets, supplied the public
offices with blank forms of all kinds, and also carried on a
general publishing business.   In 1745 she printed for the
government an edition of the "Laws," containing 340
pages.   She was assisted in the office by her two
daughters, who were also clever, capable women, and a
maid servant usually worked the press.

The Bradfords, both husband and wife, were among
the best of the early printers in Philadelphia.   He died
in 1742, having edited the *American Weekly Mercury*,
the third newspaper on the American continent.
Mrs. Bradford continued it for some years and carried on
the business with energy.

In the South, women were also proficient in the trade.
Mrs. Hassebotch, a Dutch woman, was the wife of the
first printer in Baltimore; she succeeded to her husband's
business, and conducted it with talent and industry.
Mrs. H. Boyle published a newspaper in favour of the
crown, in Virginia, during 1774: she is said to have
been a good printer, thoroughly understanding her
business.   Mrs. Timothee published the *Gazette* in
Charleston, South Carolina, for two years after her
husband's death, in 1774; and Clementina Rind published
a newspaper of the same name in Virginia, in 1773.

The present century has been equally fertile in women
journalists, and they are very numerously employed in
the mechanical art of printing.   In Chicago alone there
are about a hundred female compositors.   No physical
disqualification or inferiority to men, seems to be urged
against them: their attendance is as regular.   The
United States *Christian Register* gives it as its expe-

rience that a woman is absent from her case on the plea of sickness fewer days in a year than a man. For eight or ten years all the type-setting for the *Register* has been done by women of only average health, and it is very seldom that one of them is ill even for a day. Some are always at their posts.

In England no attempts were made to open the profession to women till, we believe, 1859, when the Society for the Employment of Women turned its attention to the pressing necessity of providing more varied, and consequently better paid occupations for women than those they are ordinarily engaged in. A small press and type sufficient for an experiment were purchased, and with the assistance of Miss Faithfull, the enterprise was started. By the next year sixteen female compositors were in training: four of these, however, had already received some degree of training in their fathers' printing offices. Encouraging letters were received from various parts of the country. At the present time women compositors are employed by several firms in London, amongst whom we may instance Messrs. Bale and Sons, Messrs. Danks, and Messrs. Boldero and Foster. The Women's Printing Society which has been lately established in temporary offices, Castle Street, Holborn, offers special advantages to girls desirous of learning the business. Many parents who would feel scruples about apprenticing their daughters to an ordinary printing establishment where most of the employés are men, might be willing to send them for instruction here, especially as several ladies of position are on the Board of Directors. In 1871 there were 741 female printers in England, according to the census.

In Scotland women were first employed in printing by Mr. Turnbull, George Street, Edinburgh, during the fifty-one hour strike, in December, 1871, when it occurred to him to try how far females might be trained to do the work. He took on a few, and being pleased with their progress brought two or three publishers to see their work. Miss Lewin thus writes in 1874: " Girls and women are now employed by Messrs. Chambers, Messrs. McNeile, and others, altogether about eighty are now

working as printers in Edinburgh. At first, Mr. Turnbull
thought they might in time earn as much as men, but he
now sees that they have not the same physical strength ;
but after two years of steady careful work a girl could well
earn from 15s. to 18s., and perhaps £1 per week. This
would also go farther in Edinburgh than in London, as
the girls would probably be able to go home to dinner,
and certainly be able to walk to and from their daily
work. The greater part of Taine's last work on English
Life was printed by girls in Edinburgh. The chief
faults their employers had to complain of were want of
accuracy and perseverance. Their spacing was apt to
be irregular, and, in some cases, their attendance. These
faults, however, he thought they were now trying to
overcome." There are no women compositors or
readers in Glasgow.

Unfortunately, now that it is fairly shown that women
can make their way in this trade, opposition is arising
in many quarters among the workmen. Mr. Gladstone,
many years ago, predicted the printer's monopoly—a
powerful combination, which has for its first principle
that no woman shall be employed ; " because women are
admirably suited for that trade, having a niceness of
finger, which would enable them to handle type better
than men." As an instance of this opposition we may cite
those Manchester printers, who, three years ago, hearing
that some girls were practising type-setting, passed a
rule ordaining a strike in the shop of any master printer
who should allow type set up by women to be sent to
his machines to be worked. A deputation of Edinburgh
operative printers deposed before the Factory Acts
Commissioners last year that they objected to the employment of women in the composing rooms ; a deputation of master printers had previously declared that
they would be glad to employ women more largely
than they do at present, but are prevented from doing
it by the legal restrictions which prevent women from
working occasionally overtime. There can be no doubt
that in this, as in other trades where women will
generally work for a lower rate of wages than men,
masters would be willing to employ them, and it is
equally natural that the work-people already employed

should resent an influx of cheaper labour. It is said that a more organised resistance to the competition of women in this branch of industry may shortly be expected; if it should prove so, the women printers must try the benefit of union among themselves, a system already found so efficacious in other trades.

Meantime it is gratifying to see that the same causes which prompt women here to seek new trades, acting in other countries, have met with like results. In Sweden, women conduct several printing offices. There are 676 male and 159 female printers, according to a recent computation; consequently more than one-fifth are women. In Prussia they are also employed.* In France, M. Martineau has a large typographical training institute for girls at Pluteaux near Paris; he has sixty women now with him whose work he reports to be highly satisfactory In Austria women are employed by the government in type-founding, which is surely a more arduous labour

---

* A printing office for women alone was last year started in Berlin, its prospectus was as follows :—

"The undersigned committee of the Lette-Union, under the protection of her Imperial and Royal Highness the Crown Princess, gives notice that by the efforts of the members of this Union, a printing-office and compositors' school for women has been established at No. 47, Ritterstrasse. The aim is to instruct women and girls as compositors, and either employ them constantly, or, after they have attained complete knowledge of their profession, to find independent situations for them in other printing offices. The success hitherto attained by the female compositors' school affords satisfactory proof of the capacity of women for this avocation. Printing of all kinds can be accomplished at the shortest notice and most moderate prices. We appeal to the directors and directresses of the girls' schools, and to the committee of the various unions to contribute to the prosperity of our establishment by confiding to us the printing for their schools, prospectuses of their unions, reports, &c., &c. We have only been able to take a limited number of pupils as yet, as owing to the novelty of our enterprise, we must employ them for a long time in our service before we shall be able to obtain other situations for them. If more work flows in more compositors can be trained. We trust that you who have always given the education of girls, and the furtherance of humane schemes your help, will give a friendly hand to our enterprise. Please direct to the Superintendent of the printing office, Herr Carl Jauke, 47, Ritterstrasse, Berlin.

"Respectfully yours,

"The Committee of the Lette-Union.

than type-setting.   In Italy, though we have not heard
of women being employed in printing, two newspapers
are now published by ladies ; *La Donna* by Mdlle. Beccari,
at Venice, and *La Cornelia* by Mdme. Faliero, at Florence,
and another in Spain, *La Violeta*, was a few years ago
published by a woman.   Finally, at the Cape of Good
Hope a few months ago girls were employed to set type
by Messrs. Saul, Solomon & Co., with such success that
now a large number are employed.

Women are fairly started in the business, but there is
still before them a long period of discouragement and
peculiar difficulty, before the trade will be considered as
naturally a feminine employment as needlework or
teaching.   Meantime we would urge upon all ladies who
require printing to be done, to inquire whether the
printer they select employs women in his office, and to
give the preference where it is possible, to anyone who
is doing his best to help on a very laborious class of
women in a comparatively new and arduous undertaking

Art. III.—AT AN ELECTION.

Scene.—*An open market place—a polling booth at one
side, groups of people gathering round it.*
Enter two ladies.

1st Lady. Can you discover for what reasonable reason I may not vote, when my tenants to a man, have
come in to perform that duty to the State ?

2nd Lady. *(Laughing.)* Oh yes, easily ; for the very
reasonable reason that women have different work from
men.

1st Lady. As if voting could alter any immutable
fact !

2nd Lady. You know it would require us to think
more about many important things than we do now.

1st Lady. Yes, but would that hurt either us or our
work ?

2ND LADY. Oh yes, we should care far less for our
worsted work and croquet; we might even prefer a
visit to that den of horrors *(pointing to the polling booth)*
than to the dress-maker.

1ST LADY. Was not the rush and crowd at the
regatta you went to last week as great as at that " den
of horrors ? "

2ND LADY. True, much greater, but elections are
not suitable topics for drawing rooms.

1ST LADY. Can you name a drawing room in the
county where Mr. A. *versus* Mr. B., and Mr. B. *versus* Mr.
A. has not been discussed for the last month ?

2ND LADY. Oh well, amateur fashion; but if it were
really taking a serious part—besides women have no
physical force, and you know the professors of history
have discovered that no one has a right to vote who
cannot back that vote by a cudgel.

1ST LADY. Glorious discovery for this age of culture !
Ah, here is poor Mr. G., how lonely he comes along.
He would make a worse figure with a cudgel than I
should, for all that he has three votes or more in different
places.   [*Exeunt the ladies.*
Enter Mr. G., leaning on his son's arm.

SON.   There is Miss F., she has driven in some of her
people to vote.

MR. G.   She has far more right to vote herself—
although she would vote for Mr. B.   She is a capital
farmer, and knows what the people want; it's a shame
she can't vote.

SON.   How can you say such things, women never
ought to vote.

MR. G.   Your reasons if you please?

SON.   They never did, and so they never should.

MR. G.   Ay, but your reasons?

SON.   It's not natural.

MR. G.   I doubt elections being natural; they are
products of political art, therefore any arrangement connected with them might just as well be styled artificial
as natural.

SON.   Politics are our affairs, women should stay at
home.

MR. G.   As the little girls stay at home from school
" to mind the baby ? "

SON. Yes, let them teach the young ideas to shoot.

MR. G. Ah! to shoot where they never learned to shoot their own.   [*Exeunt.*

Enter some country people.

COUNTRY WOMAN. There are the folks voting. What gives a vote Tom?

COUNTRY MAN. Taxes! People that pays taxes votes; I pays taxes, I am going to vote.

C. WOMAN. I pay taxes too. I'll go and vote along with you.

C. MAN. Nonsense Mary, you can't.

C. WOMAN. Can't? Why can't I?

C. MAN. Because you're a woman; a woman's vote is no good.

C. WOMAN. No good? are my taxes no good then? and it was only last Tuesday I paid them.

C. M. Oh! What has taxes to do with it? Come on Jack, we'll go and vote.   [*Exeunt.*

2ND COUNTRY WOMAN TO AN OLD MAN. What can have to do with it, if Jack can vote and Mary can't? It can't be brains, for hers are as good as his any day. It can't be work either, for she works as hard as he, and it can't be learning, for Jack can scarcely read nor write his name, and Miss F., with all her books and her farms, has not a vote either they say. What is it at all?

OLD MAN. It's what'll choose the best man; that's what it is.

2ND COUNTRY WOMAN. That's what it ought to be you mean; still how will Jack choose better than Mary could if they would let her?

―――――――――

ART. IV.—THE BERLIN HOUSEKEEPERS ASSOCIATION.

From the German of Madame Lina Morgenstern in the Frauen-Anwalt (Woman's Advocate).

THE woman's question arose first of all in the hearts of individual and solitary women like a little spring out of the hard rock of some lonely mountain; their timid complaints were unheard in the beginning, but like that stream, they have been joined by others till they have swollen to a mightier current which has forced a way for itself. Its origin was the unsatisfied longing of women who could find no sphere for their slumbering capabilities, and their misdirected efforts occasionally brought contempt and mockery upon their cause.

Then the education question arose; the future of the human race lies in the hands of the mother: the endeavour to bring up a child not only with a view to family life, but as a member of the entire whole of humanity, awakened a fire of enthusiasm in the hearts of those German women who longed for a more expanded scheme of life. It was not enough to take thought for the special needs of childhood; the whole influence of education upon human nature affecting the child's relations with the community and the State was taken into consideration. Actuated by these new views, the pioneers of the Woman's Movement endeavoured to give girls the same opportunities of acquiring practical knowledge and the power of logical thought as the youth of the other sex: not only special feminine studies, but a genuine liberal education was required for girls. But as all women are not in independent circumstances, or have others working for their support—as, more especially at the present time, nearly half of the female sex misses its natural profession of marriage, or are thrown upon their own resources as widows, it follows that self-dependence must be a woman's first aim if she will not fall a victim to poverty and contempt. Thus the bread-question became the source which gave ever renewed life to the Women's Movement.

Unions for the furtherance of industrial opportunities for women were formed, which removed one hindrance after another out of the way of women's labour, and opened to the sister members new spheres of work suited to their capabilities, and the power, earnestness and contentment fostered by these societies, secured their own welfare and that of the community. But all these efforts had to struggle against the stream of general opinion, and received sympathy and help only from a few individual women: the majority of women

housekeepers were still indifferent to the woman question
It is too frequently found that the possession of a
tranquil home and pleasant surroundings makes a woman
self-indulgent and self-seeking, looking with indifference
on the struggles and storms of the outer world. So it
happened that the women householders had for a long
time no sympathy with the woman's movement, although
mothers with growing-up daughters could not entirely
avoid recognising it as a fact that they at least must be
affected by these questions.

But the time came when housekeepers also were
drawn into the stream. It was during the hard and
unsafe year of 1873, which pressed so heavily on all
household comfort, that it became a question of necessity
that housekeepers should unite their forces for self-help.
Although the struggle appeared to be for the interest of
their individual families, yet they were in reality working for the home welfare of the whole nation, so large a
part of men's incomes (which combined, form the
national resources) go through the hands of their wives.
It was an hour of great importance when these lady
housekeepers first recognised that household discomfort could be best fought by their uniting for
mutual help. The ladies first joined together owing to
the increasing dearness of the necessities of life, and
few grasped the real issues of their combination.
Individual economy is of little value if it does not have
an influence upon the market, and the housekeepers
obtained this influence not only by combination, but by
making themselves acquainted with the prices of everything pertaining to marketing, shopping, or wages.

The Berlin Housekeepers' Association came into life
in 1873. They were, of course, aware that in a city
where such decentralization exists, as in Berlin, it would
be difficult to exercise an influence upon market prices.
They first tried to enter into an agreement with contractors, who depending on the security of all the
members of the Union, would supply their wares to the
individual members at a considerable reduction. The
ladies also met together to discuss economic and household subjects. It was admitted that one of the first
cares of the Housekeepers' Association must be to reform
domestic service.

In the course of time the former relations between
servants and employers in Germany had entirely changed.
Formerly service in a respectable family was not only
the most honourable, but the only means of livelihood
for unprovided girls.   Now with the increase of factories
and workshops, where young girls can obtain better
wages, combined with a freer mode of life, they prefer
these situations to domestic service; and mistresses are
in a difficult position, especially those ladies who look
upon their servants not as flesh and blood like themselves, but as machines, from whom only blind obedience
must be expected.   The members of the Association
established a servants' registration and inquiry office,
gratis, but only admitting those who bore a good
character.   During the two and a half years of its
existence, 10,000 female servants and workwomen have
procured situations through this registry.   The Committee, also having examined the legal regulations for
domestic service, which were enacted in 1810, suggested
to the authorities alterations in various clauses, which
have been accepted, with great advantage to all parties.

To make a propaganda of its views, the Association
resolved at one of its monthly assemblies to issue a
newspaper, "The German Housekeepers' Newspaper;
this has appeared since April, 1874, and is edited by the
President of the Association, Frau Lina Morgenstern.*
This paper, which contains price lists, &c., appears
weekly with a circulation of 4,000 subscribers, and has
not a little influence upon the furtherance of the woman's
movement in Berlin.

In July, 1874, the Association resolved, by purchasing
their provisions wholesale, to secure the advantages
of cheapness, of which hitherto they had been deprived by the shopkeepers.   The Central Bureau was
established, beginning with the small capital of 100
thalers, and it was found to supply the wants of the
members so effectually that, by the close of the year,

---

* Frau Morgenstern in 1866 had, in company with two or three
other ladies of influence, established several " People's Kitchens,"
restaurants where meals could be obtained at the retail cost of the
materials.

2,000 families were members, and shared its benefits. In January, 1875, the husband of the President, Herr Morgenstern, was chosen as Manager, with full powers, as the greatly increased business required the entire time and powers of an honourable business man. This was the more necessary as the Association is not a Corporation or Company, the members having no other responsibility than their yearly subscription of three marks (= 3/.) The office of the Central Bureau soon became too small, and in April, 1875, larger offices were opened the number of members increasing to 4,000.

In the same month the President called a conference of delegates, and this, which took place on the 14th and 17th of April, was largely attended. The recognition of the Berlin Association as the Central Association, the recognition of the *Hans frauen zeitung* as the organ of the Society, the co-operation of the branch associations and their admission to the advantages of the Central, and other similar resolutions were passed. The remaining time was taken up with establishing bakeries, and butchers' and grocers' shops, which have been since carried on in the most advantageous manner for the Association.

The great success of the Berlin Housekeepers' Association and its importance, which through the cheapness of its prices compelled the shopkeepers to reduce their own to moderation, drew down upon it the bitterest enmity of the dealers in foreign produce, who united in order to crush it. They wrote slanderous articles in the papers, distributing them wherever they thought it might injure the Association. They left no means untried to crush it, but their animosity only resulted in making the Association better known, and compelling it to import its supplies direct from China, America, and elsewhere, and thus supply its members at still cheaper rates.

The Association also turned its attention to co-operative laundries; washing machines were tested, and new methods were discussed in the *Hans frauen zeitung*.

In the winter of 1875, social evenings were commenced among the associates with artistic accompaniments of music and recitation. There are now 6,000 members in

B

the Association, which includes the highest military and
official circles, the families of professors and teachers, as
well as the middle classes. Many of the aristocracy
belong to it. Where so many ladies are joined together,
the poor and necessitous could not be forgotten,
especially as the poverty and severity of the last winter
were very great. A Committee of members attends to
the food of the poor.

The Housekeepers' Association is only at the commencement of its usefulness. It has a great object in
the future—that is, to work at the improvement of the
civil law affecting women; when the wife and mother
has assumed her due position in the house, she can no
longer suffer the miseries of the law which oppress her in
her property rights, her rights to her children, and her
marriage rights. The Association will further carry on
its beneficent work for the good of the community, and
the care of the poor and orphans, and lastly, its most
difficult but also most necessary labour, to work against
prostitution, which casts contumely upon all women,
which has poisoned every class of society in Germany,
and which makes every mother tremble for her sons, even
though she may have been able to guard her daughters
from evil. The Housekeepers' Association must finally assume that position to which the strength and good qualities of its members entitle them, employing its ever
spreading influence for the ennoblement of their sex, as
well as for the economic ordering of their homes. Their
Association works not only for the advantage of their
members, but especially for the furtherance of the women's
movement, and the time will come when its most zealous
opponents must acknowledge that the women's movement is a part of the human movement whose course
must ever tend onward.

Art. V.—EVENTS OF THE MONTH.

EDUCATION.

OPENING OF THE LEEDS GIRLS' HIGH SCHOOL.

On September 2nd, Lord Hatherley presided at the opening of the new High School for Girls, which has been established at St. James's Lodge, Woodhouse Lane. There was present a large gathering of the friends of education, including the Mayor (Ald. Croft), the Vicar of Leeds (President of the Council), Mrs. Francis Lupton (Vice-President of the Council), Mrs. Gott, Mr. F. Lupton, Archdeacon and Mrs. Anson, Miss Carbutt, the Rev. Dr. Henderson (head master of the Grammar School) and Mrs. Henderson, Mr. and Mrs. Jowitt, Mr. and Mrs. Jas. Kitson, Mr. Jas. Kitson, jun., Mr. J. R. Ford, Miss Maude, Mr. and Mrs. Schunck, Mrs. Vincent Thompson, Mrs. Heaton and Mrs. R. W. Eddison (hon. secs.), Dr. Heaton, Mr. Eddison, the Rev. Dr. Flood, Mr. and Mrs. Titus Salt, Mr. and Mrs. John Lupton, Dr. and Mrs. Greenhow. Mr. and Mrs. G. Talbot, Mr. and Mrs. F. Baines, Mr. and Mrs. Willans, Mrs. E. R. Conder, Mr. and Mrs. Scatcherd, Miss Kennedy (head mistress), Miss Ludlow (second mistress), &c.

A limited company called the Leeds Girls' High School Company has been formed to establish in Leeds a high class day school, adapted to carry out the suggestions made in the report of the Schools' Inquiry Commission, and strong endeavours will be made to provide in it, under well trained teachers, and at a moderate cost, a sound, systematic, and liberal education for girls between the ages of seven and nineteen. Within the last four years similar schools have been opened with success in various towns throughout the country. We learn from the prospectus that although the girls' high school at Leeds will be conducted on strictly business principles, and it may reasonably be hoped that there will in a short time be a moderate dividend, the company has not been formed with a view to making large profits. While the Grammar School has provided what is needed for the education of many of the boys of Leeds, the provision for the education of their sisters has not been adequate.   To remedy this unequal condition of things, which has been long apparent, the two associations existing in Leeds for promoting the higher education of women—viz., the Ladies' Educational Association and the Ladies' Council of Education. in conjunction with several gentlemen interested in the same objects, formed a Provisional Committee to promote the establishment of the high class day school for girls by means of this limited company, the members of the council being directors of the company for the first year.   The nominal capital of the company is £10,000 in 2000 shares of £5 each.   All the shares have not yet been taken up, but it is expected that when the establishment of the school is made more widely known, the whole of the capital will be soon subscribed.

The house is capacious, the premises will accommodate from 100 to 120 day scholars, but if this number should in course of time be largely exceeded it is intended to take steps towards the erection of a new building, specially adapted for a high school for girls.   No boarders will be taken at the school, but if girls from a distance choose to attend, arrangements will be made with ladies in the town for their boarding out.   Dinners for day scholars residing out of town will be provided in the school.   The council have secured in Miss Kennedy, who has had considerable experience as classical and mathematical tutor at the Ladies' College at Cheltenham, an efficient head mistress, and she is ably seconded by Miss Ludlow, who for many years has been head of the junior department at the same college.   A gentleman residing at a distance from Leeds has kindly established a free scholarship for the daughters of clergymen, ministers, physicians, and lawyers ; and it is hoped that this example will be followed by many other gentlemen. The school will be opened for the reception of pupils on the 18th inst.

LORD HATHERLEY said :—

There was one consideration which must recommend the school to all who took an interest in the welfare of that great town, which was greatly increasing in population, viz., the consideration that having done much for education, having to a great extent provided for the education of the children of the poor, having an excellent middle class school not long since built for the young of both sexes, having

also an excellent Grammar School, which was a great credit to the
town, they had hitherto provided nothing whatever for the advanced
education of girls and young ladies in a similar station in life to that
of the boys and young men who attended the Grammar School. In
London there were Queen's College and other schools whose object
was similar to that of this new school in Leeds. In Manchester there
was one which was in very favourable operation, and at present it had
260 pupils, and a similar college had recently been established in
Bradford. That the need of such colleges existed they would all admit.
In connection with them a university for women—Girton College—had
been established within recent years, where those girls who showed
an aptitude for learning might pursue a course of study still further
under able professors. He thought that they could not for a moment
doubt that what Manchester and Bradford had done in providing a
school for the higher education of girls, Leeds would not be backward
in doing. * • * * They found that in the higher classes of
society—and, indeed, in all classes—a great deal of time was often
thrown away upon many young ladies in their instruction in music,·
as to which they could never hope to attain to any proficiency, for they
never expected or hoped to employ such talents as they possessed in
that way as to make it of value to them in their homes, or any comfort
or satisfaction to themselves. The same remark applied to the teaching of drawing, for a person might have a talent for the one and not
for the other. In all those schools it might easily be ascertained
within a short time after the pupils entered the school as to how far
there was an opportunity of developing their particular faculties. In
that there was, perhaps, one advantage amongst some disadvantages
which would be presented when comparing girls with boys. Our
public schools rightly or wrongly had got into a somewhat fixed
groove. More subjects of study were being added to those usually
proposed, but still there was a certain amount of instruction in Latin
and Greek which had become almost an habitual and a recognised
necessity, whatever might be the tendencies of the young people to
that particular mode of education. With regard to girls, the field
seemed to him a great deal more open. * * * One great thing
which would result from this school for girls would be the bringing of
a great number together, and they would be able to encourage each
other, and the exertions they made would have that wholesome
amount of competition from which he thought young ladies had
hitherto been rather too much excluded, and which have been found
in the case of young men and boys to work in a very satisfactory
manner—not an illiberal competition, leading to envy and dis-
satisfaction, but on the contrary, a warm-hearted competition, in
which all would be able to assist each other, and that they might have
a fair opportunity of manifesting the particular talents in the direction
in which they could make them most serviceable and available.

Miss KENNEDY then explained briefly the scheme of education which
had received the sanction of the Council of the High School. Latin
will be the language first taught, afterwards French and German:
Arithmetic and Mathematics: Natural Science. The University of
London have expressed their opinion very decidedly on this study by
making chemistry the one compulsory branch in their examination for

women. The chief difficulty connected with this part of our work is the scarcity of duly qualified lady teachers. There are two only who have passed the natural science tripos examination at Cambridge. The younger girls will also be taught English history, geography, reading, writing, and dictation, and the elder girls English history, geography, English literature, and historical English grammar. The afternoon classes will be limited to such as involve no serious brain work, needlework, drawing, class singing, and instrumental music.

The Rev. Dr. GOTT spoke in complimentary terms of the speech just delivered by Miss Kennedy, and urged those who had not become shareholders in the company to take shares at once. He pointed out that every one was interested in the education of women, for we must all be the better or the worse according as their intellectual culture was attended to or neglected. He alluded to the advantages the school offered to the daughters of professional men, and concluded by expressing the hope that funds would ere long be raised to enable the council to provide a new building.

The MAYOR and Archdeacon ANSON having also spoken, a vote of thanks was passed to Lord Hatherley and the school was declared open.—*Abridged from the Yorkshire Post.*

Ladies' Collegiate School, Belfast.—At the recent university examinations for women, the results of which have just been declared, the progress of the higher education was evinced by the addition of Dublin this year as a new centre. The total number of candidates from the two centres, Belfast and Dublin, was 53—24 seniors and 29 juniors. It will be seen by advertisement that of these, seven seniors and eleven juniors from the Ladies' Collegiate School, Belfast, were successful. The first senior and the first junior prizes, and all the prizes offered in open competition, except one, which was won by a Portadown lady, were awarded to pupils entering direct from the Ladies' Collegiate School, Belfast.— *Belfast Newsletter.*

UNIVERSITY COLLEGE, BRISTOL: SCHOLARSHIPS FOR WOMEN.

WE sincerely congratulate the ladies of Bristol on the establishment of scholarships for women, tenable at University College, Bristol. It is the first college of the kind which offers educational privileges without distinction of sex, and we earnestly hope that a sufficient number of students in the classes, and of candidates for the scholarship, will present themselves to justify the effort that has been made in behalf of women.

The Clifton Association for the Higher Education of Women have made a wise decision in transferring their students to the classes of University College. The primary object of the college is to supply for persons of both sexes above the ordinary school age, the means of continuing their studies in science, languages, history and literature; and also to afford appropriate instruction in those branches of applied science which are employed in the arts and manufactures. It will, further, provide evening classes for those who are already engaged in active work. The Clifton Association, which for eight years has done such excellent service in the education of women, will keep up its own committee, while transferring its students to the College, believing that in doing so they combine the advantages of the new and old institutions. The lectures will be open to students of both sexes, a part of the lecture room being appropriated to women. Separate classes for women only will also be held, in which the instruction will be of a more detailed and catechetical kind. Attendance on the classes is not compulsory on those who go to the lectures, but it is very desirable for all who would study a subject thoroughly, and it involves no additional expense. Students can select one or more courses of lectures at their own option, and can attend the College as registered or unregistered students.

The Clifton Association, anxious to stimulate the zeal of students, generously offers four scholarships, to be competed for in October. Each will be of the annual value of £15, tenable for two years at the University College, Bristol. Two or more of these will be augmented up to the maximum sum of £50 each, should the circumstances of the successful candidates require such aid. Holders of these scholarships, if not residing with relations, will be expected to board in some house approved by the honorary secretaries to the Association. The examination day will be Tuesday, October 3rd. Further particulars may be obtained on application to Miss C. Winkworth, 21, Victoria Square, Clifton; or to the Secretary of the College.

It is unnecessary to dwell on the advantage of these scholarships; we know how much they contribute to

the education of men, and they are still more needed
by women, since parents who would make the
utmost effort to meet the expense of prolonged education of their sons, seldom realise the idea that education
has really any solid appreciable value for their daughters. Moreover, the university, by uniting men and
women in common study, is another step forward in
the right direction towards the goal which all real social
reformers must have in view; combined action by
workers of both sexes, which alone can give society
the full value of the qualities of both.

THE Committee of the Association for Promoting
the Higher Education of Women have issued the scheme
of lectures to be delivered at Cambridge for the Academical year 1876-7, beginning in October. This early and
complete announcement is made in order to conduce to
the greater convenience of the increasing number of
ladies who come from a distance to attend these lectures. Copies of the scheme may be obtained on application to Mr. W. H. H. Hudson, 1, Trumpington Street,
Cambridge, the Treasurer of the Association. The
lectures begin on Monday, the 16th of October.

*Yorkshire Lady Students at the Oxford Local Examina-
tions.*—The position taken by girls in these last examinations is most creditable. Of sixteen students of Yorkshire
who were candidates, eight were girls, and eight boys;
of the juniors the number of girls was fewer in proportion. In the Report the names of girls and boys are
printed with laudable impartiality. There is frequently
as much contempt as courtesy in "*place aux Dames,*" and
we much prefer, for our part, the classification to be in
order of merit, instead of order of sex. In this list of
students the girls and boys can only be distinguished by
the names of their respective schools.

SENIOR CANDIDATES.

W. Johnson, Retford, Elmfield College, York (W. J. Russell);
passed at Leeds in preliminary subjects, Scripture, with additional
books, English, languages, mathematics (11th in 1st class).

E. M. Blackburn, Huddersfield, Sandholm, Waterloo (Mrs.
Jones); passed at Liverpool Centre in preliminary subjects, rudiments of faith, English, and languages (3rd class).

R. R. Conder, Leeds, Ladies' College, Cheltenham (Miss Beale);
passed at Cheltenham Centre in preliminary subjects, English, languages (3rd class).

F. A. Crosland. Honley, Huddersfield Girls' College (Miss Cheve-
ley); passed at Leeds Centre in preliminary subjects, rudiments of
faith, English, languages, physics, drawing, and music (3rd class).

M. L. S. Dale, Leeds, Ladies' College, Wellington, Salop (Mrs.
Hiatt); passed at Birmingham Centre in preliminary subjects, Scripture, with additional books, English, languages, physics, mathematics,
music (3rd class).

E. A. Dickenson, Sheffield, Leicester Villa, Portishead (Misses
Wale & Harrington); passed at Bath Centre in preliminary subjects,
rudiments of faith, English, languages, physic, music (3rd each).

C. S. Kilham, Sheffield, High Harrogate College, (J. P. Hughes);
passed the Leeds Centre in preliminary subjects, rudiments of faith,
English, languages, and mathematics (3rd class).

G. Lamplugh, Bidlington Quay, St. Joseph's College, Clapham
(Rev. B. Alphonsus); passed at London Centre in preliminary subjects, English, languages, and mathematics (3rd class).

E. Nelson, Wakefield, The East Hays, Cheltenham (Mrs. Scott);
passed at Cheltenham Centre in preliminary subjects, English, languages, and drawing (3rd class).

J. W. Payton, High Harrowgate, Devonshire Hall. High Harrowgate (J. B. Payton); passed at Leeds Centre in preliminary subjects,
rudiments of faith, English and languages (3rd class).

W. E. B. Priestly, Apperley, the College, Harrowgate (Dr. Heigham); passed at Leeds Centre in preliminary subjects, Scripture, with
additional books, English, languages mathematics and drawing, (3rd
class).

S. Relph, Kirk Oswald, Queen Elizabeth Grammar School, Penrith (J. Gordon); passed at Leeds in preliminary subjects, rudiments
of faith, English, languages, and mathematics (3rd class).

A. Rodgers, Sheffield, The Grange, Bushey (Miss Wilkie); passed
at Watford Centre in preliminary subjects, rudiments of faith,
English, and languages (3rd class).

H. Taylor, Manningham, The College, Harrogate (Dr. Heigham);
passed at Leeds Centre in preliminary subjects, rudiments of faith,
languages, and mathematics (3rd class).

A. P. Weatherhill, Hull, Mildmay Park College (Mrs. Coles);
passed at the London Centre in preliminary subjects, Scripture, with
additional books, English, and languages (3rd class).

D. C. Winter, Barnsley, Hipperholme Grammar School (Rev. J.
H. Stork); passed at the Leeds Centre in preliminary subjects, rudiments of faith, English, languages, and music (3rd class).

THE *Women's Education Journal* says that an Examination of students of the Kindergarten System was held
in the rooms of Stockwell College, July 18-22. The
Examiners were Madame de Portugall, Inspector of
Infant Schools in the Canton of Geneva, Miss Chessar,
and Dr. Frances E. Hoggan. Sixteen candidates

presented themselves, seven of whom received a first class Certificate, seven a second class, and two failed. The following are the names of the successful candidates:—Class 1. Miss Lydia Avis, Miss Caroline Pattison, Miss Lousia Alice Scott, Miss Mary Jane Hills, Miss Fanny Franks, Miss Annie E. Wood, Miss Emily C. Avis. Class 2. Mrs. Holton, Miss Elizabeth Gamman, Miss Ursula Hawkes, Mrs. Barber, Miss Bessie H. Kernick, Miss Alice Mayoss, Miss Marion Williams. The *Journal* also reports the annual meetings of the Hastings and St. Leonards' Collegiate School for Girls.

Malvern.—An Educational Association for Ladies has been formed at Malvern, President Lady Emily Foley, and Vice-President, G. W. Hastings, Esq., corresponding Secretary, Miss Winscon, Malvern Link. The Committee are encouraged by the fact that an increased number of students have presented themselves for examination, some of whom have obtained first class distinction. They consider that the new Oxford examinations for women will be of much benefit to their students, and expect that some will attend the preliminary examinations in March. The following is the programme for the ensuing season:—Greek—The Rev. T. E. Minshull, M.A. Latin—The Rev. T. E. Minshull, M.A. Mathematics (Euclid and Algebra), Rev. F. R. Drew, M.A., Head Master of Malvern College. Physiology—T. Wright, M.D., F.R.S.E., F.G.S., Lecturer at Ladies' College, Cheltenham. Drawing and Perspective —Julius Clarke, Esq., of Malvern College. English Literature, Miss Winscon. German—A. Wachter, LL.D. of the University of Leipzig, Master of Malvern College,

BEDFORD COLLEGE (for Ladies), 8 and 9, York Place, Portman Square (late 48 & 49, Bedford square), London. Founded 1849: Incorporated 1869. The session (1876-7) will begin Thursday, October 12th. Two Arnott Scholarships will be awarded by open competition. Candidates to send their names to the Secretary before September 20th. Prospectuses, with particulars of Scholarships, Roarding, &c., may be had at the College. —H. Le Breton, Hon. Sec.

GIRLS' Public Day School Company, (Limited).   High
Schools for Girls.—These will re-open on the 19th
instant.   The Kinder-Garten will re-open at the Chelsea
school on the same date—For particulars apply to the
Head Mistress, Miss Woods, at the above address; or
to the Secretary of the Company, 112, Brompton road,
S.W.

THE WAR IN THE EAST.

AT a meeting held in Aylesbury, on Sept. 6th, to express detestation of the atrocities in Bulgaria, Sir H.
Verney said he was sorry to see so few ladies present,
as this was more a woman's question than a man's.   We
should be glad for our part to hear of women taking
part in every one of these meetings.   We believe that
one great effect of the recognition of the right of women
to co-operate with men in political life will be that the
horrors of war will in a great measure be averted, and
its sufferings alleviated.   It was a woman, Miss Irby,
who wrote a letter in the *Daily News*, which copied widely
in the provincial press, had a large share in arousing the
attention of the nation to the atrocities it related.   We
wish that all Englishwomen would join Englishmen in
raising their indignant protest against that Christendom
which

> " looks tamely on
> And hears the Christian maiden shriek,
> And sees the Christian father die."

This is not a question which women need work separately from men—their combined and sympathising help
must be given, and we believe is given, and accepted
heartily even by those men who are wont to declare that
" women have no business with politics."

We hear that a memorial to the Queen, to be signed
by Englishwomen, praying for Her Majesty's influence
in averting these horrors in future, is being circulated.
Address for particulars, Miss F. E. Albert, 18, Bedford
Gardens, Campden Hill, W.

In organising measures for relief women, too, are
active.   Lady Strangford some weeks ago declared herself willing to transmit contributions for the aid of
the Bulgarians to the proper quarters for distribution.

Englishwomen are assisting the sick and wounded in
Servia. On August 18, a telegram was received by Mr.
Lewis Farley from Belgrade, that Miss Pearson and Miss
McLaughlin, accompanied by Mr. Jackson, had arrived
at Belgrade. They were ordered to the army on the
Drina.

On August 15th, a meeting in aid of the Sick and
Wounded Relief Fund was held at Willis's Rooms. The
following letter from Florence Nightingale was read :—

" Good cheer to your efforts to help the sick and
wounded of both sides, and bring them hospital and
medical necessaries and comforts too. I hope in this
heartrendering war, a war for a cause as intensely interesting as the cause of most wars is uninteresting; a
war which will, please God, at last bring freedom, the
safety and blessing of home, of industry, of progress, all
that Englishmen, and Englishwomen, and English
children most prize; let every English child give its
mite to what are now the Valleys of the Shadow of
Death. But for this ' to execute righteousness and
judgment to all the oppressed,' we must help righteously
the sufferers on all sides. So God speed the Eastern
War Sick and Wounded Relief Fund prays

"FLORENCE NIGHTINGALE,

"From her sick bed, August 15th, 1876."

During the meeting much doubt was expressed whether
female nurses would be available, or even useful among
the privations and dangers of the seat of war. This
doubt is set at rest by a telegram from Dr. McKellar,
from Alexinatz, September 1st. "The number of
wounded from the eight days' battle is very great. The
surgical aid is now adequate; but, with the exception
of a few Russian women and one Servian, there is a
total lack of nursing, and the wounded suffer horribly
in consequence. We desire to bring this fact under the
notice of the women of England, and to tell them that
nurses are the present great requisite in the hospitals to
tend our wounded. They must be women of sound
practical hospital training, not amateurs, and, if possible,
speaking German. A few such to organize and control
a system of nursing between this place and Belgrade

would be invaluable. The means of locomotion are
primitive, but there is no difficulty in journeying up the
country from Belgrade, and no very serious discomforts
upon arrival. In the case of women, their destination
would always be sufficiently in the rear to avoid risks of
all kinds.

Miss Freeman thus writes to the *Daily News* on Sept.
9th:—Sir,—I feel sure from the many letters we have
had, that there are numbers of warm-hearted, sympathising women in England who are anxious to do all
in their power to relieve in any way the unfortunate
suffering Christians in the East. We have heard from
Miss Irby and Miss Johnston that they are going out
again towards the end of this month, and they say—
"We shall be very glad to take warm clothing for the
refugees with us. We are particularly anxious for
children's things, and are having numbers of blouses and
trousers made up for boys of from 6 to 16, and for girls
skirts and jackets. We are making the things of warm
strong serge, and shall be glad if anything warm can be
sent to us before the 24th." I trust many ladies will
try to collect working hands to assist in making up these
articles, and will transmit them to the care of Miss
Johnston, 10, Ovington Gardens, London, S.W., before
the 24th of this month. If you will kindly insert this
letter in your widely-circulated paper, I shall feel much
obliged.

ELEANOR FREEMAN:

Somerleaze, Wells, Somerset.

LONDON SCHOOL BOARD.

We have as yet only heard of one lady who is coming
forward as a candidate for election on the London
School Board; Miss Chessar and Mrs. Cowell, who were
elected in 1873, for Marylebone, are both retiring.
Mrs. Westlake, of 16, Oxford Square, W., has issued a
preliminary notice to the electors of Marylebone, offering herself as candidate at the renewal of the Board, in
November. She says :—

"I am led to this step by the conviction which the
previous elections have shown to be widely shared
among you, that the work of elementary education in

general, and more especially that of girls, demands the co-operation of women."

The first list of Mrs. Westlake's election committee of residents in the Marylebone division includes many of the best known and most respected men and women, in political, social and scientific life. This lady is the daughter of Thomas Hare, Esq., President of the London National Society for Women's Suffrage. She is eminently fitted by position and acquirements for the office she seeks. We hope that before the time of election other ladies will have come forward as candidates in Lambeth, Chelsea, and Westminster.

HOSPITAL SATURDAY.

We believe that the assistance of ladies in making collections at street corners for this charitable occasion has only dated from two years ago. The collections made by their efforts on Saturday, the 3rd of September, in London, exceeded in value those made last summer, though the amount at each individual table was less. The number of ladies who offered their services this year are 160 as against 80 last year, and 16 the year before, when the fund was commenced. Mrs. Mercier, the wife of the chairman of the fund, occupied the station she has previously held, in front of the Peabody statue in Threadneedle Street, where she last year collected over £60. Miss Linter, whose collection last year approached nearest to this, had a table at the Royal Exchange Avenue; among other ladies who had tables, there were the Hon. Mrs. Randolph Clay, the Countess di Tergolina, Mrs. John B. Marsh, Mrs. Margaret Lucas, and Mrs. Dawson Burns. It was not intended that the markets should lose the opportunity of contributing towards the fund, and Miss Napier took up her station at Leadenhall Market that morning at 5 o'clock, Miss Mercier at the Metropolitan Meat Market, and Miss Little at the Central Poultry Market, were on duty at the same hour. Captain Mercier, the chairman, and the members of the council attended at the Charing Cross Hospital at an early hour to receive the ladies. About eight o'clock the ladies arrived, and were despatched each with a table, money box, banner, and a plentiful supply of bills, to their destinations. The cabs which were chartered to convey the ladies formed a triple line along the whole length of King William Street, and this unwonted spectacle attracted considerable crowds who hailed the departure of each cab load with cordial and encouraging cheers. The lateness of the season probably militated in no inconsiderable degree against the success of the City collections. Mrs. Mercier who last year had £62., this year had only £54. odd, and there was a similar falling off at many of the City stations. The date, however, was fixed on the consideration that an earlier period the collection would have clashed with the bean-feasts, these being festivals which absorb a considerable portion of the spare cash of the employés of the large firms in London. As it was, however, the collection was very fair, averaging throughout about £5 per box, the highest being £54 and the lowest 1s. 4d. No case of insult to any lady occurred during the day, and a great many of the ladies were so encouraged by their experience of the morning and afternoon that they volunteered to go out again at night with tables illuminated by torches, and at the West-end a deal of money was collected in this way. The street collection amounted to £775; the total amount received being more than £2000.

This is not the first instance of the warm welcome which men give to women who help them in charitable work. When will men learn the great lesson that all work, political as well as social, is the better for the combined and harmonious co-operation of women with men?

MARRIED WOMEN'S PROPERTY COMMITTEE.

The Treasurer (Mrs. Jacob Bright) reports an increase in last year's subscriptions of £180 over the amount raised the previous year, and also a proportionate increase in the number of subscribers. Those interested in securing the property rights of married women are earnestly entreated not to refuse to give because they are able to contribute only a small sum. There are still only 90 subscribers, though the amount subscribed is £461. Considering the large interests at stake it is impossible not to be struck by the fact of the small number of those who have hitherto shown themselves willing to give pecuniary aid to a cause so deserving of assistance.

Husbands and Wives in Workhouses.—An important provision appears in the new Poor Law Act as to husbands and wives in workhouses. It is enacted by the 10th section that "when any two persons, being husband and wife, shall be admitted into any workhouse, and either of them shall be infirm, sick, or disabled by any injury, or above the age of 60 years, it shall be lawful for the guardians of the union or parish to which such workhouse shall belong, to permit in their discretion such husband and wife to live together, and every such case shall be reported forthwith to the Local Government Board."

Elections of Boards of Guardians.—A vacancy in the St. Pancras Board of Guardians having occurred, last month a new election took place. There were three candidates, Mrs. Amelia Howell, Dr. Pearse, and Mr. R. Newton. Miss Collett having been elected on the Board at the last election, it was anticipated that Mrs. Howell would be successful, but though she polled 816 votes, Mr. Newton who had 874 conquered. This is Mrs. Howell's second attempt; the number of her supporters has so largely increased since the last election, that she has no cause to feel discouraged by her defeat, and we hope that at the next election, she will try again and be successful. St. Pancras is a thorny parish for a Guardian, but, we believe that our poor law would be more satisfactorily as well as economically administered if women generally took their share in its management.

SUFFRAGE.

A meeting was held September 8th, in Glasgow. Dr. Cameron, M.P., presided. Captain Pim, M.P., Mr. Sharman Crawford, M.P., Miss Becker, Manchester, Mrs. Scholefield, Newcastle, Professor Lindsay, Sir T. McClure, and Miss Tod, Belfast, were also present. The Chairman referred to the erroneous notion of some

people that women's rights meant that women should be
allowed to command regiments and discharge the duties
of men, whereas it simply meant that they should, if
they had the proper qualifications, be possessed of the
municipal and parliamentary franchise. Referring to
Mr. Bright's argument that women were not a separate
section of the community but were the nearest and
dearest relatives of the male electors, and therefore
looked sedulously after their interests, he (Dr. Cameron)
said that it had been observed in America by Artemus
Ward that during the civil war a vast number of the
citizens were ready to sacrifice any number of their
relatives for the good of their country. He was not
sure that this relationship theory of representation deserved much more consideration in this country than
across the Atlantic. Resolutions declaring that this
right should be accorded, and agreeing to petition Parliament, were adopted.

EMPLOYMENT.

WE regret to hear that the "Ladies' Dressmaking
Association," established at 42, Somerset Street, Portman
Square, will be compelled to close its work at the end of
September, unless £100 can be raised immediately, to
secure future rent.

Brickmaking.—The *Labour News* says, that at Oldbury,
where an enormous quantity of bricks are made, a
woman moulder can earn from 22s. to 30s. per week, a
girl of thirteen can earn 10s., and a girl of sixteen can
earn 14s. or 15s.

Glass Grinders.—Girls wanted for glass grinding;
those accustomed to the work preferred; good wages.
—Victoria Glass Works, Canterbury Road, Hatcham.—
Echo, September 2nd.

Sericiculture and Women's Work.—Mrs. Bladen Neill
had a long and interesting letter in the *Times* of 29th
August, on the cultivation of silkworms, saying, "the
providing of work suitable to women is and will be as
necessary in the Antipodes as it is at home, and I
must state that, next to the profitable establishment of

C

silk-culture in Australia, the employment of poor
gentlewomen was my chief aim, both in the colonies and
at home. Two reasons suffice. Women are suited to
the work, and the work is admirably suited for women."
Mrs. B. Neill has opened a small dépôt in Charles Street,
Grosvenor Square, W.

THE *Women's Union Journal* makes a sensible suggestion to women workers, to co-operate together in getting
a seaside lodging at this season. The dull time for
business when a holiday can be conveniently taken,
comes of course to most working women at the close of
the London season, but the general rush of all classes
out of town, makes the cost of sea-side lodging much
heavier than most women supporting themselves by their
work are able to pay. "The success of the Saturday
afternoon excursions already organized by the Unions,
(to Hendon and Epping Forest) seems to us to indicate
that co-operation in this direction might be very usefully
extended to longer summer holidays. By putting
together their small savings in a special fund for the
purpose—a number of women might take a house in
some sea-side place, and the payments which they would
now have to make for the rent of bedrooms, would in a
few weeks cover the year's rent of the whole house.
There might be a general sitting room and arrangements
for taking meals together. We have not space to go
into details of the mode of working or to explain all the
advantages of the plan, but we strongly advise our
friends to consider whether they might not, next summer,
make a small beginning. There is no reason why such
a commencement should not grow until a Women's
Co-operative Lodging House had been established in
every popular resort."

"A Women's Hotel at New York, intend by the late
Mr. A. T. Stewart, the New York millionaire, for the
accommodation of working girls, is rapidly approaching
completion, and will probably be opened for occupation
next spring. The building has 500 rooms, which will
be neatly furnished and supplied with gas and steam
heat. It is the intention to have good meals furnished
at cost price, or at about fifteen cents a-piece."

CO-EDUCATION IN AMERICA.

The question of the co-education of girls and boys,
young men and women, is quietly settling itself in
America. Boston University, Cornell, Oberlin, Michigan
University, Colby, and many other colleges have lately
published their programme of commencement exercises,
and the names of women and men follow each other as
a matter of course in essay and thesis. In Cornell
University the degree of "Bachelor of Literature" has
been conferred on Miss Tilden; that of "Bachelor of
Science" on four ladies; that of M.A. upon Miss Foster,
daughter of Stephen and Abby Kelly Foster, and another
lady. Similar degrees were conferred upon young men
at the same time. Boston University graduated six
women as M.D., eleven from the School of Oratory, and
one from the Theological Department; in all these
departments a much larger number of men were
graduated.

The Wesleyan University, in Middletown, Connecticut,
graduated four young women; these four women were
the first who were admitted to the University. Many
fears had been expressed by the men students that the
"admission of girls would lower the standard," but these
women were all good scholars. Two were in honours
all the way through, the third took two prizes, and the
fourth one, and now nothing more is heard among the
other students about a lowered standard.

The University of Wisconsin has, for years, admitted
young women on the same footing as young men. The
Report made by the President of the University, says:
—"No difficulties have arisen from it. There were
eight young women among the graduates at the last
commencement. Their average scholarship was certainly as high as that of the young men, and they were
apparently in good health. We feel, however, that the
young women in attendance upon the University should
be sheltered from the claims of general society, and
that they cannot meet the exactions in dress, labour.
and time, incident to society, without suffering either in
health or scholarship, or in both. The ladies, rooming
and boarding in Ladies' Hall, necessarily come under

the restrictions incident to a quiet household, and we
wish them and their parents distinctly to understand
this."

PETITIONS.—In looking over the closing report (issued
August 5th) of the petitions presented during last session
to Parliament, no one can help being struck by the fact
that the largest number of signatures reached on any
subject, were those for the " Women's Disabilities Removal Bill." During the session, 1,117 petitions, containing an aggregate of 370,166 signatures, were
presented for this measure. The accusation of indifference has so often been brought forward against Englishwomen by the opponents of this Bill, that the silent
testimony given year after year of the persistent interest
which so large a number of men and women do take in
this measure to secure a fairer representation, is very
striking. The Bill in favour of extending the Household Franchise to Counties received only 209 petitions
with 129,745 signatures, little more than one third of
those presented for Women's Suffrage.

The Bill in favour of prohibiting the sale of intoxicating liquors on Sunday in Ireland, had the next
largest number of signatures (317,004), but inferior only
to this were those forwarded to the House of Commons
for the Prevention of Vivisection; 761 petitions, with
142,987 signatures were presented, and one for the
alteration of the proposed Bill. We have no means of
telling how many were presented in the House of Lords.

The Contagious Diseases Act's Repeal Bill was supported by 1,660 petitions, containing 112,383 signatures;
a large part of these petitions are from the congregations
of chapels and the conferences of ministers.

There were also presented a great number of petitions
on other subjects in which women are concerned more
or less exclusively. Thirty-three petitions, containing
2,074 signatures, were presented for Alteration of the
Married Women's Property Law, and 1,009 for extension
of that Act. Two hundred and sixty-eight signatures
were sent in against the Offences against the Person
Bill, and 2 petitions in favour of inflicting flogging in
cases of cruelty to women (a measure which we believe
would have no effect in diminishing the crime, and con-

siderably lessen the chances of a complaint being brought against the offenders).

The Medical Amendment Foreign Universities Bill had one petition presented in favour, and three against it, but also 3,235 signatures were sent in in favour of granting medical degrees to women.

MISCELLANEOUS.

POLICE INTERFERENCE WITH LADIES.

We re-produce the following letter, which appeared in th *Irish Times.*—" SIR,—I beg to bring to your notice the illegal course at present being taken by the police in stopping and interfering with females who happen to be in the street at a late hour.

I have of late frequently noticed, particularly in Grafton Street and other main thoroughfares, females who were evidently hurrying to their destinations as rapidly as they could, being stopped and interrogated by the police on duty, who persisted in endeavouring to turn them back, and in several instances I have seen the women thus molested free themselves by a violent effort from the grasp of the police and make their escape by running away, apparently in the greatest alarm. Further, this evening, while in the Rathmines Road, at about a quarter past twelve o'clock, I saw a policeman stop a female, address her in the most offensive and disgusting language, and finally, with his arm significantly raised, threaten to " make her ears smart if ever he found her on that road again." I was within a dozen yards of them the whole time, because I waited to see the upshot of the affair when I saw the policeman stop the woman, and I am quite certain that the policeman was the aggressor, as the woman could not have said anything to him that I would not have heard before he proceeded to stop her. All men—and women also—are equal in the eyes of the law; and I feel assured you will agree with me in saying that, since the police dare not thus molest men in the streets, public opinion ought to step in and protect from cruel and brutal aggression those who are not physically strong enough to protect themselves.—Your obedient servant,   R."

THE *Irish Times* says it has often received letters remonstrating against the "rude and wanton interference of policemen with ladies, who may for the moment be without a male protector." If R. had studied the English Constitution as it stands, he would have found that women are far from being the equals of men in the eye of the law, and that the police who ought to be the protectors of women, are in many English towns, such as Portsmouth, Plymouth, &c., generating into their spies and persecutors.

Civil Service—Post Office.—Miss E. Ballantyne has been appointed postmistress in Lanark.

British Association.—Miss Buckland read a long and able paper on primitive agriculture. She first adverted to the antiquity of the art and its bearing upon civilisation; and pointed out that it could only have originated among people having a settled abode. It was therefore probably first practised in a very imperfect state by the women of tribes left in tents or villages to await the return of the hunter—a probability which was strengthened by the fact that the women are still the sole agriculturists among many semi-civilised races. The agriculture of the lower races consists, she explained, in the cultivation of indigenous roots and fruits; the cultivation of the cereals being confined to civilised races, and to those who had learnt it through contact with them: She mentioned that the origin and native land of all the cereals remains obscure, although all of them, with the exception of maize, are supposed to be indigenous to the Eastern Hemisphere. Maize is supposed to be of American origin, and to have been unknown in the Old World before the time of Columbus. She disputed this supposition, however, on the ground that travellers have found maize in cultivation in various parts of Asia and Africa before any intercourse had arisen with white men. There are traces in America, China, and ancient Egypt of a time anterior to the cultivation of cereals when the aborigines of these countries fed, as the Pacific Islanders do now, upon fruits and roots, some of them poisonous, but rendered wholesome by pounding, maceration, and dessication.

The similarity in the customs, myths, monuments, and religions of China, Egypt, Peru, and Mexico, led to the conclusion that a cognate pre-Aryan race introduced the cultivation of the cereals into all these countries, and with them the worship of the moon as an agricultural deity. The absence of agricultural implements from pre-historic discoveries proves, Miss Buckland thought, their extreme simplicity, being probably only a pointed stick which still forms the sole agricultural implement in many countries. It is also not improbable that some of the stone celts were employed as hoes, and that flint flakes inserted in wooden frames served as harrows and threshing implements, as they do at present in the East. The concluding part of the paper was taken up with arguments in support of the proposition that the traces of primitive agriculture confirm the conclusions of modern ethnologists as to the early condition, gradual development, and extensive migrations of the human race. After a brief discussion, the thanks of the department were awarded to Miss Buckland for her paper, and this concluded the business for the day.

Unmuzzled Dogs.—Everyone interested in the prevention of cruelty to animals, will be glad of the order lately by the Paris Prefect of Police, abolishing the ancient practice of muzzling dogs at the first approach of warm weather, and of keeping them muzzled all through the summer months. Even the open wickerwork muzzle, though infinitely preferable to the cruel tight strap, must have inflicted great suffering on the animals in hot weather, and the Prefect of Police says, that " it has often been itself the cause of madness in dogs, who up to the time of putting it on had apparently been in perfect health."

Distressed Schoolmistresses.—The following letter appeared in the *Daily News*:—Madame Stolzmann writes to us from Lydd, Kent:—" In reading lately an interesting account of the proceedings and progress of institutions for the benefit of Church school-masters and schoolmistresses, I was painfully reminded of the non-existence of any institution to help the aged private school-mistress in her hour of need. It is hard to believe in this

philanthropic age that no institution of this kind has any
branch to minister to the necessitous private school-mistress; that it has not I learnt with grief.   But surely it
needs but to be made known to the generous rich for
the speedy formation of an institution all sufficient for
her emergencies.   As it is, the parish union is the only
asylum open to her.   What an end for one who has year
by year, perhaps for thirty or more, zealously pursued
the onerous duties of teaching!   When bereft by death
of all relatives, adverse circumstances arise, stern poverty
almost treading upon her heels, she reaches her 64th
year, and finds in her poverty no other door open to her
than the common union.   How sad, how very sad, that
she must thus end her useful life!   May I, through your
valuable medium, be fortunate enough to excite the
sympathy of those who are willing, even anxious, to
assist in the promotion of any good cause, and be in
time to avert a degradation so deplorable?   For it cannot be gainsaid that an earnest worker in a useful calling,
merits for a last earthly resting place, a more congenial
asylum than the parish union.   I regret that my pen
cannot more impressively convey the deep and heartfelt
sympathy I, with many others, have in the cause of the
private governess.

THE statue of Livingstone lately erected in Edinburgh,
is by the chisel of a lady, Mrs. Hill, sister of Sir Noel
Paton.   The likeness is said to be excellent.

THE London correspondent of the *Leeds Mercury*
writes:—" I understand that Miss Martineau had not
only completed her autobiography previous to her death,
but she had also had it printed by an Ambleside printer,
and corrected.   The work will form two volumes, and
will be illustrated by a number of woodcuts.   All that
remains to be done, in fact, is to have the sheets bound
and issued by a publisher."   The *Birmingham Post* says
that Miss Martineau's will contains an express prohibition
against the publication of any of her private letters, and
a direction to her executors to prevent any such publication by all means in their power.

THE *Examiner* says that some complaints are now

made that women will travel in the smoking carriages
of railways, not indeed for the purpose of smoking themselves, but apparently out of mere hardness of heart, and
suggesting that every railway company should make
some stringent by-laws, which will prevent the constant
incursion of the irrepressible female in carriages set
apart for the male sex.

ART. VI.—IRISHWOMEN LANDOWNERS.

THE new Doomsday Book for Ireland, which has lately
been published, gives, on examination, a somewhat
smaller proportion of women to men landowners than
the English Doomsday Book, published some months
ago. In England, it may be remembered, the proportion of women owners was as one to six men landowners, in Ireland it is in the proportion of one woman
to seven men. The proportions vary in each province.
In Connaught it is the largest, 1 woman to 5.8 men;
in Leinster, 1 to 6.7; in Munster, 1 to 7.4; and in Ulster,
1 to 8.4, as follows :—

LEINSTER.	Women.	Men.	Average of	
Carlow	74	507	one to	6.7
Dublin County	260	1314	,,	6
Dublin City	20	268	,,	8
Kildare	139	707	,,	6
Kilkenny County	120	708	,,	5.6
Kilkenny City	11	64	,,	6
King's County	137	648	,,	4 6
Longford	47	325	,,	8
Louth	100	601	,,	6
Drogheda City	6	65	,,	11
Meath	142	994	,,	6.2
Queen's County	82	541	,,	6.4
Westmeath	80	477	,,	5.6
Wexford	176	1000	,,	5.5
Wicklow	50	457	,,	9
	1,454	8,676		6.7

ULSTER.	Women.	Men.	Average of
Antrim	185	1991	one to 10.6
Carrickfergus City...	11	62	,, 5.7
Armagh	169	1373	,, 8.4
Cavan	103	613	,, 7
Donegal	99	904	,, 9
Down	267	1878	,, 8
Fermanagh	70	497	,, 8
Londonderry	98	1282	,, 9.3
Monaghan	66	571	,, 8.4
Tyrone	176	1541	,, 8.7
	12,44	10,712	8.4

MUNSTER.	Women.	Men.	Average of
Clare	114	668	one to 5.7
Cork County	384	2412	,, 6.2
Cork City	5	90	,, 16
Kerry	49	480	,, 9.6
Limerick County	90	906	,, 9.5
Limerick City	16	89	,, 5
Tipperary	216	1496	,, 6.7
Waterford County...	108	492	,, 4.4
Waterford City	12	47	,, 4
	1,000	7,482	7.4

CONNAUGHT.	Women.	Men.	Average of
Galway County	135	768	one to 9.5
Galway City	13	110	,, 6
Leitrim	35	292	,, 8.2
Mayo	38	520	,, 5.8
Roscommon	85	495	,, 5.5
Sligo	69	336	,, 4.7
	425	2,521	5.8

Total for all Ireland...... 4,123 ...... 28,891 .... one to 7
Or one woman for every eight landowners.

The total for all Ireland is therefore in the proportion of one woman owner to seven men owners, or in other terms, out of every eight landowners one is a woman, and deprived by reason of her sex, not only of all share in the election of the parliamentary representation of her country, but of all share in electing the municipal government as well. If the property qualification be regarded as an accidental test to mark out roughly where to find responsible persons to exercise franchise, still this eighth part of the landowners are responsible persons along with the other seven-eighths, and should be treated as such.

Art. VII.—CORRESPONDENCE.

The Editor is not responsible for the opinions of Correspondents.

To the Editor of the " ENGLISHWOMAN'S REVIEW."

MADAM,—Amongst the many disabilities which the unequal laws of England impose upon women, one of the most flagrant is the entire exclusion of women from juries.

Our great English boast is our trial by jury. "A criminal shall be tried by his peers," yet if a woman is criminal she is tried by men, judged by men, condemned by men; can they judge fairly of a cause of offence where a woman is arrayed against a man? or make due allowance for outraged feelings, or for desperate acts, too often the consequence of remorse and shame and abandonment?

As a witness, and still more often as a prosecutor, a woman is made to feel the indignity of such justice, and we continually see the modesty of a woman outraged in a criminal court, where not one of her own sex remains to support and console her.

I am ashamed when I read in our newspapers of the systematic indignities to which women are subjected, who have been the victims of seduction, of brutality, and lust,—I believe hundreds of women would rather remain patient under such injuries, if they could anticipate the humiliation and insult that too often await them in an open court, where not one of their own sex is allowed to remain. If it be right to clear the court of women on such occasions, clear it of spectators altogether; what is unfit for females to hear cannot be very improv-

ing for youths or men—yet every assizes sees these
scenes repeated, for such crimes are increasing, and the
counsel for the defence makes no scruple of assailing an
injured woman with vile inuendoes or infamous asper-
sions on behalf of the most atrocious criminal, and for
an ignominious fee.

I have the honour, &c.,

· J. B****.

MADAM,—I have been much struck by some observations in a Transatlantic newspaper, which I am anxious
to set before your readers. They refer to the want of
esprit de corps, which causes women to be so rarely
generous to the wants of other women.

" A wealthy, aged, unmarried lady died in Maryland
recently, who left her entire estate to found a boys'
school. There are many reasons why she should not
have done so. First, there are more schools for boys in
operation now than can be properly maintained. What
is wanted is more money for those already in existence.
and what is most wanted of all are donations from rich
women for the cause of education among women.
There is not a single endowed woman's college in
Massachusetts, where there are numberless schools for
boys; there are but few in the other States. I doubt
if there is any single school for girls endowed by women,
for they do not give to this cause when willing their
property away.

"The idea is not that boys' schools should not be
endowed, but that Woman sometimes should remember
the needs of her own sex when making bequests. It is a
noted fact that where one rich woman gives to the cause
of female education ten rich men do. Every year new
endowments are made to Harvard, rich in its great
possessions now as no college for women will ever be,
and always among the new list of givers is some woman's
name. If it is well that her name is so seen, it would
be far better were it also seen on the subscription book
of some struggling school for women."

How true this is also in England! How little women
as a rule have to give, and how neglectful they are to
the (on them) prior claims of their own sex.

My income being very limited, my subscriptions
seem ludicrously small by the side of the munificent
donations of tens, hundreds and thousands of pounds,
which are poured into our national charities; but what
I can afford to give, I give to institutions either for
women solely, or in which women and girls have, at
least, an equal share with men and boys.　This preference I think I owe to my sex, who, as a rule, are neither
burdened with superfluous cash, nor made the objects
of their fair share of alms giving.

I am, Madam,

One of the impecunious sex.

Art. VIII.—WOMEN'S RIGHTS TO DOWER.

(From the " North of England Review.")

It is somewhat singular that at a time when women
have ascended the platform to agitate for public rights,
as well as numbers of advanced reformers amongst men,
that the one material point that women now suffer from,
that they never did in the past two thousand years or
more, is never mentioned as far as we know.

The point is one that touches the feelings more generally and more deeply than any other.　The rights of
property, particularly of *dower*.　A case came very near
to us where the wife brought the principal money at
marriage, property was accumulated during coverture,
real property was purchased, and at the husband's death
his will did not contain the name of his wife, and she
has no claim on the estate that she largely produced.
Her relatives have to keep her, or she must become a
worker or a pauper—though her husband died leaving
a landed estate as well as considerable personal property.

Only a week or so ago a similar will was contested in
the law courts and overturned; but not because the wife
and children were excluded from all benefit, but because

the testator was proved to be incompetent to make a
will. That he had for some time contemplated such a
will before his last illness was amply proved. Therefore
it is quite clear that a wife is completely at the mercy
of the husband. From a temporary quarrel, or from
some influence over the mind of a husband not exactly
of a right character, a husband can exclude his wife from
any share of his property, and give it away to whom he
pleases.

The ancient laws always favoured the wife, and gave
her one-third or one-half of her deceased husband's
property.

In the earliest laws we have of Æthelberht, King of
Kent, 560-616, the provisions are thoroughly liberal for
the widow.

CAP. LXXVIII.—*Gif hio cwic bearn gebyreth, healfne
sceat agegif ceorl ær swylteth.* If she bear a live child, let
her have half the property.

CAP. LXXIX.—*Gif mid bearnum bugan wille, healfne
sceat age.* If she wish to go away with her children, let
her have half the property.

CAP. LXXXI.—*Gif hio bearn ne gebyreth, fædering-
magas fioh agan, and morgen-gyfe.* If she bear no child,
let her paternal kindred have the "fioh" and the
"morgen-gyfe."

The "fioh," the property received with the bride.
Feoh or *fioh*, one of the oldest words in all European
languages; originally cattle when they were the only
wealth. "Morgen-gyfe" was the dowry the husband
named as his gift to his wife, before witnesses, the
morning after the wedding night. It would be generally one half what he died worth.

Other Anglo-Saxon kings were as liberal. Edmund
gave all the property to the widow, except she
married again. The historian of that period gives a
striking testimony. "It is well known that the female
sex was much more highly valued, and more respectfully
treated by the barbarous Gothic nations than by the
more polished states of the East. Among the Anglo-
Saxons they occupied the same important and independent rank in society which they now enjoy; they
were allowed to possess, inherit, and to transmit landed

property; they shared in all the social festivities; they were present at the *Witema-gemot* and the *Scir-gemot;* they were permitted to sue and be sued in the courts of justice; their person, their safety, their liberty, and their property were protected by express laws.   *   *   *   *
'*Morgen-gift.*' This was the present which the Anglo-Saxon wives received from their husbands on the day after the nuptials; a compliment to the ladies for honouring a suitor with their preference, and for submitting to the duties of wedlock."—*Turner's History A. Saxons, vol. 2.*

Under the law of *Gavel-Kind,* which was instituted here many centuries before Jutes, Angles, or Saxons arrived, or even before Julius Cæsar ever saw the shores of England, the same liberality was displayed, we (Du Lambard and Tottel) have an inquiry into the law of *Gavel-Kind,* and its acknowledged authority in 1294. The costumal of Kent commences, *Ces sent les vsages de Gauyle Kend, e de Gauyle Kendeys en Kent, &c.* These be the usages of *Gavel-Kind,* and of *Gavel-Kinde* men in Kent, which were before the Conquest and at the Conquest, and ever since till now, allowed in Eire, before John of Berwicke and his companions, the justices in Eire, in Kent the 21 years of King Edward the son of King Henry.

VIII.—Et si il eit femme, meintenant seit dowe per le heir, sil seit dage, de la meytie, de touz les terres e tenementz que son baroun tint de Gauyle-Kend en fee, a auer e a tener solonc la fourme de suthdyte. Et de tiels terres le roy ne auera an ne wast, mes tant soulmët les chateux, sicome il est auätdit.

And if he have a wife, forthwith be she endowed by the heir (if he be of age) of the one-half of all the lands and tenements which her husband held of Gavel-Kind nature in fee; to have and to hold according to the form hereafter declared. And of such lands the King shall not have the year, nor waste, but only the goods as is said before.

By our common law, from all known time, a wife, except she be an alien, a Jewess, or an apostate, was entitled to one-third of all the lands and tenements of which the husband was solely seized, either in deed or in law, to enjoy as her life estate.

Magna Charta provided that the widow should not be taxed to the lord for her dower.

The Statutes of Merton stated, and made statutory what the common law had all along allowed, that a widow could have her remedy if the dower was not given and given fairly. The sheriff could appoint her dower, or she could enforce it by Bill in equity.

But all the statutory rights and common rights to dower are now gone. By the 3 and 4 William IV., cap. 105, all absolute rights to dower are destroyed. The wife is absolutely at the mercy and goodness of her husband. If he chooses to endow a paramour, and leave the wife penniless, the law of England will support the paramour in her claim, but leaves the wife without a remedy, even though the land or other property may have been originally hers, the sole gift of her relations, or of her earnings.   W. G. WARD, F.R.H.S."

The writer of the above is mistaken in supposing that women are not keenly alive to the loss of this among their former privileges. It is not in this case alone that the women of the nineteenth century are legally less well cared for, than those who lived some few centuries ago. History tells us that women have dispensed justice in courts of law; now they are excluded from all participation in (and frequently from hearing) decisions closely affecting themselves. Till 1640, on the very brink of the civil war, women voted for members of Parliament. They will shortly form the only disfranchised body in England. Up to last year they were the equals of men in parochial concerns: now by the Public Worship Act, only *male* parishioners have a claim to have their consciences injured by the doctrines preached in their churches.

It becomes a matter of deep consideration that the freedom meted out in ever "broadening" degrees to one sex, should not at the same time be taken away from the other—robbing Peter to pay Paul is not the best way to maintain a due equipoise of the scales of justice.

Englishwoman's Review.

CONTENTS FOR OCTOBER, 1876.

All Communications to be addressed to the Editor, 22, Berners Street, Oxford Street, W.

Post-Office Orders payable to Sarah Lewin, at the "Regent Street" Post-Office.

Terms of Subscription at the Office.

Per Annum (Post Free), Six Shillings.
Subscriptions payable in Advance. Single Numbers posted Free on receipt of Six Postage Stamps.

MSS. are carefully read, and if not accepted are returned, on receipt of Stamps for Postage, but the Editor cannot be responsible for any accidental loss.

Contributions should be legibly written, and only on one side of each leaf.

THE

ENGLISHWOMAN'S REVIEW.

(NEW SERIES.)

No. XLII.—October 14th, 1876.

Art. I.—A CHAPTER FROM ANCIENT HISTORY AND ITS MODERN PARALLEL.

THE struggles of a subject people for freedom are at all times interesting; most of all when they offer lessons of warning or encouragement to those engaged in similar efforts. Such lessons are, we think, to be found in the following narrative. The story of the conflict between the Roman patricians and plebeians presents so many features in common with that in which we are engaged that it can scarcely fail to afford us both encouragement and caution. Probably, very much sooner than the Roman plebs we shall obtain as complete a victory. But the record of successive steps of progress, with compromises and tricks of all kinds, is well calculated both to warn and to cheer those who may be dispirited, because of the seeming distance of the goal.

The city of Rome was originally peopled by refugees or outlaws from the Latins, Sabines, and Etruscans, at the junction of whose territories it was located. These earliest citizens constituted the three patrician tribes of Rhamnes, Titienses, and Luceres respectively; and amongs them dwelt a large number of Clientes, persons who, though not actual slaves, were in a dependant condition, attached each to a Patronus, much as by the English

D

law a married woman is attached to her husband; supposed to have a right to protection from their patrons, but excluded from most of the privileges of citizenship. The Roman State was thus composed of two classes, both nominally free; but while the patricians were governed by a king and senate of their own order, the Clientes were under the dominion of a class with which they could never amalgamate, and for the identity of whose interests with their own, they could have no security save in absolute submission.

As soon as Rome grew strong it was involved in wars with the neighbouring cities, chiefly those of the Latins. In these wars it was usually victorious, and the citizens of the conquered cities were commonly transferred to Rome, and became partakers of the Roman name. Vanquished in war, they could not expect to be adopted into the patrician tribes; and it was real generosity on the part of the conquerors not to reduce them to slavery. They formed a third class in the state, not individually attached to a patron, like the Clientes, but like them excluded from all share in the government; nominally free, but without any safeguards to their freedom, and no person being charged with the vindication of their rights. These were the plebeians; and their position at Rome, B.C. 600, was very like that of single women in England, A.D. 1850. During the latter part of the regal period, the relation of patron and Client seems to have insensibly relaxed; and afterwards the Clientes became virtually amalgamated with the plebeians. (The Clientela of a later age was a totally different institution.) The oppression impartially exercised over all classes and conditions by the Tarquins, seems to have united all in antagonism to them; and in the revolution which replaced the kings by annually elected consuls there appears nothing of patrician or plebeian; all were Romans. So it was throughout the war with Porsenna, and as long as the exiled royal family strove to regain its lost dominion. When a nation is struggling against an impartial despotism, class rights and wrongs are ignored; it was so in England on more than one occasion, and in the long struggle against the borough-mongers that preceded the reform of 1832, the special claims of

the feminine *plebs*, as against the masculine *populus*,
were scarcely thought of. But there is a curious coinci-
dence between the fact, that in the Reform Act of 1832,
, and in the subsequent Municipal Reform Act, the word
"male" was first introduced into the legal qualifications,
and the other fact related by the old Roman annalist that,
"In the year Tarquin died [B.C. 496], the patricians
began to oppress the plebeians."

The first practical question between the two orders
in the Roman state was of a pecuniary character.
During the wars of the revolution, the plebeians had
furnished the main strength of the armies, and shared
but meagrely, if at all, in the spoils. Meanwhile their
business had been neglected, whereby they naturally fell
into poverty; while the patricians were constantly
enriched by the booty which the subject order toiled and
bled to win. It was a case of Mr. Populus saying to
Mrs. Plebs, "what you earn is mine, and what I get is
my own." Necessity knows no law; the plebeians were
compelled to borrow of the patricians at usurious
interest, and the law—in making of which of course the
plebeians had no voice—adjudged an insolvent debtor to
be the slave of his creditor. By this means the plebeians
were rapidly becoming slaves to the patricians, when a
case of unusual hardship brought the question to the
front in the form of a riot. Just at this crisis Rome was
attacked by an enemy, and the plebeians refused to fight
until their grievances were redressed. Thereupon the
consul granted some small concessions, and promised
that the grievances should be investigated and redressed
after the war. The plebeians swallowed the bait, defeated
the enemy, claimed the fulfilment of the consul's promise,
and were mocked for their pains. It was the usual
trick of those who are interested in opposing popular
demands; and succeeded, as such tricks do, until their
victims grow wise by experience. The next year another
war was impending; again the plebeians refused to fight
until a dictator was appointed in whom they as a class
had confidence; then indeed they marched to meet the
enemy, whom they again defeated, and again the
patricians—in spite of the pledge given and honourably
adhered to by Valerius, the dictator—refused even to

investigate the grievances. This drove the plebeians to rebellion, and in B.C. 493, they marched out from Rome with all their belongings, and established a camp on Mons Sacer. These strong measures brought the patricians to their senses. The oppressive laws concerning debt were not repealed, but by way of concession all contracts of insolvent debtors were cancelled, and those who had been enslaved were set free. The compromise curiously resembled the "Married Women's Property Act," in that it retained in force an oppressive and unjust law, but provided a measure of partial alleviation. But another and more important result followed the "secession of the plebeians;" they were allowed, subject to the sanction of the patricians, to elect first two, and afterwards five *tribunes,* who had no direct legislative power, but were permitted to exercise a veto on the acts of the senate. Another class of plebeian officers, called *ædiles,* was established, who acted as a sort of police magistrates. These concessions have some analogy to the local and educational franchises lately given or restored to our female plebs, but were somewhat more substantial, having been extorted by stronger measures than the most "strong-minded" of our champions has yet ventured to advocate.

The first step to emancipation thus gained, the plebeians called to remembrance a tradition that one of the ancient kings had designed to establish complete equality between the two orders. A conviction thereupon grew apace that no mere concessions should be accepted as a final settlement of the question, that nothing short of the complete equality intended by king Servius Tullius would meet the demands of justice. The struggle that issued in the realization of this project continued over two hundred years, and need not be described in detail; but some of its incidents are instructive when compared with recent and familiar events.

In B.C. 491, Rome was distressed by famine; a supply of corn had arrived from Sicily, and Marcius Coriolanus proposed that the senate should compel the plebeians to sell their lately acquired rights for bread. The curious part of the story is that Coriolanus was "a just and pious man;" not the only just and pious man who has thought it an equitable bargain for Mrs. Plebs to renounce all rights and securities, as against Mr. Populus, for the price of simple maintenance. To their honour, the senate could not see the justice or piety of the proposal, and Coriolanus had to flee for his life. In B.C. 486, a large tract of land having been gained by conquest, it was proposed by Spurius Cassius the consul, that it should be divided amongst the plebeians by whose valour it had been gained, instead of, as on previous occasions, amongst the patricians only. With immense difficulty Cassius secured the passing of a law with this intention, but for many years this "Agrarian law" was so stoutly resisted as to remain a dead letter. The year after its enactment Spurius Cassius was put to death on a trumped up charge of treason, and several tribunes who subsequently endeavoured to enforce it, were either judicially murdered or privately assassinated. Two thousand years after, schoolboys were gravely taught that the "Agrarian law," the provisions of which were thus violently defied, was an attempt to trench upon the rights of private property in the interest of low people, and this is the usual interpretation which monopolists give to the acts and projects of those who resist their selfish practices.

In B.C. 484 an attempt was made to change the method of electing magistrates, so as to deprive the plebeians of the indirect influence which they had lately exercised. The English plebs, excluded from the franchise, have been told *ad nauseum* of the unlimited "indirect influence" they possess, but in fact that influence has been almost as effectually destroyed by the ballot, as was that of the Roman plebs by the election of magistrates by the curiæ. The plebeians, however, resented the injury in a novel fashion. The ruling caste having stirred up a war, they marched into the field, and then—mocking the consuls —turned their backs on the enemy. After this the old method of election was restored.

In B.C. 479 the patrician Kæso Fabius, consul for the third time, urged the execution, in the interest of the plebs, of Cassius's Agrarian law. The ruling caste thereupon reviled him as an apostate, and two years later Kæso and all his family and retainers were slain by the

Etruscans. The main army (under Menenius the consul) was at hand, and might easily have saved them, but Menenius seems to have held aloof purely out of revenge for the sympathy the Fabian family had shown towards the plebeians. There is a grim satisfaction in knowing that Menenius was soon after defeated and disgraced, and he is said to have died of shame and grief.

In B.C. 473 Publilius Volero, who had been a centurion, was ordered by the consuls to serve as a common soldier. Refusing, he was sentenced to be scourged, but a mob of plebeians rescued him from the hands of the executioners. The following year he was elected tribune; and it appears by this time the plebs had secured the right of electing their tribunes without the need of the election being confirmed by the patricians. Publilius proposed a modification of the form of electing tribunes, whereby the popular choice should be more freely expressed; and the next year he proposed that the same method of election should be applied to the ædiles, and that the plebeians assembled in public meeting summoned by their own tribunes, should be entitled to pass resolutions on all questions of public interest. These proposals were violently resisted, and only assented to by the senate after a riot, compared with which that wherein Hyde Park palings disappeared was a trifle. A similar demonstration of physical force might facilitate the assent of the English Parliament to several urgently needed measures of justice on behalf of the plebs, which have hitherto been resisted by the populus, as stoutly as the Publilian law.

This Publilian law was a great gain to the plebeians; it did not, indeed give them a direct voice in the legislature, but it secured for them the unfettered choice of their own magistrates, and authorised them to express their opinions on public matters—opinions which, in after time, acquired the force of laws. What was of still more importance, there was now at least one law which had originated with the tribune and the assembly of the plebs, an earnest of better times to come.

About B.C. 468 we get a glimpse of a curious arrangement for the election of consuls. At that time the Clientes were allowed to vote, but forbidden to vote against their patrons! Patricians and Clientes seem to have voted together, and, under such regulations, we may be sure that the voting was "All one side, like a Bridgenorth election." The plebeians, too, were expected to confirm the election; if they did so, of course their approval of the patrician choice was duly registered; if not, their disapproval went for nothing. We have heard of something like this in certain societies in which the male and female votes are taken separately, if the two majorities coincide, well; if not, the male majority carries the day, though the aggregate vote may be in the opposite direction. In 468 the plebeians at Rome refused to have anything to do with a sham franchise of this kind.

Six years later the tribune, Terentillus Arsa, proposed that a committee should be appointed to codify the Roman law, with a view of putting the two estates as nearly as possible on a footing of equality. This was not entertained until an insurrection broke out, the origin of which is obscure, but which is believed to have originated in a conspiracy on the part of certain patricians to murder the leading plebeians. The insurgents occupied the Capitol, from which the plebeian soldiery refused to dislodge them until the consul pledged himself that the project of Terentillus, if passed in the assembly of the plebs, should become law. This pledge was not redeemed for eight years longer, mainly through the opposition of Cincinnatus, him of the plough. Meanwhile, the most outrageous attempts were made to deprive the plebeians of the rights they had already gained, and even to reduce them to the state of subjection in which they had been before the secession to the sacred mount. These efforts were frustrated, and, though many prominent plebeians were assassinated, several important advantages were secured by their order; the number of tribunes was now raised from five to ten.

In B.C. 454 the bill of Terentillus became law. Ambassadors were sent to Greece to gain information about the laws of Athens, and in 451 a board of ten—the Decemviri—were appointed to draw up the new code. The plebeians had at first demanded that both orders should be equally represented on the board, but this was not insisted upon, and all the Decemviri were patricians. During their year of office—according to the custom of most ancient states—nearly all the elective magistracies were in abeyance. The administration of the board gave general satisfaction, and in the laws they enacted, the first ten of the celebrated "Twelve Tables," the rights of the plebs were more regarded than one would expect from the exclusively patrician constitution of the board. The code, however, being still deemed incomplete, it was resolved that the Decemvirate should be continued for another year. Appius Claudius, one of the first board, so insinuated himself into the favour of the plebs, as not only himself to be re-elected and to secure the election of such colleagues as were most resolute in their maintenance of patrician supremacy, but to obtain the suspension of the office of tribune. These ends secured, the new board established an absolute despotism, enacted laws of a reactionary character, convened no popular assemblies, and at the close of the year continued to retain their usurped power. They were only displaced by a revolution, which was precipitated by Appius Claudius kidnapping Virginia, who was thereupon killed by her father as the only method of saving her from dishonour. On the deposition of the board of ten, the old magistracies were revived, the new consuls being Valerius and Horatius, two patricians who had manfully stood by the plebeians during the tyranny of the Decemviri.

The legislation of the Twelve Tables was an important stage in the progress of the Roman people towards social equality. Especially was it important in that it associated the patricians and clientes with the plebeians, according to their residence, in the local tribes which before had been exclusively plebeian. Thus the *plebiscitum*, or vote of a public meeting of the tribe, became an expression of the mind of the whole people, and not of the plebeians only. The three original patrician tribes had now become practically useless, and fell into oblivion. But in the last two Tables, added to the code in the second year of the Decemvirate, were reactionary provisions of an oppressive kind. The old law of debt, which had provoked the secession forty years before, was re-enacted, and marriages between patricians and plebeians were declared illegal; the Agrarian law of S. Cassius was ignored.

The deposition of the Decemvirate took place B.C. 449; several laws were passed securing the liberties of the plebeians; two of the late usurpers, dreading the just punishment of their crimes, committed suicide, the others were banished. The following year exhibited the first indication of a closer approximation of the two orders; the patricians being now distributed among the local tribes, two patricians were elected tribunes. Three years later one of the tribunes proposed the repeal of the law forbidding intermarriage between the two orders. Another proposed that thenceforth each order should furnish one of the two consuls. The former bill was passed, the latter rejected, but a compromise was agreed upon—that in any year the senate might order the election, not of two consuls, but of an indefinite number of "consular tribunes," having the powers of consuls, but being inferior in dignity; these were to be taken from either order indiscriminately. Accordingly the next year, 444, consular tribunes were elected; they were all patricians; the plebs, content with having acquired the right to share in the highest magistracy, forbore to exercise it.

It now became evident that the dignities of the consular office could not long be withholden from the plebeians; the patricians, therefore, did their best to monopolize as much as possible of its power. Accordingly, they secured the appointment of two censors, whose business was to supervise the finances of the state; these were to be chosen every five years from the ranks of patrician ex-consuls.

After the capture of Veii, in 396, the patricians again endeavoured to keep the conquered lands for themselves. It was three years before the division was made in accordance with the fiercely resisted Agrarian law of Cassius. Six years after, the irruption of the Gauls and their capture of Rome checked for a time all further domestic progress.

In 376 two of Rome's greatest worthies were elected tribunes, L. Sextius and C. Licinius Stolo. In the dis-

tress that had followed the invasion of the Gauls, many
plebeians had been reduced to the direst poverty, and
the wealthy patricians had advanced them money at
usurious interest; in consequence, not a few of them,
under the operation of the old law, were being reduced
to slavery. Manlius, who had heroically defended the
Capitol against the Gauls, had rescued more than 400
by lending them money without interest. Sextius and
Licinius now proposed that, to meet the present distress,
any debtor might deduct the sums already paid as
interest from the principal of his debt, if he paid the
balance in three yearly instalments. They further proposed that the quantity of public land farmed by one
person should be limited by positive enactment, and
that, the "consular tribunes" being abolished, one of the
two consuls should always be a plebeian. The alarm of
the patricians at these proposals may be imagined. By
personal influence they gained a majority of the tribunes,
and thus prevented the bills of the reforming tribunes
being put to the vote. Sextius and Licinius retaliated
by using their veto, and thus preventing the election of
consuls or consular tribunes. This anarchy continued
five years, Sextius and Licinius being annually re-elected
tribunes of the plebs. At length, in 371, they permitted
consular tribunes to be elected to meet urgent military
necessities. During this time a "religious objection"
was constantly urged against the claims of the reformers;
"the plebeians," it was said, "had not the same auguries
as the patricians, and did not know how to discover the
will of the gods." To prevent them acquiring this
knowledge, the sacred books had been entrusted to the
guardianship of two patricians. It was then as now;
when an important section of the community demand
equality of civil rights, they are told that religion is
against them, and that they have not sufficient knowledge for the intelligent exercise of the franchise, though
special provisions are made for the convenience of illiterate voters of the privileged class; then, lest they
should obtain that knowledge in which they are alleged
to be deficient, the universities are closed against them,
and almost all the educational endowments of the
country are diverted from them.

" From press and from pulpit they ceased not to teach
    Our " native dependence," and fathered the libel
On Moses and Paul, by perverting their speech,
    Till we thought our subjection decreed in the Bible;
            From college and school
            They expelled us by rule,
    And classed us with lunatic, baby, and fool!"

Licinius saw the hollowness of the pretended religious objection to his proposals, and added a fourth to his list of reforms, that, instead of the two custodians of the sacred books, ten should be appointed, five from each order. For four years longer the struggle continued, until many of the plebeians became disheartened. At length Licinius only consented to be elected tribune for the *tenth.* time on condition of the people promising to pass all his four bills. This was done; on the passing of the bill about the sacred custodians the plebeians allowed consular tribunes to be appointed, and after another furious contest the patricians conceded the principles of the other three, the bills were passed in due form, and sworn to by both estates.

L. Sextius was elected in 366, the first plebeian consul. Still, the patricians could not gracefully accept ther defeat, and refused to sanction his election. At length, Camillus, the greatest general of his age, who was now for the fifth time dictator, mediated between the contending parties. The patricians acquiesced in the election of the plebeian consul; but by way of compromise a large portion of the consular power was transferred to an officer called *prætor*, not unlike our Lord Mayor, who was always to be a patrician; and two patrician ædiles were appointed to share the criminal jurisdiction in rotation with those of the plebs. There was great rejoicing over this happy settlement; but for a long time the patricians continued on every available opportunity to attempt the overthrow of the Licinian law as to division of the consulship; while the plebeians felt that their rights would not be completely secured, so long as a single office remained in the exclusive enjoyment of the aristocratic caste.

In 364, Licinius was consul, and again in 361. In the intervening year 362, Glaucius, the plebeian consul, was killed in battle with the Hernicans; and the patricians openly rejoiced at it. So much for patriotism! In 356 we find the plebeian, C. Marcius Rutilus, acting as dictator, and, in 351, the same person was the first plebeian censor. In 339, Q. Publilius Philo, the dictator, carried three important laws, by two of which the veto of the patrician curiæ, on the resolutions of the whole people (plebiscita) was abolished, and by the third, it was decreed that the censorship should always be shared between the two orders. Two years later the prætorship was also thrown open to plebeians, and Publilius was the first who filled the office. In 32ö, the old laws which condemned an insolvent plebeian debtor to slavery, were abrogated. In 300, the Ogulnian law provided that the offices of augur and pontiff should be divided between the two orders—thus terminating the ecclesiastical supremacy of the patrician caste. And in 287, the last vestige of caste distinction perished, as the Hortensian law enacted that the decisions of the plebiscitum—in which the patricians now voted on an equality with other citizens— should be binding on the whole people.

We have thus briefly traced the advancement of the plebeian order in Rome, from the position of something much resembling serfs, to an equality with the proudest patricians. It was a victory of right against prescription, won only by perseverance, watchfulness, and unfaltering resolution. It was delayed, now by the triumph of a reactionary party, now by the diversion of public attention to external dangers; and its course was marked by checks and counterchecks, and by numerous compromises. From the secession to the passing of the Hortensian law—a period of more than two hundred years—every step of progress was resolutely opposed; and falsehood, ignorance, superstition, and murder were freely used as weapons with which to resist plebeian claims. But, though slow, the progress was sure; and no reactionary measures were suffered long to be in force. And the termination of the struggle coincides with the commencement of Rome's age of greatest prosperity. We need not point the moral; the story speaks for itself; "that which has been, is that which shall be, and there is nothing new under the sun."

T. G. CRIPPEN.

ART. II.—SWEDISH PROGRESS.

A pamphlet has lately been published by the Hon. Mrs.
Rosalie Olivecrona for the International Exhibition, in
Philadelphia, which gives most interesting details of the
position of women in Sweden.   Whether we turn to the
schools and foundations for their education, both higher
and industrial, the extension of their employments, or the
improvement in the laws opening professions, and enabling them to acquire property and retain it when
married, the result is equally satisfactory.   There are
many points in which England might take a useful lesson
—her men in the generous recognition of the equal
claims of women to independence, education, and remunerative work—her women in unwearied perseverance,
and indefatigable activity in promoting the welfare of
their sex.   We may remark by the way that even so far
back as the twelfth century Swedish legislators thought
it worth their while to pass laws for the advantage of
women.   Miss Otte in her Scandinavian history tells us
that Erik the Saint, 1155-60, won the love and grateful
respect of all the women of Sweden, by the laws which
he passed to secure them many rights, amongst which
were that every wife should have equal power with her
husband over locks, bolts, and bars ; and that she might
enjoy one-third of his substance after his death.   A
century later while the rest of Europe was still governed
by the simple rule that the strongest was always in the
right, Birger Jarl, of Sweden, 1251-66, passed a law
which gave women the right to half as much as their
brothers of the property of their parents.   Before Birger's
time the daughters of wealthy men could not claim any
share in their father's possessions as long as they had
brothers living ; for, as the law put it, " where the hat
comes in, the cap goes out."   These samples of ancient
Swedish feelings of justice towards women, are doubly
interesting when we note the still greater advance in
opinion made during the last thirty years.

In 1734, by the Swedish code which was at that time
published, a woman still remained under guardianship
unable to appear at law, and only emancipated by
widowhood : she was not excluded from successions, but

not admitted to an equal share with men. She was able to be guarantee for her husband, and to make contracts, but the husband had the sole management of the common fund, and only in the event of his absence or madness did any right of administration accrue to his wife. In the country she inherited after his death one-third, in the towns half the community. She was admitted to a share of the parental power, inasmuch as she had to be consulted before her daughter could be married; and as widow, she became complete mistress of her person and property, and the guardian of her children, though she had to act with the assistance of her husband's relations. She was also allowed to appoint by will a guardian for her children (see Rights of Women. *Trübner & Co.*)

Improvements were very gradual. In 1810, women were allowed to enjoy the free administration of their separate property. In 1845, the widows of the country were placed on the same footing with the widows of the towns in regard to their rights of succession. Also in 1845, equality of inheritance for son and daughter was established, and the wife received an equal right with the husband to their common property. In 1846, women were granted the right to practise industrial professions and to carry on retail business in town or country. In 1858, a woman was permitted to claim, if she wished, the right of being of age when 25 years old; this restriction was completely removed in 1863, when she was unconditionally declared of age at 25. In 1864, her rights to trade and industrial pursuits, were enlarged, and in 1872 to a woman of full age was adjudicated the full right of disposing of herself in marriage—father's, brother's, or kinsman's consent having been heretofore necessary. In 1874, a Married Women's Bill was passed by which she was entitled (1) to manage that part of her private property, set aside for her personal use in the marriage contract; (2) to dispose of her own earnings. Through the exertions of several ladies a Society was established in 1873, the object of which is to secure to married women the right of administrating their own property. This society has subscribed a sum of 3000 Kr. to be awarded as prizes for the best essays on a projected law which adjudges to a married woman full right of administering and disposing of her own property, inherited or earned, that it may not be lost by the mismanagement of the husband or seized to pay his debts.

Legislation has not been behind-hand also in opening professions to women. In 1853 and 1859, laws were enacted to enable women to act as teachers in the primary schools: in 1861 to act as organist and to practise as surgeon and dentist after having produced proofs of competency: in 1863 to hold (with some restrictions) inferior post and telegraph offices: in 1870 admission to the Universities after having passed the students examination. Three stipends have already been founded for female students: one belonging to the University of Upsala may be competed for by female students generally: another exclusively for those studying medicine at the Carolinian Institute in Stockholm, and a third at the University of Lund. In 1867, a course of instruction was provided by the *Society of the Sick and Wounded in War* at the Upsala University, to train nurses for the sick. It is superintended by a lady who was trained for her profession at the Nightingale Institution in London. In the hospital belonging to the Deaconesses Institution in Stockholm, which accommodates 40 patients, all the attendance is performed by deaconesses with the assistance of one physician. Deaconesses are much sought after as nurses in families.

Mrs. Lea Ahlborn has been engaged since 1853 as medal stamp cutter and engraver at the Royal Mint, in Stockholm, and enjoys in this vocation a high reputation.

At the Royal Academy of Science, women are often employed to draw and paint Swedish plants for scientific purposes.

Wood carving is executed by female workers with skill and taste. The most eminent among them was Sophia Isberg (born 1819, died 1875) the daughter of a poor tailor, who early evinced artistic talent in this branch of art. Her workmanship was distinguished for a great variety of ideas, often historical, and for an elaborate execution. She had received prizes at exhibitions in Stockholm, Göteborg, Paris, London, and Vienna. Some of the best photographic ateliers are conducted by ladies: many find employment in this pursuit.

At the Archives of Swedish maps eight women have since 1860 been engaged as assistant designers, besides whom several others obtain temporary employment.

In the copying office opened 1864 through the exertions of the Editors of the Home Review (started in 1859 by two ladies and still edited by one of them, a warm and energetic advocate for woman's cause) many ladies find remunerative employment by copying and translating. Even in some of the State Departments females are employed in copying.

The first Swedish lady who in this century distinguished herself as a painter was Sophie Adlersparre (born 1808, died 1862). Many difficulties against which she had to struggle, have gradually been removed, and the Swedish female artist occupies to-day a respected position. Several female painters, such as Amalia Leudegren, Agnes Börjeson, Josefine Holmlund, Sophia Ribbing, Adelaide Leuhusen are known and respected even beyond their native country.

More than 3000 female teachers are engaged in the public schools, several of whom teach drawing and music in the boys' schools. 270 women are engaged in telegraph offices: 164 in post offices: 2 as organists— 2 dentists, and 3 surgeons. Many women are employed as clerks in private banks, savings' banks, joint stock, and life insurance companies, or as clerks at railway stations. There are instances of ladies being superintendents of branch departments of private banks; in one town the municipal treasurer is a lady. Women are even skilful mechanics; some ingenious machines have been invented by a woman; among others an apparatus for tuning organs and harmoniums. We hear of women as watchmakers, goldsmiths, shoemakers, lacemakers, glovers, hatters, bookbinders, japanners, mother of pearl workers, ropemakers, glaziers, combmakers, painters, turners, upholsterers, bakers and confectioners, all on their own account. Some printing offices are exclusively managed by women. At the china manufactories of Gustafsberg and Rörstrand, a great deal of the work is performed by women, particularly modelling and enamelling. Hairdressing is mentioned as one of the trades exclusively in their hands. Women from Dalarne, one of the northern provinces, make clever gardeners.

For such productions of female workmanship as
do not generally belong to the industrial market, a sale
room called the Beehive, was opened in Stockholm, 1870,
and has proved successful. There are similar establishments in many provincial towns and ladies' societies which
distribute work, such as spinning, weaving, or knitting
to those who cannot otherwise find employment.

Another branch of female industry is lacemaking, but
it is limited to certain parts of the country. In flourishes
mostly in Wadstena (Ostergötland) and its vicinity,
and derives its origin from old times, when it constituted
one of the chief occupations of the sisters of the far-famed
nunnery of Wadstena, founded in the fourteenth century.
By want of good patterns and proper encouragement
this industry had however, gradually degenerated, till
the late Queen Louisa, the Consort of Carl XV., tried to
elevate it by distributing new patterns and better thread
among the lacemakers. Even in Dalarne in the north,
and in Skäne and Blekinge in the south of Sweden, lacemaking, for ornamenting the national costume, is a
domestic industry. Curious embroideries, woven and
embroidered carpets, tapestries, &c., and ornaments of
hair, are all made by the peasant women.

An association called Friends of Female Domestic
Industry (Handarbetets Vänner) was organized in the
spring of 1874, to promote and develop female industry.
It encourages lacemaking and textile industry, carpet-
making, &c., and has already arranged two exhibitions
of female work. Associations for promoting domestic
industry exist all over the country, and have been very
successful in carrying out their object, *i.e.*, to promote
domestic industry among the country people, male as
well as female—basket weaving and straw work have
been developed under their care, and the making of
straw hats is now becoming a branch of industry.

With regard to what has been done to promote female
education, a list of the schools and educational establishments which are open to women will give the best
illustration. The Royal Seminary in Stockholm, for
the training of female teachers in the high branches of
education was established 1861. 288 pupils have gone
through the seminary, of whom 203 have received

E

diplomas as teachers.   Instruction is free.   The Royal
Normal School for girls, which is at the same time a
school of practice for the pupils of the Seminary was
established 1864.   There are besides of higher schools
for girls, 5 private schools, to one of which has
been added since 1870 three upper classes for the purpose
of preparing the girls for the University: three high
schools in Upsala: four in Göteborg, and one in most of
the provincial towns of importance—many of these
schools have been established by lady teachers educated
at the Royal Seminary.   As the instruction was not
gratuitous at any of these schools, the Government in
1873 asked the Diet for a grant in order to establish
higher schools for girls in four provincial towns.   This
was to be the first step for procuring for girls the
advantage of almost gratuitous instruction so long
enjoyed by boys.   The Diet rejected the proposal but
granted a yearly allowance of 30,000 Kronors to the
support of already existing female schools.

The Governesses' Mutual Annuity Fund was founded
by a lady in 1855, to secure a small annual income to aged
female teachers.   At the age of 55 the shareholders
receive an annuity of 9 per cent. on the paid investments, which have increased by the interest being added
to the capital, and by the gains derived from the investments of contributors who have died before the said age.
The number of shareholders is 218.   The institution is
entirely under female management, the board consisting of nine ladies, and 99 women now receive annuities.

Classes for the higher education of women were
established in 1865 by Miss Jenny Rossander.   The
lessons are given as lectures.   The Royal Academy of
Music admits female pupils since 1854.   There are
20 teachers, three of whom are women, instruction is
free; there were 72 female pupils in it last year.   The
Royal Academy of Fine Arts was opened to a limited
number—25—of lady pupils in 1864, but there was some
restriction as to the studies.   The Industrial School in
Stockholm, which numbers 788 female pupils, gives
almost gratuitous instruction since 1854 in drawing,
painting, modelling in clay, wax, and parian, lithography,
xylography, chalcography, lacquering, perspective and

book-keeping, besides languages.   The Telegraphic
School, established in 1873 in Stockholm by the telegraphic board of administration, gives free instruction;
the present number of women pupils is 59.   The Royal
Central Gymnastic Institution trains ladies as teachers
of gymnastics; instruction is free.   Lying-in Hospitals
for instruction in midwifery exist in Stockholm, Göteborg, and Lund, also gratuitous.   This course of instruction is 200 years old in Stockholm, but has been of late
years extended.   At the end of last year the number of
midwives all over the country was 2,043, of whom 1,156
were in Stockholm.   Free seminaries for training female
teachers for the primary schools are established in Stockholm, Kalmar, and Falun (among the subjects taught
here we may mention swimming).   Primary schools
are scattered all over the country with an aggregate
number of 2,800 female teachers, and 358,000 female
pupils.   High schools for peasant girls have also been
lately established, as a continuation of the primary
schools, but the experiment is as yet too new to be
considered as fairly tested.

There are also free industrial and sewing schools for
poor children, schools for the training of maid servants,
and practical housekeeping schools.

In Göteborg, one of these practical housekeeping
schools was established in 1865.   The number of
scholars is 25; 103 girls have gone through the school,
of whom 60 have got situations as servants.   To this
school belong a laundry and a bakery, by means of
which no inconsiderable revenue is obtained.   It contributes also to its self-support by receiving school boys
as day boarders; also a "crèche" where babies are receive
for the day, giving the maidens opportunity to get
experience and insight in the nursing of infants.
Similar schools, either established or organizing, are
also to be found in many provincial towns.   A most
practical form of instruction is given in the dairy schools,
of which there are two public ones, one at the Agricultural Institute of Ultuna, and one at Bergquara,
these receive an allowance from the State.   The girls
are taught all that belongs to the management of dairies
and cattle, and pay for their instruction, board, and

lodging by work. Private dairy schools are also provided in two different counties by agricultural societies, and in other well managed farms instruction in cheese and butter-making is given to female pupils at the charge of the Special Committee of the Royal Agricultural Society. It is not uncommon in Sweden for women to take the whole care of the dairy cattle on the farm, as well as the indoor management of the dairy.

Of course there is much in these institutions that is peculiar to the country, and could not be imitated in England with advantage, but many useful hints might be taken from a careful perusal of Mrs. Olivecrona's pamphlet. Dairy schools, for instance, might be establishing here with great advantage to girls intending to emigrate. It is impossible not to recognise that Swedish women enjoy greater opportunities in education and avocations than we do in England, and the success which has attended these experiments is very encouraging to us in our own efforts.

ART. III.—WOMEN'S MEMORIAL TO HER
MAJESTY.

IT would have been impossible for women to have stood by and taken no part in the movement which is thrilling through England, and has aroused in the mind of the people a feeling that has united all ranks and conditions, whatever their differences in religion, politics, or social station. Women have taken but small part in the numberless public meetings which have been held through the length and breadth of the land, but in order to give them a special opportunity of recording their sympathy with the sufferers in Turkey, and their horror of the inactive policy pursued by the European powers, it was proposed to prepare a Memorial to be presented to the Queen, to be signed by the women of Great Britain and Ireland.

It was felt that an address, coming from women

solely, would have a significance quite distinct from all
the other memorials and petitions which have been
signed at public meetings, not because exclusive action
on the part of women is to be preferred on any subject
to the combined action of men and women, but because
a memorial from women, framed in terms excluding all
party spirit, and addressed, not to any Member of the
Cabinet, but to Her Majesty, whom both as a Queen
whose power can sway nations, and as a woman whose
sympathy and compassion for suffering have endeared
her to every class of her subjects, was peculiarly appropriate during the continuance of a war in which women
are, more even than in civilised wars, the chief sufferers.

A meeting of ladies was summoned to meet on Sep-
tember 14th at the house of Miss Kortright, 36, Ken-
sington square, with a view of preparing the Memorial.
The following ladies were elected an Executive Com-
mittee: Miss F. E. Albert, Miss Ashurst Biggs, Mrs. S.
C. Hall, Mrs. F. Cashel Hoey, Miss F. A. Kortright, Mrs.
Anna Perrier, Mrs. Rawsthorne, Miss Arabella Shore,
Mrs. A. Sonnenschein, and Miss S. Howard Taylor. Mr.
Lewis Farley was chosen President of the Committee,
and Miss F. E. Albert as Hon. Secretary, 18, Bedford
Gardens, Campden Hill, London, W.* The Memorial
was as follows:—

To the Queen's Most Excellent Majesty.

May it please your Majesty,

We, the undersigned women of Great Britain and
Ireland, your Majesty's humble and dutiful subjects, having heard with horror and indignation
of the atrocities committed and still continuing to
be perpetrated in Bulgaria and other provinces
subject or tributary to Turkey, earnestly beg
your Majesty to use your Royal prerogative in

---

* Miss Albert is well acquainted with Eastern matters; for five
years she was governess and lady of honour, in Constantinople, to the
niece of the present Viceroy of Egypt, and from her friendship with
Mr. Washburn, head of the Robert International College in Constantinople, she had frequent opportunity of making the acquaintance
of educated men among the Bulgarians, Turks, Armenians,
and other nationalities of the East. Subsequently she went to India,
and was superintendent of a Government school for girls in the hills.

directing your Majesty's Government to adopt measures, in concert with the other Powers of Europe, to provide effectually against the continuance and recurrence of such atrocities.

As soon as the meeting was reported in the newspapers, letters were received from all parts of the country expressive of sympathy and the desire to append signatures, and before the forms of Memorial could be sent out from the printers, some hundreds of signatures had been received. Miss Nightingale thus wrote:—" It is with the deepest sympathy and interest that I hear of your and every effort for attaining the release of these young and struggling nations—Bulgaria, Bosnia, Herzegovina—from misery unspeakable, and setting them free to work their own way to order and progress. My poor personal efforts do but lie in other ways to the same end. I wish you and others ' God speed,' with all my heart and soul."

Some letters were ill-spelt and poorly worded, coming from almost illiterate classes, but expressive of the warmest wish to help; and even when, as in a few cases, there came a refusal to sign the Memorial, it arose from no want of sympathy with the cause it advocated, but from doubt as to the accuracy of its phraseology. Only three weeks elapsed from the first meeting in Kensington Square to the final sending up of the Memorial, and the rapidity with which the signatures have been collected speaks volumes, not only of the sympathy with which Englishwomen regard this political movement, but also, and in no slight degree, of the practical knowledge and organisation of such matters which women are beginning very generally to possess.

The Memorial has been signed by 43,845 women, amongst whom we may particularise Mary Carpenter, Mrs. Nassau Senior, Miss Cobbe, Miss Swanwick, Mrs. Gladstone, Mrs. Plimsoll, Mrs. P. A. Taylor, Mrs. Wm. Grey, Mrs. Garrett Anderson, M.D., Mrs. Hoggan, M.D., Mrs. Atkins, M.D., Miss Walker-Dunbar, M.D., Miss Ashworth, Mrs. Lucas, Mrs. McLaren, Mrs. Fawcett, Miss Becker, Mrs. Allingham, Mrs. Malleson, Miss Sturge, Mrs. Pease, Mrs. Westlake, Miss W. Ricketts (Brighton School Board), Miss Mary Carlyle Aitken, Miss Kortright,

Miss Arabella Shore, Miss March Phillips, Lady Constance Shaw-Lefevre, Miss Octavia Hill, Lady Young, Lady Reed, Mrs. Freeman, Miss Pearson (English Hospital, Servia), Miss Buss, Mrs. Abbott, Mrs. Haweis, Mrs. Butler (Harrow). Among the signatures was that of Mrs. Tod, of Belfast, whose sympathy and active co-operation, in spite of her advanced age, with all her daughter's earnest and self-sacrificing work on behalf of the women's cause, has caused her subsequent death, after a short illness (on October 6th), to be felt as a painful loss, even by those who were far removed from the circle of her personal friends.

Of the 43,845 names, London and its suburbs contributed nearly 10,000; Lancashire 4,734, of which Manchester sent 1876, Accrington 1,077, Liverpool 343, Wigan 340, and Rochdale 337. Yorkshire sent 1,654 signatures; among these were women of York, Huddersfield, Leeds, Ripon, Whitby, Sheffield, Northallerton, Dewsbury, Doncaster, Burton-on-Trent, Malton, and Bradford. Cornwall sent 247 names; Devonshire 1,808, of which 862 were from Plymouth; Bristol sent 1,142, Bath 710; Kent sent 1,314, Surrey 1,020, Sussex 821, Hampshire and the Isle of Wight 856, Wilts (principally from Calne and Marlborough) 443, Dorset 305, Gloucestershire 269, Oxford 160, Berkshire (principally Maidenhead and Abingdon) 431, Bucks 210, Hertfordshire 373, Essex 1,541, Beds (from Bedford, Luton, and Dunstable chiefly) 641, Northampton 789, Cambridge (from which a separate memorial had previously been sent) 97, Huntingdon 45, Suffolk 598, Norfolk 583, Leicestershire 359, Warwickshire 852, Worcestershire 417, Herefordshire 215, Wales 1,669, Salop 177, Staffordshire 678, Derbyshire 460, Nottinghamshire 543, Lincolnshire 624, Cheshire 326, Westmoreland 231, Durham (chiefly Darlington) 1,161, and Northumberland 234; Scotland sent 1,150, and Ireland 1,474. The remaining signatures were from various places, impossible to be classified.

The Memorial was forwarded to Balmoral on Friday, October 6th.

Art. IV.—EVENTS OF THE MONTH.

EDUCATION.

BRITISH ASSOCIATION. LARGE MEETING AT GLASGOW.

A LARGE meeting of those interested in the higher education of women, was held during the British Association Congress in the Medical Jurisprudence Class Rooms of the University. The Rev. Dr. Dodds, of St. George's, presided. After a few words he introduced Mrs. Daniels to the assembly:—

Mrs. DANIELS then read a paper on the subject, pointing out the great interest that has been aroused regarding the higher class education of women, and remarking that Scotland had not fully shared in the great interest of the movement. Glasgow, she considered the proper centre for a national effort in this direction. The Ladies' Association recommended to be formed, should aim at the establishment of a thoroughly good understanding with the University, in order that lectures should be provided of a nature calculated to invite students, and that certificates of ability should be obtained by teachers from the University. She then explained at length the advantages of the certificates.

Mr. HUNTER, Glasgow, who has had a large experience as a teacher, desired to speak more upon the general subject of female education than on the individual theory. The great evil of female education in Scotland, especially in the middle and lower middle, and even lower classes, was a striving after "accomplishments."

Dr. FITCH spoke highly in favour of public day schools for girls, which were superseding by degrees the old-fashioned system of small private schools. Experience had gone to prove the superiority of such public schools. There were advantages to be gained in the public schools which could not be had in private schools, against which he, however, would not say a word. In the public schools we got larger numbers, a greater amount of intellectual life, and a far better economy of teaching power. They had in them well-qualified teachers, selected on account of their interest in the work and fitness for it who could be removed in case of unfitness. The most important item in connexion with the public day school system as opposed to the purely private adventure schools was that they had a governing body responsible to the public. The movement he believed was producing a wholesome effect on the education of girls in England. It was also felt in England there should be education higher than the secondary school—analogous to that of the universities—for those young women who were not content to consider themselves finished with a little top-dressing of accomplishments. He then spoke of the establishments started for the purpose—mentioning particularly the establishment at Girton—whose students have achieved great distinctions in various branches of education.

Mr. E. H. BIGGS spoke of the progress of higher education in England and America, and thought there was nothing to hinder "the accomplishments" being taught along with a thorough education.

Professor LINDSAY referred to what had been done in Scotland in regard to the education of girls. The teaching of girls in Scotch schools had been better than the teaching of girls in English schools. In his country schools, boys and girls had been taught together, and in the Latin and mathematical classes—which he was sorry to say were changed under the new system—in these classes the daughters of the peasantry, of the farmers, and sometimes ministers, were, girls as well as boys being taught with success. It has been much more the habit in Scotland, not having boarding-schools to send girls to, to send them to day schools. He then gave an account of the Edinburgh Local examinations, the number of pupils who came up for which was largely increasing. In conclusion, he said that what was required for the success of the movement was that the ladies should be anxious for it, and should organise themselves into a Ladies' Association, and it depended also on the co-operation of the professors of the University, who had always shown themselves liberal in educational movements in the city.

Mrs. STEVENSON, Edinburgh, referring to the local examinations there during the last two years, said the number coming forward had increased enormously, and had reached 200, and these were not only women educated in Edinburgh, but from other towns all over the country. One pleasing feature was the result of the examination in arithmetic.

Miss FLORA STEVENSON, a member of the Edinburgh School Board, alluded to the success of the Edinburgh Ladies' Educational Association, which was largely due to the interest taken and encouragement given by the Professors of the University, especially Dr. Masson.

Mr. LATIMER, Plymouth, spoke of the institution which he and his friends had formed in that town about two years ago. There were now 174 girls there—a great number had passed well. The success of the school had a great influence on the private schools, and they had now all the schools of any eminence competing in the examinations. They had had associated with them the Bishop of Exeter, who had taken a great interest in the work.

Dr. JACK wished some information as to what Hutchesons' Hospital in this city was doing for female education. He understood that £20,000 had been bequeathed, and half of this, he was led to believe, was meant for the education of women.

The CHAIRMAN, who is one of the patrons of the Hutchesons' Hospital, said that in the School which had been recently opened on the south-side by the Incorporation, the number of applications far exceeded the accommodation. He thought that similar schools should be opened on the north-side as well, and also in the West-end, where there was a sad deficiency of the facilities for higher education.

Miss TOD, Belfast, said, the ladies' institute in that town was formed about eight years ago. Their first idea was to get up lectures, which they were still continuing under the direction of the professors who conducted them. The ladies memorialised the Senate of the Queen's University to grant certificates to women on the model of the

Cambridge examinations which were granted. They had also obtained prizes and scholarships. One of the most valuable results of the examinations was that they afforded an efficient test of the goodness of the schools and institutions from which the candidate came. A useful piece of work to be done by an association of ladies, such as they had in Belfast, was the promoting of the lectures for women who had entirely finished their educational course, but the most important duty of those present was to memorialise the Senate of Glasgow University to establish examinations for women, such as all the other great universities of the kingdom have already established, and which have been practically proved to be the best means yet devised for raising the standard of education. She was surprised that Glasgow was so far behind in this matter.. especially when she remembered that the Pope's Bull, under which the University was established, enjoined that it should resemble that of Bologna, where not only there were female students, but where also ladies assumed professional duties. The object should be to keep the question of the higher education of women prominently before the public, as it was one of immense importance. She dissented from the remarks of a previous speaker, who advocated the teaching of cookery and domestic economy above scholastic education. It was no more the duty of parents to educate their girls for other people than it was their duty to teach the boys for other people. Let them teach the lower things as well as the higher things, but by all means keep them in their proper place.

Mrs. FINLAY looked at the practical aspect of the meeting, and thought that the higher education of women would make them better wives and mothers, better at their own firesides, and would, above all things, supply agents for going forth to work against the darkness, heathenism, and ignorance that were unfolded every day. A higher education of women would benefit mankind and not merely womankind.

Mr. JOHNSTONE STONEY, Secretary of the Queen's University, Ireland, urged upon all interested in the question the wisdom of keeping before them as their ultimate object the opening of the universities themselves to women, which would be the only satisfactory "crowning of the edifice," and towards which all partial efforts should be considered as steps. As to the admission of women to degrees, he would say that every person who believed there were essential differences between the minds, as between men and women in other respects, should be willing to remove all artificial restrictions.

Mrs. HANCOCK and Professor FOSTER also spoke, and Dr. DICKSON, of the University, stated that there had been lectures delivered in the University on English History, Astronomy, and on various branches of Natural History, and those lectures had met, on the part of the ladies of Glasgow, with much acceptance. Whether the movement would take more formal shape would depend on it being adopted by the ladies of Glasgow. He believed his colleagues would be found ready, when the movement presented itself in a formal shape, to do their duty in the matter, and give such instruction as might be desired.

The CHAIRMAN then requested those present who might be disposed to join a local association to be formed to leave their names.

FRÖBEL SOCIETY FOR THE PROMOTION OF THE KINDERGARTEN SYSTEM.

The Committee of the Fröbel Society have arranged some Classes, extending over three Terms, to assist Students who are preparing for the next Kindergarten Examination. The Classes will be held on Thursdays, from 3.30 to 6 p.m., at the College of Preceptors, 42, Queen Square, Bloomsbury, W.C. The first Term will begin on Thursday, October 19th, and will end Thursday, December 21st, and the following subjects will be taken:

Fröbel's Drawing, ten Lessons ...	Madame Michaelis
The First Four Gifts, seven Lessons...	Miss Bishop
Relating Stories, Three lessons ...	Miss E. A. Manning.

In the last half-hour, work done at home will be inspected. Fee, £1 per Term, or £2 10s. for the whole course. Materials extra. Names need not be sent in beforehand.

E. A. MANNING,
Hon. Secretary of the Fröbel Society,
35, Blomfield Road, W.

LADIES' EDUCATIONAL ASSOCIATION IN CONNECTION WITH UNIVERSITY COLLEGE, LONDON.

THE Session of 1876-77 (the ninth Session), of twenty-six weeks, begins on Monday, the 23rd of October, and ends on Saturday, the 9th of June. It is divided into three Terms:—

Michaelmas Term, of eight weeks, from October 23rd, to December 16th.

Lent Term, of ten weeks, from January 15th, to March 24th.

Summer Term, of eight weeks, from April 16th, to June 11th.

The subjects and times of lectures are:—

GREEK.—Tuesday and Friday, at 9.45 a.m., beginning October 24th. Talfourd Ely, Esq.

GREEK.—Elementary, 4.30 p.m., Tuesday and Thursday.

LATIN.—Tuesday and Thursday, at 2.30 p.m., begins October 24th. Professor Alfred Goodwin.

LATIN.—Elementary, Wednesday and Friday, at 2.30 p.m., begins October 25th.

ENGLISH LITERATURE.—Monday and Wednesday, 11.30
a.m. Prof. Harry Morley.

FRENCH LITERATURE.—Monday, 3.30 p.m. Prof. Ch.
Cassal.

ITALIAN LANGUAGE AND LITERATURE.—Monday. Prof.
Cavaliere G. Volpe.

GERMAN LITERATURE.—Wednesday, at 2.30. Prof.
Friedrich Althans.

LOGIC.—Friday, at 2.30. Prof. Croom Robertson
(girls under 17 may join this class).

PHYSIOLOGY AND HYGIENE.—Thursday. Prof. W. H.
Corfield.

HISTORY.—Tuesday. Prof. Beesley. Beginning on
the 16th of January.

ENGLISH CONSTITUTIONAL HISTORY.—Prof. J. W. Willis
Bund.

MATHEMATICS.—Monday and Thursday. Prof. J.
Harding.

PHYSICS (Optics).—Tuesday. Prof. G. Carey Foster,
F.R.S.

Prospectuses of the Classes of Jurisprudence, Roman
Law, Political Economy, and Geology (to which respectively ladies are by permission of the Council admitted), and of the Fine Art Department, can be obtained
in the Secretary's Office at the College.

College for Men and Women. Prof. Sheldon Amos
will deliver a course of lectures on the Science of Politics,
on Friday evenings, commencing October the 20th. He
will also carry on his Class of English History on the
same day. Fees for men, 2s. 6d., for women, 2s.

Lectures to Teachers.—Women's Education Union.—
Mr. Percy Harding is giving a course of six lectures on
the Method of Teaching Geometry at the rooms of the
Society of Arts, John Street, Adelphi, on Tuesday
Evenings at 6 p.m. They began October 3rd. Mons.
Andrade will give six lectures on the Palin-Paris-Chévé's
Method of Teaching Music, beginning Nov. 14th. Fees
for each course:—Teachers, 4s.; non-teachers, 8s. For
the two courses:—Teachers, 7s.; non-teachers, 15s.—
LOUISA BROUGH, Secretary, Office, 112, Brompton Road,
S.W.

High School at Plymouth.—The Bishop of Exeter presented certificates and prizes to the successful candidates in this school on October 7th. This school, though recently established, has so increased that it has become necessary to erect another building at the cost of several thousand pounds.

THE WAR IN THE EAST.

During the past month women have not been idle in the expression of their warm sympathy with their unfortunate sisters in the East. On the 19th September a meeting of ladies was held at the Congregational Institution in Nottingham; about 200 ladies were present. Letters expressing sympathy with the movement were read from Lady Belper, Mrs. Loyd Lindsay, Mrs. Mackenzie (wife of Bishop Mackenzie), and from the Hon. Mrs. Forester. A committee was formed to decide upon the best means of getting relief, and officers were appointed. We have elsewhere spoken of the Memorial to the Queen from 43,845 women of Great Britain and Ireland, to which the names were collected with such energy and goodwill, that only three weeks elapsed between the first meeting of the ladies who drew it up, and its final despatch to Balmoral.

A similar memorial was sent to Her Majesty by the ladies of Cambridge on September 18th, and another numerously signed from the ladies of Coventry. An address of sympathy to the Christian women of Bosnia, Bulgaria, and Herzegovina, has been extensively circulated in Scotland.

A largely-attended meeting of the Women's Peace and Arbitration Auxiliary (which also took the form of a working party in aid of the distressed Bulgarians, Bosnians, and Herzegovinians) was held on October 3rd at the offices of the Peace Society, 20, New Broad street, London, at which the following resolution was proposed and unanimously adopted, viz.:—"That this meeting. sharing with the whole nation the feeling of horror at the cruelties and oppressions perpetrated by the Turkish Government and its agents upon the Christian inhabitants of Bulgaria and other countries, desires to express its opinion that the English Government in concert with

the other Great Powers of Europe, exert a prompt
decided action in order at once to prevent the recurrence
of these outrages, and to bring about an entire cessation
of hostilities, and to secure for the Christian provinces a
legislative and administrative autonomy which shall
place them beyond the reach of the arbitrary control of
the Turkish Government. That this meeting further
desires to express its conviction that these results may
be obtained by a mutual understanding between the
European Powers without recourse to arms."

A meeting of the same society for the south-eastern
district was also held on September 15th, when similar
resolutions were passed.

Miss Pearson and Miss McLaughlin are still pursuing
their work of indefatigable charity in the Servian
hospitals. Their opinion is, that owing to the expense
of carriage, it is not worth while to send anything but
medicines, instruments, and similar stores, which cannot
be procured on the spot, and that clothing for the
refugees is better bought there than sent from England.
Dr. Sandwith, however, wrote from Belgrade begging
for supplies of warm clothing as well as money for the
destitute. Acting on this suggestion, Miss Irby and
Mrs. Frank Malleson have agreed to have a central
depot for clothes and other contributions. at 29, Queen
square, London, W.C. (the College for Men and Women),
to be called "The Clothes Relief Fund for Christian
Fugitives from Turkey and the Christian Inhabitants of
the Slavonic-Turkish Provinces." The clothing will be
sent to the different points according to the discretion
of Mrs. Malleson and her committee. It is necessary to
mention, 1st, that every contribution of clothing must
be accompanied with a donation towards the expense of
carriage; 2nd, money must never be enclosed in the
parcels; 3rd, whatever is sent must be clean and in
good repair. Strong warm skirts, jackets, or garibaldis
for women, quite plain; strong trousers and jackets and
good stout coats for men; blankets or pieces of flannel
to wrap babies in, as well as any warm clothing for
children; calico clothing is not needed, but any sums
of money will be very useful to assist in purchasing
sheepskins or strong clothing on the spot. If any ladies

are unable to send ready-made clothing, but will send materials, Mrs. Malleson undertakes to have them made up at the depôt.

Miss Freeman and Miss Johnston have already set out with stores, clothing, and money. Viscountess Strangford left England some weeks ago on her way to Phillippopolis, in order to superintend personally the distribution of the funds entrusted to her.

FEMALE VOTERS IN IRELAND.

At a recent meeting of the Maryborough Town Commissioners, the Town Clerk called the attention of the Commissioners to the fact that women who had the property qualification hitherto voted at the election of commissioners. He stated his opinion that this was illegal, and, on reference to the Act of Parliament, it was found that "person" was there defined to mean "a male householder." The Commissioners struck about 27 names of ladies off the list of voters.

We do not cavil at the determination, for of course, till an Irish Municipal Bill resembling the English one is passed, women have not the legal right of voting—but that they have *hitherto* done so unchallenged, and are now struck off the list of voters, is one more instance of the tendency to restrict their political rights in favour of those of men.

LADIES' CLASS FOR DRAWING AND ENGRAVING ON WOOD.

A class for teaching the above useful profession has just been established in London by Mr. Paterson, who has conducted a similar class for several years in Edinburgh with much success. It is established with the view to open up a new and suitable occupation to women of education. It is clean, not particularly laborious, and can be carried on at home. There is generally abundant employment for competent hands, as the use of book and serial illustrations is constantly on the increase, particularly in London, while the long time necessary to become proficient prevents the business being overstocked. The return varies from £1 to £5 per week, but a higher scale of remuneration may be reached with superior skill.

Though a knowledge of drawing is not absolutely necessary, it greatly assists the pupil, and it has consequently been thought judicious to receive pupils also for instruction in drawing on wood, either with the prospect of continuing this branch separately, or in conjunction with engraving. The class meets every Monday, Wednesday, and Friday, from 2 p.m. to 3. Fees: engraving, £2 2s. per quarter; drawing on wood, £2 2s.; both inclusive, £3 3s. A small charge is made also for wood. This sum, however, is uncertain, being according to the quantity used by each pupil, and can never exceed a few shillings quarterly.

All particulars may be learned by applying to Mr. R. Paterson, 21 and 22, East Temple chambers, Whitefriars street, Fleet street, E.C.

Mr. Paterson's head assistant still carries on the class in Edinburgh.

The *Women's Union Journal* says that 45,270 women are employed in the straw plait manufactories in England and Wales, while the number of men so employed is only 3,596. It hopes soon to see a union formed among the women working in Luton and its neighbourhood, which is the principal seat of the trade.

TRADES' UNION CONGRESS, NEWCASTLE-ON-TYNE.

LAST month the Ninth Annual Trades' Union Congress, met—and among the delegates were three women, Mrs. Paterson, from the Bookbinders' Women's Society, London; Miss Edith Simcox, from the Shirt and Collar Maker's Women's Society, London; and Miss Jane Wilkinson, from the Upholsterers' Women's Society, London. A discussion took place upon the Workshops' Act. Mr. J. J. Allen, of the National Early Closing League, moved the following resolution:—

That this Congress reaffirms the unanimous decisions of previous Congresses, pledges itself to renewed exertions with the object of obtaining during next session of Parliament the simplification and consolidation and extension of the Factory Act of 1874 to all children and young persons and women employed in workshops and shops open for the manufacture and sale and repair of goods, also in bleaching, dyeing, and finishing works; and request the Parliamentary Committee to take the earliest opportunity of pressing the views of Congress upon the attention of the Home Secretary.

What they wanted was that the Government and the
nation should consent to do justice equally to all trades
where children and young persons and women were
employed, because they believed that the tendency of
restricting certain trades had the effect of inducing the
overcrowding of these trades.

Mr. PARKS, Gateshead, of the Chainmakers' Association, gave an account of that industry as carried on in
the black country, in which men, women, and children
all worked together in one shop, under often very
wretched conditions. The work was most unsuited to
women and children. The children were certainly
under the Factory Act, but the district was so well
picketed by the children and women who were not
working, that the Factory Act Inspectors had very little
chance. No Factory Act, or any other Act, would be
satisfactory unless it included them within its scope.

Mrs. PATERSON, London, said she had visited the
black country, and thought the accounts as to the state
of the women and children employed in the nail and
chain trade were little exaggerated. Speaking to the
resolution, she said she thought the extension of the
Factory Act as recommended by the Royal Commissioners would be a mistake in so far as women were
concerned. Children should be legislated for certainly,
but not women, who were now showing a disposition
to protect themselves by union. She thought that in
this matter women had a right to be heard. It was
proposed that the inspectors should be henceforth appointed by the constabulary; but she was of opinion
that it would be contrary to English freedom to put
such power into the hands of the police. It was really
too bad that a policeman should have power to enter a
workshop and turn out the young women at a certain
time, because the Commissioners proposed that the mere
fact of the presence of the workers in a workshop after
certain hours constituted an offence. She hoped the
Parliamentary Committee would·endeavour to prevent
that part of the report from being passed into law. The
most serious objection she had to urge against the report
was the suggested extension of the Factory Act to small
workshops, for that would tend to drive the work more

E

and more into the homes. And it was just that home
work the Commissioners did not propose to interfere
with. The home work where fewer than three women
were employed was the greatest obstacle to women's
unions.

Miss SIMCOX, London, advocated the extension of the
Factory and Workshops' Acts to all employments, including domestic employment, where women worked in
their own homes.

The resolution was then put and carried.

The *Weekly Scotsman* says very justly of this debate:—

The question, as to the extension of the Workshops' Acts, is one
which this year has been discussed very much after the fashion of
previous years, though, thanks to the presence of women representatives, the views expressed have not been altogether one-sided, as
they formerly were. The demand made is, that more restrictions
shall be put upon the labour of women. It pleased the Legislature
many years ago to class women and children together as beings requiring to be specially protected. That there was reason for it in
the case of children is undoubted ; but that women should be fettered
as to the hours of their work is not so easily justified. At first, only
women working in factories were dealt with ; but afterwards, the law
took in hand women who are engaged in workshops of various kinds.
The Royal Commission on the Factory and Workshops' Acts, who
reported a few months ago, found that the operations of the Workshops' Act was not satisfactory. In effect it causes inspection and
regulation of good, well-ventilated workrooms, and limits the hours
of work in these, while it does not touch small unhealthy workrooms,
or meddle with the work done there. In itself that is an anomaly of
a grave kind. Yet it is one that cannot be remedied unless inspectors be appointed for every house of every working woman. Miss
Simcox, one of the speakers at the Congress, advocated the extension
of the Acts " so that they might apply to all industrial employments,
even although, as in what were called domestic workshops, employers
only gave work to two or three, or even only one person." The proposal is extravagant enough in itself ; but its extravagance is not its
worst fault. If it could be carried out it would inevitably produce
serious evils. The workshops contemplated by Miss Simcox are
those of employers, and, presumably, for the most part not unhealthy.
What would happen if her proposal was carried out? Each woman
worker would carry her work to her own room to do, and what many
of these rooms are it is scarcely necessary to say. The working
tailors object to what they call the " sweating system," for one reason
because it leads to men and women doing work in their own unhealthy
rooms. Yet the same men who object to the " sweating system " for
this reason ask for legislation which would certainly drive many
women who now work comfortably, to work in their unhealthy rooms.
Mrs. Paterson, who also took part in the discussion, saw this, and
objected to further extension of the Acts. She said that such further

extension meant more home work. For the statement she had the
best justification in the report of the Commissioners. They got evidence in abundance to the effect that, under the law as it stands,
much work is done at home. The law limits the number of hours
that women may be kept in workshops, and when a busy time comes
they take work home with them. Everybody admits that this is not
desirable; and legislation is asked for which would inevitably increase
the evil. There is, however, something more to be taken into account than the healthiness or unhealthiness of the places wherein
women may work. Mrs. Paterson insisted that women should have
more consideration, and that they should not be classed with children.
More will be heard of such contention in time. Women must live,
and if many of them are to live honestly they must work. They are
coming into competition with men in many cases, and the men do not
like it. The Legislature is therefore invoked to put barriers in the
way of women and to handicap them as workers. Such a demand
ought not to have any response. No adequate justification has been
shown for it, and alike on sanitary grounds, and because of its injustice to women, it should not be complied with.

EMPLOYMENT.

THE *Labour News* says: Envelope makers are very
slack at present. They are mostly all women and
young girls who are engaged in this business; and
some of the principal houses employ, even at present,
over a hundred, who border, stamp, and fold. A good
hand can fold eight thousand envelopes per day; the
lowest price paid being sixpence per thousand, for some,
eightpence. Thus an experienced woman can earn
upwards of £1 per week. In some houses machinery
worked by steam is employed, and with the aid of one
female, in some instances two—the number depending
on the quality of the work to be done—each machine is
capable of making from 50,000 to 60,000 envelopes per
day.

TOBACCO AND SNUFF MANUFACTURERS.—A man, on
piecework, can earn in this trade from £2 to £4 per week;
women and girls, five, ten, or fifteen shillings, according to
the experience they have gained and bring to bear on their
work. A young girl, on first taking up this branch, as
a future means of livelihood, is paid by her employers a
small wage, and is placed under the guidance of an older
and more experienced hand, who receives, as remuneration for her attention to her pupil and consequent loss
of time on her own work, any extra profit arising from
that pupil's work over and above the small salary paid.

Pill-making.—In Crane Court, Fleet Street, a pill manufactory employs about twenty young women, who earn from twelve to twenty shillings per week. They are busy at present, and have lately sent some large cases of pills to Australia; they manufacture largely for export.

Nursing as a Profession for Ladies.—The *Standard*, reviewing the report of the Metropolitan Nursing Association, says:—"There are few, if any, schools where a lady can be taught to be a nurse without pledging herself to a religious or quasi-religious life; none in which she can be trained to nursing as a profitable occupation. The Association has, to a certain extent, but to a very small extent, supplied the deficiency. What is required is much more. We need room for the training of so many lady nurses that their number shall give credit and social status to the profession, the want of which, and the feeling of social degradation consequent thereon, constitute at present the only reason why a father who cannot provide an independence for his daughters should shrink from educating them to earn their bread, in the most charitable and the most feminine of all employments."

Loundry Work.—The *Whitehall Review* announces that Miss Elizabeth Philp, the well-known composer of so many graceful songs, has established a laundry at Paddington Green, London, W.

The jute factories about Hackney employ several hundred workpeople, principally women. Some of the more experienced women can earn at this as much as twenty-six shillings per week, but with many, twelve or thirteen is about the average.

MISCELLANEOUS.

The Female School of Art, under the special patronage of the Queen.—Instruction in drawing, painting, modelling, &c. Competition for Gilchrist £50, and other scholarships and medals. Autumn session commenced Monday, 2nd October. Prospectuses can be obtained at the School, 43, Queen Square, W.C.—LOUISA GANN, Superintendent and Secretary.

Artists' Annuity Fund.—The *Suffrage Journal* states

that though women might become members on the
same conditions as to payment and benefits as men, yet
they were not allowed to attend the general meetings
of the society, nor to vote in the election of the committee or the enactment of the rules. At the Quarterly
General Meeting of the Society, held on June 12th, 1876,
the committee stated that the claims of the female
members exceeded the amount of their premiums, and
therefore strongly recommended that in future female
artists should be ineligible as members. The recommendation was adopted by the meeting. One of the
lady artists' writes to complain of this grievance: she
says, "It does not affect me personally, as I have been
in it some years, but I think it very hard upon women
to exclude them from the working department of the
society, and then vote for their expulsion. We are not
allowed to attend the meetings, and so can make no
suggestion, but it seems to me that a fairer way of over-
coming the difficulty would be to raise the premium to
be paid by women members. But why, in this fund
more than in ordinary societies, the men's and women's
accounts should be kept distinct, I know not, nor can I
see anything in the bye-laws to justify this arrangement;
but if it must be so, surely raising the premiums would
be the best thing to do. Here is a fund for the relief of
painters in want, women are admitted on equal terms as
regards payments and benefits, but they are ineligible to
attend meetings, consequently when the men members
find the women members unprofitable in consequence of
their own arrangement as regards separation of funds,
they pass a rule excluding women members for the future,
without the existing women members having a voice in
the matter."

HOME FOR LITTLE GIRLS.—Miss Agnes Bolton writes
to the newspapers for help for the Home, which she has
established at Leytonstone, for girls from six years old
to twenty, who are liable to fall into bad courses. The
Home is said to be very successful, but though to some
extent self-supporting, external assistance is needed.

LONDON SCHOOLS' SWIMMING CLUB.—On September
23rd, the same day that the second annual fête of this
club took place, a girls' swimming fête in connection

with the same club was held at the King Street Baths, Camden Town, under the direction of Miss Chessar and Miss Richardson, and was very successful.

WIFE-BEATING.

The following instructive case occurred a few weeks since at Bow street. The right of men to beat women is a practice of long standing, and one which is said to be on the increase among the coarser and more brutal of our working classes.

John Jackson, a rough-looking man, was charged before Mr. Flowers with violently assaulting Hannah Hoblent, a woman with whom he has been living.

Prosecutrix said that on Saturday night the prisoner came home and without any reason violently assaulted her. On Sunday night he met her in the Strand, kicked her, and pulled her hair out.

Police-constable 338 E corroborated the evidence. He also said that the prisoner threatened to hang the prosecutrix when he got out of this difficulty.

Mr. Flowers—Now what do you say to this? Is it a manly thing to kick a woman?

Prisoner—I think so, when she richly deserves it.

Mr. Flowers—Oh! you think that?

Prisoner—No; I'm sure of it.

Detective Boyell, who was in court, told his worship the prisoner had already been imprisoned for assaulting his daughter and for assaulting the police.

Mr. Flowers, addressing the prisoner, said he appeared to be under the impression that he possessed the privilege of beating a woman whenever she deserved it. He might or might not possess that privilege, but at any rate he would not exercise it for six months to come, that being the term for which he would be sent to prison with hard labour.

The *Daily News* remarks on this:—We fear that man's history will show him to have been at all times a great deal too ready to accept the possession of superior strength as an authority for its arbitrary use. But while in most other ways civilization has been exercising a healthy and corrective influence over this propensity, it is only too evident that in our country there has sprung up among certain classes a disposition to treat women with a savage ferocity such as no time or class ever seems to have known before. There appears to be a large number of persons among our population who have no idea of rebuking a woman in any milder way than by the operation of a heavy boot or clog. So many women have been cruelly injured, so many have been actually killed, by the kicks of their brutal masters, that when a man now raises his savage foot against a woman he ought to be regarded and dealt with as one who does what he knows may cause death, as a criminal is who used a weapon which may obviously have a deadly operation. One of the defects, and probably the unavoidable defects of our system of criminal law, is that we cannot readily bring exceptional punishment to bear upon new forms of outrage and violence while they are still exceptional. Owing to this defect the habit of kicking women has among certain classes grown to be not exceptional. The weakness of the system of punishment applied to it has fostered it into a custom. Perhaps we can hardly feel surprised that men of the stamp of Jackson have actually come to regard it as a manly privilege and a right. It is to be regretted that his punishment could not be made severe and sharp enough to disabuse himself and all his fellows of their belief.

Lady Helps.—Mrs. Crawshay writes word that her office for lady helps at the Quebec Institute, Lower Seymour street, London, W., is doing much work since its re-opening after the vacation. Some other offices with the same object have also been opened.

Art. V.—FOREIGN NOTES AND NEWS.

France.

On the 12th of August Madame Ribard, of Nantes, read her thesis for her medical degree, in the great amphitheatre of the Medical School, in presence of fifty doctors and students. She replied in a very satisfactory manner to all the questions asked, and was complimented by the examiners. She has now received her diploma as

doctor of medicine. Madame Ribard is twenty-seven years old—she
is the wife of a physician.

At the distribution of prizes of the Society for Elementary Instruction in Paris, Madame Paulin, directress of the Commercial School
for girls, and two of the mistresses of the Institution received medals.

M. Leon Richer announces in the *Avenir des Femmes* the re-
organisation of the Society "Pour l'amélioration de sort des Femmes," which was suppressed last winter.

The Working Men's Congress was opened October 2nd, in the
School Hall, No. 3, Rue d'Arras. There were 105 delegates
in attendance from the provinces, and 255 from Paris. Several
women and a number of guests were also present, and the Press was
well represented. M. Chabert, engraver, of Paris, was elected president, and among the members of the Congress chosen to act on the
bureau, it was remarked that Citizen Andrée, a woman, was selected
for the secretaryship. The Congress was occupied the next night with
a discussion on the question of female labour. An address from the
Patriotic Club of London was received, from which we extract the
following :—We have particularly remarked the subject of woman
labour. On this point we wish to tell you what experience has
taught us : of all the scourges which strike and degrade the working
men's home there is not one which causes such ruinous and disastrous
effects in a household as woman labour. Besides destroying domestic
comfort, it produces a general fall of wages. We do not ask that
women should be unnecessarily banished from the labour market, nor
that they should be hindered from creating an independent existence
by their industry ; but we are conscientiously opposed to an abuse of
their weaker nature, by which they are pitilessly made mean competitors, and are deliberately made use of to lower the wages of real
heads of households, a circumstance which is only too common now-
a-days. On this point we are in accord with you, for here our sad
experience puts us on our guard ; in this country up to the present
time women have been unable to get justice from capital except by
the action of the law.

Two of the first three papers read on " Woman's Labour " were by
women—Citoyennes Raoult and Aubé. The women who have spoken
at the Congress are as speakers and reformers far superior to the
men, though these last have given proof of no mean talent ; but while
they now and then indulged in sonorous declamation, the women stuck
to facts and figures, and their point never failed to draw plain and
palpable conclusions from their concisely expressed statements. It
appears that the Parisian skilled needlewoman can earn on an average
no more than 1s. or 1s. 3d. a day. It may be imagined how insufficient that support is from the fact that beefsteak now costs in Paris
from two to three francs a pound. Besides she has to clothe herself
with neatness, not to say elegance, in the *ateliers*, and moreover her
lodgings still remain to be paid for. She is at the shop 12 or 13
hours a day, for her day is longer than that of the workman. When
she leaves the shop she must go and fetch her children from the
neighbours or the *asile* to which she has confided them, then get the
evening meal ready and do her housework, and on Sundays instead of
resting she must go to the *lavoir* to wash the family linen. The unfair

competition arising from the sale of convent and prison manufactured
goods particularly affects the price of female labour. Both convents
and monasteries have of late years been turned into factories ; and the
nuns, moreover, take charge of numbers of little girls whose mothers
are engaged in factories, and teach them various industries from
patterns supplied by outsiders, and the labour of these children is
thus placed in competition with that of their parents, to the disadvantage of the latter. As an illustration of the extent of this competition, it is stated that no fewer than 150 convents work for one
drapery shop in Paris alone. The nuns pay little or no taxes,
and scarcely anything to the girls they employ. The competition of
the prisons is no less injurious to the honest isolated workwoman condemned to remain at large. There are in France eight central prisons
for women. Last year these prisons produced 915,421 days of labour
with 2,933 workwomen, and this work was, of course, sold much
below the price necessary to maintain the ordinary workwoman.
Another complaint is that women leading an immoral life employ
seamstresses at low wages for the purpose of cloaking their vice,
selling the work without a profit, and that the employers of seamstresses keep their carriages, while the seamstresses fall into vice or
crime. Sewing machines, it is likewise alleged, are injurious to health
when worked for hours at a stretch, and relays of workers, with improved seats, have been suggested to remedy this evil. Citoyenne
Raoult read the next paper, which supplied a number of most telling
figures of the low rate of wages, and proved that the salary of work
girls seldom exceeds 9½d. for a day of ten hours. Many houses for
ready-made apparel get their goods made in the rural districts, and
never pay in money, but in kind. One way in which the Parisian
employer grinds down his workwomen is, when the dull season has
set in, to say to the middle-woman, "Here's an order which is not
urgent ; I paid you 1s. 2d. for these skirts last year, but I have to
deliver this order only in three months time. To keep you going, if
you like to take them, I will pay you 10d. a piece." The middle-
woman consults her *employés*, who, hoping the lowering of price is
only temporary, accept, and the price never rises again. Citoyenne
Raoult's eloquent conclusion was, that the remedy for the present
oppressed condition of workwomen was co-operation. "Why," she
asked, "should not workwomen form co-operative societies of production, and why should not their fathers, brothers, or husbands
come and buy of them what they want rather than go to those houses
whose fortunes they make, and in which their mothers, sisters, and
wives are so ground down that they cannot live by working ? " To us
this seems the only solution.

The Organisation of Sempstresses.—A sempstress named Jozon, 45
years of age, has been tried by court-martial in Paris for participation
in the Commune. It was alleged that she belonged to a women's
committee deputed to organise workrooms, its members receiving two
francs a day, that she frequented the clubs, and headed a band of
women armed with rifles, with a red flag and scarf. Her defence was
that she devoted herself to the organisation of female labour, and
received no pay from the Commune. She called witnesses to establish
this, and was acquitted.

A house has been opened for young servant girls out of employment at 85, Rue Legendre, Paris. It is under the direction of a
deaconess and a committee of ladies. The directress places the girls
in good situations, and continues to exercise a kindly influence over
them. Many of the young girls to whom this home has proved useful
are Swiss. The charge is 1 franc 25 centimes per diem, which is far
from defraying the actual cost, so that subscriptions are much needed.
—*Bulletin Continentale.*

The *Semaine Religieuse* says that fifteen young ladies in Paris, of the
wealthiest class, have combined among themselves to renounce all
superfluity of dress or ornament, and are employing the money thus
saved to the education and support of nineteen orphan children, who
are thus saved from misery and probably from vice. The paper recommends others to follow this example.

ITALY.

Signor Mauro Macchi, a deputy to Parliament, urges the necessity
of establishing superior normal schools for women.

At a meeting recently convened in Naples to protest against the
atrocities in Turkey, a lady, Matilda Caselli, was one of the chief
speakers. She is said to have spoken admirably, and received tre-
mendous applause. To express one's own sentiments, she said, in
behalf of a noble cause is not, nor ought it to be, the monopoly of men.
She said she protested in the name of the Italian women against the
maintenance of the present state of things.

GERMANY.

The General Conference of German Women's Associations was
opened, in the beginning of October, at Frankfort-on-the-Main. The
audience was so large that the rooms of the Polytechnic Society,
where the meeting was held, were found insufficient, and many that
had come were obliged to go away. Miss Augusta Schmidt, of
Leipzig, opened the proceedings by an eloquent speech, extending over
an hour. The higher education, and the opening up of new avocations for women, were declared to be the objects of the association.
The association does not, the speaker said, countenance any movement,
similar to those in England and America, for the attainment of the
franchise. At Leipzig and Gotha, schools for the further advancement of knowledge among the female sex have been established with
great success. "Evening Entertainments for Women of the People"
have also been started at Leipzig, combining the pleasant with the
useful. In some towns the branch associations occupy themselves
with the extension of the Kindergarten system, and the formation of
a staff of efficient lady teachers.

The German government has issued a report resulting from an
inquiry undertaken in the various States of the Confederation upon
the labour of women in manufactures. From this it appears that about
226,000 women above the age of 16 are employed. 24 per cent. are from
16 to 18, 42 per cent. from 19 to 25, and 34 per cent. above 25 years of
age. About one-fourth of the entire number are married. More than half
(128,500) of the total number of workwomen are engaged in textile

manufactures, 34,000 in the manufacture of cigars, the remainder in various industries. The hours of work are generally 10 to 11 hours, but some work 13 hours. The wages are usually 5 to 8 marks a week (a mark is equal to a shilling), some earn less, but—on the other hand —some earn as much as 24 marks.

The *Woman's Gazette* of September contains an interesting notice translated from a German magazine, *Die Gartenlaube*, upon the employment of women in the Berlin Telegraph Office :—

"The first impulse in this direction was given by the "Lette Union for the employment of the female sex," instituted in 1868 at Berlin ; and, taking pattern by Switzerland and the Grand-duchy of Baden, the Postmaster-General Stephan acceded with great willingness to the petition passed on to him by the Reichstag. A portion of the "Lette House," at the corner of the Konigsgrätzer street, was given up for the use of young girls who were to be trained in the necessary theoretical and practical knowledge, provided they could pass a preliminary examination in English, French, geography, and the construction of German sentences. After a three months' course in the practising rooms, where a sufficient number of apparatus is placed, they have to undergo a practical examination, consisting of the sending forth and receiving an English, French, and German despatch, for which three minutes each is allowed.

" Definite appointments are not made until after a yet longer probation of three to five months, during which time lectures upon chemistry and physics are attended twice a week. Another written and verbal examination must then be passed upon the internal management of the Telegraph Service, and the uses of the various apparatus. When all these trials have been successfully surmounted, the candidate receives an appointment with a monthly salary of twenty thalers, which increases according to length of service.

"There are about a hundred ladies employed in the Telegraph Office, and among them are women and girls of the best standing. Berlin furnishes scarcely one-half of the contingent—the greater number come from elsewhere. A good many are the daughters of officials and officers whose fathers' narrow incomes do not suffice for the maintenance of their families. Still more painful is the lot of those unhappy maidens and women who have no such support, and have to fight the battle of life for themselves. The Telegraph Service offers them a welcome shelter, and protects them from utter poverty or worse ills. Not unfrequently one is surprised to hear aristocratic names there, and to see faces well known in the best circles of society.

" The way in which the women clerks do their work appears to be highly satisfactory as to its intelligence, rapidity, and completeness. The most excellent discipline is maintained in the departments, and the intercourse between the male and female clerks is conducted in the most friendly, considerate, and decorous way. The officials appear to be entirely contented with their female colleagues, and complaints are very seldom heard. Although the work is hard, and the girls are out in all weathers in order to be at their posts punctually, there are very few absences from illness. Should a really serious case arise, the doctor has to give his certificate, and a leave of absence is granted for six weeks. All other absences are inexcusable, and are visited with penalties or dismissal. Although the pay is small—barely sufficing for the necessaries of life—yet the great demand for the service proves that it is a welcome work for women; and it is surely much the best for women of all grades in society to learn to work for themselves, if necessary, rather than allow themselves to be a burden upon others."

AMERICA.

Canada.—The Montreal Ladies' Association have instituted a Kindergarten in the Des Peres School; seventy-five children are at present in the school. It is reported to be a thorough success.

United States.—There are three first-class Medical Colleges for women; there are some others, but they do not in the opinion of the best physicians afford a thorough training. These three are the Woman's Medical College of the New York Infirmary, 128, Second Avenue; (regular) New York City; the Woman's Medical College of Pennsylvania; (regular) North College Avenue, Twenty-Second Street, Philadelphia, and the Boston University Medical College, East Concord Street, (homeopathic) Boston.

The California State Medical Society, at its recent meeting, passed, by acclamation, a resolution to admit ladies who hold medical diplomas, into full fellowship in the Society.

The right of women to vote in the election of vestries has been discussed at Episcopalian conferences in California and North Carolina, and decided negatively.

Miss Pangborn, for the last six years the capable and efficient recorder in the Probate office of Burlington, Vermont, has been lately appointed and sworn as a notary public.

Mrs. Robb of Texas, is described in an American paper as the "Cattle Queen of America." She owns 35,000 head of cattle.

ARGENTINE REPUBLIC.—The Commissioner stated that "Education was gratuitous in every province, and, still better, compulsory until the child could read or write. After the age of sixteen a yearly payment of ten (Argentine) dollars was required, with which small sum the lad could go on until fitted to begin life as lawyer, doctor, &c. Women were taught to read, write, and sew, gratuitously; "if they would learn more it must be paid for."

BRAZIL.—In the schools of Brazil, "boys and girls are rigorously separated. Women are employed and preferred as teachers in these primary schools, *receive the same salary as men*, and offer more successful results as the proof of their efficiency. While there are many Normal schools, the ranks of teachers are frequently recruited from the ordinary schools. The chirography is unusually fair. Whether these Brazilian girls will ever write for the press is problematic, but if they do it will be a day marked with a white stone for the printers. One, Luiza da Alvarenga's, composition I remember, the script of which would make a compositor's heart leap for joy. One errand of the Commission here, is to secure competent lady teachers of Frœbel's system, familiar with the Portuguese language, who will introduce it.

CAPE OF GOOD HOPE.

Some months ago we received information of the successful introduction of women, by Messrs. Saul Solomon & Co., printers, into the composing as well as the bookbinding departments of their establishment. They also imported several male employés from Europe; some of these latter having been frequently absent from work, some of the printing of the *Cape Argus,* published by Messrs. Solomon, was given to the female branch of the composing department. When this reached the ears of the men a meeting was called, and a deputation waited upon Mr. Solomon to urge that his firm should cease to employ female labour, and, as he declined to do anything of the kind, that the firm should not employ females on work connected with the *Argus, Mercantile Observer* or *Government Gazette.* This being also declined, the deputation made use of certain threats with a view to intimidate the firm as to the way in which they should carry on their business; this proving of no avail, several of the men absented themselves from work. They have thus exposed themselves to two charges under the Masters' and Servants' Law—for absence without leave, and attempts to intimidate by threats. They were summoned before the magistrates and fined. Thus the jealousy of women's labour, which impresses us so painfully on reading the records of trades' unions in England, extends to the other side of the world. Of course these men are no longer in Mr. Solomon's employment, and we trust that the prompt example made of them may deter others of the stronger sex from vindicating their exclusive right to remunerative employment. The *Cape Standard and Mail,* of August 29th, says of this: "Mr. Saul Solomon has, of late, introduced an innovation in his printing establishment which, in our opinion, is a very useful one, viz., that of employing female compositors. It is a great advantage for the girls, who generally have very few chances of getting a decent livelihood when they are not sufficiently educated to apply for a situation of governess, and too respectably connected to be fit for menial service. It is equally advantageous for the employers, especially in a country where labour is scarce and liquor cheap. But it would appear that some of the male compositors do not like the competition of the weaker sex, and that this has been the motive of a kind of strike which they lately attempted. As girls will do their work just as well as the men themselves, the latter will have a great chance of seeing every place in our printing offices taken by the former if they go on with their practices. There is no want of girls at Cape Town, and if the Africander compositors, who are rather numerous, have their daughters and sisters trained for the business, the European compositors, who are said to have taken the lead in the matter, will soon be out of employ. But besides, they should consider that of all trades those connected with the Press can boast of being among the noblest ones, and that in a printer, want of consideration for the fair sex is far less excusable than in some other walks of life.

Art. VI.—HIGH ART.

Fair marble statues are not shaped alone
    From the ideal in the sculptor's brain,
They seem already buried in the stone,
    And waiting but his word to live again.
Methinks that all true women, by high grace,
    Are artists too, they have the magic skill
Through roughest veils to see th' ideal face
    Lying beneath the surface—deep and still.
Ay, what is more, they have the power, too,
    From such mere outer growth to free the soul,
And help it to stand forth, pure, good and true,
    As the great Master dreamt at first the whole.
Woe to the woman, who, content with part,
Plays false to what should be her highest art !

                     E. Hadwen.

Art. VII.—CORRESPONDENCE.

The Editor is not responsible for the opinions of Correspondents.

To the Editor of the "Englishwoman's Review."

Dear Madam,—I have once more made my protest against "Taxation without Representation," by refusing payment of the Queen's Taxes, and allowing a distraint to be made, a man to be put in possession, and goods to be taken away and sold.

Last year I was unable to do this, as I was changing house, and was beside seriously ill. The Suffrage movement has come to that stage when argument appears to have done its utmost, and when it would be well if decided action could be taken. I have always been of opinion that nothing would be so effective as to refuse the taxes, since we are refused the vote ; and I have now acted on that conviction five times.

I consider that women owe a duty to the women of their family and country as much as to the men ; and I would ask if any one of them could tamely bear the thought of injustice done to father, brother, husband, or son, merely because he happens to be a man. Injustice to a human being merely because she happens to be a woman is no less unjust and odious; but such is the force of old custom, superstition and subjection, that, as yet, women generally seem scarcely to realize this. For my own part, when I read, as any one may daily, of the injustice inflicted, and the brutality exercised upon women, I am only able to console myself with the reflection that I have taken the most decided course I could discover for showing we are in earnest in seeking the Parliamentary vote, without which no educational or benevolent measures can do women any lasting good.

Yours faithfully

CHARLOTTE E. BABB.

September 22nd, 1876.

*Extracts from the letter of a Berlin correspondent,
July 21st, 1876.*

" The men are almost all openly opposed to Women's Suffrage, and the few who may perhaps judge better dare not express their opinion. Naturally most women now *say* that they do not wish for it, for they know that to struggle for so hopeless an end would bring bitter unpleasantnesses without being of any use. We shall, therefore, have long to wait for actual, material (pecuniary) and moral freedom for women. Still the need is so great that we are compelled to seek for remunerative occupation. But it is made very difficult for girls to fit themselves for any regular calling; it still is regarded as something exceptional and deemed derogatory for women to earn money.

. . . . . . "The bad school education of the lower classes urgently needs earnest help, and who could better give it than the many women who are now unemployed or necessitous? However, this is still far from being perceived by the upper classes, and all that has yet been done for the emancipation of woman, consists in permission to carry on certain occupations; but this permission is illusory as regards married women, for they can be forced at any moment to give up a business, established with the consent of their husbands; besides, all that a married woman earns, acquires, or

inherits belongs at once to her husband. The marriage
laws are very unfavourable to women in other particulars: the husband may introduce strange women
and girls into his business, and his wife cannot
prevent it. She must be content with the money he
gives her for housekeeping, and if he gives her nothing
she cannot compel him—"a wife cannot sue her husband,
for such a suit is inadmissible"—and she must be
separated from him before she can sue him.

· But even this profits her seldom, for a husband has a
thousand means by which he can make a separation
that he does not wish for impossible. He can only be
made liable by proved adultery and bodily violence,
and these can scarcely be proved unless he voluntarily
confesses himself.

" The separation at length obtained, the husband can
easily withdraw his wife's alimony, if he apparently
possesses no property. . . . . . In spite of everything, the husband has an unbounded right over the
destiny of his children, until they are of age, even,
though he may pay nothing for them, nor take care of
them.

" All these things make a chain of wrongs for the
wife, from which the franchise only can save her. But
it will not be thought of in Germany, until *other* countries have made the beginning. At the present time
not a soul speaks of it. . . . . : .

"A few men, sometimes write in behalf of improvements
in the marriage laws, and the laws relating to the earnings of wives, but that is as yet *all* in Germany; notwithstanding that many unmarried and married women
must work for money to obtain a livelihood. . . . .

" I know, by my own experience, that no improvement
in the social position of women can be hoped for until
they obtain the suffrage, and I hail every advance that
is made in England with the liveliest joy."

Englishwoman's Review.

CONTENTS FOR NOVEMBER, 1876.

All Communications to be addressed to the Editor, 22, Berners Street, Oxford Street, W.

Post-Office Orders payable to Sarah Lewin, at the "Regent Street" Post-Office.

Terms of Subscription at the Office.

Per Annum (Post Free), Six Shillings.

Subscriptions payable in Advance.   Single Numbers posted Free on receipt of Six Postage Stamps.

MSS. are carefully read, and if not accepted are returned, on receipt of Stamps for Postage, but the Editor cannot be responsible for any accidental loss.

Contributions should be legibly written, and only on one side of each leaf.

THE

ENGLISHWOMAN'S REVIEW.

(NEW SERIES.)

No. XLIII.—November 15th, 1876.

ART. I.—THE SOCIAL SCIENCE CONGRESS.

If the labours of the Social Science since its first
establishment were estimated only by the impetus which
it has given to the better understanding ot the purpose
and practice of education, it would still have acquired
a title to the grateful consideration not only of the
leaders but of the rank and file of the army of progress.
The furtherance of women's education has, from its
commencement, received special attention, and the
proceedings last month showed how much has been
already accomplished, and gave hope of still further
improvement.

The Congress opened on October 11th, and on the
14th Mrs. Wm. Grey read a paper by Miss Shirreff
(then absent in Italy for her health) on the Training of
Teachers. The paper reviewed the position of teachers
both in this country and abroad, and dwelt upon the
importance of a better system of training being introduced both for male and female teachers, but more
especially the latter. The subject, she said, had been
hitherto treated with strange neglect in England; in
France, also, the system is very imperfect, doing little for
the great mass of masters, and still less for women; but in
Germany neither man nor woman can obtain a licence to
teach without passing an examination which tests both
general and professional knowledge. During the past

F

year the Women's Education Union has taken up the work in England, and has definitely founded a Society for the training and registration of teachers. The first object of the Union is doubtless to obtain good teachers for girls' schools, but the Society opens its ranks to both sexes. The scheme includes classes for general culture, study of education and practice in schools, and finally an examination. As men will probably be slow to take advantage of the help offered by the Women's Education Union, female teachers will be the first to reap the advantages offered by the new Society. But gradually the numerous schools that cannot afford to compete for the services of University graduates will perceive that the Society's certificate offers a guarantee such as no employers have been hitherto able to obtain in England, and will give the preference to those teachers who hold it, and thus a great work will have been initiated which it may be hoped the University will in time come forward to complete.

A crowded meeting on the same subject was held on the 16th in the Lecture Hall of the Free Library, the Rev. Mark Pattison presiding. Mrs. Wm. Grey again gave full details of the new Society. It proposes to found institutions providing for a systematic course of training for candidate teachers. The institutions for the training of higher grade teachers should be day colleges. The first day college they would attempt to found should be one for women, because men teachers have access to the Universities, and can get at least three years' lengthened study after school, though no professional training. She hoped, however, that these institutions would not be limited to two or three, to one sex or one place, but that in time we should see in every populous centre day training colleges for teachers of both sexes, which would provide something equivalent to a University education to men, who cannot afford to go to Universities, and to women who are excluded from them. A resolution was unanimously passed—" That this meeting recognises the necessity of professional training for teachers of higher grade schools of both sexes, and desires the organisation of means to apply such training and to test its efficiency."

We have always believed that the influence of women when fairly admitted into the great moral educational and social questions of the day will not be directed towards the exclusive advantage of one sex, but, with a larger-heartedness than has too frequently been displayed by institutions founded by men, will aim at the good of men and women equally. This step of the Women's Education Union furnishes confirmation of our view. While the better education of girls is naturally their first object, that of boys will also derive a permanent benefit from their efforts, and women will be the originators of, as well as in a great measure the instruments for carrying out, a scheme for incalculable good to the future youth of the country, whether boys or girls.

The other papers read by women on the subject of education were two. Miss Foster read an article describing a girls' school which she had seen in Germany, and Miss Carpenter, on the 14th, described, in a paper on "Female Education in India," the results of her recent visit to that country. In Bombay, Surat, and Ahmedabad a movement had arisen fifteen years ago among the educated young men to establish girls' schools, and among the Parsees a very fair education was given to girls. Elsewhere they had failed from want of female teachers. Taught as the schools are at present by masters, the children, who are married at eight or ten, must be removed from school still earlier, and the teaching, therefore, is necessarily of the most rudimentary character. In the spring of 1868, Lord Lawrence, then Viceroy, made a grant for the establishment of a Female Normal School in each of the three Presidency capitals; progress was very slow, and difficulties beset the work at every step, but now the results are encouraging. In Bombay Presidency two female training schools now exist:—One at Poona for the Mahrathi language, which has already sent out seventeen native female teachers since 1872, and has twenty-three still in training; there is also a large practising school for the students to learn teaching. The other is at Ahmedabad for the Guzerathi language: it will be an important aid to the numerous girls' schools of the district. The Madras Female Normal School has attained considerable efficiency and sent out many teachers. The Government Normal School at Calcutta was discontinued, but another is being carried on by Keshub Chunder Sen with Government aid. At Hyderabad in Sind, female education was commenced about eight years ago by the devoted exertions of a native subinspector of education; a female training school has been established, which will doubtless soon lead to the spread of education in Sind. Another Normal School is at Jubblepore, under the superintendence of an English lady, and another in the North-Western Provinces, taught by two native female teachers. The help of English ladies is very necessary to the successful working of these schools, but they ought not to undertake the task unless protected by Government or by some association. The social position of women had greatly improved during the past ten years, and there were many gratifying instances of progress. A short discussion followed.

Miss Carpenter also read a paper, in the Repression of Crime Section, on " Day Industrial Schools" for those children whose neglected condition prevents them attending the ordinary elementary school. These industrial schools are now recognised by the new Educational Act as forming a part of the educational system of the country, and, moreover, they form a part of the reformatory system. Miss Carpenter gave illustrations of various cases, and then stated the results of eight months' work in a day industrial school at Bristol, which was confined to the most miserable children, who were unfit to enter any other school. Eleven boys had gone to work and were maintaining themselves; four girls had gone to a home for training girls for service; twelve had gone to other schools for which they were now fitted.

In the same section a paper was read by Mr. Serjeant Pulling on the legislation necessary for the repression of crimes of violence, especially of men towards their wives. He said the judicial statistics presented to Parliament showed that in Liverpool there was an amount of savage brutality certainly not exceeded in any part

of the kingdom, especially towards women. The lot of
a married woman in the kicking districts of Liverpool
was one of worse suffering and subjection than that of
the wives of mere savages. In Liverpool in the year
1864 there were no fewer than 3,222 charges of crimes
of violence, and the coroners' inquests were nearly three
a day. He recommended that in cases of assault by a
husband on a wife, the evidence of the wife should be
taken immediately, and that the depositions thus taken
should be received as evidence on the subsequent trial.
With regard to legislative means, he thought the appointment of a public prosecutor would be salutary as
tending to make punishment more certain in aggravated
cases of violence, and on a second conviction he would
make flogging a part of the sentence. During the subsequent discussion, the Rev. D. McLeod, of Birkenhead,
deprecated the use of flogging. He said it was a brutal
punishment which brutalised those who had recourse to
it, and it was not certain that it had a deterrent effect
on crimes of violence. Mr. P. A. Taylor had shown that
the crime of garotting had already begun to diminish
before the lash was applied to it. With respect to wife-
beaters its use was doubly questionable, as it made
affection between husband and wife impossible in the
future. No man who had been subjected to the lash
for beating the mother of his children could ever appear
among his children again except as a degraded and
still further brutalised man. The Hon. Charles Leigh,
barrister, said that a theory was mooted that a man
who had assaulted his wife should be forcibly separated
from her, the woman to have the custody of the children.
Mr. J. H. Roper believed that the chief cause of brutality
was drinking, but urged the appointment of a public
prosecutor. Mr. Foard pointed out that this officer
already existed in Liverpool and Manchester. Mrs.
Sheldon Amos and the Rev. David Morris also spoke,
the former thinking that injured women should have the
power of leaving their husbands and taking their children—the latter condemning flogging. Incorrigible
men having been thus dealt with, a paper was read on
" Incorrigible Women—what are we to do with them?"
It declared that short periods of detention were useless,

and recommended three or five years' detention in
certified prison industrial homes, where the prisoners
might have a means of learning a trade and securing
a living after their release.

In the Health Section, on October 14th, Dr. Lowndes
read a paper on "Infanticide in Large Towns: the difficulties of detection and conviction, and the means to
be adopted for its prevention." Dr. Whittle suggested
that one great preventive would be to return to the old
law, under which a child could be affiliated before its
birth, and the father be compelled to support it after
birth. Dr. Hardwicke observed that he had held 200
inquests in the course of one year on the bodies of illegitimate children, and he thought the mother should be
enabled to claim from the father of her illegitimate offspring at least twelve weeks' support for herself, so that
the child should not suffer for the mother's wants.* This
paper was referred to the Council.

On the previous day Miss Lankester (daughter of
Professor Lankester) read a paper on the "Advantage
of giving Health Lessons to the Poor and Ignorant
Classes," giving illustrations of her success in London.
A similar paper was read by Mrs. William Baines, and
another by Miss C. C. Morfit.

In the Economy and Trade Section a suggestive
paper was read on October 13th, by Mr. W. Cooke
Taylor, on "State Interference with the Industrial
Employments of Women." This paper advocated the
principle that it is desirable for the State to regulate to

---

* At a meeting of the Dialectical Society in London,
Nov. 1, Dr. Hardwicke read an essay on this subject, in
which he enlarged on the cruelty and folly of letting a
young mother and her infant go away from the workhouse
with no friend or adviser to see what becomes of her
and her child. He pointed out the probable danger to
the child's life from wilful or unintentional neglect, and
the expense to the public entailed by coroners' juries,
and an increase in the vagrant class of women and
children. He also observed that few infant homes and
nurseries are open to illegitimate children.

some extent the employments of adult women, and
sought to define the degree in which it is just and right
to do so. As the labour market is not equally open to
men and women the latter are at a forced economic
disadvantage as compared with men, and will become
still more so if left to themselves. Partly by the mere
fact of their numerical preponderance over men, partly
by the more lucrative professions and occupations being
monopolised by the dominant sex, and partly by their
defenceless position, traceable for the most part to
political causes, women are forced to the lowest and
worst paid employments, and ground down to the
minimum of endurance. It was right for the State to
step in to defend them from the consequences of monopoly;
but protection means something more than rejection or
even restriction; and protective legislation for women's
work cannot justly begin and end with its mere subjection to the work of men. There is reciprocal obligation
to facilitate women's entrance into other occupations to
recompense them for the loss of those from which they
are excluded. If the State may determine for what
occupations women are unfit, and throw obstacles in
their way in entering them, it may also determine for
what occupations they are fit, and afford them proportionate facilities, nor is the one course of action more a
breach of economic propriety than the other, while
socially, morally, and physically, women are surely
more in need of help than man. The article concluded:
" I contend, then, that if the State is justified in shutting
up certain occupations from women—and I believe it is—
that it is equally justified in opening up and facilitating
their entry into others, and that the extent to which it
exerts itself in the one direction should measure more
or less accurately the extent to which it may justly
occupy itself in the other." In the discussion which
followed, Miss Becker said there was a growing and
dangerous tendency to interfere with the liberty of
women, who might with discretion be employed in
public work and other occupations. Mrs. Grey thought
the only justification for restricting the labours of any
adult was, that which might be found in the general
interests of society, and Mr. J. A. Picton (Liverpool),

thought legal protection for women was necessary against tyranny and oppression, but that, as in the case of domestic servants, a great deal of want of employment was their own fault.

The advantages which working women would receive from a developed system of union among themselves, were ably illustrated in a paper by Miss Caroline Williams, on the work of the "Protection and Provident Union among working women." A large meeting of working women was also held during the Congress.

Other papers on miscellaneous subjects were read by ladies during the week. Mrs. Lowe read an essay on the "Lunacy Law Reform"; Miss E. A. Corlett gave a report of the Queen's Institute Art Department in Dublin, and Miss Rhoda Garrett read a paper on "How to improve the interior of Modern Houses, with special reference to their furniture and decorations." This last subject is one that begins to have great attraction for a large number of women, and its discussion at the Social Science Congress cannot fail to induce many to enter upon a profession which is so eminently suited to feminine capabilities.

ART. II.—MEETING OF THE GERMAN NATIONAL WOMEN'S ASSOCIATION.

THIS Association, which held its yearly session on the 25th of September, at Frankfort-on-the-Maine, is not to be confounded with the Union of German Women, which met some months ago in Hamburg, and whose head quarters are in Berlin. The object of this latter is to assist women to get work, increase their facilities for employment, and their efficiency when at work, and to help them to a better and more thorough education. Its tendencies are rather aristocratic, and it quite excludes from its programme the social and political side of the "women's question." But the association which

held its last meeting at Frankfort, and has its centre in
Leipzic, is more liberal in its views, and aims not only
at a higher education and better remuneration for work,
but discusses also social and political questions, and
aspires to raising the position of women, legally and
socially.

This movement in Germany has but little resemblance
to the same movement in England and America, for in
these latter countries much stress is laid on establishing
political equality with men. In Germany the general
political education of the people is far behind that of
England, and independence in politics is but little known
or practised, even by men. The woman's question is
therefore an educational one, and is called forth by
absolute necessity, the intense suffering of women giving
a stimulus to the reform. It is now about ten years
since the German women have been labouring in this
direction, and the results already achieved are worthy
of their work. When we consider the low condition of
German women in general, and how little help they get
in these matters from the stronger sex—the men in
Germany being more opposed to women's elevation
than those of any civilized country—we can, by appreciating the difficulty of their work, see what the courage
and patience of the leaders must be.

I will endeavour to give you an account of this
meeting of the Leipzic Association, which took place at
Frankfort in September. The ladies and gentlemen
composing it came from several parts of Germany; the
various branches of the Association reported what they
had accomplished during the past year, and chiefly their
success or failure in inducing the government or the
other authorities to establish better schools, or to open
a wider field of occupation.

Darmstadt was well represented by Fräulein Louise
Büchner, a well-known authoress and able worker, who
has done much to raise the position of women in her
native town. The branch associations in Stuttgard and
other southern cities of Germany reported that additional schools had been called into life, and great interest
in the work was being awakened. The Rev. Mr.
Laengin, from Carlsruhe, spoke upon the injustice of

the Government towards women. In most large cities the State establishes additional high schools for boys, but makes no provision for the higher education of girls. The present object of educational reformers is to interest the State in establishing "gymnasia" for girls, on the same principle as those which prepare boys for the Universities. He considered that it was more important to obtain these for women than even the permission to enter the Universities.*

Mrs. Emma Laddey, from Munich, a poetess and writer of books for young people, is also much interested with the advancement of women. She read a lecture on the beneficial influence which these questions would exercise upon marriage. She pictured in lively colours the evils that exist at this time, and appealed alike to men and women to unite in helping forward a purer state of society. After her lecture there was a lively discussion on the subject.

Mrs. Lina Morgenstern, one of the foremost workers in the movement, and a lady of varied capacity, great practical talent, and power of organisation, reported the success of the Volksküchen (kitchens for the people), which were established by her ten years ago in Berlin. The Volksküchen have been a great boon to the Berlin working-people, providing them with wholesome, good food for about threepence a dinner. They have been imitated in several other German towns. In Berlin there are a number of them, chiefly located in the manufacturing part of the city; 250 persons, mostly ladies, are engaged in this benevolent work, and a systematic organisation has raised the Society to great prosperity. The original capital was only 4,000 thalers

---

* These "Gymnasia" are not identical with the gymnastic exercises for girls which have been the custom for some time in a number of educational establishments in Germany, and compulsory in all the upper towns' schools for girls at Berlin. The system is now extended, since October 1, to all the commercial schools for girls in the German capital. The movement for the better physical education of the female sex is now rapidly spreading. Some opposition has for years been attempted on the part of mothers, and at present, in spite of the obligatory character of the law relating to gymnastics, nearly one-half of the girls still obtain a dispensation from it through certificates granted at the instance of the mothers.

(£600), which was raised by subscription. Subsequently the institution has not only been entirely self-supporting, but the capital has increased to more than 13,000 thalers. A school for cooking and another for training servants arose from this establishment, and in 1873 the German Housekeepers' Association arose,† which answers the purpose of a great co-operative society, buying wholesale and selling retail at wholesale prices all things pertaining to domestic economy, with a newspaper of its own, and a Registration Agency for all kinds of female work. This society also is in a very prosperous condition.

Mrs. Lina Morgenstern also read an essay upon Woman's Work in Society, which was so full of good points that I cannot refrain from giving you a short extract. She said: "The special characteristic of our times is self-help and appreciation of personal industry, but women are still excluded from the general rule. Their difficulty in gaining recognition as industrial agents is an absolute injustice done to the physically weaker sex, and what we seek to find out to-day is the incalculable benefit to humanity consequent on a reform in women's work. The objection that it is unnatural for a woman to labour outside her house, is based on a fiction. We are apt to think that which is woman's nature, the result of an artificial education and a perverted social standard, which dwarfs her natural gifts and extinguishes her self reliance. She is now neither expert in domestic management nor acquainted with the laws of health; she is seldom qualified to educate her children or to be an intelligent companion to her husband. It will only be when she is allowed to take an active part in all great movements, when she has learned the laws which govern and elevate society, and has gained an interest in the affairs of the State, that she can be the real representative of her home, a true wife and mother. Much gratitude is due to those women who have shown so much personal courage in keeping true to a noble ideal at a time when materialism and sensu-

---

† *See* also page 327, under Article " Berlin Housekeepers' Association."

ality are beginning to undermine those homes from which all noble sentiments ought to spring, and who have been praiseworthy pioneers endeavouring to elevate the condition of their sex on the sound basis of education and industry.

"Woman is deprived of her natural rights even in the position which is said to be her sole natural one, that of wife and mother; everywhere the law is against her. The marriage contract differs from all other contracts between members of the same grade of society, since it does not recognise the equality of the contracting parties. The help of pure minded women is especially necessary to withstand the terrible increase of prostitution. There is hardly a department of reform in which women's help would not be advantageous. Commerce, industry, direct and indirect taxation, co-operation, joint-stock companies, political and social affairs, transient and permanent suffering, are all more or less connected with home, and with woman as the natural representative of it." She ended by appealing to men and women to unite in this new effort after equality and independence, as it must lead to the happiness and welfare of the human race.—CLARA NEYMANN.

From *Neue Bahnen* we learn also the following particulars :—

The proceedings of the Association commenced on the morning of the first day with the re-election of the President, Frau Louise Otto-Peters, and Frau Lina Morgenstern, of Berlin, as secretary. Frau Sauerlander, Frau Diehl, and Fraulein Meck, from Frankfort, Frau Weber, from Tübingen, and Fräulein Kauffmann, from Cassel, were also elected on the council. Dr. Diehl, and Frau Emma Laddey audited the accounts.

In the evening Fräulein Augusta Schmidt made the first speech upon the objects of the Association: namely, the industrial independence of women, and the need that every woman should have a vocation whether in, or apart from, her home life: and the necessity of a reform in female education, in order that she may become better fitted to enter on such a vocation. The President, Frau Otto-Peters, then described the advance which German women had made during the last eleven

years; an advance such as no other time could show;
it was the consequence of awakened courage on the
part of women, and a resolution to help themselves,
which had procured them many helpers. In Frankfort,
as far back as twenty years ago, an interest had been
felt in women's work. She explained the part which
the Association had taken with reference to the clauses
affecting women in the new laws on Marriage and
Guardianship of Children, about which a petition would
be forwarded to the Reichstag. The President concluded with these words, " Our cause counts its friends
and opponents among all shades of social and political
parties, which affords an additional proof that this is
really the chief reform question of the day. Our aim is
the harmony of humanity which cannot be accomplished
so long as one human being is legally or socially hindered from being in union with others; and women are
hindered so long as it is rendered impossible, or even
difficult for them to develop their full capacities, and to
use their influence freely and spontaneously for the
common welfare."

Fraulein Marie Calm then spoke of the weight of
prejudice which had still to be overcome even among
the friends of the women's movement. Since the foundation of the Association in 1865, women were accustomed to meet together to discuss the most important
interests of their sex, which are identical with the best
interests of the race. It was now generally admitted
that women might take part in literature, but their right
to speak in public still aroused much prejudice; it was
considered unfeminine, though women might take part
in public concerts, or amateur theatricals, without giving
offence. She also combated the popular opinion that
it was unnecessary for women to be trained for other
than home duties. Before the last Prussian war there
were 1,827,441 unmarried women, and more than 700,000
widows, and this number was now much increased. It
was necessary for these women to find some profession,
and opportunities for attaining it should be given
them. She believed that the time was fast coming
when no occupation would be thought so disgraceful
to a woman as idleness.

Fraulein Büchner spoke of the work of the Lette-
Verein, which now includes 17 branches situated in ten
different towns.   She remarked that its aim was not so
much to open fresh employments to women, as to fit
them better for those already entered upon, and it had
therefore established industrial and training schools, of
which the most important was in Hamburg.

Frau Goldschmidt spoke upon the Kindergarten
system as the best means of educating girls.   Fraulein
Kampf gave a report of the work of the Union in Dresden
and Gotha; Fraulein Corill gave an account of the
various women's organisations in Frankfort since 1813;
the deaconesses' work and soup kitchens for the poor.
Fraulein Calm gave a report of the Union in Cassel, and
urged that a similar branch should be established in
Frankfort.   Dr. Sauerlander, who had just returned
from Munich and Vienna, reported the success of the
Art and Industrial Schools for women there, and also
urged their adoption in Frankfort.

In a discussion which took place on the introduction
of women into Post and Telegraph offices, it was remarked that in Saxony girls were first employed in this
work in 1865.   The Minister of Commerce in Wurtem-
burg is reported to be well inclined to the employment
of women.   Fraulein Buchner said that the Lette
Verein had prepared a petition on behalf of the more
extended admission of women into Post offices.

On the last day of the meeting, the proceeding terminated in the establishment of the Committee of a
branch of the Association in Frankfort.   Its primary
objects are announced to be the better education of
girls, the improvement of the industrial powers of women,
and their admission to superior employments.   Frau
Sauerlander, 18, Leerbach Strasse is placed at the head
of the members.

A prize has been offered by Herr Stiger, of Zurich,
to be awarded in six months for the best book upon the
independence of women, and upon what proportion of
influence they should possess in legislative, judicial, and
executive matters.   The book is to be printed in three
languages, German, French, and English, that its merits
may be more widely appreciated.

ART. III.—TEACHERS IN SWITZERLAND.

THE *Bulletin Continental* gives interesting statistics on the number and status of the women employed in the profession of teaching in the Swiss Cantons. This differs widely in the different States. Their salaries are sometimes the same as men, but generally inferior; the teachers' incomes are derived from several funds, and sometimes one fund is fair towards women, and another source of income may be greatly to their disadvantage.

In Zurich women are, as a rule, excluded from taking part in public education; there are 570 men teachers and only 8 women teachers.

Berne allows the parishioners of the commune liberty to employ either men or women, but the subsidy allowed by the Canton for primary teachers is less for women than for men. This has long been the case, but last year, when a general revision of the laws relating to these salaries took place, this discrepancy was made the subject of discussion. A petition from the women teachers was rejected on economic grounds, nevertheless the number of female teachers is greatly on the increase, and out of all proportion with a corresponding increase in the number of male teachers. There are at present 504 women and 1,098 men employed in instruction. The honorarium for teaching needlework was somewhat raised. The allowance made by the State is 250 francs for a man, 150 for a woman, but it increases after a long term of service, to 550 francs for a man, and only increases to 250 for a woman.

There are no difficulties in the way of women teachers in Lucerne, nevertheless in the whole Canton there were, in 1871, only 15, compared with 349 men. There is no law about their salaries.

In Uri, Schwytz, Unterwald, Appenzell, and Zug, instruction is in great measure in the hands of nuns. Taking all these Cantons together, there are 219 men and 122 women teachers; of these latter 103 are nuns. The salaries are regulated by each commune.

In Soleure, Basle, and Glaris, women are only engaged as teachers in needlework schools, with the exception of ten women in inferior classes in girls'

schools in the town of Basle; Schaffhausen only employs
two, in a school of little girls.   In St. Gallen the inferior
girls' schools are confided to women, of whom there are
13 as compared with 406 men teachers.   The canton of
the Grisons employs 388 men and only 54 women, of
whom 16 are nuns.   Argau is favourable to the introduction of women as teachers; it employs 33.   In these
two last cantons there is no legal difference made between the salaries of women and men.

The greatest proportion of women engaged in instruction is found in the Italian cantons of Ticino, there
being 266 women to 209 men.   The law presupposes
all the teachers in infant schools to be women, and
expressly suggests their employment in primary and
even secondary schools.   Their salary is one-fifth less
than that of men.   It would seem, therefore, that their
extensive employment in the State schools has been due
to motives of economy.

Vaud admits women teachers in the public schools;
there are 205 compared with 539 men, or about 30 per
cent.   In principle their salaries are the same, but in
point of fact more is paid to men than to women.
Valais authorises female instruction, and employs 169
women and 281 men; the pay is about the same.
Neufchatel is, next to Ticino, the most favourable to
women teachers; there are 172 employed and only 146
men; they are also on an average paid better than in
other cantons.   In Fribourg there are but 89 women
teachers, but in the city schools men and women are
paid alike,—in the country schools they receive less.   By
a law passed in 1872 the salaries of both were increased.

Lastly, in Geneva 54 women are engaged in tuition,
but their pay is on the whole inferior to that of men;
for instance, among other emoluments, men have a right
to a lodging of 400 francs, women can only claim one
of 250.

It is worthy of remark, from an inspection of the
whole table, that the question whether instruction shall
be left in the hands of women, appears to be regulated
chiefly by economic reasons, especially when it is committed to the nuns.   Also that German Switzerland, as
a rule, is unfavourable to the employment of women as

teachers, whereas in the French cantons they have a much better position.

The same paper, in an article on the cause of the inferior salary of women, says: "There exists on the part of the men of the working classes a settled general intention to restrict as much as possible the industrial chances of women.   Their exclusion in grounded on the dangers which the competition of female work causes to masculine labour, a danger increased by the well known fact that for the same work women consent to receive smaller wages.   Supposing this to be absolutely true, the proceeding loses none of its revolting injustice. To forbid any human being to gain his means of livelihood through work, in order to get better conditions for one's self is one of the greatest crimes which can be committed against natural rights and social interests. Surely the workman from his defective moral and economic education is unaware of the importance of the injustice he commits, or he would understand that such a negation of the freedom to labour surpasses any grievances which he may suffer from the supremacy of capital."

ART. IV.—A NEW DANGER FOR WOMEN.

A movement has recently been set on foot with the object of urging Parliament to legislate actively for "the control of the habitual drunkard;" and, according to the *Daily News* of Oct. 21st, a society has already been formed for the purpose of carrying this out, by Dr. Alfred Carpenter, which has the Primate at its head, and numbers among its vice-presidents many bishops and the Earl of Shaftesbury.

The idea is said to have emanated from amongst the medical profession, who, next to "the unhappy wives and families chiefly concerned" are supposed to be best acquainted with the "deplorable phenomena." Accounts of this movement will, no doubt, attract many benevo-

G

lent persons; but, before they give in their adhesion to
it, it would be well for them to ask themselves if the
remedy is not likely to be worse than the evil. The
danger to all the nation from touching the liberty of the
subject would be far greater than the danger to a
portion of the people from the intemperance of "a
section of humanity, happily few in numbers."

From the *Daily News'* paragraph we might be led to
think that the fact of men constituting the main body
of intemperate persons was fully recognized, and that
the legislation proposed would chiefly affect men. This
is entirely mistaken. Very few, if any, men could be
be brought under the operation of any controlling act.
A man usually gets his drink away from home, and
unless his associates would give evidence as to the
amount he habitually took, his wife and family would
be powerless to get him under constraint. Men usually
stand by one another, nor could any one wish the
horrible spy system to be further extended in this
country. The effect of this intended legislation will be
to give men yet greater power than they now have
over women. That women are the real objects aimed
at in this movement is pretty well shown by the circumstance that its advocates usually bring forward instances
of "women" who drink, when endeavouring to illustrate their views. This is well exemplified in the *Daily
News* account, October 18th, of what was said by Mr. S.
S. Alford and Dr. Shrimpton at the Social Science
Congress in Liverpool. If these gentlemen also gave
evidence as to men drunkards, it is a pity that it was
not mentioned in the newspaper, because any woman
who considers the subject seriously, will see that
legislation of this kind would be analogous to that
which has already curtailed the personal liberty of
women in many ways, even as to earning their own
bread. In the face of the fact that our police reports shew
men to be most guilty of intemperance, our legislators
may not make the measure, verbally and intentionally, to
apply only to women, as do the Contagious Diseases
Acts, which place women at the mercy of police spies,
who can cause them to be imprisoned without trial by
jury. But if the proposed legislation should be appa-

rently applicable to both sexes, it cannot fail to be wholly unjust to women. In the first place, they are allowed no voice in legislation, and to subject them arbitrarily to laws affecting them so vitally is to ignore every principle of liberty; and the mere suggestion of such legislation, without the consent of half the nation, shows only too well how completely woman is a slave where she is denied real citizenship.

It would be almost impossible for a wife to get evidence which would " control " the habitual drunkard of a husband; but it would be quite easy for the husband, who has prejudice, authority, and money on his side to get his wife condemned by the easily persuaded medical man. The greedy heirs who see a sick old lady take a glass of wine may soon get her placed in confinement, and then, with their boon companions, can riot with her money; but, though legislation by men alone may effect this, it will never save the wretched wife from the kicks and blows she will receive when, as now, she ventures to the public-house to entreat her "lord" to come home, or to give her sixpence to buy bread for the children. Let women seriously look at the fact that legislation which affects them in their homes, their affections, and their daily needs is now more rife than ever; and then let them ask themselves whether they can, in justice to themselves and to other women, submit to laws which are made without their concurrence. If no other instance were wanting, this "habitual drunkard" proposed legislation should awake us to insist, with all the power we have, that no more Acts to coerce women shall be passed until, by the possession of the suffrage, they can co-operate in the suggested reforms.   C. E. B.

ART. V.—EVENTS OF THE MONTH.

EDUCATION.

NEWNHAM HALL COMPANY, LIMITED.

THE balance sheet of this company for the last year has

been issued. It appears to be going on prosperously, for a dividend of 4 per cent. has been declared on all shares paid up before June 29th, 1875, and proportionately on shares subsequently paid up.

As appears from the subscription list, a sum of £2,800 has been raised by shares (ten of these put in trust for a Scholarship), and—exclusive of donations to the Gymnasium and Laboratory—£7,238 given in donations, of which about £4,550 has been given by Shareholders. With this total of £10,038 all liabilities for the expenses of building, furnishing, and laying out the garden, will have been met; there remain the expenses of papering and painting the inside of the house, which can be met from the balance of the Newnham Hall Company's account at Cambridge.

During the past year two most liberal gifts have been received by the Council for Scholarships, to be held by students of Newnham Hall. A Shareholder, who wishes to be anonymous, has taken ten of the Company's shares, of which the interest is to be given annually for a Scholarship, the amount depending on the rate of interest declared at the Annual General Meeting; and the Goldsmiths' Company have made a grant of £100 per annum, which is to be divided into Scholarships of £50 each.

WOMEN AT CAMBRIDGE.—The *Suffrage Journal* says: "There has been such an influx of young ladies at the commencement of this term at Cambridge that Girton College and Newnham Hall are unable to accommodate them, and many are compelled to take lodgings."

IN a letter to the *Times* Miss Shireff acknowledges the receipt of a gift of £1,000 for the building fund of Girton College from Mr. Thomas Taylor, of Aston Rowant, Oxon, as a memorial of his daughter Edith, lately deceased. His letter accompanying the cheque says: "Dear Miss Shirreff,—To you, as one of the members of the executive committee of Girton College, and as a friend of our late daughter Edith and ourselves, I send the enclosed cheque for £1,000, and shall feel obliged if you will give it to the treasurer of the building fund of the college. It was the wish of my daughter to enter Girton this term as a student, and knowing the great

interest she took in the college and her sincere desire
for its success, Mrs. Taylor and I feel we cannot better
show our respect and love for her than in making this
'In Memoriam' gift to its funds.   In doing this I feel
that I am but carrying out one of the earnest desires of
my daughter, to help forward the cause of women and
advance their higher education.—Yours faithfully,
Thomas Taylor."

LADIES CLASSES AT UNIVERSITY COLLEGE, LONDON.—
The ninth session of these classes began on October
23rd.

These classes, which have been taught from the first only by professors and lecturers upon the college staff, were first given in rooms
engaged for the purpose.   In the third session two of the classes, and
in the fourth session all the classes were taught within the college
walls, and since that time ladies have found their way to the lecture
rooms at University College in increasing numbers, and these ladies'
classes were attended during the last session by 394 individual students.
It was in the session 1871-72 that the experiment was first made of
holding all the classes at the college, with proper arrangement for the
comfort and convenience of the ladies who attend.   In that session
the number of individual students was 277, and twenty-one classes
were held.   In that year there was no examination of the students in
the ladies' classes.   In the following year the number of classes held
was eighteen, and the number of individual students in attendance
on them was 279.   In three classes written examinations were then
introduced.   In the next session, 1873-74, the number of classes
taken was fourteen, the number of individual students in the ladies'
classes was 315, and the number of classes in which voluntary written
examinations were held was increased from three to six.   In the
session of 1874-75 there was a decrease of eight in the number of
students—it became 307.   Twelve classes were formed, and in seven
of them written examinations were held and certificates of several
grades given to those who passed.   Last session the decrease of eight
was followed by an increase of eighty.   The number of classes was
seventeen.   The number of individual students became 394, and the
number of written examinations held rose to fifteen.   The number of
students entering for such examinations in the last four years has
been successively 18, 58, 66, and last year 108.   The gross receipts
from lecture fees were, in 1871-72, £560. 8s. 7d., and in 1875-76,
£791. 9s. 1d.   In addition to this work done in connection with the
London Ladies' Educational Association, which brought last session
394 ladies to classes of their own in Gower Street, University College has been cautiously trying the experiment of mixed classes, and
the ordinary classes of Jurisprudence, Roman Law, Political Economy
and Geology are those now open to students without distinction of
sex.   In the Fine Art classes this distinction never has been made,
and thus there were last session 113 ladies on the list of college students in addition to those in attendance on the ladies' classes.   The

number, therefore, of individual female students who received college instruction in Gower Street last session was 507. The number of registered pupils in attendance last year at University College, apart from the ladies' classes, was 1,606, namely, 900 in the college and 706 in the school. The 394 who were attending lectures in the ladies' classes brought the number up exactly to 2,000.—*Daily News.*

The *Educational Guide* says that at the recent annual meeting of the club connected with the Great Ormond Street Working Men's College, Mr. Thomas Hughes, Q.C., who occupied the chair, announced that the Working Men's College and the College for Men and Women in Queen's Square will shortly be amalgamated. We are glad to see that the *Educational Guide* is largely increasing its circulation.

WOMEN'S EDUCATION UNION.—Lectures to Teachers. Mons. Edmund Andrade will deliver a course of six lectures on the Galin-Paris-Chevé method of teaching music, on Tuesday evenings, at six o'clock, in the room of the Society of Arts, John Street, Adelphi. The first lecture will be given on Tuesday, Nov. 14th. Fees for the course, teachers, 4s.; non-teachers, 8s. Tickets can be obtained from the Secretary of the W. E. Union, 112, Brompton Road, or at the lecture room on the evening of the lecture.

MEDICAL EDUCATION—IRISH UNIVERSITIES.

AN important step has been taken during the past month in this hardly-fought contest. Two of the Irish Universities have resolved to give that justice to women students which has been so long denied to them in the sister countries. By a recent decision of the College of Physicians of Dublin, the Fellows of that body have deliberately determined to admit Miss Edith Pechey to the examination for the license of King and Queen's College of Physicians of Ireland, and have thus thrown open the doors of the profession to all comers, whether they be "persons" of the male or female sex. The *Medical Press and Circular* expresses its opinion that however pregnant of results this decision may be, it does not seem to them that any other conclusion was possible, and they expect the example will be followed by all other bodies; though expressing some doubt

about the ultimate success of women as practitioners,
it adds, "we deprecate strongly the exercise of any exclusiveness towards them. They are certainly entitled
to 'a clear stage and no favour' both as students and
as doctors, and if they have the energy or talent to
shoulder aside male competitors they are entitled to our
best wishes."

The Queen's University, Ireland, has imitated this
example of justice. At the meeting of the Senate on
October 10th, it was resolved, after an interesting discussion, to admit female candidates to examination for
the degree of M.D., at and after the next University
session. The following members were present:—His
Grace the Duke of Leinster, Chancellor of the University;
Sir Dominic J. Corrigan, Bart., M.D., Vice-Chancellor
of the University; the Lord Talbot de Malahide, F.R.S.;
Professor Moffett, L.L.D.; David Ross, M.A., L.L.B.;
the President of Queen's College, Cork; Professor Red-
fern, M.D.; Professor Maxwell Simpson, M.D., F.R.S.;
Sir Robert Kane, L.L.D., F.R.S.; Andrew M. Porter, Q C.;
John Thomas Banks, M.D. G. Johnstone Stoney, M.A.,
F.R.S., Secretary to the University, was also present.

It will be remembered that Miss Pechey who is now,
after six years struggle, permitted to wear her well
earned laurels, is the same who was admitted to the
examination in Arts in the Edinburgh University, and
when there obtained the third place in the Chemistry
prize list, becoming thus entitled to the Hope scholarship, which was founded for the four students who had
received the highest marks. The scholarships give free
admission to the College laboratory, and had been
founded by the late Professor Hope, from the proceeds
of lectures given to ladies fifty years ago. Miss Pechey's
claim, however, was passed over, and the Hope scholarship given to the fifth student on the list, who was a
man, the Professor announcing as his reason for with-
holding it, that, having studied at a different time, she
was not a member of the Chemistry class. With characteristic inconsistency the bronze medal which accompanies the scholarships was awarded to her, and the
ordinary certificate declaring her to have attended the
Chemistry class of the University of Edinburgh was
accorded her.

It would be ungenerous to bring forward, after this lapse of time, the discreditable injustice with which the ladies, who had been admitted as students in Edinburgh, were treated by the authorities of that University, were it not that only last summer, on the passing of Mr. Russell Gurney's Bill, when it seemed as if a golden opportunity was offered them of repairing their past injustice, they adhered to the same ungenerous policy. The *Daily Review* thus characterises it:—"One more chance was now offered to Edinburgh of redeeming her broken pledges, for on the very day of the last reading of the Bill in the House of Lords, after its passing through the Commons, a request was presented to the Senatus that the women who had for four years been its matriculated students should, under the now certain legislation, be admitted to the ensuing professional examination in the present month. It was notorious that the Senatus meeting at which the request was presented was the last that would be held before the October examinations, but the only answer vouchsafed to the petition was a calm refusal to consider the question until the bill had become law, after fulfilling the last minutiæ of formal etiquette."

Ireland has thus had the honour of first finding out how to be just and generous. There still remains the serious difficulty to women, of obtaining that acquaintance with the practical part of their profession which the London School of Medicine, in Henrietta Street cannot give; but having done so much, we may confidently hope that the Irish Universities will do yet more, and not suffer the work they have so nobly commenced to be frustrated by incompleteness of details.

LONDON SCHOOL BOARD.

THE London School Board election will take place on the 30th instant. Three ladies have presented themselves as candidates in the forthcoming election. Mrs. Westlake has every prospect of success in Marylebone. Miss Helen Taylor, step-daughter of John Stuart Mill, has come forward for election in Southwark.

A crowded meeting was held on Oct. 23rd, at the Bridge House, in support of two candidates, Mr. John

Sinclair, and Miss Taylor. Mr. E. H. Bayley occupied the chair.

Miss Taylor said:—"If she had presumed to present herself to them to solicit their suffrages for the School Board of London, it was because she felt that this was no time when any friend of education should remain inactive—and because she had been told that there were many among the electors who would not think it a disqualification that she was a woman. There were many details of management belonging to the School Board which she thought fell naturally within the department of women, for the electors would know that one-half of the children proposed to be educated were girls. These were matters not only which the ladies would perhaps manage best, but which the gentlemen would only be too glad to be rid of. But she would even take higher grounds than this, and say that she believed it would be with the School Board as it was with the home, that the interests of boys, as well as girls, would be best cared for where men and women worked together. Among the complaints with respect to the past action of the School Board, was one as to the want of thorough economy. Well, perhaps more ladies on the Board would greatly help in this matter. In the first place, "women's business is mainly the economical distribution of the money which men earn," and the training which women had in looking into details of a domestic character fitted them for entering into details on larger subjects. She then enlarged upon the responsibility resting upon electors in choosing proper persons for the School Board, so as to secure a proper education for the rising generation, and to enable this country to hold its own among the nations of the earth. Lord Bacon had said "Knowledge is power," and it was for the electors to see that their children had that power given them which should enable them to make and keep their country.

Miss Garrett Anderson also spoke the same evening, specifying the matters in regard to which women on the School Board were needed, more particularly enlarging upon the confidence their presence gave to women when appealing against compulsory attendance at school, and also with respect to the convenience it was for female teachers to have one of their own sex to whom they would refer their grievances or their views. In the course of her remarks, when speaking of the conflict of the rival parties on the Board, she said there was one party in the contest that both quite lost sight of, and that was *the child*—but so far as she could, she had looked after the child, not caring so much for the interests of denominational schools, nor the special interests of secular schools.—*Abridged from the South London Press.*

Mis Fenwick Miller is also a candidate for the Hackney School Board.

The *Daily News* in an article on the school boards thus points out the advantages hitherto obtained by having even a few women on the School Board. These successful efforts to improve the condition of girls, have often been noticed in our columns, but our readers will be glad of their repetition:

" It will be a serious hindrance to the successful accomplishment of the task that still awaits the energy and skill of the new Board if the places of the two ladies who have seats on the present Board should not be filled by suitable representatives of their sex. A single incident will illustrate how necessary it is to secure fair play for the girls of the schools, and for the school mistresses that their special interests should be represented by ladies on the Board. When the Lawrence scholarships were established it was proposed that a larger amount should be given to the boys, although the subscriptions were received freely from both sexes. There was a vague idea that boys need more money than girls, and that to give seven pounds to a boy and six to a girl is in accordance with the eternal fitness of things, and harmonises with the ineradicable superiority of the male sex. Owing, however, to the presence of Miss Chessar, who pointed out that the girls would have to pay more for their advanced education than the boys, the Board was recalled from the high regions of abstract truth or falsehood to sober facts, and it unanimously resolved that the scholarships for boys and girls should be equal. This case illustrates the special advantages of having on the Board intelligent and well-informed women. Men constantly fall into mistakes on questions affecting the other sex from sheer ignorance, because they have no occasion in their daily lives to observe and remember the facts that tell in favour of women. It is of the utmost importance that some ladies at least should be on the Board, not merely to see that the educational interests of the girls are not neglected, but to communicate with the schoolmistresses, and afford them that sympathy and support which can best be given by women to women. The advantages to the female teachers in being able to appeal to ladies on the Board for encouragement and help are obvious; while the complete withdrawal of women from the Board would be little short of a disaster to the education of one half of the scholars in the Board's schools.

"The best argument for the election of ladies of suitable qualifications to the School Board would be a record of the work done by the ladies who have been on the Board. There are, indeed, some departments of the work that almost require the attention of women. Every school has special provision for infants under seven years of age. For the benefit of these youthful attendants great efforts have been made to introduce the Kindergarten system, which provides for the eye and hand a most valuable training. The development of this part of an infant's education seems to be in a special sense women's work. For girls considerable importance has always been attached to needlework. A considerable share of time has been given to it, and great care must be taken to avoid two blunders—first, giving too much attention to mere fancy work; and, secondly, taking the girls too much away from the proper work of the schools. These are topics, however, that cannot be said to possess much attraction for men; they involve a vast deal of tedious work, which only women could be expected to undertake. The lady members of the Board have given much attention to this department, and an association has been formed to hold exhibitions and give prizes to the schools in the metropolis for the improvement of elementary needlework. The first exhibition will take place about the middle of next month, and we hope will be successful in diffusing among the poor that skill with the needle and consequent personal tidiness which are lamentably deficient among them. In other directions the presence of lady members on the Board has been most beneficial. The School Board has endeavoured, wherever it was possible, to provide good playgrounds, but it has not deemed it a part of its duty to build swimming-baths. Swimming is, however, an accomplishment that cannot be too much encouraged, and the Board was well advised in accepting the offers made to it, and making arrangements without burdening the ratepayers, for lessons being given to the boys. It is not too much to say, however, that but for the reminder of the ladies of the Board, the girls would have been forgotten, and this great boon been exclusively confined to boys. In providing also that girls should have have regular physical exercise suited to their constitution and strength, an important step has been taken to neutralise the deleterious influence of town life on the future mothers of the working class. * * * *

"In the month of November last year, the first centre was established to give instruction in cookery. Admission was given only to a favoured few; selected pupil teachers and scholars who had distinguished themselves by regular attendance and good conduct were alone permitted to enjoy the privilege. Another centre was immediately set up in Blackheath-road for scholars from Greenwich and Southwark. The experiment met with encouraging success, and in May of the present year two new centres were opened for the Eastern and South-Western Divisions of the metropolis. At present 816 girls have the benefit of the instruction. At first the lessons given were of a somewhat theoretical character, but recently a change has been made, and the girls spend half the time in preparing food under the eyes of the teacher according to the instructions given to them. As might have been expected, the practical work has possessed most interest for the girls, and has done them most good, while the cost has been very small, amounting only to 2s. per lesson for 30 scholars. Here, then, is a growing branch of work in which the superintendence of a lady member of the Board will be recognised as peculiarly appropriate. Another department that needs the care of women is the inspection of industrial schools for girls. It is only a woman who can usefully make that minute examination of the internal arrangements of the schools that is so necessary for the comfort and discipline of the girls. These are large and wide interests; they require the most sedulous attention; and that care can hardly be given except by women. We believe that if the ratepayers reflect on the special and important work that properly devolves on women, they would receive with the utmost favour the candidature of any lady for the School Board who can satisfy them of her qualifications. At present it is to be regretted that so few ladies have come before the constituency. It is all the more urgent that the two lady candidates who are in the field should receive general support from all parties among the ratepayers. It is necessary that some women should be on the Board to attend to women's special work. The electors of Southwark have an opportunity of sending to the School Board a lady who has preeminent claims to their favourable consideration. Miss Helen Taylor, the step-daughter of Mr. John Stuart Mill, is spoken of in his Autobiography as one whose practical talents are of the highest order. She has leisure, and proposes to devote her whole energies to the work of the Board. Marylebone sent Miss Chessar and Mrs. Cowell to the last Board, but neither of them on this occasion asks for re-election. Mrs. Westlake, who has done much in the northern district to establish a hospital for women, asks for one of the vacant places. It is satisfactory that any ladies should be found willing and able to take up the very heavy burden of School Board work, and it is to be hoped that the new Board will have the benefit of their assistance in its future labours."

Miss Lydia Becker is again returned for the Manchester School Board, and the Leeds and Birmingham School Boards have made no change with regard to Mrs. Buckton and Miss Sturge.

THE PROPERTY OF MARRIED WOMEN.

THE Committee have great pleasure in announcing that the Right Hon. Lord Coleridge will, early early next session, introduce a Bill to amend the law relating to the property of married women. The object of the Bill will be to secure to a married woman her own property, and to make her liable for her own contracts, as if she were a single woman.

A correspondent of the *Women's Suffrage Journal* gives
an instance of the confusion arising out of the involved
language in which the Married Women's Property Act
of 1870 is framed, which shows that the protection intended by the framers of that Act to be secured to the
earnings of married women is in many cases no protection at all.

There can be no doubt, says our correspondent, that the promoters
of the Bill intended by clause 1 to protect the earnings of married
women in any business or occupation of their own in which their
husbands were not engaged, but it seems clear that section 1, as
framed, falls short in carrying this out. The condition is that the
business or occupation shall be carried on "separately from her
husband," *i.e.*, from *him*. But, to carry out the promoters' wishes,
the section should have declared, separately from her husband's
business, calling, or *engagement.* At least one legal decision upon
the section referred to bears out this remark. Shortly after the
passing of the Act, a case in which our correspondent was concerned
was decided under the Equity Jurisdiction conferred by the County
Courts. The facts were shortly these :—The husband was a cashier,
the wife a ladies' dress and mantle maker. The latter business was
carried on by the wife and her own assistants, and the proceeds
applied by her as she thought proper, she hiring and paying assistants, making purchases and giving receipts, at no time accounting to
her husband, but contributing without any arrangement to do so to
the general maintenance of the family. The husband, for some
reason of his own, took upon himself to search his wife's boxes for
papers, and found a sum of £90, the savings of the wife out
of the business referred to. The husband kept the money,
and the wife's solicitors instituted proceedings under the Married
Women's Property Act to compel restitution to her. Of course the
allegation was that the money belonged to the wife as separate earnings. Our correspondent was acting for the husband, and his contention was, through counsel whom he instructed, that, as the parties
were living together during the carrying on of the business, the husband
having access to it and all pertaining to it as a business, it could not
be said that it was carried on separtely from *him.* It was quite true
the business was carried on separately and apart from his *business,*
but the Act did not go so far as to give the wife the right so long as
the business was not separate from *him*—the individual. The Court
adopted this view, and dismissed the wife's claim to the money.

No appeal was lodged against the decision referred to, and the
logical effect of it is, that no wife is safe in carrying on a business or
occupation if the husband can by any means have frequent access to
the place where it is carried on. If living with the wife, the husband
can scarcely be deprived of such access, and eventually he may, by
his continued wrongful interference with it, be enabled thereby to
show it has not been carried on *separately* from *him.* The section,
therefore, to give effectual protection to a wife's earnings, makes

separation next to, if not absolutely, a necessity. Of course it is a
question of fact in each particular case, to be ascertained what has
been done separately from the husband.

SUFFRAGE.

THE Women's Disabilities Removal Bill has again
passed into the hands of its early leader, Mr. Jacob
Bright, to whom Mr. Forsyth has resigned it. We
believe that this announcement will be received with
sincere congratulation by the friends of the movement,
and a renewed determination to push forward in the
work. It is far better for the dignity of the measure,
and for its maintenance as a non-party question—affecting alike women of high and low rank, and of every
sect, opinion, and degree of education—that it should
not be identified with either the Liberal or Conservative
benches, but should, three years ago, pass from the
hands of a Liberal to a Conservative leader, and be now
again resumed by a Liberal. During Mr. Forsyth's able
guidance of the question it has steadily increased in
importance; its friends have, almost without exception,
remained staunch to it, and if its declared enemies have
not in any large number come over to it, the large
neutral masses between are increasingly disposed to
discuss it in a serious light. The Bill has had two
divisions while in Mr. Forsyth's hands; in one it met
with the smallest opposition majority it has ever recorded, and though this majority was much enlarged
last session, the increase is attributable rather to the
respect paid to the Right Hon. John Bright's adverse
speech than to any lack of zeal or ability on the part of
the Bill's supporters. Mr. Forsyth deserves the best
thanks of the friends of the cause for his past services
as well as for his promise of continued support on the
next introduction of the Bill.

The winter campaign of public meetings is expected
to begin shortly. The first important one will be the
Annual General Meeting of the Manchester National
Society for Women's Suffrage, to receive the report,
the statement of accounts, to appoint the committee,
and to transact any other business which may arise,
which will be held in the Town Hall, King Street, Man-

chester, on Wednesday, November 29th, at 3 o'clock.
A few have been held during the past month. A Dun-
gannon (Ireland) correspondent writes that the Young
Men's Christian Association of that town have debated
the subject—"Should women householders have the
franchise?" On a vote being taken, the affirmative
side had an overwhelming majority. A crowded public
meeting was held on October 25th, in the Town Hall,
Brighouse; Thomas Ormerod, Esq., occupied the chair,
and Mrs. Scatcherd and Miss Becker attended as a
deputation on behalf of the National Society for
Women's Suffrage. Resolutions in support of this Bill
were moved and seconded by the Rev. Mr. Candelet and
the Rev. Mr. Galbraith. A lecture was also given by Miss
Blackburn in the Lecture Hall, Sydenham, on October
26th. The Rev. A. T. Davidson occupied the chair.

Among the pamphlets which have recently appeared
on this question, one by W. T. Blair, Esq., magistrate
for Somerset, will be welcomed. It is, in part, a reprint
from an article in the *Victoria Magazine* of 1874, but
some remarks on the last debate in the House of Commons have been added. These principally refer to Mr.
Bright's speech, which was, in fact, the only one in that
debate in which talent was arrayed on the side of moral
and political wrong and injustice. After summing up,
and concisely answering the majority of the arguments
usually brought against women's suffrage, Mr. Blair
adds:—"It can hardly be doubted, I think, that the
cause of education and of temperance, bearing as they
do on the peace and happiness of domestic life, and on
national morality generally, would be largely promoted
by the addition of the female vote to the present constituency, and it should constantly be borne in mind in
considering this question, that the connection between
votes and *laws* lies at the very root of the representative
system, and those free institutions of which the country
is at once so jealous and so proud."

EMPLOYMENT.

AUSTRALIAN SILK.—Mrs. Bladen Neill has left England
for Australia, with the intention of pushing the production of silk in large quantities in connection with the

"Ladies' Victorian Sericicultural Company (Limited)."
The directors of this company are ladies, assisted by a
board of advice composed of some of the leading men of
business in the colony. The company is formed with
the hope of in time establishing a new industry for educated women, at home and in Australia. The production of silk is, in all its branches, essentially a woman's
work; and while the women of England may be employed
in "educating" worms for "grain," women in Australia
can rear them for the production of silk. The experiment which has been tried in London with the famous
black worms, introduced into England by Mrs. Neill,
has proved successful, and the grain may now be purchased at the Australian Silk Growers' Depot, 7, Charles
street, Grosvenor square, where also ladies can subscribe
for shares in the company. These shares are only £1
each, fully paid up, and through the almost entire failure
of the silk crop in Europe, and the consequent enormous
rise in the price of silk, there is every hope that this
company, benefitting by the advantages which Australia,
in her soil and climate, offers for the production of silk,
will be a great commercial success, as well as an
inestimable gain to women; this last being the primary
object for which Mrs. Neill has striven with untiring
energy and dauntless enthusiasm.

From the *Labour News* we gather the following rates
of payment of women in various trades:—

BRUSHMAKING.—A skilled man, if regularly employed,
can at present earn about 30s. a week. Women can
earn from 8s. to 12s., but a smart and clever hand may,
by commencing early in the morning and working till
twelve at night, with the aid of two or three children,
who are paid but a few pence a week each, earn, perhaps, 18s. or £1 per week.

COACHBUILDING:—Women employed in this trade gain,
according to the class of work they do, 7s. 6d. or 15s. a
week.

BEDDING MANUFACTURE.—Men in this branch earn,
when fully employed, from 25s. to 50s. per week; women,
9s., 15s., 16s., and some a trifle more, per week.

TOBACCO-PIPE CASEMAKERS.—At this work men earn,

ordinarily, 30s. a week, and women, who cover the
cases, about 16s.; but in busy times, like the present,
when work goes on till late at night, the week's wages
are much in advance of this.

FUR-SEWING.—Women, if good hands, can earn from
10s. 6d. to 20s. on piecework; indifferent workers, of
course, earn much less. Muff stuffers and liners can
earn from 20s. to 35s. a week. Messrs. Hyman and Co.,
furriers, 151, Aldersgate street, who have now about
twenty muff hands in their employ, say they can make
room for twenty more, and give them constant employment ten months out of the twelve, at which the chances
are open to make the above money. They must know
their business and be steady. Work commences at
half-past eight in the morning and finishes at nine p.m.
Learners get 3s., 6s., and 9s., for the first six, twelve,
and eighteen months respectively.

FANCY BOXMAKING. — This trade chiefly employs
women. A girl before she receives any wages has to
work six months, during which probationary period she
manages to spoil more work than she is worth. At the
end of six months she may be in a position to earn 2s. 6d.
a week, which sum is gradually augmented as her
services become more valuable, until, if she become
really efficient, she may probably take her £1, and sometimes more, per week, and eventually become forewoman
of a room.

ARTIFICIAL FLOWER-MAKING.—Something like 3,000
women, and 1,600 girls, under twenty years of age, are
employed in this branch of industry.

MANTLE-MAKERS are briskly engaged preparing for
winter. One large firm in Islington have 200 machines
at work, making mantles, jackets, ulsters, etc., and are
sending out 8,000 per day—two waggon-loads. The
machinists—young women—earn from 12s. to 16s. per
week.

WARD-MAIDS AT THE CANCER HOSPITAL.—£14 a year
are the magnificent wages offered in a recent advertisement for the above painful and responsible posts of duty.
The mere money spent in unprofitable advertisements

H

to get candidates would probably, in the year, materially increase the wages offered.—*Labour News.*

PRINTING.—The *Workmen's Club Journal* is now printed by the Women's Printing Company, Limited, 38, Castle Street, High Holborn, London. We hope this indicates progress in the work which Mrs. Paterson and her colleagues have in hand.

A LARGE portion of a Scotch country weekly newspaper, the *Blairgowrie Advertiser*, is put in type by girls. The experiment was tried in the office of that paper about the beginning of the present year, and we understand that the proprietor considers it highly successful. He finds that the girls are more easily taught than boys, and that they are more careful and quiet.

MISS Lewin (Employment of Women's Society), writes that Messrs. Niel & Co., printers in Edinburgh, employ about 40 young women as compositers, some working as in England, and others at some composing machines invented by Mr. Fraser, the managing partner. The girls in the machine room looked much more intelligent than those in the hand room, but there was not much difference in the wages of good workers in either room. "One young woman told me she had been a compositor seven years and liked the work much. They earn from 10s. 6d. to 15s. a week, which is about equal to 15s. and £1 in London. Some of them are persevering at their work, but several are like the men, taking holidays on Mondays and Tuesdays, and then working fearfully hard the rest of the week trying to make up for it. Six firms in Edinburgh now employ women as compositors, of whom there are at present about 100. Some of a lower class are employed in feeding press as well as in binding. As yet they have no regular form of apprenticeship, but it is understood that a girl who learns the trade, serves the master who taught her, four years without seeking to change. The girls require more help in the heavy part of the work than men, but Mr. Fraser said they were quite as good, and often quicker workers than the boys. Women who are employed as binders earn from 8s. to 14s. a week."

Mr. R. Anderson, architect, Northumberland Street,

Edinburgh, employs three female apprentices, and thinks
the employment well suited to women.

HOME FOR ENGLISH CHILDREN IN PARIS.—In one of the
quiet boulevards leading out of Paris, there has stood
for ten years, in the midst of a pleasant garden, a house
which has gone by the name of the British Hospital.
But now this home of suffering has become a play place
for happy children. By the generous liberality of M.
Galignani (who instituted the hospital), the house with
all it contains has now been given over as a Home for
Orphaned and Deserted Children to the Society represented by Miss Leigh, founder of the "Mission Home
for Englishwomen," 77, Avenue Wagram. On Thursday, November 2nd, the ceremony of inauguration took
place, and 27 children were transferred from the Mission
Home, at Avenue Wagram, to their new abode. A large
number of visitors were assembled in the spacious dining
room of the house, and at a given signal the children
entered singing, and bearing the British Flag. This
was followed by a short service, in which the principal
English clergymen of Paris, and other friends, took part;
and the visitors went over the Home, and were much
pleased with its inviting and comfortable appearance.
The want of a Children's Home has long been felt, and
could be abundantly proved by the history of some of
the children present on this occasion. Two had been
brought over from England to be sold as artists' models,
others had been left in utter destitution by the death of
their parents, while two had been found, but a few
months ago, wandering deserted through the streets.
M. Galignani has known well the need which he now
seeks to relieve, and he has added to his most munificent
gift an announcement that he intends to head the subscription list with £300.

MISCELLANEOUS.

THE Manchester Sewing Machine Workers' Society has
now an office at the Temperance hall, Grosvenor street,
Manchester.

LAWS OF HEALTH.—Dr. W. H. Corfield has commenced
a series of lectures on the Laws of Health, in the large

room of the Society of Arts, John Street, Adelphi, on
Saturdays. Dr. Corfield has been giving similar lectures
for the last three years in Birmingham, at the close of
which were examinations. The "Teachers' Exhibition"
was gained by a lady who obtained no less than 465
marks out of 500.

The lady teachers of the National Health Society will
assist the lecturer by revising and correcting the written
answers, which will be invited to questions on the
lectures. These ladies have acquired experience by
conducting classes in various parts of London, since the
Society was founded in 1871, and several of them are
pupils of Dr. Corfield. In order to bring the lectures
within the reach of the industrial class, working men
and women can be admitted at a charge of one shilling
the course, and one penny the single lecture.

MESSRS. HENRY KING will shortly publish a story by
Miss M. Drummond, called, "A Study from Life." It is
a story about the London poor, and is written in aid of
the Westminster Home for Training Nurses—the memorial to the late Lady Augusta Stanley.

THE *Academy* says that the Princess Leichtenstein,
authoress of "Holland House," has in preparation a
novel entitled "Nora," taken from the German. It may
be described as preluding an entirely original work by
the same authoress.

A COOKERY school is to be opened in Dunfermline, N.B.

THE Edinburgh School of Cookery is going on well. It
is under the charge of a lady with a diploma from South
Kensington.

THE Edinburgh Employment of Women Society has
removed its office to 50, George Street.

HELP FOR THE BOSNIAN AND BULGARIAN FUGITIVES.—
Mrs. Malleson sends every week parcels of warm clothing
to be distributed by Dr. Sandwith among the houseless
fugitives from the Turkish provinces. Contributions
are received by her at 29, Queen Square, London, W.C.
The materials should be woollen or fur, as lighter fabrics
(such as linsey woolsey and cotton) are not worth the
expense of carriage. Old linen is very valuable for

the wounded. In a letter to the *Daily News,* Nov. 11th,
she says: "For the reasons given by Dr. Sandwith,
English blankets and woollen stuffs will be more than
ever acceptable for the fugitives, and I may remind the
readers of the *Daily News* that I am sending out stores
of these goods and ready-made clothes as fast as the
public enable me to do so. Miss Irby and Miss Johnston have also written urgently for further supplies of
these for the relief of very terrible suffering and destitution among fugitives along the coast of Dalmatia.
Through the kindness of Messrs. Burns and MacIver,
and the London and North Western Railway Company,
the goods are sent out to Trieste free of carriage; there
is, however, the carriage from Trieste to Belgrade, or
to some other centre of distribution, to be provided for.
I am, Sir, yours sincerely,—ELIZABETH MALLESON, Hon.
Secretary.

Central Depôt for Clothes, Relief Fund for Christian
Fugitives from Bosnia, Herzegovina, and Bulgaria,
29, Queen Square, Bloomsbury.

ART VI.—FOREIGN NOTES AND NEWS.

FRANCE.

Art Studio in Paris.—The *Academy* says :—"We understand that
a new *atelier* for lady artists has been opened in Paris by M. Krug,
an artist of known ability. The morning class begins at eight o'clock,
working on till twelve o'clock from the semi-draped figure. The
afternoon class, from one till five o'clock, is occupied specially with
the study of portraiture. In the evening there is another class for
two hours, again working at the half-draped figure. M. Krug,
besides his own assiduous instruction to the students, has secured for
them also the benefit of weekly visits from three distinguished artists
in Paris."

In France, girls and women are employed in selecting apples for
the English markets, nailing up the boxes, and loading the trucks,
for which work they only get about a shilling a day.

Women and children are said to be the best pickers in the vine-
yards, and the men are for the most part employed in carrying the
baskets to and fro, emptying the crates, and loading the wagons.

The *Avenir des Femmes* says that a free class in bookkeeping has just been opened for women by the Chamber of Commerce, at 39, Rue de Ecuries d'Artois, Paris. Free evening classes for reading, writing, arithmetic and spelling, have also been commenced for women.

A journal says that the number of midwives in Paris is 945.

BELGIUM.

According to a French paper which has recently devoted several articles to the Belgian mines, there are several in which very young girls as well as women are employed. It is stated that girls of eleven years old sometimes work from three in the morning to six or eight in the evening.

GERMANY.

BERLIN.—A lady, Fraulein Lenus, has within the last few weeks taken up her abode in Berlin as a fully qualified physician. She has studied at several German universities, but went through her qualifying examination in Berlin. She will probably soon obtain a good practice. Up to the present time there have been only two women dentists, both of whom had studied in Philadelphia; Fraulein Lenus, therefore, deserves to be welcomed as the first instance of a Prussian lady who has taken up medical work.

SWITZERLAND.

The printer and bookbinder Schmidt, in Zurich, has a class for female printers and bookbinders. For the first half year the learners receive no wages; then 6 francs a week for the next half year, and afterwards according to their ability.

ITALY.

Madame Jessie White Mario sent the following details of the education of Italian girls to the New Century for Women :— " Perhaps on the whole there has been more progress made in female than in male instruction ; with increasing liberty in general, there is springing up a belief that women are susceptible of education, and that they may even have a right to it. No country has produced a greater number of female celebrities than Italy ; in no country are the masses of women so thoroughly mediocre. In most families, the birth of a girl is looked upon as a misfortune. As a child and girl, she is the slave of father and brothers. A dowry must be eked out of the family finances, so that she may be married and got rid of. Then she becomes the slave of her husband and children. Now the mere fact of the increased number of schools, has opened a new field for women. The normal schools, the few upper class schools and colleges existing, are crowded with applicants ; women are even beginning to find their way into the post and telegraph offices, and when women become bread-winners, the male element begins to hold them in respect.

Besides the elementary female schools in every district, there are two female colleges in Rome, superintended by *Signora Ermina Tua*

Fusinato and the *Signora Milli.* These colleges for Rome have a special importance, as they enable parents to give their girls a really first-class education, without sending them to the convents or to the conservatories. So successful have 'been these colleges, that elementary schools, for parents who prefer paying for their children, to keep them select, have been opened in connection with the colleges. The evening and Sunday Schools for adults are also very much frequented. The same lessons are given, and by the same masters, gratuitously, as in the day schools. Prizes have been offered by private individuals, and have much stimulated the competitors. Then there are special schools, schools of design, technical schools, and now. in the *Collegio Romano*, where a number of museums have been united, so that it is in reality a mimic Kensington Museum, a school for the application of arts to industry has been opened.

So much for the Municipal schools, to which, of course, the mass of the population must look for instruction, and besides these, since the proclamation of Rome as Capital of Italy, many philanthropic individuals and societies have devoted themselves to lead the rising generation from darkness into light.

Foremost among these was Mrs. Emily Bliss Gould, whose Italo-American School in *Via in Arcione* was at its best when I first saw it at the beginning of 1875. To see Mrs. Gould in the midst of her "children," boarders, and day scholars, was simply to see a mother in the midst of her family, that family one of the happiest and merriest imaginable.

A personal friend thus writes of her enterprise :—"Shortly after the entry of the Italians on the 20th of September, 1870, Mrs. Gould began, on her return to Rome after the summer's absence, to take the first step towards the fulfilment of her long cherished desire. Great difficulty was found in procuring a room or a teacher, but her indomitable energy did not permit her to despair. After repeated disappointments, on the 20th March, 1871, ' with a capital of fifty francs and without a teacher,' as she herself writes, ' a school was opened in ¡which three girls were the first scholars,' herself the teacher. Two more soon presented themselves for admission, and by the first of May there were more than thirty. Many had, however, been rejected, owing to difficulties made on the score of failures in personal cleanliness, punctuality, and tolerably decent clothing. The school, commenced as an infant school, soon found such favour with the class to the amelioration of which its chief efforts had been directed, that boys of fifteen and girls of seventeen presented themselves eager for admission. Mrs. Gould's courage did not fail her ; she arranged her classes, started evening instruction for the elder among her applicants, ¸and ¸a Kindergarten, the first of the kind in Rome, for the youngest.

"¸The day schools soon numbered over a hundred and thirty children. Circumstances compelled a change of *locale,* and about half only of the original number were able to follow their directress to the new school-rooms, which were at a considerable distance from the first. The condition of some among the poorer children as to their home relations, was a keen agony to the tender mother-heart that was so devoted to them. A plan for a home, into which the most unfortunate of these might be at once snatched from corruption and misery, grew into a possibility under her active exertions, and on the 1st of June, 1873, the ' *Collegio Convitto Italio Amercana* ' was inaugurated.

" From 1872 to 1874, from one contrary circumstance and another, there were continual changes and much trial of the patience and perseverance of the directress.   *   *   *   *

" At last in the month of December, 1874, the Home and Schools were opened at 106, *Via in Arcione,* close by the Fountain of *Trevi.* In this very central situation a first-class house of four stories was engaged for a term of six years. The printing offices, wherein the children of both sexes studied daily the art of typography, under competent English and Italian teachers, were established on the first floor. Here also were the receiving room of the directress, and three large class-rooms. On the second floor, two other class-rooms, the matron's chamber, the girl's dormitory, the refectory, and the kitchen. On the third floor the apartment of the head master and wife, the sleeping rooms for the boys, their lavatory, etc., etc., the fourth consisting chiefly of a large open air play-room, attics, and store-rooms.

" The printing establishment, directed by a young Scotch printer, would, Mrs. Gould hoped, not only soon pay its own expenses, but be a source of profit to the school which it was her ambition to leave a self-supporting institution. The children were making rapid progress, and printing in both languages, English and Italian, work from without was freely undertaken. A smaller press was worked entirely by the children; the large Hoe press sent from New York required adult assistance, but the children were the compositors, and enjoyed their labour. She could not resist sending her mite to every good work that she felt promised future good to Italy, the new society for prevention of cruelty to animals, the Roman ladies' society, " *de piccoli Contributi* " a benevolent institution, for administering privately small subsidies to the very poor and needy, and others. Her private means alone were the limit of her charities, she was ever full of the cares of others as well as her own.

" All her anxieties and responsibilities and great personal exertions, weighed however upon her, body and soul. For more than a year, her more intimate friends felt that she was sacrificing her very life to the cause she had so faithfully espoused. Her health failed visibly during the winter and spring of 1875. Mrs. Gould died in June, 1875."

" The grief manifested by the children when their great loss was made known to them, was of itself a proof of the love and the respect she had inspired. Truly the children felt that they had lost their mother, nor could they at once realize how great that loss might prove. On her death it was found necessary at once to close the day-school. Untoward circumstances necessitated the breaking up of the Kindergarten, and the children of the Home have now passed into the hands of the Waldensians."

NORWAY.

Miss Aasta Hanstein, of Christiana, has lately begun to give read-
ings and lectures in public. The first reading was on the 2nd of
May, when she gave some chapters from a work of which she is the
authoress, "Woman Created in the Image of God." It was most
successful. There was an intelligent and distinguished audience, who
gave her warm applause. On June 11th she gave a second lecture
to a much larger audience than before upon the "Condition of
Women." Later on, she has spoken five times in various towns in
Sweden and Norway to very appreciative audiences. Mr. Edgvist,
doctor of philosophy in the University of Upsala, proposes to print
her first lecture and diffuse it widely through the three Scandinavian
kingdoms. The Copenhagen journals speak very highly in her praise.

RUSSIA.

A correspondent of the *Pall Mall Gazette* says that "as regards
the education of women Russia may certainly claim to be more progressive than any other country, except, perhaps, the United States.
The French *pensions* have nearly all disappeared, and their place
has been taken by girls' schools and women's colleges, in which the
teaching is quite equal to that of the colleges for male students. In
Moscow there is a classical women's college, founded under the
auspices of the late Professor Leontieff, and specially favoured by the
Minister of Cultus and the Empress.

In Russia boys and ¦girls are taught separately, except in the
Kindergartens, though both sexes were employed indiscriminately
as teachers, and *paid the same*. Here, too, women are preferred.
All the gymnasia, even the great universities, are now open to
women. The professors in these universities are paid by the Government. The primary schools, of which in 1853 there were only
3,000, in ten years increased to 35,000. Since then an effort has been
made to establish them in every district. Of all ¦pupils who enter,
the children of the former serfs are most eager and successful.

Courses for the higher education of women are to be commenced in
the University of Kazan.

ROUMANIA.

Princess Koltzoff-Massalsky, better known as the Princess Dora
D'Istria, has been awarded the first medal of the new order of Bene
Merenti, founded by Prince Charles, of Roumania, for scientists and
authors.

INDIA.

The *Journal of the National Indian Association* says: Dr. Balfour,
of Madras, in his reply to a valedictory address presented to him,
thus alluded to the medical education of women in India: "British
India has about eighty millions of women whom the customs of
many of the races preclude from seeing a medical man, and I thought
European ladies might, with general approval, study and practice
medicine among their Indian sisters. That was a wholly unoccupied

sphere, to train women doctors to enter on it was to interfere with no one's livelihood, and the liberal views of Government permitted the suggestion to be carried out. Tne Madras Medical College has already been utilized in this way, and, under Surgeon Furnell's care, it has been so in the quietest and nicest manner. Four ladies entered it as students in the bygone session, ladies from Europe have been inquiring regarding its rules, and within the past month two ladies have applied for admission from the far north-west of India—one from Meean Meer, and the other from Attock, on the Indus. I look forward to much good resulting to women of the country from this movement."

At Benares, Brahmin widows who have become well educated in the Vizianagram Schools are going through a regular medical training, and the aptitude they show leads to the hope that they may become good practitioners. At Bombay a midwifery class for women has been connected with the Medical Hospital: a number have been already sent out, and have proved very successful.

A Baptist missionary's widow, a Mrs. Thomas, has been made superintendent of a diocese in Burmah, which includes thirty-nine native Karen pastors, besides other evangelists, schools, &c.

CAPE OF GOOD HOPE.

Female Assistant-Teacher.—For the Ladies' Institute, Bloomfontein, Orange Free State, South Africa, qualified to teach English and instrumental music. Salary, £120, and £50 allowed as passage-money to Port Elizabeth.—Mr. Morrison, rector, Free Church Normal School, Glasgow.

The War in the Transvaal.—Inquiry having been made into the charge of killing women and children brought against emissaries of President Burgers, it has been ascertained on indisputable evidence that Von Schlickmann ordered two women and one child to be murdered in cold blood, after a council of war had ordered them to be released; that Von Schlickmann told those under his orders that if they did not kill the women and children he would himself go into the native huts and cut their throats; that one Englishman deliberately shot down a woman, and that another Englishman went up to her as she lay on the ground wounded and blew out her brains. Every one here asks why her Majesty's high commissioner does not interfere to stop such atrocities, as most of the perpetrators are British subjects.

AUSTRALIA.

The *Melbourne Argus* says of the candidates who presented themselves for examination in the July term at the University of Melbourne:—"The number who presented themselves for this examination was 52. Out of this number there were 36 candidates for the matriculation examination, consisting of 23 males, of whom seven passed, and 13 females, of whom six passed, making a total of 13 who passed—but none with credit—out of the 36 who presented themselves for this examination. For the Civil Service examination there were 43 candidates, consisting of 30 males, of whom nine passed, and 13 females, of whom seven passed, making a total of 16 who passed out of the 43 who presented themselves for this examination. Out of the 52 candidates, 12 passed both the matriculation and Civil Service examinations; but it should be mentioned that there were seven who presented themselves for examination in single subjects, and were not candidates for either examination, and that out of the remaining 43 who were candidates for the Civil Service there were 36 only who were also candidates for the matriculation examination. Thus it appears that one-third have passed both the examinations, that a little more than one-third have passed the matriculation examination, and that nearly the same proportion have passed the Civil Service examination. The ladies have done better than the gentlemen. Scarcely one-third of the latter have passed either examination; while nearly half of the ladies have passed the matriculation examination, and more than half the Civil Service examination."

The following are the names of the candidates who passed:—

Matriculation Examination.—Sarah Ann Fish, Joel Fredman, Benjamin Matthews French, Alice Louise Griffiths, William Parker Little, Charles Mackay, Ernest William Crofton Sadleir, Margaret Lucy Thomas, Catherine Hay Thomson, Andrew M'Clure Valantine, Ella Louise Vasey, Duncan Walker, Elizabeth Williamson.

Civil Service Examination.—Arthur William Blagdon, John Clinch, Sarah Ann Fish, Joel Fredman, Benjamin Matthews French, Alice Louise Griffiths, Thomas Hewitson, Annie Lawrence, William Parker Little, Charles Mackay, Ernest William Crofton Sadleir, Margaret Lucy Thomas, Andrew M'Clure Valantine, Ella Louise Vasey, Duncan Walker, Elizabeth Williamson.

AMERICA.

The Woman's Congress has lately closed a three days session in Philadelphia. Maria Mitchell, Professor of Astronomy in Vassar College, presided. The discussion on many subjects was thoughtful and practical. We shall have occasion to notice them subsequently.

Employment for Women.—A lady writes from San Francisco:— "Living in California for nine years, I have never paid less than twelve dollars for the making of the plainest dress, and I am not a wearer of puffs or ruffles or flounces. When I have been sick I have never paid less than twenty dollars per week for a nurse, and a very poor one at that figure. I have never paid less than twenty dollars per month for a very ordinary house servant. With these prices in gold, it seems to me that a person might lay by a comfortable little sum. I know two young lady teachers from the East, who failed to find schools. They have rented a small chicken ranch, and are making money fast and easily. They find a ready sale for eggs at seventy-five cents per dozen at Christmas time. Eggs never bring less than twenty-five cents per dozen; at this season they are fifty cents per dozen, while chickens bring readily one dollar or one dollar twenty-five cents apiece. A few days since I had occasion to employ a collector; he charged five per cent. on all money collected. I said to myself, 'Why is not this a good business for ladies?' There is

another very desirable opening for female labour in America, viz. :
the opening of restaurants conducted by able women, also bakeries on
the English plan where meat as well as pastry is cooked. If our
housekeepers could depend upon the cleanliness and good quality of
food purchased at the bakeries, it would be a great convenience, and
an invaluable help to a now overworked class."

Art. VII.—TRADITION.

We have left the city with its lights behind,
  Its gas-lit palaces and lamp-gemmed shrines,
  Where the crowd bows, and serves, and raves, and pines,
For the still night and country unconfined,
The tranquil stars and unpolluted mind.

The streets, whose every stone we knew so well;
  The thresholds—hallowed by long memories dear,
  So bright each finger-post and sign ran clear,
Swaying our hearts with old familiar spell ;
But in that city, more we must not dwell.

The night is dark : the plain is strange and wide,
  No road to guard our footsteps can we trace—
  No beacon pointing to some resting place ;
Our glimmering lanterns dazzle us, not guide ;
The steady stars our only light beside.

Which way to turn ? No light, no guide, no track ;
  Darkness in front, behind, the ruddy haze
  Of custom, use, and long-remembered ways.
One thing we know : we cannot now turn back
Into the servile city's childish pack.

Onward we must: the day will break at last.
  The world's broad highway lies beneath our feet,
  In place of walled-up court and narrow street.
Time-buried customs, all behind us cast,
We leave Tradition tranquil with the Past.

                        P. P. C.

ART. VIII.—PARAGRAPHS.

MUSICAL COMPOSERS.—The list of feminine composers
is a brief one, and most of its members are now living.
There was Leopoldine Blahetka, daughter of a professor
of mathematics in Vienna, a famous pianiste who published more than seventy songs and pianoforte pieces,
some of which were greatly admired by Beethoven;
Josephine Lang, the friend of Mendelssohn, who composed many charming songs; Madame Hensel, the
sister of Mendelssohn; Louise Puget, whose vocal
romances enjoyed an enormous popularity in France;
Elise Polko, who, carefully educated as a singer,
lost her voice prematurely, then wrote many pretty
novelettes, and now appears before the world as a song
composer; Madame Dolby, and Virginia Gabriel, the
English ballad writer. Madame Schurman and Madame
Garcia have both composed some fine works, though
few in number. But women have not hitherto realized
what long years of severe mental discipline and scientific
training are necessary in order to master the art of composition. This is not much to the discredit of their
patience and courage, for very few among musical
students of the other sex are, in America, willing to devote themselves to such self sacrificing study; too many
when they begin to understand the amount of labour
required, become discouraged, and abandon it; and
none among them yet have acquired such thorough
early training as will insure perfect development to their
talent for composition, and lasting fame to its results.
Mathematics, acoustics, psychology, foreign languages,
and literature, the theory and practice of many instruments, as well as the science of music itself, must all be
mastered by the composer, and gradually, through the
application and assimilation of long years of study and
practice, become the "second nature" of his mind.

A WOMAN MACHINIST.—The *Philadelphia Times* says:
—The women of the United States resolved to display at the Exhibition a complete representation of
their industries, art, and skill. They have accomplished
their purpose, and, in so doing, were careful to exclude
as far as possible everything emanating from the hand

or brain of the opposite sex. Though they did not
actually build the Women's Pavilion, they paid for its
erection, and their exhibits in that structure, with the
exception of the machinery, are the work of their own
hands. The same is to be said of their guests and co-
exhibitors, the women of England, Canada, and other
countries. The rule has been carried even to the engine-
house, where the Baxter portable engine of six-horse
power is run by a woman engineer. This engine is the
motor of all the spinning frames, looms, and other
machinery in practical operation within the pavilion,
and its fair mistress is Miss Emma Allison, of Grimsby,
Ontario. She is by no means a soot-begrimed and oil-
covered Amazon, but on the contrary, of neat and
cleanly appearance and a highly educated and refined
young lady. Of the brunette type, medium height,
well-formed, strong and active, possessing a gentle
disposition and much vivacity and good sense in conversation, she affords no little attraction to visitors as
she dextrously manages her iron pet and tells them all
about it. Her dress is neat, and of grayish linen, prettily
braided in black. She makes it a point to keep both
engine and room in the perfection of tidiness, and while
she would grace a parlour in a manner equal to that of
any lady, no lady in ball-room attire could grace that
engine room better than she. Her choice of this employment comes, she says, from three sources, namely:
Her delight in the study of natural philosophy gave her
a fondness for machinery which was developed into its
comprehension through the assistance of her brother, a
member of the Engineer Corps of the United States
navy; her means being limited, she must follow some
remunerative occupation, and she accepted her present
position as the one of her choice, although hitherto she
had nothing but theoretical knowledge of steam engi-
neering, and she believed it the duty of some one of her
sex to enter a "new departure" which is among those
opening out to women employment far more paying
and healthful, requiring as much knowledge and skill
for its accomplishment, and carrying with it as great
honour as teaching school, keeping books, or operating
sewing machines, copying, etc. She believes that if so

many male engineers did not find such apparent delight
in plastering themselves all over with soot and making
their engine rooms perfect specimens of disorder and
filth women would long ago have looked with favour
upon the occupation. She does not, however, intend
continuing in the work after the Exhibition, purposing
then to start a literary magazine in San Francisco.

MRS. L. MARIA CHILD ON THE INTELLECTUAL
EQUALITY OF MEN AND WOMEN.—The only argument
I think it worth while to offer on the subject is this: If
women have physical or intellectual strength sufficient
to earn property, and consequently be taxed for it, they
have intellect enough to vote concerning the use that
shall be made of their taxes; and if they have sense
and feeling enough to suffer from the effects of corrupt
or imbecile legislation, they have sense enough to try
to improve it. That women at the present time are
not, generally speaking, the physical or intellectual
equals of men, in general, is obvious. But I deem it
impossible for the wisest thinker, or the most careful
investigator, to determine how far the present inequality
is to be ascribed to natural organization, or how far to
centuries of impeded growth, and the dwarfing effects
of habitual subordination. All I ask is perfect liberty to
choose our own spheres of action, and a fair, open
chance to do whatsoever we can do well. I am very
willing to leave time to decide the degree of our capabilities, and I have no anxiety concerning the verdict.
For myself, I believe in the perfect equality of men and
women by nature, yet I think there is a difference in
their spiritual, as well as in their physical organization;
and that, generally speaking, though they might work
in all departments equally well, they would spontaneously work in a different manner.

QUEEN'S INSTITUTE, DUBLIN.—The last report of this
useful and valuable institution, contains the following
sensible hint:—"It seems requisite to call attention to
the necessity of steady application to work by those
who wish to turn acquirements to account. It is a
fallacy that a lady can make an income by working an
hour or two in a day. No doubt, if possible, it would
be very agreeable. If a lady becomes a writer for the

press, or for publishers, she finds she must go in for hard
work. If she be a governess she finds her employers
require her whole time; if she adopts music as her profession, she willingly undertakes the needed study.
But it is strange that few think of applying this diligence
to other pursuits. Those who do not think it worth
while to begin at a low rate of remuneration, may be
perfectly certain they will never reach high emolument.
The highest talent must be content to undergo sufficient
cultivation and submit to competition until proved able
to surmount rivals."

WOMEN IN BUSINESS.—Benjamin Franklin, in his autobiography, thus urges the business education of women.
Nearly a century and a half later, his hints are equally
valuable: "In 1733 I sent one of my journeymen to
Charleston, S.C., where a printer was wanting. I furnished him with a press and letters, on an agreement of
partnership by which I was to receive one third of the
profits of the business, paying one third of the expenses.
He was a man of learning, and honest, but ignorant in
matters of account; and though he sometimes made me
remittances, I could get no account from him, nor any
satisfactory state of our partnership while he lived. On
his decease the business was continued by his widow,
who was born and bred in Holland, where, as I have
been informed, the knowledge of accounts makes a part
of female education. She not only sent me as clear a
statement as she could of the transactions past, but
continued to account with the greatest regularity and
exactness every quarter afterwards, and managed the
business with such success, that she not only brought
up reputably a family of children, but, at the expiration
of the term, was able to purchase of me the printing-
house, and established her son in it. I mention this
affair chiefly for the sake of recommending that branch
of education for our young women, as likely to be of
more use to them and their children in case of widowhood, than either music or dancing, by preserving them
from losses by imposition of crafty men, and enabling
them to continue, perhaps, a profitable mercantile house
with established correspondence, till a son is grown up
fit to undertake and go on with it, to the lasting advantage and enriching of the family.

Englishwoman's Review.

CONTENTS FOR DECEMBER, 1876.

All Communications to be addressed to the EDITOR, 22, Berners Street, Oxford Street, W.

Post-Office Orders payable to SARAH LEWIN, at the "Regent Street" Post-Office.

TERMS OF SUBSCRIPTION AT THE OFFICE.

Per Annum (Post Free), Six Shillings.

Subscriptions payable in Advance. Single Numbers posted Free on receipt of Six Postage Stamps.

MSS. are carefully read, and if not accepted are returned, on receipt of Stamps for Postage, but the Editor cannot be responsible for any accidental loss.

Contributions should be legibly written, and only on one side of each leaf.

THE

ENGLISHWOMAN'S REVIEW.

(NEW SERIES.)

No. XLIV.—December 15th, 1876.

Art. I.—THE PASSING YEAR.

THE greatest revolutions generally take place silently. It is with the body politic as with the human body—growth is not marked by any sudden change, but by the gradual evolution and increase of atoms. Now and then the political world is startled by a sudden catastrophe, but the moral and social changes which affect the well-being of the community are usually slow in action, and as imperceptible in their progress as the change of winter into summer—

> The mills of God grind slowly,
> But they grind exceeding small.

We must not be disappointed, therefore, if, in enumerating the gains of the woman's cause in the past year, we do not find so much manifest progress as was made in 1875. Could we only transport ourselves in thought ten years back, we should be amazed at the wonderful progress which has been made in the education of girls, in the opening of fresh employments to women, the extension of their local franchises, their election to public offices of usefulness and the awakened lives of an untold multitude of women.

The best gift women have received from 1876 has been the satisfactory conclusion of the long struggle to obtain a medical education and diploma in the British

I

Isles. After the close of this year, a woman will no
longer be obliged to expatriate herself in order to
obtain recognition of her medical acquirements, nor
suffer the immense disadvantage of pursuing her studies
and sustaining her examination in a foreign language.
This act of justice was first accomplished when, late in
this summer, the House of Commons passed Mr. Russell
Gurney's bill to enable British Universities to admit
women to degrees. The well known sympathy of some
leading Irish Physicians induced women to look to that
country for help. A deputation accordingly presented
memorials, praying for admission, to the Council of the
King's and Queen's College of Physicans in Dublin, and
to the Senate of the Queen's University, both these influential bodies granted the application. The constitution of the Queen's University requires that a student,
however good his previous preparation, shall attend
medical or arts classes, for at least one session, at one
of the Queen's Colleges (of which there are three: Belfast, Cork and Galway.) The only College yet asked
to make the needful arrangements for the lady students
is not quite ready to do so, on such short notice; but
this is only a question of time. The King's and Queen's
College of Physicians will admit to their examinations
anyone sufficiently instructed in an authorised medical
school, and many young ladies, who have been studying abroad, are now preparing themselves to take
advantage of the recent action of the Council, in opening
their examinations and granting a licence. The example
so generously given must shortly be followed in
England and Scotland, and though much difficulty
and prejudice may still remain, they cannot be considered insuperable by the brave women who have
surmounted so much harder obstacles.

The late School Board elections have again shown
how easy it is for women to record their votes under
the ballot system. It seems almost needless to say that no
disturbance occurred at the polls which could alarm
even an old or invalid woman. Six, or even three
years ago, the question invariably addressed to a lady
householder on the day of election was, "Are you
going to vote?" It is now, "Whom shall you vote

for?" There is a world of progress between the two questions.

In education there has also been considerable progress. The establishment of the Teachers' Training Association by the Women's Education Union, marks a new era in the better comprehension of methods of tuition. The establishment of a High School for Girls at Brighton by the Company, and of the Endowed Girls' School at Leeds, offer additional advantages to those large centres of population: while the admission of women as students into the Manchester New College, and the establishment of scholarships for them in Bristol University College, will bring the means of higher culture within the reach of many hitherto deprived of it.

Among the new professional employments opened to women we may record the establishment, in Bayswater, of the first completely qualified woman pharmaceutist and chemist. Other women are now studying the science. It is the first step in these instances which is difficult: imitation afterwards becomes easy. The office for training women to trace plans for engineers and architects, in Westminster, was also opened this year—though it had long previously been prepared for. The Women's Printing Company was started, and new Benefit Societies have been formed under the auspices of the Provident and Protection League.

Another direct gain has been the extension of the term for which pauper children may be boarded out in Ireland: formerly they were compelled to return to the workhouse at so early an age that the advantages of the system were lost. This extension of age was obtained through the passing of Mr. O'Shaughnessy's bill.

We ought also to count on the side of positive gain those cases where evil legislation has been frustrated or postponed. Amongst these we may instance the successful resistance opposed by Mr. P. A. Taylor and Sir E. Watkin to the Offences against the Person Bill, which, under a misleading title, was an Infanticide Bill, calculated to make women accountable for actions which might be committed while labouring under temporary insanity. The postponement also, for another year, of any legislation extending to the Factory Acts, re-asserts the principle that adult women ought to be as free to contract or to labour as adult men.

It would be impossible to close any review of the year without reference to the war rumours with which the air is still oppressed. It may be that the new year will see us drawn into the terrors of a protracted struggle, though we may rather hope that arbitration will interpose to secure peace—not that peace which is "no peace, but gagged despair and inarticulate wrong—" but liberty to an oppressed people. During the last few months Englishwomen's hearts have pulsated with Englishmen's hearts in detestation of the brutalities practised by the Ottoman, and so long condoned by our own Government. Three months ago a memorial signed by 45,000 women went up to the Queen, praying for her interference, and many Englishwomen have gone to the East, either to nurse the wounded, or to distribute food and clothing to the starving fugitives. Whatever may be the issue of the present difficulty, we firmly believe that, if woman has a public mission distinct from man, it is that of a peacemaker, and that, when women shall have a fair share in the national representation, and a voice in the national councils, international arbitration will be more frequently resorted to, and the last deadly appeal to arms be only made after all other means have failed.

ART. II.—WANTED: MORE WOMEN.

"AN ounce of mother is worth a pound of clergy," says an old Spanish proverb, and we would add without derogation to organized civilisation, it is worth an hundred-weight of Boards, Committees, and Police. Our English social economy teems with elaborately arranged systems, but they want the vitalising warmth of woman's work, and still more, of woman's control—the *mother* influence in short, without which a society, as well as a family, grows up unharmonised and depressed.

The need of womanly influence is beginning to be felt by School Board electors. The four ladies whom London has lately elected and the other ladies returned in other towns of England, have been all chosen with the distinct feeling that when girls have to be educated and women teachers employed, the co-operation of women is absolutely essential. Still, the number of women in the School Boards, taking England and Scotland together, is ludicrously small compared with the number of female children to be educated, considering also that a large number of the boys are mere infants, and that in other cases, it is the mothers, more than the fathers of the children, whose comfort is interfered with, and who have to attend before the Divisional Committees for carrying out the bye-laws or compulsion. Women on the Boards can sympathise with domestic difficulties—of parting with an eldest girl, for instance— and suggest ways of remedying them. Much of the unpopularity of the School Boards, as evidenced in police courts, might have been prevented if the members could have given more time to visiting the parents, persuading instead of forcing them to educate their children, a work for which women are far more adapted than men. Again, more than half the teachers are women, and women on the Board can understand their difficulties. Valuable as all the work was which Miss Chessar did for the Board, there was perhaps none more useful than her giving up one afternoon in every week to teachers who came to her for advice. But on a Board of fifty members there are still only four women—while other towns have yet a smaller infusion of feminine influence—more women are wanted before anything like fairness can be obtained.

More women are wanted for the management of workhouses, as, with few exceptions, the inmates are aged, sick, or children. The arrangements for their comfort are really on a sufficiently liberal scale, as we have been assured by many Poor Law guardians, but yet there is a very prevalent sense of discomfort and unhappiness: a little infusion of motherliness in the

management of these institutions might go a long way
to make them what they are intended to be, " homes "
for the destitute.   Let us fancy what the discomfort of
a house would be if left to masculine administration, if
there were five or six children in the nursery, and one
or two invalids or aged parents to look after. Confusion
and discomfort and worse would be the consequence,
and these same defects which occur in parochial
management would stand a chance of being remedied
if there were one or two women on every Board of
guardians.   Economy in details of expenditure is essentially a feminine talent, and would in this case prove an
argument not likely to be thrown away upon ratepayers.
As an instance of feminine care for little comforts, we
may cite Lady Burdett Coutts' recent present of
spectacles to the old people of St. Pancras Workhouse.
She offered to give them to all well-deserving of the
kindness, and sent an optician to the workhouse to fit
her gift to the sight of each one.   If there were women
on the Boards of guardians similar acts of kindness and
thoughtfulness towards the aged would be more likely
to be general.   Yet there is only one woman guardian
of the poor in London.   In this office, emphatically,
more women are wanted.

The need for women comes before us specially in reading the report of a conference which took place some
months ago at Sir C. Trevelyan's house on the boarding out of young pauper children. Mrs. Senior said
of the children in workhouse schools that "they want
mothering," and the advantages of the boarding-out
system appear to be the substitution of family life,
for that collective life of the schools, which is so unfavourable to the development of childhood.   But the
very key-note of the well-working of the system is the
close habitual and indefatigable supervision which can
be given by no one so well as by a Committee of Ladies.
Sir C. Trevelyan said: " In these days when women's
work is so much discussed, can there be a work more
truly beneficent, more entirely feminine than this to
engage the energies of the wives and daughters of
England? If our ladies throughout the country, with
the aid of their husbands and brothers would take the

matter in hand in their respective unions, this would in itself be the highest safeguard." Again, Col. Freemantle said : " To any lady who undertook the task of watching over the children as Ladies' Committees are doing, it would be a great good by enlisting her in a most interesting work ;" and a clergyman wrote : " It is one of the blessings that must arise out of this system that it brings the women of our working classes into an active, self-denying work of this nature." Thus, whether it be for the well-being of the children, or for the cultivation of a higher and more noble life among women themselves, it is desirable that ladies should come forward to take upon themselves social burthens, instead of selfishly limiting themselves to the *dolce far niente* of family life.

When women do once fairly undertake the work of organisation they can compete with anything men have done in the annals of charity. Before Mrs. Chisholm took charge of female emigrants, there was no safety or comfort for any self-dependent woman in attempting a new life on colonial territory. Before Miss Rye and Miss Macpherson took out orphan children from English workhouses to Canadian homes, no one had thought of the possibility of systematised juvenile emigration. The *Maison Mère* of the Sisters of Charity of St. Vincent de Paul at Paris sends out five hundred trained women as nurses every year to all parts of the world. The other day there was published in Philadelphia a catalogue of the Charities conducted by women in all parts of the civilised world. This list which, however, was far from complete, contained 676 charitable and reformatory institutions in America, 140 from Great Britain, 33 in Germany, 37 in Russia, 31 in Denmark, and 5 in Italy. It includes hospitals, crèches, reformatories, training schools for nurses, for domestic service, and various industries ; evening reading rooms, cheap dining rooms, free soup kitchens, protection of animals and children, employment societies, refuges, and homes of all kinds. The Women's Co-operative Association in Prussia* is another instance of the organising faculty of women,

---

* See a full account in p. 397.

and the benefit that would accrue to society by their more general adoption of public duties.

A great American moralist said twenty years ago of the "Public Function of Woman" that "Woman is to correct man's taste, mend his morals, excite his affections, inspire his religious faculties. Man is to quicken her intellect, to help her will, translate her sentiments to ideas, and enact them into righteous laws. Man's moral action at best is only a sort of general human providence aiming at the welfare of a part, and satisfied with 'achieving the greatest good of the greatest number.' Woman's moral action is more like a special human providence, acting without general rules, but caring for each particular case. We need both of these, the general and the special, to make a total human providence."

Yes, we want both men and women to carry on the public work of the world: the State, which is only an aggregate of families can no more do with only masculine government than can an individual family. The household which is only ruled over by women wants breadth of interest and activity; the household which is only ruled over by men wants tenderness and consideration for diversities of temperament and powers. So it is with the State: the laws made by men, be they ever so good, cannot be made to fit comfortably a world which contains so many sick, poor, and little ones, without the help of women's insight and adaptability to special requirements. A regimental outfitter makes his coats after one size and pattern; a dressmaker fits and shapes her garment to suit individual curves. There is something of this difference in men and women's work. We need more women, not only on the School Boards, but on Workhouse Committees, in jails, on Boards of Health and Town Councils, on juries, in science, and in law. When we hear it said there is a redundancy of women in England, it means of women who cannot set their hands and brains to any particular work, who are the drones of society: there is not a redundancy, but a scarcity of women who will put aside the comfort and ease of private life for the public responsibility of being useful. Fortunately, the number

is increasing of those who recognise that there is more
womanliness in being "motherly" to the sick, ignorant,
and suffering, wherever they can be found, than in
remaining silent, and unoccupied within the four walls
of a house, be it never so secluded and comfortable.

ART. III.—FOURTH AMERICAN WOMEN'S CONGRESS.

THE greatest of modern Italians has said in enforcing
the necessity of teaching men their *duties* rather than
their *rights*, "We must convince men that they are all
sons of one sole God, and bound to fulfil and execute
one sole law here on earth; that each of them is bound
to live, not for himself but for others; that the aim of
existence is not to be more or less happy, but to make
themselves and others more virtuous; that to struggle
against injustice and error, wherever they exist, in the
name and for the benefit of their brothers is not only
a *right* but a duty—a duty which may not be neglected
without sin, the duty of their whole life."

We consider it a sign of the immense progress which
the movement for the "rights" of women has achieved
of late years in the United States, that the papers read
at the Women's Congress lately held in Philadelphia
were mainly occupied with the duties of women. It was
was necessary in the beginning of the struggle, when all
claim to independence of thought, of education, and of
action was denied to speak of the inherent right of women to be free agents in these respects, as men are; but
when a foothold has been won, when concessions have
been made, and the question of women's equality with
men legally, educationally, and professionally is steadily
gaining ground, it is necessary to consider how women
may be trained to use the power which will shortly be
in their hands for the benefit, not of themselves only,
but of the whole world; in short, it is time to speak of

women's duties rather than of their rights.   This
higher standard of thought was adopted by the ladies
who lately met in Congress at Philadelphia; the moral
elevation of women, the necessity for hard work,
thorough training, self-sacrifice, wider interests in order
that they may do their appointed work in the world
successfully, was thoroughly entered into.   The influence of the tone of thought of these papers will tell
for good; they encourage us in the belief that, as soon
as women obtain their equal share with men in social
and active life, a deeper and more earnest love of right,
for the sake of right, will be infused into the work of the
world.

Among the papers read was one by Miss (Rev.)
Georgiana Watson upon the present defective system
of the education of women.   She advocated greater
attention being paid to the cultivation of the reasoning
powers instead of merely exercising the memory for the
retention of words.   "Women," she said, "have not
been taught to think, but taught to think as they are
taught.   They are unfitted by their training, and therefore, to a great extent, unable to form an opinion upon
a question on its own merits, where authority, custom,
or usage is involved—their whole education having
tended to enforce and strengthen these.   A free intellectual life cannot be maintained under bondage to
authority; its despotism destroys such life, and its only
legitimate supremacy is in a system of education intended to make material for the control of priests and
demagogues.   There are several questions now in agitation; for example, the secularization of our public
schools, and the taxation of church property, upon
which, it is not too much to say, that the great majority
of women are not only incompetent to form an opinion
from ignorance of the facts, but they would inevitably
be influenced to vote in the negative on them by the
skilful use of sentimental and semi-religious rhetoric.

"It is owing to these defects, especially of method and
conditions, that our popular education is so barren of
results.   We are surprised that with all our education
we have no higher tone of society—that women are so
frivolous in their aims—that they make the claim to

social distinction rest on the possession of wealth, and
its accessories, dress, jewels, and equipage; that their
intellectual life asks only the sensation novel, alternated
with study of dress and watering-place gossip, with
which they fill what a distinguished speaker once
described as the "lumber-room and empty attic of a
fashionable woman's part, which she calls her mind."
We wonder at the increase of purely mercenary
marriages, at hearing our young girls measure the good
fortune of their companions who marry by the wealth
of the husband won. Our education is at fault; it is a
mass of words, with no living power, intellectual or
moral. * * * The inability of women to appreciate
the need and the nature of political and social reform is
a hindrance to reform in every country that engages in
it; that this inability is the result of historic and philosophic ignorance and of subservience to authority, is
not hard to demonstrate."

Miss Watson also urges the more frequent introduction
of political economy into the curriculum of girls' schools.
"I shall mention but one subject which is still generally
omitted from the course of academic study. Political
economy has not been made part of the instruction of
women, indeed, though of the greatest practical importance, it is limited to collegiate instruction even for
men—women no less than men need an acquaintance
with its principles. With a large class of expenditures
women have, by our social usage, much more to do
than men. Women are largely consumers of income,
not producers; the employment of servants, the purchase
of food and clothing, the use of the work of the artizan
in household decoration and utensils, are mostly under
their control. Their action must therefore have a
marked effect on the demand and supply in these
departments, and by the interlinking of production, all
that is bought and sold will be sensibly affected. Is it
not important then that they should have some knowledge of the laws of supply and demand, of value, of
wages, and the elementary principles of finance?
The ignorance of educated women was fairly represented by a lady of decided literary culture, who, hearing the general complaint of the scarcity of money, said

naïvely, 'Well, John, if there is not money enough in
the country why don't they make some more?' Those
who have made the experiment of teaching this science
to women, using the method of discussion and investigation, have found them competent to grasp and apply
its principles.

Miss MITCHELL, President of the Association, and
Professor of Astronomy at Vassar College, in an essay
on the "Need of Women in Science," urges upon young
women a course of solid scientific study in some one
direction for two reasons. 1st. The needs of science.
2nd. Their own needs.

"1st. The needs of science: For the very reason that a
woman's methods are different from those of a man, are
women needed in scientific work. All her nice perceptions of minute details, all her delicate observation
of colour, of form, of shape, of change, and her
capability of patient routine would be of immense value
in the collection of scientific facts. When I see a
woman put an exquisitely fine needle at exactly the
same distance from the last stitch which that last stitch
was from its predecessor, I think what a capacity she
has for an astronomical observer; unknowingly, she is
using a micrometer—unconsciously she is graduating
circles. Persons who are in charge of the scientific
departments of colleges are always mourning over the
scarcity of trained assistants. The directors of observatories and museums not infrequently do an enormous
amount of routine work which they would gladly
relinquish; their time and strength are wasted on labour
which students could do equally well, if students could
be found who would be ready to make science a life
work.

"Women are needed, too, as lecturers in schools; it
needs only the supply, and the demand will come.
Persons who are known to be in a line of scientific
work, are continually besieged with applications to give
lectures, to write short articles for periodicals, to translate foreign works. Such lectures and such articles
would do little directly for the advance, but much indirectly in forming taste and arousing interest.

"I am far from the intention of encouraging young

women to scientific study on account of its outward
utility ; at best its wages to-day are little above those
of manual labour, and were they those of royal revenues,
I should still raise the objection that it is an ignoble
following of nature, which looks for gain. But, for
themselves, for young women who have a love of nature
and a longing to study her laws, how shall the taste be
developed and how shall they be encouraged ? * * *
The laws of nature are not discovered by accident—
theories do not come by chance, even to the greatest
minds ; they are not born of the hurry and worry of
daily toil; they are diligently sought, they are patiently
waited for, they are received with cautious reserve,
they are accepted with reverence and awe. And until
able women have given their lives to investigation, it is
idle to discuss the question of their capacity for original
work."

Mrs. CHURCHILL read an address on Industrial Education. She took occasion to express regret at the fact
that the true cause of Woman's Rights is so materially
injured by narrow-minded women who push themselves
or are pushed into positions of leadership, and bring
merited ridicule on themselves and unjust contempt on
the cause they misrepresent by their denunciations of
men. Mrs. Churchill was of opinion that woman can
only lift herself out of helplessness by labour, shrinking
from entrance into no honest avocation that her physical and mental abilities fit her for. She thought industrial schools offered a powerful means for the elevation
of women into positions of strength and independence.

ELIZA SPROAT TURNER contributed an article on
" Woman's Clubs," urging that clubs would be a valuable help to hundreds of women, not only for the
physical comforts of rest and refreshment but for the
facilities they offer for reading newspapers and magazines, for the certainty of meeting congenial acquaintances, for making appointments, and for co-operation
in matters of mutual interest, "I have said," she continues,
" a club should be instituted primarily for convenience ;
but, in addition, the possibilities for mutual counsel, for
co-operation, for the furtherance of all our women's
projects, seem to me worthy of very serious consider-

ation. Scattered, we do so little; united, we become, as has been proved, a power. If we could succeed in establishing a centre to which would gravitate intellectual, gifted, and enterprising women, in the expectation of meeting other such, we should gain the advantage which men esteem so highly; namely, the mental stimulus that comes from contact with active and varying minds   And we should be helped to correct the mental narrowness which is one of the faults of our sex."

Mrs. E. B. DUFFEY, of New Jersey, in an article on " Women in Literature," urges a more solid training and harder work. She said that many women believed they could enter a literary career even if they had no experience, no study, no opportunities for self-improvement. Careful thought and hard work were as necessary to form a literary woman as a literary man ; and a woman who adopted literature as a profession must not expect to find it play; a professional writer leads a life of *bonâ fide* drudgery. Only amateur writers possess the inestimable privilege of waiting till they are inspired before they begin to write ; the professional writer must compel the inspiration or write without it. On the subject of " Want of Time," so frequently urged by women as a reason for not undertaking serious study, she said : " Who read one-half, if not three-fourths, of the hundreds of thousands of sensational newspapers which are weekly published in this country—immense sheets of finely-printed matter, which must require noticeable time for their perusal? Women. Who flock to public libraries as soon as a flimsy, sensational English novel is re-published in this country, and make such demands for it that a large number of copies cannot supply their wants? Women. Who buy the editions of fourth-rate stories that are constantly issued from the American press, the very reading of which vitiates the taste and the perceptions concerning a correct literature? Women—at least two-thirds of them, women! But women tell us that they have no time for Huxley, or Darwin, or Tyndall, or Herbert Spencer, or Agassiz, or Max Muller, or Froude, or Washington Irving, or Bancroft, or Gibbon; no care

for Ruskin; no appreciation of George Eliot or Anthony
Trollope; while they turn with undisguised disgust
from theologians, ancient and modern, orthodox or
heterodox.   Alas! women think they have no time for
anything; but if they would devote the same time to
solid, profitable reading—which should enlarge their
views of life, and give them grander ideas of science, of
nature, and of God—which they now give to the lightest
literature, they might every one of them become at
least comparatively wise.   An hour a day—and there
is scarcely a woman in the world who cannot, on an
average, secure at least that much time to herself—
would, in ten years, turn an ignorant woman into a
wise one, provided the capacity for wisdom is there.   If
a woman has no taste for this kind of reading, that is
quite another matter.   She may let it alone; but let her
drop the pen also.

One of the most interesting papers, however, was a
report of the Committee on Reform, which was read by
Ellen S. MITCHELL.   The number of charitable institutions founded and presided over by women in the
United States is astonishing.

The Committee have distributed during the past year
the following circular, which has been productive of
good :—

To secure the best practical results from reformatory measures
organized efforts among women is most earnestly desired.   Will you
aid in the endeavour to secure this by sending back this circular with
its questions answered?

1. Is there a Reform School for girls in your State?

2. In your community are there institutions established by women,
and in their charge, for the protection and reclamation of the class
generally called "Magdalens"?

3. Are there Prison Associations of women for the improvement
of the condition of female prisoners while under sentence, and to
take charge of them upon release, for the purpose of affording them
opportunities to obtain an honest livelihood?

4. Are there Children's Aid Societies of women, intended to seek
out the children of vicious parents, and secure for them the instruction and proper training necessary to make them good, honest and
useful citizens?

5. Are there Homes for inebriate women?

6. How far have these organizations justified the theories of their
founders by successful practical results?

Information with regard to existing reforms intended to raise and

advance the condition of women, will be most helpful, and is solicited.
Circulars may be returned to the chairman of the committee. Communications may be addressed to any member of the committee.

ELLEN MITCHELL,
922 Wabash Ave., Chicago.
CLARA P. BOURLAND,
Peoria, Illinois.
MARY J. STAFFORD BLAKE, M.D.,
16 Boylston Place, Boston.

Among recent institutions on behalf of women the Report mentions :—

"The Magdalen Asylum of San Francisco has added a wing to its building for the accommodation of the class of girls who would fill Reform Schools if such schools were provided by the State. At present there are about fifty girls in the building. They are kept apart from the unfortunate women.

"The Magdalen Asylum, San Francisco, is under the charge of the Sisters of Mercy (Catholic). Of the six hundred women received since its opening, six per cent. only have proved utterly irredeemable.

"The Ingleside Home, Buffalo, New York, is under the charge of ladies entirely, and is for the care and reformation of women. By an act of the Legislature passed May 27, 1875, the Police Justice has discretionary power to send to it with their consent, girls between the ages of fourteen and thirty—to be under the care, custody, and instruction of the managers. This act is designed to benefit those who having taken the first steps in an immoral life would become hardened by contact with vice in workhouse or jail. For the maintenance of these girls one dollar and a half a week is allowed by the county. Its annual report states that the results of this work are encouraging.

"The Woman's Guardian Home, St. Louis, has for its object, 'to protect the unprotected, house the homeless, save the erring, help the tempted and aid destitute women to obtain an honest livelihood,' it is under the charge of women with an advisory committee of men, has cared for eighty-five girls the past year (1875) admitted eighteen babes—six have been born in the Home; has furnished three hundred and ninety-five meals to women seeking employment. The annual report for 1875 concludes with these words : ' As year by year we go on with this work we grow to feel that many reforms which we have recommended as efficacious, such as the better education of girls that they may be self-sustaining, the provision of better homes for working-girls, etc., etc., are merely palliatives; they do not strike at the root of this great evil. We have come to see very clearly that men must come to the rescue; they must accept for themselves the same standard of virtue demanded of women."

Another association productive of much good was the Women's Prison Association in New York, which was incorporated 1845. Thirty years ago a little band of earnest benevolent women formed an association for the amelioration of the condition of female prisoners for the enforcement of prison discipline, and the government of prisons in respect to women, and for their support and encouragement when released. This was the Women's Prison Association, an organisation which was for a time a department of the Men's Prison Association, but which has been for more than twenty years entirely distinct from that, in no way connected with it, or dependent upon it. This institution after various vicissitudes in the struggle for life, and in spite of numerous obstacles, overcome mainly by the faith and persistent devotion of its few friends, has at length found a firm footing. The whole number of women received from 1845 to 1854 was 1,371, making the average per year for ten years 137, the number admitted for 1875 was 377, and sent to service 237. Part of the duty of the Executive Committee is to visit the female departments of various houses of detention and endeavour to save and elevate the women as soon as discharged.

Three useful societies in San Francisco were also mentioned :—The Boys' and Girls' Aid Society, incorporated 1874, has a building containing lodging, bath, reading and assembly rooms, library of more than one thousand volumes, and gymnasium ; it has found homes for forty boys during the past year. The Ladies' Protection and Relief Society, incorporated August 9th, 1854, has a Home in which are about two hundred

K

children—girls between two and fourteen years of age, and boys between three and ten years, are admitted, educated, and cared for till suitable homes can be found for them. This society has a firm hold on the sympathies of San Francisco, and is doing a noble and successful work. The Little Sisters' Infant Shelter, incorporated March 10th, 1874, takes care of the young children of working women during the hours in which the mothers are out at daily labour; it has spacious, pleasant rooms. These three societies are all under the care of women, and have been successful in realising the idea of their founders. The Ladies' Protection and Relief Society, from its greater age, has given time for wider observation of its beneficial results, and very many of the children trained there are now useful and respected members of society.

We must congratulate the ladies of Philadelphia on the able manner in which not only this congress, but other women's meetings which have taken place in their city during the summer and autumn have been arranged.

ART. IV.—EVENTS OF THE MONTH.

SCHOOL BOARD ELECTIONS.

THE London School Board elections have resulted very satisfactorily to the cause of women. Four ladies were candidates, and all were returned, one of them, Mrs. Westlake, being at the head of the poll, and registering more than 20,000 votes. In the first School Board election—now six years ago, only two ladies were elected,—Miss Garrett for Marylebone, and Miss Davies for Greenwich. During the same election Mrs. Wm. Grey failed of being elected for Chelsea by a very small number of votes. This was the first time that women had ever been elected by popular votes to a public position of trust and importance. Three years later, the second School Board election resulted also in placing two women on the Board: that time, Marylebone was the only district which kept true to the principle of having women to manage women teachers and girl pupils. Miss Chessar and Mrs. Cowell were the successful candidates. Chelsea failed to send Mrs. Arthur Arnold, and Westminster was unable to carry Mrs. Wm. Burbury's election. The number of lady members therefore remained the same, miserably disproportionate to the female interests legislated on by the Board.

This year London has done better. Of the four candidates Mrs. Westlake was first in the field, issuing her programme in October. The successful result of the election is due no less to the admirable organisation of her committee than to the qualities of the candidate which so excellently qualify her for the post she now fills. As before stated, she polled 20,231 votes—being more than 2,000 in excess of the next successful candidate on the list. It would be impossible and unnecessary to enumerate the many meetings which were previously held in Marylebone in support of Mrs. Westlake's candidature. At a crowded meeting in St. George's Hall, on November 16, she thus gave her reasons for seeking election. She said:

The electors had shown at two previous elections that they desired the return of women to the School Board. They had shown that, in their opinion, for the training and management of the pupils in the girls' and infants' schools, even for the boys at the tender age at which they are received into the classes, there was no one more suitable to direct and guide than a woman. Among the teachers, too, were women; and they required a woman on the Board who could advise them in their perplexities and be their advocate with the Board. With the very best intentions in the world, men were rather apt to forget the claims of girls. There was an instance of that when, it was proposed to devote smaller Scholarships out of the Lawrence Fund to girls than those given to boys. But Miss Chessar (their own representative) was on the Board to point out that the secondary schools for girls are even more expensive than those for boys, and the Exhibitions were made equal in amount. In the battle of systems and creeds men were apt to fight for ideas which passed harmlessly over the heads of children. Women would think first of the wants of the child. During the early days of the first Board, there was a question as to the establishment of a school in that district. One gentleman said the school was too near to one in which he was interested, and others made other objections. But the site would have been selected had not Mrs. Garrett-Anderson (then Miss Garrett) shown the Board that the spot where they intended to place their school was by the side of a great thoroughfare which the children would have to cross on their way to school, so that they might be disposed of in a way not contemplated by the Education Act. Then there were the compulsory clauses. The law would appear less harsh to the mothers who were summoned for not sending their children to school if they found upon the Committee women, who could enter into their difficulties. They would see that they found sympathy, and were not drily told,—"We are here to carry out the law." It was after all on the mothers that depended the success of the best system of education, for they could make or mar any plan. They could cause endless expense in compulsion, they could reduce the grant by inducing failure in attendance and an absence of the disposition to learn. In fact, a father recently complained to a magistrate that he was fined for not sending a child to school, although the mother was the true cause of non-attendance, and when he beat her he was fined again. On the point of economy the presence of ladies at the Board, their custom at looking at details would lead to the checking of waste. It was in details that economy could be practised alone, for the great principles would not be altered. The matter of compulsion, the way of dealing with the religious question, must be taken to have been settled. The duties of the Board are now mainly administrative ; the management of schools, the building of new schools from time to time as the want arose, the purchasing of sites—all these were details in which the co-operation of women might be useful. She had had the advantage of addressing the electors of the Paddington Division in a meeting at which all the candidates were present ; and one gentleman was kind enough to say he should support her, because she was a lady and would look after the needlework. She would indeed do her best, if she were elected, to look after the sewing. Like all housekeepers, she knew and suffered from the bad work which was called sewing, the botching and mending which went under the name of darning. But she did not appeal to their suffrages merely as a woman * * * *

Miss Helen Taylor came third on the list of the Southwark candidates; she polled 6,081 votes—the highest being 6,568. She supports the general policy of the Board, but personally is in favour of secular, compulsory, and gratuitous education; her reason for desiring election was to promote the efficient instruction of girls. The meetings held in Southwark in support of her candidature, and that of the Rev. Mr. Sinclair were numerous and enthusiastic. Miss Taylor is an accomplished speaker and writer, and London may congratulate itself on having the step-daughter of John Stuart Mill on its Educational Council.

Miss Florence Fenwick Miller was the third lady candidate who came forward, and she now stands fourth on the list of Hackney members, having polled 15,011 votes. Miss Miller has been known for some years as a popular lecturer on Women's Suffrage, the medical education of women, and other subjects of interest to her sex. She has herself received a medical education. At the meetings which were held in Hackney in support of her candidature she explained that " one of her reasons for desiring a seat at the Board was that, as a woman, she necessarily had a special knowledge of what was required for the education of girls. She approved of Bible reading in schools, and on the subject of economy she thought that, although there was a general feeling adverse to the expense which had been incurred, it had not been excessive. Women, she maintained, were needed on every School Board in the country, because more than half the children who had to be educated were girls." When the result of the poll was made known, Miss Miller was warmly congratulated upon her success.

Mrs. Elizabeth Surr, who is fourth on the list of the five Finsbury members, having polled 13,098 votes, is known as the author of several children's books—" Our Children's Pets," " Sea Birds," and other works. So far as we know this is the first public work she has been engaged in. Mrs. Surr came forward on the ground that the education of girls required women's guidance and care; she is in favour of giving sound secular teaching and unsectarian Bible instruction. At one of the meetings held in support of her candidature, in Myddleton Hall, her chairman, Mr. W. T. Paton, said he was no advocate of what were termed "Women's Rights" (we wonder what this bugbear of "women's rights" is, if the election of women on the most important of local Boards be not part of it), but he thought the Legislature had wisely determined that ladies should be eligible to assist in the management of public schools, in which there must be a vast number of girls. As to the remark that woman's place was at home, that was the very sentiment which Mrs. Surr wanted to help to carry out in the Board schools. The resolution passed at that meeting practically pledges the Finsbury voters, always in future to have one of their members a woman. " Inasmuch," it said, " as there are more girls

than boys in attendance at the London Board schools,
and a larger number of female than male teachers are
employed, many questions—educational, social, and
domestic—must constantly arise which can only be
dealt with suitably by ladies, this meeting, therefore
pledges itself to use every effort to secure the return at
the coming election of a lady candidate for Finsbury."
Mrs. Surr has received everywhere in Finsbury a de-
servedly hearty reception, and from her able, clever
and thoughtful speeches, it is predicted that she will be,
a most useful member of the Board.

BRIGHTON.—Miss Ricketts has again been re-elected
on the Brighton School Board.

BIRMINGHAM.—By an error in last month's edition, it
was announced that Miss Sturge was a member of the
new Birmingham School Board. Miss Sturge did not
seek re-election.

NATIONAL UNION FOR IMPROVING THE EDUCATION OF WOMEN OF ALL CLASSES.

PROCEEDINGS OF THE CENTRAL COMMITTEE.

Teachers' Training and Registration Society.— The
Teachers' Training Committee of the Union was constituted on the 12th of July, the Provisional Committee
of the proposed Teachers' Training and Registration
Society. The Committee at present consists of the
following members :—

Provisional Committee—Rev. E. A. Abbott, D.D., Miss
Buss, Miss Chessar, Captain Douglas Galton, C.B., Mrs.
William Grey, Miss Gurney, Mrs. Hertz, Rev. W. Jowitt,
M.A., C. H. Lake, B.A. (Lond.), J. M. D. Meiklejohn, C.
Kegan Paul, Rev. Mark Pattison, B.D., Rev. R. H. Quick,
M.A., Rev. Dr. Rigg, Miss Shirreff, R. N. Shore, James
Stuart, M.A., and the following persons have become
Vice-presidents of the Society :—The Dowager Lady
Stanley of Alderley, Rev. Dr. Montague Butler, Right
Hon. W. E. Forster, Professor Liveing, and Sir John
Lubbock. The Committee has been engaged since its
formation in drawing up the Memorandum and Articles
of Association of the Society. These being now defi-
nitely settled, application has been made for a license of
the Board of Trade, which it is expected will be granted

immediately, and the Society will then issue its prospectus to the public.

Scholarships—The Women's Education Union Scholarship, given at the Edinburgh University Examinations this year, was awarded to Miss Dora C. E. Clark, who continues her studies in the classes of the Edinburgh Ladies' Educational Association.

That given at the Queen's University (Ireland) Examination, was awarded to Miss M. Nicholl, who continues her studies in the classes of the Ladies' Collegiate School, Belfast.

Funds are now much wanted to supply the amount necessary for Scholarships. This year five, of the value of £25 each, were given by the Union, and from correspondence the Union is convinced that much good has been done by this means. Donors of Scholarships, donations and subscriptions towards forming Scholarships, will be gladly received by Miss Brough, Secretary, 112, Brompton Road, London.

The City Companies.—The Cloth-workers' Company has sent a subscription of £10 10s. to the funds of the Union. *Women's Education Journal.*

CAMBRIDGE HIGHER LOCAL EXAMINATIONS.—The number of candidates who presented themselves for mathematics was eleven, of whom nine were women and two men. Of these, all were examined in Euclid and algebra, 9 in trigonometry, 4 in conic sections, 9 in statics, 1 in astronomy, and 4 in dynamics.—*Times.* Experience goes far to prove that mathematics instead of being the study most uncongenial to the feminine mind, as was formerly supposed, is one which women select by preference, and in which they may be expected to excel.

MIDDLE SCHOOL FOR GIRLS AT EXETER.—Pursuant to a scheme framed by the endowed Schools Commissioners for the management of the Exeter episcopal schools, the govenors (of which body the Bishop of Exeter is chairman) will open a new middle school for girls next January in buildings in the centre of the city. The scheme of secular instruction will comprise the usual subjects of elementary education—history, geography, English, the elements of mathematics and natural science, French or Latin, or both, drawing, vocal music, household management, the laws of health, and needlework. The religious instruction will be in accordance with the doctrines of the Church of England. Provision is made, however, for the exemption of any scholar from receiving religious instruction whose parent or guardian shall require such exemption by notice in writing addressed to the head mistress. The admission fee is 5s. and the tuition fee £3 a year, payable quarterly in advance. Exhibitions are attached to the school, carrying the advantage of free education and other privileges. The examination for admission will be graduated according to the age of the candidate, who will be admitted as young as seven years of age. There will be an annual examination of the scholars by examiners appointed by the governors. The new school is likely to be very popular. We understand that, subject to the approval of the Charity Commissioners, Lady Hotham, Mrs. Temple, and Mrs. H. S. Ellis, have been appointed co-operative governors of Maynard's Girls' School.

A PLEA FOR GIRLS.

Under the above title the *Daily News* published an eloquent appeal from Mrs. Wm. Grey, on behalf of scholarships for girls :—

"In your article to-day on the report of the Committee of the London School Board on the endowments of the City of London, you commend as one of the best uses that could be made of such of them as were specially intended for the poor, the creation of scholarships which would enable poor boys to rise from the elementary to the higher grade schools, the scholarships being of sufficient amount not only to cover the tuition fees, but enable the scholar to live during the time he was continuing his education. Will you let me remind your readers that there exist poor girls as well as poor boys to whom similar scholarships would be no less a boon than to their brothers, and that the ultimate benefit to the public from this disposal of the funds might be equally great ? It is notorious that one of the great obstacles to improving the quality of teaching in our elementary schools arises from the miserably low standard of education among the pupil teachers. How could such scholarships as those I have mentioned be better employed than in providing the abler pupils of both sexes equally with the means of carrying on their education to a higher standard ; and if some of the girls, as well as the boys, should be able and willing to rise higher still on the educational ladder, why should their sex be made a reason for denying them the use of the ladder? In any redistribution of educational endowments girls might put in some claim on the ground that much that was intended by the founders to be shared by them has been monopolised entirely by boys, and that at the best they have but the crumbs which fall from the boys' table—witness the fact stated in the report of the endowed schools Commissioners, that the annual revenue of school endowment for boys amounted to £177,000 a year; that for girls to something under £3,000. One would suppose that girls were provided for by the operation of some law of nature, so completely are they ignored in most schemes for the education or improvement of the young of any class. The other day there was a great meeting at the Mansion House, for the purpose of founding institutions for giving to boys between 13 and 18, working for their livelihood in the day-time, places of instruction and wholesome amusement in the evening. Now, although the fact was passed over at the meeting, many such institutions for boys exist already in London, and are doing an excellent work. But why did no one suggest that similar institutions would be equally good for girls of the same age, thousands of whom are earning their bread like their brothers by their daily labour away from home, if they have any home— girls whose temptations are far more dangerous, and whose fall, if they do fall, is irretrievable? Noble efforts are made for women when they have fallen. Would it not be better to try and prevent them from falling—to bring them during the perilous passage from childhood to womanhood under the nightly influence of good and refined women, who would do for them what good and refined men are doing for their brothers, and surround them with that best of safeguards, the belief that they are cared for by those better and higher than themselves, to whom their well-doing will be a joy, their ill-doing a grief? If the interest of the poor girls themselves are not sufficiently worthy of consideration, let it be remembered that they are in the end inextricably bound up with those of the boys; for never shall we succeed in permanently and thoroughly improving the men of a class or nation, unless we raise the women to an equal level. Nature, in making women physically the weaker sex, gave them the superior force of attraction; and where the woman stands, be it high or low, thither in the end she draws the man."

KINDERGARTENS.

THE FRÖBEL SOCIETY.—The second annual meeting was held on the evening of December 5th, in the theatre of the Society of Arts. After some preliminary proceedings, Mrs. W. Grey, who presided, read an address explanatory of the objects and history of the society. The main object was, she said, to introduce and make general in England the kindergarten system of education, of which Fröbel had been the inventor. The society as yet numbered only 150 members, but she had a firm faith that in due time its objects would be generally recognised and accepted. There were already many kindergartens in England, but not in all equally were Fröbel's principles worked out. The worst kindergarten was, however, a vast improvement on the old system of education. But in Fröbel's kindergarten the child was dealt with as being the father of the man, and the mind was prepared for the great intellectual battle of life. The first principle of Fröbel was to present to the child the thing instead of the word, which was its verbal symbol, and which could convey no solid practical idea to the child's mind. The lecturer proceeded to give the details of the system, beginning with the wooden ball exercise, in which any peculiarities of substance and motion as regarded the ball were made manifest to the observation of the child. The sphere followed next, and the third lesson was given on a cube composed of eight smaller cubes, upon which the child, aged between three and seven, was taught the elementary principles of geometry and arithmetic. Such lessons could not, however, be properly given by an untrained teacher. Mrs. Grey proceeded to compare the kindergarten with the ordinary school system, and concluded by strongly recommending the principles of Fröbel to the serious attention of all the teachers of children, at the same time stating the means by which the society sought to train suitable teachers by examinations conducted by Mdme. Du Portugal and Miss Chessar.

BRIGHTON KINDERGARTEN.—Classes for children and adults will be held on and after January 15th, morning and afternoon respectively, by Miss Ridley at the kindergarten, 29, Duke-street, Brighton. A teacher's class, in a course of ten lessons, will be held on Monday and Thursday at three o'clock, and a similar class for parents on Tuesday and Friday afternoons.

FRÖBEL SOCIETY FOR THE PROMOTION OF THE KINDERGARTEN SYSTEM.—An examination of students of the kindergarten system will be held in London, July, 1877, conducted by examiners appointed by the committee of the Fröbel Society. Those students who satisfy the examiners will receive first or second class

certificates of their qualification to become kindergarten teachers. No candidate will be admitted to the
examination under the age of eighteen. The examination fee will be £1. Names of candidates should be sent
(with the fees) on or before June 1st, 1877, to Miss E.
A. Manning, honorary secretary of the Fröbel Society,
35, Blomfield road, Maida Hill, W. The fee will be
returned if, through unavoidable circumstances, the
candidate cannot present herself for examination. Candidates will be expected to produce a certificate of
having passed some recognised public examination in
English subjects. For those who cannot produce such
certificates, a preliminary examination will be held in
the following subjects *this year only:*—Arithmetic (to
end of decimals), physical geography, English history,
English composition. The candidates will be examined
in the theory of education, theory of Fröbel's kindergarten system, practical knowledge of the occupations,
kindergarten games, music, art of relating stories,
elements of geometry, elements of science, and practice
in teaching. In the latter case candidates will be expected to have had not less than six months' practice in
class teaching of young children, and to give a lesson
in the presence of the examiner.

WOMEN'S PROTECTIVE AND PROVIDENT LEAGUE.—On
November 23rd a conference to consider the recommendations of the Royal Commission on the Factory and
Workshops' Acts concerning new laws affecting women's
work was held at the rooms of the Women's Protective
and Provident League, 31, Little Queen Street, Holborn.
The Hon. Auberon Herbert took the chair, and there
was a good attendance of ladies interested in the question of women's work. The Chairman said the Commissioners proposed to place workshops on the same footing
as factories, the hours in which were $10\frac{1}{2}$ per day and
not to exceed 60 hours per week. Also, when overtime
was worked it was not to be paid for extra in money,
but allowed for in succeeding weeks. For his part he
thought it was far better that the work of women should
be just as free as the work of men, and he could not
understand why women should be reduced to the level
of children. It must be much better for women to be

free and able to work shorter and longer hours as they chose. On the other hand, when there was legislation it prevented women from finding out what was best for them. Mr. Pennington, M.P., having pointed out some of the principal proposals in the reports, Miss Whyte moved: "That this meeting, recognising the usefulness of factory legislation for children, and also for factory operatives generally at a time when, as in the past, the working classes were not organized and were consequently unable to protect their own interests, believes that any legislative interference with the work of adults has become less and less necessary, and would earnestly deprecate a further extension of special restrictions on the work of women." She thought further restrictions would not be wise, and for her part she would have liberty to work extra hours when the employers, from press of work, required it. Women, in her opinion, ought to be allowed to do as they chose, and not be legislated for as a separate class: they might be supposed to know what was best for them. Miss Downing, in seconding the resolution, urged that the restriction of women's work would unduly handicap them in their contest with men. If men could work twelve and fourteen hours a day, and women only ten, of course the employer would prefer men. She was not in favour of long hours; but, at the same time, women should be free to work as they pleased; they had had enough of paternal legislation. Miss Smith, Miss Mitchell, Miss Sinclair, Mrs. Paterson, Mr. Idle, the Rev. J. W. Horsley, and others continued the discussion, in the course of which approval was expressed by more than one speaker of the operation of the Factory Acts in the past. Professor Sheldon Amos summed up the discussion by a review of the report of the Commissioners, in which he urged that the result of legislation was to impose an iron rule which bore more or less hardly upon all women. Why should not women be allowed to vindicate their right to make their own arrangements in the way which would best suit themselves and their children? The resolution was then agreed to. Miss Mears moved and Mr. Wood seconded a resolution condemning the proposals of the Commis-

sioners to abolish payment for overtime, as an instance
of the inevitable tendency of such legislation to con-
travene all sound economic principles, and to return to
the exploded system of the State regulation of wages.
This having been carried, a third resolution was agreed
to, proposing a memorial to the Home Secretary object-
ing to further legislative interference with women's
work.

NATIONAL UNION OF WORKING WOMEN.—The Executive Council met on Nov. 18th, Mr. Alan Greenwell
presiding. The secretary reported an increase of members in the branch, since the soiree was held, and read
numerous letters of inquiry which he had received relative to females joining the union. Mr. Phillips, Brynmaur,
Brecon, writing from the above place, stated that there
was a good opportunity for a branch to be formed in
that locality. The deputation appointed to inquire into
the brushmakers' strike as it affected women's labour,
reported that they found that one of the chief causes of
the strike was that women's work was being done in
Birmingham, and the men struck against it. Messrs.
Greenslade had, since the strike, fitted up a factory for
female labour exclusively. Upwards of 80 women were
now employed by the firm, and were receiving very good
wages. The factory had been visited, and every facility
was given for obtaining information. The report was
considered satisfactory, and the council, whilst expressing
pleasure at the opening of a new sphere of industry for
working women in Bristol, regretted that the men had
not adopted another course than that of striking against
female labour. With regard to one case of assault which
was alleged to have occurred, an unanimous determination was arrived at that should any attempt be made in
future to insult or annoy the female brushmakers, the
council will do its utmost to have the offender prosecuted.
The first benefit to a sick member of 5s. per week was
ordered to be paid promptly. Dr. Eliza Walker-Dunbar
was invited to act as medical attendant to the union.—
Western Daily Press.

WOMEN'S SUFFRAGE.

THE annual meeting of the Manchester National Society

took place on November 29th, in the Town Hall. The Mayor of Manchester presided. A letter was read from Mr. Forsyth expressing his satisfaction that Mr. Jacob Bright had resumed charge of the Bill, and his assurance that he would continue to support the measure to the best of his ability, whenever it should be brought forward in the House of Commons. Mr. Jacob Bright, in the course of his speech, said that it appeared to him that there were just as signal marks of progress in the year that had just closed as could be found in any year in the course of that agitation.

A LARGE meeting was held at Keighley on Nov. 6. On the 14th another meeting was held in Tewkesbury, under the presidency of the Mayor, J. H. Boughton, Esq., and letters were read expressive of sympathy with the movement from J. R. Yorke, Esq., M.P., and Capt. W. E. Price, M.P. Another crowded meeting took place at Failsworth, near Manchester, on Nov. 28th; another at Dover on December 6th, Rowland Rees, Esq., presiding; and another at Deal, on Dec. 7th, when the Rev. W. D. Payne, D.D., took the chair. Meetings were announced to be held in the Victoria Hall, Sunderland, on Dec. 11th, the Mayor, S. Storey, Esq., presiding; in Halifax on Dec. 13th, in the Town Hall, the Mayor taking the chair; and in Southampton on Dec. 14th, Major-Gen. Tryon taking the chair. At all these meetings deputations of ladies have attended.

DEBATING societies have also frequently taken up the subject. In the Scarborough Society the question was put to the vote, and was carried in favour of women's suffrage by a majority of one. The Manchester Grammar School Debating Society and the Manchester Literary Society have also discussed the question.

VIGILANCE ASSOCIATION.

THE annual meeting of the Vigilance Association was held in the office of the Society on December 4th, for the purpose of adopting the Report, and re-electing the Committee for the ensuing year. The Report was read by the Secretary, M. E. Marsden, Esq., and the amount of work done during the past session which it summarised shows fully how important it is for women

that such a society should exist. Through the kindness of the Secretary we have been enabled to reprint
a great portion of it.

The Committee report that they promoted petitions in
favour of Mr. P. A. Taylor's amendments on the Mutiny
Bill, but they have again to regret the rejection of those
amendments. The first amendment was rejected by
199 votes to 82, the second amendment by 195 votes to
80. Their scope and intention were to render
it impossible for a soldier or marine to evade the
obligation to maintain his wife and children. Mr.
Taylor has expressed his intention of renewing his
efforts next session.

OFFENCES AGAINST THE PERSON BILL.—Mr. Charley,
M.P., having introduced a Bill into the House of
Commons, which, although bearing the title of "Offences
against the Person Bill," was in its scope and object
entirely different from the Bill which had previously
borne that title, the Committee promoted petitions
against it. The Bill was almost identical with the
Infanticide Bill of last year, against which vigorous
action had been taken by the Vigilance Association.
Towards the end of the session, and mainly in consequence of the persistent opposition of Mr. P. A. Taylor
and Sir E. Watkin the Bill was withdrawn, and should
it be reintroduced next year, the Committee announce
that they will again take such action as may be necessary to ensure its defeat. In reference to that Bill the
Lancet wrote as follows:—

Under the law as it at present stands cases have occurred in
which justice has miscarried in a marked manner, and in which the
punishment has been in great excess of the offence. The effect of
the above clause will be to make the law still more stringent, and to
render criminal, women who should, in many cases, be held blameless.
It is a well-known fact that the injuries enumerated in the above
clause are almost invariably committed by women *while in a state of
mental alienation*, which may last for some time or be of the most
transient character. Transient as this state may be, however, there
can be no doubt that while it continues women are not responsible
for their actions, and to make mothers answer for and expiate acts
committed under such conditions appears to us cruel and inhuman.
We are glad to find that a committee of ladies has been formed with
a view to draw up and present a petition to the House against the
passing of the Bill. We trust that their efforts will prove successful.

In the course of the debate Mr. P. A. Taylor showed (1)
That the Bill did not, as at first sight it appeared to
do, mitigate the penalty for infanticide—for the capital
character of that offence was specially retained in cases
where murder, wilful or premeditated, were proved.
(2) That it sought, by establishing a lower penalty in
cases where wilful murder could not be clearly brought
home to the unhappy mother, to induce juries to bring
in a verdict of guilty in cases where they would not
otherwise do so.   (3) That it was a fact recognised by
competent medical authority, that women, at other
times sane, were frequently in an absolutely irresponsi-
ble condition of mind during labour, and incapable of
mental self-control.

A BILL with the title of "Homicide Law Amendment
Bill," was introduced into the House of Commons by
Sir Eardley Wilmot, but was found to contain the same
objectionable clause which had previously been embodied
in Mr. Charley's "Offences against the Person Bill."
That clause sought to make a mother responsible for
injuries inflicted on a child during or immediately after
birth. A statement of "Reasons" against the Bill was
prepared, printed, and circulated among members of
Parliament and others. The Committee promoted
petitions and took other action against that clause, and
ultimately the Bill was withdrawn.

EARLY in the year a congress was convened at Bristol
by the National Early Closing League, and the Vigilance
Association made application to the Council for permission to send a delegate, but their permission was
refused. Miss Lilias Ashworth, however, raised a discussion upon the Shop Hours Regulation Bill, and
moved an amendment recognising the fact that the
hours of labour of shop assistants are excessive, but
expressing an opinion that combination and mutual
agreement with their employers would lessen their
hours of labour, while the proposed legislative enactment would have the effect of depriving women of one
mode of employment. That amendment was seconded
by Mr. Mark Whitwell, and supported by the Rev. Dr.
Percival, but was lost by a small majority.

THE Vigilance Association also supported Mr. P. A.

Taylor's motion in the House of Commons for the
abolition of flogging in the Navy (which was defeated
by 120 votes to 62—a defeat which almost amounted
to a victory) and Mr. Russell Gurney's Medical Act
Qualification Bill, which became law. In the early part
of the Parliamentary session, the Committee drafted a
Bill with the object of procuring a legislative declaration
of the parental duty of the proper maintenance of
children, and of furnishing a more effectual remedy for
the breach of it. Lords Redesdale and Shaftesbury
were invited to bring it forward in the House of Lords,
but after consideration declined to do so. Efforts in
this direction are to be continued.

That part of the Report which deals with the Factory
Acts' Commission is yet more interesting.

Your Committee are glad to believe that the action taken by them
in this matter, and especially by bringing working women to give
evidence before the Royal Commission, produced a very considerable
effect upon the minds of the Commissioners, and tended greatly to
modify their Report, which was far less opposed to the principle of
women's right to labour than your Committee had previously had
reason to anticipate.

Your Committee cannot leave this subject without expressing their
deep sense of obligation to the O'Conor Don, M.P., for the great
service rendered by him to the cause of free labour and self-help
among women, by the issue of his separate Report. That Report ably
summarizes the reasons of his dissent from the recommendation to
extend to all the workshops the factory system, which limits the work
of the protected classes, *and especially of adult women*, within a
certain fixed period, as well as to "the proposed local and police
assistance to the inspecting class." The O'Conor Don objects to the
so-called protective restrictions upon women's labour, upon the same
ground as that taken by your Committee, viz., that they "show a
continued disposition to regard adult women as children, and to interfere with their freedom of contract." He shows that the aim of the
workmen who desire further restrictions on women's industry, is not
protective, but oppressive, and points out that "the men tell us that
one of the first effects of the change would be to eliminate women's
and children's labour," and that "that is the object they have in view
in recommending restriction." The O'Conor Don then alludes to the
evidence of the 63 female witnesses—"philanthropic ladies, factory
hands, and working women"—before the Commission, and remarks
that "nearly all of these came to protest against restriction, at least
as far as they themselves were concerned." He further notes that the
existing Women's Trades' Unions "deprecate interference with their
labour by law," and says that "the moment a girl is responsible for
her actions, she ought to be allowed freedom of labour," and he adds
these remarkable words: "to my mind it is a most striking fact that

L

the evidence which was strongest against this very restriction of confining the working hours within strict limits, is the evidence of those in whose interest it is nominally proposed.

That part of the Report which records the case of Anne Agnew, merits the serious consideration of thoughtful Englishwomen.

In December of last year the attention of your Committee was directed to an outrage committed in the North of England on a young girl named Anne Agnew, who was charged with having concealed the birth of her illegitimate child. After her apprehension on that charge, she was, according to her own statement, compelled by the police to submit to a personal examination by a medical man, in order to ascertain whether the suspicion of the police was borne out by her condition. * * * * * *

An action has been brought against the magistrate, the police inspector, and the doctor, and, on the advice of the solicitors, the cause has been removed to London, it being thought more likely that a verdict could be obtained against the local authorities out of their own neighbourhood. The action is set down for trial, and it is hoped, will shortly be disposed of.

Your Committee instituted these proceedings in no spirit of vengeance against the coroner, surgeon, or police. They are willing to believe that all the persons implicated in this gross assault, may have acted rather from ignorance than from deliberate brutality, but your Committee felt it to be an imperative duty to seize this occasion of re-asserting the principle of the inviolability of the personal rights of the meanest citizen, and of enforcing observance of the law, because, notwithstanding the distinct utterances of the Lord Chief Justice and of several eminent Counsel, the utter illegality of such proceedings does not appear to be generally understood, and it is absolutely necessary for the protection of other women (whether innocent or guilty), that the limits of the coroner's powers should be clearly defined and publicly ratified by the decision of a Court of Law.

A CONFERENCE was held at the Westminster Palace Hotel of the representatives of the several associations affiliated with the British and Continental Federation and the National Association for the Suppression of Regulated Vice. Mr. Stansfeld, M.P., presided; he said they intended to hold a conference in Geneva in September next, to discuss the hygienic results of the system throughout Europe generally, and they expected eminent medical and scientific men to take part in it. Only a few days ago the municipality of Paris had by a majority refused to vote the money for keeping up the system, and similar opposition was taking place throughout France. A newspaper war was going on in Paris on the subject, and several of the leading journals were taking the part of the opponents of this system. One newspaper editor had been fined and imprisoned for having boldly attacked the system. He had no doubt that in the course of a few years it would be abolished in England ; and he should not be surprised if in Paris—the cradle of the system—it should receive its death blow. Mrs. Josephine Butler read letters from France descriptive of the intense excitement which is beginning to prevail there.

EMPLOYMENT.

THE *Agricultural Gazette* says, on the subject of the hirings of farm servants in the north of England, which take place at Whitsuntide and Martinmas: " Both male and female servants are hired for the half year, and they live in the house of their employer, receiving board, lodging, and washing, and so much money for the six months, payable at the expiration of the engagement. They are required to work well, and consequently their employers, as a rule, realise that they must live well The diet is plain, but strengthening ; and they are a hardy, contented, and happy peasantry; labour agitations being as yet unknown amongst them. For years wages have been on the increase. With regard to women servants, the high wages they can command in gentlemen's and tradesmen's families, coupled with their easier work there, is year by year thinning the ranks of agricultural women servants, and, as a consequence, is yearly compelling farmers to pay higher rates." The *Gazette* proceeds to give the following rates :—" *Appleby :* Girls, from £6 to £8 the half-year ; women, from £10 to £12. *Brampton :* The demand for women servants was brisk; dairy women, &c., from £10 to £11 10s. ; young girls, from £7 to £9 (the wages are calculated by the half-year). *Carlisle :* Women, £9 to £11. *Cockermouth :* Women, £7 to £10 ; girls, £3 to £7. *Penrith :* First-class women servants, £11 10s to £12 10s.; second class, £8 to £10. *Kendal :* Female servants commanded from £7 to £15 for the half-year, the latter, of course, being exceptional. At *Malton* female servants very scarce; for the first time for many years these had to " stand the market," the Corn

Exchange not being open for their accommodation.
(We are ignorant of the reason of this change; its hardship is manifest.) In *Howden*, Yorkshire, very young
girls got £8 to £10; older ones, £15 up to £18 and £20,
according to age and capabilities. Considerable difficulty was experienced in getting girls for farm houses
where they had to milk. (It is a pity that we have not
in England agricultural schools for women similar to
those which have worked so well in Sweden. The
healthy country life, though combined with hard bodily
work, would be a welcome change to many of our little
town-bred girls.)

FEMALE CLERKS.—The *Civil Service Review* says:—

The asserters of Women's Rights gained last year a somewhat important point in that addition to the force of the General Post Office
which is recorded in the following very brief paragraph of the Postmaster-General's Twenty-second Annual Report:—"The force of
the Savings' Bank Department was augmented last year by the addition of a staff of female clerks; and I am glad to be able to report
that the experiment has been attended with very satisfactory results."
The world is well aware that the Post Office has long employed
females in the provinces; that from time immemorial young women
who were not covenanted Civil Servants have assisted London Letter
Receivers in the small duties of their small offices; and that, on the
transfer of the telegraphs to the State, a great staff of Female Tele-
graphists became covenanted servants of the State, entitled in all
respects to rank as Civil Servants. But it is not so well known that
the young women who conduct the various businesses of the department in question behind the counters of the district and branch post
offices, and who appear to be called Counterwomen, have now for
some time been subject to the general laws of entry into the Civil
Service and employment therein. Still less, perhaps, is the general
public aware that, in a quiet nook of the City, in a building formerly
devoted to the purposes of a central telegraph station, the not unim-
portant branch of the Post Office formerly known as the Dead Letter
Office, but now called the Returned Letter Office, is carried on with
the assistance of a staff of young women, who are gradually superseding the male officials to whose lot it has heretofore fallen to open
and deal with undelivered letters."

WOMEN DYERS AT PERTH.—Miss Lewin (Employment of Women's Office, 22, Berner's Street) writes:—
We went to Messrs. Campbell, an older though smaller
establishment than Puller and Co. (who admit no
strangers); after waiting a few minutes we were shown
through various rooms where girls were stitching, folding, and ironing clothes, shawls, tablecovers, cushions,
&c., of all colours. The rooms were well ventilated,

and the girls looked healthy and very neat. About 160 girls were employed, earning from 5s. to 12s per week. In the linen factory of Messrs. Shields at Perth, many women are employed; the wages are higher, but the women are not so healthy looking. A few were tracing patterns, and we were told that some were employed as designers.

BOOK-KEEPING.—Mr. George Frazer is giving practical instructions in book-keeping at the College for Working Women, 5, Fitzroy Street, Fitzroy Square, London, W.

THE LADIES' GUILD.—The "Working Ladies' Association" is henceforth entitled "The Ladies' Guild," in consequence of a conference held by Lady Mary Fielding, November 8th, at 30, Onslow Square, at which she read a paper which began as follows :—

The designation is chosen on account of its true meaning—that is, a society or fraternity for mutual help, and engaged in united work. The object here proposed is to link together persons connected with the institutions and centres of industry which already exist for the benefit of ladies.

By so doing these institutions will obtain increased sympathy and support, and isolated efforts be strengthened and enlarged. For want of some such link, *workers*, and those requiring work done waste both time and trouble in seeking for each other. Also helpers and those needing help fail to find each other out. *Union is strength*, and many helpers now apart and unknown to each other would find it so if they were formed into a living chain of help, extending far and near, but connected with the definite work of existing institutions."

The Guild suggests that the members might give aid in many ways; such as—Aid in obtaining employment of all kinds. Aid in instructing workers. Aid in obtaining materials and new designs. Aid in disposing of work. Aid in procuring recreation or country air. Aid in sickness or in obtaining advice from doctors and other professional men gratis. Admissions to convalescent or other homes. Aid in obtaining suitable and respectable lodgings. Aid in obtaining articles of dress. Small loans to be repaid in instalments, chiefly for the purpose of obtaining instruction. Aid in saving or investing money. The Guild is at present affiliated to three institutions—the Royal School of Art Needlework, South Kensington; the Ladies' Dressmaking and Embroidery Association, 42, Somerset Street; and the **Employment of Women Society, 22, Berner's Street**

Ladies willing to become members are invited to send
their names to the secretary at the *Woman's Gazette
Office*, 42, Somerset Street, W. Till a treasurer is appointed Lady Mary Fielding undertakes to receive and
acknowledge subscriptions.

PROPERTY OF MARRIED WOMEN.—The *Suffrage* Journal gives the following instance of the inefficient protection which the present law gives to women :—

WOOLWICH.—A middle-aged woman asked the magistrate to grant
her protection for her furniture. She said she had been married five
weeks to a man who had turned out badly.—Mr. Patteson : Has he
deserted you?—Applicant: No, I wish he would; he is selling off
my goods.—Mr. Patteson : He has a right to do that, for by marry-
ng him you have endowed him with all you possess, and you can
only have protection for the property which you acquire after he
deserts you.—Applicant said she feared that he would not desert her,
and left the court.

LADY LAWYERS.—The Council of University College,
London, have awarded the Joseph Hume medal to Miss
Orme, who has already taken the first place in all the
classes that women are permitted to attend at this institution, and who is now making her way in such active
business at the law as is allowed to persons who are not
called to the bar. The *Athenæum* says : "It may be a
long time before the Benchers' of the Inns will grant
the "call" to women, but if they prove themselves
worthy of it, it can only be a question of time.

RELIEF OF THE DISTRESSED BULGARIANS AND OTHER
REFUGEES IN SERVIA.—The necessities of these unfortunate refugees, whose houses are burnt, whose flocks
are stolen, and whose clothes have been taken, continue
to increase as the severity of the winter increases.
Though Lady Strangford is working mostly in Bulgaria, there is but little hope of remedying the miseries
of those who remain there until a change in political
circumstances has taken place, because as fast as English
charity gives, Turkish rapacity again takes away. But
crowds of fugitives from every province are in Servia,
where Miss Irby and Dr. Sandwith are distributing food
and clothes as fast as they can procure them. All who
can send even a trifle at this season should do so, either
to Mr. Freeman, or to W. J. Stillman, St. Helen's Cottage,
Ventnor. Mrs. Malleson forwards every week bales of

old and new clothing from the office, at 29, Queen Square, W.C.; Mr. J. J. Jones (of the Homerton Mission), who has just returned from Servia, receives and forwards new and cast off clothing from 9, Water Street, Blackfriars Bridge, E.C. In both these cases a small contribution of money is urgently requested to help to defray the cost of carriage.

The work of the Birmingham Ladies' Committee deserves special record for the splendid organization it evinced. Having obtained money by assiduous collection, and laid in wholesale stores of the most serviceable materials, a large hall in the Exchange were assigned to them; one manufacturer presented them with twelve sewing machines, another lent them the services of two professional cutters-out, and in two days many hundred garments were made.

MISCELLANEOUS.

A SOCIETY called, after the Man of Ross, the Kyrle Society, has been started in London with the object of beautifying and improving the homes of the poor. Miss Octavia Hill, 14, Nottingham Place, W., is treasurer of the Society, which is a certain guarantee for its practical character. Officers of working men's clubs, reading rooms, or schools are invited to make known their wants to the above address.

A THIRD edition of the "Year Book of Women's Work," under the title of the "Handbook of Women's Work," with additional chapters, has been issued by Messrs. Hatchards, 187, Piccadilly, London. It is edited as heretofore by L. M. H.

"SUGGESTIONS FOR HOUSE DECORATION," by Rhoda and Agnes Garrett: Macmillan. The authors know their theme thoroughly and treat it practically and clearly. The little volume is very suggestive to all desiring to be made acquainted with the principles of ornament.

NATIONAL TRAINING SCHOOL FOR MUSIC.—A competition among the scholars of this school for the musical scholarships which have been founded by the Queen and other members of the Royal Family, commenced on

Monday, the 13th inst., and terminated on Wednesday,·
the 16th, when the following students were elected to
be Royal Scholars:—Eugène d'Albert, to be the Queen's
scholar; Minnie Eliza Webbe, to be the Prince of
Wales's scholar; Eva P. Pidesch, to be the Duke of
Edinburgh's scholar; Hélène Heale, to be the Duchess
of Edinburgh's scholar. Proxime Accesserunt: Anne
A. Marriott and Mary Thomas, æquales. The examination was conducted by the Principal, Mr. Arthur S.
Sullivan, Mus. Doc., Cantab., assisted by all the members
of the professional staff. The scholarships which become
vacant by these elections are—one of the Society of
Arts, two of the Fishmongers' Company, and one of the
county of Northumberland. The founders of these
scholarships have the privilege of electing new scholars
to fill the places of those who have become Royal
scholars.

HOME FOR NURSES.—Miss Firth, whose Association of
Trained Nurses, 74, New Bond Street, W., has already
been so useful, has opened another home for the same
purpose in Kensington.

ART. V.—THE LATE CYCLONE.

Calcutta, November 16th, 1876.

THERE has occurred in Bengal a terrible cyclone, of
which you have probably already heard by telegraph.
I may be able to give some details which will help your
readers to realize better what has happened.

The district of Bákarganj in south-east Bengal has
suffered most severely, and in it the "eastern and
southern portions of the island of Dakhin Shabazpur
and the islands on the south and east of it, and the
thanas (police divisions) of Bowfal and Golachupa, have
been almost entirely destroyed. (Report of Mr. Barton,
officiating collector of Bákarganj). The area of the
cyclone was much greater than the district here named,
but its fury centred in these places. It has done great
damage and caused considerable loss of life in the ships

which it overtook in the Bay of Bengal, and also in districts bordering on Bákarganj.

On the night of the 31st of October there was a hurricane from the north-east, accompanied at the time of the tidal wave (bore) by a succession of storm waves driven from the south-west up the Titulia river and over the neighbouring land. When it is remembered that the delta of the Ganges is in this district only a few feet above the sea it will be seen that there is no protection for the villages. In places where there are no masonry houses a rush of water, estimated in various places as from 9 feet to 30 feet in height, must sweep everything before it. Complete destruction of property—houses, fruit trees, cattle and tanks, has occurred in many villages; it is to be feared that the loss of life has been appalling. Of Dowlut Khan, the principal mart of Dakhin Shahbazpur, nothing remains but a few mounds, the raised foundation of houses. It is said that Manpura, an island with a population of 5,000, is submerged; that an officer who was sent to report upon it was unable to find it. The same story is told of other smaller islands.

The following is the substance of a report sent to Mr. Barton by Babu Dino Nath Sircar, police inspector in Dowlut Khan:—

The storm began by a strong wind from the east, which at 10 p.m. veered to the north-east and became a hurricane, in which the police station was soon blown down. Babu Dino Nath Sircar gathered together the prisoners and placed a guard of constables round them. At 11 p.m., while they were looking at a house which had taken fire, they felt that water was rising under their feet, and then saw that water was rushing towards them in the space between the "lock-up" and the guard-house. They lost all hope, and the sub-inspector told the prisoners to save themselves. The water rose quickly to their waists. Some of the party climbed to the roof of the prisoners' work shed; the water rose and carried away the roof and some six or seven men who clung to it. Stronger waves rolled in, which tore the thatched roof to pieces and threw the men into the water. Dino Nath Babu now began to

swim, and was drifting to the south, when he came
across a " half drowned" Balam boat, which he seized
with two or three others, who were also swimming.
Just as all had scrambled into it, it was struck by a
floating roof and sank. The sub-inspector found a
mádár tree floating—a wild tree armed with large
thorns—he took hold of it, and with it was carried into
a garden of "mango and cocoanut and betel trees."
" I was, however, obliged to relinquish my hold, as the
mádár tree was full of thorns, and each time that it rose
with the waves the thorns pricked my sides, hands, and
feet." He let go, and was able with great difficulty to
cling to a mango tree until morning, when he found by
measuring with a bamboo that the water was still 9
feet deep. It receded rapidly, and at 8.30 a.m., when
he descended, it had ebbed to $4\frac{1}{2}$ feet. We called out,
and found that there were perched on other trees, and
one on a roof, four other men in the garden. He made
his way to the police station, where everything had
been carried away, a few bricks from the floor of the
deputy magistrate's cutcherry alone remaining. He
says : " Under the circumstances in which I was placed
and from what I saw of those whom I met, I believe
that few of the population could have saved themselves.
No one expected such a catastrophe, and none were
provided with a means of safety. We found a few bags
of rice, wet, lying in the open bazaar space, and helped
ourselves, a handful each, to preserve ourselves from
starvation. No one has been able to save anything,
and those who are saved must be in an utter state of
destitution."

The following account of his escape and losses was
given to me by Babu Uma Charan Banerjèa, deputy
magistrate of the island (Dakhin Shahbazpùr). On the
night of the storm he and his wife and family were in
the Sub-Divisional Buildings. With them, after the
hurricane began, were sheltering some hundred other
persons, amongst them a number of "manjhis" (boat-
men), whose boats had been destroyed in the early
part of the storm. They expected that the bore would
be unusually high in consequence of the violent wind,
and prepared for it by piling up tak-ta-poshes (a kind

of bedstead) to raise a safe place for the children: One son of Babu Uma Charan Banerjèa, a boy of eleven, climbed with some constables to the roof, but the hurricane tore it down, and the boy was killed in its fall. The great waves came suddenly upon the ruined house. Uma Charan Babu and his wife, who had each a child in their arms, were carried away and saw no more of their companions. He knew nothing further until he was found by a relief party next morning lying on a mass of floating *débris*, which had become entangled amongst some trees. His wife was near him and alive; but both the children were lost. They had been carried across a river for the distance of half a mile. In these few hours they lost four sons, their only daughter and her two young children, besides other members of the household, numbering eleven in all. The unhappy parents left Dowlut Khan on the following day, partly on account of the cholera-breeding smell consequent on the destruction of so many human beings and cattle, and partly to visit Gya and there make the "shraddh" to ensure the salvation of the souls of their dead. Happily their eldest son was at Dacca and so escaped; so also has another boy who had been given in adoption to a cousin.

I copy the report (dated 4th Nov.) of a court sub-inspector of Patuyakhali; as its hurried sentences sum up the horrors of a cyclone :—

"Mr. Jackson of Golachupa came here at about 4 p.m., his body cut into hundred ways; he has lost his wife, sons, and servants; only the corpse of the servant is obtained. Others washed away. With a dhooty on he appeared before Mr. Gupta, who has given him his travelling expenses to his home; he asked me to apply to the district superintendent for leave.

"News from Bowfal exceeds all horrors. Inspector Gunesh Bose, sub-inspector Chandra Kumar Ghosh, head constable Mohima Chundra Mookerjea, wife, son, and daughter of head constable Gupta washed off. The number of men died cannot be ascertained. Half the population gone. Carcasses of dead animals float through rivers and canals. Famine widespread. More persons are dying from hunger. Buildings have come down. It is impossible to de-scribe them. . I myself have narrowly escaped death. Had I not had the help of Madhub Babu, the sub-inspecting postmaster, I would have surely died.

"Outpost Chaltabonia washed off. Where the head constable is gone, and where his family, nobody can say. Radhakant Babu was at Parda Kuja within Golachupa. After three days' fasting he is

come here, and tells us that he has heard there is nothing left at Chaltabonia. I wish to know whether my brother is alive ; if any news of
his living has come to the head quarters, I pray the district superintendent will inform me about the matter."

These melancholy histories doubtless resemble many
hundreds of others. In many places where the loss of
human life has been inconsiderable, the destruction of
property has been enormous. At Barisál 90 per cent. of
the houses were levelled with the ground ; timber and
fruit trees were torn up. The 31st was fortunately a
moonlight night, so that the people were enabled to find
their way to the masonry houses, and there take refuge.
Hundreds of natives found shelter in the houses of the
European residents of Barisál. Dowlut Khan had no such
asylum. Even the deputy-magistrate's cutcherry (sub-
divisional buildings) was only in part masonry.

The loss of little children has been cruel. In Noakhali alone 35 are said to have been drowned. Here,
too, a delicate lady was able to escape only by wading
for 1½ miles in water to the waist, over fallen trees.
Mr. Porch, the officiating magistrate of Noakhali says
that the place on the morning of Nov. 1st, looked " as
though it had been cannonaded and then inundated. I
waded from my house door through the bazaar to the
thana, through 3½ feet of water." "The roofs of the
pakka buildings were crowded with the inhabitants, and
the streets were canals with strong currents running
north and carrying along the débris of houses and
shops." In Chillagong there were few deaths but much
injury was done to the shipping, and large quantities of
rice and tea were destroyed. The commissioner, Mr.
A. Smith, reports that 24 people, mostly women, had
reached his compound, who had been carried over an
arm of the sea at least 10 miles wide, on the roofs of
houses, on pieces of wood. One woman tells a melancholy tale of how "she was obliged in her extremity to
let two of her children perish to save herself."

The after consequences of such a flood are famines
and cholera. To meet these dangers relief measures
were immediately taken. Food, money, and clothes
have been sent from the head quarters of each district ;
decaying rice thrown into the sea or rivers, tanks cleared
of dead bodies and carcasses.

At present it is not possible to tell the number of the dead. It is variously reported at from seventy thousand to two hundred thousand. Possibly I may be able to send you further particulars for your next issue; and to tell you the fate of several islands and villages which it is feared are destroyed. The breaking up of boats made it at first difficult to obtain information from the more distant places exposed to the storm.

ANNETTE S. BEVERIDGE.

ART. VI.—CORRESPONDENCE.

The Editor is not responsible for the opinions of Correspondents.

To the Editor of the "ENGLISHWOMAN'S REVIEW."

DEAR MADAM,—I am sure you will be glad to learn that the Ex-Collegio Medico Schools in Naples, instituted by Mrs. Salis Schwabe, of my first visit to which last spring I sent you an account, are now in a more independent and flourishing condition than I could then report them to be.

The present liberal Government in Italy has promised, and begun payment of, a yearly subvention of 6,000 francs, and the Municipality of Naples has promised 4,000 francs yearly, thus making an assured income of 10,000 francs, besides the children's fees and subscriptions from the supporters and friends of the institution.

Though these yearly gifts from the Italian Government and the Municipality of Naples are but small, yet, added to the previous loan of the buildings for the institution, they enable the benevolent foundress and her devoted coadjutors to work with a cheerful hope and confidence in the future which mere donations from friends could not give. The support of the National Government, moreover, proves that Mrs. Schwabe's work is in harmony with Italian feelings, and is appreciated by the intelligent among the Italian people, both points which I had heard disputed by English travellers whose interest I had besought for these schools.

With such hopeful confidence has this secured yearly income inspired Mrs. Swabe and Miss Baermann that they have now ventured on a step, long urged upon them by Mr. and Mrs. Quarati, the directors of the schools, and have ceased to admit pupils *gratis* to the school, or to feed them daily with warm soup, as at first. This daily *dinner*, you may remember, attracted many of the poorest and dirtiest children of the crowded streets of that quarter, whose parents cared nothing for the teaching, indeed under the influence of bigoted priests, viewed it with suspicion, but were glad their little ones should be saved for a time the sufferings from hunger which their own idleness brought on them. The poor little creatures brought such dirt into the school, as well as low habits and breeding, that the better brought up were driven away by them. *Now*, 25 orphans, without at least one parent, are taken into the house, when, well fed, washed, and clothed, they regain the brightness natural to childhood, and are taught and cared for with loving assiduity. All others coming to the Kindergarten and the progressive schools have to pay sums varying from 2 francs to 5 francs a month. I need not again repeat how admirably they are taught by Mr. and Mrs. Quarati and their assistants, or how quick is the progress of these bright, clear-headed children of the south.

As soon as possible, it is now proposed to organize a normal school for teachers on the Kindergarten system. Of course, this is principally intended to train young Italians for Italian schools, where the need of good teachers is almost universal as yet. But I understood Miss Baermann to say that young ladies from England or elsewhere, wishing to study Fröbel's system, and at the same time enjoy a mild climate, would be received into the house on certain fixed terms. I cannot but think were this known some of our young English girls would be anxious to take advantage of such an opportunity. Not only those who wish to gain their livelihood by teaching systematically well might do so, but those who look forward to the more general life of woman, as wife and mother, might here learn usefully the best plans for developing the intelligence of children thoroughly and happily. They would be gainers, not only in the future but in the present, substituting the interest of useful, happy work among little loving children for the wearisome search after excitement in dress and amusement, which is so painfully characteristic of too many young women in our social circles. Of course, to learn Fröbel's system one need not go so far as Naples; it is the beauty of climate and situation there which would be attractive, and the facilities for learning Italian and for promoting international friendliness. The more the beauty and usefulness of Fröbel's system is appreciated, the more I feel sure will healthy young women study and teach it; and its spread, for a time, must come through the voluntary efforts of the educated classes.

I am living at present in the neighbourhood of a small seaport and fishing village, and in the fresh healthy air which circulates all round, children seem to spring up as fast as the mosses and furze which form the principal vegetation on the coast. There are excellent School Board schools provided, but children are not obliged to enter them till they are five years of age, and the parents think even that too young to shut up little creatures to lessons for several hours daily. The active movement, the singing, the constant variety in the children's garden, so satisfy the imperious demand for activity at that age, that the little ones like school, and relieve the parents of all need of pressure to get them to go. Both parents and children delight, too, in the little works they learn to do there, so that early and constant attendance are secured, and the formation from the first, of cleanly, orderly, refined habits. On the contrary, the child left to tumble about till five years of age, has already formed habits of dirt and idleness, and has inevitably learned low and coarse language and ideas, poor little thing, from its surroundings. So that at school there is first much to undo, much that can never be effaced, to *dim*, before the habits of order, obedience, industry, and cleanliness can be formed. The work is doubled both for teacher and child, and is never so hopeful as it might have been, had the baby of two years entered the bright precincts of the children's

garden. And yet, how little are these admirable institutions known! We need such an enthusiast as was
Mr. Wilderspin for infant schools, to go as he did, forty
years ago, from town to town, to explain, insist, and
prove their utility and practicability, until he roused
the interest, and called out the liberality which ensured
their formation wherever he went. Though not come
yet, I think the day is near, when all our little ones will
be gathered in from the earliest years, to feel first in
Fröebel's schools, and then in others, the influence of
common sense and kindness, preparing them from the
first dawn of reason, for the wise use of the life that
lies before them. May, it but come quickly.

C. M. JOHNSTON.

Nov. 22, 1876.

MADAM,—I have read the paragraph on *Musical Composers* in the November number of the *Englishwoman's
Review*, with much interest, the more especially as some
years since I began collecting materials for a biographical work on the subject.

May I say that instead of being *brief*, the list of
female musical composers is a surprisingly long one,
from the times of St. Cecilia, Lamia, and Sappho to the
present day. I could not venture to trouble you by
even an outline. Many ladies, especially among the
French and German, have composed operatic pieces, but
the greater part have composed for the voice and
pianoforte. Among English composers of modern
times, you have overlooked Claribel (Mrs. Brown), Anne
Fricker, Mrs. Worthington Bliss (Miss M. Lindsay),
Elizabeth Philp, Alice Smith, Mrs. John Macfarren
("Jules Brissac"), and several others, chiefly song
writers. Anne Fricker's "Fading Away" is one of the
most admired songs in modern repertoire, and Claribel's
songs are world-famed.

I hope you will pardon me for trespassing on your
attention.

I am, Madam, obediently yours,
ELLEN C. CLAYTON,
(*Author of Queens of Song, English Female
Artists, Notable Women, &c.*)

To the Editor of the ENGLISHWOMAN'S REVIEW.

TABLE OF CONTENTS, 1876.